THE
NEW
KGB

Books by William R. Corson

The Betrayal
Promise or Peril
Consequences of Failure
The Armies of Ignorance

THE NEW KGB

ENGINE OF SOVIET POWER

**WILLIAM R. CORSON and
ROBERT T. CROWLEY**

WILLIAM MORROW AND COMPANY, INC.
New York

Library of Congress Cataloging in Publication Data

Corson, William R.
  The new KGB, engine of Soviet power.

  Bibliography: p.
  Includes index.
  1. Intelligence service—Soviet Union. 2. Espionage—
Soviet Union. 3. Soviet Union—Politics and government—
1917–   . 4. Soviet Union. Komitet gosudarstvennoĭ
bezopasnosti.   I. Crowley, Robert T.   II. Title.
JN6529.I6C67   1985   327.1′2′0947   85-2911
ISBN 0-688-04183-3

Printed in the United States of America

First Edition

1 2 3 4 5 6 7 8 9 10

BOOK DESIGN BY BERNARD SCHLIEFER

To the Memories of
John W. McConnell
and
Justin E. O'Donnell
Men of Courage, Truth,
Integrity, and Intelligence

CONTENTS

PREFACE

We began working on this project more than four years ago. The newspapers of the day were reporting that IBM 370 mainframe computers, plus third- and fourth-generation microchips and other electronic devices, were disappearing from U.S. firms. The reports said there was evidence that the material had been stolen by the KGB or, possibly, by agents of one of its Warsaw Pact surrogates and shipped to the USSR. Each of the stories treated the thefts as isolated, aberrant events.

Robert Lindsey's book *The Falcon and the Snowman* had also reached the best-seller lists. It described the treason of Christopher Boyce and Andrew Dalton Lee in conspiring to sell to the Soviets extremely sensitive and highly technical data. The book did not discuss, however, the anticipatory steps and new methods used by the KGB to reap immediate benefit from the secrets taken from TRW. (Only recently has this data been used by the USSR to blind U.S. surveillance satellites.) Soviet exploitation of the espionage opportunity presented by Boyce and Lee succeeded because of a combination of factors, the most important being that the Soviets had prepositioned skilled technical officers in the United States to seize, "control" (direct), and analyze "targets" of opportunity such as those presented by Boyce and Lee.

This prior planning by the Russians, which included the assignment of trained scientific and technical personnel to the United States, enabled the KGB to get, in a minimum time span and at little risk, all the highly classified, relevant data concerning a major satellite system designed and managed by TRW for the U.S. government. The TRW cupboard of secrets was just about bare before the activities of Boyce and Lee were discovered.

Today, the same kinds of stories are still being reported by the media, and they are still being presented as newsworthy but unrelated events. Most recently there have been stories about large shipments of sophisticated computer equipment being intercepted en route to the USSR by last-minute customs inspections in Sweden. But for every success in thwarting the Soviets' industrial-scientific-technological espionage campaign against the West, twenty-five to thirty illegal shipments elude detection.

In 1983, extended congressional hearings demonstrated that Western technology can now be found in more than 150 of the main Soviet weapons systems. This means that the Soviets have built missiles and aircraft, including a clone of the American AWACS, which are based on nearly exact copies of U.S. equipment. The rapid Soviet catch-up in the military and naval fields is possible only because of a broad strategy to "borrow," by illegal, clandestine means, the essential Western design and engineering data if not the object itself.

Another recent major Soviet military advance was made possible by their "acquisition" of armor-piercing technology which directly threatens British and American tanks in Western Europe. The effect of this technological theft has since become evident in the Iraq-Iran war, in which Soviet-provided armor and tank ordnance has enabled the Iraqis to hit and destroy an unusually high number of the American and British tanks that comprise Iran's armored force.

In addition to the loss of advantage in armor, NATO nations are now forced to spend untold additional millions of dollars developing countermeasures to defend against electronic developments originally created by the NATO countries and either "sold" to the Soviets or illegally diverted to the USSR or Warsaw Pact countries. The equipment, including more than three thousand of the most sophisticated minicomputers, is identical to that currently used by the U.S. Defense Department and is sufficiently advanced to target nuclear weapons and to direct cruise missiles to their intended targets.

In the fifties the KGB was primarily seeking conventional military secrets. Today, its targets are specific industrial, scientific, and technological secrets with direct military application. Soviet weaknesses in areas of design, engineering, miniaturization, and advanced electronics are compensated for by this theft of Western efforts. The Soviets' demonstrated inability to innovate and effectively apply new technology to weapons development has been offset, if not overcome, by the KGB's massive industrial-espionage strategy. The Soviets depend on the continuation of this source of Western technology and equipment to develop and manufacture most of their advance weapons systems—and virtually all of their countermeasure systems. Additionally, powerful economic incentives are involved. The USSR is incapable of supporting the multiple, broad, and exceedingly costly research and development programs of the West. Any attempt by the USSR to compete in this area would further depress their present low standard of living and introduce the real risk of destroying the Soviet economy, with concomitant loss of control.

For example, the Soviets and their Warsaw Pact allies have derived significant recent military gains from their coordinated theft of Western technology. This disciplined, multifaceted Soviet strategy has allowed the USSR to:

- Save, in the past six to seven years, an estimated $12 billion to $15 billion in research and development costs, and five to seven years in research and development lead time.
- Modernize critical sectors of their military industry and reduce engineering risks by following or copying proven Western designs, thereby limiting the rise in their military production costs.
- Achieve weapons superior to what would have resulted if they had to rely solely on Soviet technology.
- Incorporate countermeasures to Western weapons early in the development of their own weapons program.

To understand where we are today, and to comprehend the Soviets' *modus operandi,* in Chapter 7 we have traced, examined, and analyzed the phenomenon of Soviet industrial espionage. The chapter is historical in its treatment because there is no way to appreciate the present without an understanding of fundamental decisions, made in the twenties, which continue to guide the process today. In Chapter 7 we underscore the fact that "trade"—i.e., a fair exchange—with the Soviet Union is a basic though popular delusion. It has trapped many American and European industrialists and confused an equal number of politicians about the virtues of détente.

A number of excellent books have been written about the KGB in recent years. Among them are *The Secret World* by Peter Deriabin, which aims at describing the psychological burdens of working in the Soviet intelligence services. There is *Inside a Soviet Embassy* by Alexander Kaznacheev, which points up the internal bureaucratic competition within the KGB for prestige, honors, and promotions. Also, *The KGB* by Brian Freemantle, and *The KGB: The Eyes of Russia* by Harry Rositzke. Then there are *KGB: The Secret Work of Soviet Secret Agents* and *KGB Today: The Hidden Hand* by John Barron. These last two titles are noteworthy because they attempt to strip away some of the romantic nonsense that has grown up about the KGB. However, none of these books has tried to do what we have: to describe, explain, and analyze the changes in the KGB from its beginnings in 1917 to the present day.

We have focused on the sixty-eight-year background of Soviet intelligence and security operations in order to supply the connective tissue that lends coherence and meaning to the actions of today's "new KGB." The results of our examination are alarming. This book documents how the organs of Soviet state security and intelligence have attained their dominant role in the Soviet government.

Our research is new and, in many ways, constitutes a spy story in itself. We were seeking the truth about Soviet operational failures and successes rather than undertaking conventional historiographic research. As authors, we combine more than seventy years of experience in the field of intelligence, most of them spent in attempting to counter, thwart, identify, and understand the activities of our contemporaries in the KGB. And as we note in the acknowledgments, advice from former colleagues led us to obscure and previously undiscovered documents and files. Thus, our view of Soviet history, and our analysis of Soviet behavior, are sharply at odds with the traditional academic positions held by many American scholars who, to maintain their access to the USSR, have had to temper their critical instincts or risk being denied visas by Moscow.

The significance of the KGB's "newness" is twofold. When Yuri Andropov became the KGB chairman in 1967, it was evident to him that the USSR was gradually losing status in the world; and within the Soviet Union, the government was losing its ability to cope with a growing series of intractable internal problems. If the Soviet state intended to continue its competition with the West, the need for change was critical. American and European breakthroughs in military technology and science were widening the gap of Western superiority at an ever-increasing rate. In consequence, Andropov initiated administrative, operational, and personnel changes designed to modernize the KGB and to prepare the way for its eventual assumption of full control of the Communist party and the Soviet government, both of which had become corrupt, grossly inefficient, and weak. Second, the KGB's "newness" was concealed by a program of disinformation and other active measures to promote the appearance of business as usual and to encourage the view, especially in the West, that it was an unimaginative, totally predictable organization, without real authority.

The impact on the West of this deception is as genuine as the threat posed to Western Europe by Soviet nuclear missiles. By underestimating the new KGB, the West has been induced to regard it in a conventional (though wholly mistaken) context. For example, in the face of hard evidence, the hemorrhaging of Western industrial, scientific, and technological secrets into the USSR's industrial base is dismissed on the grounds that it isn't significant, not necessarily KGB-directed (because of the other nationalities involved), and further, that it is *impossible* to erect barriers to stanch this flow. KGB disinformation specialists have succeeded in insinuating the notion that the technology of microelectronic circuitry is like the ideas of pure science: i.e., it knows no boundaries and none can be established.

The question of a new KGB is extremely vexatious, especially to the Western intelligence services and Western politicians. It requires rethinking basic premises and predilections about the Soviets as well as our expectations in dealing with them. It does not, however, mean the recognition of Soviet virtue. It means the recognition of Soviet power and how it is applied.

Sometimes this takes on subtle forms. For example, before Andropov assumed control of the state security, its KGB residents (members of the foreign embassy staffs and various "trade representatives") were distinctive, almost caricatures, in that they dressed like Soviets, spoke like Soviets, and acted the way we expected Soviets to act. Today, the new KGB officer in the United States and the Western democracies wears custom suits and can easily be mistaken for an account executive or a corporation lobbyist on Capitol Hill. The new (unseen) KGB officer is among us in a new form and in numbers never previously approached. When the Church and Pike congressional committees alleged excesses by U.S. internal and external security and intelligence services, the Soviet Union detailed sixteen senior KGB and GRU officers to intensify their "work" in the halls of Congress. These sixteen officers are identified in this book, as are their efforts to infiltrate congressional staffs and committees.

The expansion of the KGB through utilization of the satellite nations' intelligence services has not been written about in great detail before. Yet the KGB controls operations and assigns functional roles to various bloc government intelligence services, all of which remain under Soviet KGB control. Thus, the Bulgarians handle "wet affairs" or assassinations. The Poles and East Germans concentrate on ultrahigh-tech espionage. (The East German service has been monitored sending enciphered messages into West Berlin and West Germany every six and a half minutes, twenty-four hours per day, for the past twenty-five years.) The Czechs, whose intelligence service has been rebuilt by the KGB since the Soviet invasion of that country in 1969, have now been put on a steady diet of operational support missions. We describe how this process evolved and its effect in multiplying the KGB's capacities by creating a controlled, multinational intelligence and security service. Here, the corporate analogy of the multinational firm is far more appropriate in describing the new KGB than the popularly repeated nonsense that "it is sort of a cross between the CIA and the FBI."

During Andropov's short term as General Secretary of the Soviet

Communist Party and chairman of the Defense Council, the Western press interviewed their expert sources and confidently reported that he was considered by some to be a closet liberal. It was reported that he was an urbane, cultured gentleman with a taste for modern music and an ear for the plight of the dissatisfied. Andropov was also praised for his program to modernize Soviet industry (here again the carrot of East-West trade was dangled before the Western business community to deflect attention from Soviet realities). His anticorruption program was widely hailed in some newspapers as though he were the newly elected Reform candidate who would soon clean up City Hall. What was not noticed was that within his fifteen months in power, Andropov "removed" (a euphemism for arrest and, in some instances, execution) more than 20 percent of the Cabinet and the same percentage of oblast party chiefs. Though no exact U.S. analogue exists, an oblast is a regional area based, much like a U.S. congressional district, on population. In turn, the oblast party chiefs are the political power in each area and, as such, are responsible for maintaining work norms, party loyalty, and discipline, and for keeping the domestic peace. During the Brezhnev era, they were also entitled to take their graft off the top of the system. Unlike Brezhnev, Andropov rewarded the more corrupt of the oblast party chiefs with speedy trials and even execution. Conservative estimates are that, during his short term, more than thirty-five thousand members of the CPSU were ousted from the party and that several thousand executions, including those of the chairman of the State Committee for External Economic Relations and his deputy, were carried out. Both of these men had been appointed by the former Communist Party boss, Leonid Brezhnev.

Andropov then named one of his own loyalists to take over control of the Ministry for Internal Affairs (the MVD), a reversal of a thirty-year-old decision, taken after the execution of Beria, that had separated the MVD's police and investigative forces from the KGB. Four Andropov nominees were also appointed to the Politburo. Instead of the enlightened new leadership envisaged by the Western press, Andropov achieved significant control of the Politburo and the Central Committee. This occurred in the first seven months of Andropov's term and before he became debilitated by illness. The effect of his strategy has been augmented by subsequent internal changes, and the results are gradually becoming felt. There has been a return to neo-Stalinism, government promotion and sponsorship of anti-Semitism, harsh repression of dissent, and the suspension of emigration, betraying many of the hallmarks of the old tyrant's techniques.

This process is accelerating. Andropov's nominees are now the most powerful influence on the future of the Soviet state. The selection of the least qualified man in the Kremlin, the ailing Konstantin Chernenko, to serve as General Secretary of the party was an essential stratagem intended to convey the illusion that Andropov's "confrontational policies" had been abandoned, and that there was a retreat toward the more comfortable status of a Brezhnev-like rule. At the time of this writing, in reality, Chernenko is without power or support. He serves only to buttress the deception that the continuity, collegiality, and control of the system still reside in the Soviet Communist Party. Andropov's men are clearly in charge and control of the Soviet state.

This is our story of how this situation has come about.

ACKNOWLEDGMENTS

We are indebted to the Honorable Loy W. Henderson, for his generosity in allowing access to his unpublished memoirs; to Ruth Levine, whose contributions were unique and of great value; to Mrs. David Nimmer, who filled in a mysterious blank; to Dr. James D. Atkinson, who provided important advice and comments.

To the staff of the National Archives and National Records Center, especially John Taylor, Tim Nenninger, George Chalou, Ron Swerzek, Kathy Nicastro, Sally Marks, and the others who assisted with competence, good humor, and valuable suggestions.

To the FBI's FOI/Privacy Section, for the patient and efficient assistance in processing hundreds of requests for data relating to the Soviet personalities who "worked" the United States in the twenties and thirties.

To Thomas F. Conley, chief of the FOI/P Office of the U.S. Army Intelligence and Security Command, for providing guidance and highly professional help in acquiring essential documentation.

To the FOIA elements of the Departments of State, Justice, Navy—our thanks. Also, the Secret Service, the Immigration Service, the Bureau of Prisons, the Passport Office, all of which aided, materially, in the search for basic documents.

To those former Soviet "workers" who later agreed to extended interviews and consultations, we are most grateful. Their strong encouragement, detailed knowledge, and, in some instances, their own personal records relating to events described, were essential to understanding the motivations and rationales of the Soviet services.

To a few unnamed widows who, though not themselves disciplined "workers," held astonishing data, which they freely shared, relative to the roles played by their husbands in Soviet espionage operations in the thirties.

To a large number of former U.S. intelligence officers with direct Soviet experience, who encouraged the authors and provided advice and special insights "peculiar to the trade." As indicated in the Introduction, some facts relating to Soviet operations must be regarded as "unknowable," and even if the Center's files were open to perusal, the truth could not be ascertained because of the Soviets' compulsion for unending historical revisionism.* No doubt the British government would share our interest in knowing the identity of the Englishman who recruited Beria on the behalf of M.I.6.

*Where the USSR has followed a policy of constantly revising "history" in the form of publications issued by the state publishing house, the United States has, without conscious effort, fallen into a policy of "nonhistory" or "missing history." Events that occurred fifty years ago (i.e., predating the delegation of domestic counterintelligence responsibilities to the FBI and twelve years before the establishment of the CIA) are still not generally available to scholars. Two factors appear to influence the "nonhistory" policy.

The first is the assumption that the release of such documents would endanger sources and methods, and the second is the general notion that the decision to release official documents of that era (mainly the period prior to recognition of the Soviet Union by the United States) might in some way be interpreted as giving offense to the USSR or putting at peril our current relationships with the Soviets.

A group of documents that fall into the "nonhistory" category are those that have been removed from official files or destroyed. Among these are a Secret Service file entitled "Counterfeiting by the USSR Government," which was deposited in the National Archives and later withdrawn—that is, permanently "lost." The Van Vliet report on the Katyn massacre, which was removed or "lost" from the Pentagon, is another example. This category can be expanded to include records in the Departments of State, Treasury, Commerce, the National Archives, and the Library of Congress, which were removed or ordered destroyed by "friends of the Soviet Union" who held high positions of trust in the U.S. government during the late twenties, thirties, and forties.

It is the assumption of some that methods used fifty years ago, if known, would handicap America's ability to cope with the Soviet problem. Among the methods are accounts of foot surveillance, direct interview, and recourse to government files and public records (not truly esoteric techniques to be forever husbanded in closed files).

Among the "sources" are former Soviet agents who testified before congressional committees and congressional staff members in the twenties and thirties and provided detailed accounts of their personal involvement in espionage in the United States. For the most part, these disclosures remain inaccessible.

A last category of unreleasable documents are those that are more accurately described as "embarrassing" rather than properly classified. Included in this group is the personally penned, enthusiastic (and almost certainly unwitting) sponsorship of a Soviet agent's application to enter the United States. The man who successfully intervened with the Immigration Service by giving his personal guarantees, served as a member of the U.S. Congress and, within the last year, offered himself as a prospective candidate for the office of President of the United States.

"Embarrassing" documents lend themselves to out-of-context exploitation and take on a political weight far in excess of what is warranted. Several of the U.S. government elements involved in various aspects of intelligence and counterintelligence have produced "classified histories," which are unreleasable and designed only to meet administrative fiat. Such court histories, for the most part prepared by incipient retirees, effuse a golden glow undiminished by the intrusion of accounts of errors, betrayals, and unprofessional judgments.

In the beginning it was necessary to concede the high probability of errors in tracking the careers of "workers" in several continents, who used multiple identities and were associated with diverse sponsors. Faulty transliterations, party names, work names, aliases, etc., added formidable barriers to the full resolution of some true identities. In this connection we can only urge others to take up the quest and mine the growing accumulations of unexploited documents, which will buttress and add to a broader and deeper appreciation of the role of the Soviet services' activities in the United States.

We are indebted to our editor Bruce Lee for his encouragement, patience, and personal support along the tortuous trail leading from the Cheka to the *The New KGB*.

Vice Admiral Rufus Taylor, USN (Ret.), Col. H. A. Aplington III, USMC (Ret.), and the late Justin E. O'Donnell and John W. McConnell all gave valuable advice and special, educated, perspectives to the narrative.

Finally, we want to thank our wives, Emily Crowley and Judith Corson, for their great patience and remarkable forbearance as well as the Corson sons, Adam, Zachary, and Andrew, who helped by their willingness to accept the fact that the "book writing" would someday end.

WILLIAM R. CORSON
Potomac, Maryland

ROBERT T. CROWLEY
Washington, D.C.

INTRODUCTION

The Soviet intelligence and security services have been functioning for almost seventy years, but their true nature and role remain unknown. It is frequently suggested that the Soviet services are analogous to the national services of other countries, with the possible exception that they are merely more numerous and more energetic. The popular assumption—that every nation's intelligence and security services are organized, staffed, and directed along certain conventional lines—has aided the Soviets by giving the false impression that comparative examination of bureaucratic differences is a tedious and unrewarding line of inquiry.

This popular acceptance of the notion of "comparability" is another reason we have written this book. We believe it essential to demonstrate that the Soviet services are truly unique in function and mission. Failure to recognize the special role of these intelligence and security services, in every aspect of Soviet life, tends to obscure and trivialize the issue. It makes rational comprehension of the Soviet state impossible.

From their beginnings in 1917 to the present, the Soviet secret political police have been used to provide "solutions" to the problems confronting the USSR. They have sealed the frontiers, built and operated the gulags, tamed the citizens, subdued the Red Army, and preserved the ruling oligarchy's authority. In return for these services, the present KGB has achieved prominence and, finally, primacy in the Soviet government. To accept that the "traditions" of the KGB are conventional, ordinary, and "comparable" is to accept the corollary notion that Soviet leaders, though sometimes seemingly erratic, are ordinary men, guided by Marxist-Leninist principles, who are simply trying to operate a conventional government.

A bureaucratic decision can be measured only by its effect. The application of a decision to its intended purpose requires compliance. Compliance either results from voluntary acceptance or must be exacted by enforcement. Because the Bolshevik "revolution" was actually a military coup d'état by a highly organized minority element, and because it did not have popular support, compliance with the Bolsheviks' subsequent decisions was entirely based on the ability of the newly organized secret police to enforce Lenin's version of the minority's will.

To accomplish this vital task, Lenin established, in the month following the coup, an Extraordinary Commission to Combat Counterrevolution, Speculation, and Sabotage as the enforcement arm of the Bolshevik government. With an appetite for acronyms and sinister-sounding allusions, the commission soon came to be referred to, euphemistically, as the "organs."* The term, denoting the various Soviet state security services, is still used by the Soviet government.

The effects of Bolshevik decisions can be measured, in retrospect, by noting some of the organs' dramatic successes in enforcing them:

Under Felix Dzerzhinsky, the secret police saved the Bolshevik armed coup of 1918 and destroyed the only representative government in the history of Russia. Their draconian internal-security actions eliminated *all* non-Bolshevik political parties as "counterrevolutionary." They crushed the Kronstadt rebellion, when soldiers, sailors, and workers who had supported the Bolsheviks in the 1917 coup rose against the "three-year-old autocracy of Communist Commissars."

They invented mass arrests and mass executions, enforced the Great Famine and collectivization, and facilitated Stalin's rise to absolute power. They murdered Sergei Kirov (a putative rival to Stalin) and, at Stalin's direction, produced the theatrical trials in Moscow that ended with the liquidation of every leader who had direct knowledge of Stalin's crimes. They set up the forced-labor camps and pioneered new methods of coercion. They murdered and abducted émigrés, political opponents, and the disaffected in every part of the world. They assassinated Leon Trotsky, recruited Kim Philby and Sir Anthony Blunt, and executed hundreds of thousands of Russian POWs who were forcibly repatriated at the end of World War II.

The secret police became the instrument that produced, over a period of sixty-eight years, 40 million deaths from slave labor, starvation, exposure, and execution. Demographers who have studied Soviet-produced data relating to the USSR's population have been confounded by contradictions. When earlier and more reliable Russian statistics are projected into the present, it becomes apparent that there have been millions of

*The commission's Russian acronym, VChK, led to the use of the term *Cheka,* which came to include all of "the repressive organs of the state."

additional casualties among the unborn. The most conservative estimates support the likelihood that more than 3 million Russians *were never born,* as a result of Stalin's famine. Another 3 million children were abandoned and died during the same period.

On November 26, 1939, and at Stalin's direction, Red Army artillery shelled Soviet soldiers on the Karelian Isthmus, killing four and wounding nine.

Radio Moscow accused the Finns of provocation, and three days later a special Red Army group—the Seventh, Eighth, Ninth, and Tenth armies, twelve rifle divisions, a tank corps, and two separate tank brigades—supported by naval gunfire and units of the Red Air Force, made simultaneous attacks along the Finnish frontier.

The "war" ended at noon on March 13, 1940, with sixty thousand Soviet dead and two hundred thousand wounded. Uncounted additional casualties included the thousands of Red Army officers sent into forced labor camps for failing to secure an easy victory over the Finns.

Of the estimated 20 million Soviet military and civilian casualties resulting from World War II, at least 2 to 4 million died as a consequence of Stalin's policy decisions, enforced by the NKVD, and are not ascribable to enemy combat operations.

After almost seven decades of Bolshevik rule, extrapolations of reliable census data call for a Soviet population of nearly 400 million and not the 262.4 million claimed in 1979. The secret police, more than Stalin alone, are to be credited with this disparity.

The organs continue to keep the Red Army docile, the Soviet populace in a bovine state, and, most importantly, the Communist Party of the Soviet Union (CPSU) in power. Since the beginnings of the Soviet government, much of the world has wanted to see the USSR as a comprehensible modern state that would one day grow tired of Lenin's notion of "continuing war," the subsidizing of international terror, the repression of captive populations, and the menacing of other nations by military aggression. The prospect of such a metamorphosis seems unlikely if one understands the role of the Soviet secret police.

Because they have no analogue elsewhere in history, examination of their role is essential to any understanding of the USSR.

It is generally accepted that Adolf Hitler was a mad, demonic slayer of millions. Proof of the Holocaust includes 32 million captured Nazi documents, miles of German photographic film, and thousands of survivors and first-person witnesses who can attest to its scope and barbarity. The Nazi crimes are all the more dramatic because they are so exhaustively documented. Before embarking on mass slaughter, however, Hitler drove thousands of highly credible witnesses to the West. And at the time of the German nonaggression pact with the Soviet Union, he sent hundreds of

German communists to safe haven in the USSR. Those loyal adherents of Stalin who were returned to the socialist homeland, with few exceptions, died there at the hands of the secret police. As a matter of Soviet policy, witnesses to Soviet crimes seldom survived.

There is no dispute about the enormity of Hitler's Holocaust. But it is equally important to be as aware of the accomplishments of the Soviet secret police, which brought death to at least four times as many Russians, Poles, Jews, Latvians, Lithuanians, Estonians, Japanese, Koreans, Chinese, Gypsies, and Romanians as Hitler did in his eleven years as leader of the "1,000-year Reich."

As a minority, the Soviet Jews have been most consistently victimized by the Soviet government. In the early days, however, the Bolsheviks' guarantee that anti-Semitism was a criminal offense, and that fairness and equal justice would protect against recurrent repression, brought the first ray of hope to many Central-European Jews. Some of these achieved prominence in the days following the coup, when the secret police were quick to recruit those among them who spoke foreign languages, had traveled abroad, and knew something about the outside world. The obvious importance of Trotsky, Grigori Zinoviev, Lev Kamenev, Maxim Litvinov, Rosengoltz, and others gave substance to the hope that anti-Semitism finally would be rooted out of Russia.

With the ascendancy of Stalin, a special kind of anti-Semitism began to reappear. Soviet NKVD documents, captured by the Germans and later taken by the United States, detail cases in which orthodox Soviet Jews were arrested for anti-Semitism in the late thirties. Since the orthodox Jews had encouraged other Jews to observe religious holidays, the Soviets took the position that they were trying to induce the non-religious Jews to refuse (for religious reasons) to fulfill their "work norms," thereby making an economic attack on the socialist state. That the orthodox Jews had addressed the call only to nonreligious Jews was clearly an attempt to cause them harm, and hence proof of the deliberate commission of an anti-Semitic crime. The orthodox Jews were arrested and sent into the coercive labor camps to die.

In the early thirties the Soviets organized and subsidized various militant antifascist organizations, which were represented as acting in the interest of the European Jews who were being menaced by Hitler. The strategy was predicated on the broad assertion that, among all the nations, only the USSR had the prescience and courage to speak out against Hitler's attacks on the Jews. Begun as a Soviet propaganda effort, the campaign won broad support and succeeded in deflecting world attention from the fact that the secret police under Stalin had already extinguished more human lives than Hitler was to account for in his entire career. The nonaggression pact of 1939 instantly reversed the polarity of Soviet strategy. Support of the antifascist organizations went from open Soviet sponsorship to clandestine manipulation. The antifascist campaign had never been intended as an instrument for helping persecuted Jews but as a means by which the USSR could benefit from associating with a humanitarian cause and, at the same time, gain access to previously denied political areas.

When the new state of Israel was established in 1948, Golda Meir was sent to Moscow as its first ambassador. The spontaneous demonstrations that attended her arrival infuriated Stalin. He saw the warm welcome as confirmation of his basic conviction that the Jews were "insufferable nationalists" and did not deserve his trust. He directed that Jews be removed from sensitive positions in the Soviet government, especially in the state security apparatus. At the time of his death in 1953, there were none remaining in important posts within the Soviet secret police.

The emigration of Soviet Jews to Israel and elsewhere has fallen off sharply. Soviet writers have once again been advised by the KGB that it is permissible to produce new "studies" reflecting discredit on Jews. Press accounts following the death of Donald Maclean in Moscow noted a curious sign on the wall of his apartment declaring that anti-Semites were unwelcome in his home. It is odd that a British ideologue of yesteryear, in the capital of the socialist camp, felt compelled to warn his visitors of his continued upholding of a principle that, if it ever existed, was abandoned long ago by the Soviet government.

In the thirties, as a part of the antifascist campaign, the USSR was also promoting the "united front" coalitions in Europe. Simultaneously, the USSR applied for admission to the League of Nations. Once granted, Soviet membership in the League was of short duration. The decision to exploit the Nazi attack on Poland by sending Soviet troops to seize and occupy eastern Poland, and the unprovoked attack on Finland in 1940, resulted in expulsion of the USSR from that body. These Soviet "victories"—occupying part of a militarily defeated neighbor and waging wholly unwarranted bloody war against a tiny and nonthreatening adjacent state—reflected the insecurity of a leadership characterized by the now well-established technique of preying on the weak and the wounded.

The performance of the Red Army in the Finnish war was pitiable. There were terrible Soviet losses because of poor leadership, lack of training, inadequate supplies, starvation, and freezing. The secret police, through the political officers in the army, meddled in the command structure and countermanded military orders. The Red Army leadership was blamed for failing to win an easy war; they were arrested and sent off to labor camps. At the time of the German attack on the USSR, the surviving troop leaders were released from the prison camps and put back into the Red Army to fight in defense of the motherland.

Although the alliance with Hitler brought certain rewards, in the form of a large part of eastern Poland, the betrayed and stunned party faithful throughout the world were given whispered assurances that it was only a stratagem to gain time. Having gained a little time, the secret police spent some of it executing the twelve thousand Polish officers who had voluntarily surrendered to the Soviet forces occupying eastern Poland after the German attack in September 1939. Their graves were later discovered by the Germans, who, for their own propaganda purposes, called for an international commission to verify and document Soviet authorship of the massacre in the Katyn Forest.

The trials, the nonaggression pact with Germany, Stalin's reinstitution of brutal postwar repression, the forced repatriation of Russian war prisoners, the USSR's chronic inability to achieve even pre-World-War-I levels of agricultural production (86 million tons of grain in 1913, against an annual average of 80 million tons during the last four years of Stalin's rule, 1949–1953), and a crushing military economy have combined to make a telling indictment of the Soviet system. Other Soviet-originated statistics indicate that the infant death rate is climbing, life expectancy is falling, and alcoholism (the state being the only distiller and seller of alcohol in any form) is rising steadily. These grim factors suggest that the life of the average Soviet citizen is less than it should be. Modern Russians have been habituated to low expectations, and after almost seventy years, only a rapidly diminishing number of citizens still live who can recall life, however barren, without the Bolsheviks.

The USSR's economic, agricultural, and ideological problems are basically what they were fifty-five years ago. The burdens of central planning, operating inefficiencies, low productivity in the labor force, and major inadequacies in resource allocations still prevent the Soviet Union from elevating its standard of life. Although there have been impressive statistical improvements since Stalin's early days, most of the hard-won gains have been lost to endemic, institutionalized corruption. The practice of misrepresenting, at every level, data relating to inventories, costs, production norms, and the like dates back to Lenin's New Economic Policy, in which the central planners set unattainable goals that could be achieved only by adulterating the product or falsifying the statistics. (Although the Greeks might not have had a word to describe this activity, the Russians do: It's called *tufta,* and is a part of the common vocabulary.)

The inherent weaknesses and vulnerabilities of the Soviet system, which the KGB is bound to defend, have naturally affected the KGB. More is known about the organization, its personnel and methods, than ever before. This body of evidence is not a tribute to any Western success but is the simple and direct consequence of persistent Soviet failures.

To illustrate the role of the Soviet secret police, it is essential to outline the internal and external political factors that affected their growth and direction, and to present accurate, documentable facts about several types of operations that bear their characteristic imprint. The means and the methods described in this book are wholly consistent with known Soviet practices of the day. Publicly available documents are cited in the Chapter Notes. An effort has been made to convey a sense of the extent of the Soviet secret policemen's reach and the broad nature of their "work," including covers, subterfuges, disinformation strategies, technical deceptions, and agent recruitment and handling techniques. The process is complicated by the fact that all secret services devote much energy to safeguarding their methods and, to whatever degree possible, their sources. Still, the salient personalities who played important roles in these operations are known, by at least one name. Their methods and accomplishments are also known—too often after the fact and through testimony of victims.

Internal Soviet political events have played a role in producing waves of important Soviet deserters to the West, particularly in the period before and during the Great Purges. The undocumented parts of this book are based entirely on information derived from interviews and papers, including unpublished manuscripts provided by former Soviet "workers." Among this group are men and a few women who served in Germany, Spain, Britain, France, and the United States, some of whom were arrested and imprisoned during the purges. Former service officials, confined to the gulags, attempted to reconstruct their own histories of the events and personalities that brought about their arrest and imprisonment. Because many of the "workers" spoke languages other than Russian, they were able to learn from Polish, Latvian, Japanese, and German prisoners about the fate of colleagues who had served in foreign intelligence and security assignments.

In some instances the beginning, middle, and end of a case is known. In other cases, the event was not recognized as a Soviet operation until years later, when the participants on both sides were long dead. Since these events occurred before the Great Purges, in which OGPU case officers themselves deserted or were executed, it is unlikely that any reliable Soviet versions still exist. Reconstruction of the older cases evokes the *Rashomon* effect, in which we find first-person witnesses in absolute contradiction. Sources of great personal integrity have found later that they played unintended roles in furthering Soviet deceptions. In conventional historical research, one finds deliberate deception, assumed identities, false "legends," and continuous clandestine support of a major world power as occasionally engaging exceptions. Here, they are the rule.

Valid Soviet documents are not accessible at present. And it is not reasonable to expect that they will become available for research, so long as the organs exist. It is known, however, that even internal Soviet documents have been selectively withdrawn or altered to allow the "rehabilitation" of various Chekists who were executed as Japanese, British, or Zionist spies during Stalin's time. (A rational mind must balk at Stalin's insistence that at least three of the heads of his most powerful bureaucracy were in the employ of Tokyo and London, and that his Red Army marshals worked for Berlin.)

In the main, Soviet military-intelligence (GRU) officers have been better educated and of higher quality than their counterparts in the state security (KGB). Contrary to expectations, GRU officers have also exhibited a greater loyalty to their superiors than have the more highly politicized state security officers. An analysis of cases that produced important data for the USSR indicates that GRU professional abilities in the intelligence field have been generally superior to those of the KGB. The GRU does not have responsibilities in the areas of abduction and assassination operations, safeguarding party loyalty, suppressing the populace, guarding the borders, or operating the gulags. GRU officers consider themselves the professional as well as the moral superiors of their cousins in the KGB.

It is useful to bear in mind that the state security organization has co-opted many important GRU cases, as well as some of its more gifted officers. In every instance, the KGB has the authority to preempt the GRU. Case after case has had its inception in the GRU, only to be taken over by state security. To ensure that no GRU or satellite service independently develops a promising operational lead, all file checks are made in Moscow by the state security. The Center* can and does exclude all subordinate service interests at will.

The practice of borrowing GRU officers for "special tasks" has been extensively documented. In the past, technical and scientific cases employed GRU officers because the secret police had very few officers of sufficient education and competence to handle these demanding cases. In the last twenty years, the state security has begun to rectify this weakness by instituting a program devoted to the development of technical and scientific specialists within its ranks.

In improving the educational level of the state security, new vulnerabilities have become evident in the form of intellectual corruption and indiscipline. Cynicism and careerism have completely replaced the ideals, however skewed, of some of the early "Honored Chekists." An

---

*The term "Center" is not to be considered slang, but is the usual and appropriate term applied to the directing level of the state security. Although it is a "headquarters" and has been moved to different locations at different times, Soviet defectors do not refer to it as anything other than the Center.

incentive-and-reward system has replaced the ideological cement that bound the early zealots. Today, privileges, possessions, and perks are the carrots that make the donkey run. However, the growing venality and corruption of today's state security organs in no way diminish their ability to discharge their principal functions. For all its internal problems, the KGB is no less dangerous.

There are obvious comparisons to be made between the accomplishments of Stalin in 1927 and the Andropov of 1983. Both were committed to the accretion of absolute power. Stalin's early actions were concerned with ridding himself of Trotsky and, later, the Old Bolsheviks who made up the corporate memory. Yuri Andropov, on assumption of office in 1982, set in motion the eradication of all residual traces of the Brezhnev *banda* (or "gang"). Stalin didn't completely control the organs until he put his own men in charge in the early thirties. But Andropov had control of the KGB on the day he took office. Stalin had to wait years, until the mid-thirties, to gain absolute control of the Red Army. Andropov achieved this goal within a few months. Early in his reign as General Secretary, he allowed a few, muted signals that he might be preparing to use the costly adventure in Afghanistan as the basis of a thorough "investigation" into military corruption, bad generalship, narcotics smuggling, desertions, disaffection, and the unforgivable crime of failure.

Now, rather than being shot, as they would have been in Stalin's day, the generals could be encouraged to retire, leaving vacancies to be filled with loyalists of the new regime. If necessary, official inquiries would find whatever evidence was required to prove malfeasance or worse. The guilty would not be forced to confess in public. And should Red Army defendants speak out against the state, they most likely would be found, as was General Grigorenko, to be "mentally ill" and taken off to a state-security-run psychiatric hospital for treatment and rest. Securing the absolute subservience of the army is the last step necessary for any KGB chairman and his state security acolytes in achieving the power of Stalin.

There can be no doubt that the Soviet secret police are more sophisticated than before. In 1971 one of Andropov's senior KGB officers explained to an arrested dissident the KGB's enlightened policies for dealing with such criminals: "We will break some of you, we will buy others and throw the rest to the West." With the KGB controlling the security of all Soviet nuclear weapons, nothing can happen without KGB participation. In fact, *nothing* starts or stops in the USSR without the KGB's retaining the power to intervene.

This book, then is a chronicle of the Soviet secret police and of some of the men and women who pioneered therein. It is also intended to make it clear that there can be no rational analysis of the Soviet state that omits consideration of the overwhelming authority of the Soviet secret police—the secret that drives the engine of Soviet power.

1 · The Cheka

On a bitter gray Thursday, Lenin signed the document that established the Extraordinary Commission to Combat Counterrevolution, Speculation, and Sabotage. This ordinary act of December 20, 1917, marked the birth of a malign organizational creature of vast and terrible implications. With the Bolsheviks' taste for efficiency and modernity, the ponderous formal title of the commission was soon reduced to VChK, or simply "Cheka." To chair the new commission, Lenin had selected a widely experienced forty-year-old Polish revolutionary radical named Felix Edmundovich Dzerzhinsky, a man who combined high intelligence with fierce dedication to the revolution. Dzerzhinsky's selection later proved to have been an inspired choice for the regime and a calamitous one for the Russian people.

Within a week of his appointment, Dzerzhinsky gave a reception at his Petrograd headquarters in the Gradonachalstvo building at Gorokhovia #2 to celebrate Lenin's decision and to toast the founder.[1] In addition to a number of his revolutionary comrades and former fellow inmates of the Czar's prisons, where he'd spent more than a quarter of his life, Dzerzhinsky invited two Americans. They were John Reed and his declared wife, Louise Bryant.[2] As the evening progressed, the vodka-induced collegiality gave way to sentimental recitations of the emotional impact of the October coup d'état. The reception also marked the end of "the ten days that shook the world," about which Reed would later write.

Dzerzhinsky called for attention and surveyed the now silent crowd. Most were later to fill important posts in the Cheka, and it seemed appropriate for him to speak briefly about the future and to put them on unmistakable notice that theirs was the responsibility to "save and protect the revolution." In explaining the way in which the responsibility was to be discharged, he said quietly, but with great force: "To save the revolution, we must first destroy the counterrevolutionaries." At the time, no one could have realized that the discharge of this simple-sounding mission would take thirty years and as many as 40 million lives.

John Reed's presence at the gathering was neither accidental nor without significance. Although the October coup that catapulted Lenin and the minority Bolshevik faction into power had been successful, Dzerzhinsky knew that their grip on that power was tenuous at best. He also knew that Reed was a revolutionary communist idealist who could be counted upon to extol and propagate the abstract virtues of the Bolshevik regime. Dzerzhinsky's confidence in Reed's willingness to act as an evangelist for the cause was not misplaced, nor was it based on whim. It was, rather, the result of extensive inquiries, a kind of positive vetting, which Dzerzhinsky carried out before the coup.

During those first fateful days and until his appointment to head the Cheka, Dzerzhinsky had been commandant of Smolny Institute, a huge building on the eastern edge of Petrograd, which had been seized in February 1917 as the headquarters of the Petrograd Soviet and the All-Russian Central Executive Committee of the First Congress of the Soviets.[3]

As such, Smolny was the hub of revolutionary activity and the provisional government's command and control center. It also served to bring together under one roof, though in separate wings of the great gray building, leaders of the various factions who tirelessly schemed and vied for control over the revolution and the new government that might finally eventuate.

As commandant of Smolny, Dzerzhinsky was responsible for the physical security of the building and its occupants. More importantly, he also controlled the building's internal and external communications system, which enabled him to keep Lenin and Trotsky fully informed of their opposition's plans as well as the actual progress of the revolution elsewhere in Russia.

Reed's later relationship with Dzerzhinsky, following his return to Russia in 1920, is not known. However, in the early days prior to and following the coup, Reed enjoyed considerable privilege. The fact is reflected in the issuance of a pass to Smolny, signed by the commandant and made out in the name of "John Reed, Correspondent of the American Socialist Press."[4] At the time, access to Smolny was carefully restricted, and special guard battalions were deployed inside and around the building to prevent assassination attempts and attacks against the headquarters itself. Reed's pass to enter the building at will connoted a level of trust. Implicit in the permission to use Smolny as his exclusive newsbeat was Reed's collateral reporting function. No other foreign journalist was afforded similar treatment by the revolutionary authorities.

Although Reed's role in the October coup is not directly acknowledged in official Soviet references, it's clear from contemporary accounts,
as well as Trotsky's writings, that the Bolsheviks received and acted on
information that only Reed, with his press "cover," and Dzerzhinsky,
with his band of wiretappers, were in a position to acquire.[5]

Thus, from the time of the Cheka's creation, Dzerzhinsky looked on
John Reed as a potentially valuable intelligence asset. Reed could be
depended on to put a benign interpretation on any act, however brutal,
that served the Bolshevik Party. It is probable that Reed can be counted
as the first U.S. citizen to act as a Soviet disinformation agent and, certainly, the only one to have been issued Soviet credentials certifying his
role.

Reed's subsequent writings attest to the fact that he was a "witting"
Bolshevik asset. Whether he remained a convinced supporter after observing Dzerzhinsky's counterrevolutionary excesses during the civil war
is not known. At the time of his death in 1920, several of his contemporaries claimed that his revolutionary zeal had waned appreciably.[6]

The role of the Cheka and its successor organizations—from the
GPU, OGPU, NKVD, etc., down to today's KGB—has remained an
internal contradiction in the characterization of Marxism-Leninism as a
palliative for social and economic ills.

Although it has been demonstrated that an organized and disciplined
militant group can initiate a revolution, it has also been shown repeatedly
that it cannot hold power without the will and capacity to beat back any
and all residual counterrevolutionary forces, including the power it initially deposed.

Further, if a revolutionary group attempts concurrently to impose a
new or alien ideology, the intensity of the counterrevolutionary opposition is expanded to include otherwise passive segments of the population.
Revolutionary theory is clear on both these points. Counterrevolutionary
theory and practice is much less precise.

Certain parallels exist among the counterrevolutionary actions taken
in the French, Chinese, and Russian revolutions. However, only in the
Russian experience were the counteractions an integral component from
the beginning. These aggressive and absolute counterrevolutionary principles governed Soviet actions and, more than any other single factor,
made it possible for the Bolshevik minority to seize, expand, and continue control of all of Russia, its people and institutions.

At the inception of the Cheka in December 1917 it was seen by some
as a temporary expedient, and its original mission—i.e., to deal with
counterrevolutionary elements—was not seriously questioned. If there
was any popular assumption regarding the Cheka, it was that the commission would gradually but certainly disappear with the establishment of a

stable government. It was not fully recognized at the time that the Cheka was the Bolsheviks' only means of protecting the power they had captured and that the Cheka, in an evolved form, was a permanent, enabling instrument of Bolshevik rule.

In the beginning, the Cheka had a staff of only twenty-three, in addition to a teen-aged female secretary and a collegium of five representatives from the various revolutionary factions who were expected to oversee operations and to prevent Dzerzhinsky's abuse of the commission's vague authority to "protect the revolution."

From December 20, 1917, to November 2, 1918, the Cheka existed and operated in a bureaucratic netherworld. According to N. V. Krylenko, chairman of the Supreme Revolutionary Tribunal: "Up to November 1918 it [the Cheka] existed without any statutes or laws."[7] The absence of officially mandated restraints or specifically delegated authority enabled Dzerzhinsky to do with the Cheka what he and Lenin judged to be in the Bolshevik Party's best interest.

The detailed day-by-day history of the Cheka's first year makes an engaging study in the use and abuse of bureaucratic power to gain dictatorial control over a nation's people.[8] It was during this period that Dzerzhinsky began to construct the organs, which eventually converted Russia into what Vladimir Petrov termed the "Empire of Fear."

How and why did Dzerzhinsky succeed where others failed, in the creation of a system of awesome power which survived his death and the turbulent successions from Lenin to the present? A part of the answer lies in a combination of fortuitous circumstances which Dzerzhinsky recognized and exploited with telling effect.

The first of these was the unexpected success of the largely spontaneous uprising in February 1917 that toppled the Romanoff regime and left no institution in its place. Neither the czarist secret police (the Okhrana) nor the Russian Imperial Army was able to assert, or reassert, an effective central government. The rot of the Romanoff regime was so pervasive that when it fell it collapsed in its entirety. The event produced a devastating effect on the whole of the institutional fabric of Russia: its bureaucracy, business, courts, and especially the army and police. It also gave Dzerzhinsky a valuable roster of "counterrevolutionary enemies," bound to the Romanoffs and their patronage.

The second circumstance favoring the Bolsheviks was the chaos that existed in Russia during the Cheka's first year of existence. Disorder flourished in the first revolutionary government and in the society at large, creating a mammoth diversion of public interest and enabling Dzerzhinsky to go freely about the task of building an extralegal organization without significant resistance from any quarter.

"As originally conceived, the Cheka was an administrative organ whose purpose was primarily investigative, and certainly not judicial."[9] Dzerzhinsky and Lenin skillfully nurtured and publicized this view among the Bolsheviks' opposition in the revolutionary government. It was a further diversion to conceal the activities and intentions of the Cheka.

The stratagem worked extremely well. Reports of Cheka excesses were deflected by Dzerzhinsky and Lenin as aberrational acts of individuals who, in their revolutionary passion, had acted without or exceeded their proper authority. The "rogue Chekists" explanation was badly worn by the summer of 1918; however, it gave Dzerzhinsky sufficient time to establish the Cheka firmly within the bureaucratic structure. It also allowed time to build an organization, which was now expanding at a rapid rate.

In March 1918, Lenin secretly moved the revolutionary government from Petrograd to Moscow by armored train. Coincident with the move, Dzerzhinsky and his growing band of Chekists, now augmented by their own combat detachment of Cheka troops (drawn largely from the ranks of Czar Nicholas's personal bodyguard), traveled overland to establish their new headquarters in Moscow. The selected site was Bolshaia Lubianka #11, which they occupied on March 30.[10]

The headquarters remained at that location until early December 1920, at which time it was moved to Bolshaia Lubianka #2, a building once occupied by the All-Russian Insurance Company.[11] Both buildings were imposing examples of the fortresslike architecture that then characterized Moscow. "Within two months of arrival in Moscow the Cheka had so increased in size that it spread into an adjoining house."[12] The scope of expansion during its first year is made more impressive by the fact that it was matched by a similar enlargement in the number and size of the Cheka's combat detachments. The military units gave Dzerzhinsky the added means essential to make the Cheka a more credible Shield and Sword of the Revolution.

By August 1918 the burgeoning size and increasing actions of the secret army of Chekists provoked calls from Lenin's opponents for a commission to investigate the Cheka.[13] Although a commission was formed, it had little or no restraining effect on the Cheka, or on its subsequent evolution and practices—not because of the conventional ineptitude ascribed to most governmental commissions, but because of an unanticipated event: an unsuccessful attempt on Lenin's life by Fania Kaplan on August 30, 1918.[14]

Kaplan's attack was fortuitous opportunity. At the time, the revolutionary leaders, including Lenin, were partially hoist on the petard of their socialist rhetoric. How could the system deal with a person such as Kaplan when it publicly called for a classless society governed by rule of law, and widely trumpeted an abhorrence of the death penalty?

Although the Cheka had carried out illegal "liquidations," the idea of fair and open trials without the prospect of capital punishment was still part of the socialist creed. But now that an attempt had been made on Lenin himself, it seemed appropriate to use the Kaplan attack as a pretext to abandon the revolution's idealism and to loose the Cheka. In a small voice, without detail or amplification, *Izvestia* reported on September 4, 1918: "By decision of the Cheka, the execution took place of the Right SR, Fanny Roid Kaplan, who shot at Comrade Lenin."[15]

The disposition of Kaplan quite literally endorsed the Cheka's license to kill. It also marked the start of the organs' program of mass terror. Hitherto, the Cheka had been selective in its liquidation of "counterrevolutionary enemies of the state," but now the moderate approach to murder was abandoned in favor of one designed to eliminate all potential opposition. The Chekists, in essence, became Lenin's avengers in a fratricidal class war.

The use of terror is a two-edged sword. Although summary executions, torture, illegal imprisonment, or exile can be used to eliminate a regime's opposition, these tactics have been known to engender further opposition where none existed before. Terror also produces a climate in which essential activities are suspended and little gets done. The Cheka's terror tactics, although apparently random, were actually aimed at those segments of the population that represented the "resistance potential," i.e., incipient counterrevolutionaries. The Cheka chose its targets according to their vulnerability and the effectiveness of their opposition to Lenin. The intellectuals and liberals who had advocated reform, rather than destruction, of the Romanoff regime were the first to go. From Dzerzhinsky and Lenin's point of view, the intellectuals and liberals, as a class, had to be extirpated. The revolution had to speak with one voice, and that voice was Lenin's. There could be no "middle way," no multiple interpretations of Marx's ambiguous doctrines, only endorsement of Lenin's wisdom.

As a group, the intellectuals and liberals were particularly vulnerable. They hardly constituted an organized political force. Most were encumbered with records of little or no effective opposition to the excesses of the former autocratic regime. Because many had benefited and been subsidized by the Court in the prerevolutionary period, they were slow to take an antimonarchical political stance. Their passivity was, to a degree, predicated on the false assumption that they would be called upon to contribute to the cultural pretensions of the new rulers. Having supped at the Czar's trough, they were now regarded as hypocrites of the lowest order. As the Cheka terror mounted, fewer and fewer among those classed as intellectuals and liberals were willing to come forward in defense of their friends, associates, or co-ideologists; to do so was to invite the Cheka's vengeance.

With the voices and pens of the intellectuals stilled by arrest or death, the Cheka turned on other societal elements. A few, like Maxim Gorky, were allowed to continue to write and speak in order to promote the myth of the open nature of the Soviet state. The new targets were the bourgeoisie, the decamped professionals of the Imperial Russian Army, dissident peasant groups, and, in Lenin's words, the "slothful and lazy bureaucrats."[16]

The time of the first terror was marked by unprecedented and vicious bloodletting. The techniques of brutal assassination, the primitive forms of torture, the barbarity of the prisons and the instruments of coercion employed against the "enemies" of the Bolshevik state were sometimes equaled but never exceeded by even the most inventive sadists of the Gestapo and SS.[17]

Because the terror tactics were inconceivable, morally abhorrent, and beyond the experience of most, only a few Western scholars have been willing to examine the process in terms of the intentions of those who designed and executed the terror and the appalling results derived from its application.

Lenin's prerevolutionary writings foreshadow nothing about the employment of mass terror in the postrevolutionary consolidation phase, unless it can be interpreted as a subsidiary function of "conflict." His references to the problem of counterrevolutionaries suggest that such persons are more consistently seen as needing rehabilitation and reeducation rather than liquidation.[18]

Also, the counterrevolutionaries are described as a minority element in the total, "just" socialist society. Once Trotsky delivered the successful coup, Lenin was immediately beset by fears that others were actively conspiring to take it from him. Lenin's personal dread, and his growing conviction that the revolution could not be directed and controlled by committee, compelled him to opt for dictatorial powers. In this context it is not surprising, given the pretext of Kaplan's attack, that the Cheka was empowered to eliminate *all* opposition to Bolshevik rule.

Dzerzhinsky saw nothing wrong with mass terror as a means to advance and protect the revolution. He reportedly wept as he signed the death warrants of hundreds and thousands of persons who had committed no crime. But his alleged lamentations did not deter his pen.[19]

Although the Kaplan attack sparked the first program of mass terror, it was clearly the political efficacy of the method that brought about its permanent inclusion among the Bolsheviks' weapons of control.

By the end of the bloody civil war, the Red Army, led by Trotsky, certified the Bolsheviks' continuation in power, at least for a while. The intensity of the war itself excused the exercise of summary justice upon those who violated the regime's martial law decrees.[20] The Cheka's victims were, again, mostly those who had been marked previously by Lenin

as belonging to classes of "enemies of the state." Even though many of
the victims were sympathetic to the Red cause, their elimination was
thought warranted by their prior associations and prerevolutionary status.
Not surprisingly, many members of the Red Army who believed that
their service in the civil war was sufficient to overcome objections to their
earlier allegiances were summarily eliminated by the Cheka once the war
was won.[21]

The victory of the Red Army was another tribute to the organizational genius of Trotsky, who, in the face of great obstacles, succeeded in
raising and fielding an effective force. The Imperial Russian Army, in
every respect, had ceased to exist as an organized military force at the
onset of the civil war. The "People's Army," which emerged in the immediate wake of the October Revolution, was a conglomeration of ragged,
disorganized military and quasi-military groups, some no more than
armed mobs. Others of these motley organizations were residual units of
the Imperial Army that now, without their former czarist officers, remained haphazardly mobilized. Some units consisted of self-selected revolutionary militia that alternately practiced brigandage and their own
version of revolutionary vigilantism. With truly remarkable administrative skill, Trotsky was able to organize and redirect these elements
into a force sufficient to defeat the White Armies.

It is essential to note that the White Armies were also made up of
patchwork organizations based on Imperial Army units that had remained relatively intact when Russia left the World War in 1917 and
subsequent to signing of the Brest-Litovsk Treaty in early March 1918.[22]
The leadership of the anti-Bolshevik forces included many of those commanders who had already demonstrated their ineptitude against the Germans. The troops were exhausted and hardly motivated by the prospect
that, even if they were victorious, the best that could happen would be
institution of another harsh, autocratic rule.

Out of necessity, Trotsky turned to many former czarist officers to
lead units in the Red Army. Unfortunately, however, neither their military professionalism nor heroic service spared them from successive
purges in the immediate postwar period. Lenin did not oppose the continuation of the Red Army, once the Whites had been defeated, even
though he recognized that it could pose a potential threat to him personally as well as to the Bolshevik Party. In theory, the Revolutionary War
Council controlled the army, but in fact Trotsky's highly personalized and
dynamic leadership had made him the personification of Soviet military
might, which in the post-civil-war period loomed as another potential
source of political danger.

Lenin knew that Trotsky had the military power to oust him from
leadership and to take control of the party. Aside from the real or imag-

ined threat of Trotsky's personal ambition, the Red Army had to remain a disciplined element, subordinated to Lenin, or it would become an immediate and grave danger.

Lenin, with the aid of Dzerzhinsky, approached the problem of gaining and maintaining a politically reliable Red Army in an innovative manner: Responsibility for the security of the Soviet armed forces was assigned to the Cheka's Special Department (*Osobye Otdel* or OO). The authority for this enormous extension of the organs' powers was detailed in a Cheka directive, signed by Dzerzhinsky on February 3, 1919, adopted by the All-Russian Central Executive Committee on February 6, and published as a statute on February 21, 1919.[23]

From the outset the OOs had their work cut out for them. They watched over the loyalty of the officers (and in particular the "military specialists," those former Imperial Army officers who had been recruited by Trotsky and who still outnumbered officers with appropriate proletarian backgrounds). The OOs were not to interfere with the conduct of military duties (unless treason was suspected), but they were to take charge of party work in the Red Army and to carry out political propaganda and educational work among the peasant conscripts. The primary OO role was to ensure the political loyalty and obedience of the armed forces to the Bolshevik regime.[24]

Appending the OOs (or, as they were sometimes called in the West, "political commissars") to the Soviet armed forces does not at first glance appear to be unique. Other despotic regimes have used similar techniques to maintain the political reliability of their legions; however, the power and control of the OOs, which continue to exist in the KGB's Third Chief Directorate, have never been approached.

Some Western military analysts contend that the OOs were (and continue to be) a dead bureaucratic hand on the initiative of the Soviet armed forces. They have been credited with destroying innovation, prohibiting the delegation of authority, and creating a climate in which responsibility is avoided.[25]

According to a former Red Army officer who served during World War II, the OOs trailed the troops into battle, and if a soldier lagged behind during the advance, the OOs would shoot him on the spot. This fact, coupled with complete disregard for recovering battlefield casualties until long after action (another OO-directed solution), made the lot of the Russian soldier especially grim. "The OOs drove the men forward like a herd of cattle and, if wounded, the troops prayed that their wounds would be fatal."[26]

There is obvious truth in the contention that OO methods have adversely affected the Soviet armed forces' performance, but it is also a fact that, from the civil war to the present, the OOs have succeeded in maintaining a degree of political reliability in the forces.

At Dzerzhinsky's direction, the OOs were installed in the Soviet armed forces down to, and including, the platoon level. This pervasive presence was dictated by two major considerations: (1) the genuine need to educate the conscripts in the tenets of Marxism-Leninism and (2) the collateral requirement to project the coercive power of the party as a ubiquitous force. The OOs made it clear that political heresy would not be tolerated and that poor military performance would be regarded as a grave political crime.

The process worked reasonably well. Essentially it replaced the usual means of ensuring military viability—notions of patriotism, appeals to soldierly virtue, comradeship, caring leadership, provision of creature comforts, etc—with the motivational force of fear. The OOs have always been a credible threat.

Implicit in all this was Dzerzhinsky's conception of revolutionary power, which entailed recognition of the fact that the Bolshevik Party required two pillars of support in order to survive. No matter who controlled the party, continuation of power was based on the organs and their ability to control the military forces. In this scheme the OOs, from their inception to the present day, have succeeded in keeping the Soviet armed forces under control. A measure of this division of labor in the Cheka under Dzerzhinsky was that one third of the budget went to the OOs. Current estimates of the present cost of the OOs remains at about the same percentage of a total budget that has increased by several orders of magnitude.[27]

The organs' control over the widely divergent Russian populace of some 130 million (c. 1918) who lived within the fifteen republics required tactics of a different nature, but the methods were related to those used by the OOs. Terror remained the most utilitarian method of control. Three varieties were systematically employed: (1) individual, uncoordinated assassination attacks against dissidents; (2) programmatic acts of terrorism directed toward a specific objective, such as the elimination of "counterrevolutionary" guerrilla groups; and (3) indiscriminate mass terror used to consolidate Bolshevik power.[28] Under the third method, entire classes of Russian society such as the bourgeoisie, landowners, and "capitalists" were completely exterminated by the Cheka. Other minorities, including many Jews and most of the religious, were described as falling into "multiple" class designations and were also targeted as enemies.

A senior KGB defector who, as part of his official training, was required to study the actual results of the organs' terror tactics said that the organs "annihilated some 20 million innocent Soviet citizens in their prisons and forced labor camps."[29] In the prison in the basement of Cheka headquarters at Lubianka #2, the preferred method of execution was a single bullet fired, without warning, into the base of the skull.[30]

The Western mind has trouble coping with the enormity of 20 million executions or murders. Even Stalin said, "One man's death is a tragedy; 10,000 deaths is merely a statistic."[31]

Revolutionary theory is consistent in its insistence that revolutionary success carries within it the seeds of counterrevolution. The Bolsheviks' preemptive attacks on those who *might,* at some future time, have reason to oppose them was without precedent. It was the impeccable logic of terror.[32]

Lenin's revolutionary rhetoric concerning the use of mass terror does not constitute a clear endorsement of its automatic use in the consolidation phase of the revolution.[33] Lenin did not oppose mass terror on tactical or moral grounds, but he was acutely aware of its costs and risks. Encouraged by Dzerzhinsky, the organs moved to traumatize the populace. Where Trotsky had given Lenin military victory, Dzerzhinsky gave him a more enduring gift, the Soviet police state.

Dzerzhinsky's *tour de force* in creating the mechanism to control the Russian populace was not an accident. Just as the organs were effective in using the OOs to control the armed forces, they were equally able to exert absolute mastery over the populace. Their technical success can be attributed to their sound conceptual basis and their exceptional knowledge of the behaviorial responses of their targeted enemy, the Russian people. The principal component of the concept was a new kind of coercion. Not based merely on fear, torture, and terroristic acts, it had as its objective the elimination of mutual trust.

By creating an atmosphere in which all persons, especially friends and close relatives, became suspect provocateurs, the organs left no one in whom a victim could confide. A neighbor picked up by the organs in an indiscriminate mass-arrest sweep would not survive "investigation" without accusing close friends as well as casual acquaintances and family members of "counterrevolutionary" crimes. To have made any kind of adverse comment about the government or its leaders was a guarantee of eventual arrest. Children were encouraged and rewarded by their teachers for giving "evidence" of their parents' anti-Soviet sentiments. The process—one arrest leading to the incrimination of eight to ten additional individuals, no one of whom could hope to survive without implicating still more innocent people—devastated trust. Failure to contribute new suspects to the ever-growing list of those to be arrested simply comfirmed to the organs that the arrestee was protecting others who held anti-Soviet attitudes. It was not possible to extricate oneself once in the hands of the Cheka without becoming a denouncer of innocent people. A corollary form of coercion was expressed in direct threats against immediate family members. Torture and the deprivation of food, water, and rest simply accelerated the process. In prison holding areas, the organs made extensive use of provocateurs who tried to gain knowledge of the arrestee's greatest fear so that the information could be used against him in later interrogations.

As trust and confidence were destroyed, so were the prospects of seditious behavior. It was clearly not possible to consider joining an underground resistance organization, because those that existed were known to be already under the control and direction of the organs. The result of the mass-arrest campaign was a national near paralysis born of fear. To a remarkable degree, Dzerzhinsky succeeded in eliminating any counterrevolutionary potential that might have existed among the Russian citizenry.

The process of tightening constraints on the Soviet populace continued with the imposition of additional internal controls. One of the more effective means of reducing the internal security problem to negligible proportions was to prevent free movement of citizens within the country. The Russians were about to become participants in the first phase of what would later come to be called "population control."

Like most of Dzerzhinsky's designs, the plan reflected a capacity for malign minutiae. A new identity document was prepared for issuance to all Soviet citizens. The massive program was presaged by assurances from the government that, by this measure, a prompt end would be put to the counterrevolutionary wreckers responsible for the visible failures in the Soviet economy: inadequate food supplies and the persistent shortage of habitable dwellings. The Russians were once more psychologically prepared to cooperate with the organs in surrendering more of their limited freedom in the belief that, by their willing compliance, living conditions would improve.

To a significant segment of the population, the internal identity document was recognized for what it was: a way of isolating those who, by reason of birth or prior service, would fail to qualify as Soviet citizens. Among this large element of the population were those with ties to the outside world, those who were, even in distant degree, relatives of "political criminals," and of course those who had been identified with previous non-Bolshevik political factions. Also in this group were thousands of conventional criminals, many of whom had been released under the benign amnesty of the first moments following the coup. For them, the application for an identity card meant the likelihood of immediate rearrest. The socialists' precept that criminals were the natural product of corrupt and exploitative societies had since been revised to exclude burglars, forgers, and most other chronic malefactors.

In the early twenties there were bands of veterans who had fought against the Bolsheviks and had later moved to remote areas and changed their names, simply trying to survive the consolidation phase of the new government. They lived outside the society in the fragile hope that someday they could return to their towns and villages as peaceable citizens. Now that prospect disappeared, and with no alternative, they waited for their eventual capture.

In obtaining an identity document, it was essential for the applicant to respond to a lengthy series of questions relating to family, education, work experience, and political status (party member, candidate, aspirant?). As a part of the control mechanism, it was also required that each person produce a "guarantor," prepared to give assurance of continued good conduct. Soliciting guarantors proved to be very difficult, since in this dangerous and distrustful period few were prepared to attest to the loyalty of another. Having once given written assurance about someone's future behavior, the guarantor, in the view of the organs, assumed responsibility for any subsequent criminal acts. If the guarantor himself was later arrested in connection with a "crime," his relationship with the former applicant could be construed as incriminating to both individuals.

Possession of a valid identity document became an imperative. To tighten the cinch, giving aid, solace, shelter, or support to an undocumented Russian became a crime. All means of travel were controlled and free movement ceased. The identity document, then as now, was the *sine qua non* of a Soviet citizen's existence. Without it, there were no jobs, no food, no housing, and no escape.

In the scheme for population control, identity documents represented an important step in closing the internal security loop. It was gratifying indeed to have the citizenry come to the police and disclose their frailties rather than to sustain the tiresome necessity of continuing the mass arrests.

As an obvious adjunct to the controls already in effect, the organs added two subordinate organizations, the Frontier VChK (border guard) and the Railway VChK. The frontier guard had been founded originally to seal off the border between Russia and Germany, consistent with the terms of the Brest-Litovsk Treaty. The railway guards were initially charged with protecting from theft by starving peasants the food shipments en route to the cities from the countryside.

The organs took over these elements in the midst of the civil war, and the harsh new actions that followed were thought essential to ward off collapse of the Bolshevik government. Rampant, endemic disorder was everywhere; food riots were occurring within all the major cities. Large-scale smuggling was rife on the borders and millions of uprooted Russians attempted to flee the country, just to get out of the battle zones.

These perilous conditions warranted strong control over the borders and the transport system. For the most part, the populace was disposed to approve such measures, considering the alternatives. Once the wartime controls were in effect, they remained in effect. Instead of temporary expedients, they became permanent fixtures that would only grow stronger in the years to come. In most countries, the peacetime patrol of borders and protection of railroads is performed by a conventional customs service or the transport ministry, but, as Dzerzhinsky recommended, these two functions remained under the firm hand of the organs. Once again, the shield and sword (*shchi i mech*) had been adroitly burnished and extended in the protection of the party.

In the last sixty-eight years, the Frontier VChK has evolved into what is now called the KGB Border Troops. It is a formidable deterrent to anyone seeking to escape the USSR. Present strength of the KGB Border Troops is estimated to number between 750,000 and 1 million troops.[34] This force has its own naval and air arm as well as ground combat units to back up the fixed border outposts. With the military VChK (OO) in the Soviet armed forces, and the border forces deployed through the country, even the Red Army's capacity for decisive independent action is no more than slight. (Today, in Afghanistan, for the first time since World War II, the Soviets are engaged in a military incursion into a foreign country. However closely monitored, the troops are direct witnesses to what the extended hand of fraternal socialism means to the pathetic Afghan towns and villages they see destroyed. Despite the efforts of the OOs, Soviet troops have deserted to the "enemy," an odd choice to make in light of the desperate circumstances of the anti-Soviet Afghanis.)

During the several years following the civil war, the Frontier VChKs took few prisoners, in their own way contributing to that organization's direct death toll. Those who managed to escape from the USSR in that period have confirmed, in grisly detail, that at the borders there was little turning back of refugees by the frontier forces. Those captured were frequently killed outright or, if physically able, were dispatched to long, indeterminate sentences in penal camps. With the forced-labor colonies also under the command of the organs, the administrative burdens of dealing with deserters from socialism were conveniently minimized.[35]

The Russian émigrés, as distinguished from the emigrants, were those compelled to take refuge outside Russia, principally in Western Europe and the Far East. Many settled in Germany, some in the Balkans, and the largest concentration in France. By the arbitrary standards of Lenin, all émigrés were counterrevolutionaries, for he feared that the once-defeated Whites would somehow regroup, unite, and return to depose him.

The Cheka, from its inception, monitored the activities of these groups, and in response to a terse order from Lenin on December 5, 1920, Dzerzhinsky issued a directive to expand the surveillance and to initiate provocation operations against the émigrés. A primary objective was to induce the émigré populations to return home, where they could be disposed of quickly and without notice.[36] To discharge the task, the Cheka formed the Counterespionage Department (*Kontrarazvedyvatelnyi Otdel,* or KRO). The KRO detachments sent abroad in the early twenties were the forerunners of the later OGPU and NKVD "wet" squads used by Stalin in his seventeen-year-long campaign to extirpate émigré leaders throughout the world.[37] (The present-day lineal descendants of the KRO and wet squads are under the direction of Department V of the KGB's First Chief Directorate, headed by Lieutenant General Alexandr Mikhailovich Sakharovsky.[38]

Dzerzhinsky's conception of foreign counterespionage was not significantly different from the methodology he had used to impose controls on the internal population. Both systems reflected a special effort to understand human nature and ordinary behavioral responses, in order to identify the attitudes, motivations, and vulnerabilities of "imperialist" enemies. The particular targets were (1) leaders of incipient opposition (counterrevolutionaries), (2) foreign socialist parties, and (3) tourists, businessmen, and, especially, members of foreign diplomatic and trade missions.

Concurrently, the KRO's domestic surveillance mission was broadened to include such "active" tasks as the entrapment, subornation, and coercive recruitment of foreigners. These techniques became the classic tools of Soviet operations. The distinction to be made, however, is that not until Dzerzhinsky were these methods employed in such a broad, systematic manner against virtually all non-Soviet targets. The scope of the Soviet effort in this regard is without parallel and reveals the staggering demands of this most labor-intensive program. Since sex, in any of its various forms, has been employed with effect in the recruitment process, Dzerzhinsky (a model of monogamous orthodoxy) established a training facility to ensure that the Cheka would be able to meet the appetites of all prospective recruits, however bizarre.[39]

On a practical level, in the Soviet Union today no foreigner, male or female, can avoid contact with the KRO. Cab drivers, busboys, charwomen, waiters, and the ever-present, effusively friendly Intourist guides who want to "improve their English," long-lost relatives who turn up at the visitor's hotel, and particularly "friends of friends" are integral parts of the KRO system.[40]

In the early days the KRO operated abroad under the "official" aegis of the ministries of Foreign Affairs and Trade. In the Soviet official communities it is customary to staff the embassies and trade missions with Soviet personnel who perform all of the housekeeping tasks, interpret, drive official cars, act as receptionists, and manage the telephones. Later, other nationalities were occasionally employed in these tasks, but only when their political reliability and party discipline could be certified by the organs.

In the Soviet Union, the foreign embassies were completely dependent on the Soviet government's selection of personnel to drive, translate, and provide other necessary services. Refusal to accept a chauffeur offered by the central Soviet hiring hall, Burobin (which was entirely operated and staffed by the organs), simply meant that the job went unfilled. The consequence of this intense penetration of foreign embassies was that all official and personal activities of all diplomatic staffs were under daily surveillance by multiple Soviet-managed agents.

Each of the Russian employees so placed was coerced into cooperation with the organs. In the aggregate, the Cheka came to have a more precise appreciation of an embassy's personnel and functions than any ambassador did. When surveillance in the streets became too obvious and the diplomats complained, the Ministry of Foreign Affairs (Narkomindel) simply explained that the men who dogged the trails of the diplomats did so not because there was interest in where they went or whom they contacted, but only to "protect" them. The effect of the internal observation and reporting within the embassies, the heavy street surveillance, and the forced co-option of cooks, maids, and nannies in the personal quarters of the diplomats guaranteed that nothing that was said, done, or planned by the foreign families went unrecorded. Russians attempting contact with a foreigner in the streets were taken into custody by the surveillants and hustled away. The foreigner was then advised that the stranger had confessed his intention to attack the foreigner, and that only the prompt intervention of the organs had saved the foreigner's life.

At first, foreign embassy personnel regarded the blatant attempts by the Soviets to spy indiscriminately as annoying; after a while, they were amused. The foreigners ridiculed the sometimes clumsy efforts, attributing them to the Soviets' having only recently come to power, being inexperienced, frightened, and above all insecure. It was considered a temporary condition that would pass as soon as it became widely accepted within the Soviet government that the diplomats had no malign intentions. Sixty-eight years later, the same process (though enormously more effective and now supplemented with modern technological gewgaws) continues to produce recruits, penetrations, and complete intelligence coverage of the foreign official community in Moscow.

The policies of surveillance, penetration, and provocation paid off early in a major case involving an American whose assistance had been importuned by the U.S. Department of State. It was Dzerzhinsky's first major case involving a foreign government. Its effects reverberate to this day.

The U.S. citizen bore the improbable name of Xenophon Dmitrevich de Blumenthal Kalamatiano. He was the first American "secret agent" to cross swords with the Cheka, to lose badly, and in the process to face execution. For a variety of reasons of state, once captured, Kalamatiano was abandoned in a Soviet prison and all but forgotten. The Kalamatiano case is of importance because of its effect on the Soviet government and because it demonstrates the utility of the Cheka's tools of provocation, deception, coercion, and penetration.

Kalamatiano was born in Vienna in May 1882. His father was a Greek trader and businessman of uncertain ancestry. His mother, on the other hand, was the only daughter in a family with close ties to Czar Nicholas I and other members of the Romanoff family. Her father had been admiral of the Imperial Black Sea Fleet, and her mother was the daughter of a Russian count in Bessarabia. These antecedents were to bear heavily on what happened.

In 1894, Kalamatiano's father was killed in a carriage accident. His death produced a marked change in young Xenophon's life. Though not impoverished, the family could no longer afford for Xenophon to continue his education in the elite schools of Switzerland and Russia. In 1895, the widowed Mme. Kalamatiano married Monsieur C. P. de Blumenthal, a Frenchman with some pretensions to nobility. The newly formed family moved to the United States and for the next several years De Blumenthal eked out a modest living by teaching Latin and Greek at a small academy in Bloomington, Illinois. It was there that young Xenophon developed the intellectual prowess that complemented his previous continental education and gave him an unexpected *savoir-faire*. Though still an adolescent, he was a most exceptional young man.

The academy at Bloomington failed, and De Blumenthal was forced to take up another appointment, teaching Latin and Greek at the Culver Military Academy in Indiana. Young Xenophon's performance at Culver was impressive. A skilled horseman, at a school that exalted equestrian skills, he adapted well and was wholly accepted by his classmates. Although a recently arrived transfer student, he graduated from Culver with honors in 1899. Culver was then, as now, considered an elite prep school, especially for those destined for West Point or the Ivy League schools. Rather than pursue a military career, Xenophon decided to attend the newly founded University of Chicago, from which he was graduated with an A.B. degree in 1903. By then he had acquired a reputation as an engaging raconteur, linguist, and enthusiastic member of the Sigma Alpha Epsilon fraternity.

From 1903 to 1907, Kalamatiano held the position of "First Tutor of Russian" at the University of Chicago. His teaching time was well spent, as it led to his being discovered by J. I. Case, president of the farm implement company that bore his name. The Case Company headquarters were in Racine, Wisconsin, with offices in Paris, Bucharest, and Odessa, and it was Case's intention to use Kalamatiano as his foreign representative. The company was in the business of manufacturing, selling, and leasing tractors, combines, and reapers. Although Kalamatiano knew little about such machinery, he knew a great deal about Europe and Russia. Case, with a reputation as a flint-hard businessman, hired the twenty-five-year-old Xenophon to bring Racine's technological know-how to the steppes of Russia.

Both Kalamatiano and the Case Company prospered. From 1907 to 1912, Kalamatiano made significant contributions to Case's "bottom line." Unfortunately, Case didn't think them enough. The two men disagreed on the issue of compensation, and Kalamatiano left Case to form his own firm, the Pan Kivel Company, with headquarters in Moscow. Soon afterward, Kalamatiano became the sole representative of thirty American and European farm implement and machinery companies, all eager to sell their wares to the czarist government. Business prospered and Kalamatiano became a wealthy and well-established commercial success. He moved in the highest of Moscow's social circles and, in late 1913, married a beautiful Russian woman who was a member of the Czarina's court.

In early 1914 he returned to the United States because of the accidental death of his stepfather. While in the country, he was approached and discreetly asked if he would perform a service for the United States government. The man who made the contact was an emissary of Secretary of State Robert Lansing; he made it clear to Kalamatiano that it was his duty to keep Woodrow Wilson's administration informed of developments in Russia. It was, in conventional terms, a "soft" recruitment. Implicit in the nonthreatening suggestion was the unstated premise that Kalamatiano, because of his foreign background, might have a "greater responsibility" to demonstrate his fidelity to the American system.

Kalamatiano was vaguely flattered and accepted the suggestion. In his view it was perfectly usual to expect that businessmen, on request, assisted their governments. Lansing didn't want to know anything that wasn't common gossip in Moscow, at the Winter Palace in Petrograd, and in the other watering holes frequented by the Romanoffs and their extended courts. A few weeks later, when he returned to Moscow, he recalled the emissary's encouraging words: "Do not worry. If anything goes wrong we'll take care of you and yours." It was in this casual, deliberately indefinite sort of allusion that Kalamatiano's career as a secret agent began.

When the World War started a few months later, Kalamatiano's role as an informal, unsupervised, and unpaid volunteer agent became increasingly important to Lansing and the Wilson administration. Because of his access to the higher stratum of the Russian government and the Czar's court, Kalamatiano's mission soon evolved into what might have been called that of "an agent of influence." He not only listened for the worth of what he heard, but more importantly, when appropriate, he nudged Russian government officials in directions favorable to the United States.

To communicate information to his State Department "controller," Kalamatiano opened a New York City office, which was described as necessary to handle correspondence between his Moscow office and his many client companies. The real purpose of the New York office was that of "mail drop" for the information Kalamatiano dispatched to Secretary Lansing. The system worked reasonably well in the first years of the war, but with the February Revolution and the near-collapse of postal and telegraphic service from Russia, it had to be abandoned.

In April 1917 the United States joined the war against the Central Powers, and Kalamatiano's information-collecting role became more important. After the revolution in Russia, Lansing and members of President Wilson's war council had new and pressing needs for information about conditions and, in particular, the new government's intentions to continue in the war. To meet these demands, a change in Kalamatiano's status was thought necessary. Secretary Lansing offered and Kalamatiano accepted a confidential position in the State Department's "Russian Bureau: Special Duty" at an annual salary of $2,400.

Special funds were made available to Kalamatiano to hire informants and "unknowing" information sources (i.e., those not permitted to know that Kalamatiano was actually an agent of the U.S. government). Other funds were provided to rent a "safe meeting house" and to cover the incidental expenses of running a clandestine intelligence network. Kalamatiano was also issued an additional authentic U.S. passport in the name of Sergei Nikolaevich Serpukhovsky. He was directed to accept orders from, and pass his reports back to Washington through, the U.S. chargé d'affaires, De Witt Poole (later to head the Foreign Nationalities Division of the OSS during World War II).

To justify his frequent travel between Moscow and the U.S. consulate in Petrograd, Kalamatiano added a "news service" to his business activities and provided the service to the U.S. consulate and other foreign missions. It was a rather transparent device although it seemed to be effective in providing a broader base to his widening areas of concern.

In this almost casual manner Kalamatiano was transformed from his unpaid volunteer "singleton," quasi-secret agent status to that of a "confidential employee." Far too much was expected of him by his Washington employers. In the first place, he was to live as a businessman and, concurrently, be prepared at any time to slip into and out of his "legend" identity. He was to build up a clandestine intelligence organization and respond to an increasing number of widely divergent requests for information. It wasn't an easy set of tasks, especially in view of the chaotic conditions in Russia that flowed in the wake of the February uprising. Although the hazards were multiple and severe, there are no indications that Kalamatiano hesitated or, for that matter, questioned the sometimes conflicting demands of his assignments.

The need to be away from Moscow on intelligence-gathering tasks, as well as the unpredictable post-uprising violence then sweeping Russia, made him fear for the lives and safety of his wife, Katherine, and their young son, Dmitrevich. Although Kalamatiano was a U.S. citizen, he had neglected to provide similar status for his family. The nationality issue became critical because, under the then-current regulations, his wife and son were considered to be citizens of the new Russian "revolutionary state" and therefore ineligible to leave the country. Kalamatiano asked Secretary Lansing for help. It was immediately forthcoming. His wife and son were accorded U.S. citizenship, issued passports, and immediately left Russia to take up residence with Kalamatiano's mother, Vera, in Pasadena, California.

With his family out of danger, Kalamatiano redoubled his intelligence work. His success is verified by the quality of his reports back to Lansing—excellent examples of what one might expect but seldom get from a field agent. They had the distinctive quality of not confusing the truly significant with the distractingly obvious.

The Bolsheviks' acceptance of the Brest-Litovsk Treaty with Germany in March 1918 added to Kalamatiano's mission. Secretary Lansing was concerned, and rightly so, that Russia's bilateral treaty with Germany might enable the Germans to redeploy troops on the Western front. Kalamatiano was also directed to make an additional detailed assessment of the Bolsheviks' political situation with an eye to determining how secure was their hold on the reins of power.

His reports made it clear, in the summer of 1918, that the Bolsheviks were vulnerable. How important these reports were in the American decision to join with the British, French, and Japanese in dispatching troops for the intervention in Russia cannot be judged. A later decision did, however, result in the United States' sending troops to both Siberia and Archangel, beginning on August 2, 1918. Beyond denying the Russian Baltic Fleet to the Germans, the Allied Task Force's mission was uncertain. But Kalamatiano's mission was clear. It involved energizing his intelligence net and attempting to persuade others that the Bolsheviks' day had come and gone. Where possible, he proposed that responsible Russians take whatever action they could to depose the Bolshevik minority.

The failure of Kalamatiano's dual and conflicting roles (i.e., confusing an intelligence-collection activity with a vague covert political-action mission) might have carried an important signal to Washington, though there is still no evidence that it has been received. Kalamatiano, ever the good soldier, attempted to discharge his brief and to marshal forces in support of the Allied landing in Archangel. Simultaneously he was to attempt to organize other pro-Allied support in Moscow and Petrograd. It is necessary simply to conclude that he was unsuccessful and that his covert-action efforts brought him under hostile surveillance.

Kalamatiano's failure was due to two important factors: first, the assignment by Washington of two incompatible missions, and second, Dzerzhinsky's effective methods for defeating the Allied objectives.

In the spring of 1917, following the February uprising and Dzerzhinsky's release from prison, Dzerzhinsky moved quickly to gain some semblance of control over the revolution's internal-security situation. It was a very complex, highly volatile political climate in which the Bolsheviks' power was unified by a fragile bridle of threads. Dzerzhinsky, having given much thought to the problem while in prison, acted with purpose and, by December 1917 (when the VChK was formally established), had already organized a highly effective counterintelligence and counterespionage system which gave Lenin a markedly superior advantage in the area of counterintelligence and party security.

By co-opting the Okhrana's system of informants and agents, Dzerzhinsky was able to function on a broad scale in an exceedingly short time. Most of the Okhrana informants were motivated by money and welcomed the VChK as their new employer. Dzerzhinsky exhibited considerable wisdom in bringing them into the VChK without regard to their politics and past association with the czarist secret political police. Their employment by the VChK was to prove temporary even though they fulfilled a vital tactical role in the early days of the organs.

As invariably happens, some informants prove to be more valuable than others, and among the newly acquired confidential sources (*seksot*), one proved to have been the closest friend of Kalamatiano's wife when she attended the Czarina's court. This particular woman, who feared for her life in the hands of the Chekists, was more than willing to share with the organs the confidences and indiscretions of Kalamatiano's wife. This information, coupled with that held in captured Okhrana files, was sufficient to bring Kalamatiano under suspicion. Dzerzhinsky, with his sophisticated turn of mind, immediately saw the advantage to be gained in increasing surveillance on Kalamatiano while he went about his collection mission, so that his sources and methods would be disclosed.

Dzerzhinsky's position was enormously strengthened by a second discovery. This time it was another Okhrana informant who happened to be employed by the U.S. consulate. It was not difficult to coerce the man into providing (from approximately October 1917 on) copies of Kalama-tiano's intelligence reports. So armed, Dzerzhinsky was able to play a game of intelligence chess with the unsuspecting American. Kalamatiano received his instructions about the Allied landings at Archangel, and the plans for the countercoup, at about the same time that identical messages reached Dzerzhinsky, in late July of 1918.

While Kalamatiano was checking the perimeter and trying to verify that there was a basis for a popular revolt, Dzerzhinsky was making an inventory of the physical means available to the anti-Bolshevik forces should they attempt an insurrection. Dzerzhinsky concluded that the Bol-sheviks were safe, at least for the moment. To make doubly certain, Dzerzhinsky dispatched two Chekists, Ian Buikis and Ian Sprogis, to Pet-rograd to infiltrate another espionage net run by the British naval at-taché, Captain F.N.A. Cromie.[41]

Cromie's primary mission was to foil any attempt by the Bolsheviks or the Russian naval commanders to turn the Russian Baltic Fleet over to the Germans. If necessary, Cromie and his net were prepared either to blow up the ships or to engineer their scuttling by crew members who had been bought off by the British. Though Lenin had proclaimed "All Power to the Soviets!" there was considerable uncertainty in the Bolshevik hier-archy, as well as among the Allies, as to whether the Russian Navy, noto-riously independent and highly political, intended to surrender all or any of its power to the new Soviet state.

The "Dual Ian" mission was complicated. Dzerzhinsky was also trying to learn the intentions of the Russian Navy, and in this case he was at-tempting to get the information by operating under the aegis of another nation's clandestine intelligence operations. At the same time, he wanted to set a trap for the Allies if they proceeded with their projected plan to stage a popular uprising against the Bolsheviks.[42]

The Chekists were successful in penetrating the British operation. In addition to insinuating themselves into Cromie's net, they dangled the prospect of two disaffected Lettish battalions in Moscow which were de-scribed as prepared to revolt against the Bolsheviks. Cromie rose to the bait like a hungry trout and provided the Chekists with letters of intro-duction to the British diplomatic agent in Moscow, Robert Bruce Lock-hart. The endorsement by Cromie set in motion what came to be known as the "Envoys Plot." It is worthy of note that Dzerzhinsky had the pres-cience to order the shooting of Captain Cromie, on August 31, 1918, to assure that no one survived to challenge the Bolshevik version of what actually happened.[43]

The main thrust of these events was to strengthen Bolshevik allega-tions that the Allies had conspired to: (1) assassinate Lenin (the Kaplan attack was attributed to the Allied powers); (2) organize the projected coup and the involvement of the disaffected Lettish battalions, thereby proving the Allies' hostile intentions toward the Bolshevik regime; and (3) plan to organize a "stay-behind" operation to work against the Soviet state from within. Since plans 1 and 2 failed, the third charge was to be proved in open court. Xenophon Kalamatiano was to be the centerpiece in the first of the now famous Soviet spy trials.

It is clear that there was some substance in the Bolsheviks' allegations. The Allies had indeed contemplated toppling the Bolshevik regime as well as establishing stay-behind espionage operations in the event the Archangel occupation failed, or the Germans succeeded in bringing the Russians into the war on their side. Unfortunately, Kalamatiano became odd man out in the legal proceedings, which established the Allies' perfidious actions toward Russia and, inferentially, the infant Soviet state.

In retrospect, it can be said that the Bolsheviks were seen by the Allies in a German context. The Allied forces were exhausted from their military efforts on the Western Front when their Eastern ally, Imperial Russia, collapsed. The Bolsheviks were regarded as pro-German simply because Germany had engineered Lenin's return from Switzerland to promote revolutionary actions—which, incontestably, served the German interests. The Brest-Litovsk Treaty removed Russia from the war and tended to confirm the Allies' assumption that the Germans were now free to move new troops to the Western Front to oppose the British, French, Italian, and recently arrived U.S. forces. In the view of the senior military commanders and Western political leaders, the Bolsheviks had already contributed to Germany's ability to continue. Consequently, anti-Bolshevik sentiment was understandably high.

The spy trial, sometimes referred to in Soviet publications as the Lockhart Case or the Envoy's Plot, was heard before the Supreme Revolutionary Tribunal in Moscow from November 28 to December 3, 1918. In modern terms, it was a major media event. The Bolsheviks used the trial to demonstrate their thesis that the capitalists were out to destroy them.[44] Although more than sixty-seven years have passed, the same theme continues to dominate, with great effect, the training and motivation of Soviet intelligence personnel.

The trial and the summation by the Bolshevik public prosecutor, N. V. Krylenko, whom Lockhart described as a "degenerate,"[45] served Dzerzhinsky's purposes. The Allies' falsity was unmasked and the organs' role as the protector of the revolution was enhanced. The dramatic nature of the trial is seen in its verdict: Four of the principal accused were sentenced, in absentia, to be shot as enemies of the state. (The four had already been exchanged for Bolshevik diplomats, most notably Maxim Litvinov, whom the British had prudently incarcerated when Lockhart was first arrested.) Of the others, eight were pardoned (these were

Dzerzhinsky's penetration agents), eight were committed to five years at hard labor in prison, and two were sentenced to death: Xenophon Kalamatiano and his principal assistant, a Russian officer in Soviet government service, Lieutenant Colonel Alexandr Friede, who was executed on December 14, 1918.[46]

On several occasions Kalamatiano was dragged before a firing squad, given a last cigarette, blindfolded, subjected to the deadly tension of the commands *Ready! Aim! Fire!*—and then returned to his confinement without explanation. At times, Chekists posing as fellow prisoners were thrown into his cell to try to elicit information that would in some way compromise him. Despite these methods, Kalamatiano persisted in his version of events. Although the Bolsheviks knew what he had been doing, he resolutely refused to confirm their knowledge or to make any admission of use to his captors.

The decision not to kill Kalamatiano, the "master spy," was apparently made by Lenin.[47] Though the Bolsheviks were at odds with the United States, Lenin was sufficiently astute to realize that Kalamatiano might have future use as a hostage. Dzerzhinsky agreed, and Kalamatiano was confined in Lubianka #2 as a pawn to be used in subsequent negotiations with the United States.

Kalamatiano, by now an intelligence professional, spent his time in prison observing the internal activities in the Lubianka. Like Dzerzhinsky before him, Kalamatiano tapped into the prisoners' communications system—the clandestine, informal transmission and receipt of information concerning events in the outside world. Although unable to communicate with any U.S. authorities, he continued to collect intelligence information regarding the VChK and, in particular, data relating to the activities of Dzerzhinsky himself.

Months passed. The civil war waxed, waned, and eventually ended in the collapse of the anti-Bolshevik forces. The end of the war compelled the Allies to alter their stand with regard to the Bolshevik government, as it was realized that, after two years in power, the Bolsheviks had consolidated their domination over Russia and were growing stronger each day.

As early as November 8, 1919, Britain's Lloyd George declared that the Bolsheviks could not be conquered by arms, and on January 16, 1920, the Allied Supreme Council voted to withdraw the economic blockade of Russia. A little later Archangel was evacuated, and soon thereafter all Allied troops were withdrawn from Russian territory. During this period Kalamatiano languished in the Lubianka with no apparent hope of release. Although his death sentence had been commuted by mid-1920, his fate was still uncertain.[48]

The U.S. government—that is, the Wilson administration—was unwilling to acknowledge that Kalamatiano was one of their own. Petitions from many organizations, including the newly founded American Legion, had no effect. The Department of State made several low-key diplomatic attempts to secure his release. Wilson's incapacity, and the departure of Robert Lansing from the administration following the disappointments of Versailles, left Kalamatiano without a single consequential U.S. official still in government who had firsthand knowledge of his activities.

One person, though not a member of the Wilson administration, was a personal confidant of Lansing's and in that way became aware of Kalamatiano's contribution to the cause of U.S. national security before and during the war. He was a man of remarkable memory, later to become the thirty-first President of the United States, Herbert Clark Hoover.

Hoover, perhaps one of the most underrated of all American Presidents, was personally incensed by the fact of Kalamatiano's incarceration. He decried the lackadaisical efforts of the Wilson administration to secure his release along with other Americans held by the Bolsheviks. Hoover, who had supervised the production and distribution of food for America during the World War, felt strongly about the case of Kalamatiano and was positively aggrieved when his protestations to Colonel Edward M. House and Mrs. Wilson failed to produce an effect.

Official indifference might have sealed Kalamatiano's fate but for two external events. In mid-1919, President Wilson appointed Hoover to head the American Relief Administration (ARA), through which the U.S. government intended to distribute massive supplies of food throughout the famine areas in Eastern Europe and Russia. Famine and the ensuing epidemics of typhus and influenza did not respect either the Soviet border or its new ideological barriers. The ARA, under Hoover's leadership, was solely committed to save lives, and Kalamatiano's was one Hoover did not intend to lose.

A second unanticipated event was the catastrophic drought of 1920, which greatly enlarged the already devastating famine and directly threatened 30 million people in the Ukraine, the Crimea, the Caucasus, and the Volga and Ural regions. Lenin tried to deal with the crisis using meager Russian resources, which proved grossly inadequate to the task. By the spring of 1921 the crisis was so severe that he was forced to turn to the United States and ask for ARA assistance.[49]

His petition for aid resulted from a difficult and complicated decision. Acceptance of outside help was thought to threaten the Bolshevik regime in subtle ways. Dzerzhinsky argued against taking ARA aid because, by the terms under which it was given, the food distribution mechanism would entail a sizable American presence on Soviet soil. The purpose of the ARA supervisors was to guarantee that the food went to the intended recipients and was not used for Bolshevik political purposes. Although Lenin overruled Dzerzhinsky on the principle, he compensated on the means. The only Russians allowed to assist the ARA representatives would come from the ranks of the VChK.[50]

Despite the agreed terms, the Bolsheviks continued to insist that they, as the sovereign government, must have the right to distribute the food. Their proposals were rejected by the United States, and Hoover, now Commerce Secretary in Warren G. Harding's administration, refused to renegotiate the terms of relief. Lenin was left with no alternative as internal conditions in the USSR became increasingly desperate.

In late July, when all the protocols seemed to be in place, Hoover instructed his emissary, Walter L. Brown, the European director of the American Relief Administration, to inform Lenin's representative, Maxim Litvinov, of a new, nonnegotiable demand. There would be *no* food without the prior release of Kalamatiano and the other Americans held in Bolshevik prisons. Brown conveyed the essence of Hoover's message: The Americans are to be freed or you will suffer the consequences of 30 million Russians' dying of starvation. The political implications of refusal were not lost on the Bolsheviks.

These were terms of a kind that Lenin and Dzerzhinsky understood. For the first time in their Marxist-Leninist revolutionary careers, they had encountered a capitalist enemy who rejected any inhibitions of guilt in the use of power. There was credibility in Hoover's mien, and Dzerzhinsky, for one, believed the demand was not a bluff. Hoover clearly meant what he said, and it was known that President Harding had given him carte blanche in the negotiations. Lenin concurred in Dzerzhinsky's opinion that perhaps they had finally met a courageous capitalist. Lenin instructed Litvinov to accede to the new conditions.

It was a U.S. negotiating coup that was disremembered in the later policies of conciliation. It is evident that Hoover recognized that the Soviets were driven less by compassion than by the politics of food, and treated them accordingly.

Lenin acted without delay, and on August 10, 1921, ten days before the first ARA representatives entered Russia, Kalamatiano and the other Americans were removed from their Moscow prisons and transported, by special car, to the Estonian border at Narva. On their arrival, the barbed-wire gates defining the boundary swung open, allowing the special car to enter Estonian territory.[51] Though exhausted, worn, and disheveled from his long imprisonment, Kalamatiano was not beyond making a telling point to the Chekists who had accompanied him to freedom: "Observe the contrast, comrades. Your Bolsheviki brothers guarding the east side of the line are starving and the well-fed uniformed Estonians on the west side are keeping you out because you are the example of what communism does for people." One of the escorts took advantage of the moment and escaped. The others returned to the special car and were shunted back across the border to dismal prospects in the land of Lenin.

Kalamatiano, after a long bath, shave, and a change to more suitable clothes, "was the most composed and best dressed among the group of released prisoners. He resembled the conventional American tourist. In his new raiment he showed little effects of his imprisonment."[52]

Kalamatiano was careful in his comments to the press. He knew all too well the reach and grasp of the organs. His fellow prisoners described Kalamatiano as their "chief comforter" during the long days and nights in the Lubianka and Butkyri prisons. Kalamatiano acknowledged their appreciation and praise, but said little more. It was his intention to give a full report at the formal debriefing, which he expected as a matter of course.

From Narva he was transferred to Riga, Latvia, and finally brought under the protection of the American authorities there. The U.S. commissioner in Riga, Evan E. Young, was discomfited by the presence of Kalamatiano, and even the Secretary of State, Charles Evans Hughes, was not particularly enthused by his release. Hughes had previously ordered the release and deportation of some 150 Bolshevik agents rounded up by Wilson's Attorney General, Mitchell Palmer. At the time Hughes ordered their release, he failed to insist on reciprocity. Now Hughes could see no merit in affronting the Soviets further. He expressed the possibility that future trade with the USSR might suffer if undue attention were given to Kalamatiano.

Young was directed to take Kalamatiano's statement, forward it to the State Department, arrange his transportation, and instruct Kalamatiano to hold his tongue until he later met with Department of State officials in Washington.

Kalamatiano's report on the Lockhart Trial in Moscow during December 1918 was written in Riga and forwarded on August 22, 1921. The verbatim text reveals much detail about the VChK and its effectiveness. Kalamatiano wrote:[53]

. . . When I returned to Moscow from Samara, on September 18, 1918, I found that, already on the second day of the month, my premises had been searched and a guard left at the house to arrest me, should I return. The interesting point about that search was that the VChK men looked for me under my real name, as well as the name under which I lived at this particular time. This is of interest, because my stay in Moscow under an assumed name was known only at the Consulate, and then only to a few people, as far as I know to Mr. A. W. Friede and to Lieutenant Reilly.*

I knew, before leaving Samara, on the 13th, of various arrests, that of Friede among them, but I knew of none of the other

*Ed. note: Reilly was an important figure during this period. See p. 87.

complications and I still hoped to be able to find Consul General Poole for whom I had some information and letters. So, having escaped from this first trap (at my rooms), I called at Friede's and found that he and his sister were still under arrest and their house closely watched. I decided to take no more chances before I delivered the letters in my possession and walked to the Consulate, where I found the Norwegian flag floating and everything looking very peaceful. To make sure, I walked back and forth several times and then entered the courtyard. There was, however, an armed guard, concealed in the janitor's small house and I was surrounded and covered before I could get to the main entrance. Not knowing the exact situation I thought that I could bluff my way through by declaring that I was an American going to the Consulate for my passport, but this did not help and I was taken to the VChK.

My case was in the hands of Peters, at that time chief of the Moscow Division, Kingissep, an Esthonian communist, and I was also examined by Karachan. I quickly found that before my arrest, in the first days of September, Friede and his sister had been arrested and, later, the following men: Potemkin, Chvalinski, Ivanoff, Zagriazhiski and Solius, who were all arrested, at different times, when coming to see Friede, by the guard stationed at his house after his arrest.

The details of the various interrogations to which I was submitted are unimportant, but their purpose was the following: to get from me an admission that at the meeting held in the American Consulate on the 25th of August there had been discussed a plot against the Soviet Government, and especially the blowing up of the Zwanka bridge.

I took the following stand: My presence at the meeting, my identity and my connection with Friede and the others were established quite definitely, this I very quickly discovered, so I considered it useless and even harmful to deny something which they could prove. In regard to the meeting I testified, however, that I knew of no special meeting called for any particular purpose, and that whereas I was present I heard nothing of any plots or any bridges, that I had met Reilly and Vertement there and knew that they were going to remain in Moscow, and that we exchanged addresses, that I knew nothing of their business, that I had never seen Marchand and that I was in no way connected with the Consulate. I stated that I had been in Russia for many years representing business houses and that this could easily be proved. That in view of the present situation it had been impossible to do actual business but that I had remained believing that eventually business would be resumed. That for the same purpose I had some time previously organized a small force of men whose business it was to travel and report on such conditions as could immediately affect business. That my own firm in New York, as well as other firms were interested in the information thus obtained, and that this information was gotten out in the shape of bulletins. I admitted that I furnished such bulletins to the American Consulate, and also that I had arranged to supply Reilly and Vertement with them.

This statement was worked out by me because (1) they knew of the organization and my connection with it, (2) the first arrest had been that of Miss Friede, while she was entering the place Reilly was supposed to be, and at that time she also had in her possession a report for Vertement and one for the Consulate (Sept. 1st). (3) As above stated, they evidently had inside information about the meeting at the Consulate.

All this information I received, partly when I called at Friede's just before my arrest, and partly from statements which Peters and the others let slip.

The interrogations lasted about ten days (two to three interrogations during each night, every time by one or the other of those previously mentioned, using different systems, Peters bullying, Kingissep arguments, and Karachan promises or rather suggestions of immunity, etc. if my testimony was satisfactory). It was stated that they had inside information from the Consulate, upon which I demanded to be confronted with the informant, something which they evidently found to be undesirable, or impossible. I was told all about a statement by Marchand (for there is no question but what Marchand deliberately gave information to the VChK and his letter to the President, which was supposed to be found in his lodging, was just a blind). I asked that Marchand be called in, and this they did not do, so at the end of ten days we were in the same dead-lock.

To me it was quite evident from the importance the Bolsheviks were attaching to the whole matter that they were trying to make out a big case against the Allies and to mix the American Consulate up with it, but that they really had very little actual proof and it was up to me to block them if possible. Also, I was trying to save the lives of Friede and the others, so I believed that my stand was the only proper one to take under the circumstances.

During this time I had been kept alone, with the exception of what I believe to have been spies, but in the end I and all the other people arrested in this case were transferred to the Butyrka prison, and after the trial to the Lubianka. Although we were all supposed to be in solitary cells there were possibilities of communication so that I got in touch with the others and told them exactly the stand I had taken and suggested that they better stick close to that same position. With the exception of Friede and his sister on whom I relied absolutely and of General Zagriazhiski, none of the others knew anything about my connection with the Consulate anyway. I was called out by the VChK twice more and each time examined along the same lines, and also they were trying to establish some further connection between me and Reilly and some of his friends who had been arrested, two women and a business man.

At my home was also arrested Pshenichka, a Czech who had come with me, according to an arrangement made with Consul Williams at Samara. The VChK tried to establish some connection between us, but found this impossible, as we had reached a previous agreement in case of trouble.

During one of my trips to the VChK I met Consuls Bury and Leonard, who were under arrest, and whom I also saw later in Butyrki. In view of the possibility of their release I supplied them at the time with all the information I have given above, for transmission to Mr. Poole.

On November 20th we were all read an act of accusation, a copy of which was unfortunately taken away from me later. I was accused of being an agent of the American government, organizing a spying organization for the Allies, and taking part in the Lockhart plot. The others were accused of being spies.

At this trial there were still present seven judges (now three) and ordinary lawyers were allowed (since then only lawyers registered by the government are allowed to act, and are not engaged but appointed by the tribunal).

I presented my case to the lawyers and insisted that this was the only defense possible (I say insisted, because Muravieff wanted to present an entirely new line of defense, and as a lawyer, could not quite get my point, which I also could not very well explain to him in detail).

The trial was most interesting because of the Lockhart side. During the previous two months the papers had published a great deal about the Lockhart conspiracy as well as of my arrest and connection with it, so naturally one expected some definite statements in regard to this famous plot.

Peters stated that Berzin, the other witness, had at all times been in touch with the VChK, and that he, Peters, was continually in touch with the plans concocted by Reilly and Berzin, and that in fact Berzin was an employee of the VChK. (This very fact proved that Berzin was practically what is known as an agent provocateur, and that his testimony could not be particularly relied upon.) Peters next said that about the end of August a French "officer" had come to him with tears in his eyes, and had confessed to a dreadful plot against the Soviet government which had been discussed at the American Consulate on August 25th. Evidently referring to Marchand. Further, the famous Marchand letter was produced as evidence.

Berzin, the other witness, testified that he was a Colonel of a Lettish regiment and that at all times kept in touch with the VChK. He said that he had at various times met Lieutenant Reilly of the British Army, and that Reilly had made him an offer to pay him ten million roubles for the purpose of starting a mutiny among the Lettish troops (which at the time were the Bolsheviks' only strong support). The troops were to mutiny in Moscow, Lenin was to be hung, and Allied troops were to march down from Archangel.

According to Berzin's own statement, however, he had had only one actual interview with Lockhart, on whom he called with Reilly and with whom he found Grenard. Also, at that meeting no plots of any kind were discussed, but the freedom and future independence of Latvia was spoken of in a general way, and that either Lockhart or Grenard made the statement that the Allies sympathized with the Letts and would help them regain their independence.

All actual plotting was therefore done by Reilly and Berzin, and about this plotting there was no more actual proof than the Marchand letter and Berzin's own statement.

The most interesting part of the Berzin testimony was that about the end of August he made an appointment with Reilly to meet him in Petrograd, in order to become acquainted there with some of the other men in the "conspiracy." Berzin went to the address given by Reilly and waited for the latter in his room. While waiting in his room he stated that he found a card with my name and address and also the addresses and names of the people who were afterwards arrested in Moscow (among them the woman to whom Friede was to deliver messages from me to Reilly).

He saw Reilly later in Petrograd on the same day but met no one else, and returned to Moscow, where a search was made for me and a trap at once laid at one of the addresses found in Reilly's rooms.

In cross examination I asked, why Reilly was not arrested himself as long as the VChK knew just where he was to be found, but received no satisfactory answer.

In regard to the Marchand letter I made a formal demand to the tribunal that Marchand be called as a witness, but it was stated that he could not be found, although at the time he was often writing articles in the Moscow papers.

The testimony of Reilly's friends, two women and a business man, brought out nothing whatever except that they knew Reilly.

The testimony of Mme Morens, a French lady at whose house Captain Vertement roomed also brought out nothing.

The testimony of Pshenichka brought out only that he had come to Moscow from Samara, on his way to Bohemia, that he had been given my address by some friend in Samara.

My own testimony was given along the lines already mentioned, and the testimony of the others connected with me quite coincided with mine, with one exception: Friede under cross examination stated that he did know Consul General Poole. (This slip I lay entirely to a very long and tiresome series of cross examinations, but I believe that if it had not been for this slip he might have been saved.)

The whole trial lasted from the 25th of November until the 3rd of December, with many interesting incidents (all the way from hysterics of the women to the calling of Brusilloff as a military expert).

I can state with satisfaction that nothing was proved either in regard to any conspiracy, or in regard to any connection of myself or others with the Consulate of the United States, and that after the trial was over all newspaper talk in regard to the famous Lockhart trial ceased.

In his closing speech, Krylenko, attorney for the State (accuser for the people, according to his official title) paid me the compliment of warning the judges against my "cleverness" in concealing our "tracks," and stated that proofs were not necessary, that they, the judges, should let their revolutionary consciences decide if we were enemies of the people and act accordingly.

The verdict was: Lockhart, Grenard, Reilly and Vertement, to be shot whenever caught. (As far as I know none have been captured.)

Myself, shot within 24 hours (taken out to execution twice, and under death sentence until May 1920 when it was reduced to fifteen years, and later to five years).

Friede, shot on December 14th, can say of him that he was a gallant gentleman, did what he considered his duty to his country, assisted me tremendously in keeping up the spirits of the others, and was shot, first because of the slip I spoke of, and also because he tried to take some of the blame on himself. I understand his stand, and yet it was not necessary, because at the worst it would have been better to have only one man shot, and besides there was more chance of my escaping, as a foreigner. I must especially emphasize his conduct as opposed to that of General Zagriazhiski, who at one time, with the idea of saving himself, almost told everything he knew and more, too.

The points that interested me particularly, were the position of Reilly and the other sources of information to the VChK. In regard to the latter I am quite certain in my own mind that there was a leakage in our Consulate. In regard to Reilly, I have been able to get some information about him personally from people who knew him previously, in the Far East, then in Petrograd, and then in New York where he had offices in 1916–7. I was told in Moscow that Reilly was a "professional." On the other hand he showed criminal carelessness in leaving around secret addresses.

Also, why was Reilly not arrested, when the VChK knew just where to lay their hands on him, and why were people connected with him all released, whereas people connected with me all sentenced, with the exception of one. I should say a further inquiry into his actions should be of interest. The whole thing looks very much like a piece of "provocation." Marchand, in conclusion, was undoubtedly a traitor, from the very start.

Kalamatiano returned to an indifferent Washington. His report from Riga was seen as an oddity bearing on events long past. He, too, was made to feel an awkward relic. He was philosophical about the official indifference and the fact that the U.S. government seemed to have no interest in what he had learned about the Bolsheviks during his three years in prison. Among the warnings Kalamatiano brought from his stay with the VChK were that the United States would eventually replace Britain as the "main adversary" and that our vulnerabilities invited further attack.

After several desultory weeks in Washington, Kalamatiano was paid off and given a train ticket to Chicago, where he took up his former role as a Russian tutor at the university. So far as is known, he made no effort to reestablish relations with his wife and son. He simply subsided back into university life. During December 1921, in response to a request from a colleague of his stepfather's at Culver Military Academy, he gave several lectures on his experiences in Bolshevik Russia. No record of the talks now exists. The head of the academy offered him the post of professor of modern languages; he accepted and joined the Culver faculty in the following school year.

On November 19, 1923, Kalamatiano died of blood poisoning, which resulted from a hunting accident the previous winter. His death was given little notice in the local papers. From an official standpoint, Kalamatiano was a "spy who never was."

While Kalamatiano was forgotten in the United States sixty years ago, his is still a familiar name in the KGB.[54] The Kalamatiano case continues to be used in training KGB officers. It is presented as proof that the United States has engaged in aggressive assaults on the USSR for six decades. It is cited to make and reinforce basic counterespionage themes that support and explain the USSR's continuing conflict with the United States. The most important of these, according to former KGB officers who studied the case, are:[55]

1. All Americans on Russian soil, regardless of their ostensible vocation or position, must be considered enemy intelligence agents and treated accordingly.

2. In any intelligence operation directed against the Soviet Union by the Western powers, especially when it involves the cooperation of the United States, France, and Great Britain, it is possible to play one ally off against the other and thereby counter their operations.

3. The capitalists' greed is sufficient to excuse, overlook, or otherwise justify the Soviet Union's counterespionage activities.

4. The United States is weakest and therefore most vulnerable in the area of counterespionage because its intelligence officials are (a) unable effectively to exploit those who have deserted the Soviet services, and (b) incapable, unwilling, or fearful of acting on the basis of information acquired by their own agents. This mistrust of those who have deserted our cause must be encouraged.

Dzerzhinsky's counterespionage doctrine has proved a useful and enduring guide.

Since the Kalamatiano case appeared to hold no lessons or opportunities for the West, it was treated in isolation as a nonrecurring phenomenon. Dzerzhinsky, however, saw it as an important illustration of a malevolent United States, pursuing a determined course of action to destroy the new Soviet state. The inculcation of this legend has preserved a residue of distrust that has effectively beclouded all subsequent relations between the two countries.

The deliberate cultivation of distrust, and promotion of the idea that the USSR is continually under attack by Western agencies, make a proposal for coexistence or the advocacy of détente seem positively sinister attempts at deception. A policy that insistently asserts the destructive aims of all others has great value in facilitating Soviet counterintelligence and reinforcing the KGB's control of the populace.[56]

Although the KRO was a most favored element of the Cheka, Dzerzhinsky did not neglect its other, more conventional intelligence activities. The KRO had performed its assigned duties in a most effective manner. Lenin expressed his general satisfaction with the expanded VChK, but noted his disappointment that its operations did not extend to the United States.[57]

To correct this inadequacy, Dzerzhinsky immediately ordered the formation of a new unit, the Foreign Department or *Inostrannyi Odel,* better known by its acronym, INO. The directive authorizing its beginning, approved on December 20, 1920, charged the INO with responsibility for the direction of foreign intelligence operations,[58] plus the added function of collaborating with the KRO in penetrating and destroying resistance nuclei outside the USSR and destabilizing émigré opposition elements throughout the world.

Collateral and exclusive functions of the INO were its supervision of Soviet officials stationed abroad and the physical security of Soviet foreign missions. Initially the INO's intelligence-collection function was carried out by "singleton" agents, some of whom were dispatched personally by Dzerzhinsky.[59] The singletons, who operated under aliases and with false identities, were spies in the classic sense. With the aid of "confidential associates" (*seksots*), they collected information by stealth and cunning.

At the time the INO was launched, there were few official Bolshevik embassies or missions. After the civil war, Lenin made a strong effort to establish diplomatic relations with many of the major powers and, where possible, to normalize trade relations. The success of his efforts was much reduced by the Bolsheviks' repudiation of all war debts incurred by the Imperial government. The United States refused to recognize the Soviet government until 1933, while most European countries forgave, forgot, or overlooked the debt issue in the twenties.

With the acceptance of diplomatic relations came the Soviet embassy, and with the embassy came the INO. A usual precursor to full diplomatic recognition was the establishment of a Soviet trade mission or purchasing mission, also internally controlled by a large INO complement. INO operators in the embassies adopted the titles associated with diplomacy and were described as having come from the People's Commissariat for Foreign Affairs. Those assigned to the trade missions were represented as experts drawn from the tractor, electrical, mining, or heavy industrial combines.

In each Soviet facility, the first requirement was the maintenance of strict party discipline and absolute security of the assigned personnel. This primary function closely resembled the OOs' mission within the Soviet armed forces. The senior INO man was known as the "legal resident." In the diplomatic missions, the resident was generally designated in the diplomatic lists as a first or second secretary or attaché.

Completely disassociated from the official Soviet community was the "illegal" resident, who commanded parallel networks that functioned independently of the official Soviet structure. A "legal" is one who enters a foreign country with documentation—visas, passports, etc.—that meet the foreign country's formal requirements for admission. An example would be a KGB officer (often carrying an alias passport issued by the Soviet Ministry of Foreign Affairs), who has been assigned to a Soviet embassy or trade mission and has been granted a valid entry visa by the host country. An "illegal" enters a foreign country using stolen or forged non-Soviet documents. Once in the foreign country, the illegal generally uses a different identity and nationality supported by a second or third set of documents. Illegals eventually try to acquire genuine documentation issued by the host country that supports their assumed identity.

The military, naval, and (later) air attachés were usually drawn from appropriate elements of the GRU. Staffing of these posts with bona fide military officers was not, however, a rigid rule. Many senior organs officers served outside the USSR in the guise of military officers.

Failure of an individual to perform effectively or refusal to submit to the resident's discipline constituted a serious political crime. From the first, those who served in the Soviet state's foreign representation were forcibly compelled to absolute orthodoxy. The assignments, however, held certain special advantages that helped compensate for the many risks.

Customarily, each appointee had a guarantor who attested to his loyalty and competence. If the sponsor subsequently became implicated in any matter under investigation by the Cheka, scores of arrests followed, ending the careers if not the lives of all those remotely associated with him. There are numerous documented instances of the widespread effects of a fall from grace in Moscow. In the mid-thirties, hundreds of OGPU and GRU officers were abruptly recalled from their foreign stations and, on returning to Moscow, were arrested and executed as "accomplices" in "crimes" of which they had no knowledge and to which they certainly had no direct connection.

Initially, selection for service in a foreign post was heavily weighted in favor of party loyalty. It soon became evident to the leadership that education, competence, and skill were not to be treated as liabilities. It is only in the last twenty-five years that the organs have focused on the recruitment of better-educated and more-accomplished candidates. The need to augment loyalty with ability became essential only when the Center recognized two major shifts in the world: First, after World War II the pool of those who were susceptible to ideological recruitment evaporated;

second, the need for scientific and technical knowledge among people conducting espionage abroad became imperative.

An important innovation of the early period was a duality of systems operating in foreign areas. To have several unrelated elements focusing on the same target was wholly consistent with Dzerzhinsky's concept of the most effective means of reducing vulnerability to penetration, limiting loss in the event of compromise, maintaining tight cellular security, and of course, providing a critical cross-check on information collected. The system has proved sound for the Soviet services in the intervening years and is still used extensively.

Lateral coordination between "illegal" and "official" elements is handled by Moscow, and no contact can occur without the approval of the Center. The same discipline applies to the Czech, East German, Romanian, Bulgarian, Polish, and most recently, Cuban services. It is possible to reduce conflicts and casualties among the disparate subordinate services by requiring that *all* operational proposals first be submitted to the Center.

The main files, which Dzerzhinsky preserved and Mikhail Trilisser (later chief of the Foreign Department) expanded, are the most critical element in the process. A Czech intelligence man in Copenhagen cannot undertake the development and recruitment of a Danish official without requesting approval from the Soviets. In the same regard, a Turkish radical assassin in Rome, under Bulgarian sponsorship, can't fire a pistol at his assigned target without Sofia's prior coordination with Moscow. The methodology of Soviet operations' using subordinated services is well founded. There is no evidence of a relaxation of Soviet control to the degree that uncoordinated operations can occur.

By insisting on discipline and absolute compliance, it has been possible for Soviet official elements to be expelled from a country without implicating the illegal nets. Poor operational security, especially the failure to disassociate minor agents who had become known to the police, caused grave damage to the Soviet clandestine networks in Germany during the years 1933–1941.

In most situations the legal resident is known to the illegal resident, though the reverse is not always true. Emergency procedures are established to cope with an occasional arrest of an illegal by the local security forces. The previously planned insulation of one element from another makes it possible for Soviet espionage to continue despite arrests and expulsions.

The expulsion of a "legal" state security officer from a trade mission or Intourist, Aeroflot, Novosti, Amtorg, or Tass office has not been a serious detriment to either the individual's career or subsequent assignment to another country. Replacement of an illegal is more costly, is time-consuming, and requires special protection to ensure the integrity of the illegal's net and its ability to continue to operate.

Dzerzhinsky's basic precepts continue to serve the Soviets:

(1) Build while there is peace against the certainty of war.

(2) The "officials" are less able to assist at precisely the time they are most needed (periods during which the risk of hostilities is most imminent).

(3) Highly developed nets of illegals are important and reliable sources of intelligence information.

"Do not depend on the assumption that the exposure of the legal INOs and the expulsion of INO personnel with diplomatic cover marks the end of espionage."[60]

The history of the sinusoidal curve of Soviet diplomatic experience during the last fifty years has vindicated Dzerzhinsky's strategy.

The expansion of the Soviet organs into foreign countries raised awesome technical problems regarding the need for timely clandestine communications. Although the early codes and ciphers were weak and extensively read by the unauthorized, the concept of communications security was relatively advanced for the period. Dzerzhinsky demanded that all communications be enciphered, but in addition he directed that they were to be handled as if they were highly incriminating and written in clear text. He was convinced that an intercepted cryptic communication, even though it could not be read, still conveyed the dangerous information that the originator and the addressee could be assumed to be involved in activities inimical to the interests of the countries in which they resided. Simple disclosure of the use of any clandestine means was a serious breach. Under his direction, new techniques for the concealment of such communications were brought to a high level of development.

VChK technicians devoted great effort to experimentation with the various kinds of secret inks that had become common during World War I. The Dzerzhinsky contribution to the security of these systems was his demand that the cryptic message be enciphered as well as concealed. This was in addition to the early practice of giving each officer with net responsibilities a cipher system unique to him or to his net. This was accomplished by using "book ciphers," in which the same techniques were used in conjunction with a different and commonly available book as the key. The use of a book cipher requires special techniques, such as (1) selection of an appropriate book as the source of the "key text" and (2) the ordination of the different sequential steps to be used in the exchanges. Both are thought to be techniques commonly used in clandestine communications. "Codes" have not been in use for fifty years. It was also customary in the early days for each officer in an official facility, when he left the secure area, to assemble his documents in a cloth bag which he then *sewed* shut with a distinctive colored thread, protected further by the imprint of a peculiar device applied to hot sealing wax.

Dzerzhinsky's recognition of the necessity for controlled, secure communications led to the development of a cumbersome, rigid system which, for all its inefficiencies, was generally successful. The ever-increasing use of the wireless and cable introduced new vulnerabilities which the Soviets were slow to grasp. As long as the *fact* that communications were flowing from point to point was concealed, their weak cipher system gave a degree of protection. However, once the messages were transmitted by wireless, they became fair game for the black chambers of Europe, not one of which found the early Soviet ciphers beyond their abilities to decrypt. (The term "black chamber" derives from the seventeenth-century *cabinet noir* in France, which was a secret center for decryption. "Black chamber," although deservedly archaic, is still used occasionally to denote facilities dedicated to cryptanalytic attacks on foreign codes and ciphers.)

The Italians, Japanese, French, and British read Soviet ciphers for years. It wasn't until the late twenties that the OGPU recognized the transparency of the methods then in use. Dzerzhinsky had insisted that the VChK communications system be independent of all other Soviet systems. Later, as experience suggested, the sole responsibility for the generation of ciphers and the enforcement of communications security came to rest in the Ministry of State Security, where a Chief Directorate of the KGB still controls these critical functions.

Clandestine communications systems, to include ciphers, methods, means, security, and discipline, are exclusive present-day KGB responsibilities. All personnel directly involved in the control of clandestine communications, starting with the earliest of the KRO and INO illegal agents, have been Chekists. By instituting a carefully thought-out and fully integrated internal system, the organs have been able to maintain a better than average level in communications security, which has been relatively effective against large-scale, current, and continuing cryptanalytic penetration by other services.

In addition to new high-grade ciphers, Soviet messages are further protected by the unfailing use of cryptic references and by a strict prohibition of the use of true names. By requiring strict compliance, the Soviet service has been able to protect its intentions, activities, and, to some degree, the identities of personnel engaged in clandestine work.

The control of information within the system is governed by scrupulous observance of the "need to know" principle. In this regard, Stalin gave a long-running, bloody demonstration of just how dangerous it can be to "know" when he executed virtually all of the service members who had guilty knowledge of his own crimes. Anyone who survived his purges of the organs came away with the conviction that, although information might confer power or advantage, it could also be a lethal commodity.

Today, more than ever before, there is no casual exchange of information among service officers. In the more collegial days of the ideologues, it was not uncommon for Comintern, OGPU, and GRU operatives to make disclosures of some aspect of the "work" to others within their organization. Today, without the small bonds of trust born of common conviction that previously existed, confiding in a friend or colleague has become highly dangerous.

All of the rules governing security were derived by the VChK's founders from their own extensive prison experience. By trial and deadly error, rules governing clandestine activity were developed and refined. On the assumption that communications would be infrequent, briefing for a mission was very broad in its content. Agents dispatched to the field had a clear understanding of the mission's objectives and were given the latitude to make adjustments in the field. The Center, prior to dispatching agents, devoted careful consideration to the kinds of problems that might reasonably be expected. Alternatives were examined and provisions made for documentation, funds, escape procedures, danger signals, and the like. The stress given to pre-mission planning and the granting of near autonomy to some operators was a tribute to the intensity of the operator's ideological commitment (in other words, his trustworthiness), a reflection of the infrequency and unreliability of communications, and because there was no satisfactory alternative.

Extraordinary results were obtained by early Soviet agents who single-handedly achieved monumental objectives in espionage operations. With the development of improved means of secure communication, the Center devoted less time to planning and more to supervision and management. By 1927 and the arrival of Stalin as the effective head of state, the operator's freedom of action was gradually reduced to zero and the ideological drive diminished to a point at which desertions began to occur.

Under Dzerzhinsky, agent selection, briefing, training, and dispatching were based on sound principles buttressed by revealing exchanges of mutual confidence. The shared goals, dedication to a set of revolutionary ideals, and general reverence for Lenin's near-divine leadership made mission failure unthinkable. This mix of psychology, commitment, and absolute faith in their historic role made the early Chekists remarkable in any context.

Official Soviet histories of the VChK take note of the fact that Dzerzhinsky prohibited the creation of files on the activities of many of the singleton agents he personally operated. Some of these agents were later identified by Soviet historians. His observance of his own rules governing clandestine activity ensured that there would be no record of their "time behind the lines" in the VChK archives.[61]

From its inception the VChK operated on the assumption that there could be no neutrality in the pursuit of revolutionary goals. One was either wholly absorbed in actively advancing the Bolshevik cause or one was an enemy. The proposition of perpetual siege or eternal war was used effectively to sustain the VChK's mission and excuse its excesses. With an endless supply of internal and external "enemies," it has been possible to generate a permanent state of acute paranoia, which characterizes the Soviet organs to this day.

Until the replacement of the famed Article 58 of the Soviet criminal code (which was devoted to arming state security with "extraordinary" powers in suppressing anyone the service determined to be an enemy of the state), the charges against those arrested invariably included "counterrevolutionary" activities. The present laws, which empower the KGB to operate with the same latitude, are now aimed at "anti-Soviet" activity. The change of euphemism suggests that the revolution is no longer at risk. But the Soviet state, despite its absolute dominion over the populace, continues to promote the fiction that it is menaced by internal enemies who threaten its existence. Thereby it fully justifies the KGB's vast authority.

It was decided that foreign visitors to the USSR must be accorded treatment that would reinforce their view of the government as truly engaged in making a workers' paradise. The task of reinforcing favorable opinion was seen as an internal-security function, and congenial Chekists saw to it that visitors were carefully isolated from the realities. Today, Intourist performs these escort functions and maintains the essential connections with the state security organs.

The KGB also supervises the propagandizing of tourists and scholars, and maintains a subsidiary school system for training foreigners, especially Third World terrorists and those who will participate in the theft of scientific and technical information in the West.[62]

The organizational nature of the VChK is characterized by its coherent integration. The scope of the Soviet service, unlike those of other nations, is a continuum of related missions and objectives. Non-Soviet services have tended to organize and develop in reaction to perceived threats: For example, by extension, Britain's M.I.5 and the Special Branch can claim to be lineal descendants of the Irish Branch of the 1880s, just as the U.S. Army's G-2 can claim derivation from the Indian scouts who served with the cavalry in the western territories prior to the Civil War. "The House that Felix Built," however, bears evidence that the architect and builder was able to anticipate future needs at the time of construction.

The intended inefficiencies of the democracies fortunately prevent the development of a Western analogue to the KGB. The concept of an intelligence community in which responsibilities are shared, an oversight role for the legislative branch, and a President's Foreign Intelligence Advisory Board make it impossible for the United States government to equal the awesome power of the KGB—for which we must all be grateful.

Having marked these distinctions of choice, it is essential to add simply that no Western service can be compared in any way with the KGB. To suggest comparability is to reveal a gross misconception of the reality. The conventional Western problems of bureaucratic "turf," the conflicts, both personal and institutional, between and among bureaus, agencies, ministries, legislators, and heads of state, all operate to prevent the creation of a truly integrated internal-security and national intelligence apparatus.[63]

The elements that still define the Soviet system of internal security and intelligence were, initially, devised by Dzerzhinsky. Other derivative functions, such as the highly organized propagandization of foreign tourists and scholars in the Soviet Union and the training of Third World terrorists, were added in later years.

The *raison d'être* of the system was and is to establish and maintain rigid control over the entire Russian populace. The totality of the control, and enforcement of absolute discipline, have the additional advantages of reducing the regime's vulnerability to penetration by other national intelligence services. It is a most effective counterintelligence method and has substantially contributed to the furtherance of some conventional Soviet intelligence activities outside the USSR.

Dzerzhinsky's success in controlling the Russian populace and the Soviet armed forces assured Lenin's complete political dominance over the fledgling revolutionary state. The decision to adopt the tactic of mass terror exemplified the way in which the idealistic content of the rhetoric of the revolution was ignored. "All Power to the People" came to mean all power to Lenin and the party—which consisted only of those subservient to Lenin.

Lincoln Steffens, who had "seen the future and it works," and John Reed, both of whom fancied themselves as the main American explicators of Soviet mysteries, were strangely silent about Lenin's arrogation of power. The writings of both men failed to include any suggestion of condemnation. They and other liberal advocates who had preached the social democratic dogma were uniformly reserved on this point. By their silence they betrayed that faith and, in so doing, indirectly facilitated the imposition of the police state.

When Lenin dissolved the Constituent Assembly on January 5, 1918, he set a precedent for Hitler's 1933 dissolution of the Reichstag. The true nature of the Soviet state had become evident. As Professor Leggett notes, "Thus ended the sole parliament in the history of Russia to be freely elected on the basis of universal, unrestricted franchise and secret ballot. The only blood spilled was that of some seven or eight persons killed when the Bolshevik soldiery fired on a crowd of demonstrators."[64]

Although the Western press took little notice of the event, the significance of Lenin's arbitrary action was not lost on Maxim Gorky, who described the incident on January 9, 1918, in *Novaia zhin:*

> On January 5, 1918, the unarmed Petersburg democracy—factory and white-collar workers—demonstrated peacefully in honour of the Constitutent Assembly. For almost a hundred years the finest Russians have lived by the idea of a Constitutent Assembly, a political institution which would give the entire Russian democracy the opportunity to freely express its will. In the struggle for this idea, thousands of the intelligentsia and tens of thousands of workers and peasants have perished in prisons, in exile and at hard labor, on the gallows and by soldiers' bullets. Rivers of blood have been spilled on the sacrificial altar of this sacred idea, and now the People's Commissars have given orders to shoot the democracy which demonstrated in honour of this idea. . . ."[65]

With the Constitutent Assembly out of the way, Lenin proceeded to pick off the political opposition groups one by one. Some individual members of the opposition were allowed to join the Bolshevik fold; these were mainly technicians with essential skills. Most of the opposition leaders were later "investigated," arrested, and imprisoned or executed by the organs. A relatively small number managed to escape Russia and become active in various anti-Soviet organizations.

The Russian émigré colonies in Western Europe became more numerous, though no more united in their consensus about the USSR. The monarchists, the veterans, and now the various shades of socialists, anarchists, and radical syndicalists found they had nothing in common but their exile. Despite the disunity of the factions, the émigrés were of continuing concern to Lenin. Surveillance and monitoring of émigré activities became an important mission for the VChK, and on December 5, 1920, Dzerzhinsky, in response to an urgent order from Lenin, issued a secret directive to expand the effort and to initiate provocation operations designed to repatriate or otherwise neutralize the émigrés.[66]

The fact that the émigrés posed no real threat to the Bolshevik regime was not relevant. Lenin believed that the million or more who had fled during the revolution and the civil war constituted a danger to the Soviets. His preoccupation with the émigré threat was the motivating factor in the establishment of the Counterespionage Department (KRO), which sent detachments abroad to hunt down émigré "counterrevolutionaries."

The use of mass terror by the organs proved an effective tool in eliminating individual trust. Its indiscriminate application conveyed the message that everyone was vulnerable to arrest, detention, and worse. In *The Edge of War* Professor J. D. Atkinson quotes N. V. Krylenko, the public prosecutor and later minister of justice, as the latter captures the essence of the Soviet government's intent: "We must execute not only the guilty. Execution of the innocent will impress the masses even more."

Dzerzhinsky was among the most complicated of the Bolshevik revolutionaries. Unlike Lenin, Trotsky, and Stalin, who were revolutionaries from afar, Dzerzhinsky fought at close range. In the years before the successful uprisings in 1917, he had already "made his bones" by killing in the name of the revolution. He was no simple pamphleteer but a dedicated communist who allowed nothing to stand in the way of the revolution. His single-mindedness was not without cost: He had served twelve years in various czarist prisons.

Usually, Dzerzhinsky is dismissed with the marginal notation that he was the "founder of the VChK." Although the statement is true, its import is seldom noted. The success of the Soviet coup and the continuation of Soviet power to this date could not have occurred without the VChK, and the VChK *was* Dzerzhinsky.

Without the VChK, Lenin would have failed and Stalin would have drowned in the sewers of Bolshevik politics. The ascendancy of the KGB recently neared its zenith with Andropov's assumption of control. The USSR, long regarded as a prison in which 264 million inmates are confined, appeared to have made the metaphor a reality when it put a professionally trained jailer in charge.

Although Dzerzhinsky's career suggests much about the nature of the man, the official Soviet biography of him, as well as the many official histories of the VChK, are sufficiently nonspecific as to obscure or omit reference to his early life.[67]

His family background, personal demeanor, and physical characteristics provide no portent of his adult life and revolutionary behavior. Felix E. Dzerzhinsky was born on September 11, 1877, near Svenchtani, in the province of Vilna, now part of the Soviet Republic of Lithuania. Vilna was formerly the center for the ancient kingdom of that name which was merged with the kingdom of Poland in 1386 following the marriage of the reigning Polish queen to the grand prince of Lithuania. In 1772, when Poland was partitioned among Frederick the Great of Prussia, Maria Theresa of Austria, and Catherine the Great of Russia, Lithuania was absorbed into the Russian Empire. But its population, part Polish, part

Lithuanian, and strongly Catholic, never became reconciled to Russian domination, and the Lithuanians were characterized by their continuing antipathy to Russian imperialism. Resentment of czarist Russian attitudes formed a constituent part of Dzerzhinsky's historical legacy and of his emotional baggage.

Dzerzhinsky's family belonged to the Polish *drobna szlachta,* the landed gentry or lesser aristocracy. In Russia, Dzerzhinsky was regarded as *dvorianin,* or member of the minor nobility. The family's landholdings were not vast by the period's standards, but neither were they modest. The family was a respected element in what might be called an upper-upper-middle-class stratum. His father, in addition to being an absentee landlord, belonged to the intelligentsia by virtue of a university degree in mathematics and physics and a post as professor at the Vilna *gymnasium.*[68]

Most accounts describe young Felix as a precocious if not brilliant student. His scholastic aptitude, however, did not extend to mastery in the fields of mathematics, physics, or the Russian language. His principal interests were in logic and the political and economic sciences of the late nineteenth century. Raised a Catholic, during his formative years he considered a career in law or the priesthood. A part of his character was engaged by the authority and order of the Church, but he did not commit himself for reasons undiscovered by his biographers.[69]

Two events suggest possible influences on his decision not to seek holy orders: In 1895 he joined the Lithuanian Social Democratic Party, an organization that first exposed him to the heady doctrines of Marxism. His family indulged his forays into the area of social justice, much as Japanese families once allowed their male children one radical fling before going on to university and a lifelong career in the military or business. In young Dzerzhinsky's case, he decided to complete his studies in Moscow despite his poor command of Russian (he was required to repeat the first year of Russian at the *gymnasium* because of his difficulties with the language), and in the fall of 1896 he became a university student in Moscow.

There are two versions of the second event. One is that he had "trouble with the school authorities" and then opted to devote himself to revolutionary life.[70] The other version implies a different motivation: namely that, like Lenin, whose older brother was executed for his participation in a plot to assassinate the Czar, Dzerzhinsky saw his tubercular younger brother executed by the Okhrana for writing seditious and revolutionary poetry.[71]

There are no means of measuring the effects of these events on Dzerzhinsky's revolutionary motivation, but it may be that a combination of the two forces prompted him to seek vengeance in radical politics. The account of his younger brother's execution has been depreciated by Soviet writers because it calls into question his acceptance of the objective correctness of Marx's explanation of the world. In the Bolshevik scheme of things, no person can be exalted by an action based on emotional response.

Dzerzhinsky was an unlikely revolutionary. Slightly built, quiet in demeanor, and open in his dealings with others, he lacked the assertiveness of those who proclaimed the inevitability of the new order. At that time Marxism was only a leitmotiv, not yet a complete religion.

For the next several years Dzerzhinsky was active in social-protest movements. These ineffectual organizations were known to the Okhrana but were allowed to continue as safety valves for the steamy exhalations of the young. Members of the groups were identified and carded. The group leaders in many instances were Okhrana agents charged with distinguishing between the many who merely talked a good rebellion and the few who posed a genuine threat to the Czar.

Dzerzhinsky, becoming impatient with street-corner exhortations, pamphleteering, and endless debate, led a few ill-planned attacks against the Okhrana. The raids were singularly unsuccessful, and for his leadership role he was arrested. On July 17, 1897, two months before his twentieth birthday, he was accorded an indeterminate sentence for "crimes against the state." The charges included pamphleteering for the release of political prisoners. His insistent quest for reform of the system caused the authorities to decide it would be best to cool his radicalism with a penitential visit to Siberia, where his sentence was changed to five years' hard labor.

It was in prison that Dzerzhinsky began the most important phase of his education as a revolutionary leader. Like most other members of his socioeconomic class, Dzerzhinsky had no prior experience with the criminal element of Russian or Polish society. The criminals were "different," whether they were in prison for stealing a loaf of bread or for murdering an unfaithful wife. Dzerzhinsky, on the other hand, was a "political" and was so marked the day the prison gates closed behind him. To his credit, he adapted quickly, and he successfully challenged the convict hierarchy as well as the ancient system of coercion and repression used by the guards. He gradually established himself as a leader, asserting the principle that all prisoners were simply victims of an inhuman system, imprisoned because of the underlying political and economic rot of a society built on a foundation of economic exploitation.

He was physically courageous and seemed able to bear harsh punishment. His apparent indifference to pain made him a moral leader among the convicts. He endured the most brutal treatment the Okhrana devised and emerged with no diminution of his ideological fervor. This notable behavior earned him the respect of his fellows, many of whom were later to serve under him in VChK. The personal loyalties he won in prison would count for much in the early days of the Cheka.

Dzerzhinsky's effect on his prison associates was dramatic, as evidenced by his ability to inspire common criminals to political activism. On August 28, 1899, Dzerzhinsky, not yet twenty-three, escaped from his Siberian penal camp. The escape succeeded only because of the support of the nonpolitical prisoners, who had come to accept him as a peer, and was sufficient to put Dzerzhinsky very close to the top of the Okhrana's list of dangerous enemies of the Czar.

By now he was the subject of an intensive police search, and five months later, on January 23, 1900, an Okhrana informant betrayed him. He was recaptured and sent to a different prison to serve the remainder of his sentence. He caused no initial disturbance, but since his reputation was established, he was regarded as a convict celebrity. He had considerable influence among the prisoners, and the authorities found it difficult to oppose or ignore him without arousing unwanted confrontation.

Dzerzhinsky was more resourceful and usually more intelligent than those who held him in confinement, and he used these advantages to achieve nominal gains for his fellow inmates. On his second prison tour, Dzerzhinsky was very much wiser in the ways of the system and understood precisely how best to exploit it.

Having been an attentive prisoner with an intensively focused mind, Dzerzhinsky learned from his criminal tutors how to operate with impunity in Moscow, Petrograd, and elsewhere. He developed a wide knowledge of clandestine methods and an even broader range of criminal contacts who could be trusted to provide assistance. He had been accepted by the criminals in prison and, in effect, was an honorary member of that select caste with a valid visa to the Russian underworld. He had demonstrated the attributes of a journeyman felon, with his contempt for informers and his strength and resolution in resisting coercion.

His ability to withstand interrogation won him the respect of his fellows. His adamant refusal to give useful information and his growing dialectical skill led the Okhrana to conclude that he knew much more than they had originally suspected. Their baseless assumption of Dzerzhinsky's importance greatly augmented his already imposing prestige, but it also made him a target for further investigation, interrogation, and torture.

After his 1902 escape, Dzerzhinsky was a much warier fugitive. He had learned an important lesson: not to underestimate the Okhrana's power or competence. He later imparted this caution to his VChK subordinates. Too often, in the past, revolutionaries had assumed that the regime's decadence reflected a similar decay in the Okhrana. Dzerzhinsky's point was that an intelligence service is not necessarily a mirror image of a nation afflicted by corruption. Though the distinction was subtle, it was one Dzerzhinsky emphasized.

A second point he insisted on as he struggled to build competence in the VChK was that even though the security service was bound to protect the party, it must remain, within its own organization, completely apolitical. Despite the contradictions, the senseless havoc, and the terror, Chekists sustained and justified their misguided actions as the simple execution of the omniscient party's will. It was exactly the acceptance of this myth as an article of unshakable faith that most facilitated the rise of Stalin.

In September 1912, again through the agency of an Okhrana informant, Dzerzhinsky was recaptured and sent to yet another penal colony, in this instance a copper mine located east of the Ural Mountains. In mid-1916, Dzerzhinsky was again transferred, this time to the infamous Butyrka prison in Moscow.

Butyrka was a maximum security prison reserved for the most hardened and incorrigible political prisoners. Though Dzerzhinsky had long held that status, the Okhrana had not previously sent him to Butyrka for fear he might try to organize its inmates. His confinement in the Urals, however, had created a crisis of sorts which made the transfer necessary.

Dzerzhinsky's health was failing. He had tuberculosis, and the authorities feared that his death would establish his martyrdom. Then, too, his organizational flair had produced a band of "Soviets" in the Ural penal colonies which, the authorities reasoned, would explode in violent resistance if he remained there. It was therefore thought better to separate him from his criminal "revolutionary" troops.

From his first imprisonment in 1897 to his release from the Butyrka in February 1917, he enjoyed only two periods of liberty: June 1902 to July 1905, and late 1909 to September 1912.[72] During these brief interludes, two events occurred that had a lasting effect on his subsequent life.

The first was in 1906, when he met Lenin and Stalin in Stockholm, where they were attending the Fourth RSDRP (Russian Social Democratic Labour Party [Bolsheviks]) Unity Congress. Lenin was fascinated by Dzerzhinsky, whom he saw as his intellectual peer as well as a genuine revolutionary capable of carrying out the plans Lenin was exhorting others to accomplish. Stalin, being neither an intellectual nor more than a vicarious revolutionary, was impressed by Dzerzhinsky, though fearful of his abilities.

When the conference ended, Lenin reverted to his role of the revolutionary from afar—that is, safely out of the dangers of the class struggle. Stalin resumed his career as a minor functionary (with hidden Okhrana connections), while of the three, Dzerzhinsky alone took up the burdens of producing, smuggling, and distributing revolutionary literature, and organizing strikes and demonstrations. Of the four most important Bolshevik figures, only Trotsky was absent from the Stockholm meeting.

The second event occurred in November 1910, at which time Dzerzhinsky married Sofia Sigizmundovna Mushkat. Like Felix, she was a dedicated revolutionary. They first met when Sofia was on a clandestine assignment in Poland under orders of the SDKPil (Social Democratic Party of the Kingdom of Poland and Lithuania). Her mission had become compromised, and in later years they would tell friends that their lives as "socialist lovers" had begun when Felix was sent to her rescue.

Although Dzerzhinsky was a fanatical revolutionary, he was not an ascetic. Before he met Sofia, two other women greatly influenced his life: Julia Goldman, who died of tuberculosis in 1903, and Sabina Feinstein, with whom he lived intermittently. These liaisons were not unusual in themselves, as Dzerzhinsky, aside from his revolutionary predilections, was a normal, almost pedestrian man. What was unusual was that later, as head of the VChK, he held a strong anti-Semitic bias, which, however, did not cloud his mission or result in his exclusion of capable Jews from important positions within the organs.

The personal cost of Dzerzhinsky's pursuing the life of an active revolutionary can also be seen in its effect on his wife and son, Ian, who was born on June 23, 1911, in a crowded women's prison in Warsaw.[73] Dzerzhinsky saw Ian for a few minutes on one occasion in 1912, before he was sent to the Ural mines. Similarly, eight months after Ian's birth he, too, was separated from Sofia, who was sent into perpetual exile in Siberia.[74]

After the February uprising, which secured the release of the czarist political prisoners, Felix, Sofia, and the seven-year-old Ian were briefly reunited. But once more the revolution came before the family, and Sofia and Ian went to Berne, where she took up an important post in the new Soviet diplomatic mission.[75] Dzerzhinsky was named commandant of the Smolny Headquarters and set in train the events leading to the October coup d'état and the formation of the VChK.

They remained separated until October 1918, when Lenin directed Dzerzhinsky, who was in poor health, to visit his family in Switzerland. They then remained apart until 1921, when Sofia and Ian returned to Moscow and the Dzerzhinskys took up family residence in the Kremlin apartments.

Lenin realized that Dzerzhinsky lent to the Bolsheviks a kind of legitimacy that neither he nor many of the others who labored on behalf of the cause could ever claim. Dzerzhinsky's sole observed affectation, if it can be called that, was to advertise his revolutionary commitment by wearing a three-quarter-sleeved Cossack tunic that left exposed the deep manacle scars on his slender wrists. These marks of revolutionary honor were a silent reminder to the schemers and Bolshevik bureaucrats that Dzerzhinsky had endured great physical pain in the service of the revolution, an experience shared by few of those who later rallied to the Bolsheviks' banner.

Dzerzhinsky's cruel physical experiences only intensified his revolutionary commitment. With his unprepossessing appearance, it was difficult to accept that he could have survived the tortures and deprivations of the Czar's prisons—until one looked into his hard blue eyes. He had the icy gaze of Dostoevsky's Grand Inquisitor. One of his captives, held by the Cheka, later remarked, "Dzerzhinsky's personal interrogation was the most feared because his eyes made you feel that he could see into your very soul."[76]

No matter one's political orientation, Felix Dzerzhinsky was a remarkable man. His dedication to the Bolshevik cause was without equal. He was a brutal, brilliant pragmatist who, in building the Cheka, showed extraordinary adeptness at innovation in the exploitation of opportunities. The resultant organization was a highly integrated system for internal security and intelligence which had as its primary objective the preservation of Bolshevik power. His energetic efforts to build the Cheka were formally recognized on February 6, 1922, when the "temporary" organization was converted into the all-too-permanent State Political Administration (*Gosudarstvennoe politicheskoe upravlenie*), the GPU.[77]

The name change was more than symbolic. It confirmed that the functions, missions, and authorities arrogated by Dzerzhinsky in the preceding three years were now legitimized. In the future, he would operate with the full authority of the Soviet state and continue to provide his own direction. With the formalization of status, the first developmental phase ended. The organs were intact and the GPU was secure in the service of the party.

2 · The Communist International

In March 1919, before the Bolsheviks achieved complete control of the Soviet state, Lenin and Trotsky convened a casual group of some forty foreign sympathizers in Moscow and proclaimed the assemblage to be the founding congress of the Third or Communist International. The acronym *Comintern* came into general usage as a substitute for Third International. The *Third* denoted that there had been two previous congresses: Karl Marx's "International Workingmen's Association" in London in 1864 and the Social Democratic Second International in Paris in 1889.

Before proceeding, it is useful to dispose of a popular myth: the assumption that the Comintern was basically an intelligence organization. It was not. Like every Soviet organizational creature, it served Soviet intelligence. This chapter deals with the Comintern as a curious political artifact and points up the ways in which it identified recruitable talent, performed minor intelligence collection, and most significantly, deflected attention from the more dangerous and important Soviet intelligence.

Unfortunately, the Comintern's importance in Soviet intelligence has been elevated (by a few historians) to a level it never attained.

The Comintern's initial manifesto, written by Trotsky, summoned all victims of imperialism, proletarians and colonials, to rally to the communist cause.[1] The substantive content was little more than a paraphrase of Marx's initial *Communist Manifesto,* issued seventy-two years earlier. The victorious Allied powers were occupied with the complexities of the aftermath of Versailles and paid little heed to Lenin and Trotsky's dramatic imperative: WORKERS OF THE WORLD, UNITE! YOU HAVE NOTHING TO LOSE BUT YOUR CHAINS!

Although the egalitarianism expressed by the Comintern attracted widespread support among fledgling foreign Communist parties, there was never a moment that the Comintern wasn't under absolute Soviet control. In the best Orwellian sense, all Communist parties were equal, except that the Soviet party was always more equal. The Comintern was designed to act as the general staff in the coming world revolution, and it could not function without a chief.

Grigori Zinoviev, as Comintern chairman in 1919, had the task of resolving the organizational chaos implicit in a self-proclaimed "democratic" body made up of independent headstrong elements whose organization was, in fact, secretly operated by the Soviets. The Comintern's early years were devoted to the Soviet objective of splitting the European Socialist parties into warring factions and bringing the radical left-wing elements under Comintern discipline and control.

To this end, the Second Comintern Congress of August 1920 laid down "twenty-one conditions," drafted by Lenin, to which member Communist parties were compelled to subscribe.[2] The adoption of all twenty-one by the national parties of the Comintern signaled the end of the pretense of collegiality contained in Trotsky's initial manifesto.

Discipline became the watchword. It meant simply that henceforth there would be absolute obedience to Bolshevik dictates. Comintern members were required to commit themselves to the political pattern of Soviet rule that had emerged in Russia. It meant acceptance of the tactic of violent revolution under the exclusive leadership of a strictly "disciplined" Communist party—i.e., one that acted only on direction from Moscow. Additionally, the Comintern members were required to accept without question all decisions of the International and to accept the overriding interests of the Soviet Union in all matters relating to the "world revolution."

Western reactions to the Comintern's publicly proclaimed objective of world revolution were predictable, though mixed. Winston Churchill, for one, who believed communism to be malign, found the Comintern's statement of objectives to be patent confirmation of his own fixed opinions. Pragmatists and political moderates tended to dismiss Comintern rhetoric on the grounds that economic reality would compel the Bolsheviks to modify, or even abandon, their world revolutionary goals.

The sincerity of the Bolshevik leaders' faith in the efficacy of world revolution of the proletariat is difficult to conceive. The problem was simply that the success of the Bolshevik coup had contradicted the basic revolutionary dogma of Marx, which held that the vanguard of the revolution would be the proletariat and that revolution would first occur in an advanced industrial (capitalist) state. In their post-1918 writings, both Lenin and Trotsky took special pains to avoid acknowledging the discrepancy between the facts of the Bolsheviks' armed coup and the revealed "truth" of Marx. It was not practical politics to admit that the coup had been a fluke and that the sainted Marx was wrong. Further, it was false to pretend that its success was "historically determined by the fundamental contradictions of capitalism."

Aside from Lenin's Marxian dilemma, there was another and perhaps more comprehensible basis for the Comintern's demand for world revolution. The Armistice of 1918 marked the ceremonial end of the First World War, but the conflict continued in other areas and for reasons other than those for which it was initially fought. The Comintern correctly noted that the social fabric of the *anciens régimes* had not adapted to the shape of the new world and that the war had had the effect of thrusting societies, particularly in the industrial countries, into a new social and political context.

Lenin and Trotsky had some understanding of the phenomenon but were disabled by their insistence on the literal truth of Marx and their predisposition toward the radical left—which blinded them to the possibility of an equally strong appeal from the radical right. In the early years of the Comintern, Lenin and Trotsky overlooked or dismissed as infeasible the possibility that the proletariat would opt for a Hitlerian rather than a Marxist Nirvana. For the Bolshevik apostles, it proved a costly error.

While the Versailles Peace Conference lumbered on, the excluded Bolsheviks were not unaware of the serious dislocations and near-chaos in Germany. The punitive reparations that were being exacted by the Allies were certain to complete the destruction of the war-weakened German economy. The Bolsheviks were beginning to gain the upper hand in their own civil struggle, and the Allied withdrawal from Soviet territory, plus the Red Army's 1920 defeat of the "invasion" of Russia by Poland, were the factors that convinced Lenin and Trotsky that the propitious moment for export of their revolution had arrived.

The comments of Comintern Chairman Zinoviev about the 1923 decision to set the world revolution in motion have a familiar ring:

> . . . German events are developing with the certainty of fate. . . . Soon everyone will see that the autumn months of 1923 mark a turning point not only for Germany, but also for the world in general. . . .
>
> The social basis of the coming revolution is absolutely clear. In the cities the workers are definitely numerically superior [to the rest of the population]. These workers have followed the counterrevolutionary German Social Democratic Party in one way or another . . . [but] this worker-giant is now convinced that the country and the working class can be saved only by revolution.
>
> From the moment the German working class turns its back upon

the German Social Democrats and follows the Communist Party, the fate of Germany is sealed. . . .

The forthcoming German revolution will be a proletarian class revolution. The twenty-two million German workers who make up its army represent the cornerstone of the international proletariat. They will meet the capitalists with an international revolution. According to the highest estimates, in 1917 Russia had eight to ten million workers among a population of 160 million. Germany, with a population of sixty million, has more than twenty million workers. With us, the working class was only a small minority; in Germany it is the principal element, the majority of the population. . . . Lenin was correct when he said: "In Western Europe, and especially in a country such as Germany, it will be much more difficult to start a proletarian revolution than in Russia. But it will be much easier to continue and finish it."[3]

Zinoviev's estimate of the political situation with Germany, with which Lenin concurred, resulted in the Comintern's ordering the German Communist Party (KPD) to initiate an insurrection. The German party tried to carry out the Comintern mandate. At a crucial moment the main attempt was canceled, but isolated party groups, not informed of the reversal in orders, launched their attacks only to be savagely put down by loyal Germans who favored "law and order." Following the abortive uprising, the German party went on the defensive until it was finally obliterated by Hitler.

The failure of the German party to carry out a proletarian revolution raised serious doubts in the minds of the Bolshevik leaders about the Comintern's ability to manage a single national insurrection, let alone a world revolution. The Comintern hierarchs appeared to be more dedicated to the preservation of their own positions than to the pseudoidealism of Marxism-Leninism. Lenin's failing health caused him to pay less and less attention to the Comintern and Trotsky's grandiose plans. Instead, his dwindling energies were directed toward solving the most recent set of problems posed by the New Economic Policy (NEP) and arbiting the unremitting struggles for power among his own lieutenants.

In his final years, Lenin, a tireless advocate of criminal behavior, began to realize that he had accumulated subordinates who were similarly disposed toward criminal conflict but tended to direct it at one another, without the restraints of the lofty idealism he professed.

During the years of the Comintern's "world revolution" phase, Stalin focused on building his now-extensive patronage and let the party intellectuals collide with one another in the debate of abstract issues. Although Trotsky had displayed organizational and command ability at the time of the coup, his persistent advocacy of world revolution rendered him vulnerable to attack. The failure in Germany suggested that the policy of promoting uncoordinated uprisings was demonstrably ineffective and that the Comintern was far from being a general staff.

Like Stalin, Dzerzhinsky had strong reservations about the utility of the Comintern in achieving revolutionary aims. At the time, Dzerzhinsky was deeply involved in the growing problems, economic and ideological, that resulted from the NEP as well as the GPU's expanding operational role, especially in the Western democratic states. Dzerzhinsky still maintained tight control over Comintern activities that might impinge on or impede the objectives of the organs' intelligence missions.

Of particular concern to Dzerzhinsky was the counterintelligence problem of the Comintern and its foreign member participants. To ensure that this critical mission was effectively discharged, he appointed Mikhail Abramovich Triliser to be chief of the GPU's Foreign Department (later to become the KGB's First Chief Directorate). Triliser was authorized to veto any Comintern activities that affected Soviet security in any respect. He was also given authority to co-opt Comintern elements and personnel to carry out intelligence activities. In this way, if an operation went wrong, the organs had the advantage of "plausible denial" and could conveniently attribute the event to spontaneous enthusiasm on the part of the national parties.

The techniques of disavowal bedeviled the West, especially the United States. The Comintern's relationship with the organs was certain, though the Soviet Union insisted there was no connection. Further, the Comintern was not an official part of the Soviet government, but "just a collegium of communist parties who shared common objectives," in the words of Foreign Minister Maxim Litvinov.

At the time of Lenin's death, on January 21, 1924, the Comintern was a discredited revolutionary vehicle, having failed to bring about a successful uprising in Germany. It continued to exist because the principal Moscow actors were too preoccupied with the intrigues of succession to focus on the fate of the "fraternal parties." While the contending leaders maneuvered, the Comintern drifted.

Trotsky, the inveterate revolutionary idealist with messianic overtones, remained an exception. His vision of world revolution was unimpaired by the realization that the world still wasn't quite ready. Trotsky also ignored the fact that the USSR was not yet a significant world state, and he refused fully to accept that the Bolsheviks, though in control, had only a tenuous hold on their ownpower. These factors were to contribute to his eventual downfall.

A significant weakness in the Comintern structure was that various national party leaders advanced extravagant claims in order to enhance their own importance. Later, when ordered to execute a Moscow-originated plan of action, the local parties had neither the strength nor the discipline to carry out the action. It was an unintended result of the Comintern's failure to recognize and deal with the weaknesses in the national parties.

After the Soviet Union had finally succeeded in establishing diplomatic relations with Great Britain, an event occurred that inflicted serious damage on the Soviets' image. The Soviet Foreign Office (Narkomindel)[4] expressed one foreign policy, and the Comintern seemed to be advancing another. The incident involved the notorious "Zinoviev letter," a mysterious document that in 1924 helped topple Britain's first Labour government. It simultaneously weakened—if not all but destroyed—Great Britain's tiny but vocal Communist Party (CPGB). Relations between the Soviet Union and Great Britain were greatly strained by the event. Although widely publicized, more is known about the effects of the "Z" letter and less is known about the attendant facts.

In early 1924, Sir Hugh Sinclair, head of British Secret Service, came into possession of a letter purportedly written by Zinoviev, then chief of the Comintern. The letter was addressed to the leaders of Great Britain's minuscule Communist Party and called upon the "Dear Comrades to have cells in all units of the troops, especially those based in big cities or near munitions plants . . . etc." The letter was incendiary, though it stopped short of calling for armed rebellion.

Sixty years later, the authenticity of the "Z" letter is still mooted in some scholarly circles in Britain. Essentially, there were three salient possibilities: 1) It was a genuine Comintern document of conspiratorial instruction; 2) it was a forgery constructed and introduced by British intelligence; 3), the least likely, the letter was the product of a third party—Russian monarchists, Poles, French, or one of the flourishing European "forgery mills," which customarily manufactured documents for sale to various intelligence services.

As in most Comintern manipulations of schemes for world revolution, the facts are elusive. In the case of the "Z" letter, the issue is further clouded by the fact that Sinclair himself wrote to Sir Eyre Crowe of the Foreign Office that the letter had come to him from "an absolutely trustworthy source."

Subsequent investigation established the reasonable probability that the absolutely trustworthy source was Sinclair's "master spy," the chameleonlike impersonator and compulsive adventurer Sidney Reilly. Reilly had been a principal player in the Lockhart Affair in 1918. It was at that time that he came under suspicion by Xenophon Kalamatiano, who believed him to be a Soviet agent. Born in Russia as Sigmund Georgevich

Rosenblum, Reilly operated for both the British and the VChK. He was finally ordered executed by Stalin in 1925, having outlived his usefulness to the organs.

Educated speculation has advanced the theory that the "Z" letter might have been deliberately introduced, through Reilly, by Stalin and his conspiratorial associate Dzerzhinsky. The purpose of such a ploy would be to discredit the Comintern; its inspirer, Trotsky; and its chairman, Zinoviev, who at the time was one of the USSR's post-Lenin ruling triumvirate.

Another version contends that the "Z" letter was a clever fake produced by British intelligence and the Foreign Office to bring down Prime Minister Ramsay MacDonald's Labour government. It is further asserted in this version that Donald im Thurn, a former M.I.5 officer, introduced the forgery and was paid £10,000 for his efforts by the Conservative Party Central Office.

Whatever the facts, the "Z" letter had a dramatic effect on Britain's 1924 elections. The letter was published four days before the elections, and the public reaction stripped Labour of fifty seats and ruined those Liberals who had supported MacDonald's minority government. The "Z" letter was the denouement of a massive anti-Soviet campaign by the Tories that was supported by most of the British press.

MacDonald, who paid the price at the polls, had incurred the double enmity of Britain's Tory establishment not only for his recognition of the Bolshevik government but also for having negotiated trade agreements favorable to the USSR. From the Tories' perspective, these were heinous crimes; the "Z" letter was confirmation of MacDonald's malefactions as well as his naïveté in treating with the Bolsheviks in the first place.

Available documents tend to support the likelihood that Reilly gave the letter to im Thurn, who gave it to Sinclair, who gave it to Crowe, who "leaked" it to the friendly press. Later, Crowe insisted that he was helping, not hurting, MacDonald by releasing the "Z" letter. Crowe's protest was not persuasive, because simultaneously he fired off a protest to the Soviets without getting the customary MacDonald initialing on the draft of the note. Crowe's precipitate actions also provided the basis for subsequent press speculation, which served to keep the issue alive during the immediate pre-election period. For the rest of his life MacDonald complained about what he regarded as "indecent haste" in releasing both the letter and the protest note to the press.

Any approach to the "Z" letter incident requires asking the basic question: Who benefited from the act? The response is apt to be unsettling, since Stalin, Dzerzhinsky, and the Conservative Party were the significant winners, with the British Communist Party, the Comintern, Trotsky, and especially Zinoviev most hurt.

In another sense, the Tories and Trotsky both got what they wanted: the discrediting and downfall of a British Socialist government. To Trotsky, the ultimate leftist communist, socialism achieved at the polls in a free election was even more of an anathema than capitalism. Trotsky's doctrinal mind excluded any prospect of a middle way on the route to the dictatorship of the proletariat. It was the Trotskyite tone of the "Z" letter that led many to concede it was genuine (i.e., produced in the Comintern, at Trotsky's direction).

The most conclusive evidence is to be found in the recent release of Soviet messages of the day, which were intercepted and decrypted by the British. The messages reveal discussions among the Soviet leaders about an "actual" Zinoviev letter.

Further confirmation is to be found in the posthumously published memoirs of Aino Kuusinen, a Finnish Bolshevik who later spent years in Soviet prison camps.[5] Her husband, Otto, was secretary of the Comintern's Presidium, and his signature, along with Zinoviev's, was on the letter. According to Mrs. Kuusinen, the "Z" letter was genuine; however, she contends that the British Communists handled it carelessly and that parts of it were leaked to certain journalists. Aino Kuusinen further insists that the "journalists" concocted a new letter, which was the one read out in Parliament as the original and authentic one.

Additional doubt was cast on the innocence of the Soviets in the matter when the British envoy in Moscow reported "the somewhat similar case" of a letter from the Soviet Communist Party, intercepted by the Finnish government in 1922. Its authenticity had at first been denied by the Soviet government. "When it was established, by means of examination of the typewriting, that it was the work of the same machine as that on which various undoubtedly genuine circulars had been typed, the Soviet authorities took the fresh line that it was the work of a typist, Miss Eva Korhonen and that the committee of the party had nothing to do with it. The matter was dropped, as so many of these matters are."[6]

Aino Kuusinen adds: "It was clear to Otto from the outset that the letter which was made public was a forgery, even though it contained a few of the instructions . . ."[7] In this, Aino Kuusinen might have been correct except for her view that the original letter was altered by "journalists." It now seems more likely that if the material was in some instances paraphrased for purposes of clarity,[8] it would have been done by Reilly, im Thurn, and/or one or more of Sinclair's aides attempting to "enhance" the original letter to make it even more alarmingly seditious.

On the Soviet side, the letter reveals something of the Comintern's unrealistic empiricism in its early days. The "Z" letter unquestionably hurt both Trotsky and Zinoviev and, in so doing, advanced the interests of Stalin and his view that policy must now focus on internal control ("building socialism in one country,") rather than dissipating energies in the cause of world revolution.

Following Trotsky's internal exile to Siberia in 1927, Zinoviev, L. B. Kamenev, and Stalin made up the triumvirate that initially ruled the country in the wake of Lenin's death. The former two, like Trotsky, soon found themselves eased out by Stalin. While Stalin shinnied up the greased pole of Soviet power, the neglected Comintern turned its attentions from world revolution to augmenting the Soviet intelligence services in foreign areas.

The final fiasco in the world-revolution phase was the attempted use of the Comintern as the vehicle to lead an armed revolution in China in 1927. Once more, enthusiasm based on poor intelligence led the Soviets to believe that they were succeeding in the manipulation of Chinese political factions. When Chiang Kai-shek, without warning, purged his Kuomintang Party, expelled the Soviet advisers, arrested and executed communists, and broke with the Comintern-sponsored "united front" government, it became clear to Moscow that something had gone awry.[9]

Chiang's effective, if bloody, act ended the fiction that the united front government in China was anything other than a tactical approach by the Soviet-directed Chinese Communist Party (CCP). In the united front the CCP participated in the government; under Chiang's abruptly revised system the Chinese Communist Party was proscribed and the surviving members hunted down.

In Moscow, the remaining Trotskyites in the Comintern were outraged, claiming that the Soviet Central Committee (an unambiguous reference to Stalin) had disapproved the proposal to arm the Chinese Communists and initiate a Bolshevik-type revolution. The rhetoric surrounding this event is bewildering and difficult to reconcile with reality. "The Declaration of the Eighty-four," a Trotskyite document of May 1927, reflects a perverse rejection, on the part of the Comintern, of the united front policy by advancing the misconception that the small, weak Chinese Communist Party was a truly effective instrument capable of launching the world communist revolution without the need to develop additional strength.[10] Trotsky's insistent advocacy of premature violent revolutionary activity by the national communist parties only hardened Stalin's determination to purge the Comintern of the Trotskyites and their bankrupt policies.

The expulsion of Trotsky and Zinoviev from the Soviet CP in November 1927 was predicated on Stalin's charge that they were fragmenting the party and endangering the future of the Soviet system. The news of their expulsion evoked serious disagreement in foreign communist parties. In the ensuing months, the schisms resulting from Stalin's action caused serious strains throughout the International and gave Stalin a new pretext to tighten Soviet control over the Comintern. Many of the Trotskyite dissidents were sent to Siberian coercive labor camps for socialist "reeducation and rehabilitation."

By 1928, Stalin turned his attention to initiating attacks on the adherents of Nikolai Bukharin. Coincident with his assault on the Bukharinites, Stalin proposed a new ultra-left line for the Comintern and ordered a purge of the leadership of foreign communist parties. As a result of the purges, most of the foreign party founders were removed from their own parties and driven out of the Comintern.

From that time forward, the Comintern was under absolute Soviet control. It was harnessed completely to the support of the USSR's foreign policy and intelligence objectives. The Comintern's role in these matters has never been in dispute, although assessments of the Comintern's effectiveness in carrying out Soviet aims vary considerably.[11]

Without the complete support of the organs, Stalin could not have disposed of his growing opposition. With the organs, he was empowered to move on to the next phase.

A collateral aim of the Soviet government's use of the Comintern was the furtherance of Soviet policy by seemingly independent foreign national groups. A case in point was the exploitation of the American Communist Party (CPUSA) for intelligence collection, political action, and the provision of prospective recruits for the Soviet intelligence and security services. The CPUSA, like other indigenous Communist parties, slavishly adhered to the Moscow party line.

CPUSA leaders William Z. Foster, Eugene W. Dennis, and Earl Browder made repeated pilgrimages to Moscow to reaffirm their loyalty to Stalin and to revalidate their status. The CPUSA leaders, even in Moscow, were considered anti-intellectual, brawling boors who denounced each other in jealous attempts to secure Stalin's favor.[12]

Under Foster, Dennis, and Browder, the New York *Daily Worker* ran the party line in a strident editorial voice, which over the years afforded much unintended comic relief. The inadvertencies and embarrassments of contradicting or misinterpreting Moscow's dicta gave rise to long silences, ninety-degree editorial turns, and an occasional full reversal of yesterday's sentiments.[13]

The *Worker's* unintended silliness was a poor measure of the effect of Soviet propaganda, because its readership consisted mainly of native-born Americans. The foreign-language press in New York (principally German, Finnish, Russian, and Yiddish) was more effective because it was addressed to a highly sensitized and politically sophisticated readership with European and Russian connections.

Foster, Browder, and Dennis imagined themselves as obvious national leaders who would assume control of the United States "when the revolution comes."[14] The impression made on the foreign communists by the Americans was more Marx Brothers than Marx. The CPUSA never achieved any useful political power. Its chief contributions to the Soviet services were the collection of basic encyclopedic data and the names of a wide selection of prospective recruits.

The CPUSA's antics also deflected attention from the genuine internal-security threat posed by Soviets in the United States in the time prior to diplomatic recognition of the USSR in 1933. During the period, scarce internal-security resources tended to be devoted to observing the CPUSA and trying to fathom the labyrinthine structure of the Comintern.

During the thirties, when the Comintern was at its peak, thousands of American communists made the trek to Moscow to pledge their support of the world revolution. While such a pilgrimage might have produced a sense of well-being in the individual travelers, the Soviets' pervasive suspicion kept the Americans from ever achieving status as wholly acceptable international communists. It is interesting to note that in all the years since, no American has been rewarded by appointment to a position of authority or influence by the Soviets. None of the U.S. leaders enjoyed the prestige, power, or international repute of Wilhelm Pieck in Germany, Palmiro Togliatti in Italy, Maurice Thorez in France, or Harry Pollitt in England. The Bolsheviks apparently could not accept the premise that Americans, with their bourgeois background and demonstrated lack of discipline, were capable of sustained belief in Marxism-Leninism.

After the International's debacle in China, the question arose—Why did Stalin, who by then had consolidated his political power, permit the Comintern to continue in existence?—particularly when the Comintern kept alive the polemic exchanges between the Stalinists and the Trotsky "oppositionists." Although Stalin had succeeded in expelling Trotsky from the CPSU and banishing him and his followers to Alma-Ata, exile had not stilled Trotsky's pen, which continued to exhort world revolution led by the Comintern parties.

Trotsky was out of sight, but he was never out of Stalin's thoughts. By 1929, Stalin felt secure enough to exile Trotsky from the USSR and arrange for his dispatch to Turkey. There, Trotsky continued to oppose the Stalinists and their perversion of Lenin's ideals and the Comintern's mission. Trotsky's writings were proscribed in the Soviet Union after his expulsion from the party, and their propagation within the USSR was by copies, passed hand-to-hand in much the same clandestine manner as the present-day *samizdat* writings.

In light of later events, it is likely that Stalin allowed the circulation of

Trotsky's tracts as a means of identifying Trotsky's secret supporters. Stalin's own writings do not answer the question of why he allowed the Comintern to continue. Former Comintern officials have confirmed his contempt for its utility and his usual references to it in terms of ridicule and disdain.

The Comintern failed to achieve its primary role as the engine of the communist world revolution, and by late 1927, Stalin simply used it as a political cat's-paw and a means of monitoring national Communist parties in the search for exploitable revolutionary talent.

Many of those selected in the Comintern's development programs were ordered to the Soviet Union, where they were given instruction in communist doctrine and practice. (The procedure of inducing "progressive" foreign nationals to further their studies in Moscow continues today, especially among Third World leftists. The process is not to be confused with the somewhat similiar techniques employed by the Soviet intelligence services in sending foreign nationals to the USSR for intensive espionage training by the KGB and GRU.)

From the time of the Cheka to the present-day KGB, the Comintern and the "independent" or national Communist parties have provided occasional recruits of high quality. Today, because there are serious security risks involved in the use of individuals who have been overtly active on behalf of the USSR, the Soviet services no longer rely to the same degree on the national parties' nominees as other than incidental support agents. It is also increasingly difficult to find Marxist-Leninist ideologues who are qualified to meet the needs of the Soviet security service.

In its best days, the CPUSA did produce useful results and valuable talent for the Soviet services, but it must be remembered that the ease of recruitment (through self-selection) and the reliability of the recruits in the early period can be attributed to the fact that theirs was a genuine, though naïve, conviction about advertised Soviet aims.

In late 1927, Stalin was convinced that a capitalist-inspired assault on the USSR was in train. He was certain that immediate steps had to be taken to prepare for survival in the face of a blockade and to ward off imminent military attack. His *idée fixe* on the external threat brought strong measures into effect. His personal concerns only reaffirmed the Bolsheviks' convictions about the world outside the USSR. By reading the political tea leaves in his own way, Stalin was able to reinforce his mind-set and disbelieve contrary evidence.

The political rhetoric of the Western nations and Japan, when subjected to Marxist interpretation, revealed unmistakable antipathy toward the Soviet Union. The fact that the Soviets were castigated for their political manipulations in China, India, and throughout Western Europe and the United States was officially regarded in the Soviet press as unwarranted, hostile criticism. The Bolsheviks maintained that if indeed there were peasant revolts, strikes, riots, and guerrilla military actions, they were simply inevitable, according to Marxism-Leninism. Further, the local Communist parties that made up the Comintern and fomented the unrest were not subject to Soviet control, and their actions could only be viewed as "spontaneous expressions of the will of the oppressed masses."[15]

Inversion of the facts was essential in extending internal control within the USSR. Prosaic transgressions became monstrous crimes when committed in the fevered climate of sustained alarm about the imminence of war. The cumulative impact of converting the ordinary turning of the world into issues of direct menace to the Soviets had had regrettable if not irreversible effects on successive Soviet regimes. As a product of Stalinism and as a young, intense observer of the day, Yuri Andropov soon learned that terms such as *peace, peaceful coexistence,* and *détente* were important weapons in the Soviet armamentarium. When liberally used with non-Bolshevik audiences, they never failed to evoke responses favorable to the Soviet Union. He also learned that the frequent use of these words invariably gave rise to the hopes of foreigners that the Soviet Central Committee had abandoned its *raison d'état* and seized on the advantages of sharing common goals with the rest of the world. Since Lenin, the Soviet leadership has fully comprehended the fact that repetitive utterances of moderate, reassuring terms can be relied upon to assuage and disarm reasonable people everywhere.

Since each of these terms has an esoteric Bolshevik connotation, they do not necessarily mean what we think they mean. Soviet bellicosity is easier to deal with than Soviet cooperation. Direct threats are more handily met than feigned friendliness, bearing in mind that the exchanges are limited to world opinion on the one hand and the Soviet Central Committee on the other. The Russian public plays no role in the generation of policy and is usually not aware of policy beyond the official explications appearing in *Pravda.*

The preemption of evocative words, and the calculated encouragement of misperception on the part of the world as to Soviet intentions, wreak havoc with attempts to rationalize relations with the USSR. In any exchange in which the terms do not have an agreed meaning among the parties, there is no communication nor can there be any true negotiation. The historical record suggests that the well of East-West relations has been poisoned over many decades and has produced the acute distrust that governs current attempts at resolving dangerous issues.

Stalin's draconian measures of 1927 did much to distort the realities of the day. By focusing attention on the enemy without, he was better able to suppress and control the citizens within. The Comintern was directed to deliver messages on several levels. Prospective enemies were informed of the Soviet Union's growing military capacity, which, owing to enlightened leadership, was approaching astonishing power. Soviet friends were informed that the USSR, though strong, could not withstand attack from any quarter and that all who hoped for a socialist victory were to redouble their efforts and increase their own contributions to preserve the Soviet state.

The true vulnerabilities were masked. The Comintern was charged with keeping the international facade intact. Stalin's strategy to meet the imagined threat was to order a simultaneous revolution in industry and agriculture. Again the Comintern was put to work dramatizing the successes of the Five-Year Plan, which had been decreed in 1928. The plan, which demanded radicalization of all industrial activities as well as the total collectivization of agriculture, was seen by the outside world as impracticable. It was too grand, too extensive, and it failed to give appropriate consideration to the millions of Russians of all degrees whose lives would be affected by the drastic changes envisioned. Here again, Stalin's capacity to inflict barbarous treatment on the Russian people was not fully comprehended.

To accomplish the plan's objectives, Stalin made immediate resort to terroristic tactics against both the farmers and the industrial workers. Farms were destroyed, the farmers driven off the land, the granaries emptied, and the grain sold in the export market. Throughout this mad cycle of hunger and human suffering, the Comintern kept the world informed of the great "progress" in the plan's fulfillment. Reports of Stalin's terror were branded capitalist lies. Good people everywhere who hoped for the best gradually came to believe that Stalin, the fair-minded, just "little father," was at last leading the Soviet Union into a modern version of advanced socialism. The Comintern's propaganda efforts, along with the comprehensive program of calculated disinformation, biased much opinion in favor of the Soviets. Conscientious liberals everywhere were influenced by the reports of betterment of the lot of the workers and peasants, and critical judgment was suspended in hopes that the USSR would emerge from the experiment as a model state demonstrating the reality of Lenin's promise. By filling the information void with mass promotions of the success of collectivization and industrial reform, the Comintern played a vital role. Stalin was consistently portrayed as a firm, compassionate "builder" at the very moment he was embarked on destructive rampage.

The worldwide financial collapse of 1929 gave Stalin an additional reason for continuing the Comintern. He was certain that the economic chaos in the West gave the Soviets exploitable advantages. But the hoary exhortation to the workers of the world—"Unite! You have nothing to lose but your chains!"—failed to produce desired results, as most workers were more interested in reemployment than in chain-breaking and proved deaf to ideological sloganeering.

An example of the Comintern's support of Soviet foreign policy and its ability to harness world sympathy is seen in the case of "Hilaire Noulens" and his wife, which warrants brief notice:

A European named Ducreux, arrested and imprisoned in Singapore on June 1, 1931, carried the notation "Post Office Box #206, Shanghai, China" among his papers.

The arrest in Hankow of a "Chinese," Nguyen Ai Quac, [16] led to a Shanghai cable address—"Hilanoul, Shanghai"—which he identified as a communications center for communists.

The Shanghai municipal police soon established that both the post office box and the cable address were held in the same name: Hilaire Noulens.

A man and woman were arrested for their clandestine activities on behalf of the Pan-Pacific Trade Union Secretariat (PPTUS) of the Red Trade Union International, or Profintern, and the Far Eastern Bureau of the Comintern.

When first approached, the man used the name Hilaire Noulens. As the investigation proceeded, he was found to be using, concurrently, the additional names Samuel Herrsens, C. (for Charles) Alison, and Marcel Motte. He had documentation to establish his identity as Fernand Vandercruyssen, Donat Boulanger, Alfred Julien, Edward Briggs, and Rudolf Bergman. In addition, he used the names Henry, Coty, and Wales in his communications.

His "wife," known in Shanghai as Mrs. Marcel Motte, was also documented as Marie Vandercruyssen (nee Duson), Mrs. Sophie Louise Herbert (nee Dorent), and Mrs. Adele Ruck. In financial records she used the names Frau Coty or F. Coty, and at no time did she use the name Mrs. Noulens. After their arrests, the names Mr. and Mrs. Xavier Alois Beuret, and Paul and Gertrude Ruegg were introduced as aliases for Mr. and Mrs. Noulens.[17]

A massive accumulation of files and documents seized and examined by the police disclosed conclusively that Mr. and Mrs. Noulens supervised a group of Europeans and native Chinese who were collecting information; that they administered a large organization; and that they were communicating intelligence information to Moscow.

Among his effects Noulens had ciphers and codes, as well as clear-text messages, encoded and decoded cables, and telegrams and letters written in coded languages. He maintained a log of post office boxes in different names, and registered telegraph and cable addresses in still other names.

He kept the keys to the many mail boxes he serviced, and another log indicated that he was also responsible for the operation of a courier service consisting of many local associates.

He was charged with communicating to Moscow and Berlin the many personal and operational problems of the people in his net, usually by encoded letter.

He leased, furnished, and maintained many safe houses and accommodation places. He kept the financial books and inventories of the furniture in the various houses. In emergencies or periods of disuse, he liquidated the houses and sold the furnishings. Additionally, he subscribed to many magazines and received books, newspapers, and other materials for use by his agents.

He kept large sums of cash, in many currencies, on hand in safe-deposit boxes and in several local banks, each account in a different name. He also converted large sums of money given to him for operational purposes into workable currencies of small denominations.

He paid the salaries and travel and medical expenses of agents and staff personnel. He also bought and took charge of stamps and maps, and paid cable costs and charges for advertisements in the local press.

Additionally, he maintained financial records for both the Comintern FEB and the PPTUS.[18]

When news of the case broke in the international press, the Comintern was in trouble. Grave implications of the arrest of the Noulenses were reverberating in Moscow. When caught in such a situation, the predictable Soviet response is to go immediately on the offensive.

Moscow proclaimed in loud tones and many languages that the arrests were "foul provocations" by the British imperialists. As "the conscience of freedom-loving people everywhere," the USSR pledged its full support to the many millions who were already clamoring for the release of the Noulens couple. (Until the Moscow declaration on the case, no one, least of all the British, was aware of any "worldwide clamor.")

Mrs. Noulens, arrested separately, insisted that she was a French national. The police, according her every courtesy, were escorting her to the French consulate when she suddenly realized that en route she had become a Belgian. She was then escorted to the Belgian consul, who, on the basis of the Vandercruyssen passports, had no choice but to assume jurisdiction. (It took many days of urgent cable exchanges with Brussels to establish that the Vandercruyssen passports were forgeries.)

In one of the lockboxes kept by Noulens was a Canadian passport in the name of Donat Boulanger. Noulens denied all knowledge of the passport and did not explain how a recent photograph of himself happened to be cemented to the passport under a Canadian seal bearing the signature *Donat Boulanger*. A few days later Noulens admitted that his name was

Beuret and that he was really a Swiss. When the Swiss consul failed to take jurisdiction, Noulens waited a few more days before confessing that he now recalled that his *real* honest-to-goodness everyday true name was Ruegg.

A German lawyer was dispatched (by the Comintern) to Shanghai to lead the defense of the Noulenses. He was retained by the newly formed International Committee for the Defense of Paul and Gertrude Ruegg. A lawyer in Geneva sent a cable to the Swiss consul general in Shanghai which said that Madame Barth Ruegg had called at his office and told him that her son, Paul Ruegg, and his wife, Trude, had been arrested and asked that the consul general intervene. The lawyer later appeared in Shanghai as part of the defense team. The Swiss consul general, after much dithering, finally informed the court that the Noulenses were most assuredly *not* the Rueggs.

Moscow allocated $100,000 (Mexican) for the defense. The Tass man in Shanghai (S. Slepak) and the head of the United Petroleum Trust of the USSR (B. S. Zimen) formed the liaison link between the Soviet diplomatic wireless and the defense team operating out of the Shanghai law firm of Musso, Fischer, and Wilhelm. Zimen was able to "enlist" the aid of the Chinese section of MOPR (The International Society for the Aid of Revolutionaries) to effect clandestine contact with the prisoners then held in Nanking. It was through this tortured communications link that Noulens was informed of his ever-changing identity.

"This is an Imperialist plot to murder Noulens"; "Workers, close your ranks"; "Defend an intrepid friend of the toiling masses" were among the shorthand slogans used throughout the world. Noulens was said to be a "hardworking trade union organizer. The documents were British forgeries and what's more, the whole thing was a Kuomintang-Imperialist plot." The League Against Imperialism joined the chorus and organized noisy demonstrations in London.

As frequently happens, many high-minded U.S. citizens (Norman Thomas, Clarence Darrow, Theodore Dreiser, Lincoln Steffens, and others) were led to believe, in the absence of the facts, that the British had connived with the Chinese government to decapitate a liberal couple whose views were judged inimical to His Britannic Majesty's Colonial Empire. In this case it was the redoubtable Roger Baldwin, founder of the American Civil Liberties Union and liberal partisan extraordinary, who, being disposed to impute the worst to the colonial-minded British and the despotic Nationalist Chinese government, agreed to chair a committee, raise funds, and organize an international campaign to "free the Swiss nationals," whom he insisted on calling by one of their several aliases, Paul and Gertrude Ruegg.

The committee that Baldwin was asked to chair had already set up shop in room 412 at 70 Fifth Avenue in New York City with secret money from Soviet sources. The "International Committee for Political Prisoners (ICPP), organized in the interest of freedom of opinion" joined the roster of similar groups that were hastily and unwittingly put to work by the Soviet government.

Failure to insist on knowing the details of the charges against the Rueggs, coupled with reliance on others for the facts, frequently led otherwise reasonable people to play speaking parts in the Comintern's world theater.

(Carlo Tresca, a member of ICPP's general committee at the time, was later murdered in New York City after giving anti-Soviet testimony at a U.S. congressional inquiry.)

The Rueggs, Noulenses, Vandercruyssens, et al. were sentenced to life imprisonment. They survived the Second World War, and the last public reference to them was in March 1951, when it was suggested, in an elliptical manner, by the Chinese communist radio that an individual thought to be Noulens was en route to the United States or Canada on an espionage mission for the USSR.[19]

The accomplishments on behalf of the USSR by the Anti-Fascist League in the thirties, the Stockholm Peace Committee of the fifties (which investigated germ warfare in Korea and found the United States guilty), and some of the variant forms* of the Nuclear Freeze movement of the eighties tend to confirm Lenin's pronouncement on the tactical utility of "useful fools" who appear ever ready to sacrifice intellect to emotion.

Hitler's rise to power in 1933 gave the Comintern a new and important role. The Soviets had mixed reactions toward Germany. The Brest-Litovsk Treaty of March 3, 1917, had enabled the Bolsheviks to withdraw Russia from World War I and left them free to turn their energies on their own people. The Treaty of Rapallo (April 16, 1922) gave the Germans a most favored status with great new benefits accruing to both sides.

---

*For example, the Soviets own and operate the World Peace Council (WPC), which received $63 million from the Soviets in 1980 alone. The U.S. subsidiary of the WPC is the U.S. Peace Council (USPC), which, according to the FBI, is led by Mike Myerson and Sandra Pollack of the Communist Party of the U.S.A.

The USPC has a number of affiliates, among them: Women's International League for Peace and Freedom (WILPF), Mobilization for Survival (MFS), Women Strike for Peace (WSP), Women for Racial and Economic Equality (WREE), and Women's International Democratic Federation (WIDF).

All of these organizations have provided organization, direction, tactics, and graphic "evidence" (films, photos, etc.) calculated to influence American foreign policy in a manner favorable to the Soviets.[20]

The Nuclear Freeze movement has no effect within the USSR, yet its very existence is essential to give an air of spontaneity to the movement in the United States. One reason for this is that U.S. disarmament is a primary objective of Soviet policy, both overt and covert.

(From the German standpoint, not the least of these was an opportunity to manufacture new weapons in the USSR in violation of the Versailles Treaty.) In Germany, the failed, Soviet-backed "revolution" in 1923 produced sharp, enduring antagonisms and gave the extreme right a basis for engaging in its own kind of excesses.

By the early thirties, the cancerous effects of the Great Depression had spread from one country to the next. The Comintern, on Stalin's orders, stood aside, waiting for the final collapse of the capitalist system as predicted by Marx. Stalin's decision was tempered by his innate sense of caution in matters beyond his control, and nonalignment of the Comintern seemed a prudent course. In the West, governments were weak and aimless. Germany, following the fall of the Weimar Republic, saw the worst inflation and political extremism. The suggestion that Stalin, by his passivity, actually aided the rise of fascism in Germany is without basis and fails to take into account the pragmatic nature of Soviet foreign policy of the day. Stalin could not have prevented Hitler's rise to power, though the Comintern did much to unite opposition to him by advocating coalition among other anti-Nazi elements and arranging for the circulation of strident warnings about Nazi intentions.

Now, with Hitler as chancellor, the Soviets had good reason to be alarmed. Stalin was presented with a classic dilemma. From Rapallo on, the Soviets had enjoyed many special advantages including the introduction of expert German industrial and engineering assistance essential to realization of the Five-Year Plan. On the other hand, a Nazi or National Socialist was no more a socialist than were the Bolsheviks. Hitler had won much of his support by brawling in the streets with communists, who, he insisted, were just another manifestation of the malign influence of the Jews. His threatened repudiation of the Treaty of Versailles would surely mean that the Germans would no longer require the secret rearmament arrangements with the Soviet Union, and the terms of Rapallo would cease to be of benefit to the USSR.

Stalin was awed by Hitler's political skills and the manner in which he used violence, first against his own followers,[21] and then against his political opposition. The "special relationship" between the Soviet Union and the discredited German government that had preceded Hitler was about to come to an end. Once in office, Hitler moved swiftly to disavow the Versailles Treaty. German advisers and technicians were called home from the USSR, and Germany embarked on its own course of open, defiant rearmament.

A resurgent Germany led by Hitler was a fearsome prospect for Stalin's faltering regime to contemplate. A new and wholly revised strategy was in order, as Stalin, more than anyone else, understood the danger. At first he would attempt cautiously to cultivate the new Hitler, being careful, as always, to conceal his own weaknesses. He would probe the Germans for signs of opposition and simultaneously begin a quiet search for possible allies. The year 1933 was one of great danger. With a new Germany rising in the West, the Japanese stalking in the East, and the USSR in a weak and disorganized state, Stalin saw the survival of his regime as being questionable.

The Comintern was directed to put great energy into the formation of a propaganda strategy that would rouse world opinion against the German and Japanese threats. Two proposals were advanced and, after consideration, approved by Stalin. The first represented a reversal of prior policy. It demanded that the national Communist parties drop all previous antipathy toward other political factions so long as the common aim was antifascism. It was the beginning of the "united front," the formation of coalitions to oppose fascism. Where effective, the strategy won new friends, tempered attitudes toward the USSR, and in some instances allowed communists to achieve positions of power and influence in otherwise conservative states.

A second proposal was to contrast the Nazis' racial policies with the USSR's loudly proclaimed "democratic" insistence on human rights, and sharp public focus was directed toward the Nazis' depredations against "liberals," political dissenters, "progressives," and especially all Jews.

Anti-Semitism, a vague and ill-defined concept at best, requires comment. Its most abhorrent manifestation is to be seen in Hitler's singular focus, which not only identified Jews as intrinsically evil and inherently corrupt, but went on to adduce their eradication as an Aryan imperative. The absolutism of the Nazi policy, coupled with the energy and even enthusiasm with which it was carried out, brought into being a modern German industry, employing advanced technical innovations, whose sole purpose was the production of the deaths of captive Jews and others who failed to meet the minimum standards for survival in the Third Reich.

If the Nazi form can be taken as an extreme example of anti-Semitism, certain characteristics warrant note: First, Hitler was unequivocal in his determination to eliminate the Jews. Second, attacks on German Jews, commencing in 1934, made credible his commitment to their eventual destruction. And third, being a Jew was in itself cause for arrest and removal from German society.

This declared, overt, genocidal intent was a calculated policy, and in this context, *anti-Semitism* becomes an inadequate descriptive term. With the rapid expansion of German-controlled territories, more Jews were sent to the extermination camps. In this regard, the Nazis' war against the Jews was clearly indiscriminate. Polish, Russian, Lithuanian, Czech, and Rumanian Jews who could not have been guilty of the charges Hitler had levied against the German Jews were also destroyed.

The policy was predicated on the pseudoscientific notions that Jewish blood somehow polluted racial "purity" and that Jewishness was a biological "trait." Many of the assimilated German Jews who had served in the German forces in World War I found it difficult to comprehend that they were regarded by the new state as Jews and not as Germans. Orthodox Jews who held to strict religious observance were the most visible and, for that reason, the most immediate victims.

The condition of East European Jews near the turn of the twentieth century was indeed grim, if not hopeless. The authorities in the Austro-Hungarian Empire, Poland, Lithuania, Latvia, Estonia, and Imperial Russia were, with varying degrees of intensity, devoted to officially sanctioned anti-Semitic policies. It is not possible to overstate the need of the East European Jews for relief from the increasing dangers to which they were subjected.

In the abstract Marxist ideals relating to the elimination of class were appealing, as were other "socialist" reforms. However, association with any political element antithetical to the continuation of autocratic rule was an act of treason against the state. The only alternatives were to emigrate, become a clandestine activist, or submit to intensifying repression by the governments.

Those who joined political opposition groups were hunted down, arrested, and imprisoned or killed. The survivors exacted lessons from the experience, and techniques of survival evolved rapidly: Aliases, false documentation, disguise, indirect communication, encryption and signaling, compartmentation within organizations, all had to be used, and in a disciplined manner or the groups were doomed.

Those who had emigrated were frequently proselytized and occasionally coerced to provide money or cover, or to act as post boxes and procurement agents. Identification with the radical left was represented as the only means of survival, and the high incidence of prominent Jewish intellectuals in the International was cited in confirmation of the legend. All governments were said to be dedicated to the repression of the Jews; only the Bolsheviks offered safe haven as publicly promised by the Soviet state.

In the twenties, the Comintern was able to generate and sustain a belief among the people that there was likely to be reactive repression from the right. Yet despite the Comintern's antifascist campaigns, the USSR's repressive policies regarding dissidents were in no way moderated. The distinction was simply that while Hitler's crimes were observed and reported, Stalin's were not. Soviet victims were either dead or dying in the camps. As early as 1929, the Russians knew that in the Soviet Union everyone belonged to one of three classes: those who had been in prison, those who were in prison, and those who would be in prison. It was rare indeed to have witnessed the organs at work and lived to tell about it.

Isaac Don Levine, who had fled Russia as a boy, returned as a young reporter (with social-revolutionary convictions) to report on the Russian Revolution. Levine witnessed the destruction of the Provisional government and the Bolshevik coup and immediately recognized that the disciplined Soviets, by violence and deception, had stolen the future of the Russian people.

In 1923, Mussolini caught the attention of Western Europe with his march on Rome (the inspiration for Hitler's later and unsuccessful "beer hall putsch" in Munich), and Levine reported on the growing threat of fascism. Levine saw the fascists as German and Italian variations of the same totalitarianism that wielded all power in the USSR. He made no distinction among the three except to call the Nazis and fascists Brown and Black Bolsheviks. If there were notable differences, it was in the colors of their shirts.

Levine knew Albert Einstein and his family and visited with them in Berlin in the early twenties. It was in this period that Levine, under the aegis of an international committee headed by Roger Baldwin, was preparing a volume of documentary evidence on the Soviet persecution of political opponents.[22] Albert Einstein wrote a prefatory note in which he praised the successful effort to reveal the nature of Soviet repression.

In 1932, Levine presented to Einstein a copy of his biography of Stalin. A month later Einstein wrote:

S. S. San Francisco
March 15th, 1932

Dear Mr Levine:
During my voyage I was at last able to read your book on Stalin. It is undoubtedly the best and most profound work on that great drama that has fallen into my hands. . . . I have the impression that you are unimpeachably objective. I am truly grateful to you for the fine piece of knowledge which you have provided for me. . . . The whole book is to me a symphony on the theme: Violence breeds violence. Liberty is the necessary foundation for the development of all true values. It becomes clear that, without morality and confidence, no society can flourish. . . .

With greetings and high regards
Your,
A. Einstein

In 1934, Einstein's property was expropriated by the Nazis; he was deprived of his German citizenship and forced to leave the country. In the same year, Sergei Kirov was assassinated in Leningrad and Stalin ordered the summary execution of sixty-six political prisoners who had no connection whatever with Kirov's death. A public protest was organized in New York, and Levine sent a copy of the appeal to Einstein for his endorsement and signature. Although written forty years ago, Levine's questions are relevant today:

> Where are the hundreds of liberal and radical voices which so properly raised a storm of protest last June upon the bloody Hitler "purge"? Why are these professed champions of human rights so inexplicably silent in the face of the medieval bloodbath improvised by Stalin?
>
> Where are our humanitarians who flooded the press last summer with letters of protest against Hitler's detention without trial of the Communist leader, Thaelmann? I recall one long and powerful plea which appeared in your pages [*The New York Times*] from the pen of Waldo Frank. Have these spokesmen of our public conscience one standard for Russia and another for Germany? Are they ready to admit that they can condone the Red Terror and condemn the Nazi Terror without outraging the fundamentals of civilization?
>
> Is there not a single public body in this country to express American indignation at the barbarous "purge" just consummated by the Soviet government?

In an accompanying note, Levine wrote to Einstein: "I know you will agree with me that it is important to have a great Jewish voice raised against the terror in Russia in order to make the protest against the Nazi terror more effective."

Einstein responded promptly but, to Levine's astonishment, expressed this extraordinary reversal of his previous stance:

> Princeton, N.J.
> 2 Library Place
> December 10, 1934
>
> Mr Isaac Don Levine
> 400 East 52nd Street
> New York City

Dear Mr Levine:

You can imagine that I, too, regret immensely that the Russian political leaders let themselves be carried away to deal such a blow to the elementary demands of justice by resorting to political murder. In spite of this, I cannot associate myself with your action. It will have no effect in Russia, but in the countries which directly or indirectly favor Japan's shameless aggressive policy against Russia. Under these circumstances I regret your action and suggest that you abandon it altogether. Take into consideration that in Germany many thousands of Jewish workers are driven to death systematically by depriving them the right to work, without causing a stir in the non-Jewish world. Consider further that the Russians have proved that their only aim is really the improvement of the lot of the Russian people, and that they can in this regard already show important achievements. Why then direct the attention of public opinion in other countries solely to the blunders of this regime? Is such a choice not misleading?

> With highest respect,
> A. Einstein

Levine was stunned by Einstein's reply and wrote immediately to clarify and expand on his initial letter:

> . . . I am grateful to you for your kind and frank reply to my invitation to join in a protest against the Red Terror, but feel that you have raised a number of points which require answers. I wish I had an opportunity to discuss these points with you in person. In the meantime I pray that you will give your earnest consideration to the following propositions. . . .
>
> The modern phenomenon of the state becoming an instrument of social hatred, as exemplified under the Nazis, is the consequence of the Bolshevist successful experiment in organizing hatred against all classes except the proletariat, a small minority in Russia. Hitler's anti-Semitism is patterned after the Bolshevist state persecution of all elements the social origin of which is nonproletarian.
>
> The only known effective weapon against such hatred and oppression is the Anglo-Saxon system of justice, theoretically the only classless system of justice yet devised. In practice, it has been frequently abused. In theory, it remains unexcelled. It is the shield of civilization and has been the salvation of the Jew in the Western world.
>
> I was grieved to read your statement that the only aim of the Soviet rulers is the improvement of the people's condition. How can one reconcile that belief with the fact that in 1933 from three to five million peasants were deliberately starved to death by the Stalin regime? (W. Henry Chamberlin's *Russia's Iron Age* contains the

latest and most authoritative and undisputed testimony of that man-made catastrophe.) The dominant motive of the Soviet rulers is not humanitarian, but mechanistic; not love of people, but a love of power; and the salvation they would bring is more like that of Torquemada than that of Hugo, Zola, Tolstoy.

It is this fear of losing their power that makes the Soviet rulers so cruel and so haunted by shadows. Such a shadow is the belief that other powers are inspiring Japan's aggression against Russia. At a moment when the United States is selling secret war planes to the Soviet government, when France concludes an entente (if not an alliance) with Moscow, it is difficult for sane observers to believe in the propaganda that Russia is a victim of Western imperialism. . . .

Nor can I agree with you that the horrible policies of Hitler against the Jews have not aroused a storm of protest in the Western non-Jewish world. That this storm has not been great enough is perhaps due to the fact that the Western intelligentsia has dulled our sense of indignation by condoning the Red Terror and by falling for the Leninist dogmas instead of adhering to the old cries of justice, human rights and freedom.

Jewish emancipation owes its birth to these issues. The modern Jew owes his present status of a freeman to the English concept of the state, a concept which the American Revolution helped make a reality in half the world. Even the comparative rights won by the Jews in Germany under the Kaisers and the pitiable liberties allowed the Jews in the last years of Czarism were all due to the triumph of the English libertarian idea of the state.

How then can the Jew fail to fight for that idea to the last drop of blood in him? How can the Jew serve two masters at once? I fear that the fact that so many advanced Jews swear by liberty and condone dictatorship is a grave omen for our future. I fear that the American Jews may make the same mistakes as some of the German Jews did—the mistake of not foreseeing events when the handwriting is already on the wall. . . .[23]

Einstein did not respond. The ten-year friendship with Levine died. The Comintern's antifascist wave not only engulfed Einstein (and Roger Baldwin) and thousands of other truly dedicated humanitarians, it also successfully altered the world's external perception of the USSR and ensured that a criticism of Stalin came to be heard as an encomium of Hitler.

It has always been characteristic for the KGB to have Soviet Jews play the role of antagonists to Zionism and Jewish nationalism. This perversity is readily accomplished by coercion. The Public Committee Against Zionism, established in 1983 in Moscow, for example, is the latest of these sham organisms. It purports to be spontaneous and completely staffed by Soviet Jewish leaders who are indignant about Zionism and Jewish nationalism.

The Public Committee Against Zionism is currently used to convey an unambiguous signal to all remaining Soviet Jews that emigration has stopped. It has charged that a number of Soviet Jews are known to be in communication with various foreign organizations (Hebrew Immigrant Aid Society, Amnesty International, etc.) and that these organizations have conveyed instructions calling for actions inimical to the Soviet state; and that the continuation of Hebrew classes is a cultural penetration of the Soviet Union with the intention of serving a foreign interest and spreading subversion. In the thirties, the European Jews were induced to believe that the Comintern's "antifa" campaign against Hitler had something to do with relieving their threatened positions. The fact was that the USSR needed the Anti-Fascist Committee (and the support of prominent Jews in the West) for political purposes quite apart from any serious effort or intention to aid the Jews.

Since there is no spontaneity in anything that happens in the Soviet Union, the appearance of anti-Semitic attacks in the Soviet press and government-published books is a clear manifestation of official Soviet policy. Observers have been aware since Stalin's time that a "Zionist" is a "Cosmopolitan," and a Cosmopolitan is a Jew. The anti-Semitic campaign started by Stalin in 1949 was abandoned in the confusion after his death. It is now being revived as the basis of further repression of the Jews and as a Soviet bone to be thrown to the USSR's radical Arab clients.[24]

The issues that fueled the internal wrangling of the Comintern member parties in the period 1930–1935 are best characterized as Swiftian debates over which end of an egg should be opened first. The political disputes had much the same content and produced interminable arguments on the several ways to define left sectarianism and right deviationism. While the upper reaches of the Comintern were splitting hairs, the bottom was hard at work on practical matters.

Stalin rarely pretended interest in the Comintern's polemical disputes. He kept his own political counsel. When necessary, he used the organs to tidy up heretical dissenters by converting the troublemakers into "nonpersons." Stalin's cautious international style reflected his uncertainties about the course of political and economic events in Europe.

Stalin had originally thought that the close relations between the Red Army and the Reichswehr (the German Army) would constitute an effective bar to Hitler. His view was buttressed when, in April 1932, Kurt von

Schleicher, Hindenburg's defense minister, emphatically assured the Soviet ambassador in Berlin that the Reichswehr would "never tolerate" Hitler as Chancellor or President.[25] The context in which the statement was made implied a continuation of the secret military agreements.

Similarly, in the summer of 1932 the Soviet intelligence officer Walter Krivitsky reported a conversation with a staff officer of the Reichswehr who was firmly committed to the policy of German-Soviet cooperation. Of Hitler's rise to power, he said: "Let Hitler come and do his job and then we, the army, will make short work of him." According to Krivitsky, Stalin was much gratified by the report.[26]

Stalin's belief in the efficacy of the Soviet-German military connection was dealt a sharp blow on the night of June 30, 1934—known as the Night of the Long Knives—when several hundred persons thought to constitute a danger to Hitler's personal rule were shot on his orders. Included were Ernst Röhm, commander of the Nazi paramilitary Sturmabteilungen (SA); Gregor Strasser, once Hitler's rival as the head of the Nazi Party, and of course Schleicher, the former Chancellor and head of the Reichswehr who had depreciated Hitler to the Soviet ambassador.

The first communist reaction to the Hitler purge was to declare that the "monopolist big bourgeoisie" had crushed the "petty bourgeoisie strata."[27] This interpretation of the event underscores the tyranny of the Comintern's Marxist-Leninist language and the doctrinal Bolsheviks' inability to deal with political reality outside the rigid confines of dogma.

In commenting on Hitler's June 1934 purge of enemies and possible rivals, E. H. Carr states:

> . . . More significantly, perhaps, Hitler had surrendered his private army, the SA, into the control of the Reichswehr in return for the recognition by the Reichswehr of his supreme authority. The murder of Schleicher, and the acquiescence of the other Reichswehr generals in it sealed a relation between the Reichswehr and the dictator which was undisturbed for several years. What now haunted Moscow was the vision of a well-integrated Germany where military and economic power were welded into an iron, popular dictatorship. The safeguard on which reliance had so long been placed by Soviet leaders, of the secret bond of sympathy and cooperation between the Reichswehr and the Red Army, was now subject to the unpredictable will of the Nazi dictator."[28]

In 1934, Hitler's abrupt termination of the "special military relationship" between Germany and the Soviet Union forced Stalin to reconsider the role of the Comintern. Among the first casualties was the notion that Hitler's actions against the KPD (*Kommunistische Partei Deutsch-*

lands) and the SPD (*Sozialdemokratische Partei Deutschlands*) were "internal German affairs" having no effect on German-Soviet relations. This was consistent with the Soviet Union's pretense that it had no influence in regard to the Comintern and that the local Communist parties were autonomous. By sustaining this fiction, the Soviet government was able to use the national parties with relative impunity. Member parties soon came to realize that in critical situations the Comintern was quite prepared to sacrifice the local communists in the interests of the USSR. The CPSU was always *primus inter pares,* and egalitarianism went out the window when Soviet interests came in the door. In Stalin's world view the national parties, as well as their leaders, were expendable.

Comintern assets, no matter how weak, were now directed to alert the world to the menace of Hitler. At first the anti-Hitler campaign disoriented the propaganda audience. The same people who had been stressing the evil of the democracies and tolerance toward Germany suddenly reversed themselves and called for worldwide opposition to Hitler by all who represented democratic causes. By some political alchemy, the USSR proclaimed itself in the van of the democratic forces. Like the little boy who cried wolf, the Comintern's alarms made little impact, because only weeks before, the same voices had been loudly condemning those to whom their appeals were now directed. A less strident and more effective tactic was then brought into play: The Comintern's new approach called for coalitions of like-minded opponents of fascism in the "popular front" campaign.[29]

As might be expected, Stalin's *volte-face* evoked vicious recriminations in the Comintern's member parties. But the rigid enforcement of Moscow's discipline by the Soviet organs very swiftly and certainly brought about full compliance within the local parties. It was axiomatic in the Comintern that one "went along to get along." Like the Queen of Hearts, a Comintern member could believe and articulate any number of ridiculous things before a figurative noon without any qualms of conscience. The late Arthur Koestler put the explanation another way by invoking the *"Credo Quia Absurdum:* It is right to be wrong with the party, but it is wrong to be right against the party."

Many years later, General Heinz Guderian expressed the opinion that Stalin's later purge of the Red Army generals in 1938 was specifically directed against those Soviet officers who had been closely associated with the secret German-Soviet military arrangements. According to Guderian, the taint of association with the Reichswehr was sufficient to place an individual officer on Stalin's personal hit list. On the German side, Hitler acted in a similar manner. General Guderian was too junior at the time of the secret agreement to have warranted the punishment visited by Hitler on some of the senior Wehrmacht officers.[30]

The Comintern's attack on Hitler drew mixed reviews in the West. For example, in the United States, Earl Browder stopped charging Franklin Roosevelt with being "a fascist imperialist warmonger" and instead referred to him lovingly as a sensible opponent of the genuine fascist, Hitler. Because the *Daily Worker* preached only to the converted, the major policy switch and its many implications were lost on the American public. The fact that the U.S. economy was just beginning to improve made Hitler too remote a threat to be considered. In 1932–1933 most Americans had a limited understanding of the issues at stake in Germany, and foreign news was at best an incidental part of the coverage of the major newspapers.

The Comintern's "united" or "popular" front tactic enabled the Soviets to place disciplined assets in various Western governments but was ineffectual in stopping Hitler. In summarizing the first sixteen years of the Comintern's history Professor Carr notes:

It is tempting to dramatize the Franco-Soviet pact and the declaration of May 16, 1935, as marking an abrupt abandonment of the aim of world revolution inherent in Marxist and Bolshevik doctrine in favor of the diplomacy of defensive alliances sponsored by Litvinov—the decisive victory of Narkomindel over Comintern. But this would be an undue simplification. Faith in imminent revolution in Europe foundered in the German debacle of 1923. Events in China in 1927 showed up the limitations on the aid which the Comintern could or would render to revolution in a semi-colonial country. Henceforth, world revolution became an article in a creed ritualistically recited on solemn public occasions, but no longer an item of living faith or a call to action. The place left vacant in the ideology of the Comintern was taken by defence of the Soviet Union. The "twenty-one conditions" of 1920 had imposed on communist parties an obligation to give "unconditional support to any Soviet republic in its struggle against counter-revolutionary forces". The principle of the defence of the USSR was inscribed in the programme of Comintern after the war scare of 1927 at its sixth congress in 1928; the argument that, since the USSR was the one country where the socialist revolution had been victorious, the prime duty of communist parties everywhere was to defend it against the assaults of its enemies, became common currency. When the world economic crisis of 1930 provoked fresh confirmation of the impending bankruptcy of the capitalist order, and revolution in central Europe seemed once more a possible or even likely contingency, Comintern soon began to sound a note of caution, and impatient revolutionary enthusiasm became a "Left" or "sectarian" deviation. As the early prospects of world revolution receded from view, the theme of the defence of the USSR gained strength and prominence, and was well established at the twelfth and thirteenth IKKI in 1932 and 1933. What was new in 1934 and 1935 was the recognition that the defence of the USSR could be assured through the support, not of foreign communist parties too weak to overthrow, or seriously embarrass, their national governments, but of the governments of capitalist countries exposed to the same menace as the USSR, and that the best service which parties could render would be to encourage governments to provide that support. It was an unexpected, but logical development, a product of the weakness of the existing communist parties and of the miscalculations by the early Bolsheviks of revolutionary prospects in the capitalist world. After 1935 the defence of the USSR was the highest common factor in the programme of the Comintern and the diplomatic manoeuvres of Narkomindel."[31]

Professor Carr's *Twilight of the Comintern, 1930–1935* lays bare the curious posturings of the Comintern's member parties. Although not especially mentioned by him, another consequence of the high visibility and vocality of the Comintern parties was their utility in soaking up the energies of various local internal-security and police forces. This red-herring function was not a conscious strategy, but the Soviets were quick to recognize it as an effective diversion of police scrutiny. In places like New York City in the early thirties, much police attention was directed to public demonstrations by radical elements in Union Square rather than to the more important Soviet agent operations out of Amtorg, the Russian Red Cross, and other Soviet intelligence facilities. Thus the Comintern performed a useful role of some importance to the Soviet intelligence organs.

From 1935 on, Stalin kept the Comintern's eye focused on the dangers posed by Hitler while attempting to gain some sort of accommodation with his threatening new neighbor. The growing German diplomatic and military consonance with Japan heightened Stalin's anxieties, and in the end, it might well have been the British "peace in our time" agreement at Munich that suggested the Soviets' most audacious move.

It was clear to Stalin that the Soviet Union could not withstand even a brief military collision with the Germans. He had just obliterated the command structure of the Red Army and thoroughly traumatized the populace with the Great Purge. Not since the first few weeks following the 1918 coup had the USSR been in such a state of disarray. It was imperative to buy time, and Munich suggested a method. Stalin concluded that the time had come for a "crossed fingers deal" with Hitler.

In 1934 the Soviet government had reversed its foreign policy abruptly and called for "collective security" against Germany and Japan. To give credence to its new concerns about the world outside, the USSR joined the League of Nations and, in 1935, concluded a military alliance with the French. To make sure that these actions were properly understood in the Comintern, Stalin sent "instructions" to its seventh (and last) congress in August 1935. The members were directed to work for, and actively promote, cooperation with liberal and socialist groups wherever such Popular Front alliances with Comintern member parties could be arranged. The abandonment of revolutionary rhetoric did much to enhance the appeal of the communists, and, partly due to their efforts, Popular Front governments achieved power, temporarily, in France and Spain.

Of the instructions issued by Stalin to the Comintern, items 1, 2, and 5 are of particular interest:

1. The defense of the immediate economic and political interests of the working class, the defense of the latter against fascism must be the starting point and form the main content of the workers' united front in all capitalist countries. In order to set the broad masses in motion, such slogans and forms of struggle must be put forward as arise from the vital needs of the masses and from the level of their fighting capacity at the given stage of development. Communists must not limit themselves to merely issuing appeals to struggle for proletarian dictatorship, but must show the masses what they are to do today to defend themselves against capitalist plunder and fascist barbarity. They must strive, through the joint action of the labor organizations, to mobilize the masses around a program of demands that are calculated to really shift the burden of the consequences of the crisis onto the shoulders of the ruling classes; demands, the fight to realize which disorganizes fascism, hampers the preparations for imperialist war, weakens the bourgeoisie and strengthens the positions of the proletariat.

2. Without for a moment giving up their independent work in the sphere of Communist education, organization and mobilization of masses, the Communists, in order to render the road to unity of action easier for the workers, must strive to secure joint action with the Social Democratic Parties, reformist trade unions and other organizations of the toilers against the class enemies of the proletariat, on the basis of short or long term agreements. . . .

5. Joint action with the Social Democratic Parties and organizations not only does not preclude, but on the contrary, renders still more necessary the serious and well-founded criticism of reformism, of Social Democracy as the ideology and practice of class collabora-

tion with the bourgeoisie, and the patient exposition of the principles and program of Communists to the Social-Democratic
workers.[32]

Stalin's other instructions (there were six in all) dealt with methods to
be used in election campaigns and so on. Although tactically important,
instructions 1, 2, and 5 above convey the conceptual framework of the
Popular Front strategy. It was an adroit plan, and in accordance with its
principles, the Spanish communists gave their full support to the Republican government in the civil war that followed General Francisco Franco's
rebellion of July 1936. The "united front" in Spain enabled the Soviets,
many of whom who were dispatched from Moscow, to exert strong influence in the Republican government until it was overwhelmed by Franco
in March 1939.

The Spanish Civil War produced a major sea change in the operations
of the Soviet intelligence services. Hitherto, the organs had operated
within the personnel constraints established by Dzerzhinsky: i.e., keep
the overseas elements small and use only our own (Soviets) to run them.
Spain changed all that.

As progressives and liberals from all over the world flocked to the
Spanish republic's banners, it was evident to the OGPU chief in Spain, L.
L. Felbin ("General Alexandr Orlov"), [33] that here were new, limitless
opportunities to recruit ideologues of all nationalities for use in the
"work." Orlov was quick to recognize the angst, vengeance, and guilt
that drove many of the highly educated who came to Spain in expiation of
their own social advantages and affluence. Many of these emotional adventurers were already psychically prepared to accept OGPU discipline
and anxious to revenge themselves on their own countries.

The Spanish Civil War bought Stalin some time and enabled Red
Army officers, like their Wehrmacht opposites, to test new concepts and
equipment in the military phase. To Soviet intelligence, the more important result was the successful recruitment of new agents from capitalist
bourgeois backgrounds. Dzerzhinsky had warned against but had not prohibited the recruitment of Western intellectuals. Had he lived to witness
the moral disillusionment resulting from the Great Depression, he likely
would have applauded Orlov's proposal.

The Republican government proved to be a weak Soviet client, and as
the war progressed, the Soviets assumed increasingly dominant roles in
the Republican government and army. The International Brigades were,
in fact, the Comintern army and subject to Soviet rather than Spanish
discipline. As the Soviets became the disciplinarians of the Republican
cause, the hand of Stalin grew more apparent. Executions and abductions
by the organs became commonplace and the military situation worsened.

In late 1938 the USSR began the withdrawal from Spain with several serious dents in its reputation. On the positive side, the Soviets gained some time, expanded and variegated their intelligence services, blooded some Soviet military leaders, and to Stalin's delight, made off with all the Spanish gold reserves.[34]

Following the Spanish Civil War, and in the wake of Hitler's uncontested occupations of Danzig, Austria, and Czechoslovakia, Stalin decided that the Popular Front ties with France were not particularly effective in arresting the Nazis' accretions of land and people and that a different approach was essential. Without prior consultation with the Comintern, Stalin directed the Commissariat of Foreign Affairs to commence negotiations with Germany. The resultant nonaggression pact (with secret protocols) of September 1939 burst on the world as an unthinkable consequence. No rational observer could have predicted that the antithetical tyrants would embrace. The shock rattled the faculties of the sane and positively pulverized the Comintern.

The Comintern parties were incredulous when the pact was announced. The international wire services flashed the news to the rest of the world while the Comintern struggled to square the Marxism-Leninism circle. Hitler had been castigated and denounced tirelessly in the communist press, and now, without any warning, it was imperative to get the message out to the faithful that he was *really* an admirable fellow with whom the Comintern was proud to associate. Because Moscow was unable to get the full text of a digestible scenario out and down to the troop level, this mad reversal of long-standing Soviet policy hung in the air like a giant concert of Nazi-Soviet political wind-breaking.

The local parties for the most part went mute. The hiatus between the event and the later explanation was a precise measurement of the time it took to get instructions from Moscow. Never before had the Comintern so exhibited in public its absolute subservience to the USSR. The pact itself was another overt demonstration of the Soviets' willingness to betray the national parties in the interests of the USSR. It was a bitter pill for the Comintern to swallow, and the triumph of political hypocrisy over ideological ideals was too much for some of the party members to endure. Many of the party prominent deserted the Soviets and publicly prayed a pox on both houses. To others, who had given their lives to "building socialism in one country," there was no turning back. Many of the local, individual party members could not bring themselves to concede that their selfless efforts had been made in the name of a false and undeserving cause. Especially confounded were the self-selected party intellectuals who consciously rejected reason, disregarded all evidence, and set about rationalizing the impossible.

As Molotov put it:

August 23, 1939, the day the Soviet-German Non-aggression Pact
was signed, is to be regarded as a date of great historical importance. The Non-aggression Pact between the U.S.S.R. and Germany marks a turning point in the history of Europe, and not only
of Europe. Only yesterday the German Fascists were pursuing a
foreign policy hostile to us. Yes, only yesterday we were enemies in
the sphere of foreign relations. Today, however, the situation has
changed and we are enemies no longer. . . .

The art of politics in the sphere of foreign relations does not
consist in increasing the number of enemies for one's country. On
the contrary, the art of politics in this sphere is to reduce the
number of such enemies and to make the enemies of yesterday good
neighbors, maintaining peaceable relations with one another.[35]

Less than two years later, following the German attack on the Soviet
Union of June 22, 1941, the communist view of the world was once more
turned on its head. Stalin stressed that Russia was fighting a "patriotic
war" to defend the sovereign rights of nations and hailed the positive
actions of his new British allies. The proletarian revolution was abandoned and ignored. The operational reality that animated Stalin was
dread that the Nazis might win. The palpability of this threat, coupled
with his fervent desire to survive, made it easy for Stalin once more to
desert all ideological pretensions and ally himself with the USSR's historic enemies.

Stalin's later actions with regard to the Comintern are of significance.
In May 1943, professedly on the grounds that it no longer served the
interests of the working-class movement, Stalin ordered the dissolution of
the Comintern. Victory over Germany was made the supreme goal of the
world communist movement. At the time, there was an unwarranted collective sigh of relief. Gone were the ominous portents the name invoked.
Instead, the red banners were furled, the *Internationale* went unsung, and
the periodic conferences were canceled.

Postwar events were to demonstrate that the national parties, with
few exceptions, remained under Moscow discipline. The reality was that
in the war-changed new world the International was an anachronism. But
despite Stalin's assurances, there were no changes, except in name. The
few important functions continued as before. The national Communist
parties are still courted, and money and propaganda still flow through the
old circuits like the Neva at crest. For a brief period following the war,
the Soviets promoted another organization, the Cominform (Communist
Information Bureau), which operated with little success and poor reviews, and after a few expensive years, it was deposited in an unmarked
grave.

The influences that resulted in Stalin's decision to end the Comintern remain unclear.[36] The reason most frequently advanced is that his certification of the Comintern's death would be greeted with glad cries by his new allies. Since final victory in Europe seemed assured, the USSR could emerge from the war as a great power, having renounced the subversive adjuncts of a weak political pariah. It was not characteristic of Stalin to bow to external pressures or to seek the approbation of others, especially at a time when his enemies were in retreat.

By any standard the Comintern had ceased to be vital to Soviet interests, and the world communist movement was no longer the simplified "us against them" that had been the International's stock in trade. Sociopolitical conditions were more complex and didn't fit the conventional Marxist model of the Comintern framework. Hitler had been the *raison d'être* of the Comintern since 1934, and with his defeat there seemed no further need for the International.

Throughout the Comintern's twenty-four years of existence, the Soviet government consistently disavowed its own paternity of, and authority over, the organization. The facade of Comintern autonomy was a bureaucratic expense that rankled Narkomindel and greatly complicated the modalities of Soviet foreign policy. The Foreign Ministry looked on the Comintern as wasteful and inefficient. Advice from this internal quarter might have had a bearing on Stalin's decision.

By mid-1943, Stalin began to consider the shape of postwar Europe and the new role of the USSR. The traditional enemies were now allies and the German threat was receding. It was time to think of China, Poland, Czechoslovakia, Romania, Bulgaria, a defeated and occupied Germany, Yugoslavia, possibly Greece, and all the other opportunities that might present themselves to a conquering Red Army. Beyond the security of the USSR and the armed acquisition of new lands and people, it would be tactically wise to focus on the current allies as tomorrow's enemies. With much hard fighting still ahead, Stalin looked farther west and directed the then head of the NKVD, Lavrenti Pavlovich Beria, to step up NKVD espionage operations in the United States, United Kingdom, and Canada.[37]

The end of the Comintern gave added emphasis to Stalin's pressure on his allies to open a second front in France and to discourage the alternatives under discussion—which included an attempt to land British and American troops in the Balkans. Stalin's vision of postwar Europe did not include Western troops anywhere except in the West. In this calculus, once victory was won, the NKVD's Foreign Department would be free to tidy up Eastern Europe and, using residual local Communist parties backed by the Red Army, gain political control.[38] According to Beria,

"Those parties that did so would be supported to the fullest extent of the Power still left to the Soviet Union."[39]

Beria's remarks set the tone and form of "cooperation" among the "fraternal socialist parties" that persist to the present day. Since 1943 there have been challenges to Soviet hegemony (from Yugoslavia, Albania, and China, for example) but for the most part and until recently, the national Communist parties have been relatively faithful adherents to the Soviet line.

In a sense, the ghost of the Comintern lives on in a more modern guise. The next time Aeroflot rolls out the carpet in Moscow and some unheard-of citizen—whom *Pravda* identifies as a "popular Leftist leader" from a less well-known country—deplanes, he'll more than likely be met by the usual Narkomindel functionaries. The senior among the greeters will present the forty-pound floral bouquet and hastily explain that the boss was disappointed he couldn't be there himself. Perhaps the regent of Lumumba University (a sinecure for semi-retired KGBniks) or the Central Committee hack in charge of national party affairs will also be present to give the visitor appropriate fraternal greetings.

The Soviets still put a premium on capturing foreign dissidents in elaborate snares of flattery, mock respect, and—the great persuader—money. Of course arms can be provided by the Czechs; the Libyans will happily give safe haven; if you send your lieutenants, we'll train them to assassinate policemen and government officials; here's a little something to use in setting up a clandestine radio; we'll do the scripting and the folks over at Tass will show you how to start an underground press operation in just a few short lessons; the faculty at the terrorist training center can show you how to bomb, burn, and shoot your way into international prominence. But most of all, welcome to the USSR, home of the peace-loving people of the socialist camp.

The deputation at the airport, in their three-piece suits, may not resemble Lenin's lieutenants, but these gray bureaucrats are the last men on the barricades of the seventy-year-overdue world revolution. Their primary objective remains the merchandising of the illusion of "world revolution of the proletariat" under the leadership of the USSR. The skills, resources, and dedication of the new Soviet leaders bear no relationship to those of yesterday's ideologues. The present leaders operate a highly successful, oligarchical business, solely concerned with the preservation of power. Their successes are a tribute to their devotion to controlled terror. Soviet advanced techniques of oppression, intimidation, and coercion, pioneered by the Bolsheviks and brought to a current state of high refinement by the organs, have created cancers in every part of the globe.

The skeletal remains of the Comintern, bereft of all past pagentry, still hang in the Kremlin closet—except when needed at the airport.

Felix Dzerzhinsky (left), the man who constructed the system of techniques that enabled the Bolsheviks to seize and control the Russian people. An intuitive master of predictive, human behavior, Dzerzhinsky succeeded in eradicating the mutual trust among Russians of all classes, thereby destroying all capacity to resist. *(National Archive photo 306-NT-91956, April 1924)*

Taking the oath (above) to the new Cheka flag. General Klimenti Voroshilov and Mikhail Trilisser (second and fourth full figures from the left, behind the table), are seen returning the salute. *(National Archive photo 306-NT-10640)* This photograph (below), taken by a French photographer in Moscow in 1936, is captioned: "Arrest by the Cheka." *(National Archive photo 306-NT-160706C)*

N. V. Krylenko, prosecutor in the "envoy's plot" (Lockhart/Kalamatiano trials) and minister of justice, was arrested and shot by Stalin in 1937. Krylenko served the Bolshevik regime by officially "endorsing" and "legalizing" various extensions of power by the organs. In the end, he also found himself trying to buy his way out of prison by implicating others in fictional conspiracies. *(National Archive photo 306-NT-166366)*

Nikolai I. Yezhov became head of the NKVD when he succeeded H. Yagoda in 1937. (Yagoda had been tried and executed as "an enemy of the people.") Two years later, after killing more people than Hitler, Yezhov was relieved and reportedly committed suicide after confinement in a mental hospital. Stalin then named L. Beria as head of the NKVD. Beria continued to head the then-massive secret police organization until his own death by execution in 1953. All three chiefs of Stalin's huge intelligence bureaucracy were officially alleged to have been in the pay of the British. *(Personal collection)*

"Hans" (actually Hans Galleni alias Joe Pirelli, etc.), the Soviet illegal who entered Britain in 1930 to attempt the recruitment of the British Foreign Office clerk, who had "walked into" the Soviet embassy in Paris. Despite his personal courage and exceptional operational skills, Hans was recalled to Moscow in late 1933 (after the Foreign Office clerk was discovered dead in his home kitchen), and was himself executed. The line drawing of Hans was produced from memory by an artistic, former "working" colleague of Galleni's, who dropped out of espionage at the time of the Hitler-Stalin pact and, somehow, lived to tell about it. *(Private collection)*

"Cilly," a German OGPU officer, worked in the Arcos office in London. Her area of specialization was "making friends." After the May 1927 raid, Cilly was assigned to Paris. As an active recruiter, she involved a number of French officials in Soviet espionage, and at the time of Stahl-Switz arrests, the numerous copies of this photograph among the possessions of arrested French officials were the only remaining trace of her in Paris. *(National Archive photo 306-NT-163438C)*

"Mysterious Paul." As a senior OGPU officer serving in France under the name "General Muraille," he was arrested and served three years for espionage in a French prison. His true identity was not established. On completion of his sentence he was deported to the USSR where, under Stalin's dictum, he would have been regarded as a "turned" agent (i.e., working for the French) and shot. *(National Archive photo 306-NT-166710C)*

Moishe Stern in his regalia as "General Emil Kleber, famous former Canadian commander of the International Brigade" (April 24, 1937). In 1933 Stern "worked" in New York as "Fred Stern," "Mr. Herb" (in the Arma engineering case), "Kotasky," and "Fred Stein." *(FBI file 95-52. Department of State decimal file 861.20211/52. File photo)*

Arvid Jacobson (above left), an American recruited by Alfred Tilton, claimed to have accepted the Soviet offer because he "could use the money." Jacobson was convicted on a charge of espionage and jailed in Finland. *(FBI photo)* "Mary Louise Martin" (above right), the name used by the organizer and leader of a major Soviet espionage net operating in Finland. She was the wife of Alfred Tilton, a long-established GRU officer serving in New York City at the time of her arrest. *(FBI photo)* Lydia Chkalov Stahl (right) was arrested in the roll-up of a major Soviet net operating against French military targets. The French convicted Stahl but released the Switz couple because the latter had assisted in the prosecution of Stahl. *(FBI photo)*

Robert Gordon Switz (above left), recruited by the Soviets in New York, was the mysterious "Harry Duryea" of the Osman case in Panama in 1932. After arrest and confinement by the French, both Robert and Marjorie returned to the United States upon their release. *(FBI photo)* Marjorie Tilley Switz (above right), an American recruited by the Soviets, was later arrested in France along with her husband and Lydia Stahl. *(FBI photo)* George Martin Mink (below left), a former Philadelphia cab driver who personally executed two Americans serving with the Abraham Lincoln Brigade during the Spanish Civil War. Mink was one of the more memorable thugs who served the Profintern and NKVD. He was later arrested and convicted of the rape of a chambermaid in a Copenhagen hotel. On his release from a Danish prison, Mink returned to the USSR and was reportedly executed. Dr. Gregory Rabinowitz (below right) was a successor to Dr. Dubrowsky as head of the Soviet Russian Red Cross in New York. Rabinowitz used the names "John Rich," "Dr. Schwartz," and "Roberts." His wife was an Amtorg employee who appeared on the company's rolls as "Mrs. Schwartz." Rabinowitz's primary mission in New York was a highly compartmented NKVD operation, which had as its sole objective the assassination of Trotsky. *(FBI photo)*

Armand Labis Feldman (with numerous aliases) was an NKVD officer who worked in the United States and Canada at the direction of Ovakimian. He was interned by the Canadians in 1940 and his arrest led to the discovery of a major, Montreal-based net that provided fraudulent documents to the Soviet services. Feldman also arranged the cover and financing of several NKVD operatives in England. While in the United States, Feldman maintained links with the Amtorg Trading Company in New York. *(FBI photo)*

Willy Brandes (alias Brandeslovsky, Hoffman, Stevens, and Nathan Green), an experienced NKVD officer who served in the United States under Ovakimian and later ran the Woolwich Arsenal case in England. Brandes eluded the British police and escaped to France and thence on to the USSR. It is doubtful that he survived after the British publicly disclosed the degree to which his activities had been penetrated. In New York, Brandes was supported by funds from Amtorg. *(FBI photo)*

3 · The GPU–OGPU Era

(1922–1934)

When, on March 1, 1922, the Cheka became the GPU (*Gosudarstvennoye Politicheskoye Upravleniye*), the personnel and functions remained the same except that now each republic formed its own subordinate element. On November 23, 1923, the separate GPUs were unified and placed under the central control of the *Obiedinyonnoye Gosudarstvennoye Politicheskoye Upravleniye* (Unified State Political Administration), or OGPU.

The purpose of the reorganization was to unite all the revolutionary forces of all the republics to "combat the political and economic counterrevolutionary movements, espionage, and banditry." The mission statement was a carryover from the one previously assigned to the Cheka. Felix Dzerzhinsky was appointed chief of the OGPU by the Presidium of the Central Committee of the USSR in which he participated as a voting member.

As chief of the OGPU, Dzerzhinsky was also a member of the Supreme Court. The chief prosecutor, N. V. Krylenko, was charged by the Court with producing a wholly cosmetic certification to the effect that all the acts of the OGPU were legal. It was another extension of the Cheka, except this time there were broader powers and fewer restraints. Because of its unbounded authority, the OGPU was the most feared of the Soviet agencies. It wasn't until 1934 that Stalin moderated the license of the OGPU when he directed that it be brought under the Ministry of Internal Affairs and renamed the *Narodni Kommissariat Vnutrenik Del* (People's Commissariat of Internal Affairs), or NKVD.

The formal establishment of the GPU in 1922 amounted to official acknowledgment that the organs of state security had emerged as the power without which there would be no Soviet state.[1]

Lenin's health was failing, and the question of succession had not been resolved. Of even greater concern to the party leadership was the pressing question of the Bolsheviks' ability to continue their control of the government in the wake of his imminent death. The only reliable guarantor against loss of power was the GPU/OGPU. Dzerzhinsky had anticipated the crisis; the organs were fully employed in choking off incipient cabals within the government, the army, and the insignificant private sector that had come into being with the New Economic Policy. Discipline and authority were to be maintained, whatever the cost. By a combination of Marxist doctrine, ideological zeal, and broad-based selective terror, the organs saved the Soviet state. Neither Lenin nor Dzerzhinsky foresaw the long-term consequences of this decision.

Lenin had achieved his one-man rule in a series of carefully orchestrated steps. In publicly deferring to the concept of democratic socialism, he stressed the fiction of his personal subordination to the party's collective will. Lenin was a deceptor *sans pareil*. His reversal of the polarity of truth is most evident in his success in creating an absolute political autocracy in which failures only enhanced his own authority and prestige.

By simply attributing every success to the Bolsheviks and every failure to the invidious "enemies of the state," Lenin was able consistently to deflect the attention of the populace. Turgid expositions of Marx and the constant invocation of conspiratorial demons, foreign and domestic, who were attempting to subvert the revolution were effective means of putting to rest any suggestion of incompetence or malfeasance on the part of the government.

The security organs and the sole-source press worked in absolute harmony to buttress the illusion of danger. Each day the organs uncovered new plots to explain why bread was not available or why production norms had not been met. The published "truth" was that a secret organization of White guardists had been discovered destroying the wheat crop, or that "owing to the vigilance of the security organs," a major sabotage unit in the pay of the British had been thwarted. All of the arrested men had confessed and implicated others. And now for the good news: A heretofore unknown peasant in a distant (unnamed) village chopped wood continuously for three days as a measure of his gratitude to the state. Statistics just received from a renamed (and therefore unrecognizable) factory show that the output of manufactured products (unidentified) has risen (from what level?) dramatically in the last six months.

Three basic themes were invariably present and insistently repeated in the Soviet press: (1) Any failure is caused entirely by malign counterrevolutionary elements; (2) the government is making breathless advances in other areas; (3) the security organs are heroically rooting out subversion, sabotage, and economic wrecking.

By 1922 few remained to challenge Lenin's preeminence in the Bol-shevik hierarchy. To do so would have assured nocturnal retribution from the organs in the form of arrest, expulsion from the party, internal exile, or worse. The offender was effectively cut off from further participation in the revolution's spoils. The Cheka guaranteed an uneasy status quo among those who aspired to Lenin's power, and none save Stalin had a strategy for succession.

In the Central Committee, Stalin's reputation was that of peasant clerk: minor, tough, and thoroughly anti-intellectual. His mere presence was looked upon as a personal indulgence of Lenin's. Stalin worked at nurturing his image as a technically competent secretary, totally subser-vient to the will of the party. He was also the man who could provide the members with additional, unwarranted "perks" and bits of confiscated treasure.

But Stalin had a clear, unaffected, peasant's understanding of the me-chanics of power. While the prominent aspirants to authority vied for Lenin's consideration, Stalin went about his essentially clerical respon-sibilities of appointing functionaries within the growing bureaucracy. Be-cause the appointments did not seem consequential at the time, the process was not subjected to scrutiny by others.

Stalin intuitively knew that each nominee proposed for a government position, however insignificant, must first be made to understand that his office was given in exchange for personal loyalty to Stalin. It meant that the appointee undertook to keep Stalin aware of information that came to his attention. In this gradual but certain manner, Stalin's strategy of power through patronage was effected.

The placing of personal loyalists in key positions gave Stalin the beginnings of a political machine. These minor, though essential, func-tionaries formed an invisible infantry for his march to power. His manip-ulations provoked little concern at the upper reaches of the Bolshevik regime because his intellectual superiors were fully engaged in matters of grand strategy and policy.

Stalin's personal appointees were invariably party members who had become more dependent on Stalin than on the party. Stalin hired and fired these officials with impunity, often making use of the organs to re-move those who failed to serve his interests.

As Stalin busied himself with the creation of a personal bureau-cratic army, the others, most notably Trotsky, Zinoviev, Kamenev, and Bukharin, maintained a curious deathwatch in anticipation of Lenin's de-mise.[2] In their periodic public statements they maintained the fiction of collective leadership, disavowed personal amibitions, and restated that the party was bound by the principle of majority rule. Trotsky was able to lend himself to this display of unanimity because he was satisfied that the party would be compelled to turn to him when Lenin died. His superior intellect, demonstrated ability, and past contribution to the success of the coup made him the obvious choice. His complacent arrogance in this regard was not without a rational basis. Most of Lenin's revolutionary sycophants were not competent to deal with the problems now faced by the Bolshevik state.

Trotsky and the others grossly underestimated the cunning, tenacity, and patience of Stalin. Unlike Trotsky, who should have known better, the others had no grasp of what was needed to maintain a modern state. Stalin's understanding of these problems was not much better, but his comprehension of the use of terror, coercion, fear, and ambition to maintain personal political power was highly developed.

Dzerzhinsky, having accepted the twin concepts of collective leadership and party majority control as articles of communist faith, gradually became an even closer ally of Stalin. The cooperation of these two men— Stalin with the burgeoning bureaucracy and Dzerzhinsky with the organs—might have suggested more caution among those who pretended to Lenin's mantle.

As the manuevers in the Central Committee went on, the GPU continued to expand and consolidate its powers. It was during this period that several major deception operations were developed and the GPU began to expand its overseas bases. Dzerzhinsky played a direct role in the recruitment of GPU personnel. We are told, by impeccable Soviet sources, that he was guided in his selection of recruits by his demand that "the intelligence officer must have a clear mind, warm heart and clean hands."[3]

In building a permanent structure for the GPU, the problem of staffing was of primary importance. The Chekists who had functioned in the immediate postcoup era and those who distinguished themselves during the civil war were, in many instances, unsuited for inclusion in the now formally established GPU. A new generation of Chekists was needed to carry on the work of the state. In subtle and unarticulated ways, Dzerzhinsky, although an anti-Semite, resisted pressures to reduce the number of Jews holding important positions in the GPU. It is not possible to know his intentions, though it is evident that he anticipated the certainty of an eventual reaction to their disproportionate presence in the GPU. Among these were the men who had helped to make the coup and had shown extraordinary dedication to the principles of the Soviet regime. The Jews who were, by their intellect and courageous behavior, in the revolution's forefront were encouraged to lead elements of the GPU in the war against the people.

Allowing some Jews to become powerful as well as highly visible brought several benefits to the GPU. The chief advantage was that it was publicly manifest that the Soviet regime held no prejudice and that Jews could achieve importance commensurate with their abilities. Since there were remarkably few Chekists who spoke a second language, had traveled abroad, or were educated beyond the most rudimentary level, the more cultivated Jews, objectively, were essential to the organs.

Dzerzhinsky knew precisely the kinds of recruits needed. They must be resilient enough to accept the vagaries and contradictions of Soviet socialism. They must be rigid enough to apply untempered terror. But, of prime importance, they had to submit to political control while remaining political neuters. They must be willing to enforce Bolshevism in any of its varied forms and to devote themselves wholly to the protection of Soviet power.

Dzerzhinsky's personal zeal gave him what was taken to be moral authority. Service in the early GPU was indeed characterized as a form of knighthood in which dedication to party aims was the highest virtue. The only more modern counterpart is found in the Nazi SS formations of the mid-thirties, where purity of purpose and honor were suborned in the name of the state. The GPU became a collegial and thoroughly elitist band.

Those selected to carry out the GPU's mission did so in the belief that they were simply agents of the historical imperative. Bolshevism would inevitably prevail, and they only hastened the day by dispatching to the hereafter those who by reason of birth or circumstance were doomed never to know democratic socialism.

The GPU, like the SS, had a self-purging mechanism that removed those who lost their enthusiasm or sense of total commitment to the party. The rigid code of conduct did not measure degrees of brutality, avarice, or lust, but only subservience to the party. Backsliding in the GPU was a capital crime, and such a betrayal of organizational trust was regarded as the most serious offense one could commit. Trust, in this regard, referred to state secrets. The members of the organs had as little mutual trust among themselves as the rest of the citizenry had in one another.

Chekists were encouraged to recommend others who, they believed, had the skills and motivation to warrant consideration as new recruits. If a proposed recruit demonstrated appropriate fervor, it reflected favorably on the sponsor. If he proved unadaptable to the work, the sponsor was put at risk. This spurred the less able to find the better qualified so that they themselves would benefit. Dzerzhinsky's approach to staffing the early GPU was a then-innovative and effective manipulation of a system of rewards and punishments to achieve organizational goals.

Witnesses who survived in the organs and later escaped abroad confirm that investiture in the GPU resembled induction into a band of

Thugs, the highly organized Indian assassins, only without the religious consecration of the dagger or garrote. The oath, the internal code of behavior, and the elaborate system of reprisals would be familiar to highly developed criminal organizations. Like the Mafia, the GPU had all of the malevolent features that attend a novitiate who must "make his bones." By obediently carrying out passionless acts of murder and brutality, the candidate proves his worth. Service in the organs was a lifetime commitment. Although it did not assure cultural development, it was the most certain opportunity for social and economic improvement in the Bolshevik state.

Status, privilege, and power were the chief attractions of the security service. To bind the participants more strongly to the cause, a system of separate schools, commissaries, and apartments was open to Chekists and their families. The pact was explicit: GPU members who did what they were told to do, without revulsion or pause, enjoyed the privileges promised by Marx. Their children were given preferred treatment and promised more. Dzerzhinsky's "Guardians of the State" were bought at a reasonable price and have since repeatedly proved their worth to the state.

Candidates selected for the GPU who later failed to measure up to the organization's strict standards were culled and destroyed much as a breeder might dispose of animals unworthy to perpetuate the stock. The second-generation Chekists were willing to control their fellow citizens in a manner and degree that no other totalitarian society has achieved. Although it is not generally recognized, the GPU's unequaled capacity for contriving the death of millions was fully functional ten years before Hitler came to power. At no subsequent time did the Nazi death squads under Himmler exceed the Soviet organs in the systematic destruction of humans.

In assessing Dzerzhinsky's contribution to the preservation of the Soviet state, it is evident that, without the organs, the Bolshevik regime could not have continued beyond the death of Lenin in 1924. Dzerzhinsky's dedication, zeal, and intellect forged a shield and sword that went on to subdue the populace, secure absolute dominion in the name of the minority party, and in 1982, succeed in elevating its former chief to the highest and most powerful political position in the USSR.

Dzerzhinsky had the good fortune to suffer early death and immediate elevation to the revered status of demigod in the Soviet pantheon. Had he survived, he would not be remembered today in the USSR as the White Knight, but more likely as a fiendish spy in the pay of Warsaw. Although Stalin used the mighty system Dzerzhinsky built, he could not have endured the threat of Dzerzhinsky's dedication to those revolutionary principles that Stalin freely debased. Almost as important was the fact that Dzerzhinsky was present at the birth of the Bolshevik regime and knew Stalin as a minor figure. As was learned later, accurate recollections of the early Stalin were apt to be fatal.[4]

It is useful to note that Dzerzhinsky's personnel algorithm (i.e., the predictor and profile of the successful Chekist and the basic criteria for candidate selection) was essentially intuitive in its origin. His innate understanding of human behavior, greatly extended by his prison experience, gave him a remarkable appreciation of the needs of the organs. Unfortunately, his insights were institutionalized before his death in 1926, and his governing precepts still affect the selection of candidates for today's KGB.

In the interim, successive leaders of the organs, by a process called "longitudinal evaluation," have been able to identify and track potential recruits for the KGB, from infancy (privileged sons and daughters) to their eventual investiture in the KGB ranks, in a thoroughly scientific manner. Today, the young Soviet man or woman who is "invited" to become a member of the KGB is a predictable commodity. Each has been observed and tested in numerous ways.

Few Westerners are fully aware of the immense prestige conferred by induction into the state security organs. It is certainly not a model for emulation, but it is a distinctive characteristic of the Soviet service.

The aims and objectives of the Bolshevik leadership have been clear from the time of the October coup in 1917. Their strategy and tactics have been consistent. Opportunities are exploited when presented and where effective. The system has been flexible enough to respond by modification and extension when appropriate. Although the tactical minutiae might be unknown, the strategic objectives are never mysterious. The Soviets put great store in the West's boundless capacity to disregard contemporary history and to sustain the absurd hope for their eventual conversion into benign nationalists.

A day-to-day narrative of the development of the Soviet services obscures more than it reveals. Some activities and operations were carried out on a strategic basis; others were essentially tactical in nature. The differences between long-range efforts and those born of immediacy are not always evident to observers. It is wiser to treat Soviet intelligence operations in a conceptual context rather than by the conventional case method.

Because the Soviet services undertook simultaneous, parallel, and duplicative operations in many parts of the world, a strict sequential narrative would not reconcile intelligence events abroad with the internal issues and concerns of the USSR. Some Soviet operations have had remarkable longevity and continue, in modified form, into the present.

Furthermore, if one presents Soviet operations in individual episodes, the facts are obscured and distorted. Realities are not seen coherently. One response to episodic treatment of Soviet operations is that counter-measures tend to be reactive, and consequently ineffectual.

Public response to disclosures of specific instances of Soviet intelligence activity ranges from indulgent amusement to national paranoia. Neither is appropriate to the problem. The hazards associated with So-viet-directed espionage are real, and it appears that Sir William Stephen-son's question—"Will the democracies consent to their own survival?"—requires a timely answer.

The varied operations and aims of the Soviet services are sometimes presented as having the impenetrability of a polynomial equation with a thousand unknowns. In light of the masses of documents now available to interested scholars, this view is insupportable.

Three persistent factors have contributed to the problems faced by the democracies' counterintelligence efforts: (1) an institutionalized policy in the U.S. of deliberate discontinuity in the counterintelligence area (usu-ally with the aim of providing general experience rather than expert spe-cialization). (2) Chronic shortages of trained personnel; because even the most effective counterintelligence fails to provide a steady stream of dra-matic, short-term benefits to bureaucratic managers, it is frequently slighted in favor of more "productive" activities. (3) A depreciation of the need to understand what has gone on before in the development of the Soviet intelligence and security services. One Western officer put the problem succinctly when he asked the question: "Why should I read his-tory when I could be out there making it?"

Just as no solution can be found to a problem whose terms are not known, no thoughtful countermeasures against the Soviet services can be derived without a deeper knowledge and better appreciation of their phil-osophical predication.

Bolshevik intentions have been clear from the beginning. So have their strategic and tactical applications. Where effective, they have per-sisted. When countered, they have been modified and readapted. Under-standing Soviet intelligence is a function of historical analysis. There are no great mysteries associated with it as a whole; it is only when one attempts to draw conclusions from isolated cases that erroneous judg-ments result. Every operation run by the Soviets is made to appear to originate with another sponsor. Elemental deception is an organic prop-erty of all operations.

A wide variety of deceptions have been used to cloak the criminal activities of the Soviet organs and to conceal origins. Murder remains murder, no matter what euphemisms are employed to obscure the event. The same is true of kidnapping, counterfeiting, and other felonious undertakings exhaustively documented in official archives. Such crimes are committed in a political context and become more comprehensible, if not less contemptible, once the official motivations are understood.

The Soviet organs have had an ally in the short attention spans of their adversaries. Thus they have come to rely on the probability that earlier, similar events are either not known or have been forgotten.

The procedures and methods generated in the Cheka were extended in the GPU, refined in the NKVD, and brought to their present high state of effectiveness by the KGB. Although there have been major changes in the techniques, the underlying rationale of Dzerzhinsky remains constant.

Recruitment is a term used extensively in intelligence literature. For that reason, it warrants comment. In one sense it is the process of inducing another, by whatever means, to act in your stead: that is, to cause someone to act as your *agent* or, in a legal sense, to act in agency. In the idealized intelligence usage, it is the process of gaining the full cooperation of an individual who has continuing access to *foreign, classified* information. The word *recruitment* is frequently associated with other descriptive words intended to qualify the term.

In the most elemental sense it can be said that there are two kinds of recruitment. The first can be regarded as ideological—that is, those instances in which shared interests motivate the agent (as in the cases of Guy Burgess, Donald Maclean, Sir Anthony Blunt, and others). There is no question that ideological recruitments have been accomplished by the Soviets. However, they have become statistically quite rare. An analysis of known Soviet operations indicates that while ideologues made the most significant contributions in the earlier period (1918 through World War II), every important recruitment since the end of the Second World War has been coercive in nature. In 1976, at a meeting in the Soviet embassy at Bonn, the chief of the Czech intelligence service in that city complained, "Nobody works for us for ideological motives anymore."[5]

The factors accounting for this startling change are several. Before and immediately following the October 1918 coup, there was a broad response to the dynamism of change throughout the world. In the closing days of World War I, the whole bloody conflict was beginning to be seen as a war among commercial interests seeking to rationalize their colonial economies. When the Germans retired from the field of battle, the Japanese picked up the former German concessions in China and a few islands in the Pacific Far East. Britain took title to the former German colonies in Africa, and France and Italy gained the forfeit lands in North Africa that had marked the Western reaches of Germany's wartime ally the Ottoman Empire.

Russia had no foreign colonies to lose. The collapse of the Romanoffs, her withdrawal from the war, and the separate treaty with Germany left Russia with no claim against the Central Powers. In the first half of 1917 the new Russia had no allies and no enemies. By the end of that year the Bolsheviks' coup had destroyed the weak attempt at representative government and was in the process of gaining complete control of the new state.

The most immediate problem confronting the Bolsheviks was the prevention of a *third* revolution. Two imperative actions had to be taken simultaneously: The first was to destroy the threat of the White armies and their foreign sponsors by confronting them with a strong and resolute Red Army. The second action demanded the institution of means to ensure absolute command of the population and resources. By December 20, 1917, such a mechanism came into being in the form of the Extraordinary Commission to Combat Counterrevolution, Speculation, and Sabotage.

Outside the Soviet Union the world was deluged with dramatic reports of how the working-class heroes humbled the mercenary bandits of capitalism while defending the ideals of revolutionary socialism. The Soviet government presented the consistent line that everywhere "people" were marshaling to defend "freedom," expel "oppressors," and secure "peace."

In the early days, those who paused or dissented were arrested under the VChK's broad interpretation of "counterrevolutionary activity" and were imprisoned or shot.

Foreign observers and a few reporters were provided access to Lenin so that their readers could learn more about the man who had wrought the great miracle of social change. To the occasional question about alleged excesses of the Cheka, Lenin, with simulated candor, called on the auditor to visualize an imaginary kitchen in which an omelet couldn't be made "without breaking eggs." This unfortunate and overused irrelevancy, coupled with his confidential admission that in the confusion a few mistakes had been made, satisfied most that he was a compassionate man beset with overwhelming problems which he was laboring to solve.

The world press depended on Soviet government handouts, dispatches from a few foreign reporters in the USSR, and various stringers who gave detailed amplification to the glowing accounts. Occasional contradictory reports emanated from those who had fled the Soviet Union. Because they were branded as members of the "exploiting class," as counterrevolutionaries or political criminals, their firsthand accounts of Soviet barbarity were judged to be biased and exaggerated. The world was getting its first taste of "managed news." The consistent, enthusiastic reports from the USSR produced powerful empathetic responses everywhere.

Initially, the foreign Socialist parties considered the Soviet Union a gratifying fulfillment of their own political advocacy, and their intellectuals regarded the Soviet "experiment" as daring and deserving of uncritical support. Others raced to be publicly identified with the "people's revolution." Among these were some who suffered from the delusion that their own disappointments, inadequacies, and failures were the result of discriminatory political factors that interfered with their intellectual freedom. It was a comfortable notion, but as the world was later to learn, it did much harm. J. M. Thompson put the case of the bogus intellectual succinctly when he pointed out that "a private grievance is never so dangerous as when it can be identified with a matter of principle."

These people were never "recruited" by the Soviets because there was no need. Each foreigner who rallied to the Red banner brought his or her own engine of motivation. The Cheka's job was to assess their utility, measure their influence, and find the buttons—culture, politics, money, or fame—that made them jump.

Americans who visited Moscow in the immediate postrevolutionary phase, with few exceptions, deliberately blinded themselves to the realities of life under Lenin. They had previously proclaimed the USSR a paradise. Vanity, arrogance, or naïveté did not permit retreat from error. The additional expectation that things must inevitably change for the better was born of the same cast of mind that afflicts compulsive gamblers. They bet their reputations and, in some instances, their lives on the conviction that their faith would be vindicated. The Soviet Union remained an exciting game for dissatisfied political adventurers and irrepressible romantics. Their emotions betrayed them and their judgment was faulty because they neglected to take into account the fact that, in the Soviet game, the house made and suspended the rules at will. Further, the house owned the table, dice, and cards, and every tie went to the dealer.

Millions who lived outside Soviet Russia admired and supported what they *thought* was taking place within the country. The millions who lived inside knew that they were barely subsisting under the harshest tyranny the world has ever known. The internal and external views of Soviet Russia had been manipulated into positions diametrically opposed. An escapee or deserter who tried to describe life under the Soviets found people unwilling to believe accounts that conflicted with their preconceptions, acquired through reading *objective* accounts propagated by the Comintern and the official releases appearing in the Soviet-controlled press.

In one of the few major errors committed by the Cheka, some preliminary recruitments were made among foreign Communist parties. These were not true recruitments, because the CP members had already self-selected themselves to perform any task calculated to advance the interests of the USSR. It was an error in that many, if not most, of the foreign

CP members were known to the police or security services of the countries in which they resided. It is obviously poor clandestine form to participate in demonstrations and street brawls on Monday and hope to go unnoticed for the balance of the week. This fundamental error, which was not corrected by Dzerzhinsky prior to his death in 1926, became most evident in Germany when Hitler came to power. Although a number of German CP members, in anticipation of Hitler, had broken with the German party (KPD) and gone underground, the effusively detailed German police records had not been amended to reflect this information. There was a consequent roundup of Soviet agents who, though operating covertly, were still obvious to the police. In later years, as Hitler's power became more pervasive, the Soviets made a special effort to insinuate their own agents into the Gestapo and police, with good results.

In the early days of the Soviet services, loyalty and willingness to submit to discipline were of paramount importance. Assiduous pursuit of these characteristics, however, tended to produce an army of eager aspirants without access to useful information. Since the Soviet approach to espionage had been labor-intensive from its inception, there were many useful support tasks to be performed. Surveillants, couriers, and communicators drawn from this vast pool of volunteers were then discreetly detached from association with the visible, sometimes overt national Communist parties.

The next phase in the recruitment process was to locate those who had access or influence that could aid the Soviet cause; the "target" was first identified, and the search for prospective agents was then begun. In this context, recruitment of an agent who could perform a specific function was the objective. The prospect was examined like a used car, utilizing every available technique except tire-kicking. Assuming the nominee to be recruitable, responses to a questionnaire were required, with key questions working backward from the target to the prospective agent:

- Can the individual approach the target directly in the normal course of work or social activity?
- If not, can such access be generated? How?
- What are the anticipated technical demands (photography, communications, other)?
- What kind of person should "handle" the recruit? How should the individual be approached? What will motivate the individual to act for us? Who should attempt the recruitment?
- With respect to the individual: Is he "progressive," venal, vain, alcoholic, homosexual? (In countries where homosexual liaisons are deemed criminal, this fact represents a powerful lever to the recruiter.) Is there something about him, his wife, family, friends, or associates that can be used to exert pressure?

None of the questions were addressed to the prospect. Instead, the information was gradually developed in the course of surveillance, elicitation, pretext inquiry, and other techniques that did not disclose particularized interest. If possible, the prospect was maneuvered into a social or mock business situation in which he could be observed and met. Throughout the process, the critical factors were: First, if recruited, could the agent get or do what was wanted? Second, what apparently motivated the agent and how could he be "controlled"?

The most dedicated ideological recruit, one who was prepared to commit any crime in the name of the party, was always suspect to the experienced Chekist. They knew, mostly from their own experience, that ideological drives wane and are replaced by doubts. Even if the prospect was prepared to make great personal sacrifice without any reward, it was not permitted. It was an absolute imperative that the Soviet recruit be "corrupted" with money or gifts. To the high-minded, money degrades the worth of the service offered. To the Chekist, it *had* to be done. It was simply one of the many controls that exacted performance, coerced compliance, or compromised a later desertion.

When money was given, a receipt had to be signed—another imperative. Sometimes the exchange took an innocent form, such as payment for a translation service, the editing of a few pages of text, preparing a comment on a published article, or reviewing a book. If the prospect expressed willingness to contribute his services without payment, the Chekist might have to resort to mock humility and explain that he must take the money and sign a receipt so that no subsequent issue could be raised about what had happened to the money: "If you will please take it, then I can submit evidence that the money was paid. If you wish to return it, you can make arrangements to do so later." When the status of the prospect or agent was elevated and money seemed inappropriate, an expensive gift was substituted and the deliveryman could take the receipt.[6]

The operating principles first introduced by Dzerzhinsky remain in force in the KGB today. It is as though Dzerzhinsky understood that ideologues could not sustain long-term interest in a set of ideas that were becoming more irrelevant each passing day. Coercion, intimidation, and blackmail also did away with the tedious necessity to discuss all forms of human activity in the opaque language of Marxist-Leninist believers. There are other methods of making spies that don't demand the invocation of dialectical materialism.

As experience added to sophistication, the Chekists developed indirect approaches that are still in daily service. One of the most effective of the techniques that came into prominence in the mid-twenties was the one referred to as the "false flag" method. In its elemental form, it is a more modern version of a very old Okhrana provocation technique brought to a higher level by the Chekists. As the name suggests, the operation is based on the assumption that even the most militant opponent of Soviet communism might be willing to join an ultra-secret organization if it was dedicated to the obliteration of Soviet communism (shared objectives). Therefore, the recruiter takes on the coloration of an extreme antagonist of the Soviet Union and approaches the target from downward. Coming from an unexpected quarter, and knowing the biases of the target, a skilled operator might succeed in gaining his or her cooperation in a bogus anti-Soviet operation.

The technique is used extensively in the Soviet Union and in selected situations elsewhere. Milovan Djilas gives a firsthand account:

> First, upon the suggestion of party functionaries, the party police (KGB) establish that someone is an "enemy" of existing conditions; that if nothing else, his views and discussions with close friends represent trouble, at least for the local authorities. The next step is the preparation of the legal removal of the enemy. This is done either through a provocateur, who provokes the victim to make "embarrassing statements," to take part in illegal organizing, or to commit similar acts; or it is done through a "stool pigeon" who simply bears witness against the victim according to the wishes of the police. Most of the illegal organizations in communist regimes are *created by the secret police in order to lure opponents into them and to put these opponents in a position where the police can settle accounts with them.* The communist government does not discourage "objectionable" citizens from committing law violations and crimes; in fact it prods them into such violations and crimes.[7]

In the later GPU–OGPU era, Stalin gave as much attention to the prospect of organized opposition abroad as he did to the possibility of rebellion at home. The expulsion of Trotsky and his brief exile in Siberia gave Stalin an opportunity to gauge Trotsky's influence and measure his ability to rally anti-Stalinist forces. The OGPU handled every detail of Trotsky's life in Siberia. His mail was intercepted and his visitors carefully noted. From Trotsky's voluminous correspondence, Stalin learned precisely who was supportive of the former minister of war and, of course, the identities of those who expressed the hope that Trotsky would be restored to both the party and the Soviet government.

Stalin continued to regard the internally exiled Trotsky as a threat. Though on the verge of absolute dominion, he was himself not yet sufficiently assured to order Trotsky's death. A formal trial would certainly be embarrassing and might prove dangerous. Trotsky, with his oratorical skills, his revolutionary credentials, his long association with Lenin, and most importantly, his detailed knowledge of Stalin's insidious role in subverting the revolution, made the outcome of such a trial unpredictable.

It would therefore be better to expel Trotsky for his crimes and to use his name as the new term for the most heinous political offenses. To be a Trotskyite, to profess Trotskyism, or to know or have known Trotsky was now considered unforgivable. The OGPU, which had come to know "deviationists" and "revisionists," did not have to engage in doctrinal hairsplitting, but went immediately to the core of the matter. Trotsky had opposed Stalin, and in the prevailing climate, there could be no more serious offense. Djilas distilled the essence of the process: "Communists settle accounts with their opponents not because they have committed crimes, but because they are opponents."[8]

To a degree, national intelligence and security services reflect the intentions, personalities, and wills of those who have founded and initially directed the organizations. Just so would one see the influences that affected the British service under Sir Francis Walsingham and Queen Elizabeth I, or the United States' OSS under William Donovan and Franklin Roosevelt. Strong personalities with conviction and will usually leave a lasting mark on their handiwork. In this regard, it is useful to consider the relationship between Dzerzhinsky and Stalin. With Lenin, and later with Stalin, Dzerzhinsky built a modern service of unique character which over a span of more than sixty-eight years has become an imperial power in its own right.

When the OGPU moved into foreign areas, new and special problems developed. The Soviets' perception of the outside world was (and is) predicated on the conviction that all non-Soviets are aggressive and hostile to the USSR. Direct evidence to the contrary is no more than a clever form of deception, and all manifestations of friendship are poorly concealed attempts at provocation.

However absurd these notions seem, it must be remembered that the promotion of these fears has been a demonstrably effective counterintelligence technique. The security of Soviet personnel and facilities rank as the organs' first priority.

Within each facility, an officer of the organs is charged with the supervision of the *sovetskaia koloniia* (Soviet Colony), or SK. His functions are of an internal-security rather than an intelligence nature. He conducts bed checks, interrogates Soviet personnel about their local contacts, and prays to the ghost of Lenin that no member of the staff defects during his tour of duty.

To the amazement of the early foreign staffs, local citizens voluntarily called at the embassies and trade missions to seek information, express support of the USSR, and try to solicit business. It became evident that some of these well-wishers might be of considerable service to the embassy's intelligence mission.

In the early days, selected members of the local CP were directed to conduct investigations of these people and, in some instances, to place them under surveillance. The rudimentary system for vetting embassy callers sometimes led the GRU and OGPU officers to seek subsequent clandestine contacts, many of which proved extremely valuable. Gradually a policy evolved of having a seasoned officer meet with *all* callers to make some preliminary estimate of their possible utility in espionage. It marked the recognition of the as-yet-unarticulated First Principal of Espionage ("Most intelligence coups are the result of unplanned events") and its equally apt antithesis: "Most intelligence debacles are also the results of unplanned events."

In 1928, a furtive little man approached the Soviet embassy in Paris. He said that he was an employee of the Italian government and asked if the Soviets would be interested in buying some Italian ciphers. The Soviet officer who dealt with him noticed that the caller had something under his coat and was exhibiting great anxiety. The OGPU man asked to see the "merchandise," and the Italian offered a folio of documents for his inspection. After quickly scanning the material, the OGPU man turned to the now thoroughly frightened Italian and declared that the ciphers were fakes. When the Italian rose in protest, the OGPU man threw the documents into the fireplace, and two other Soviets, standing by, seized the Italian's arms, roughly escorted him to the embassy door, and shoved him out into the street.

It was correctly assumed that the Italian had no recourse. If he went to the French police, they would probably inform the Italian police, and in due course he would be arrested. Since selling documents is not a political crime, he might find himself extradited to Italy on a charge of theft and tried before an Italian court on a charge of treason. Not a very promising prospect.

After the Italian was forcibly expelled from the embassy, the ciphers were recovered from the fireplace and sent off to Moscow by courier. A few weeks later, the OGPU officer[9] who had organized the little drama was rewarded by a congratulatory message from the Center. The ciphers were genuine and had been found most helpful. The fact that they had been acquired without cost only added to their worth.

Within the year, a second stranger made a similar approach to the Soviet embassy in Paris. This time it was a cipher clerk from the British Foreign Office who was temporarily in Paris with a British trade delegation. The consequences of his visit were to have grave long-term implications.

The case is useful because it illustrates the point that unplanned events and unexpected visitors warrant careful professional examination. That the case eventually became extremely valuable to the Soviet service is a testament less to Soviet competence than to dogged perseverance.

The British clerk, like the Italian, approached the Soviets believing that he had something of value to sell for cash, and that one simple transaction would meet whatever financial need drove him to the act. Without attempting to divine the complexities of either man's motivation, let it be conceded that the most obvious likelihood was avarice. A second possibility was vengeance, a desire somehow to embarrass, intimidate, or even get rid of a superior.

The case of the British clerk was a mixture of both. He had joined the Foreign Office in 1913 and, with the exception of one year in the army during World War I, had served continuously in the Communications Department of the Foreign Office. His entry salary was less than £100 per annum, and after seventeen years of service he found himself earning only a few pounds more. It is likely that he was as resentful of his employers as he certainly was poor.

The Soviet embassy in Paris was then (1929) on the Rue de Grenelle.[10] It was an imposing structure with many outward signs of deterioration, looking a little like a beleaguered fort. The lower windows were barred and shuttered against the world, and from a standard on the roof, an outsized red flag fluttered in the June breeze. On two sides of the embassy, over large ornamental windows, the stone facing appeared to be painted white. A fanciful design had been applied in poster colors incorporating a hammer and sickle imposed on a representation of the world. The whole was surrounded by a wreath in which a new sun was rising. The defacement seemed to characterize the occupants: garish, bold, and defiant.[11] At the embassy entrance, instead of a burnished brass plate, there was a crude handmade sign that added nothing to the structure's dignity.

The clerk went to the main entrance and asked for the military attaché. Once admitted, he was subjected to a search and put into a waiting room, along with two attendants. The room had once been a magnificent library but was now given over to the disordered storage of excess furniture, file cabinets, and rolled carpets.

Soon the OGPU man Vladimir Voynovich, using the name "Major Vladimir," entered the room. The clerk explained that his name was Scott (which it wasn't), that he worked in the British Foreign Office, and that he had a cipher to sell for $2,000 in American currency. Voynovich asked to examine the material, took it, and without further comment rose and left the room. The clerk protested but was restrained by the guards. In twenty-five minutes Voynovich returned. He was visibly angry and threw the documents into the clerk's lap, denouncing him as a provocateur and swindler. A moment later the clerk, in a state of paralyzed shock, found himself in the courtyard of the embassy as the great entrance door slammed shut.

The dazed "Scott," drenched in perspiration and gasping with fear, picked his crumpled hat from the pavement and moved swiftly to the courtyard gate. He tried to compose himself as he walked away. His efforts to reconstruct the events of the last hour were clouded by alternate waves of humiliation and fear.

He was oblivious to the fact that an OGPU surveillant was following him as he made his uncertain way to a small *pension* on a narrow street one third of a mile from Rue de Grenelle. He had earlier rented a room there, reassured by a small hand-lettered sign in the window of #163: ENGLISH SPOKEN. The surveillant noted the number, then waited nearby for twenty minutes while trying to discern if Scott was met by others or if the *pension* seemed to have any special significance. The OGPU customarily used surveillants to help identify "unknowns," and Scott qualified under that heading. It was also a Soviet conviction that callers of Scott's kind were apt to be provocateurs employed by the French police, the British, or any one of a number of anti-Soviet émigré organizations in Paris.

When the OGPU man was satisfied with his observations, he made his way back to the embassy by another route so that he could be certain that *he* was not being followed. When he prepared his report, he inadvertently recorded the *pension* number as 168 rather than 163. It was a consequential error.

By his visit to the embassy, Scott had compromised himself, failed to get the expected money, and was now in an exceedingly vulnerable position. Within three months of his humiliation at the Soviet embassy, when he was back at the Foreign Office processing enciphered traffic, he received a second blow. The British representative who maintained liaison with the French security service sent a cable from the Paris embassy describing the recent defection of the Soviet chargé d'affaires in Paris. His name was Bessedovsky, and he was reportedly giving the French highly detailed accounts of Soviet espionage and subversive activities in Western Europe. Scott feared that Bessedovsky might be "Major Vladimir" and that his own visit to the embassy might now become known to the British service.

At the time Bessedovsky defected, Valerian Dovgalevsky, the Soviet ambassador to France, was in England attempting to persuade the British that diplomatic relations, broken as a result of a Special Branch raid on the Soviet "trading company" Arcos, ought to be restored. While away from Paris, Dovgalevsky had designated Bessedovsky to act in his stead, a routine previously approved by Moscow.[12]

Bessedovsky, knowing that he would soon be recalled to Moscow for questioning about financial irregularities, had climbed over the wall of the embassy garden and presented himself at a French police post. In his hand he carried an automatic pistol that had been fired recently. He claimed he was in danger and that his wife and daughter were being held captive by OGPU thugs in the embassy.

The matter was promptly reported to the ministries concerned, and the police were instructed to disarm him and protect his person until further instructed. With Gallic precision, the Quai d'Orsay concluded that Bessedovsky was indeed in charge in the absence of Dovgalevsky. Further, at the time of recognition, the French had pledged to take all steps necessary to protect the physical security of Soviet diplomatic personnel. French honor had to be upheld even if it meant husbanding a deserter from the Soviet embassy.

Later in the day, Bessedovsky, escorted by representatives of the Quai and twenty gendarmes, descended on the embassy and in an impressive theatrical display, demanded the release of his wife and daughter. The Paris press dubbed it "l'Affaire Bessedovsky," and editorials in the great dailies called into question the worthiness of any nation whose embassy held hostages. The émigré press saw it as the beginning of the collapse of the Soviet Empire, and Bessedovsky, who a week before had been a contemptible Bolshevik lackey, was instantly transformed into a far-seeing, clear-eyed ally in the fight against international communism. The French security service was also very active: Within a week of the event, more than twenty Soviet apparatchiks and an equal number of *seksots* fled France.

Dovgalevsky received word of Bessedovsky's flight while he was closeted in a hotel room at Brighton, secretly parleying with British Foreign Secretary Arthur Henderson.[13] He returned to Paris immediately to prepare a message explaining the debacle. He knew his report would go directly to Stalin and desperately sought extenuating factors that might in some way mitigate the embassy's blame in the matter.

The French, in exchange for asylum, relentlessly exacted information from Bessedovsky. Exaggerations, dissimulations, and outright lies were dealt with quickly and effectively. At the end of the first week of intensive interrogation, most of the bluster, feigned indignation, and self-righteousness had gone, leaving a humbler Bessedovsky in their wake. He was shown hundreds of furry photographs of furtive men and women taken without their knowledge, and he was able to identify many of the subjects as OGPU apparatchiks posing as diplomats, secretaries, translators, and aides assigned to the embassy or the trade mission. He was impressed with the extensive French knowledge of the official and quasi-official Soviet community in Paris. His respect for the French security service went up sharply as his confidence in his ability to tell them something they didn't know declined.

Near the close of a long morning session, Bessedovsky volunteered what he thought was an entertaining anecdote. His purpose was to amuse the French interrogators, who in the course of their intensive sessions had become his friends. It was a thirdhand account of an Englishman named Scott, who had recently called at the Soviet embassy and attempted to sell some British ciphers. His interrogators froze. No one moved. Everyone looked expectantly to him to go on. He explained that Scott was obviously without experience and no match for Voynovich and his brigands, who had quickly separated him from his folio of cipher material. The ciphers were photographed, and then Voynovich ordered that Scott be thrown bodily out into the street while Voynovich denounced him as a swindler trying to exploit the Soviets by selling patently bogus information.

Bessedovsky looked about in expectation that England's embarrassment would cheer the French. He was mistaken. Instead, lunch was postponed while, with new energy, the French pressed him for every detail of the event. What was told as a divertissement had become the focus of intense interest.

That evening Bessedovsky met with a British officer for the first time and retold his account of the Scott affair. It was alarming news, and throughout the afternoon Bessedovsky was asked to repeat the story again and again and again.

On the following morning the British officer took Imperial Airways' cross-channel flight from Le Bourget to Croydon, assuaging his nervousness by draining his flask before boarding. (The import of his message for London made it imperative that he sublimate his personal aversions in the name of duty.)

Bessedovsky's revelations were stunning in their implications, the most important of which was that the Scott case couldn't be trusted to the Foreign Office cables. Within an hour the liaison officer was closeted with Capt. Guy Liddell and several senior officers of the security service. The Bessedovsky story was again detailed at length. He asserted his conviction that Bessedovsky's apostasy seemed genuine. Regrettably, since Bessedovsky hadn't seen the Englishman "Scott," there was no physical description, and the name Scott was almost certain to be bogus. Bessedovsky had, however, an insistent point of fact: Voynovich had twice referred to the visitor as "B-3." The obvious conclusion was that the "B" stood for Britain, and the "3" implied at least two other possible Britons who were undiscovered and under OGPU discipline.

Ten days after the meeting the Special Branch interviewed more than forty individuals named Scott who had entered or departed England, by sea or air, during the period of the Soviet embassy visit in Paris. Not one of those interviewed appeared to warrant further investigation. A team was sent off to Paris, over the objections of the Foreign Office, to determine if a clerk or local employee could conceivably be suspect. (Although the team did not find a likely suspect, they did establish that the registry clerk's records were in disarray and the security of the vaults was inadequate.)

The Foreign Office permanent undersecretary reacted to the information on Scott with all the enthusiasm he would accord an invitation to tea at a railway buffet. Liddell's summary was there on his desk, he'd read it twice, and each time his annoyance grew. The Foreign Office was not moved by indistinct allegations made by people who themselves had just committed treason. Further, there was no Scott on the Foreign Office list who could in any way be considered suspect.[14] And the criticism of the Paris embassy's housekeeping still rankled. Sometimes, it seemed, the rampant imagination of the police mind went too far. In sum, the suggestion that a member of the Foreign Office would even consider betraying confidential information to the Bolsheviks was, in and of itself, preposterous. After all, there was absolutely no evidence to support the allegation. It was also important to keep in mind that these people from the War Office and Scotland Yard were the same ones who had proposed the Arcos raid. They seemed to thrive on alarums and excursions, and seldom took a longer view of the consequences of their actions. He returned the note to its protective envelope, sealed it, and on a covering slip wrote one ambiguous word—"seen"—and added his initials.

In Moscow, the cryptanalytic branch at the Center was satisfied that the material they had just received from Paris was the key to opening up the British cipher system. Intercepts of recently dated Foreign Office messages were beginning to surrender to their attack. With continuing assistance from the new Paris asset, several avenues that had been blocked were now open. The counterintelligence branch might find the spoor of British penetration agents. The Ministry of Foreign Affairs could negotiate from a superior position, with advance knowledge of the intentions of the British Foreign Office. The whole of the southern tier, British India, Afghanistan, Persia, and Turkey could be viewed through British lenses. It was a triumph for Paris.

Trilisser initialed the telegram to Paris commending Voynovich and put special stress on the importance of securing Scott as a premier agent—worth any demand for money he might make. It was a great coup for the OGPU Foreign Department and would no doubt please Stalin immensely. Stalin had an *idée fixe* about the British; he considered them extraordinarily adept at black arts and quick to employ any means to weaken or destroy any threat to the Crown.[15] No people could have built such an empire without frequent and easy recourse to clandestine means. He was satisfied that sufficient evidence had been found to implicate Britain in a succession of extravagant plots against the Soviet Union. The possibility of seeing their anti-Soviet intentions laid bare by decryption was a tantalizing prospect.

Voynovich was warmed by the fraternal greetings from the Center and was elated to learn that Scott's materials were genuine. The last paragraphs of the cable, however, were unexpected. They noted that he should have met Scott's request for money and given him at least enough to ensure his continued interest in the promise of more. A minor point, but important. The last paragraph stated that Scott was to be recontacted and given $2,000. Arrangements were to be made at that time for sustained contact. Extraordinary care was to be taken to protect his identity, and Paris was directed to bend every effort to safeguard this most valuable new source.

Voynovich was made uneasy by the Center's focus on Paris. When he had forwarded the photographs, he had expected that the Center would find the information useful in only a marginal way. Once this view was officially confirmed, he had planned to send a second message saying that the Center's appreciation of the worth of the material coincided with his own, and for that reason no money had been given to Scott. His irrepressible guile had led him to believe that his reputation for cleverness would be enhanced by this adroit cheating of a cheat. Now the matter had taken on an unexpected complexity. He sent his secretary to the cellar vault to retrieve the surveillance report made following Scott's expulsion from the embassy and called a meeting of his Paris staff. The officer who had written the report was in Berlin on another assignment and not available to lead the search. Two men were dispatched to #168 to make immediate contact with Scott. Others were sent to set up observation posts at British offices and residences in and around Paris. If Scott was not found in his rooms at #168, the OGPU men were to wait. While waiting, they would give the concierge a substantial bribe to provide access to Scott's rooms, which were to be carefully searched. Every effort was to be made to reestablish contact. Whatever the difficulty, whatever the cost, Scott must be found.

As a result of Bessedovsky's desertion, Paris was flooded with new OGPU men. Some were replacements for the apparatchiks who had been compromised and others were to augment the staff in anticipation of possible "wet" operations against Bessedovsky and another defector, Boris Bajanov.[16] The OGPU knew that Bessedovsky was talking with the British and had, under obscure auspices, met with Bajanov. The liquidation of the two traitors in Paris would do much to reinforce Stalin's instructions regarding deserters: "We must show them that our arm is longer than their leg." OGPU agents in the repatriation offices and even a few Comintern agents were ordered to join in the search.

No one seemed to know Scott. The concierge accepted the bribe with considerable pleasure and cheerfully arranged for the search of every room at #168. Not quite knowing the purpose of the searchers, she offered to act as an informant, to intercept mail, and to perform any other such useful services as they might require, at reasonable cost. The street teams watched the British embassy by day and by night. There was no trace of anyone who resembled Scott. Voynovich put off sending his telegram to Moscow as long as he could, hoping that the Englishman would reappear. Moscow, assuming that Paris was in contact with Scott, put a number of technical questions in a telegram, which arrived the next day.

It was at this point that Voynovich had to decide on a course of action: He could venture that Scott had been arrested by the British and bundled off to London to stand trial *in camera;* or that Scott had been killed in a motor accident en route to a meeting with Voynovich. In either case, Moscow would want to know Scott's true name in addition to all details relating to the fictitious incidents. Too dangerous. The fact that Voynovich did not know Scott's true name was the cause of burning professional embarrassment. He couldn't give another false name because the ferrets at the Center could prove it a lie in a matter of days. If Scott had indeed been arrested by the British, it was entirely possible that the Center might have other Foreign Office penetration agents who could be set to identify him. Since none of the options was feasible, Voynovich was compelled at least to consider telling Moscow the truth.

Voynovich's telegram came a few hours after Trilisser had sent a note to Stalin claiming that the Foreign Department had a new source who was positioned to provide access to British Foreign Office communications. The note, once sent, was not retrievable. Voynovich's account of the Paris OGPU's handling of the case made Trilisser shudder. Voynovich had compromised Trilisser by his errant stupidity. What could have prompted him to act in such a mindless way? His ridiculous attempt to save $2,000 had cost the loss of a priceless asset. The man was a halfwit at best. A matter to be raised with E. Y. Pauker and L. I. Studnikov.[17]

Now there was no trace of Scott in Paris. Perhaps, Trilisser reasoned, Scott was not resident in Paris. It was possible that he had come from London with the sole purpose of contacting the Soviet embassy. It was not an unreasonable speculation, since there was no official Soviet presence in Great Britain. When he was rebuffed by those fools in Paris, he might have returned directly to London. It was entirely possible that he worked in Whitehall itself. Pursuit of Scott in England was a task that could be undertaken most efficiently by the "illegals." At least they were more disposed to think than to act, unlike the OGPU's pseudodiplomats who lounged about the embassies.[18]

Scott's physical description, abstracted from the Paris surveillant's report, and the blurry photographs taken in the Paris embassy's courtyard were sent by the Center to The Hague for action. The Hague was selected because several important Soviet illegal nets were concentrated there, and many of the agents were Europeans working against Germany, France, and Great Britain.

After careful consideration of the task, the resident at The Hague selected an apparatchik called Hans for the job.[19] Hans, an old hand at illegal work, posed as a businessman specializing in artists' supplies. He bought bristles in China, rare earths in Africa, and oils in the Levant. He had fluent command of five languages and was widely traveled. His documents were tested, and his cover was of such substance that he was well known and respected in local commercial circles as an ardent promoter of Dutch trade. He operated a long-standing place of business, and his credit and reputation were verifiable through the main banks and trade associations. A second advantage in using Hans was his nationality. The British continued to regard the Dutch as a diminished colonial power with whom they still shared some common interests.

Several weeks before his departure for England, Hans wrote carefully composed letters to various small British firms trading in art supplies. The letters stated that Hans would be traveling to London soon and that he planned to call on the firms following his arrival. Within a week the dependably correct British companies wrote in return that they would welcome his visit. He took his sample cases, which in addition to sable brushes, pigments, and oils, included a vial of colorless liquid that could be mixed with distilled water to make an effective ink for concealed-message writing.

Although there was no official Soviet presence in Britain, there was an illegal resident living quietly in a housing block in Lewisham.[20] In the normal course, he would be notified of Hans's visit, in order to ensure that if Hans had an unforeseen incident involving the police, the resident could notify the Center by his own means.

Hans shared the OGPU's dread of the British police. It was widely believed that Scotland Yard and the War Office people had the most advanced internal-security system ever devised. The failure of the energetic Germans to accomplish anything significant in England during the four years of the Great War was a testament to the exceptional skills of the police and other special groups. Even those rare instances in which the British were, or seemed to be, publicly embarrassed gave little real comfort. Stalin, for one, held to the firm conviction that these displays of inadequacy were really calculated deceptions. The Zinoviev Letter was a good example of the British government's remarkable manipulation of a forgery for internal political effect. How else could it be explained? One had to conclude that the British were very strange people and, in spite of their calculated dissimulations, very dangerous.

Within a day of his landing in England, Hans became aware of a surveillant. It could be the police, but, he reasoned, it was more apt to be one of the resident's people. Hans began making his commercial calls and filled his days with discussions of calligraphers' nibs and canvas grounds. After a few days he was convinced that his shadow was not the police. The process of confirming his judgment was elemental: While walking west along the Embankment from Blackfriars, he suddenly reversed direction and walked toward the surveillant with a broad smile of feigned recognition. Flummoxed, the surveillant rapidly changed direction and began to walk quickly to the north, crossing through a stream of moving traffic and disappearing up Carmelite Street. No Special Branch man would have made such an ill-planned disengagement. Hans turned and resumed his course, which eventually led to the Charing Cross Underground station. There he took up a position, half-hidden by an afternoon newspaper. At the end of ten minutes he was satisfied that he was unwatched and, with a quick movement, boarded a departing train for Westminster. En route he decided that to obviate further attention by the resident, he would move to another commercial hotel and send a messenger for his bags. The ineptitude of the resident's surveillant was just one more threat to his own precarious safety.

In the late afternoon in St. James's Park, Hans saw fifty men who matched Scott's physical description: They wore bowlers and almost identical gray-black suiting, and all carried umbrellas. It was a hopeless task. After forty minutes of close watching, Hans returned to the Westminster tube station convinced that no technique of observation would assist in identifying Scott on sight. He took the next train to Sloane Square and walked by a circuitous route to the Gerald Street police station a few blocks away.

Enlisting the aid of the London Metropolitan police was a high-risk method of achieving his objective, but he saw no alternative. If, however, the resident's man observed him speaking to a British police officer, no subsequent explanation Hans could offer would be accepted by his superiors. In Stalin's time, there was always the presumption of guilt. Even the illegals, whose lives and liberty were without the protection of diplomatic status, were subjected to restraints that made their tasks more dangerous and difficult. Hans was experienced enough to know that he was in greater danger from the resident than he was from the British police. (Witnessing a traffic accident, or becoming the random object of a bellicose drunk—anything, in fact, that brought a Soviet citizen to the attention of the foreign police—was considered treasonable activity under the current broad interpretation of the Soviet law known as Article 58.[21] Anyone charged under Article 58 was automatically convicted. If you weren't executed, you could be assured of fifteen to twenty-five years in the camps.)[22] That was another excellent reason for getting rid of his surveillant.

At the police station a very young constable manned the reception counter. Hans assumed his most affable, puzzled, and exceedingly Dutch persona and in almost impenetrable English explained his purpose: His sister, married to a Frenchman, was living in Paris. An Englishman who visited Paris on June 28 had been present at the time her young son, Hans's nephew, was struck by an automobile. The driver of the car had continued on without stopping. The Englishman acted very bravely and took the boy to a nearby pharmacy, where he was given medical aid. The Englishman gave his name and a description of the automobile which, regrettably, went unrecorded in the confusion. One of the other witnesses later said that the Englishman was an official in the British Foreign Office. In the meantime, the boy had suffered complications. He was recovering very slowly, but the expenses were great, and his mother, on learning of Hans's intended visit to London, had implored him to find the hero, to thank him in the name of all and to learn if he could still describe the car or the driver. Hans had already called at the Foreign Office to ask for assistance, but his inadequate English prevented him from making his request understood. Several times he was referred to the police, and he had come to them now to put his problem to them and to ask their help. Was it possible that the London police, whose reputation for efficiency was well known, could assist in this matter?

An older police constable, standing to one side monitoring the conversation, suggested to the younger man that a call to the Foreign Office staff secretary might produce the information. Hans interposed that he had tried to telephone but his request was not understood. He had come to the police to ask that they make the call, the cost of which he was prepared to pay.

The young P.C. turned to the older man, who nodded his assent. Hans put a number of coins on the counter along with a few ten-shilling notes. Beneath the nearby public telephone were the London directories. The young P.C. found the Foreign Office number and made the call.

Hans heard him give his name and slowly spell it. He identified himself as a police officer assigned to Gerald Street and explained that he was trying to locate a Foreign Office employee who was a witness to an accident in Paris on the twenty-eighth of June. After a pause he stated his name again and gave the Gerald Street number, which he repeated several times. He hung up the receiver and, turning to Hans, indicated a rock-hard oak bench intended for public use.

During the first ten minutes, events seemed to be favoring Hans's boldness. It must have occurred to him that the resident would be stunned to know that one of the illegal Chekists was taking his ease on an oak bench in the Gerald Street police station at the invitation of the constables there.

Fifteen minutes later his sense of well-being was beginning to give way. Under such circumstances even an experienced illegal begins to know dread. The extended delay began to raise some disturbing questions: What's taking so long? Did the constable really call the Foreign Office? Or did he signal the Special Branch that a suspicious foreigner was making inquiries about a British official? The two police officers betrayed no nervousness. Was it because they were so well trained? But how could they know?

As a Soviet illegal, Hans knew that if he was arrested, there would be no publicity. The British would simply take him into custody and try to use him as bait to catch the resident. The Hague did not anticipate his return in less than six to eight weeks. In the meantime they would have no indication that he was held by the British. A good Chekist must be prepared for such an eventuality. The standard method was to resist interrogation, then to admit in final desperation that he was an agent—a German agent. Hans knew the names of a few Abwehr people in the Low Countries;[23] these names he would confess, with great reluctance, to the British. On that score, his story might hold if he came up against a less than seasoned interrogator.

The Soviet side was a different matter. His running-off of the resident's man might have been a mistake. At least the resident could have warned The Hague. In any case he knew he wouldn't be believed. The best he could hope for if he got out of England was an endless sentence to a Soviet coercive-labor camp. If he stayed, he could count on seven years or more in Brixton or the Scrubs. Then there was always the real danger that the Soviets would kill him while he was in a British prison, on the assumption that he'd betrayed Stalin. There was another grim possibility—

The ringing telephone interrupted his morose reverie. It was the Foreign Office. The young constable took the call and Hans could hear little of what was said. The constable was making a note of the information. He gave his name again and thanked the caller. Turning to Hans, he reported that there had been four people on temporary duty in Paris on June 28. Their names were noted on the slip of paper he handed to Hans.

With appropriate formality Hans expressed his thanks. He picked up his sample case and backed out into the hall, where he put on his hat and moved quickly through the heavy doors.

That evening, Hans telephoned his commercial hotel and told the proprietor he was returning to Holland because of illness in his family. He added that he would send a messenger for his bags and listened patiently while the proprietor expressed his sympathetic sentiments on the subject of illness. Later, he met the messenger with the bags at St. Pancras Station. Again he deliberately mentioned that he was returning to Holland because of an emergency. When the messenger left, Hans called a porter and asked his help in getting his bags into a taxi for transfer to the Liverpool Street Station, again repeating his intention to travel on to Holland. Once in the taxi, he made a point of telling the driver that he was in a hurry to catch the boat train.

At the Liverpool Street Station he checked his two bags at the left-luggage office and retired to the men's room, where he quickly shaved off his moustache. From his pocket he took a pair of eyeglasses, which gave him the appearance of an older man. He changed clothes in a stall and emerged five minutes later as a French middle-school teacher. His field of interest was British diplomatic history and he had come to London on a subscription raised by his students to research public records of Napoleon's unfortunate day at Waterloo. Because his visit was between terms, he planned to be in London only a short time. He scrutinized his image in the mirror and carefully reexamined the contents of each pocket. The French passport carried a photograph of himself made only sixty days ago, yet, like the passport, it appeared to have been made on the issue date, March 14, 1928. He had two left-luggage checks for the bags he'd deposited earlier and one more check for another bag in the left-luggage office at Euston Station.

Euston was an easy walk from the University of London and the British Museum. Inexpensive rooms were available in a wide variety of small houses, just right for a frugal French researcher on a short sabbatical. He took the Underground to the Bank station and there changed to the train that would take him to Euston. He got off the train at Moorgate, and again at King's Cross. Each time he bought a paper, walked across the platform, and assured himself that he was not under continuous observation.

At Euston he bought a packet of colored postcards showing London's most memorable sights. The cards were connected by paper hinges so that they could be easily separated, or the whole collection could be posted in its heavy paper folder, which had a conveniently gummed seal. He noticed that this particular book of cards was displayed at virtually every kiosk and newsstand. The cover bore a montage of Westminster, George V, St. Paul's, and Buckingham Palace. On the other side, above the address plate, were the words "Souvenir of London." He inspected one carefully, decided it was suitable for his later use, and bought it.

He then redeemed his bag and left the station on foot. Off Chalton Street, between Euston and St. Pancras stations, he found a room in an old transient hotel that showed evidence of hard usage. The proprietress, though not of the same age, was equally worn. He was struck by the number of neatly lettered small signs in the reception area and lounge, each prohibiting some form of human activity: NO COOKING. NO SMOKING IN ROOMS. NO ANIMALS. NO EXTENSION OF CREDIT. And, of course, NO UNREGISTERED GUESTS. He paid in advance and was shown to a cubicle containing a broken box spring topped with a thin mattress and gray sheets. It was difficult to know if this room was set aside for French passport holders or if it was the best a late arrival could expect.

Before extinguishing the bare ceiling light, Hans studied the list of four names the constable had given him. At last the search was narrowing. Until now it had been a maze of abstraction. Thanks to the London Metropolitan Police, it was taking on substance.

In the morning Hans registered at the British Museum as a researcher. With that card, his passport, and bogus letters of academic endorsement, he was able to pick up cards at the Westminster Library and at St. Catherine's and Somerset House. Documents of any kind, in any name, were of great interest to the cobblers who supported the illegals.[24]

In the late morning he went to the British Museum's Newspaper Library at Colindale. The distance was much greater than he had imagined and he made only a cursory visit, but long enough to get an impression of the holdings and the uses to which the library might be put. He was anxious to leave Colindale because of the intense RAF activity at the Hendon aerodrome to the east. It wouldn't do to be questioned as a suspicious foreigner when his real task lay elsewhere. Accident, chance, and the unplanned event had taken a toll among his comrades over the years; it wasn't their failure to take proper precautions but, more often, something that could not have been foreseen that brought about their arrest.

In Brussels once, a colleague had been waiting for a contact to pass material to him in a railway station when a woman reported to a nearby policeman that he looked very much like the man who had stolen her purse a few days before. The police kept him under observation. In a few minutes the contact appeared and the two men exchanged small parcels. In a moment the police had both in separate custody. Their stories had not been sufficiently worked out, and when they were searched, additional incriminating evidence was found. They were charged with passport irregularities and, later, espionage. One was deported, the other was sent to prison for seven months. The woman who had brought them to the attention of the police then announced that she had been mistaken in identifying the man in the first place.

In the very late afternoon Hans was back at the Westminster Library, examining the Foreign Office lists to find the functions of the four men who had been in Paris on June 28. One was a king's messenger, two were senior officials, and the last was found listed under "Communications Department." The librarian was giving unmistakable signals that the facility was about to close. As his eyes raced down the list, he saw that there were two men with the same surname in the Communications Department. He memorized the entries, apologized to the impatient staff, and went quickly out the door.

Early next morning, Hans took the twenty $100 notes and counted them again. They were the older series of 1914 notes, bearing a distinctive, if unflattering, likeness of Benjamin Franklin.[25] It was a currency most Europeans recognized and cherished. He located the checks for the luggage he had left, in his Dutch persona, at the Liverpool Street Station. In an emergency, he would try to go immediately to the station, change identities, and leave Britain by ferry to the Hook of Holland. His "French" belongings, sans passport, would be checked at Euston. The luggage check and French passport would be posted in the "Souvenir of London" envelope, from which he'd removed the postcards. He applied double postage to the envelope and addressed it to a mail accommodation in Antwerp.[26] The currency, in a locally purchased envelope, went into his inside right-hand jacket pocket. If things went awry he would have to depend on the envelope and chit in his left pocket. (His rule, left over from a forgotten childhood game, was that the good things were *right* and not-good things were *sinistra*.)

Before leaving the hotel he ordered tea in the dingy ground-floor room that the landlady grandly called the lounge. With the same extravagance, she referred to the baked object glistening in its own grease on his plate as a continental breakfast bun. Perhaps, like the failed mattress, it was a concession to his assumed nationality.

At the library he returned to the task of reconciling the names on the list with similar or identical names in the London telephone directories. The Foreign Office list gave full Christian names followed by abbreviated orders, decorations, degrees, and the like. The telephone directories more frequently gave initials, surnames, and nothing more. Instead of resolving the matter, he ended the first hour by adding two more names and addresses to his brief list.

He left the library a little before noon and took a taxi to the first of six addresses. It was a grand structure on Bayswater Road overlooking the park. Most improbable. He paid the driver and walked to the Hyde Park Gardens nearby. He struck Bayswater from the list and hailed a second cab.

The next address was in Pembroke Gardens, a crescent lined with modest, attractive small houses. It was a possibility. He told the driver to drop him at Pembroke Road, explaining that the address must be wrong because he was looking for a store that sold used textbooks. The driver offered to assist him in his search, but Hans paid him off and began walking toward Earl's Court. When the taxi was out of sight he doubled back and made his way through Pembroke Gardens. If this was the address of his man, it was likely that he took the Underground from Earl's Court to the Foreign Office. Very convenient and quick. He decided to come back later to see who returned to the house at the end of the working day.

He hailed another taxi on the High Street and gave an address in Brompton. It was a small block of flats with a common entrance. The name he was looking for was carefully pasted above the mail box marked 2-B. The name, cut from an engraved calling card of ancient manufacture, unequivocally identified the "J. C." of the telephone directory as *Miss Josephine Charlotte* of Hasker Street.

At three-thirty in the afternoon, Hans had exhausted his list. The most promising possibilities were the two names appearing on the roster of the Foreign Office Communications Department. One gave a military club as his address, the other was in Pembroke Gardens. He decided on the latter. It would be easier and less dangerous to approach the man in the street, especially if there was a crowded high street nearby to facilitate disengagement should there be a scene.

This time he took a taxi to the Earl's Court Underground, where he bought a ticket to Wimbledon and, from another teller, one to Finsbury Park. The destinations didn't matter, only the cost-related distance. If he had to use the Underground, a prepaid fare might make for a speedier departure. He bought another newspaper and began a methodical reconnaissance of the platforms, exits, conveniences, and stairs. Aboveground, he walked from the station exit northwest along Warwick Road, keeping to the east side of the street. He crossed Cromwell Road and continued to Pembroke Road. Once across Pembroke, he turned right and, within a short block, entered the gardens on his left. The walk took thirteen minutes. To avoid the evening crowds—and possibly missing his man—Hans took up station at Long Ridge Road and waited.

The late afternoon sun was unusually strong and Hans was beginning to feel the accumulated stresses of the last ten hours. He'd been over much of London, yet had seen very little. He'd eaten several small meals during the day but was unaccountably hungry. His legs were weary and starting to ache. While his body signaled a desire for bath and sleep, his mind began to stimulate his adrenal glands in the familiar fight-or-flight process he'd experienced earlier at the Gerald Street police station.

He concentrated on his approach to the target: Assuming the man would take the route Hans had just surveyed, he planned to wait until the target was in the Cromwell Road intersection and then come toward him from the rear. This would, in all probability, put him close enough to his man to call him by name. Then, once the pedestrian traffic had begun to move, he would say, "I regret that we didn't meet in Paris. I know of the grave error made by Major Vladimir. He has since been removed and punished. I have come to give you what is rightfully yours." He would take the "right" envelope from his pocket and give it to the man, adding; "There is a note inside concerning the time and place of our next meeting and instructions for contacting me. My name is Paul." Once the target had the envelope in his hand, Hans would turn and walk rapidly back to the Earl's Court station and leave by the first available train.

Automobile traffic was gradually increasing, the pedestrians becoming more numerous and purposeful. Gone were the casual shoppers of an hour ago. These were mostly men returning home at the end of the work-day. From this distance, the Earl's Court station seemed to pulsate, every few minutes disgorging a new crowd of pedestrians.

At twenty past six Hans saw a likely target following the expected route. Approaching Hans from the southeast, walking with his furled umbrella on his left arm, was a pleasant-looking man in his late thirties. Hans ran over the familiar Paris description once again. Height, weight, color of hair, style of clothing, all seemed to match. The target was now crossing Long Ridge Road. When he reached the opposite curb, Hans folded his paper and fell in behind him. By the time they reached Cromwell Road, a small clot of pedestrians had accumulated, waiting for the signal to cross. Hans had the envelope in his hand. He called quietly to the target.

At first there was no reaction. Hans called again. This time the man turned and Hans began his prepared speech. At the mention of Paris, the target reacted suddenly, moving away in panic. Hans persisted, careful to give emphasis to the removal and punishment of Vladimir. The man re-acted a second time, obviously frightened, even in mild shock.

Hans knew he had made a match. Without another word he pressed the envelope into the man's hand and darted across Cromwell Road just as the traffic resumed.

He hurried to the station and took the first train. It was bound for Wimbledon, in exactly the opposite direction from his room near Euston. He got off the train at East Putney and made his way back across the narrow walk on the Putney footbridge. The Thames had a golden glow, and a cool evening breeze was starting up the river. From the bridge he watched a man bailing out his small boat. It was a view that might have been included in his "Souvenir of London" photos. By the time he found a taxi at the start of New King's Road, his physical and mental exhaustion was all but complete. He told the driver to take him to Euston Station and fell into a heavy sleep.

His landlady, seeking further advance rent, met him coming into the hotel. He submitted with grace and made his effortful way to his room.

Before subsiding into sleep, he thought about the target and the $2,000. Sleep might not come easily to the Foreign Office clerk this night. Whether he realized it or not, he had become the newest soldier in Stalin's secret army. Even a hardened old ideologue like Hans was moved by the pathos of the struggling creatures caught in the OGPU's grip. Hans enjoyed combat with the enemy and took strength from battle, but the clerk was a victim, not an enemy. Perhaps with development and careful nurturing he would find satisfaction in the "work." Hans closed his eyes, remembering the expression of terror on the target's face, and recalled what Scott would later learn: There were no live deserters from Stalin's secret army.

Scott stood on the kerb at Cromwell Road staring at the envelope. He absently tore at the flap and, when he saw the currency, realized that he hadn't imagined the man who mentioned Vladimir. There was such a man. Scott shoved the envelope into an inside pocket of his jacket. In the awkward maneuver his umbrella fell to the pavement. When he tried to pick it up he dislodged his hat. A nearby man saw him clutch at his chest and, thinking he was suffering a heart attack, moved quickly to assist him. Scott recoiled from the man's touch and fell to his knees. Several others saw the distressed man kneeling on the pavement and tried to be helpful. He struggled to regain his feet and forced an embarrassed acknowledgment of thanks. He adjusted his hat and, with one hand still under his jacket pressed against the envelope containing the currency, resumed his route to Pembroke.

Once in the house, Scott put the envelope in the center of the kitchen table and lit the gas under the kettle. His wife, Lucy, would not be home for another hour. He noticed that his hand trembled when he tried to extract a cigarette from its package. As a man of habit, he carefully removed his jacket and hung it up. Returning to the kitchen, he stared at the envelope with the fascination of a rabbit confronting a snake. The water was coming to a boil, and he readied the teapot without taking his eyes from the center of the table. While the tea was brewing, he picked up the envelope and tentatively enlarged the tear.

The bills were neatly tied with cloth tape and double-wrapped in a light tissue, with only the ends of the notes visible. He removed the wrapping and arranged the notes on the table. He counted them several times, studying each bill for any sign that it was marked or counterfeit. He had very little experience with American Federal Reserve notes and was fascinated by the color and texture of the bills. With a start, he realized that both he and the pile of bills could be seen by anyone looking in through the kitchen windows. He got up quickly and drew the curtains. It was a furtive act—the kind of thing a spy might do.

He turned on the light, gathered up the bills, and stuffed them back into the torn envelope. He put the money into a niche in the wall beneath the gas geyser and with electrical tape taken from a box under the sink, secured the envelope to an exposed pipe. Again, the kind of thing a spy might do.

Returning to his seat at the table, he poured a cup of now cool tea and loaded it with sugar. His copy of *The Telegraph* carried a brief table of foreign-exchange rates, a feature previously without interest to Scott. He found, after hasty calculation, that the contents of the envelope were valued at more than £400. For the first time in almost a year, he felt a wave of pleasure and satisfaction. With the money in his possession he vowed to himself that if he was somehow extricated from the frightening aftermath of the events in Paris, he would lead a more ordered existence as a most loyal servant of the Foreign Office.

He opened the note that had been enclosed in the envelope and studied the instructions for recontact. The note was signed *Paul*, the name given by the man in Cromwell Road and had to do with a meeting to be held weeks later. The instructions reinforced his determination to convey, in the most unequivocal terms, that he wanted nothing more to do with the Soviets.

Politics had played no role in his original decision to approach the Russians in Paris. Indeed, he was basically hostile to what he thought the Soviet Union stood for. His plan had been to sell some cipher texts for money, nothing more, but that first unhappy transaction had convinced him he wanted no further involvement. The business of selling secrets was far more complicated and dangerous than he had originally thought, and though his career prospects were no better than they had been, still, his finances were now much improved by the $2,000, and he had no intention of reliving the terror he had felt over the Bessedovsky defection. He conceded to himself that Paris had been a rash act, never to be repeated.

Scott realized that the only way he could explain his irreversible position was to meet with the Soviets once again and break the relationship that Paul seemed to presume existed. But this time *he* would control the conversation. He would make it clear that the Soviets were the ones at a disadvantage in London and that, as a native-born British subject, he was free to exercise his own will. The tables would be turned.

Hans's impressions of Scott were mixed. The clerk had seemed to be slightly deranged. It was possible that his extreme reaction was the product of severe self-generated pressures; if so, his actions would be very difficult to predict. It was also possible that Scott had confessed his Paris adventure and that M.I.5 was now using him as bait, knowing the Soviets would attempt recontact. The British had a reputation for unusual skill in the manipulation of opportunities like this one. It was a possibility worthy of careful consideration.

In the end it was decided at The Hague that Hans, as "Paul," was best suited to make the recontact with Scott and to enlarge on his initial appraisal of the man. Further, it would have the advantage of not requiring the introduction of still another new face to the already frightened Scott.

The note that had been passed to Scott in the street near his home contained precise meeting instructions: He was to travel by Underground, arriving at the Hyde Park station at 6:25 P.M., forty-five days after the first encounter in Cromwell Road. The long interval was necessary to allow Hans sufficient time to visit The Hague, give his personal report, and assist in planning the second meeting.

As with all instructions of Soviet manufacture, there was no accommodation for spontaneity. Details were presented to the Center in Moscow for review. All names, dates, places, and persons were described. A tentative *parol,* or password exchange, was proposed to the Center in both Russian and the language in which it would be spoken. The parol usually consisted of a statement or a question asked by the Soviet officer and an improbable rote response by the agent. The officer would add a second remark or question, the agent would make the approved rejoinder, and both parties could then assume that the other was who he purported to be.

Before the verbal exchange, each party was to display certain agreed-upon visual signals. Books, newspapers, briefcases, and, in one notable instance, a tennis ball served as signals.[27] An imperative requirement in the preverbal phase was the danger signal: If either of the parties sensed hostile scrutiny, then the blowing of a nose, the scratching of an ear, the tying of a shoelace would convey, prior to contact, that the meeting was to be deferred to another date and place.

If for any reason the two parties failed to meet as arranged, the instructions included alternative dates, times, and locations. The routes governing approach to and departure from the meeting points were also meticulously prescribed. There seemed to be no limit to the minutiae required by the Center.

One obvious reason for the Center's demands was discipline and control. Another was that in the event of a serious operational casualty or compromise, Moscow would have sufficient data to launch a clandestine counterintelligence audit. If the operation failed for any reason, the Center could always manipulate the details to discover incompetence or betrayal. Incompetence, as in the case of Major Vladimir's frugality, was measured against past performance and the degree of support that could be garnered among influential officers who would plead his case. Betrayal, on the other hand, unleashed the terrible forces of revenge by terror which, once in train, might involve hundreds who were guilty merely of acquaintance with the offender.

The parol selected for the second meeting with Scott was prepared originally in German, translated into Russian for approval by Moscow, and finally rendered into a kind of English. The banality of the parol and its stilted language were embarrassing to the urbane GRU officers who worked in Western Europe. This was an OGPU case, and the GRU was simply acting at the direction of the Moscow managers, few of whom had ever traveled more than twenty miles from Moscow.

Scott had read the instructions in abject puzzlement, feeling as if he had been invited to participate in a game designed by small boys who had misread Lord Baden-Powell.

The clerk's contact was to approach him approximately thirty-five feet from the entrance to the Hyde Park Hotel. The contact would recognize the clerk, who would carry his umbrella in his right hand with the ferrule next to his right ear as if it were a saber. In the event of rain, the umbrella was to be open, with the shaft resting on his right shoulder. In his left hand Scott was to carry two books, one green, one red. The contact would ask him to indicate "the way to Hans Crescent." The clerk was to reply, "It's convenient to Sloane Street, a quarter mile from here." The Soviet would respond, "I see you have a copy of Milton," and the clerk would end the parol by saying, "No, it's an illustrated guide to Andorra."

Scott couldn't conceive of saying these things to a stranger on the street. It all seemed so contrived, yet it was imperative that he meet the contact to explain that he had no intention of further aiding the Soviet Union.

The instructions provided that, on the appointed day, Scott was to take a train from Westminster to Charing Cross, there to change for Piccadilly, and there to change again for Hyde Park Corner. On arriving at Hyde Park Corner he was to cross to the north side of the street, turn left, and continue toward the Hyde Park Hotel with books and umbrella appropriately arranged. If contact was not effected according to instructions, he was to cross Brompton Road and walk south along the east side of Sloane Street for the half mile leading to Sloane Square, and there to reenter the Underground. The next contact would take place six days later and one hour earlier.

Once Moscow put its imprimatur to the plan, Hans returned to England as the commercial Dutchman. His moustache had reappeared, and there was very little resemblance to Paul, the French researcher who had given Scott the envelope. If Scott had informed the police of the approach to him in Cromwell Road, he could not have given a description sufficient for the British to make an identification. Hans's appearance was so altered, that he felt he could confront Scott directly without Scott's realizing, at first, that he was the same man as Paul.

On his first day in London, Hans settled into a room in a small hotel in Holborn frequented by commercial travelers. With the assistance of the telephone clerk, he spent the first hour calling various prospective customers who traded in art supplies. He gave the clerk ten shillings and the promise of more if the clerk would be particularly attentive to any telephone messages intended for him. That afternoon he took one of his smaller sample cases and left the hotel with the announced purpose of calling on a client. He walked to the tube station at Russell Square and rode the creaking, wood-paneled cage down to the platform. The purpose of this late-afternoon sortie was reconnaissance.

At Leicester Square, he boarded the train for his destination, Westminster. En route, Hans studied the passengers and route maps. The Underground system might be a convenience to the London public, but it was a certifiable boon to a Soviet illegal. He liked London. The people seemed disciplined and almost alarmingly polite and helpful. On the leg to Leicester Square he listened carefully to the animated conversation of two London University students who sat opposite him. He had had little occasion to speak English for almost two months and found it difficult to adjust to the tone and inflection of their accents.

At Leicester Square he bought an afternoon paper and walked slowly to the platform where he would board the train to Westminster. He was attentive to the presence of others making the change and studied each one as a possible surveillant. At Charing Cross he watched the most likely subjects either walk toward the exits or remain on the train traveling south. Scott's instructions required that he begin his approach to the meeting at Westminster. Hans planned to travel the precise route that Scott would travel. He had selected the Underground because it gave certain advantages. As the unrecognizable Dutchman, he could observe Scott entering the station at Westminster and judge whether Scott was being watched. He planned to board Scott's train and to make the first two changes with him. When Scott detrained at Hyde Park Corner, Hans would continue to the next stop at Knightsbridge; once more aboveground, he could watch Scott making his way on foot to the Hyde Park Hotel. Without assistance from any other source, Hans planned to run an effective counter-countersurveillance. If his observations aboard the trains and at the various changes revealed no trace of watchers, he would move on to the next phase at Knightsbridge.

From his post on the south side of Brompton Road, Hans would have a panoramic view of Scott's approach, including any surveillants at or near the hotel. If he sighted anything amiss, he could simply step back into the Knightsbridge station and leave the area. Scott's instructions clearly stated that if contact did not occur thirty-five feet from the hotel entrance, he was to cross the street and walk south. In Hans's plan, that contact would not occur. He would wait on the corner as Scott approached, to assure himself that it was indeed Scott, and then direct his scrutiny to those who crossed the street with or slightly behind him. Satisfying himself that Scott was not under surveillance, Hans planned to cross to the west side of Sloane Street and take up a position three hundred feet behind Scott.

Hans timed the trip, including the two transfers and the long walk. It worked out to seventeen minutes, point to point. Westminster was only an eight-minute walk from Whitehall. If Scott left his office promptly at six, he would arrive at the contact zone exactly on time.

Hans had worked out every contingency. He spent the remainder of the afternoon, like the professional he was, calling on a prospective customer in Brompton Road in an attempt to sell him a newly introduced line of German-made gum spirits. The outstanding feature of the new product was that it left no telltale traces.

For several days before the meeting, Hans scoured the vicinity of Victoria Station for a meeting place that would allow both privacy and anonymity. Hotels were not suitable because of the routine requirement that guests present their passports at the time of registration. He investigated the possibility of renting temporary accommodations and found the passport demands on foreigners even more stringent than in the better-class hotels. An outdoor meeting would not do because of control problems, the vagaries of London weather, and the impossibility of avoiding observation.

The essentials were three: a room to which he had easy and direct access, a lock on the door to prevent intrusion, and a prepaid arrangement that did not require the presentation of identity papers. The search led him back to Victoria Station.

On an earlier visit his attention had been drawn to two men in the waiting room. At first he took them to be detectives, but after a few minutes of observation he concluded they were homosexuals looking for contacts. He was surprised at their boldness; in England, public soliciting was almost invariably rewarded with swift and severe penalties. At the time, he had simply noted his error and put the incident in a remote part of his memory.

The day before the planned meeting found Hans still without a satisfactory meeting site. As his anxiety increased, it occurred to him that the homosexuals might lead him to a solution. He returned to Victoria and began a careful inventory of the men in the waiting room, particularly of two who were seated on end benches feigning interest in newspapers. Their locations gave them an opportunity for eye contact with arriving passengers. Occasionally one or the other rose from his bench to speak to another male who had seemed to return a friendly glance. One offered a cigarette to a new arrival and engaged him in urgent conversation. The newcomer smiled and nodded his head. A few moments later the two were walking arm in arm toward the exit.

Hans followed them out onto Wilton Road. From the rear, they looked like old friends reunited. There was much physical contact—so uncharacteristic of the British, Hans thought. They turned at Gillingham and walked into the entrance of a disheveled gray building. Hans took up station nearby and, within half an hour, saw two other male couples enter the house off Gillingham. Forty minutes later the two men he had followed reappeared. After a brief conversation on the street, they parted, the first man strolling lightly back toward the station.

Hans walked through the adjoining streets to familiarize himself with the immediate locale. Returning to the gray house, he walked up the few steps to the entrance and opened the heavily glazed door. There was a dreary small lounge off to the left and a makeshift registration desk to the right. The entry was poorly lit, and Hans did not notice the man behind the desk until he moved. The first impression was startling: a parched white face with two spots of rouge, topped by a jet-black wig. The clerk's shriveled hands were ornamented with rings that only invited attention to the corrugations of age. As Hans moved toward the desk, the man greeted him in a deep, worn voice with exaggerated sibilance.

Hans began to explain his purpose in a defensively awkward manner. A friend from the country was to arrive in London tomorrow and it was important for Hans to meet with him privately for a few hours. Would it be possible to reserve a room and pay in advance so that no time would be lost? The clerk studied Hans for a moment trying to decide if he might be a detective from the vice squad or a representative of some order of self-anointed saviors on the lookout for errant souls. But Hans's accent made the first possibility unlikely, and his general demeanor did not reflect the aura of rectitudinous superiority that usually cloaked the latter.

No, the clerk explained, it was not customary to book rooms in advance, because they were let by the hour. Hans paused to consider. Would it be possible to pay for the hours in advance to be assured of holding a room? He quickly calculated the requisite number of hours and asked for a quote of the hourly rate. Thirty-six hours times 10 shillings: It came to £18 even, slightly more than a luxury suite at the Savoy. The clerk, beginning to see Hans in a new light, pointed out that with the maid and linen charges, the grand total would amount to eighteen pounds, four shillings, and sixpence.

Hans, no longer the petitioner, acted the patron. He wished to inspect the room, he said, and if it was satisfactory, pay the advance and take the key with him. The clerk led the way to the second floor rear and showed Hans a mean, dirty little room. The door had both a conventional lock and a sliding dead-bolt. A bed, a chair, and a clothes tree made up the inventory of furnishings.

Hans tried the key in the lock, slid the bolt, and looked out the grime-coated window into a dark areaway. He satisfied himself that unless a better alternative came along, he would bring Scott here for the meeting.

Back at the registration desk, he paid the advance with four new, £5 notes. The clerk stored them carefully in his tin cashbox and put Hans's change, a single pound note and some coins, on the desk. Hans hesitated and then made an effort to smile as he indicated that he regarded the change as a gratuity for the clerk.

On the day of the scheduled meeting with "Paul," Scott told his wife that he would not be home at the usual time because he planned to attend an informal supper with some of his old army friends. As he embroidered the story, he found that he lied easily and with some imagination. The reunion was to be held at the Hyde Park Hotel, and to reinforce the deception, he added that he was looking forward to an evening of reminiscence about the Great War.

He arrived at his office a few minutes early. As the other clerks on the shift came down the iron stairs, he saw them as men who had lost their way and become subservient, broken to the Foreign Office wheel. His anticipation of a meeting with a Soviet agent and the deception of Lucy had stimulated his mind as only secret knowledge can. It was, he imagined, a little like having a mistress, except much more affordable.

During the morning he considered the tactics he would employ: He would dominate the interview, explain his position, and give his contact twelve hours in which to leave England before Scott would provide the police with the agent's detailed physical description.

If by some rare chance his contact proved to be the "Major Vladimir" of the Paris embassy, he was resolved to call Scotland Yard and demand his arrest as a Bolshevik agent. The police would doubtless take the Soviet in manacles to Bow Street, where a stern magistrate would dispose of him. Scott was confident that Vladimir's papers would not be in order and that his earlier assault on an English civil servant would warrant a substantial fine and a few days of confinement awaiting the issuance of a writ of deportation by the Home Office. Public exposure and deportation in such circumstances would ensure that Vladimir could never return to England, and might very well end his usefulness to his sponsors. Scott's resolve exhilarated him and made the morning's work go quickly.

Twice during the day, Scott reread the meeting instructions. He had the two books with appropriately colored bindings and had memorized his part of the spoken exchange.

At four o'clock he shared a pot of tea with Bert King, one of his colleagues. Bert was an older man who had been sorely affected by the war; having survived four years in the trenches, he had returned to England to find he was unable to get a job. Unemployed for several years, he could not support his American wife and their young son, who both returned to the United States to live with relatives. Some months later, Bert was finally successful in securing a probationary appointment, at £95 per annum, in the Communications Department of the Foreign Office. Since he had no status, he did not appear in the Foreign Office lists.

A few minutes before six, Scott secured his safe and set out on the first leg of his new adventure. As instructed, he boarded the Underground at the right place and the right time. He was not aware of Hans, who boarded the same car, nor would he have recognized him. Scott made the change of trains and seemed to be following the prescribed routine. At 6:12 he detrained at the Hyde Park station, and Hans continued on to Knightsbridge to take up his countersurveillance.

From the crowded Underground entrance on Brompton Road, Hans watched Scott walk toward the Hyde Park Hotel. The clerk carried the books and umbrella in the exact manner instructed. At the entrance to the hotel he paused and looked about expectantly. After a few moments he brought his umbrella ferrule into sharp contact with the pavement in a gesture of visible annoyance. He crossed the street toward Hans in the midst of a group of pedestrians.

He passed within a few feet of Hans and continued along Sloane Street. Hans stayed where he was, alert for any indication that Scott might be under surveillence, until the clerk was three-hundred feet down Sloane Street. Then he took up the trail. Midway to Sloane Square, Hans crossed the street and hailed a passing taxi, giving Victoria Station as his destination. When the taxi was about to overtake Scott, Hans told the driver to stop. He jumped from the taxi and, approaching the clerk from the rear, spoke the first line of the parol. Quickly he thrust an envelope into Scott's hand. He ordered the clerk to enter the cab and to remain silent until they reached their destination. Once in the taxi, Hans told the driver to proceed and silently indicated to Scott that he should open the envelope.

Scott tore the end from the envelope and saw the now-familiar green of American bank notes. He realized that once again he had lost the initiative, and with it his confidence. Hans didn't speak, but smiled warmly and winked at him.

At Victoria, Hans paid the fare and, holding Scott by the elbow, began to walk briskly toward the house on Gillingham. He said urgently, "It is important that we do not speak as yet. Also we must not be observed." Fearing that Hans was alluding to the police, Scott was compliant. They walked to the entrance of the gray building and Hans held the door for Scott to precede him.

The man with the jet wig was behind the counter, smoking a small cigar. Hans offered no greeting but held the room key in the air like a talisman and proceeded up the stairs to the reserved room. Once inside, with the bolt set, Hans began to explain to Scott that his sponsor wished to convey his deep appreciation. The contents of the envelope were simply tokens given in recognition of Scott's brave and selfless action on behalf of the working class.

Scott's planned repudiation speech went unspoken. He was flattered by Hans's sincerity and considerably heartened by the envelope in his pocket. At the end of ten minutes he was beginning to believe that perhaps Vladimir was an aberration; Paris had been a Soviet blunder and Moscow hoped to compensate him for his humiliation and pain. In the future, Hans guaranteed, he would be treated with appropriate respect.

The meeting lasted less than thirty minutes. By the end of it, Scott had agreed to accept two tasks: first, to prepare a list of employees of the Foreign Office Communications Department with notations about their politics, experience, families, rates of pay, years of service, etc., and second, to make a schematic of the operations of Foreign Office communication links in the Northern Department along with representative signal protocols. Considering the rewards, the effort would be minimal. Scott knew the personnel and worked almost exclusively on Northern Department cables.

Hans quickly gave Scott new meeting instructions and set a date and an alternate. He then told him he would leave the room first and that Scott was to wait five minutes and then depart himself without speaking to anyone. As Hans moved toward the door, Scott asked, "Is that person—that strange-appearing man in the reception—one of yours?"

"No," replied Hans, "I regret to say he is one of yours."

The recruitment of "Scott" marked the first penetration of the British Foreign Office. For two years he provided the Soviets with detailed information relative to cryptographic procedures and communications security methods. Hans and Scott worked well together, and on a few occasions Hans, posing as a successful Dutch businessman, took him and his wife, Lucy, out to dine at expensive restaurants. By the end of the second year Scott introduced Hans to Bert King, whom Hans later cultivated. The relationships with both men continued to develop.

In the fall of 1932, Scott suddenly informed Hans that he could not continue in the work. Hans was unable to determine exactly what had caused his abrupt change of heart. Gradually, Hans began to suggest that Scott really had no alternative and that Hans's superiors would react badly, maybe dangerously, if Scott persisted in his determination to withdraw. At that moment Scott announced that he had anticipated such a threat and had already, ten days before, resigned his post at the Foreign Office.

Hans extended the meeting, using every possible point of leverage to dissuade Scott from his decision. He made particular reference to the fact that Scott had received more than £5,000 for his efforts, roughly fifty years of his present salary. Perhaps more money would change Scott's mind? The session became acrimonious, and Hans broke it off. Scott would not agree to another meeting and was adamant in his resolve. Hans knew that the Center could not abide a deserter from the work, particularly one who continued to live in the locale of an important operation. For that reason he made one last effort to convince Scott that his refusal might mean his life.

Exactly one year after their last meeting, a man was discovered unconscious on the floor of the kitchen in the little house in Pembroke Gardens. He was not identified by name, though his shirt bore a three-letter monogram. Rushed to Saint Mary Abbotts hospital on Marloes Road, he was pronounced dead on arrival. The coroner's report noted the cause of death as "coal gas suffocation, unsound mind." Scott's death was simply one more occasion to recall the familiar black joke of the organs: "Anyone can commit a murder, but it takes an artist to commit a 'suicide.'" Scott's estate, amounting to £5,000, went to Lucy.

Bert King was later recruited and served the Soviets intermittently until he was identified to the British by Walter Krivitsky in early 1940. The "Scott" and King cases grew out of an unplanned event. Scott, for whatever reasons, was "self-selected"; he took the initiative in approaching the Soviet embassy in Paris. The OGPU's eventual success was highly exploitative and left a number of casualties in its wake:

"Scott" was a suicide-murder on September 29, 1933, in London.

"Walter G. Krivitsky" was a suicide-murder on February 10, 1941, in Washington.

As far as is known, Hans was recalled to Moscow in 1936 and was probably executed in the Great Purge.

"Paul Hardt" (Theodore Maly) was serving the first of two tours as the illegal resident at the time of Hans's visit. Hardt returned to London several years later as the illegal resident in connection with the Woolwich Arsenal case. In 1936 he, too, was probably recalled to Moscow and executed.

"Major Vladimir Voynovich" was recalled from Paris, and was executed by the NKVD in 1937.

John Herbert (Bert) King was convicted of espionage and served a prison sentence in England.

Bessedovsky survived World War II, and as late as 1951 was living in the South of France. At the time of his disappearance, he was thought to have returned to Soviet control.

4 · The NKVD

NKVD is the acronym most commonly used to designate the *Narodnyi Kommissariat Vnutrennikh Del* (The People's Commissariat of Internal Affairs). The compound abbreviation *Narkomindel* is used frequently in publications of Soviet origin.

At the time of the civil war, each of the republics organized a Commissariat of Internal Affairs, which controlled its militia, conducted criminal investigations, and operated prisons. The commissariats of the republics were disbanded in 1930, and in 1934 a new NKVD was formed. It was called the *All-Union* Commissariat, and it was empowered to carry out the following functions and missions:

(1) preservation of revolutionary order and state security
(2) protection of public property
(3) registration of civil acts and vital statistics
(4) protection of the border

Other administrations were subordinated to the new NKVD:

(1) state security (hitherto the OGPU)
(2) militia
(3) border security and internal protection
(4) fire protection
(5) corrective labor camps and settlements
(6) Department of Civil Acts
(7) Administrative Economic Administration

The All-Union NKVD, in its elevated status, proceeded to reform subordinate NKVDs in all of the republics with the exception of the

RSFSR (Russian Soviet Federative Socialist Republic), which, because of its linchpin importance to Bolshevik control of the USSR, remained directly under the All-Union NKVD. The same administrative pattern was organized in each of the subordinate elements, down to and including cities, districts, and sometimes villages.

Mass terror had already been established as a means of intimidating the populace, and once again, it was believed essential to provide the citizenry with a visible reminder that it could recur at any time. The broad presence of the uniformed NKVD man was intended to convey that threat. After centuries of oppression by the ruling authorities, the Russian people tended to accommodate the new police in the belief that since they, too, were "locals," they would act as their predecessors had. (To avoid, or at least defer, the problem of familiarity, an effort was made to employ police from distant locales.) Virtually no one understood that the new NKVD was a radical departure from anything previously known. It was difficult to accept the fact that the NKVD was a manifestation of the Bolshevik central government, which was, for the first time, quite able to extend its writ throughout the USSR.

Concurrently, the NKVD collegium within the Soviet Supreme Court was abolished. Cases of treason and espionage were referred to the Military Collegium of the Supreme Court, or the military tribunal having jurisdiction. Cases coming within the purview of the State Security Administration (OGPU) were all referred to the Supreme Court. The form of trials in the Soviet Union during the NKVD era does not lend itself to conventional analysis, although it is obvious that the "guilty" were brought before tribunals and given sentences that had been foreordained on the basis of political principles and the fact that the defendant had, after all, been arrested.

A Special Advisory Council within the All-Union Commissariat took over all other court functions of the NKVD collegium. The council consisted of five members and functioned as a court. The establishment of the council gave the NKVD even more power: It was now possible for the NKVD to try its own cases. Stalin approved the changes because it was another step intended to guarantee "good order and discipline."

In November 1935 the NKVD took over the surveying and cartographic administration of the USSR along with all of the technical agencies necessary to carry out its purposes. (That authority was removed in 1938 and included in Sovnarkom.) In October 1935 the administration of highways was brought into the NKVD. With the ratification of the new Soviet Constitution in December 1936, the NKVD became a Union Republic Commissariat. In February 1941 the State Security Administration was removed from the NKVD and formed into a new commissariat, the

NKGB, which remained separate until July 1941, at which time it was reintegrated into the NKVD, where it remained until March 1946.[1]

This tedious and arcane slice of Soviet bureaucratic history is not without relevance to the modern KGB. When the OGPU, as the instrument of state security, was absorbed into the NKVD, Stalin was concerned that it was becoming too powerful and was still outside his complete control. Many of the old Chekists were not direct beneficiaries of his patronage and owed their status to the departed Lenin and Dzerzhinsky.

Stalin had no fear of sedition on the part of the OGPU, but he recognized it as a potential long-term threat and as a future alternative power base. That was a prospect he could not tolerate. In part, his apprehensions about the OGPU were based on the fact that its head, Vyacheslav R. Menzhinsky, was so unlike Dzerzhinsky. He lacked the zealous convictions of his predecessor. He was weak and wholly unsuited to his role as chief of the organs. Pianistic talent, a sensitive nature, and highly cultivated tastes were hardly the qualifications essential to carrying out Stalin's will. Menzhinsky also suffered from chronic respiratory ailments that occasionally incapacitated him. Though Stalin had appointed him to head the OGPU after Dzerzhinsky's death, he never deluded himself about Menzhinsky's capabilities.

Menzhinsky was a weak administrator. Unable to keep abreast of his job, he was subjected to continual abuse by Stalin for his inadequacies. Many assumed that he might have qualified for the post on the basis of his subservience. It was a period when Stalin was measuring putative enemies and rivals. Menzhinsky was neither, nor was he equipped to lead the organs into any unwelcome adventurism.

Although Stalin now enjoyed considerable political power, absolute power still eluded him. With Trotsky, Kamenev, Zinoviev, and Bukharin out of the way, he moved to bring the Commissariat of Internal Affairs under central control. When the republic NKVDs were abolished in 1930, it was largely because Stalin was convinced that some of them were in business for themselves. A second reason was his determination, when the opportunity came, to staff the new commissariats with his own loyalists. In the immediate term, he focused on staffing the more important posts in the vast and growing Soviet bureaucracy.

The elimination of the old NKVD republic commissariats marked the beginning of an interim of four years during which Stalin made do with the OGPU. It was a compromise decision. Many OGPU officials considered themselves members of high calling and resented the mundane duties of administering internal affairs.

The need for a gigantic police force would seem to fly in the face of accepted Bolshevik lore. It is not possible for conventional crime to exist in the premier socialist state. Human motivations to inflict harm, as well as all other criminal tendencies, were supposed to have yielded to mass participation in improving the commonweal. To murder, rape, burgle, or otherwise transgress is characteristic of the human behavior found in the reactionary capitalist states. According to Marxist-Leninist dogma, crime is the consequence of corrupt capitalism, and criminals merely victims of oppression by the owner class. But after the owners (kulaks) were disposed of and every trace of capitalist exploitation obliterated, it seemed there were still crimes and criminals.

Fortunately, the original sociological conclusions were soft enough to permit adducing yet another "truth" without offending Marx. The new criminals were clearly "counterrevolutionaries," whose capitalist sponsors were bent on destroying the Soviet state. (Every Soviet regime has compulsively reported statistics that purport to prove socialist achievement. Perhaps of interest to serious sociologists is the remarkable fact that none of the successive statistical reprises admits that *any* criminal rape has taken place in the Soviet Union since 1918.)

The Soviet notion of crime is another anomaly. It is difficult for Westerners to understand the difference between public pronouncements by the Soviets and the realities of life in the USSR.

Although Marx's criticisms might have been trenchant with respect to nineteenth-century capitalism as an economic system, he was wide of the mark in his sociological and psychological theories about the motivations and attitudes of the individual workers who made up the proletarian masses. His understanding of the industrial system stands as a remarkable bit of analysis, but his uncertain grasp of human nature degrades its utility.

The assumption that crime is purely an economic consequence of a faulty system still flourishes. Until 1960, Soviet criminals tended to be labeled "anti-regime" (i.e., counterrevolutionary) or insane. If one Soviet citizen robbed or assaulted another, he might plead that he was insane at the time. How else could one explain the need or justification for such behavior in a socialist society? Similarly, if the crime was against property, which was theoretically owned in common, the rationalization was that the culprit had been corrupted by counterrevolutionary elements or was an agent of capitalist provocateurs.

Socialist non sequiturs about criminal behavior were obvious to the local internal-affairs personnel, who, like police officers the world over, understood human nature far better than Marx did. The internal-affairs NKVD personnel kept the peace, intervened in domestic-relations crises, and generally enforced the law. As sometimes happens, these NKVD officers were not averse to accepting or extracting "take" from those they were expected to protect. They ran protection rackets and extortion schemes, and by their avarice compounded the Soviet Union's very real economic problems. Stalin understood these practices well because of his own experience as a political extortionist, revolutionary brigand, and petty miscreant.

Three centuries of Russian tradition made the likelihood of finding an honest cop improbable. In 1934, when the NKVD was formally reconstituted, Stalin finally had enough loyalists available to assume control of the local republics' internal-affairs operations. In effect, Stalin had become the USSR's "godfather." His own *capos* controlled the NKVD, which in turn controlled the republics' internal affairs, while the state security organs controlled the Red Army. There are no indications whatever that Stalin used the system for personal enrichment; all his bureaucratic innovations were undertaken with the sole objective of increasing and protecting his personal power.

A fundamental operating principle of the Soviet government requires that power in the Kremlin always goes to the group that controls a second group, which controls a third. Over time, and with changes in the top leadership, the groups have changed. But the principle remains valid. (It is instructive to note that where it took Stalin six and a half years to achieve complete dominance of the Soviet Union's internal affairs, it took the late General Secretary Yuri Andropov only six months to achieve much the same degree of control.)

With the formation of the NKVD, Stalin decided to rid himself of Menzhinsky, who had served as the titular OGPU chief since 1926. Stalin's personal power was by now sufficient for him to appoint his own man, thereby assuring absolute command. Stalin needed a man who would execute his will without rationalizations requiring tiresome recourse to what Lenin said or wrote. His growing concern with real and imagined enemies led him to select Genrikh Yagoda, an enthusiastic Stalinist. Yagoda's reinstitution of mass terror and his doglike devotion to Stalin gave him a monstrous role to play in the purges that began in 1934, the same year he took over as chief of Stalin's terror machine.

Random terror is a curious sociological phenomenon. It can in fact engender mass panic and widespread fear. Yagoda's version had its introduction following the murder of Sergei Kirov in Leningrad in 1934. Kirov, as head of the Leningrad party, was young and handsome, and appeared to have personal traits of integrity and honesty not found in Stalin. Kirov's popularity grated on Stalin, who saw him as an incipient rival.

Kirov was respected and liked by members of Stalin's own entourage, making it impossible to cast him in a counterrevolutionary or Trotskyite role. While Stalin examined the problem of removing Kirov from the

Soviet political scene, he went to some lengths to pretend hearty, if bogus, personal affection.

Yagoda was secretly directed by Stalin to cause an "assassination" of Kirov, and Yagoda, in his efforts to please, made a hash of the affair. Kirov was most certainly killed, but the details of the murder and the inexpert preparations led to the unmistakable conclusion that the NKVD had arranged the event.

On learning of Kirov's death, Stalin immediately entrained for Leningrad, where he made a public display of his personal grief. Simultaneously, he considered announcing that renegade elements of the Leningrad NKVD, along with some White Guardists, had shot Kirov and that he was demanding the maximum penalty for those involved. For the occasion, the NKVD went into the streets and prisons and arrested sixty-six men, who were declared to be White Guardists and were executed. For a period of twenty-four hours Yagoda himself was under arrest while Stalin considered the advantages of throwing him on the mercy of the outraged citizenry.

Since just about everyone believed Kirov's death to be the result of a plot, Stalin took advantage of public sentiment and ordered the NKVD to begin arresting hundreds, then thousands, who had no conceivable connection with Kirov's murder, and to charge them with complicity in the "plot."

Thousands, including a great many Soviet officials, were arrested and sent into the penal camps. Many of the officials believed—until they finally died of malnutrition and overwork—that their imprisonment was the result of administrative error and that if Stalin knew they were in the camps, they would be released forthwith and restored to their positions of authority.

While his political rivals were being sent off to the death camps, Stalin saw to it that Yagoda included hundreds of others who had at one time or another slighted Stalin personally. During the whole process, Stalin appeared remote from the terror. The NKVD was represented as hot in pursuit of a massive conspiracy against the state, while Stalin simply posed as the arbiter who ensured that the "people's will" was served.

At last it began to occur to the public that the purges were actually being carried out with Stalin's full knowledge. It was time again for a tactical change, and this time it was Yagoda's turn to absorb Stalin's full attention. In September 1936 Yagoda was dismissed from his post, then arrested, and subsequently found guilty of conspiracy, espionage, and treason. He was finally shot in March 1938.

This obvious attempt by Stalin to disassociate himself from Yagoda's excesses—such as the alleged "medical murder" of Yagoda's predecessor, Menzhinsky—succeeded only among those who wanted to believe in the fundamental goodness of Stalin. Yagoda was a broken tool to be discarded. Even his execution was used by Stalin to reaffirm the grim message to Soviet officialdom that Stalin's rule was absolute.

The public was urged to believe that Yagoda had exceeded his authority and abused his high office. Once "discovered," he had paid the "highest price" for his betrayal of the people. The benign Stalin, in his near-divine wisdom, had not interfered with the application of the law. However improbable it seemed, there were many who persisted in believing that Yagoda's execution helped prove Stalin's noninvolvement in the actual bloodletting. Stalin was generally satisfied with the results of the first purges. At relatively insignificant cost, he had eliminated potential opponents, traumatized the Soviet party, and enormously enhanced his own power.

With his taste for retributive action, Stalin next appointed Nikolai I. Yezhov to replace Yagoda. Yezhov was publicly given the responsibility of curbing the NKVD "excesses." In doing so, he began a reign of terror that surpassed Yagoda's best efforts. Stalin was again able to avoid direct responsibility for a barbarous campaign, to the extent that Soviet history continues to refer to the period as the *Yezhovshchina* rather than by the name of its inventor and director, Stalin.

The NKVD purges turned inward, and the purgers were themselves "investigated," sent to the camps, or executed. The effect on the organs was devastating, particularly among the intelligence officers serving in foreign areas. International intelligence objectives were all but abandoned at this critical time, and the Soviet Union's major intervention in Spain was not supported to the degree required for success.

Stalin's obsession with the idea that he was the target of innumerable conspiracies had led him to believe that the NKVD was penetrated by Trotskyites who had to be ferreted out and destroyed. The deaths of 15 to 20 million Russians might have served to assuage Stalin's paranoia, but the effect of the grisly campaign on the Soviet intelligence services was corrosive. By turning the NKVD into a massive death squad, Stalin severely weakened the means required to keep the Soviet Union apprised of what was going on in the rest of the world. It was not possible to devote virtually all resources to domestic internal security without reducing the capacities of the organs to function abroad.

At the direction of Stalin, Marshal Tukhachevsky was publicly accused of spying for a foreign state. On that date, June 11, 1937, a purge of the military began. Three of the Red Army's marshals were murdered, and all 11 deputy commissars of defense, 13 of 15 army commanders, 110 of 195 division commanders, 220 of 406 brigade commanders, and tens of thousands of other officers were imprisoned or executed. The killings were on a scale much greater than that experienced by any army officer corps, of any nation, in any war.

The slaughter in the army left the USSR with a skeletal officer corps, intimidated and inexperienced at every level. Stalin's act of madness in gutting the Red Army had its basis in his conviction that the senior officers had been corrupted by their association with the Germans during the period between the signing of the Rapallo Treaty in 1922 and the rise of Hitler. This explanation, while convenient, assumes a pan-Europeanism on the part of the Soviet officer corps that is not supported in any non-Soviet histories of the Red Army.

Though meticulous in carrying out Stalin's hidden agenda, from the day he assumed office Yezhov was just another of Stalin's incipient victims. Like Yagoda before him, Yezhov was eventually removed from his post and confined to a mental ward where he committed "suicide" in December 1938. Stalin then named his deputy and fellow Georgian, Lavrenti P. Beria, to succeed to the perilous job of heading the NKVD. Beria was an inspired choice. He had already demonstrated an extraordinary flair for cruelty, coupled with genuine administrative skill.

Beria, who directed the service from the end of 1938 until shortly after Stalin's death in 1953, moved quickly in the period preceding Hitler's attack on Russia in 1941 to restore some order and coherence to Soviet intelligence operations. The purges had taken their toll, not only in human lives but also in the NKVD's ability to carry out its diverse missions. Under Beria, a better balance was struck between the intelligence resources committed to internal security and those invested in external intelligence operations. New recruitment and an expanded utilization of non-Soviet intelligence assets occurred during the 1938–1941 period. Beria paralleled this with an attempt to carry out a new, selective purge of certain key NKVD and GRU officials. Soviet failures in Spain made those who had served there most vulnerable, and several of the principal officers, knowing they could not survive an "investigation" of their roles in Spain, deserted.

Among these were L. L. Felbin ("General Alexandr Orlov") and Samuel Ginsberg ("Walter Krivitsky"), both of whom had been summoned to Moscow for "consultation." They immediately recognized the euphemism as a thinly disguised promise of execution and fled the service to which they had devoted their adult lives.

The "selective" purges were based on Stalin's newly acquired distrust of the "honored Chekists"[2] in foreign assignments, whom he believed to have fallen prey to the Trotskyites. Unlike Yagoda and Yezhov, who were eliminated because of their guilty knowledge linking Stalin directly to heinous NKVD acts, the Honored Chekists were now suspect because they *might* engage in anti-Stalinist acts.

Beria's task was to rid the NKVD of its mid- to upper-level ranks of old Chekists and to replace them with Stalinists. The task was carried out with a reasonable degree of efficiency. The younger officers did not mourn the passing of the old guard, because the "selective purge" offered new opportunities to those who were not its victims. The elimination of senior Chekists produced no morale problems. More importantly, it served to rejuvenate the organs, which by now were becoming more active in the foreign field.

As Dzerzhinsky had made clear, the Chekists were the servants of the party, and by 1938 Stalin was the personification of the party. (In 1967, on the fiftieth anniversary of the founding of the Cheka, many of the Honored Chekists who had been sent to die in the gulag or execution prisons were posthumously restored to their former status. The rehabilitation process began before Yuri Andropov was named to the post of KGB chairman by Leonid Brezhnev. There were virtually none living who could claim the benefits of rehabilitation, except for a few widows who were granted retroactive pensions for their husbands' services.)

Beria and Stalin were an odd team. Stalin was a misanthropic thug without redeeming social virtues or graces; Beria pretended erudition and intellectual cultivation. In his biography of Beria, Thaddeus Wittlin makes the point:

> Beria was not impressed by Stalin at all. Such feelings as admiration or devotion were alien to Beria's cold and calculating nature. In his (Beria's) opinion the great Comrade Stalin was a vulgar, pockmark-faced Georgian peasant, Iosif Dzugashvili, a chauvinist bastard from the filthy outskirts of the Gori community in the Tiflis area, the son of a drunkard cobbler, and a dropout from a deacons' seminary, a frustrated candidate for Orthodox priesthood, an activist more lucky than clever, a conspirator rude, ruthless and unscrupulous enough to be on top. To boot, he owed his position to Lenin, whose close aide he was. Being an educated young man, Beria despised rather than adored Stalin.[3]

Beria, though equally ruthless in ambition and tactics, was superficially more urbane and intelligent. From Stalin's point of view, Beria was a worthy colleague and co-conspirator because he was patient and had the wit to cloak his contempt with subservience.

It is useful to recall that the current Soviet leaders, though relatively junior in Stalin's time, were Stalinists. It was their devotion to him that put them in a position to rise within the power structure. To believe that Andropov, Chebrikov, Aliyev, and the others were "closet" anti-Stalinists is to disregard the facts. Although they might not have had personal affection for Stalin, they survived and flourished on the basis of their unswerving support of Stalin and his methods.

Eventually Beria might have been just another of Stalin's victims, had Stalin not died in 1953. Beria obviously thought of himself as the heir apparent, and there is much incontrovertible evidence that he attempted to seize control following Stalin's death. At best, he was Stalin's default candidate as a successor, since there is no evidence that Stalin had anyone else in mind.

Unlike Lenin, who warned the party against allowing Stalin to rise beyond his level, Stalin left no final testament or political will insofar as is known. Stalin knew that Beria possessed the power and necessary ambition to take over once he was dead, and perhaps he felt that no personal endorsement was required. By 1953, Stalin resembled an ancient despot who took a last small pleasure in frustrating his aging progeny by continuing to live. In the end Beria did fill Stalin's shoes, but he never lived to walk in them.

Nicholas Dozenberg as he appeared in 1940. At the time, Dozenberg testified that he had given his naturalization papers to his first wife in 1921 with instructions to give them to Earl Browder so that Browder could apply for a passport in Dozenberg's name. Dozenberg was later convicted of passport fraud and confined at the federal prison at Lewisburg. *(FBI photo)*

Dr. Valentin Gregory Burtan (Borstein) at the time of his arrest in 1934. Burtan's faith in Stalin led him to remain an uncooperative federal convict for ten years. After the German attack on the USSR in 1941, Burtan broke silence and petitioned his release by writing to the director of prisons and volunteering his service "in defense of his country." Despite his late surge of patriotism, successive parole boards declined his requests. *(National Archive, RG 87, case file CJ-9-34)*

The *Dalstroi* (originally *Arnelo*), built in Flushing, New York in 1918, was one of the ships bought by John G. Ohsol on the concealed account of Amtorg. Robert Conquest lists her as carrying 6,000 to 9,000 prisoners during the period 1937–38 and 7,000 prisoners in 1939. She was blown up in Nakhodka harbor in 1946, probably by Baltic prisoners loading ammonal, an explosive, used in the Kolyma gold mines. The *Dalstroi* is seen in San Francisco harbor in late 1943 awaiting repairs under Lend-Lease. *(National Archive, NNVP, 26-San-1-50)*

After Beria's execution, Colonel General S. N. Kruglov was appointed to reorganize the NKVD. The resultant new and greatly reduced organization became the Committee for State Security (KGB). *(Official Soviet photo)*

Beria (below left), NKVD chief, executed in 1954. *(Official Soviet photo)* Yuri Andropov (center), as the first KGB chief to achieve political control of the USSR, is the father of the new KGB. *(Photo is a Soviet handout.)* Vitaly Fedorchuk (right) was appointed KGB chairman by Andropov. A few months later, Fedorchuk was named Minister of Internal Affairs (and as such became the controller of the MVD).

Dr. Philip Rosenbliett, a long-serving GRU officer in New York City, and his sister, Mrs. Cannon (above). In 1936, the doctor made a secret contact with his sister, the wife of Joseph Cannon, a prominent Trotskyite. Rosenbliett was observed entering the Cannon home, recalled to Moscow, and executed on Stalin's order. *(FBI photo)*

Dr. David Dubrowsky and some like-minded friends at a conclave near Mexico City in the late thirties. The photograph was taken at the time that all Soviet officers had been directed to focus on the assassination of Trotsky. Dubrowsky is at the center of the photo wearing a white suit. *(FBI photo)*

Adolphus Arnold Rubens (alias) (above left), Donald L. Robinson (alias), work name: "Richard"; true name: Ewald. He was a Lett who was charged by the GRU with the collection of U.S. passports for use by the Soviet services. Responding to an invitation from his chief in Moscow, Ewald made an ill-advised trip to the USSR in 1936, where he was arrested and charged with the then-familiar crime of having come under the influence of Trotskyites while in New York. Ewald did not survive the "investigation" in Moscow. *(Department of State photo)* Ruth Norma Robinson (alias) (above right), Ruth Marie Rubens (alias), true name: Ruth Boerger. She was identified as a trained Soviet officer assigned by the GRU as Ewald's "wife." Ruth renounced her U.S. citizenship at the United States embassy, Moscow, in 1936. No subsequent information regarding her is reflected in any official U.S. files. *(Department of State photo)*

Paul Yurevich Oras (right), the first Soviet naval attaché to be assigned to Washington. Because of his aggressive espionage efforts, Oras had been declared *persona non grata* in four countries before he was posted to the United States in 1934. Oras was later relieved and returned to the USSR, where he was arrested and charged with "Trotskyite sympathies" and shot on Stalin's orders in 1936. *(National Archive photo)*

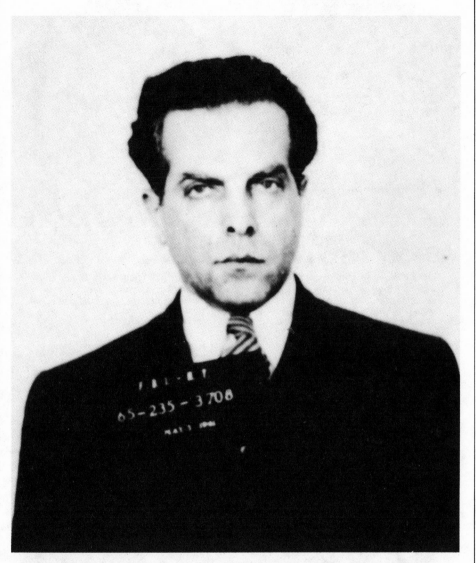

Gaik Badolovich Ovakimian arrived in the United States in 1932 and remained until his arrest by the FBI in 1941. As the senior OGPU/NKVD resident, he used the facilities of Amtorg to interview various Americans (e.g., Thomas L. Black and Harry Gold), who were thought to be prospective recruits for the Soviet service. Ovakimian supervised *all* NKVD operations in the United States during the period and is credited with coordinating and directing the multiple operations against Trotsky. Though arrested, he was never brought to trial. At the time he was in custody, the Soviets arrested three U.S. tourists in the USSR and charged them with espionage. The United States opted to trade the NKVD resident in New York for the return of the arrested Americans held under bogus charges. *(FBI photo)*

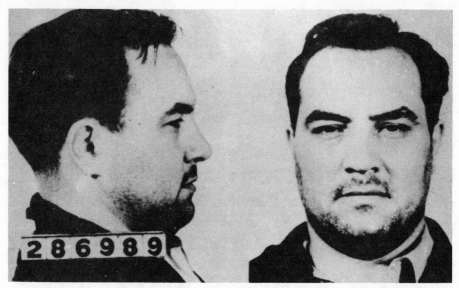

Hafis Salich, an employee of the U.S. Office of Naval Intelligence who was "false flagged" into cooperating with Soviet intelligence on the basis of "shared concern about Japanese military expansion." Salich was convicted in a federal court and sentenced to prison. His Soviet recruiter, although arrested by the FBI, was allowed to leave the United States. *(FBI photo)*

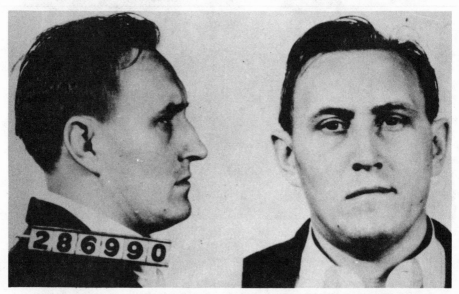

Mikhail Nicholas Gorin, the Soviet recruiter who ran Salich. Gorin was the Intourist representative on the West Coast. After his arrest, an attempt was made by Amtorg and the Soviet embassy in Washington to confer diplomatic immunity on Gorin. Despite the fact that Gorin did not qualify, the United States elected to release him rather than complicate U.S.-USSR relations at a critical moment. (The Soviet Union was then allied with Hitler.) *(FBI photo)*

Joseph Dorn (Hans Fischer) (right), confidence man and promoter of bogus securities, was an "officer" of the Sass & Martini bank of Berlin, which tried to wholesale counterfeit U.S. $100 Federal Reserve notes produced by the Soviets. He later served a term at the Lewisburg Federal Penitentiary concurrent with Nicholas Dozenberg and Dr. Valentin Burtan. *(National Archive, RG 87, case file CJ-9-34)*

BELOW Margaret Undjus (alias) (top left), James H. Dolson (top right), Judea Codkind (below left), Isador Dreagen (below middle), and A. E. Edwards (alias Sinkevitch) (below right), a few of the Shanghai net smashed by the arrest of the Soviet agents "Paul and Gertrude Ruegg/ Noulens." Exposure of the net can be attributed to disclosures made by Ho Chi Minh who, under the alias of Nguen Ai Quac, confessed details to the Chinese Nationalist police. Ho's official biography makes no reference to his role in the case. *(National Archive photos from Shanghai Municipal Police files)*

Office of the Amtorg Tractor Factory in New York, c. 1936. *(National Archive photo 306-NT-163035C)*

5 · The Beria Era

(1938–1953)

On the night of July 28, 1938, Lavrenti Pavlovich Beria, then first secretary of the Transcaucasian Party Committee, received a personal phone call from Stalin ordering him to Moscow immediately. Stalin gave no explanation, nor did Beria expect one. On the three-day train ride from Tiflis to Moscow, Beria had much to consider. Stalin's abrupt summons was part of a familiar pattern: The official, party bureaucrat, member of the state security, or military officer was called into Stalin's presence and then abruptly dragged to the Lubianka prison to be shot in the back of the head or sent to the gulag for an indeterminate period. Neither prospect excited Beria. He knew that the survivability of all officials in Stalin's USSR had become very uncertain, and could not be altered or guaranteed by exhibiting slavish loyalty to Stalin or even by fervent professions of belief in Marxist-Leninist dogma. "Crimes" were whatever Stalin said they were, and yesterday's commendation for success could easily form the basis of today's indictment.

On the morning of August 1, 1938, the train carrying Beria and his bodyguards arrived at the Kazan Railway Station in Moscow. Nothing seemed amiss. Detraining from his private car to the nearly deserted platform, Beria recognized his one-man welcoming committee as Colonel Bobrov of the NKVD. At Bobrov's suggestion Beria dismissed his bodyguards, directing them to meet him later in the day at the Select Hotel. The Select was the hotel most favored by high party officials when in Moscow on business. Colonel Bobrov led Beria out of the station to a waiting limousine.

Entering the limousine, Beria found General Alexander Poskrebyshev, Stalin's confidential secretary, there to greet him. The two men shook hands, and the car sped off. The trip passed in complete silence.

On arrival at the Kremlin, Poskrebyshev reported their presence to Stalin, and shortly thereafter a guard appeared in the anteroom where Beria
was waiting and announced that Comrade Stalin would like to see Comrade Beria. This was the moment of truth.

Stalin spoke briefly about the inconvenience of the journey and the
contrast between the climate in their native Georgia and that of Moscow.
Then, "with the same courteous air, Stalin announced that he had decided to transfer Beria from his high post in Tiflis to the Lubianka
Prison—to the front office. He would become the first deputy to Yezhov,
the present commissar of internal affairs and head of the NKVD. Beria
was to start his new job the next morning. The audience was over."[1]

Thus began the Beria era in the evolution of the Soviet security services. It was a tumultuous period, in which Dzerzhinsky's organizational
creature was put to its sternest tests. It was also the beginning of the
changes that would elevate the fragile Soviet state, under the erratic leadership of Stalin, to the status of a superpower. In retrospect, the causes of
these changes appear to have more to do with the errors of enemies and
the maladroitness of allies than with any planned course of Soviet action.
The most consistently reliable agent for change, however, was the Soviets' timely exploitation of chance. It was in this area that the organs made
their most important contribution.

Beria, an accomplished Bolshevik bureaucrat, settled into his new
post as Yezhov's deputy like a moray eel into a reef. He carried out his
assigned tasks with diligence and efficiency. Although some of the duties
were not commensurate with his rank, he played the role of the good
soldier to the limit. Beria's behavior was not lost on the enigmatic Stalin,
who in less than three months reassigned Yezhov to a new position as
people's commissar of water transport. The significance of Yezhov's
"promotion" was in its subtle signal to Beria to begin the systematic identification and elimination of senior NKVD officers who had enjoyed the
now-discredited Yezhov's patronage. Beria's action was not indiscriminate bureaucratic bloodletting but the near-surgical excision of those who
had made up Yezhov's cabal of confidants and trusted lieutenants. Stalin
monitored these proceedings with the same practiced detachment with
which he had watched the purging of those who carried out the orders he
himself had given to Yezhov.

Stalin's intentions can only be surmised, although it is clear that his
inaction was an unambiguous signal to Beria to rid the regime of Yezhov.
Beria found the task congenial, because only three years before, Yezhov
had attempted to purge him. At the time, Beria had responded by making the case that convinced Stalin that Yezhov was mentally ill and, as a
frustrated man, could be as dangerous a lunatic as was Leonid Nikolaev,
who had assassinated Kirov. Yezhov was dismissed from his post as com-

missar of water transport. Then, in the middle of the night, an ambulance stopped in front of his apartment. Two hospital attendants got out and entered Yezhov's home. Soon they brought the "bloodthirsty dwarf" out in a straitjacket, put him into the ambulance, and whisked him to Moscow's Serbsy Psychiatric Institute, where he was locked up in an isolation cell. Yezhov did not stay long at the Serbsy. One morning a nurse entered his solitary cell and found him dead, hanging from the window bar with a noose made from his underwear around his neck. His death was stated officially as a suicide. No explanation was offered of how, in a mental hospital, where the patients are watched constantly, Yezhov could tear his clothes, make a noose, and hang himself.[2]

With Yezhov and his adherents out of the way, Beria moved to consolidate his new position as commissar of internal affairs and head of the NKVD. A portion of this activity involved the customary placing of political loyalists in commanding positions in the NKVD headquarters. Those appointed fully realized that their personal loyalty to Beria was indistinguishable from their fidelity to Stalin. The imperative rule for survival of every rank in the NKVD was that one must be a "good Stalinist," no matter how often or how rapidly the criteria defining that status changed. The internal convolutions in the organs were a direct consequence of Stalin's need to exert absolute control. Bureaucratic maneuvering had been a part of life in the organs since the death of Dzerzhinsky. None of his successors—Menzhinsky (death by "heart failure"), Yagoda (executed as a foreign spy), or Yezhov—seemed able fully to comprehend the vagaries of Stalin's rules. Then Beria came along.

For several apparent reasons, Beria was more successful in avoiding Stalin's wrath than his predecessors had been. Under what might have been called Beria's Law, he spared no effort and missed no opportunity to make Stalin appear heroic. Among his most effective and pleasing achievements was his rewriting of the official history of the Bolshevik revolution, giving Stalin credit for the accomplishments of others and, most importantly, elevating him to slightly more than coequal status with the sainted Lenin.[3] This successful stroking of Stalin's ego reinforced Beria's personal security and increased his power. As an added compliment to Stalin's eminence, Beria eschewed all publicity for himself, insisting that every Soviet achievement was due to Stalin's "inspired" leadership. When failures occurred that could not be wished away or rewritten into triumphs, Beria could be depended upon to be at the ready with a sacrificial scapegoat who was made to confess, bear the blame, and accept whatever kind of public punishment Stalin judged suitable.

The legerdemain of historical revisionism has always been an important component of totalitarian societies. Under Beria, however, the process was raised to new heights. The incessant revising, the reselection of facts, the manufacture of any that were missing or needed, coupled with the chronic inhibitions of pervasive security considerations, make it impossible to measure the truth of contemporary Soviet accounts, whether they concern infant mortality rates or the production statistics of the state industries.[4]

While Beria played the role of Stalin's sycophantic toady to perfection, he knew that his obsequious behavior was not sufficient to ensure Stalin's continuing favor. As a means of making himself more useful (and thus more secure), Beria began to equip himself and the NKVD to do more than conduct purges and operate the now greatly expanded internal-security mechanism. The organs were still the shield and sword of the party, but the party was now Stalin himself. That the organs now answered to one man certified that Stalin's sway was complete.

Beria's plans were accelerated by the growing prospects of war, and from 1938 to 1941 he moved with speed and remarkable administrative skill to expand the NKVD—to put it on a wartime footing and to upgrade the quality of its personnel. He was especially selective of those assigned to the KRO, as he was acutely aware that much would depend on the NKVD's "illegals," who operated outside the Soviet Union without diplomatic protection or overt identification as Soviet citizens. He was convinced that in time of war these officers were likely to become the only sources of intelligence available to the USSR.

Both Japan and Germany posed genuine, direct threats to the USSR. In the Far East, there had been intermittent collisions on the Manchukuo frontier, and in the West, Austria and Czechoslovakia had already fallen into the Nazi camp. The ten-year nonaggression pact the USSR made with Germany on August 24, 1939, mitigated the German threat for the moment and, simultaneously, allowed the USSR to continue diplomatic relations with the Western powers. Beria, while maintaining the NKVD legal residents in Soviet embassies and trade missions, accelerated the expansion of the illegal nets, particularly in Western Europe and the United States. The concept of agents who would "stay behind" and later emerge to operate in newly occupied areas was not new. However, the scale on which Beria proposed to use stay-behinds was more extensive than previously known. From 1938 to 1941, an estimated 120 NKVD officers, of many different national origins, were insinuated into Germany, Italy, France, Belgium, Portugal, Spain, and the Netherlands. The national communist parties (where they still existed) selected promising candidates for disassociation and nominated these potential clandestine assets to the NKVD, usually through the Comintern representatives. Hitler's initiatives were unconventional and daring. Reliable intelligence on German intentions was of the highest priority, and of course, in the East there was always Japan.

To meet the personnel needs posed by these uncertainties and other threatening events, Beria established in late 1938 the NKVD's first special school, the so-called Academy for Spies at Bykovo some forty miles north of Moscow.[5] Prior to 1938, the training of NKVD personnel for both legal and illegal resident assignments was carried out as a personal tutorial—that is, the novice was apprenticed to an experienced officer who was responsible for teaching the pupil the rudiments of clandestine operations. Concurrent with the training was a continuous probing to test and verify the student's ideological commitment to "Great Stalin." The curriculum included special instruction in surveillance, communications (e.g., radio construction), ciphers, hand-to-hand combat, silent killing, and more. The embryonic Chekists were individually hand-tooled. Without abandoning the principles laid down by Dzerzhinsky, the academy at Bykovo was founded on Beria's twin convictions that it was both necessary and possible to mass-produce capable foreign field agents.

To shorten the period of gestation required to deliver a KRO agent, Beria upgraded the recruitment criteria by instituting a sort of *levée en masse* among the most talented officers of the Soviet police and the brightest students at Moscow University as well as the most attractive of the young stage and screen actors and actresses.[6] The selectees for Bykovo comprised a true elite. In the normal course some would have sought careers in the organs, but the rising threat of Hitler did much to spur patriotic fervor for the defense of the motherland, a motivation that was artfully exploited.

Whatever the recruitment approaches or techniques of coercion used, Beria got the personnel he wanted and needed. The training at Bykovo was intense and thorough. Though overt hostilities had not commenced, each student was imbued with the Bolshevik interpretation of history, which is based on the assertion that the Soviet Union is continually at war and that the "military phase" (armed conflict) is merely a change in form. Indoctrination went beyond the traditional ideological communist opposition to capitalism and the inevitability of unending class war, to an understanding that all alliances forced upon the Soviet Union were essentially tactical and wholly temporary. Theirs were missions of espionage and subversion, as important as the more obvious one of defeating Hitler by force of arms.

In pursuit of the dictum "Know Thy Enemy," the novitiates at Bykovo were extensively schooled in the language, customs, and culture of the countries in which they would work. In the case of those selected for dispatch to the United States, Britain, or Canada (major targets in the pre-World War II period), a special effort was made to teach them to speak like natives, with accents that conformed to the specifics of their individual "legends." The linguistic training went beyond acquiring vernacular vocabularies, grammar, and appropriate syntax; they should be able to read, write, and speak a second or third language with native fluency.

The training required that the students also learn the kinesics of their new languages so that they could imitate the body and facial movements of native-born speakers. No matter the student's intellectual or ideological commitment, this was an exceptionally difficult task. Actors and actresses with extensive role-playing experience, in addition to English language and verbal imitative skills, proved adept recruits.

Underlying the training of the illegals at Bykovo was the need for those destined to serve in the United States or Canada to do more than simply pass as Americans or Canadians. They were also expected to enhance their legends by actual participation in American or Canadian society. Based on age, sex, education, physical abilities, etc., and the projected purpose, an individual might be directed to matriculate at an American university that was known to be engaged in military or scientific research for the federal government. After acquiring legitimate academic credentials, the individual might be ordered to seek a post in the U.S. government, the armed forces, or with a specific commercial firm such as IBM, AT&T, or G.E., with the obvious objective of making a lasting deep penetration of the technical areas of greatest importance to the USSR.

Beria's decision to pursue this approach was prompted by previous experience with locally recruited espionage assets. The weaknesses and hazards of a system that relied exclusively on native-born agents had become evident: They tended to be less reliable and less emotionally stable than recruited Russians. This is not to say that the KRO apparat became solely dependent on Russian staffing. Rather, there was a need for increased control and discipline in the NKVD in order to meet a dramatically changing world situation.

Dzerzhinsky's KRO illegals had been drawn largely from a small core of ideologues, most of them born in Russia. In addition to this group were some recruits drawn from the military prisoners who had been captured by the Imperial Russian forces during the Great War. Among these Austro-Hungarian and German soldiers were many who became ardent converts to Bolshevism while in the POW camps. They were particularly useful to the KRO because their education, travel, and business activities reflected the cosmopolitan nature of pre-World War I Europe rather than the parochialism of czarist Russia. Dzerzhinsky was aware of the weaknesses of nationalism in the prewar era and consequently did not rule out the recruitment of foreigners as illegals. He knew that French, German, or Balkan nationalism was at best very shallow, and he had no illusions about the long-term utility of recruited foreigners. They were to be used, exploited, and discarded when they no longer furthered the aims of the organs.

According to General Orlov, Beria was aware of the controversy surrounding the suggestion (sometimes credited to Ivan Maisky, then Soviet ambassador to Great Britain) that a serious attempt should be mounted by the OGPU to recruit upward-bound, dissident, left-wing intellectuals attending the prestigious British public schools.[7] Maisky's suggestion was not enthusiastically received by Stalin, partly because of the dictator's chronic distrust of all things English, but mostly because he believed that anyone who could be taken in by the nonsense of Soviet communism would not be a very good spy.[8] Andrei Gromyko of the Foreign Office argued that the idea was at least worth exploring, if only to get a second opinion that might challenge the information then being provided to the Kremlin by legal and illegal residents in England and elsewhere. Gromyko's view prevailed, not so much from logical and pragmatic considerations, perhaps, as because Stalin saw a chance to pit his subordinates against one another.

Like Stalin, Beria never fully trusted the foreign illegals recruited under the Maisky proposal. The Philbys, Burgesses, Macleans, Blunts, et al. were, in Beria's view, erratic in their behavior and without the "steel" it took to be a real Stalinist spy. As long as they delivered, Beria tolerated their continuation and indulged their eccentricities. But once their usefulness was ended—as in the cases of Burgess and Maclean, who fled to the USSR in 1951—they became cultural artifacts of no further utility to the organs. When Burgess and Maclean "came in from the cold," they were put on display as propaganda curiosities. The institutional distrust of the Cambridge spies was such that none of them, regardless of prior performance, was allowed to take up a substantive position in the Soviet security services. Philby has often been described as a colonel in the organs who continues to provide wise counsel to the KGB managers. Another popular fiction is that Philby holds a position in the KGB commensurate with his prior service. Soviet KGB defectors who departed Moscow after Philby arrived insist that there is persuasive evidence to the contrary. No independent Western observer (except his son) has seen the man for several years.

At Bykovo, the section concerned with the United States ran a demanding course in American "culture." The curriculum in the thirties included learning how to jitterbug and listening for hours to recordings of American radio before being examined on the story line and characters in the early soap operas. The novices were required to memorize batting averages of the current baseball heroes as well as data on which team won what, where, and when. The faculty understood the importance (for legend purposes) of baseball, radio, hot dogs, and apple pie.

The students were given detailed briefings on the cities in which they were supposed to have lived. Much of this information was provided by the CPUSA (which must have broken party discipline occasionally to wonder about the purpose of the collection effort). The physical setting in which the training took place was not unlike a movie set for an Andy Hardy film. The only thing lacking in the Bykovo American village (built in 1938 and sometimes referred to as Little Chicago) was a roller-skating rink. One was added in 1940 after a recent graduate complained that he had been seriously injured when, for cover reasons, he had had to go to a roller-skating party. It was, he insisted, a necessary social skill, and successive Bykovo novitiates were thus taught how to roller-skate as well as how to play softball and touch football.

Serious study of American and Canadian societies was also required. Beria knew all too well the futility of trying to square the official party line about life in the United States with the conditions the agents would actually encounter. Consequently, the students were advised that they would be faced with "contradictions " and temptations. Such occasions of socialist sin were to be shunned, because the agents were Stalin's soldiers in the class war that might have to be fought over several lifetimes before the final socialist victory. Theirs was a high calling and demanded much sacrifice. The same motivating argument, used successfully by Dzerzhinsky, was no less successful in the NKVD. Properly indoctrinated, man has an almost infinite capacity for self-deception, particularly if he can be made to believe he has been selected into a societal elite. The prospect of "differentness" and a dedicated life has always had the same appeal in the classless Bolshevik system as it does in more conventional political organizations elsewhere.

The American and Canadian security services were ill-prepared for the arrival of the Bykovo graduates in their midst. The tide of events leading toward World War II left in its wake increased population and social mobility. People began to move about, and the threat of war gave business an economic boost. More young people entered college, and families moved to take advantage of the revival in business and manufacturing. In this ferment, people were generally who they said they were. The Bykovo graduate who presented himself for admission to a western state university, armed with a diploma from an Ohio high school (accompanied by forged letters of recommendation), was accepted at face value.

By adding legitimate detail and subsequent experience to their legends, the Bykovo graduates were able to make their covers almost impenetrable. For example, consider the hypothetical, though not atypical, case of a Bykovo graduate, agent X, who matriculated at the University of Washington in September 1940.[9] Upon graduation in June 1943, agent X, like his genuine American peers, faced the rather certain prospect of military service. In X's case, having a degree gave him more options than most. Accordingly, X was directed by his NKVD control to select the option most likely to be of both immediate *and* long-term advantage to the Soviet intelligence services. With X's training, background, and aptitudes, he might choose to seek a commission in the Signal Corps, military intelligence, the Quartermaster Corps, or Ordnance. The point was to have agent X in place and in a position to acquire intelligence information of direct interest to the Soviets. In the case of the military intelligence option, he might provide information about what the Americans knew about the Soviets and, more important, how they came to know it.

Following the war, the hypothetical X was faced with a new set of varying options, any of which could be of advantage to the NKVD. For example, X could have elected to serve in the occupation of Germany or Japan, thereby giving the NKVD an important set of eyes and ears in the enemy camp at the inception of the Cold War. Other nonmilitary options were also open, such as a possible appointment in the expanded postwar State Department's Foreign Service. These and other career options were precisely what Beria had in mind when the academy at Bykovo was established. Although the overwhelming majority of persons who sought continued government service following World War II, whether in the military, the State Department, or the new CIA, were loyal Americans, there is no doubt that the Bykovo graduates, by centering themselves in the herd of applicants, attempted to conceal their infiltration of these organizations. Wartime service gave added preference and implied a certain kind of loyalty. As William Colby, former director of the CIA, noted, he was one who didn't take a polygraph examination at the time he joined the CIA in 1950, because of his wartime service with the OSS. Although Colby is in no way impugned, his authority is cited to underline the temporary conditions prevailing at the time which admit the possibility of a Bykovo graduate getting a free, if not full, entry into the system.

Bykovo was, and is, real. Unofficial estimates by U.S. internal-security professionals support the view that Bykovo and its sister academies have, over time, managed an annual infiltration of KRO illegals into the United States, Canada, and elsewhere of approximately one hundred to two hundred. The figure may be even higher.[10]

The numbers include dispatched agents and not only those who have achieved functional status within a targeted university, industry, or security agency. No one can determine who or how many of the Bykovo graduates were able to achieve functional status, though it is a matter of documentable fact that they have been found in sensitive areas. To insist that none has been successful is to ignore the evidence. On the other hand, one can only speculate about how many of the Bykovo graduates created their own additional legends and opted out of the organs to live their lives as ordinary Americans or Canadians. Some certainly did, but this was expected by Beria. Others who were caught, usually as the consequence of unplanned events, or otherwise persuaded to defect confirmed the essential facts of the Bykovo operation. The few who have extricated themselves from the system have been able to provide valuable data concerning methodology, though regrettably little information about the identities of other Bykovo Academy almuni.[11]

As an aside to the Bykovo operation, which was initially directed to produce KRO illegals for the United States and Canada, several sister academies were set up in the post-Beria era. They were intended to provide KRO illegals in other countries that emerged as important targets in the Cold War. Because there were very few native-born Russians who could pass as Japanese or Tanzanians, foreign personnel were recruited, either in the POW camps (especially Japanese) or in their native countries, and then dispatched to the USSR for intensive training. Elaborate care was given to creating their legends. Like the Bykovo graduates, according to counterintelligence specialists, these illegals are expected to legitimatize their legends further before being assigned foreign espionage missions.[12]

Though Bykovo was a long-term, low-risk operation with a potential for high payoffs, it is uncertain how effective it was in the period from 1938 to the end of World War II in gaining intelligence information about the United States. It was in this period, however, that Beria had a piece of luck without which he might not have been able to survive. It involved applications of the old axiom that war and politics make strange bedfellows.

From Beria's point of view, the bedfellows had their first test on August 23, 1939, when Nazi Germany and the Soviet Union signed a ten-year nonaggression pact. Preliminary negotiations were handled by the NKVD both at home and abroad. The announcement of the pact devastated the Comintern and thoroughly rent the Internationals. Beria and Stalin both knew that the pact might provide some months in which to get ready to face Hitler.

Signing with the Germans raised a series of significant and thorny intelligence questions for Beria. Not necessarily in order, they included: How much time do we have? Will Japan as signatory to the Anti-Comintern Tripartite Pact use the pretext of a German attack on the USSR to launch an invasion of the Soviet Far East? Will France and England honor their commitments to Poland? What role, if any, will the United States play in a war in Europe that involves the Soviet Union?

None of the initial answers were encouraging. According to Peter Deriabin, the GRU estimated that if the English and French failed to honor their commitments to Poland, Hitler could turn the Wehrmacht against the Soviet Union as early as the spring of 1940. This worst-case scenario prompted the rapid "rehabilitation" of thousands of low- and mid-level Red Army officers who had been consigned to the gulag in connection with Stalin's military purge of 1938.[13] Though the dead marshals, generals, and colonels couldn't be revived, the GRU estimate did provide justification for reinstatement of some officers who could be expected to bring a trace of professionalism to the defense of the motherland.

The answer to the Japanese question was carefully hedged by Richard Sorge, the Soviets' principal agent in Japan.[14] Sorge contended at the time (the summer of 1939) that Japanese intentions were unclear, adding carefully that they were likely to depend on the extent and speed of Hitler's success. Sorge didn't rule out the possibility of a Japanese attack in the Soviet Far East or a resumption of the recently concluded two-year border war between Japan and the USSR. Sorge's message that "it was too soon to know" about a major assault was not encouraging to Beria, who was loath to convey such a "nonreport" to Stalin.

The reports that Beria received from England were equally discouraging. Philby, Burgess, Maclean, et al., perhaps due to their ideological biases, misunderstood their own countrymen—those who would respond to Churchill's exhortation of "blood, toil, tears and sweat" without caring anything about the subtle nuances of fascism. Churchill personalized the war for the average Briton by making it a battle between free men and women and the bully Hitler. That brand of "ideology" was lost on the Cambridge spies, who looked upon individual freedom as a quaint archaic notion that had been replaced by a more vital one: service to mankind (via a foreign state). In defense of Philby, Blunt, Burgess, and Maclean, much of the misinformation they unintentionally provided served in the beginning to confirm Stalin's low opinion of foreigners as agents. And Beria was as much deflected by the unpredictability of a reemergent Churchill.

In the late thirties, reports from the NKVD resident in the United States and from Colonel Boris Bykov, a senior GRU officer in New York, were even more foreboding. Isolationism seemed a dominating force. Hitler was the least of America's worries. Anti-British sentiment was strong, and Russia was a far-off place about which most Americans knew or cared little. The only promising thing in Bykov's reports was the information that the dreaded FBI appeared more interested in tracking down German spies than in focusing on the NKVD.[15]

Taken together, the answers to the burning questions added up to a very gloomy picture. They indicated a strong possibility of the Soviet Union's being left to stand alone against Hitler, plus the added threat of having to face Japan's military might at the same time: that is, a two-front war with catastrophic implications for the Soviet Union. In such a situation, Beria's lot was not a comfortable one. The NKVD could not, as if by magic, pull allies out of a hat, nor could it with certainty foil the principal enemy, Hitler, by tactics of propaganda, espionage, and sabotage. These means were useful but would not be decisive in heading off what lay ahead.

The rush of events from September 1, 1939, when the German Army invaded Poland, to June 22, 1941, when Hitler invaded Russia, are beyond the scope of this account. Suffice it to say that these events gave further, albeit still partial, answers to Beria's intelligence questions. Though some contend that Beria had hard intelligence in hand concerning Hitler's intention to invade Russia,[16] this contention, like many of those surrounding the Pearl Harbor controversy, is not likely to be resolved. It is entirely possible that Beria did provide Stalin with the intelligence, but that Stalin, like many political leaders who act as their own intelligence officers, disbelieved it or evaluated it in wholly subjective terms. The latter case is supported by several factors:

Hitler delayed the attack from the Wehrmacht's recommended date of April 7–10, 1941, until June 22, 1941, in accordance with a horoscope cast for him by his personal astrologer. The June 22 invasion date was the first of three mistaken decisions Hitler made that led to his final defeat. The second error was the refusal to arm the "liberated" anti-Soviet peoples of Estonia, Latvia, Lithuania, and the Ukraine, against their Soviet masters. The third astounding error was the declaration of war against the United States on December 11, 1941, which flowed from the first mistake and provided Beria with an opportunity to bring the full force of the NKVD to bear on "The Great Patriotic War."

Germany's blitzkrieg assault on Russia knocked the Red Air Force out of the war within the first thirty-six hours and plunged the Kremlin into chaos. Stalin was traumatized by the event and went into seclusion. His most immediate fear was that the millions still in the forced-labor camps would be liberated by the Germans and would tear the flesh from his living body. His second fear was that the military, who had suffered humiliation in Finland and defeat on the frontier, would stage a coup and execute him. The German armored columns then racing into the heart of the USSR could claim no more than a part of Stalin's attention.

Reports from the front merely added to his conviction that he, too, was about to become a victim. Like millions before him, he could claim that the anticipated bloody reprisals could be attributed to only one man: Iosif Vissarionovich Dzugashvili, the now-frightened tyrant who called himself "Steel."

Like Stalin, Hitler considered the Estonians, Latvians, Lithuanians, and Ukrainians subhuman, a misperception for which both would pay dearly. Stalin's view was based on his recollection of the antagonism shown by the little Baltic states at the time the Bolsheviks were trying to stitch together the diverse elements that would eventually make up the USSR. Because several large forced-labor camps were certain to be over-run by the German advance, Stalin ordered the NKVD to begin mass executions of the prisoners while simultaneously moving other armies of prisoners to new camps east of the Urals. When battle conditions pre-cluded the transportation of prisoners, they were executed on the spot by NKVD border guards and the guards of the forced-labor camps.

As the German advance continued, some of the Reich generals advo-cated arming those who had been "liberated" for use as cannon fodder to wear down the Red Army's infantry. Hitler demurred, allowing his eth-nocentric vanity to obstruct the commanders' sound, albeit bloody, mili-tary advice. Among other considerations, Hitler was determined to defeat the despised Stalin with the force of German arms.

The refusal to utilize the enormous anti-Soviet potential, not only in the Baltic states but also in the western reaches of the USSR, was to prove a costly mistake. In a sense, the Nazis' absurd convictions about racial inferiority both disabled the German military commanders and gen-erated new and disastrous problems in the rear areas. Many of those liberated by the German armies initially were so fiercely anti-Soviet as to be pro-German. In other locales attitudes ranged from detached neu-trality to wholesale volunteering to join in the fight against Moscow.

The preclusive racial attitudes extended to the German Army, which, despite its efficiency and organization, was wholly unprepared for irreg-ular war. The professional officers could not conceive of untrained, non-uniformed—in a word, unconventional—forces offering more than symbolic resistance to the Wehrmacht. It was only later in the Russian campaign that the Germans allowed the formation of the first anti-Soviet guerrilla units, led by German officers and manned by disaffected former Soviet citizens.

In retrospect, Hitler's lunacy in deferring the attack date from April to late June and his exclusion of the potential resistance force represented by the captured peoples changed the course of history. Had the Germans attacked in early spring and had they utilized the Balts, Ukrainians, and other anti-Soviet populations, it is highly probable that the Bolsheviks would have been destroyed. As it happened, even with Hitler's self-in-dulgence, the Wehrmacht came to within nineteen miles of Moscow.

Like Stalin, Hitler found it difficult to accept that his intelligence ser-vice could provide him with information he had not taken into considera-tion when he conceived his grand strategies. The competitiveness that so gravely affected German intelligence also tainted the product. Hitler had no appetite for the maunderings of his senior military commanders be-cause he had consistently demonstrated that their judgment on the conduct of war was inferior to his own. As the campaign progressed, he found the German High Command's recommendations, which called for a tactical withdrawal and regroupment during the winter, clearly defeatist. He had come to expect nothing more than cautionary bad news from his intelligence services and tended to reject all that was inconsistent with his own *Fingerspitzengefühl*.

Stalin's convictions on intelligence were simply that much of the reported material was disinformation, insinuated into Soviet intelligence channels and probably intended to deceive. He had a comprehensive grasp of the NKVD's capacity to handle internal-security matters but was less confident of their ability to produce useful intelligence. Several of the GRU's most significant operations in Japan, Britain, and the United States were discounted as "provocations." In the Kremlin's climate of mutual distrust, Stalin was extremely cautious, almost pathologically so, in his response to advice proffered by his intelligence subordinates. In a sense, they were a kind of enemy, too, by the very fact that they bore bad news.

Reporting from the front confirmed the worst of Stalin's fears. Particularly disquieting was the news that anti-Soviet partisan groups, unable to win German sponsorship, were spontaneously engaging in small-scale attacks behind the Red Army's fragile lines. According to Beria, these anti-Soviet actions were becoming widespread and threatening the entire defensive strategy of the Red armed forces.

With remarkable consistency of thought, a proposal was advanced that met with immediate approval. It was old wine in a new bottle, and once more the most reliable weapon in the arsenal was examined for its application to a problem. The proposal called for the controlled use of provocation as the deus ex machina.

Special units, under the NKVD, were charged with recapturing or at least neutralizing the wayward and disaffected. The initial proposal provided that an NKVD officer would be dropped by Soviet aircraft for the purpose of making contact with the partisans. The parachute agent would carry several radios and, in his first contact with the partisans, would try to persuade them that the people of the USSR were aware of their courageous efforts *against the Germans*. The agent would add that the partisan leader was wanted in Moscow to assist in the planning of comparable irregular units and to receive a medal from the General Staff in recognition of his heroic efforts. The parachute agent would then propose that he conduct an inventory of the partisans' needs and radio the requirements to Moscow. The NKVD controlled the Moscow transmitter and promptly arranged for the identity of the partisan leader to be mentioned repeatedly on Radio Moscow as the leader of a group that had fought the Germans with conspicuous bravery.

A second effect of the broadcasts was to convey the wholly false impression that all of the partisan elements were made up of brave Soviet citizens, willing to oppose the Germans with their bare hands. Faked messages were also transmitted to nonexistent resistance groups suggesting that Soviet partisans not only were operating in every locale but were winning. The broadcasts were a powerful disincentive to those tens of thousands who were actually fighting against the Soviets.

If the partisans could be persuaded that they were under Moscow's scrutiny, their sense of purpose would be devastated. Some, believing they were viewed as anti-German resisters, considered their best survival avenue to be cooperation. The radios brought a stream of detailed information relating to the Red Army's new victories and the probability of an imminent German collapse. In the case of a cooperative group, arrangements were made to drop arms, ammunition, food, and medical supplies, and if the local leader believed what he was hearing, he might be induced to agree to be airlifted to Moscow, where he would act as a bemedaled consultant to the General Staff.

The fact that the planes, which were much needed elsewhere, came and actually dropped supplies and congratulatory messages was sometimes taken as proof that the tide of battle had turned. With the local leader gone to his certain execution in Moscow, the NKVD man assumed control of the partisan band using every psychological weapon at the NKVD's command.

Receiving decent treatment from Moscow was in itself a disorienting experience and had its effect in confusing the motivations of the partisans. If there was no prospect of true liberation from Soviet control, many felt their best course was to accept the reality of its reimposition. They were encouraged to believe that their sacred duty was defense of the motherland and that most political issues were subsidiary to that objective. Opposition to the Germans was made to seem a duty that transcended all others, and the battle was adroitly converted to the multipartisan Great Patriotic War.

On the next airdrop, additional NKVD officers arrived with decorations and commendations for the partisans. They also brought messages from Stalin himself, stressing the importance of continued resistance to the invaders. By now, Beria could consider the group neutralized. The next step was to turn the partisans to engage their new enemies, the Germans.

It is essential to note that many of the parachute agents were shot immediately on contact and that many of the resistance groups refused the NKVD's repeated efforts to herd them back into the Soviet fold. But there was another way of dealing with the recalcitrants: In areas of special sensitivity, the NKVD dropped punitive platoons of bogus partisans, who appeared to be fighting the common Soviet enemy. Once on the ground, the impostors made daylight raids on small Red Army detachments, which were directed to simulate casualties. The bogus band would then withdraw and attempt to make contact with other independent resistance elements. If successful, they were to approach the legitimate partisans, offer to join forces, and then, once mutual confidence was established, destroy the anti-Soviet elements. There are documented instances in which the charade of bogus partisans, in battalion strength, "defeated" NKVD-controlled battalions just to establish the bona fides of the punitive force.

In other areas judged to be vulnerable to German occupation, NKVD forces, *frequently in the uniform of German SS units,* entered the towns and villages and, in a shocking display of barbarity, murdered, raped, burned, and pillaged the community, always mindful of the need to leave survivors who would endure as eyewitnesses to the fact that the Germans could not be seen as saviors. The same techniques were used in areas in which the Soviets were attempting to reestablish control. An NKVD-operated mock-German unit would wantonly destroy communities immediately prior to the arrival of the heroic Soviet partisan recruiters. Having just witnessed "German" atrocities in their midst, the locals tended to be responsive to the Soviets who were attempting to organize anti-German resistance.

Once NKVD authority was imposed, a partisan band was forced to engage the Germans without its customary tactics of surprise and mobility, the weapons that had enabled the groups to fight again. The predictable result was that partisans were killed by the thousands.

In the cases of relatively well armed and disciplined anti-Soviet partisan groups whose leaders refused all Soviet attempts at neutralization, the favored NKVD tactic was to provide spurious intelligence to the Germans, identifying the group as Soviet-controlled, describing the unit's location and strength, and usually referring to an impending attack against a specified German target. The signal contained enough plausible information to provoke the Germans into a major effort against the partisans. Then the NKVD simply monitored the very efficient Germans as they destroyed the recalcitrant partisan group and served the Soviet interest.

Any members of an original band who survived the war were shot in 1944–1945 for their betrayal of the motherland in 1941.

On the fiftieth anniversary of the founding of the organs, hundreds of books were published that cynically commemorated the "brave partisan bands who fought the Nazi hordes." The few who had survived to write the tear-stained recollections were, almost without exception, those who had been coercively drawn into the organs or were NKVD men at the time.

The most distinguished practitioner of the art of neutralizing and destroying partisan warfare was a bull-necked little man named Pantelymon Kondratevich Ponomarenko. He had joined the party in 1925, was educated as an engineer, served in the Red Army for three years in the early thirties, and displayed a marked aptitude for counterpartisan provocation. As a member of the Central Committee, he was named to head all partisan (and counterpartisan) operations during World War II.

Ponomarenko's bloody provocations and deceptions were extraordinarily successful. As a tribute to his innovative leadership, he was promoted to the rank of lieutenant general.

In recognizing Soviet competence in the field of betrayal, it is also necessary to observe that the Germans were exceedingly slow to learn about irregular warfare. This point is dramatically underscored by the fact that, at the height of partisan operations against the German rear areas, the senior counterguerrilla officer was a mere major in the German Army. In an interview, Field Marshal Heinz Guderian, who later served as chief of staff of the Wehrmacht, observed that the German High Command was not prepared to accept the intelligence that indicated the NKVD's intention of developing partisan warfare. The Ponomarenko scheme was so bizarre that the German General Staff discounted reports about its activities and doubted that such a tactic could succeed. Guderian said, "If we had paid attention and forced the information on Hitler we could have defeated the Russians." (Note: Guderian's comment relates both to the use of the "liberated people" and to German support of irregular partisan activity. It suggests that if the Soviet armies had been defeated and the USSR thus driven out of the war, the U.S. aim of "unconditional surrender" might have been impossible to achieve, both physically and politically.)

In addition to his promotion, Ponomarenko was also awarded the Order of Lenin, certifying his superior contribution to the winning of the Great Patriotic War. After the war, Ponomarenko, as improbable a diplomat as any other apparatchik, was named as the Soviet ambassador to Poland, then India, and finally the Netherlands. It was in the last post that he reverted to type and engaged several Dutch police officers in a fistfight moments before he boarded Aeroflot for Moscow. His last post was as senior representative to the International Atomic Energy Agency in Vienna. He died in Moscow in January 1984.

A consequence of the Ponomarenko operation was that the NKVD, using the information it had acquired about people in the "liberated" countries during the war, was able to extend with great efficiency its internal-security operations. Although the postwar purges in the liberated countries were less extensive than those carried out in the USSR in the thirties, they were extremely effective in selectively eliminating much of the potential for "counterrevolutionary" activity. The Ponomarenko operations provided the Bolsheviks with a new and improved means of exerting population control. The principal victims were those in the Soviet Union and elsewhere who believed that the leopard had changed its spots.

A second wartime creature of Beria's was the organization *Smert Shpionam,* or Smersh. The name conveys the purpose of the organization: "Death to Spies." Under the command of Lieutenant General Viktor Semenovich Abakumov, a senior aide to Beria, Smersh operated from April 1942 to March 1946.[17] The title suggests a limited operational mission, which is deceptive. A collateral function of Smersh was to enforce Stalin's dictum: "Not one step back." To discharge its mission, Smersh rounded up all Soviet citizens who had been earlier overrun by the Germans and had lived for any period under German occupation. These were all considered, prima facie, German sympathizers or worse. Thousands were shot on the basis of "investigations" held in the field, and hundreds of thousands more were transported to the East.

With the Red Army on the attack, Smersh infantry, armor, and artillery units, of battalion or regimental size, were positioned behind Red Army units to kill those who fell behind or tried to retreat in the face of local German counterattacks. In a sense, the Smersh units were the logical extension or combat augmentation of the individual OOs assigned to the Red armed forces in earlier times; the OOs, who also shot "laggards," had advanced with the Red Army units to which they were assigned as political officers. The new order limited choices for the individual Russian soldier: He had a chance of survival if he continued the straight-ahead attack, but none if he retreated or refused to advance.

To tighten the noose around the Russian soldier's neck, Beria added a further order: All Russian POWs were deserters and would be shot if returned or recaptured. The basis for this fiat was the hard conviction, shared by both Stalin and Beria, that *any* Russian exposed to the West while not subject to NKVD control and observation was a potential security threat to the Bolshevik regime. It was wholly consistent with the hated Trotsky's prescription: "The Communist Party is maintained by recourse to every form of violence."

Although these facts were known to the handful of American advisers in the USSR during the war, they were unpleasant truths and, like other manifestations of Bolshevik methodology, were ignored, disavowed, or generally went unmentioned in official Washington. Some U.S. officials insisted that the United States had no right to question the way the Soviets treated their soldiers; however, this assertion ignores the fact that we had the means (in the form of Lend-Lease aid) to demand that Stalin and

Beria treat our true allies, the Russian fighting men, as human beings and not Bolshevik automatons. Rampant, organized inhumanity was not an abstraction; it was presumed to be the fundamental reason the war against the Nazis was being fought. America's relationship with her professed Soviet allies was explicitly predicated on acceptance of the principle that human life was precious and that we shared a common perception about the dignity and value of mankind.

In late July and early August 1941, as the German armies continued their apparently inexorable advance toward Stalingrad and Moscow, Richard Sorge reported on Japanese intentions. Sorge's reports contained two salient points, of which the more important at the time was word that Japanese forces were being withdrawn from Manchukuo and moved south in preparation for attacks on the Philippines and Southeast Asia. A second report, which was less precise and could not be confirmed by other means, was that the Japanese navy, in conjunction with other aggressive military operations, was preparing to attack British, Dutch, and U.S. naval forces in the Pacific.

Evidence to support Sorge's first point was sufficiently compelling for Stalin to order redeployment of the bulk of Soviet forces in the Far East across thousands of miles to the Soviet western front. The assault elements of those forces were first used to break the siege at Leningrad on December 7, 1941. Stalin's chronic distrust of intelligence agents was in this case suspended. He was disposed to believe because Sorge, on a visit to Moscow in 1936, had reported that Japan intended to move against China, not Russia. Sorge told Stalin that he would stake his life on the information. A year later, Sorge's prediction came true. This exchange impressed Stalin, who elevated Sorge to the rare distinction of "believable" spy.

The German armies continued to press their attack against the Soviets at terrific cost. This was especially true in the Stalingrad area. The tide of battle turned, and finally, in November 1942, the Russian forces encircled Stalingrad. The German armies, under Lieutenant General (later Marshal) Friedrich Paulus, surrendered on January 31, 1943.

The events leading to the Soviet victory at Stalingrad provided the final answers to Beria's intelligence questions cited earlier. Without depreciating the heroic efforts of the Russians in defeating the German armies, it must be stated that some advantage derived from Hitler's insistent blunders. The official Soviet history of the Great Patriotic War not improperly gives credit to the courage, skill, and tenacity of the Red Army.

The Russian conscripts were "citizen soldiers," led by an officer corps that had been all but destroyed in Stalin's mad purge of the Red Army.

Lacking professional leadership, the Russians still overcame the highly trained and wholly professional German forces, stemming their advance and eventually forcing their surrender. The undue credit given to Stalin in the earlier version of the history can be accounted for by the fact that Beria was still serving as the Kremlin's court historian. He saw to it that Generalissimo Stalin was credited with planning every phase of the Soviet victory. Western military historians tend to emphasize Hitler's obstinacy in refusing to allow his forces to withdraw to defensible positions for the winter so that they could resume the attack under more favorable conditions in the spring. Although Soviet and German explanations of the campaign differ, neither concedes that the most influential single factor in the Soviet success was the provision of U.S. military assistance, which enabled the Red Army initially to hold on and later to go over to the attack.

Official Soviet military histories denigrate the importance of U.S. aid, maintaining that it was minimal and didn't arrive until after the German surrender. Soviet deception on this point coincides with the Bolshevik party line. The facts are quite different.

President Franklin D. Roosevelt announced the decision to extend Lend-Lease aid to the USSR on November 7, 1941. This was exactly one month before the Japanese attack on Pearl Harbor and, fortunately, the same day that a reluctant U.S. Congress approved, by only one vote, the extension of the peacetime Selective Service Act. Had the act not been extended, all who had been conscripted, along with the federalized National Guard and the reserve components called up in 1940, would have been released automatically from the armed services. There would have been no legal basis, or money, to pay more than 75 percent of those in uniform on the day of the Pearl Harbor attack.

From November 7, 1941, to VE Day, May 7, 1945, the United States provided the USSR with more than 17 million long tons of cargo valued at over $9.5 billion (in 1940 dollars).[18] The mammoth volume of aid was no less important than was Roosevelt's decision itself.

Politically, Roosevelt's action in assisting the Russians was one of high risk. Winston Churchill thoroughly concurred in the decision and publicly supported Roosevelt. Congressional critics, mainly isolationists who opposed Lend-Lease in any form, were vociferous in their opposition. The U.S. military was deeply troubled, as they had been by the earlier decision to provide Lend-Lease assistance to Britain, at the prospect of additional war material being diverted to the USSR when it might be required for the U.S. buildup. Subsumed in their apprehensions was the conviction that the Russians were goners anyway, and that the much-needed equipment and supplies would eventually end up in German hands. The memory of Russia's 1917 exit from the First World War was also much in the minds of American military planners. In November 1941, the argument was not without merit. Roosevelt's countervailing claim was that the Russians were the only ones currently killing Germans.

Roosevelt prevailed, and the massive Lend-Lease supply line was opened. To a demonstrable degree, it was U.S. aid that enabled the Soviet Union to stop the Germans, contain them, and finally bring about the reversals that began with Stalingrad.

On December 7, 1941, the Japanese attacked Pearl Harbor and moved against the Philippines and other points in Southeast Asia. It was at this time that the stage was set for Hitler's third grave mistake, which was to be the greatest imaginable boon to the organs. It gave Beria his main-chance intelligence opportunity.

On December 8, 1941, Roosevelt addressed a grim and angry joint session of Congress. He called upon the members assembled for a declaration of war against Japan. Beria was unsure what effect such a declaration would have on the Soviet Union, then besieged by powerful German forces that were extending their penetrations deep into the Caucasus. Stalin had directed the preparation of an immediate plan to remove the seat of government from threatened Moscow to a point east of the Urals. It was the nadir of the Soviet Union.

Washington on December 8 was no less chaotic than Moscow had been on the day of the German surprise attack. The fact of war was obvious, but its vast implications were not. Much has been written about the effect of Pearl Harbor and its immediate aftermath.[19] Of these many accounts, few have examined the curious fact of Hitler's declaration of war on the United States on December 11, 1941.

Under the terms of the Tripartite Anti-Comintern Pact signed by Italy, Germany, and Japan, each had the obligation to come to the defense of the other signatories should they be attacked by a fourth power. When the Japanese attacked the United States, neither Italy nor Germany was bound to respond, since Japan had initiated the hostilities and was not, by definition, a member nation attacked. Similarly, Japan was under no obligation to join Germany against the Soviet Union, because Germany had launched the assault.

On December 11, Hitler made the still inexplicable decision to declare war on the United States. Instantly, the Soviet Union's status as a mere recipient of Lend-Lease assistance was transformed to that of de facto ally with Great Britain and the United States, with Germany as the common enemy. The Soviets were at war with Germany but not with Japan, and while the rest of the Allies fought Japan, Italy, and Germany, the Soviets stayed out of the Far Eastern conflict.

No rational explanation has been advanced that adequately accounts for Hitler's action. The documented record of events in the period 1938–1941 reflects instead a deliberate and clearly articulated policy on Hitler's part to avoid any action that might give Roosevelt a pretext for providing more extensive military aid to France and England. Even the *Abwehr* was enjoined against major intelligence operations in the United States.[20]

In September 1940, Roosevelt succeeded in effecting an exchange with Britain, by which the United States would acquire the use of British-owned Caribbean island bases and Britain would receive fifty overage U.S. destroyers. By March 11, 1941, the President had persuaded the Congress to pass the Lend-Lease Bill. Neither of these actions presented a grave or immediate threat to Hitler.

With the British Expeditionary Force's retreat from Dunkirk in the bleak period between May 26 and June 4, 1940, and the collapse of France on June 22, 1940, neither belligerent remained a military menace to Germany. France and Britain had been defeated on the Continent at a very modest cost in German blood and treasure. The German campaign in the West, once Hitler opted to end the "phony war," was swift and decisive.[21] Hitler's main enemy was the Soviet Union, and he rightly concluded that few Western tears would be shed if he moved east and eliminated for all time the Bolshevik cabal in Moscow.

From 1941 to the end of January 1943, the fate of the Russians hung by a slender thread. The North Atlantic convoys carrying U.S. Lend-Lease aid to the Soviet port of Murmansk were repeatedly attacked by packs of German U-boats and aircraft flying out of occupied Norway. At enormous sacrifice of men and ships, enough material got through to the Soviets to make possible the tide-turning victories after Stalingrad. The Soviet official history of the Great Patriotic War carefully avoids mention of the thousands of U.S. and Allied seamen who went to their deaths in the icy waters of the northern seas in support of the USSR.

By 1943, though much hard fighting still lay ahead, victory was assured. Allied successes were beginning to be determined, in large measure, by the overwhelming preponderance of military supplies produced by U.S. industry. Although the American contribution to the Soviet war effort is no secret to Western historians, a factor generally forgotten, if known at all, is the extraordinary exploitation of the Lend-Lease effort by the NKVD. In scale and scope it can be considered among the most remarkable undertakings in the history of espionage.

When Lend-Lease Aid for the USSR was approved, the Soviets had its commercial mission, Amtorg, in New York, and a relatively small mission in the Washington embassy. These two elements were charged with the task of buying whatever U.S. military supplies they could on a cash-and-carry basis. Prior to the approval of Soviet Lend-Lease, Amtorg and the mission operated on an *ad hoc* basis because of continued American uncertainty about the USSR's ability to pay its bills. The repudiation of past debts by the Soviet government twenty years earlier was still reverberating in the halls of Congress, and the Johnson Bill (forbidding the extension of credit to nations that had repudiated debts to the United States) was still on the books. The extremely fluid combat conditions in the Soviet Union did little to reassure American observers that the Soviets could endure to fight another day. Once Lend-Lease was approved and the combat situation somewhat stablized, it became feasible to begin to rationalize the USSR's military requirements. Instead of frantic calls to send "everything," an effort was made to resolve the requirements on the basis of need and availability.

The burgeoning mission in Washington (which was established and augmented by a staff from Amtorg) gave Beria the opportunity to perform the most astonishing feat imaginable to a leader of the organs. It had huge appeal because it combined deception, bad faith, misappropriation, and all the other characteristics that would appeal to Stalin. The prospect of simultaneously betraying trust, pulling off the largest programmatic theft in history, cleaning out the capitalist larder, and paying for it with a bad check was truly an opportunity to boggle the mind.

The early emergency transfer of U.S. military assistance had staved off imminent Soviet defeat. Now that the Congress had approved Lend-Lease, the Soviets could plunge headfirst into the American cornucopia of industrial know-how, an intelligence opportunity of rare and staggering dimensions. Beria grasped the import at once and, in early 1943, ordered that the Washington embassy's "Lend-Lease Coordinating Group" be disbanded and replaced by the "Soviet Purchasing Commission." To head the new organization, Red Army General Leonid Rudenko was dispatched to Washington. Rudenko, an old Honored Chekist, was a Beria loyalist with twenty-five hard years of service in the organs.

To assist Rudenko in his labors approximately one thousand GRU and NKVD officers were assigned to the commission in Washington as "purchasing specialists," along with "experts" from Amtorg. Their mission was to buy anything and everything thought necessary to win the Great Patriotic War. Along the way they were to collect, borrow, or steal anything they could carry. As a collateral duty, the Soviet "buyers" were to bribe and attempt the subornation of any interesting, influential, or powerful American with whom they came into contact. To suggest that this omnivorous approach to intelligence collection was ineffective is to fail to comprehend the scale on which it was carried out. Industrial processes, entire turnkey refineries, strategic raw materials, scientific instruments, radio-manufacturing plants, glass, steel, natural rubber, and thousands of designs, drawings, patents, and proprietary secrets sluiced

out to the USSR by air and sea. In addition, garnering detailed maps of
the United States and aerial photographs of major cities (hardly useful
against the Germans), plus "inspection" visits to aircraft, tank, and weapons manufacturing facilities, rounded out a busy schedule for Rudenko's
battalions of foragers.

The Soviet Purchasing Commission abused and exploited every extension of good faith and trust by Americans who were anxious to aid
the Allied cause. Rudenko himself was perfectly cast in his role as
the friendly Russian who enjoyed an occasional drink with the boys. At
the National Press Club, where he relaxed from his exertions, he told
jokes of which he was the butt while teaspooning subtle deceptions into
the gaping maws of willing American journalists. Rudenko, who understood English and spoke it with unusual fluency, posed disarmingly as the
smiling peasant thrust into the company of superior beings and hoping
only to be accepted as a simple, though inferior, man.

Today, forty years after the fact, it is still difficult to understand how
it was possible for the corporate United States to have been so unknowing, uninformed, and unconcerned about Rudenko and his commission.
The Soviets, too, must disbelieve the improbable tales told by the "old
boys" at the Center who served in Washington during the war.

The acceptance of the USSR as a bona fide ally, the willingness to
ignore all previous direct experience with the Bolsheviks, and the insistent repetition of the guiding motto of Father Flanagan's Boys Town—
"There is no such thing as a bad boy"—contributed to the popular light-
headedness. The misperceptions were greatly aided by an enthusiastic if
undiscerning press, ignorance, and a widely shared, monumental naïveté.
In every respect, a form of incredible national arrogance led us to sus-
pend all critical faculties and to embark on this high-cost excess of prof-
ligacy.

The Soviets' reputation as inveterate political criminals was hard-won
over a long period of time, yet simply because they had been attacked by
Hitler, they had been transformed as if by magic into Jeffersonian democrats. Then, as now, it was not very stylish to speak of their bloody trail
in Spain, the man-made famines, the forced-labor camps, the murders
and assassinations, the Great Purges, the cowardly attack on Finland, the
occupation of eastern Poland, the cynical nonaggression pact with Hitler.
To mention such past transgressions was prima facie proof of fascist tendencies. Early Soviet efforts to influence the major U.S. news outlets
were beginning to pay huge dividends. An afternoon spent in a public
library reviewing the newspapers of the day confirms the point with compelling evidence.

It would not be fair to suggest that this wave of uncritical acceptance
of Soviet intentions engulfed everyone. There were many who under-

stood the dangers and gave timely warning. As early as 1934, one such summary of Soviet intentions was advanced by Captain William Dilworth Puleston, director of Naval Intelligence. Puleston, after meeting the first Soviet naval attachés to Washington, Paul Yurevitch Oras and his assistant Alexander M. Yakimichev (neither of whom were naval officers), was repelled by their patent dishonesty and arrogant demands, their boorishness, overbearing manners, and manifest contempt for the United States. The Soviets demanded free access to navy yards, ships, bases, and civilian factories producing defense material. They insisted on visits to the Naval Air Station in San Diego and copies of the engineering drawings of the fast new battleship *North Carolina,* as well as a several-volume register of the specifications for the aircraft carrier *Saratoga.* These "requests" were not those of conventional naval attachés but the attempted extortions of agents of a totalitarian state.

Oras, born in Reval in 1897, had joined the Imperial Navy as a fireman in the Baltic Fleet. At the time of the Soviet coup, "he corralled his officers in fire rooms and bunkers, imprisoned them and then disposed of them by throwing them into the boilers. . . ."[22]

Having established his worthiness, Oras was brought into the Cheka, trained, and sent to Turkey as a "naval observer." Shortly thereafter, the Turks expelled him for complicity in espionage. His next assignment was to Riga, but the Latvian government, knowing his field of specialization, refused to accept him. By 1926 he was accredited to the Scandinavian countries and based in Stockholm, where he played a significant role in the Norberg naval espionage case in Sweden. By 1928 both Norway and Sweden demanded his recall. After a brief return to the USSR, Oras was dispatched to Greece as naval attaché, then quickly withdrawn for his involvement in the subornation of Greek sailors. Four months later he arrived in Rome to practice his art and was there notified that he had been selected to serve as the first Soviet naval attaché in Washington. There is much evidence to suggest that Oras was better prepared for his assignment than were the Americans.

In June 1934 Oras, Yakimichev, and Sokoloff of the Amtorg Trading Corporation descended on the Norfolk Navy Yard and demanded a limousine to travel around the base. When informed that no such privilege would be extended, they became loud and abusive. Their purpose was to make a reconnaissance, to identify objects of interest, and to verify the locations of buildings in which sensitive work was under way. The first attempt failed, but ten years later the Soviets had their own office at Norfolk with parking places, rationed gas, and all the access credentials they could carry.[23]

Puleston's warnings went unheeded except within the U.S. Navy, where he was preaching to the converted.

Roosevelt's initial decision to alter U.S. relations with the USSR was based on tainted evidence. During the presidential campaign prior to his first election, anything that sounded like a repudiation or reversal of Herbert Hoover's administration was effective politics. But Hoover's view of the Soviet Union was based on direct knowledge, while FDR's understanding of the Bolsheviks came from a highly questionable quarter, *New York Times* correspondent Walter Duranty. The celebrated promise of "Soviet trade" was disinterred and again trotted around the course. It was not a bad issue in the depths of a depression with millions of Americans unemployed.

Roosevelt, armed with extraordinary manipulative skills, exuded reassuring confidence in his ability to cope with gargantuan problems. He was bold, imaginative, and chief victim of his own patrician arrogance. The Department of State was divided on the issue of recognition of the USSR. The older, more experienced officers who had been exposed to the Soviets were uniformly against a dramatic reversal in policy without a number of important preconditions. This group included Robert Kelley, Loy W. Henderson, Breckinridge Long, and others.

The younger, more aggressive men who saw new career opportunities were enthusiastic proponents of change. Chief among this group was George F. Kennan, who eventually rose to be the U.S. ambassador to the USSR. He was assigned to Riga in 1933, and when the new Roosevelt administration began to discuss details of the proposed diplomatic exchange with the USSR, he returned to Washington to lobby for his inclusion in the new mission staff that William C. Bullitt was organizing. Bullitt was confident that a new, open policy might succeed in overcoming the damage done by sixteen years of U.S. refusal to accept the reality of the Soviet state. Initially, Bullitt had boundless goodwill, energy, and a strong personal conviction that once a U.S. mission was established in Moscow, the earlier mutual antagonisms would soon evaporate. Instead, it was Bullitt's own fervor that eroded. The Soviets' chronic intransigence, suspicion, and refusal to credit the Americans with good faith gradually persuaded Bullitt that he had completely misinterpreted the true intentions of the Kremlin. However, many of the younger officers remained optimistic about the prospects for improving relations. When Joseph E. Davies succeeded Bullitt in 1936, there was a sense among the junior officers that the problems required new and different solutions. Among these was the possibility that the Soviets' obduracy and uncooperativeness might be justifiably attributed to their fundamental fear of insincerity on the part of the United States. Davies accepted the position that if the Americans exhibited a more positive attitude, the Soviets would be reassured and responsive. Davies was prepared to overlook or depreciated the same signals that had led to Bullitt's conviction that it was the Soviet government that was insincere.

Many years later, when Kennan returned to Moscow as ambassador in 1952, he again dedicated himself to improving U.S.-USSR relations only to find the same intractable Soviet resolve to obstruct his efforts. During a visit to Germany while he was ambassador to the USSR, Kennan made a public statement that seemed calculated to give deliberate offense to the Soviets. The Soviet interpretation of Kennan's remarks resulted in their refusal to allow his return to Moscow. During this period when he was under great stress, Kennan informed a U.S. official on June 26, 1953: "I fear that there is a good possibility that I will wind up someday before long on the Soviet radio. I may be forced to make statements that would be damaging to American policy. This letter will show the world that I am under duress and am not making statements under my own free will."[24]

Recently, Kennan has used his considerable prestige in support of the nuclear peace movement. He has attacked U.S. policy, pointing out that after all, the United States made and dropped the first atom bomb and the Soviets have every reason to fear that we'll do it again.

To go back in time: U.S.-Soviet relations, under the influence of the younger experts, regrettably failed to effect policies that were anything more than genteel accessions to the continuing extortions and abuses of the Soviets. In a sense, it really didn't matter. Roosevelt had no intention of consulting the Department of State on such an important foreign affairs issue. He was more attentive to whispered insights from internationalists within his own entourage. As President-elect, he was briefed at length by Walter Duranty, the Moscow correspondent for *The New York Times* and a close personal friend of Stalin's.[25]

Duranty achieved his preeminence as Stalin's favorite foreign correspondent by his willingness to report Bolshevik blather with scrupulous attention to detail. It must have been an entertaining pastime, made more enjoyable by the fact that his sponsor, *The New York Times,* paid high prices to run it. When not taking dictation from Stalin, Duranty entertained the Moscow press corps and saw to it that the more deserving of the members received cordial receptions from Soviet officials and the less deserving did not. As a result of his tireless exertions on behalf of Stalin and *The New York Times,* Duranty was awarded the Pulitzer Prize in 1932 for his Moscow reporting. With that award, he became the Western world's foremost certified "Soviet expert," and he was ideally prepared to give FDR advice.

The chief of Naval Operations, Admiral William H. Standley, later U.S. ambassador to the USSR, described the Russian successes in the thirties: ". . . Russian attachés, military, naval and commercial, picked up everything, copies of all technical and trade magazines, military and professional journals, blueprints, and everything else including nuts, bolts and washing machines, tractors and combine harvesters."[26]

When these rapacious acts were reported, the Soviet apologists would explain that the USSR was a "struggling nation" and that the United States was at fault for its lack of forgiveness. It was essentially the same argument advanced when an ax murderer is represented to the jury as having been motivated by flaws in the society. The implication was that lack of tolerance and insistence on the enforcement of certain arbitrary rules (laws) could only produce a wave of similar crimes. It will be remembered that prior to the revolution, the Bolsheviks, made the same sort of public representations. However, once they were in power, the all-purpose sociological genie who could explain everything was put back into the bottle while the government built the greatest array of coercive labor camps and penitentiaries in the world.

Although the Great Patriotic War was expensive in that it cost many millions of Russian lives, it was a profitable investment for the organs. The war was a positive force in the modernization and development of the NKVD and GRU. It seemed that each crisis provided new opportunities for expanding and extending the services. The United States, in an effort to strengthen the Soviet military, provided technical data of immense worth. The OSS Research and Analysis element produced studies that were pioneering efforts at using multidisciplinary approaches to major problems. These R&A reports provided the Soviets with an extraordinary base on which to build a strong analytical capability.

Simultaneously, Beria was able to broaden the avenues of penetration owing to the ecumenical dizziness that prevailed. To a remarkable degree, the success of the organs was directly related to our misperceptions of our new ally. Major General Edwin L. Sibert, chief of intelligence to General Omar N. Bradley, and later to the Allied supreme commander, General Dwight D. Eisenhower, addressed the subject directly. Sibert wrote about counterintelligence problems in 1944–1946, during the campaign in northwest Europe and the following occupation of Germany:

> As our intelligence operations developed, we began to see that there was an intelligence service in Europe—a substrata of society would be an accurate term for it—far more proficient and omnipresent than that of the Germans.
>
> That was the apparat of the old Communist International, which Lenin formed back in 1919 to spread the world revolution of the proletariat. Those apparats were everywhere, even in our own ranks and those of the Allied Armies.
>
> It was plain to me that the members of the apparats were loyal not to their own leaders or capitals but to Stalin and the Kremlin.
>
> They became a matter of concern to me because they were

armed, disciplined, and experienced underground fighters. We had to consider the possibility that if there was a war between Russia and the United States at the conclusion of WWII, as many thought there would be, we would find these people fighting us in our rear as they had fought the Germans.

I brought the matter to the attention of both Bradley and Eisenhower, and Bradley asked me to prepare a paper on the Communist International in a hurry. I gave the problem to the chief of counterintelligence, but when we began to look for people who knew anything about this phenomenon, we found that there was nobody in the higher command who knew very much about the International.

In the end, we had to go to British intelligence and to the records of the German intelligence services and to employ two Belgian trade unionists who were familiar with the problem. We had four million men, and we could not find one who could write a five page report on the International.

Well, the report was prepared, and we paid for it, but when I put the bill in to the fiscal people, they wrote back to me to ask why I had found it necessary to make a report on an Allied organization![27]

At the time General Sibert was attempting to take some minimal measurements of the threat, the British were conducting an independent audit of their own. A number of operations, mounted by the British Special Operations Executive (SOE) in the Low Countries, Italy, and most particularly France, had come undone with varying degrees of misfortune. Betrayals, communications compromises, and undue casualties suggested that operational security had been breached.

The study concluded that *no* SOE operation involving contact with local partisans was not subject to monitoring by disciplined Communist Party members who kept the Soviets informed. *No* escape and evasion net operated without the participation of CP members. (In many instances, the communication links and escape and evasion nets had been originally organized by the Communist parties.)

The dispatch of OSS paramilitary teams into Yugoslavia was conducted on the suspect premise that all armed resistance to the Germans served the Allied cause. In fact, aid to Tito was encouraged and facilitated, while Mihajlovic's Chetniks found themselves on a thin diet. Long before the end of the war, the Soviets began to circulate charges that Mihajlovic was colluding with the Germans and that only Tito was deserving of assistance. The various missions dispatched to Yugoslavia were airlifted by the "Balkan Air Force," a joint British-American team. Some of the crews wore red stars on their caps, which boded ill for any Americans scheduled to be dropped into the Mihajlovic areas. On a night drop, putting a jumper out over the Adriatic or into German-held territory was an easy and cost-effective method of assuring that Tito would eventually prevail. Among those overseeing the dispatch of the various missions was Major James Klugmann, a luminary in the British CP and school chum of Philby and Burgess. Klugmann and others promoted Tito and denigrated the Chetniks. As hostilities were drawing to a close, the British Foreign Office agreed that Mihajlovic should be turned over to the victorious Tito as a war criminal. Mihajlovic and many of his staff were subsequently "tried" and executed. Klugmann's office helped engineer a few more political murders and another successful coup for Stalin. Whatever satisfactions came of his efforts, Klugmann had to revise his notions of the historical imperative in 1948 when the beloved Tito broke with Stalin.

Meanwhile, Soviet penetration of the U.S. government was extensive and included a number of medium-level OSS personnel and others assigned to the departments of State, Commerce, Navy, Interior, War, and Treasury. (A partial listing appears as an appendix.)

Espionage on behalf of the Soviet organs held very little serious risk for an American citizen. In many instances there were strong reservations about prosecuting Americans. For the first time the "graymail" issue arose to becloud the scene. (Graymail is a tactic used by the defense in a trial with national security implications, to call on the government to make disclosures of data that are, in fact, of little relevance to the trial. The object is to pressure the prosecution into agreeing to scale down the charges rather than to disclose sensitive information.) Because of a reluctance on the part of the government to produce sources and disclose methods, the Justice Department opted for prosecution on charges other than espionage. Alger Hiss and Mark Zborowski were convicted of perjury, William Weisband of contempt, and others were not brought to trial because a public hearing would have been of too great assistance to the Soviets in planning new penetrations. The government had to resort to scaled-down but—as in the case of Al Capone's conviction for income tax evasion—no less effective means of arranging for the convicted to see the inside of a federal prison. However, although justice was perhaps served by the successful convictions, the sentences imposed were invariably shorter than would have resulted from espionage prosecutions.

By way of contrast, Soviet trials in matters relating to "internal security" have always been conducted along different lines. The fact that an individual has even been charged is evidence of guilt. (The organs don't make mistakes!) The courts may be open (for propaganda purposes) or closed. The trials may be conducted by the military or by civilian authorities. The judge's principal function is to attempt to reconcile the sentence with whatever punishment has already been decided upon by the organs. If appeals are permitted, it is because the defendant has agreed to confess publicly in exchange for some unstated grant of privilege by the government, such as false assurance that family survivors will not be punished for the same crime.

Some of the theatrics observed in the Great Purges of the late thirties set the tone. The defendants were permitted to believe that their confessions and their willingness to corroborate the complicity of others would be exchanged for the safety of their families. Following their charges, confessions, and disclosures in open court, they were executed. The families immunity, so expensively bought by the victims and so freely given by the organs, was promptly repudiated, and the wives, children, and parents of the deceased were shipped off to die in the camps.

There can be little doubt that the lack of suitable sanctions against American citizens, and the uneven application of those that did exist, made it easier for the Soviets to recruit U.S. intelligence assets to their cause. Even in cases where convictions were achieved, it has been invariably true that a stream of books, articles, and essays protesting the court's action followed immediately. This is not to say that all those who were and are critical of U.S. handling of these espionage cases are Soviet agents. What is evident is that the Soviets were actively engaged in programs of propaganda and disinformation in order to discredit the U.S. government in any way possible. Their seeds of discord found especially fertile ground among many intellectuals abroad, whose writings have often been translated and published in the United States. The Soviets learned long ago that the public memory of events seldom retains factual data for more than a few weeks. They also comprehend the arithmetic of demography, and can count on the fact that there are many new millions who never heard of Julius and Ethel Rosenberg, Alger Hiss, Harry Dexter White, or Harry Gold. The purpose is to convey the impression that they were victims of hysteria, McCarthyism, or anti-Semitism, and that all U.S. institutions, in varying degrees, colluded in falsifying the record, intimidating witnesses, and abusing or suspending the law. These charges are made with the certain knowledge that very few Americans are interested in much more than a single declarative sentence to summarize the facts. The cases are inherently complex, making it possible to substitute irrelevant but memorable points for the public.

By the end of the war, Beria, like a latter-day Silas Marner, had "gold" in a great many scattered accounts. The postwar climate in the United States was very favorable. In October 1945, President Harry Truman disestablished the OSS, signaling the end of the flow of valuable Research and Analysis reports from which so much had been gained. In addition to this loss, was the emotion-driven rush to demobilize the U.S. armed forces, which meant a corresponding dismantling of U.S. intelligence resources in Europe. As suggested by General Sibert, the United States became dependent on the British for information about the Soviets.

The British M.I.6 was also undergoing an abrupt transition from large wartime organization to small peacetime establishment. In the process a few of the outstanding war-temporary officers were asked to remain on in the service. Two of the most promising among these were Harold Adrian Russell Philby and George Blake. Anticipating problems with the USSR, the British had organized a new section in 1944 to focus on the developing issues and growing threats posed by the Soviets now that their strategic borders had moved to the edge of Western Europe. Philby, who had previously been concerned with counterespionage operations in the Iberian peninsula, headed the new section. His selection for this critical position warmed many hearts at the Center. Philby and Blake were *nash*.[28]

Philby's recruitment by the Soviets had occurred in the early thirties when, having left Cambridge, he went off to inspect depression-ridden Europe. While in Vienna he was caught up in the clash between the conservative Austrian government and the Moscow-manipulated "oppressed workers." It was adventure time for young Harold, and his six weeks of romantic pretense as a revolutionary groupie put him into close contact with a young communist woman, Alice (Lizi) Friedman, to whom he was briefly married.

Returning to a highly structured England, the new Mrs. Philby took her derivative British citizenship and passport and departed for the Continent. His father, St. John Philby, was a practicing eccentric who wrote indignant letters to *The Times* when he wasn't sharing roast camel hump with Arabian royalty in the Saudi desert. St. John abhorred convention, converted to Islam, and did what he could to give young Harold a bizarre patrimony.

With war imminent, M.I.6 was on the lookout for prospective officers. Guy Burgess, a sodden, sodomitical schoolmate of Philby's, set up an interview with Miss Maxie of M.I.6. Her father had been the head of the Northern Department of the Foreign Office and was considered an authority on Russia and, later, the USSR. Miss Maxie found Harold a self-effacing, bright young man with an engaging stutter. After the interview, Burgess reinforced Maxie's favorable impressions, and in time, Philby was taken into M.I.6. Burgess was also *nash*.

The U.S. occupation authorities in Germany under General Lucius Clay looked to the denazified, ex-*Abwehr* experts to lend a hand on the Soviet problem. The element most experienced in dealing with the Soviets was the group that had served under General Reinhard Gehlen in the Foreign Armies East. As the Eastern Front crumbled under the growing force of the Red Army's offensive, Gehlen had had the presence of mind to look to the future. He judged, with great accuracy, that someone with his rare skills and knowledge would be useful to the Americans at a later date. As the confusion in the German forces mounted, Gehlen, with a small staff and vital files, moved into an area where he was certain to be overrun by U.S. forces.

Following his capture, he proposed to the authorities that he might be in a position to assist them in Soviet matters. His plan was carefully examined, and after a year, Gehlen was encouraged to organize the outline of a West German service. The Soviets' insistence on the permanent partition of Germany raised grave political, economic, and military problems, which the Soviets deliberately aggravated.

In the custom of most chiefs, Gehlen sought recruits among his wartime officers and succeeded in persuading many that they had an obligation to lend their talents to the emerging Federal State. It was not until many years later that several of these *alte kameraden* recruits also proved to be *nash*.

Beria had good reason to feel that he had done a workmanlike job of penetrating the British and, by surrogate, the Americans. In every respect it had been a very good war for the NKVD.

Stalin, meanwhile, always suspicious of success, pressed Beria to get at the atomic target, pointing out that the NKVD had failed to keep the USSR abreast of developments in the secret British-American research programs. Stalin dismissed Beria's accomplishments to date and suggested that Beria justify his continuing worth by demonstrating some success in the nuclear field. Through many and varied sources the Soviets had become acutely aware of the major British effort, known as Tube Alloys, and the massive, highly classified Manhattan Project in the United States.

Klaus Fuchs, a German political refugee and very able scientist, was recruited by Tube Alloys and taken into the heart of the British effort. When Fuchs realized that the British had excluded Soviet participation, he took the initiative and made contact with the Soviet embassy in London. Fuchs, as a youthful ideologue, had been active in the KPD but on his departure to England had dropped all ties to the party. The Soviet embassy arranged for a clandestine contact with a very experienced GRU officer "married" to a Briton who, with her brother, managed him until his departure for Canada in the early forties.

The Soviet government had been excluded from participation in the atomic weapons programs primarily because, aside from a few distinguished Russian theoretical physicists, the Soviets were not competent to contribute to the work. Further, by their adamant refusal to honor commitments, they had lost the trust and confidence of the British and Americans directing the programs.

Stalin wanted the organs to bring the Soviets up to speed on the new technology and looked to Beria to get a clear indication of every aspect of the work being done in the United States and Canada. To avoid more of Stalin's humbling attacks, Beria organized a major effort designed to penetrate the programs and to rob the West of its advantage in the field of atomic research.

Donald Maclean, a British member of the U.S.-British-Canadian atomic projects, provided the NKVD with important information about refinements in the program subsequent to the successful detonation of the weapons at Hiroshima and Nagasaki. To exploit the technical data Maclean was able to steal, the NKVD had the exceptional scientific abilities of Bruno Pontecorvo, an Italian nuclear physicist who had worked in the Manhattan Project. Both Maclean and Pontecorvo were *nash,* and later, when security forces moved to arrest them, they used their Soviet-planned exit routes to escape to the USSR.

Fuchs, serving as a cross-check, gave Harry Gold samples of the barrier material developed for use in the gigantic U.S. gaseous diffusion plant. The material was a porous membrane needed in the enrichment process to separate the heavier from the lighter particles of the $UF6$ gas circulating through the system. In an independent circuit, but again using Harry Gold as the contact, a penetration by David Greenglass of the facility at Los Alamos, New Mexico, provided data on the "lens" that was the reliable engineering basis for the trigger, or detonating device, in the weapon.

Associated with David Greenglass was his brother-in-law, Julius Rosenberg, who was an electrical engineer. In time Gold, Rosenberg, his wife, Ethel, and her brother, Greenglass, were arrested. Gold and Greenglass cooperated with the federal authorities and implicated both Rosenbergs. All were tried and convicted for espionage. The Soviets moved quickly to broadcast their version of the event. The Rosenbergs were cast as victims of resurgent anti-Semitism, and Gold, Greenglass, and even the federal judge who tried the case (all of whom were Jewish), as paid betrayers of the innocent.

The Soviet service directed one of their illegals in the United States to place $5,000 in a tin can and bury the can in a New York state park; it would be picked up later and used in support of the defendants. It wasn't until the same illegal defected much later that it was learned from him that he had not buried the money but instead had converted it to his own use.[29]

The incontrovertible evidence of the Rosenbergs' complicity was never used. It consisted of NKVD cipher traffic, intercepted and decrypted by the United States, which identified the members of the net by name. The former chief of the FBI unit that handled the case has unsuccessfully sought the public release of the intercepts so that the Rosenberg case might finally and conclusively end. In the absence of these proofs the case is still being tried in campus lectures, Public Television docudramas, and revisionist tracts from the progressive press.

A recent book, based on a meticulous and scholarly study of the vast accumulation of documents on the subject, concluded that despite a variety of defects in both the defense and the prosecution, the Rosenbergs were, undeniably, Soviet agents.[30] The researchers, Ronald Radosh and Joyce Milton, were rewarded for their efforts in a letter from Julius Rosenberg's sister that was printed in *Time* magazine on September 26, 1983, pointing out that "the lies and smears prevalent to this day have blinded Radosh and Milton to the truth of the Rosenbergs' total innocence." The real criminal, we are informed, was "J. Edgar Hoover, who was desperately searching for radicals in the early 1950s and was falsely accusing left-wing dissidents of espionage." The letter accuses David Greenglass of lying, and for those who do not take the time to examine the facts, the legend of the Rosenbergs' innocence lives on.

In addition to Pontecorvo, who could judge the value and explain the significance of the material Maclean acquired, Beria was able to bring Dr. Alan Nunn May, a distinguished Canadian physicist, into the NKVD's band of brothers. In France, Frédéric Joliot-Curie, an ardent Stalinist, contributed his abilities. With such a talented roster of players on the NKVD team, Beria was able to report to Stalin that the Soviet effort to acquire nuclear weapons would be achieved forthwith, and on a very cost-effective basis.

The NKVD's performance in the area of atomic espionage was remarkable. Although many scientists rationalize cooperation with the Soviets on the popularized notion that "ideas know no boundaries" the cooperation greatly exceeded trafficking in ideas. It took the form of detailed drawings, samples of enriched material, the barrier substance, the trigger mechanism, and flow charts of the manufacturing process.

Perhaps the most significant "secret" was the precise data regarding failures in the program. The United States was able to support *concurrent* research and development in many different approaches to the enormously expensive and complex methods of enrichment. The cost in money, material, and extraordinary scientific talent would have made it impossible for the Soviets to replicate these efforts. Because the Soviets had detailed accounts from suborned scientists, they were able to avoid the costly and inefficient routes that the United States had explored and found unproductive of a reliable, continuous method of enrichment.

After weighing the alternatives, the United States embarked on the most likely course, gaseous diffusion, and built the great facilities at Oak Ridge, Tennessee, and Hanford, Washington, which consumed almost one quarter of all the electrical energy generated in the whole of the United States at the time. Through espionage alone, the Soviets were spared the unaffordable costs of experimentation. The detonation of the Soviet weapon as early as 1949 was a tribute to the NKVD's espionage and to its foresight in rounding up the German scientists in the eastern zone and coercing their participation in the early design work.

After the fact it was estimated that the NKVD's contributions, including the Germans, enabled the Soviet program to shorten the development and manufacturing process by three to four years.

Though Stalin kept Beria on a short leash, Beria's awesome bureaucratic powers were not curtailed. They are worthy of note:

As the people's commissar of internal affairs, Beria was a member of the cabinet, and as commissar of state security, he was the supreme commander of his own NKVD army, comprising more than 1.5 million officers and soldiers. His troops consisted of divisions of infantry, cavalry, motorized troops, artillery, tanks, and an independent air force. With these forces, Beria kept order and control in all the republics, among the nationalities and remote tribes in the Soviet Union. In addition, he operated the OO political officers who permeated the Red Army, Navy, and Air Force.

As chief of the militia, Beria controlled every individual in the USSR, including all members of the CPSU.

As chief of intelligence, counterintelligence, and espionage, Beria supervised the entire foreign operation of the Ministry of Foreign Affairs, including diplomats, trade delegates, ambassadors, and Soviet participation in all multinational meetings and conferences.

As chief censor, he directed the Soviet press, radio, theater, film industry, and book publishing. Further, he controlled the entire communications system—all telegraph, telephone, and postal services (which were all under constant surveillance) in the USSR—and supervised the monitors who governed all contact by these means with every foreign area.

As chief supervisor of religion, he opened a few churches for the edification of wartime foreign visitors to Moscow. The reopening of the churches was also in support of another deception: Stalin's effort to survive by making the Great Patriotic War a Russian rather than a Bolshevik war. This was widely praised as new evidence of liberalism under Stalin.

As head of the gulag (the administration of the forced labor camps), Beria also controlled the mechanism that manufactured prisoners, who were in constant demand. The prisoners made up the low-cost work force that kept the country running while the Red Army fought the war. The courts, judges, prosecutors, and lawyers—in fact, the whole judiciary apparatus that hurried them on to the camps—was operated by Beria.

As the head of transport (chief of transportation, communications, and road construction), he controlled all movement within the country.

As head of propaganda, Beria directed the foreign Communist parties, particularly those in the United States, Great Britain, France, and Italy.

As chief of Smersh, Beria's control over the Red Army was extended to the battlefield; in the Navy, it went to sea; and it also went into the skies with the Air Force.[31]

Beria's enumerated burdens were only collateral functions to the main task of pleasing Stalin and meeting all of the Generalissimo's demands. His survival was a measure either of his genius or of his single-minded pursuit of power. Beria, like Dzerzhinsky, was an exceedingly complex individual who defies simple analysis.

Unlike Dzerzhinsky, who was disposed to be an ascetic, Beria is sometimes dismissed as a power-driven degenerate who routinely used his position to abduct and forcibly deflower teen-aged virgins. Although the charges are true, they deflect attention from the real essence of his ability to grasp and exploit the weaknesses and vulnerabilities of the Western democracies, which were so ill equipped to protect themselves from a dimly perceived ideological enemy. Beria brought the organs into the international field as a powerful weapon. By his unquestioned skills, he used them evenhandedly against the USSR's armed enemies as well as her generously trusting allies.

The Soviet resident in the United States reported from New York, in 1945, that America was firmly committed to a policy of complete demobilization, which conveyed the unequivocal message that the United States thought the war was over. To the Soviet mind, however, the war had simply moved into a new phase. The American abandonment of overwhelming military power was incomprehensible to Beria and Stalin, and neither of them was fully convinced that this was fact. Stalin, with his paranoid view of the world, saw the complete demobilization as a possible deception by Truman to induce the Soviet Union into an action that could produce a punitive atomic attack by the United States. Stalin's marshals, however, did not share this view. In May 1946, they were able to convince Stalin that they could and should seize and occupy their feeble neighbor Iran.

Stalin approved the plan, but with strong personal reservations. President Truman immediately communicated, through the U.S. naval commander on the scene, that if the Soviets crossed into Iran, they would be met by atomic weapons. Stalin, as was his custom, retreated in the face of force. The Red Army was directed to strike tents and vacate any thought of direct challenge to the United States.

This particular interchange, which has long since been obscured by other history, was important primarily for its effects on the NKVD. It was now obvious that the American President was acting on the basis of intelligence, and the organs were charged with identifying the sources. Once identified, a massive effort would be undertaken to eliminate, compromise, co-opt, and otherwise reduce the credibility and effect of these sources.

It was at this point that a curious congruence of events occurred. The Soviet resident's reporting was clear in insisting that the U.S. wartime intelligence elements were being disbanded. Truman's executive order abolishing the OSS was a matter of public record. Major General William Donovan, who had organized and led OSS, was bluntly dismissed by Truman. All the signs pointed in confirmation of the resident's reports.

The U.S. service, which had not quite lost its reputation as an enthusiastic though amateur intelligence agency, was going out of business. The end of the OSS and the departure of Donovan persuaded Beria that the United States was indeed engaged in unilateral intelligence disarmament. It was another unanticipated opportunity for exploitation by the organs. But Beria's assumptions were suddenly contradicted by Truman's direct and resolute stand on Iran, plus his subsequent authorization of the Central Intelligence Group (CIG). Beria paused to consider whether he had underestimated U.S. intentions.

Soviet reporting from Washington was not particularly illuminating. CIG was engaged in planning and not operations (or was it?). There were plentiful reports attesting to its excessive secretiveness and efficiency on the one hand, and its bureaucratic and operational silliness on the other. Beria knew enough about bureaucracies to predict that any new organization, to survive, must first fight off the old-line organizations that stood to be most affected by the change. He knew that his unwitting allies in the first phase would be the U.S. Army, the U.S. Navy, and the FBI, none of which would willingly endorse a new and weak competitor. Wartime spending had stopped. Once again, the squabbles over limited resources might very well starve the CIG into an early grave.

The jury was out until 1947, when the Congress enacted the National Security Act, which established the new Department of Defense, the U.S. Air Force, and the Central Intelligence Agency. Although creation of the CIA was something of an afterthought in the National Security Act, the Agency did provide a bureaucratic home for the interim CIG and its personnel. Many of these people were "detailees" from the armed forces. Others were ex-OSS agents who had retained their World War II cover assignments to other government agencies, such as the Department of Commerce, after President Truman had officially disbanded the OSS.

The defection of Igor Gouzenko from the Soviet embassy in Ottawa had occurred almost exactly one year before. Gouzenko gave the Canadian authorities documents confirming the growing suspicions that the Soviets had engaged in widespread espionage against Britain, Canada, and the United States throughout the war. The Gouzenko disclosures and the subsequent prosecution of Canadian nationals who had been recruited by the organs shocked the citizens of all three countries. At the same time, the FBI was beginning to move against the Soviet surrogates who had participated in NKVD operations against the United States. The investigations were greatly aided by veterans of the organs who became apostates after seeing Stalin's reinstitution of harsh repression following the Great Patriotic War.

Beria reasoned that the new CIA would probably begin at the beginning and recruit new staff. Since the main thrust of the organization was to blunt the Soviet Union's expansion, it could be termed "anti-Soviet" in nature. "Anti-Soviet" was an important pejorative: It meant that whoever was so accused was automatically "fascist," although the real fascists were still on display at the War Crimes Trials in Germany. Being fascist also conveyed an unalterable flavor of anti-Semitism.

Without moving from his chair, Beria launched the first attack on the CIA. It was a creature of Wall Street, staffed by privileged sons from the Ivy League. It was controlled by the "establishment," well known for its anti-Semitic biases. The CIA's purpose was to make the world a colony operated for profit by U.S. business and dedicated to the suppression of freedom-loving people everywhere. It was not a bad start for a propaganda campaign.

On the basis of Soviet reporting, Beria continued to view the CIA with disdain. He did not dismiss the possibility that it might one day become a significant opponent. To preclude this eventuality the new organization was examined, dissected, and analyzed in terms of what it might do and how it might be thwarted in achieving its objectives.

Similar studies were made of the special conditions in the UK and France, where earlier NKVD penetrations of the older European services had contributed much information. For instance, "Kim" Philby was uniquely qualified to provide insights into the way American intelligence operated (based on his extensive contacts with the OSS in London) and, more important, into the character of U.S. personnel with whom he had served. There were instances of truly remarkable successes based on the peculiar talents of such individuals as Van Deman, Yardley, and Friedman, but there were an even greater number of failures based on anomalies in the U.S. government's decisions not to act but to defer, to neglect, or otherwise to lose advantages. In the main, the history of U.S. intelligence gave very few reliable indicators of what could be expected of the CIA. According to a senior Soviet defector, Beria confessed that the

Americans eluded him because they were "like turtles who ventured out and then returned to their holes in the sand."[32]

Beria's incomprehension is difficult to fault since President Truman, when he approved creation of the CIA, stated that it was to be "an analytical organization."[33] Beria could not have foreseen at the time that this new, rather weak organization would mature with surprising speed.

The rapid expansion of the CIA suggested to the Soviets that it would be worthwhile for them carefully to review former OSS personnel whom they had recruited (as ideologues), along with those who might be recruited coercively on the basis of information already gathered by the organs. Many of those who had made early penetrations of the OSS (e.g., Duncan Lee and Helen Tenney) had been publicly exposed and were now useful only as "consultants."

Feeding untainted recruits into the CIA was the most likely way of assuring that some would float near the top in a reasonable period of time. It was also logical that there would be some emulation of the predecessor organization, and a very great deal was known about the methodologies of OSS. The forces were now engaged: the United States racing to build, and the organs moving to destroy.

In prior years the Soviets had made very effective use of penetration agents. In the course of events, these operatives had been able to provide early warning of impending actions, the rationale behind certain decisions, and the vulnerabilities of individuals who held views inimical to Bolshevism.

When an audit of the personality of a Soviet antagonist revealed no clear avenue of coercive leverage, two other possibilities were examined: (1) the origination of disinformation that would suggest the presence of hidden character traits (of the kind searched for in the first instance and not found), which would raise questions relative to the target's suitability to continue in his primary function, and (2) the possibilities of removing the opposition irritant by inflicting injury, illness, or even death.

General Wladislav Sikorski, the Prime Minister of the Polish Government in Exile, presented the Soviets with a classic example of such a problem. On July 30, 1941, after Stalin had petitioned the Western powers for military aid to stop the German advance on Leningrad, Ivan Maisky, Soviet ambassador to Great Britain, signed a solemn agreement with General Sikorski in London. By that agreement the Soviets abrogated their prior treaties with Germany and averred that the Soviets' territorial gains in eastern Poland (the price the Germans paid for Stalin's neutrality) were null and void. Further, the USSR agreed to permit the formation, on Soviet territory, of a Polish army with a Polish commander appointed by the Sikorski government.

The unprecedented concessionary tone of the agreement was a measure of Stalin's desperations and fears. For him to have consented to the inclusion of Poles in the forces opposing the Germans was, indeed, startling. He needed troops, and the surviving Poles who had been interned by the Soviets after the start of the war in September 1939 were sitting in Soviet cages. It was difficult for Stalin to propose the plan because he was fully aware that Beria's NKVD already had murdered twelve to fifteen thousand "interned" Polish officers and noncoms held in the Smolensk region and had buried the corpses in vast common graves in the forests outside Katyn.

Much later, Winston Churchill described the scene:

> A considerable number of these prisoners, of whom more than 8,000 were officers, were members of the Polish intelligentsia, including university professors, engineers and leading citizens, who had been mobilized as reservists. Until the spring of 1940 there had been intermittent news of the existence of these prisoners. From April 1940, silence descended upon the three camps. Not a single sign or trace of their occupants ever appeared for thirteen or fourteen months. They were certainly in Soviet power, but no letter, message, escapee, or scrap of information ever came from them.
>
> Early in April 1943, Sikorski came to luncheon at No. 10. He told me that he had proofs that the Soviet Government had murdered the 15,000 Polish officers and other prisoners in their hands, and that they had been buried in vast graves in the forests, mainly around Katyn. He had a wealth of evidence. I said, "If they are dead nothing you can do will bring them back." He said he could not hold his people, and that they had already released all their news to the press. Without informing the British Government of its intention, the Polish Cabinet in London issued a communique on April 17 stating that an approach had been made to the International Red Cross in Switzerland to send a delegation to Katyn to conduct an inquiry on the spot. On April 20 the Polish Ambassador in Russia was instructed by his government to ask for the comments of the Russians upon the German story.[34]

The stage was set for a diplomatic effort in which the International Red Cross refused to participate without Soviet agreement. The resulting impasse produced the improbable effect of allowing the Germans to pose as the exposers of Soviet atrocities in an attempt to propagate their mock indignation and disgust. The Western press had no appetite for anti-Soviet news, particularly from Nazi sources. It was ready to accept almost any explanation the Soviets might wish to give. After all, the Katyn murders were merely allegations and, as a service to the readers, were represented as likely Nazi propaganda.

A few months later, in September 1943, after the Red Army had recaptured Smolensk and the Katyn Forest, the NKVD ran a press campaign to "prove" that, because of the rapidity of the German advance, the Polish prisoners fell into German hands and were slaughtered by the SS.

The matter might have ended there except for the vocality and political importance of Polish-Americans, who demanded to know the truth. In an attempt to close off the damaging speculation, Beria selected a number of foreign correspondents accredited to Moscow (including eleven Americans) to visit the site. The U.S. ambassador to the USSR, W. Averell Harriman, asked that his daughter, Kathleen, and John F. Melby, third secretary of embassy, be included as his representatives.

It was like a scene out of Russian historical lore. The story is that Catherine the Great's adviser, Prince Grigori Potemkin, ordered that impressive village facades be built along the Czarina's route of inspection in the Crimea. Peopled by peasant "actors," these Potemkin villages were meant to convince Catherine that the peasants were indeed happy and well cared for. With artful stagecraft, due attention to the details of the set, and rigid adherence to the script, Beria had a hit on his hands. The press conceded that there were some ambiguities that took the issue from stark black and white to the more acceptable subdued tones of gray. For the moment the Soviets were off the public-opinion hook.

Harriman informed Roosevelt on January 25, 1944, "None of the party was able to judge the scientific evidence of autopsies which were performed in their presence. Moreover, they were not permitted to make independent investigations except for formal questioning of the few witnesses made available. Correspondents filed reports telling what they saw without expressing opinions, but for some reason censor has held up these stories . . ."[35]

Kathleen Harriman got close to the truth in her own detailed report:

> On January 23, 1944, members of the foreign press were taken to Smolensk to get first hand the evidence compiled by the Commission on the Katyn incident. [Ed. note: The Soviets helped the observers to reach an objective finding by salting the Commission's official title with a few evocative words: "Special Commission for Ascertaining and Investigating the Circumstances of the Shooting of Polish Officer Prisoners by the German-Fascist Invaders in the Katyn Forest."]
>
> The party was shown the graves in the Katyn Forest and witnessed post mortems of the corpses. As no member was in a posi-

tion to evaluate the scientific evidence given, it had to be accepted at face value.

The testimonial evidence provided by the Commission and witnesses was minute in detail and by American standards petty. We were expected to accept the statements of the high ranking Soviet officials as true, because they said it was true.

The witnesses were very well rehearsed, and they appeared subdued rather than nervous, their pieces having been learned by heart.

When the last witness had been heard, general questions were asked, some of import to the Katyn incident, others not. Shortly, however, the representatives of the Foreign Office Press Department got up and said we'd better break up as our train was due to leave shortly. I got the distinct impression that the Commission was relieved. They had been told to put on a show for us—the show was over—and they did not want to be bothered any further. The meeting broke up without any informal chatting.[36]

The results of the Katyn Forest tragedy and its successful cover-up by the NKVD were revealing. There was only one known eyewitness to the shooting and killing of the Polish prisoners by Beria's troops, a Russian peasant who later escaped to the West. A few months after reporting what he knew to the Allies, the man was found dead, hanged in the dilapidated workshop of a deserted orchard on a farm outside London.

Another report about Katyn was filed by U.S. Army Colonel John H. Van Vliet, Jr., who, as a German prisoner of war, was forced to witness the exhumation the Germans performed at Katyn. This report was prepared in a single, original, longhand copy, classified "Top Secret," and locked in a Pentagon strongbox. When the Congress finally began its investigation of the massacre, it was discovered that Colonel Van Vliet's report was missing from the War Department files. Since the report had consisted of an unduplicated original manuscript, the content was lost forever.[37] The removal of the Van Vliet report surely reaffirmed Beria's faith in the worth of penetration agents.

In spite of the haunting legacy of Katyn, the Free Polish Army was formed under the command of Lieutenant General Wladislav Anders and fought courageously in North Africa. The Poles later crossed the Mediterranean and led the assault force that broke the bloody stalemate at Monte Cassino, Italy, greatly enhancing the Poles' reputation as fierce combatants. But it wasn't the Polish army that worried Stalin or even the growing Western suspicions about Katyn; it was a postwar Poland led by General Sikorski. The prospect of a free Poland headed by able leaders has always been anathema to the Soviet Union.

Russo-Polish history includes a long catalog of accounts of Russian disasters at the hands of Poles who were unified and led by strong leaders. General Sikorski was such a charismatic leader and a warrior in the bargain. He was seen as a dangerous threat, since he had both the will and the capacity to obstruct Soviet expansion to the West. It was easy, then, in the wake of the general's public charges about Katyn, to persuade Stalin that Sikorski had to be elminated. Although the decision was simply made and the order issued, the execution promised to be exceedingly difficult.

The security surrounding Sikorski in London was thorough and extensive. An attack on Sikorski was not feasible despite the presence of numerous NKVD officers and a few Britons under Soviet control. Killing Sikorski was not beyond their abilities; it was the problem of Soviet spoor that defeated them. Timing was another critical factor, and the pressures were mounting. A sudden German collapse might result in Sikorski's triumphant return to Warsaw at the head of Anders's Free Polish Army and with the support of Britain and the United States, a consequence that was wholly unacceptable to the Soviets. It was imperative that Sikorski die before the Western allies began to plan for such an event. It was to be a straightforward political assassination, except there could be no traces that would lead back to the NKVD. While the act was being planned, the Soviets began to stress the fact that the USSR had not been at war with Poland and that the Soviet occupation of eastern Poland, under the terms of the now repudiated pact with Germany, really hadn't occurred. While thumping the tub of Polish-Soviet amity, the NKVD proceeded to plan Sikorski's death.

An informant in the British government reported a significant bit of intelligence to his NKVD handler. General Sikorski was scheduled to make a secret inspection and morale-building visit to the Free Polish Forces in North Africa. The import was that, although he would still be protected by his own forces, he would not be in the London cocoon. An air journey in wartime was widely accepted as hazardous in itself. Sikorski's plan now seemed to present the Soviets with the possibility of causing an unattributable "accident" somewhere along the route, either on the way to North Africa or on the return leg to England. Such a plan would require exact knowledge of Sikorski's detailed itinerary.

The whereabouts and travel plans of the heads of the exile governments in London were carefully guarded secrets. As nominal head of the Polish state, Sikorski came under the protection of the British government, and in this context his safety was the specific charge of the Special Branch of Scotland Yard.

Sikorski's biographer, General Marian Kukiel, writes:

> . . . the departure from England and the trip to North Africa went off without incident, nor were there any indications during his in-

spections and conversations with General Anders to suggest any breaches of security along the way. However, unknown to Sikorski, his staff or the British Secret Service, the NKVD was in possession of the detailed itinerary. It had been provided to them by H. A. Philby of MI6. Sikorski's return trip plans called for a departure from North Africa on the night of July 3/4, 1943, to Malta for a refueling stop, thence to Gibraltar for a similar stop and then, on to England. The stop at Malta was selected since the NKVD had an active organization there.[38]

The worth of penetration agents and agents in place was again demonstrated. The fact that the arrival and refueling of Sikorski's aircraft would take place during the hours of darkness added to the security of the plan. The NKVD-operated agent placed a bomb aboard the aircraft. The bomb was of the type developed by the British Special Operations Executive (SOE) and tried, unsuccessfully, against Hitler. Once set, it was detonated by changes in the air pressure within the aircraft. The bomb went off as planned when the aircraft was approximately eighty miles from Gibraltar, killing Sikorski and his personal retinue. There was only one survivor, the Czech pilot of the aircraft. He was unable to provide any explanation of how the bomb was introduced onto the aircraft.

Thus, on July 4, 1943, the one man who was most likely to challenge the Soviet designs for postwar Poland was "rendered harmless." (The case stands as a telling reminder that little has happened to change the Soviet's perceptions of Poland today. The attempt on John Paul II carried out by the Bulgarian surrogates of the KGB and the continuing plight of Lech Walesa, both regarded as strong charismatic leaders capable of uniting the Poles against Soviet repression, are more recent illustrations of the determination of the organs to take whatever steps are necessary to prevent the development of Polish resistance.)

Because penetration agents had accounted for many earlier Soviet successes, there seemed to be no compelling reason why the techniques couldn't be used effectively against the embryonic CIA. The wartime activities of OSS (and many of its personnel) were an open book to the NKVD. Under the impression that the Soviets were, indeed, allies, OSS Director Donovan had provided the NKVD with more important intelligence information than Beria believed possible.

In the postwar period it was obvious that Donovan was out of favor and that American intelligence was undergoing a dramatic shift. NKVD reports of disorder and confusion in the U.S. intelligence elements were largely accurate. But as said earlier, the reports also had the effect of raising in Beria's mind the specter of deception. He knew from old Cheka files that Donovan had, immediately after the First World War, set up a clandestine U.S. intelligence operation focused on the Bolsheviks. Now he was fully prepared to learn that Donovan's publicized departure from Washington was a stratagem intended to cover the same purpose.

Beria knew enough about some of those who were joining the CIA to realize that it would be a serious error to underestimate the new organization. Some of them had learned much during the war and had exhibited some of the qualities essential to the development of a professional service. To keep the United States from becoming a serious threat, Beria began to examine the task of determining how best the NKVD might penetrate and, if possible, co-opt the newly formed CIA.

The task began as a massive clerical project in which the data collected by all Soviet sources on Americans and U.S. institutions were assembled. Records on some individuals were comprehensive, but many others were "unknowns." The Soviets' Washington embassy bought 400 out-of-town telephone books through the local company and secured city directories for reconciliations.

In New York Amtorg subscribed to several credit checking firms and maintained numerous banking contacts that provided added information on "prospective employees" and possible "customers." Local investigations and surveys were conducted by "friends of the family," even the poor, all but abandoned USCP was given a few odd library chores. It was a mammoth market survey intended, in the end, to reveal the identities of those who would buy, those who might buy, and those who could be made to buy. The NKVD was selling its cancer, and candidates were needed who could cooperate, be co-opted, or coerced into recruitment.

Within the Truman administration there were still debates about the CIA's role, as officials attempted to rationalize the new agency within the government. Truman looked on the CIA as a "news service" and coordinator of intelligence estimates; others in the administration hoped that it would become a resurrected OSS with a clear anticommunist mission.

In staffing the new agency it was necessary to request the assistance of the already over-burdened FBI to do the preliminary investigations while the agency built up its own investigative unit. J. Edgar Hoover, who had never posed as an advocate of the CIA, imposed limits on the FBI's investigations of CIA applicants, since a full investigation of a great many new employees within a short time would have overburdened the Bureau's capacities.

The preliminary investigative step was the "national agency check," consisting of a routine inquiry of other U.S. government agencies to determine if they held any information about the applicant. Initially, a few former OSS staffers moved into the new agency with only a superficial preemployment check.

The process must have confused the Soviets. It appeared to them that the United States was constructing a central intelligence organization without exhaustively vetting the personnel who would run it. (Note: By 1948 the CIA's Office of Security was functioning effectively, and the very few who had escaped previous notice in the first year were promptly separated).

At this time the American public was just becoming aware of the aggressiveness of the Soviet organs, and there was apprehension in Congress that the Soviets might have used the twelve-month "window" to try to insert a Bykovo-trained agent into the new agency. The extent of Beria's penetrations of other U.S. government agencies formed the basis of the likelihood that the NKVD had targeted the CIA.

In the Far East and Europe, the NKVD had been gently probing the residual post-OSS intelligence elements, which until the CIA was chartered had been operating on an indeterminate basis with no clear impression as to their future.

With the disbanding of the OSS, many elements of the U.S. intelligence apparatus ceased to exist. Others were moved to the Department of State, and the operational units, greatly reduced, were subordinated to the War Department and designated as the Strategic Services Unit (SSU). What remained was not much more than a hollow shell of the wartime OSS.[39] The NKVD was more concerned with pressing its intelligence-collection operations against the U.S. forces in Europe than with mounting major operations against the apt-to-be orphaned SSU. Successful "work" against the U.S. forces involved no great effort, and detailed intelligence flowed from a vast variety of nets, including a significant number of informants in the U.S. Army.

A few agents in the U.S. Army's counterintelligence and criminal investigation units were suborned by the Soviets. One man in particular aided the organs by forcibly abducting Germans who lived in the U.S. sector and who were on the Soviet arrest lists. To facilitate his "work," he used a U.S. Army jeep to transport the victims to a Russian exchange point, where he sold them for cash. At his trial he insisted that he was an entrepreneur, not an ideologue.

The flourishing black market, the PX, booze, women, and the surreal climate of the occupation contributed to the Soviets' ability to bring in new recruits by compromise and coercion.

At the Russian headquarters in Karlshorst, in the Soviet zone of Germany, thousands of officers from the organs were directing cases in Berlin as well as in the French, British, and American sectors. Throughout Soviet-occupied Germany, the organs collected police records on the civilian population and military records on those who had served in the

German forces. Gestapo, SD, RSHA, and Abwehr files, along with *all* police records, were then shipped to Moscow.

Freight cars loaded with millions of German documents were moved east by high-priority trains. The records were unloaded by special detachments of the organs and distributed among ten or more temporary screening centers, where hundreds of translators, working under close supervision, reviewed them. The purposes of this massive program were: (1) to establish the identity of any Russian, Pole, Estonian, Latvian, or other citizen of an occupied country who might have assisted the Germans in anti-Soviet operations; (2) to catalog information concerning the hundreds of thousands of German prisoners then held in the USSR (such information might reveal intelligence connections that the POWs would want to conceal and, in other cases, help to identify those who had shed their rank and were posing as privates under different names); (3) to identify POWs by place of origin (particularly those from the non-Soviet zones); (4) to watch with especial care for information relating to those with connections to, or knowledge of, senior contacts in the Western Allies' governments and military commands. Such information might prove useful in a great variety of ways. For example, a young German woman serving as a secretary in the British zone could be approached by an East German agent and advised that her father's release from a POW camp in the USSR was dependent on her willingness to assist the Soviet service.

Information falling into categories 3 and 4 was immediately returned from Moscow to Karlshorst for operational exploitation. Of particular interest were leads to individuals serving in foreign intelligence services.

The Soviets had enjoyed a lateral view of the U.S. services in London through their controlled British penetrations. In Paris, former U.S. military intelligence officer Lieutenant George Zlatovsky and his wife, ex-OSS officer Jane Foster, were in a position to contribute much to the Soviets' understanding of changes in the U.S. organizations. Both Zlatovsky and Foster were indicted in the United States for espionage, but the French refused to extradite them. The stations in Rome and Cairo were off the more important communications routes, and Shanghai already had an impressive concentration of both Chinese communist and Soviet agents who had survived the Japanese occupation and were well placed to continue to monitor the U.S. elements.

The operating climate in Switzerland was inviting. During the war the Soviets had run large-scale espionage nets in Switzerland with dramatic success, owing to the fact that Swiss espionage laws applied only when the spying was directed toward Switzerland. However, a few Soviet agents who deserted the organs approached the Swiss and were granted asylum. At the end of the war the Soviets demanded their return, but the Swiss refused. Later, in an effort to correct this inadmissable behavior, the Soviets simply arrested two Swiss diplomats in Budapest (at about the same time that the Swedish diplomat Raoul Wallenberg disappeared from the same city). The Swiss diplomats were exchanged for the deserters, and the Soviets reconfirmed that it was usually possible to make a deal with the businesslike Swiss.

Allen Dulles had been the OSS chief in Switzerland during the war, and by the early fifties he was being touted as most likely to be the first nonmilitary head of the CIA. President Truman's abrupt dismissal of General Donovan in 1945 had the effect of advancing Dulles's prospects. After Donovan, Dulles was the best known of the senior OSS officers. As the chief in Bern he had been a vigorous advocate of action and an enthusiastic chief. The German retreat in Italy clearly presaged the end of the Nazis, and Dulles was drawn into contact with various German general officers who purported to be emissaries of the commanders still fighting the British, Polish, and U.S. armies south of the Alps.

The German military had devoted some thought to deposing Hitler since 1934. Before any such vagrant thoughts coalesced in a plan of action, however, Hitler always managed to throw the military a bone in the form of increased funds, weapons procurement, or, as in the cases of the Sudetenland and Austria, cheap and bloodless victories. After 1939, the lightning campaigns in Poland and France induced some of the more senior of his commanders to concede that by audacious action Hitler had achieved at small cost what few of them would have thought possible. The imputation of "special" Hitlerian insights that resulted in a succession of audacious victories diminished their sense of urgency to depose him. But then the delay of the attack on the USSR and the stalemate followed by the surrender of von Paulus at Stalingrad once again raised the issue of Hitler's competence. Some of the senior German commanders, plagued by irresolution, entertained the view that they should somehow join forces with the Western Allies so that the "more important war" could be successfully prosecuted in the East.

As chief of station in Switzerland, Dulles was exceedingly active. He was on familiar ground, having served there during his brief career as a diplomat in World War I, when he was posted to Bern by his uncle, Secretary of State Robert Lansing. Throughout his later life, in referring to Switzerland, he was given to tell the story of his missed opportunity to meet with Lenin, which occurred when he opted to play tennis instead. The anecdote was usually followed by an enigmatic stare and a puff of pipe smoke. The auditor was left to imagine the myriad implications of the nonevent.

When Dulles agreed to meet with the first German emissaries, he took especial pains to institute the most rigorous kinds of security. Despite his efforts, somehow the Soviets were immediately informed of the clandestine meetings. The speed with which the Soviets protested to Washington about OSS's unilateral contact with the German military representatives can only be described as telegraphic. Stalin feared that Britain and the United States might be planning an arrangement by which the German Army would arrest Hitler, ask for an armistice in the West, then move their European forces (with secret British and U.S. support) to the eastern front, thereby producing the "final solution" to the Bolshevik problem.

Since double-crossing was an acceptable Bolshevik technique in diplomacy as well as war, Stalin saw no reason why the Western Allies might not leap at the chance to support a reequipped and greatly reinforced Wehrmach if it meant the destruction of the USSR. In Stalin's view such a betrayal was nothing more than a reasonable course of action.

One of Dulles's successes was the case of "George Wood" (Fritz Kolbe), a German official who brought Foreign Office and other documents to Switzerland and gave them to Dulles. "Wood" had been rebuffed initially by the British, but Dulles found the documents comprehensive and most revealing of the German High Command's capabilities and intentions. With barely suppressed pride Dulles made the "Wood" submissions to Washington, prefaced by his judgment of their import. When the "Wood" material arrived, it prompted two powerful and opposite reactions.

Those who were not receiving British-American intercepts of German traffic under Ultra—the top-secret project that had broken the German code—were immediately persuaded that OSS had finally opened the sluice on high-grade German secrets. Down the hall the Ultra element was shocked that Dulles was repeating, in his own cipher, the full text of German documents that they had already processed and distributed to the few British and American commanders having the "need to know." On reflection, however, it was realized that Dulles had performed a valuable, though unwitting service. Now, for the first time, Ultra had a collateral source of high-level, hard-copy, genuine German communications. And should the Germans begin to reexamine their communications systems for compromises and leaks, "George Wood" could be offered up now as a live explanation of how and where the system was hemorraghing.

When Dulles returned after the war, he was a convinced advocate of a permanent central intelligence organization for the United States. Dulles offered advice, wrote letters, and testified relative to the national need for a coordinated intelligence service not subordinated to the Pentagon or the Department of State. Concurrently, he maintained extensive contacts within a claque of OSS veterans who shared his views and spoke reverentially of his special abilities to head such a service.

By the time of Truman's unexpected return to office in 1948, three men had already served in the new post of director of central intelligence (DCI). Admiral Sidney Souers, a Missouri businessman who was deputy director of the Office of Naval Intelligence (ONI), was the first to be appointed DCI by Truman in 1945 at the time of the establishment of the National Intelligence Authority (NIA). Souers was quickly succeeded by General Hoyt Vandenberg and, later, by Admiral Roscoe H. Hillenkoetter, who became the first DCI to serve after the enactment of the National Security Act of 1947.

Following his 1948 election victory, Truman offered the job to George K. Bowden, a Chicago attorney who had been close to both Roosevelt and Truman. (Bowden had been associated with OSS during the war; at one point he was dispatched in great haste via Pan-Am clipper to Lisbon and then on to Switzerland to inform Dulles of the unintended consequences of both the "George Wood" and German surrender negotiations.) Bowden declined Truman's offer and counseled against any serious consideration of Dulles, whose name had been advanced by Robert Lovett two years before. Although Lovett did not know Dulles personally, he had been told that Dulles had "organized the best job for the OSS in Switzerland."[40] Truman eventually decided to keep Hillenkoetter in the job, but in 1950 replaced him with General Walter Bedell Smith, Eisenhower's wartime chief of staff who had been ambassador to Moscow, 1946–1949.

Washington was still reeling with the astonishing revelations of Soviet espionage in Canada, Britain, France, and the United States. Deserters from the CPUSA who had operated on behalf of the organs came forward and testified as to the extent of the Soviet penetrations of government, labor, the armed forces, and the scientific community. Congressional hearings, trials, and public debate focused on the realities of Soviet wartime operations against the United States. The Truman administration came under heavy criticism, and by June, 25, 1950, when the North Koreans launched their attack on the South, the Democrats were in broad retreat, having been charged with the "loss of China," "coddling communists in government," and failing to recognize, let alone counter, the aggressive growth of Soviet power. In every respect Truman reaped the harvest of Roosevelt's ill-founded and basically arrogant assumptions that the Soviets could be indulged and manipulated without peril.

Truman retired from office at the end of his term and was succeeded by Dwight D. Eisenhower. Following the election, the new administration's nominee for DCI went unnamed. General Walter B. Smith, a man of great integrity who was then serving as the fourth DCI, was in indeterminate health and quite prepared to accept a less demanding post under Eisenhower.

When Smith was asked to propose a successor, he recommended General Lucien K. Truscott as his personal preference. Eisenhower offered the post to Truscott, who declined on the basis that he could be more effective in the administration as a "troubleshooter" than as DCI.

When Allen Dulles was finally nominated on February 11, 1953, well after all of the Cabinet posts and many of the sub-Cabinet appointments had been announced, the delay suggested strongly that there were reservations within Eisenhower's inner circle regarding the appointment of Dulles. Later it was learned that the demurrals were overcome when Allen Dulles, at the urging of his brother, the secretary of state, agreed to accept an Eisenhower-Smith approved deputy director rather than one of his own choosing. Once that point was agreed, Dulles was named DCI, General Charles P. Cabell was nominated as DDCI,[41] and General Smith became undersecretary of state.

Dulles took over an organization that still had not found its feet. The war in Korea had bolstered the military's case that the CIA was unable to meet the intelligence demands of combat forces. General MacArthur, whose antagonism for OSS throughout World War II was well known, held the same disdain for CIA in Korea. To remedy the problem, General Smith was dispatched to Tokyo to inform MacArthur that his autocratic refusal to comply with the administration's wishes ran counter to the national plan for the prosecution of the war.

Since 1945 the U.S. Office of Special Operations (OSO) and the Strategic Services Unit (SSU) had been bureaucratic orphans, receiving their sustenance at the sufferance of the War Department. The units under the Army's G-2 had, at best, a two-star voice, which was all but inaudible in the presence of MacArthur's five stars and regal title as Supreme Commander Allied Forces, Pacific. MacArthur's long-time intelligence chief, Major General Charles Willoughby, a lofty, imperious man who, because of temperament, isolation, and long service in the MacArthur court, needed (like MacArthur) to be reintroduced to the concept that the U.S. chain of command originated in Washington.

In point of fact the war in Korea, which had begun in June 1950, was not going well for the UN forces, commanded by MacArthur. In late fall, after the Chinese had joined forces with the North Korean invaders, MacArthur complained that the enemy had an uncanny knowledge of his strategic maneuvers. "That there was some leak in intelligence was evident to everyone," he later wrote. One of his senior commanders, General James Gavin, was certain that the Chinese were able to move "confidently and skillfully" into Korea because they were well informed not only of U.S. tactical moves but also of the limitations placed on the military by the political leaders in Washington and at the UN.[42]

During this early period of the war H.A.R. "Kim" Philby was first secretary of the British embassy in Washington and chief liaison between the British Secret Intelligence Service (SIS) and the FBI and CIA. Guy Burgess was second secretary at the embassy, and Donald Maclean headed the American desk in Whitehall. According to Dean Rusk, then Assistant Secretary of State for Far Eastern Affairs, "It can be assumed that (1) anything we in our government knew about Korea would have been known at the British embassy and (2) that officers of the rank of these three would have known what the British embassy knew."[43]

In May of 1951, in the wake of investigations into possible leaks, Burgess and Maclean defected to the Soviet Union. U.S. intelligence officers were staggered not only by the defections of these high-level civil servants but also by the seemingly casual manner in which the British government reacted. After consultation with the FBI and the White House, Walter Bedell Smith demanded that the British recall Philby from his post in Washington.

After the Burgess-Maclean defections, the ever-present stresses in the relationships within the British intelligence community were greatly intensified. Sources reported that during his Washington assignment Burgess had written a memorandum, to which he gave wide personal circulation, asserting that the United States was using the Korean War as a means of provoking the Soviets into World War III. Furthermore, according to Burgess, the MacArthur proposal to "bomb north of the Yalu River" had been advanced not for tactical reasons but as the first step in the atomic annihilation of the Chinese and a strategic confrontation of the Soviets from both the east and the west. The evidence for the latter was the U.S. pledge to NATO of "atomic support."

Critics who had been insisting that the OSS and CIA were dominated, and probably penetrated, by the British were in full cry. The substantive fact was that the U.S. government itself had been broadly penetrated by Soviet agents and that corrective actions had been slow and incomplete in their scope. Senator Joseph R. McCarthy, a Republican from Wisconsin, attempted to publicize this issue in 1953–1954 by dramatic public hearings and, eventually, won more enmity than praise. The hearings were characterized by inadequate homework and increasingly indiscriminate pursuits. McCarthy was labeled by the press as an irresponsible "witch hunter" who used the hearings to destroy the reputations of the innocent by his undocumented charges and reckless methods. The substantiated facts relating to the penetration of the U.S. government by Soviet agents were obscured and eventually lost in the mounting ad hominem attacks on McCarthy himself. The McCarthy hearings simply underlined the obvious by demonstrating that a Senate investigative committee is not an effective body to attempt counterintelligence operations. Thirty years later it be-

comes possible to make a preliminary assessment of the net effects of
Senator McCarthy's efforts.

The basic signal emanating from the committee, that the U.S. government had been penetrated by the Soviets, was lost in the volume of the
noise generated by the errors, confusion, methodology, and indiscipline
of both the chairman and the staff. McCarthy came under attack not only
from the liberal left but also from within the most conservative elements
of his own party. The committee's engagement with the U.S. Army
caused such adverse public reaction that even McCarthy's better-in-
formed adherents, who understood the objectives, abandoned him because of the means used to attempt their realization.

After his early death McCarthy's reputation formed the basis for easy
extrapolation. He became known as a sodden, irresponsible, vindictive
man who had used his high office to destroy the lives, careers, and reputations of innocents. Any subsequent suggestion that, indeed, there was a
long history of Soviet subornation within the government was dismissively
ridiculed as "McCarthyism." Anticommunism became the creed of the
caricature anti-intellectual.

The year 1953 produced several important events that had serious
long-term implications. First, the signing of the armistice at Panmunjom
marked the end of America's first inconclusive foreign military operation.
The imposition of political restraints on those charged with the conduct of
battle caused wide divisions among the White House, the Pentagon, and
the Department of State. The FBI and CIA were still attempting a *modus
vivendi,* colored and still deeply affected by wisps of mutual distrust. The
United States, and particularly the CIA, was seen as having been betrayed by the British. At the FBI the British defections only confirmed
Director Hoover's fixed opinion of the probable behavior to be expected
of homosexual intellectuals in government.

In the USSR the aging despot Stalin ordered the arrest of nine physicians who were accused of causing the deaths of Zhdanov and
Shchrbakov. The "doctors' plot" was broadly interpreted as Stalin's decision to reinstitute a formal, Soviet-government-sponsored anti-Semitic
pogrom. The Stalin who had accreted unexceeded power was, with illness
and age, reverting to his most basic self. It was a period of unremitting
terror for his subordinates, all of whom, having enjoyed his largess, were
now to know his vicious, unpredictable, and wholly capricious abuse, humiliation, ridicule, vindictiveness, and murderous vengeance.

Survival during the period was characterized by slavish obse-
quiousness, flattery, and fear. There were no discussions or debates; the
USSR was governed on the basis of casual imperatives issued by Stalin.
The same men who groveled in his presence were almost equally fearful
of what would happen once the Generalissimo succumbed.

Beria's operatives had succeeded in gaining the essential scientific and technical data to create the hydrogen bomb, but the NKVD lacked the capacity to organize its production. Beria's great industrial failure and his eventual recourse to dependence on abducted German scientific prisoners and *zeks* from the gulag gained him only Stalin's contempt for his previous efforts to build the bomb by using only trusted Soviet personnel.

When, in late 1949, Stalin had ordered the removal of all Jews from sensitive positions in the government and, in particular, the MGB, many close associations that had been built up over the years were abruptly broken. Beria recognized at once that Stalin's arbitrary and baseless order would cause resentment and, perhaps, a counterintelligence threat where none had previously existed. To the affected officers it could only be seen as conclusive evidence that Stalin, like the czars before him, was not the head of a "classless society" but was simply an anti-Semite in the old Russian tradition.

On March 5, 1953, the international press was informed that "the world's greatest fighter for peace," Generalissimo Joseph Vissarionovich Stalin, had died. His violent and wholly erratic behavior during the previous months fueled speculation that he might have been helped into the hereafter by one or more of his esteemed associates.[44] The MGB then moved abruptly into the next stage of its evolution. (Note: Although Stalin actually died on March 2, the information was kept from the world and the Russian people until March 5, which was announced as the "official date.")

In the wake of Stalin's death Beria acted instantly and, perhaps, too boldly to consolidate his power and to seize control of government. On March 15 the MGB was disestablished and reconstituted as the MVD. As head of the new MVD he was able to do much, but without the army and party, he was certainly bound to fail. The party was the symbolic seat of an unstable, two-legged stool. Without the army *and* the organs, the government must certainly collapse. Following Stalin's death the military remained neutral on the basis that Beria was a known factor with whom they could coexist. The Central Committee and the Politburo, on the other hand, were deeply antagonistic toward, though not united in opposition to, Beria.

Though it was reasonable to believe that Stalin would eventually die, the fact of the event startled a number of Western "Kremlinologists" who had exhausted themselves positing the rhetorical question: "After Stalin, who?" Most fixed their gaze on form and missed the substance of the Soviet state. Virtually all before-the-fact analyses of succession to power in the Soviet Union were off the mark because they were, for the most part, predicated on the assumption that Stalin's power was legitimate.

A more striking parallel would have been found in studying the processes of succession in the Mafia. It then would have been easy to see Beria taking charge of the funeral arrangements. The Family gathers to project an image of continuity, strength, and control. The *Vozhd* is dead, but the party lives on. A few Western observers noted that, among the hundreds of thousands of Muscovites who came to view the body of Stalin, many seemed to have come to express their grief and the rest wished only to verify the fact that he was dead.

The funeral protocols and precedence in the processions confirmed that the new administration consisted of Georgi Malenkov as premier, Beria and Vyacheslav Molotov as vice chairmen of the Council of Ministers, and Marshall Kliment Voroshilov, Nikolai A. Bulganin, Anastas Mikoyan, and Nikita Khrushchev as members of the collective leadership.

The ceremony itself was a parody of a parody in which grim-visaged Central Committee members, with mock-somber cynicism, recited Stalin's extraordinary accomplishments in the socialist revolution and his mighty labors in the building of the USSR. All were simultaneously and independently positioning themselves for the power struggle that was about to begin. Beria put the MVD on alert, and forces were at the ready to consign Malenkov and his ally of the moment, Khrushchev, as two of the first to go to the Lubianka cellars.

Beria directed the Center to order all foreign stations to continue with current operations but to avoid high-risk activities that might produce adverse reaction in the Western governments and press. The meaning was clear: power was changing hands. The MVD was to lie low until Beria had dealt with his potential rivals. His alleywise colleagues fully understood Beria's tactics and realized that their individual and collective power bases were no match for his.

Beria launched a campaign of psychological warfare against the aging dons of the Moscow mafia. By cutting them off from information about what was under way in the MVD and some major elements elsewhere in the Soviet bureaucracy, he made their isolation all but complete. The bureaucratic survivors of the Stalin era could sense the imminent death of Beria's rivals.

There were no meetings of the Central Committee or Politburo because Beria had declared an emergency and imposed new and severe controls. Voroshilov, Malenkov, and Khrushchev were paralyzed by the fear that MVD troops would come to their apartments and drag them off to prison. The lethal stalking game went on for several months. As the stresses increased, a few of the Central Committee members broke ranks and signaled their willingness to kiss Beria's ring. Beria didn't seek their obeisance because it was his intention to dispose of all who had hesitated on the point of his primacy. These few instances did, however, demonstrate to Beria that the route to Stalin's power was going to be an easier road than he had expected.

Then a totally extraneous event occurred that destroyed Beria's plan. On June 17, 1953, there was a violent uprising against the Soviet forces occupying East Berlin. The street skirmishes in no way threatened the Soviets, but they did focus the world's attention on the fact that all was not well in the Soviet system. By some means a report was circulated within the MVD stating that Beria had planned a coup d'etat at six o'clock on the morning of June 19. Several ranking officers of the Ministry of State Security, who were concerned about the reported outbreak in East Berlin, informed members of the Central Committee of their concerns. With the report as justification, an emergency Central Committee meeting was convened, and Beria was summoned to account for his actions.

There are several credible versions of what actually happened at the meeting. One that enjoyed much currency holds that one of the Soviet dons shot and killed Beria in an act of old-aged machismo. Although this act in the interest of "humanity" has been attributed to Nikita Khrushchev, there is no authoritative evidence to support the claim that he pulled the fateful trigger. Regardless of who shot Beria, the fact remains that he was killed by his Bolshevik peers. The Stalin era was ended, and the organs were once again headless.

The public charade attendant to Beria's demise was directed by Malenkov and his uneasy political allies of the moment. It was a model of Bolshevik deception. In the book *Khrushchev Remembers* several variations of the "official" version are advanced. Officially, so the story goes, from the 18th to the 23rd of December in 1953, the Special Judicial Section of the Supreme Court of the USSR tried Beria in camera and sentenced him to be executed on the last date. The fact that Beria had co-conspirators who were also defendants in the trial and were also executed seems to conflict with his more dramatic though much less than judicial departure in the middle of a Central Committee meeting.

The "Beria trial" disposed of his still mighty lieutenants, including V. N. Merkulov, V. G. Dekanozov, B. Z. Kobulov, S. A. Goglidze, P. Y. Meshik, and L. E. Vlodzimirsky.[45] These men comprised the "Beria *banda*" that had controlled the organs of the People's Commissariat of Internal Affairs (MVD), the Ministry of State Security, and the Ministry of Internal Affairs. With the organs temporarily decapitated it was now possible for Malenkov and Khrushchev to reassert party control.[46] The survivors acted with resolution to protect themselves from the threat of the massive power of the NKVD under the control of one man.

6 · Between Beria and Andropov

(1953–1967)

The explosive end of Beria and his senior acolytes shook the foundations of the Soviet state security organs.[1] Without the organs, the Bolshevik state would collapse. Nowhere was this fact more evident than among Stalin's collegial successors. Malenkov and Khrushchev, acting for the Central Committee, directed General Sergei Nikiforovich Kruglov to take charge of the MVD and ordered him to bring the organs back under the party's control.

Kruglov was exactly the right man for the task. He was an Honored Chekist with a long career in the organs, having served as the head of the NKVD from July 1945 to March 1946 and as the head of the MVD from March 1946 to March 1953. He'd been Stalin's "watchbird" in the MVD, spying on Beria and identifying those who evinced a greater loyalty to Beria than to Stalin.[2] On Stalin's death, Beria had forced Kruglov out of the MVD post, taking it for himself.

Kruglov was a humorless bureaucrat and staunch Stalinist. He had a reputation for ruthless determination and was fully dedicated to the perpetuation of the party's absolute control over the Soviet state. His ideological convictions included the belief that what the "Great Stalin" had wrought, must endure. The same notion was shared by Malenkov and others, because they were without alternatives and in fear of their lives in the wake of Stalin's death. Only by imposing the strongest controls could they hope to survive.

Kruglov's appointment had little or no portent in the West. The United States was in the process of a change in national administration and with it, the appointment of a new Director of Central Intelligence. Preoccupation with change prevented appropriate weight being given to the fact that Kruglov, who had enjoyed Stalin's trust and confidence, had come to his new post with a surprisingly accurate perception of the West's political strengths and weaknesses.

Kruglov's insights were acquired in the course of his attendance at the Yalta and Potsdam summit conferences in 1945. Kruglov, in charge of Stalin's security, posed as the caricature of the comic Russian bear while he plumbed for weaknesses in the U.S. and British advisers. Like Rudenko of the Purchasing Commission, Kruglov disarmed the attendees by his pretended, primitive English-language malapropisms. In fact, he was fluent in English and did not miss a word of conversation between those who carried the papers and wrote the memos for FDR and Churchill, Truman and Attlee.

At Potsdam, for example, Kruglov put on his "mad Russian" act for President Truman and Great Britain's Prime Minister Attlee by eating packages of chewing gum—paper, foil, and all. Kruglov was the life of the party. Truman was highly entertained by his antics and presented him with the Legion of Merit. Attlee, not to be outdone, made Kruglov an honorary Knight of the British Empire.

Kruglov's low comedy may have helped to relieve the tensions at both Yalta and Potsdam, but behind his posturing was the deadly serious business of measuring the resolve and purpose of those who were advising the President of the United States and the Prime Minister of Great Britain.

An American Marine, Colonel David R. Nimmer, who was at both conferences and who had fluent command of the Russian language (which he concealed) watched Kruglov and overheard most of his remarks to subordinates. Alarmed by what he heard, the American tried to inform FDR and, later, Truman about Soviet deceptions in the conduct of the negotiations. Regrettably, his efforts were unavailing because the official U.S. position was one that did not admit the fact that the Soviets and the Americans had differing views about the "Four Freedoms" and the planned postwar world. Nimmer's direct experience in dealing with the Bolsheviks on their own terms was without equal in the U.S. government. Nonetheless, like the messenger who brings bad news, his warnings were ignored by political leaders and advisers who thought they had the knowledge and the ability to deal with the Soviets. His reports that cover both conferences are still classified. Reference is made to this instance for the sole purpose of registering the fact that in 1953, when Kruglov took up the task of putting the organs back on track, the United States had information that should have set off alarm bells. In the confusion, without institutional memory and governed by the assumption that little can be learned from the past that has relevance to current issues, the United States was encouraged to reject the facts in favor of accepting the more comforting belief that the USSR, without Stalin, would take on a new form and become less belligerent.

In addition to removing Beria loyalists from key positions in the organs, Kruglov had to bring about some structural changes in the bureaucratic organization to preclude the possibility of the rise of another Beria (or, for that matter, another Stalin). The Central Committee members' concerns were not based on a desire to establish democratic procedures for control of the party, but on their individual and collective fears that without such immediate changes there might be another one-man rule in the Soviet state.

These men of the party had in common the wits, guile, and deceit that had enabled them to avoid the unpredictable wrath of Stalin as well as the manipulations of Beria. Since none wanted a return to the *status quo ante*, restraint of power was an organizational reform on which they could all agree. The reinstitution of party control of the organs was imperative. Collectively they did not deny the need for a leader, titular or actual, who would assume the role as the USSR's official spokesman. But they were insistent on procedures that would prevent one individual from ever again gaining a monopoly of control over all the levers of coercive power in the Soviet state—that is, the organs, the military, and the party.

Reorganization of the organs was not a trivial task. Under Beria, the elements had been integrated in a manner so as to facilitate his attempt to seize power. It was Kruglov's task to reverse the process without weakening or damaging the effectiveness of the organs in carrying out "legitimate" (i.e., officially designated and approved) missions.

Back in mid-1943, for example, Beria had expanded the NKVD's writ to such a broad extent that it became virtually impossible to provide central management and control. In addition to the security apparatus, the NKVD was actively involved in administering the forced labor camps as well as much of Soviet industry. These multiple functions were carried out under the centralized direction of Beria, producing administrative chaos that could only be relieved by the transfer of the security elements into a separate organization.

The new organizational name was NKGB (*Narodyni Kommissariat Gosudarstvennoy Bezopasnosti*), or People's Commissariat for State Security. This division of labor left the NKVD in control of police administration, the secret service, and civil administration. The NKGB was charged with internal security, counterespionage, frontier security, administration of the gulag camps, and guerrilla and underground activities against the Germans. Beria retained the chairmanship of the NKVD, and the NKGB was placed under the control of a Beria loyalist, General Vsevolod Nikolaevich Merkulov, who was later to share Beria's fate.

After the war, the NKGB and NKVD were elevated to the status of separate ministries. The NKVD was renamed MVD (*Ministerstvo Vnutrennikh Del*), or Ministry of Internal Affairs, and the NKGB became the MGB (*Ministerstvo Gosudarstvennoy Bezopasnosti*), or Ministry for State Security. In 1946, subsequent to these changes, Beria was appointed deputy chairman of the Council of Ministers, a post that in essence made him Stalin's deputy premier. By virtue of this appointment, he was able to maintain overall control of the organs. His control, however, was not complete because Stalin named Kruglov to head the MVD. As a sop to Beria, Stalin permitted Merkulov to remain in charge of the MGB.

The new arrangements did not signal the end of the organs' political and bureaucratic perturbations. In 1950 Stalin, believing that the phlegmatic Merkulov had misled him or otherwise failed to anticipate the U.S. reaction to North Korea's invasion of South Korea, fired him. In his place he put General Viktor Semenovich Abakumov, the wartime head of Smersh and a favorite of Stalin's, in addition to being an unabashed critic of Beria's.

Another event that contributed to Merkulov's fall from Stalin's favor occurred in 1947, when Stalin directed the establishment of the KI (*Komitet Informatsii*), or Committee for Information. Stalin had become impatient with the MGB's dilatory execution of his grand designs for "active measures."

> The KI absorbed all the foreign sections of the Ministry of Foreign Affairs, and much to the outrage of the army, also took over the GRU, or the military intelligence service. The KI which answered directly to Stalin was headed successively by Molotov, Valerian Aleksandrovich Zorin and Andrei Yanuarevich Vyshinsky. The proliferation of Soviet espionage and subversion in the late 1940s created a need for more personnel in foreign posts. The KI drew them mostly from the internal divisions of the MGB.
>
> Beria regarded both Abakumov and the KI as threats to his own influence, and his enmity contributed to the demise of each. With his support, the army recovered the GRU in 1948 and thereby weakened the KI. In 1951, Beria, abetted by Georgi Malenkov, destroyed Abakumov by convincing Stalin he had suppressed evidence of a plot. Stalin arrested Abakumov and abolished the KI. In the autumn of 1951, Semen Denisovich Ignatiev became director of the MGB, which now regained responsibilities for clandestine operations abroad.[3]

Soon after Stalin's death in 1953, Beria tried to turn back the clock on the bureaucratic changes that had taken place in the organs since the end of the war. He deposed Ignatiev and Kruglov and remerged the MVD and MGB into one ministry under his personal control. This ill-fated merger, and its aftereffects on the organs, gave added urgency to Kruglov's damage-control mission after Beria's death. Though Beria's absolute control of the organs only lasted three months, he had used the time to poison many wells of considerable importance to the Soviet state and the members of the Central Committee.

Kruglov immediately saw to it that Beria and those "convicted" at the trial presided over by Marshal Konev were hastily converted into "nonpersons."[4] With the villains safely lodged in the hereafter, he began a selective purge of Beria loyalists considered beyond rehabilitation. The surgical nature of the operation reassured the professional officers, who were hoping for a less stressful atmosphere than they had known under Beria. It seemed likely that Kruglov would be more consistent in his techniques of measuring one's ideological purity than had been Beria. Kruglov's appointment signaled to many in the organs that the Stalin-Beria capriciousness had come to an end and that, under Kruglov, they could get on with the job at hand.

In March 1954 the state security organization was denoted by the name it bears today—the KGB (*Komitet Gosudarstvennoy Bezopasnosti*), or Committee for State Security. It was assigned the traditional political police functions; responsibility for all clandestine operations abroad (except those allowed to the GRU); and the securing of the national borders.[5]

Under the Kruglov reorganization, General Ivan Alexandrovich Serov was named as the KGB's first chairman. Kruglov, reportedly, suffered a heart attack during the period July 1953-March 1954 and was thus unable to continue in the post himself.[6]

Initially, Serov appeared to be an excellent choice. He had served with distinction since 1941 as a deputy chairman of the NKGB, earning a reputation among state security officers as a thoroughly competent intelligence professional. It is important to note that such a compliment, attributed to such a source, cannot be interpreted to suggest that Serov was a "fine fellow" or "a crypto-liberal" waiting for the first opportunity to lift the yoke of Bolshevik oppression from the necks of the Russian people. Quite to the contrary. Serov was a true Honored Chekist.

Born in 1905 at Sokal in western Russia, Serov came from a peasant family. During World War II he "made his bones" as the officer in charge of deporting hundreds of thousands of people from Eastern Europe and in carrying out the Katyn Forest massacre on orders from Beria.

Serov was not considered an intelligence hack despite the fact that his ascent through the bureaucracy was systematically aided by Georgi Malenkov. As in the case of Kruglov, it was Malenkov's sponsorship that propelled Serov into the role as Beria's successor. The organs have never operated on the merit system. Selection for higher appointments has always required the confidence of the political leadership as well as ability to perform the work. Serov brought the right mix of malevolent competence and single-minded ruthlessness calculated to reassure the Central Committee. Of course, as the beneficiary of a political sponsor, his own expectations were always a function of the sponsor's political mortality.

The KGB was moved into the same relationship to the Politburo as Dzerzhinsky's VChK had with the Council of People's Commissars under Lenin. In addition to changes strictly defining the KGB's roles and missions, Kruglov, at the direction of the Central Committee, established the areas of functional responsibility for the MVD, which retained the conventional police function, firefighting, and the direct responsibility for guarding the transportation system and all industrial sites. The industrial functions that had been taken over by Beria during the war were now in the process of being restored to the more appropriate ministries.

Responsibility for physical and personnel security of the Soviet Union's atomic energy and weapons programs was originally an NKVD function, and the derivative authority rests with the present-day KGB. After a near disaster in the mid-sixties, the KGB's control over the USSR's "nuclear trigger" was modified to admit the need for technical competence as well as ideological purity in preventing future accidental discharges of the nuclear arsenal. The technicians and scientists are still vetted by the KGB, but those without the necessary specialized training have been removed to a safe distance. The near-catastrophic event of the sixties is best described as a "bureaucratic nuclear accident."

Though it was subsequently described as an approved nuclear test detonation, in fact, the KGB controllers had "ordered" the device to be fired despite objections by the scientific and technical personnel, who warned that the appropriate safeguards were not in place.

As the Soviet leaders learned, adherence to the precepts of Marxism-Leninism does not alter in any discernible way the laws of physics. The discovery simply acknowledged that atomic weaponry is a specialized field that requires scientific knowledge and highly developed technical skills. Physical control of the weapons continues as a KGB function.

Kruglov's imposition of change gave the Soviet leadership a much needed breathing space in which to recover from the successive shocks of the post-Stalin era. It was a first opportunity to begin to examine their own circumstances and to decide the organs' future role. Although the missions of the organs had been defined, the means and the methods to be employed were still to be decided. By early 1954 the KGB had been given more responsibilities than it could conceivably discharge.

Kruglov's efforts at reorganization of the security and intelligence organs revealed stark inadequacies in the personnel resources needed to carry out the many and varied assigned missions. Particularly deficient were the techniques of inducting and training suitable candidates for assignment in foreign areas. Part of the problem could be attributed to Kruglov's removal of Beria loyalists. For the most part, however, it was because of the turmoil generated by Stalin's earlier *levées en masse* at the time he intended to project the KI into foreign intelligence operations.

Many of those occupying supervisory positions were ill suited to espionage work. Their operational ineptitude frequently resulted in the compromise, capture, or defection of talented personnel. The shortage of acceptable agent prospects was acute and not susceptible to a "crash" solution. It was not feasible simply to double the intake at the various training centers.

Under careful study, the problem directed its own solution. The East European states that had been forcibly incorporated into Soviet strategic considerations each had intelligence services, though they were seen as extremely junior adjuncts to the organs. Unlike the Soviets, the Poles, Czechs, East Germans, et al. had pools of worldly-wise, educated, and highly cultivated men and women who, with proper training and guidance, could perform much of the donkey work for the organs.

The old security and intelligence services of Eastern Europe were destroyed at the time of the Soviet occupation, and new Soviet-controlled services were organized. The original cadres for the new satellite services consisted of East Europeans who had spent the war in the USSR and whose loyalty to the Soviet Union already had been certified. To each of the satellite countries, the organs also dispatched senior Soviet "advisers," who then used the controlled nationals to construct a micro-replication of the Soviet service. The UB in Poland, the AVH in Hungary, the STB in Czechoslovakia, and all the others became KGB franchises with *all* lines of authority originating in Moscow.

The senior Soviet adviser in each of the satellite services designated targets, transmitted specialized intelligence missions, selected promising young officers for further training in the USSR, and kept a steely grip on all operational traffic. Since it was an inflexible rule that the names of all prospective recruitment targets first be submitted to Moscow for approval, the Soviet organs stood astride a river of promising leads and operational opportunities. By the simple imposition of Soviet standards for reporting, file checks, and communications, the organs multiplied by manyfold their ability to expand without delay.

The Soviets' distrust of anyone who had contact with the outside world had reached its apex under Stalin. He believed that even those extraordinary Soviet intelligence operatives who had demonstrated their loyalty to the USSR (e.g., Leopold Trepper and others) were considered suspect. The chronically insecure Stalin seemed to believe that those who had fought the hardest to defeat his enemies were the most dangerous and the least trustworthy.

With Stalin safely, or so it seemed, out of the picture and a new group of Bolshevik *apparatchiks** in charge, Serov proposed that the bloc services be elevated and given some limited foreign intelligence responsibilities. The KGB would control the operations as a matter of course, but the personnel carrying them out would be drawn from among the Czech, Polish, East German, Bulgarian, and other intelligence assets now available.

The decision to proceed with this experiment marked a major change in the basic operational philosophy of the organs. In the turgid language of business, the organs were transformed from a "domestic" company to a "fully integrated, multinational" corporation. It was a bold gamble. The bloc states' intelligence services had proven their ability to maintain internal security in their respective countries; however, their capacities to operate effectively against Western targets were essentially unproven. Though Serov's proposal did not command unanimous support in the Central Committee, the KGB's personnel situation and the necessity to get on with the various missions compelled its acceptance. Thus began the next and perhaps most productive phase in the organs' evolution.

The initial targets levied on the bloc states' intelligence services were as much designed to build confidence and experience as to acquire needed intelligence information. In many instances the penetration of NATO became a kind of graduation exercise for intelligence personnel before they moved on to more difficult assignments, including the United States and Great Britain.

NATO was an enticing target for the KGB. It had also proved to be an elusive one. Some Soviet successes occurred during the 1949–1954 period, although most of the Soviet penetration operations proved to be dry wells. A major cause of the failures against the Western European targets could be traced to the bizarre antics of Soviet KI personnel, who "showed up in Western capitals with their baggy suits and belligerent manners, these veterans of the prewar purges reinforced the gangster-like reputation Soviet intelligence had acquired in the 1930s."[7]

Such operatives were particularly ill suited to attack a sophisticated intelligence target like NATO. Similarly, though the young, newly trained Soviet illegals were capable of carrying out such operations, they were few in number and had been trained for more important, long-term missions. Beria had correctly decided not to spend such talent at NATO.

NATO's importance as an intelligence target diminished during the

*In the West *apparatchik* has come to mean "secret agent." In Soviet usage it means an official concerned with planning, administration, and supervision.

first few years of its existence. The Americans, French, and British were all involved in armed conflict in, respectively, Korea, Indochina, and Malaya. These national military commitments served to limit NATO's credibility as a serious threat to the Soviet Union. As these foreign military operations were brought to a close, however, and the NATO nations began to upgrade the number and caliber of the forces assigned to Western European defense, the importance of NATO as a Soviet intelligence target increased.

On October 23, 1954, a change took place that forced the Soviet Union to reappraise NATO. The event was the Paris agreement, which provided sovereignty for West Germany, including rearmament and entry into NATO as well as the Western European Union. It now appeared that Serov's proposal to use the bloc intelligence services had finally been rationalized, and the East German service was poised to act.

To demonstrate the worth of his plan, Serov had to find an East German chief for the new service who had the skills, instincts, and intelligence to direct the expanding State Security Service, or SSD (*Staatsischerheitdienst*).

Although the SSD leadership of 1954 was capable of ensuring East Germany's internal security, they were Chekist types of the old school, not particularly well equipped to run modern foreign operations. Many of the older Germans who had functioned in the twenties and thirties on Stalin's behalf had been killed by the Nazis. The few who were still living in prison at the time of the nonaggression pact were turned over to Stalin, who promptly had them executed. These prisoner exchanges highlighted Stalin's conviction that to have spent one hour in the hands of foreign police invariably meant that the prisoner had been "turned," therefore deserved only to be shot.

The first head of the SSD was Wilhelm Zaisser (aka Zeisser), whose Bolshevik pedigree was superior to his ability to cope with problems. Like many of the men who had spent their lives attacking governments, he found it difficult to make the transition to being a government official. Zaisser was an early convert to Bolshevism, winning recognition for his work with the Spartacus Bund and in the 1923 abortive revolt in Germany. In the early twenties, he became a naturalized Soviet citizen and was given extensive training in the USSR. On graduation, Zaisser was dispatched to China under the control of the GRU, then later served in Manchuria. In 1936, he was in Spain with the new and lofty title of "General Gomez," commander of the XIII International Brigade. His military competence was called into public question when his brigade attacked Teruel and suffered 50 percent casualties in the Chapiev battalion. The XIIIth was the only brigade that did not later fight in the battle for Madrid.[8]

Zaisser returned to the USSR after the bloody defeat in Spain. In the later stages of World War II, he, along with Walter Ulbricht and Ernst Wollweber, formed the rallying point for what was planned as the Soviet-owned government of postwar Germany. They followed in the wake of the Soviet armies and built the political structure for East Germany, with Ulbricht as the Soviet proconsul and Zaisser as the head of security and intelligence.

On June 17, 1953, a spontaneous popular revolt broke out in East Germany. Zaisser failed to give advance warning of the revolt, and Ulbricht's regime was almost toppled. Soviet troops and tanks had to intervene to restore order, and Zaisser was summarily dismissed.

His immediate successor was Wollweber, an old KPD strongarm man, heavy drinker, and "practician par excellence."[9] Under the most charitable construction, Wollweber deserved an endorsement no stronger than "not unfit." His appointment was made in the absence of a better qualified candidate who could invoke the notion of socialist continuity. (Despite their declared antagonism to sentiment, the Soviets seldom fail to produce elderly barricade fighters in an effort to provide living testimony relative to the "struggle." For example, Marshal Voroshilov's principal value, aside from his ability to absorb abuse, was that he had served with Stalin, under Lenin, during the civil war and was one of the very few creatures still living who could make that statement. The purpose of sustaining Voroshilov was to enhance Stalin's pedigree as the obvious lineal descendant of the revolutionary leaders, rather than to add to Voroshilov's questionable prestige.)

Wollweber was out of his depth and incapable of directing a modern, sophisticated intelligence service, even though he had attended advanced espionage and sabotage training in the Soviet Union. Temperamentally, he was always more comfortable with a truncheon than a pencil in his hand and made his reputation with the Soviets as an "old-style" man of action.

In one sense Wollweber was like so many of the maladjusted, violence-prone men and women who, unable to cope with the economic chaos in Germany following World War I, drifted into the communist movement. Many of these were simply advocates of dramatic change, and had it not been for a friend, geographic convenience, or pure chance, they might have joined Hitler.

After Moscow, and at Soviet direction, he put some distance between himself and the German Communist Party (KPD) and worked exclusively for the organs. In the early years, much of his activity was concerned with the establishment of "seamen's clubs," the recruitment of sources of maritime intelligence and others who could be trained to act as saboteurs of vessels and cargoes bound for Soviet enemies.

He first worked as a minor Comintern functionary—specifically, as Secretary of the International of Seamen and Harbor Workers (ISH), a Comintern-operated organization. Even after Hitler came to power, Wollweber returned to Germany to serve the cause, while most of his colleagues fled. His decision to remain in Germany and to continue trying to generate new nets won the enduring admiration of his Soviet controllers. The last group in Germany with which he maintained contact continued to provide excellent maritime reporting from Hamburg until it was discovered by the Germans in 1940. Of the twenty-odd men and women who made up the group, twelve were beheaded by the Germans.[10]

At the time he was ordered to leave Germany, Wollweber was directed to continue his work in Denmark, where he organized sabotage teams devoted to "neutralizing" German, Italian, and Japanese ships. The Anti-Comintern Pact had served to define the "enemy." The distinctive mark of Wollweber's maritime sabotage group was the concealed placement of dynamite charges in the bilges of selected ships, with mechanical timers set to detonate the explosives once the ships were again at sea.[11]

When Hitler invaded the Low Countries, Wollweber fled to Sweden, where he tried to continue the attacks on shipping. He was arrested by the Swedes while carrying a passport in the name of Fritz Koeller and was sentenced to six months in prison. Just before his release, his subordinates made an unsuccessful attack on a Finnish ship in a Swedish port. The bombers were arrested and in their confessions implicated Wollweber as the chief planner of the outrage, so his sentence was then extended three more years.

While Wollweber enjoyed the cleanliness and good food of a Swedish jail, the Soviet ambassador at Stockholm informed the Swedish authorities that the man they were holding in jail was a notorious Soviet citizen and well-known swindler who was wanted in Moscow in connection with the embezzlement of Soviet funds. The Swedes, ever anxious to be gulled by the Soviets, released Wollweber, who fled to Moscow in November 1944. By 1945 he was back in Germany.

In the years following the establishment of the SSD, several major inventories of East German personnel were conducted by the head of the KGB's First Chief Directorate, General Alexandr Semenovich Panyushkin. His objective was to find someone qualified to head the East German foreign intelligence elements. The search yielded a dozen or more prospects whose names were forwarded to Moscow for the consideration of Serov and the KGB Executive Council (sometimes referred to as the KGB Collegium). None seemed to meet the Soviet standards.

Panyushkin was directed to continue the search and eventually found Markus Johannes ("call me Mischa") Wolf. Though he was not an ideologue, Wolf knew all the words necessary to recite the cant of Marxism-Leninism. He was young, aggressive, intelligent, and unencumbered with the boring baggage of the Comintern's bad old days which burdened the personas of the prewar survivors. His memory was extraordinary, as was his intuitive grasp of operational concepts and essential detail.

Serov considered his alertness and youth to be advantages essential to the energizing of the East German service. Since Wolf was respected by his peers and subordinates, there seemed to be no reason why his nomination should not be passed to Moscow with Panyushkin's own strong recommendation.

Wolf began to ascend over the aging comrades, and after five years, in March 1951, he succeeded Wollweber as SSD chief. Wolf's first act in emulation of his Soviet supervisors was to conduct a minor purge that sent most of the ineffectual "comrades" back to the socialist equivalent of the hiring hall. His action pleased Serov (since such changes were called for in Serov's plan), and the Soviets found themselves in indulgent admiration of Wolf's applications of "typical German efficiency."

His winnowing of the SSD, coupled with an energetic recruitment program, gradually moved the service to the point where it began to pay its own way. With the time-servers and hacks gone, Wolf was able to begin to match personnel to assigned missions.

According to the chief of U.S. counterespionage operations in Germany, Wolf's appointment to head the SSD produced little or no reaction in the Western intelligence community. The British disparaged him on the grounds that he had been a member of Hitler's *Jugend,* the French contended that he lacked an adequate academic background, and the Americans, based on an appraisal by General Gehlen (now head of West German intelligence), dismissed Wolf as just another opportunistic German who had made his peace with the Soviets. When Wolf later saw these evaluations, he was encouraged because it was evident that his enemies had underestimated him on irrelevant grounds.

He made haste slowly, recruited carefully, and, after an extended visit to various KGB training centers, returned to East Germany to establish an even more rigorous tutorial for SSD agents. To avoid criticism, Wolf arranged to have senior KGB officers from the Center pass final judgment on his graduate agents. This added to Wolf's credibility because it indicated his acceptance of the unalterable fact that "the Center knows best." Serov observed Wolf's activities and progress with considerable pride, knowing that Wolf was exactly what the Central Committee had ordered. Once the SSD was in train, Serov tasked him with the NATO target. The objective was simply to learn any and all things that were under contemplation at NATO, the means of executing actions, and a full and complete audit of the physical as well as personnel weaknesses in the

Atlantic Alliance. It was a major program with heavy emphasis on penetration operations. The SSD intelligence offense was launched in December 1958, just at the time that Serov was unexpectedly relieved by Khrushchev.

Serov's successor, Alexandr Nikoloevich Shelepin, was not an old Chekist but a former Komsomol organizer with no experience in state security work. His appointment gave Khrushchev the best assurance he could get, for the moment, that the organs wouldn't turn on him. Shelepin's focus was on the preservation of Khrushchev. The SSD operation, with Wolf in charge, went forward with its offensive in the West.

Wolf assessed the NATO target with precision. It was an extended multinational bureaucracy laboring under the fiction that the principle of "unity of command" applied. The reality, however, was that the factional nationalism that pervaded NATO made a mockery of the principle. Wolf knew that each element of NATO was committing too much to paper in sanctification of its own position with more than adequate specific criticisms of all other viewpoints. NATO was waging an internal war of paper, generating oceans of analytical critiques. The key to understanding how effective NATO was seemed already to have been typed in multiple copies within the Alliance.

To respond to the opportunity presented, Wolf initiated what came to be called the "secretaries' offensive." He dispatched carefully trained SSD gigolos into West Germany with the mission of compromising, suborning, and recruiting NATO secretaries who could be led to resent the West German military officers assigned to NATO. The cases of West German secretaries who succumbed to the blandishments of Wolf's agents were, to a degree, made more numerous because of the skewed male-female ratios among Germans following the war. The secretaries' offensive succeeded to an astonishing degree, as the West was later to learn.

Besides the obvious benefits of turning NATO officials' confidential and private secretaries into knowing and unknowing SSD and KGB sources, Wolf understood the more pressing need to begin the process of recruiting high-level penetrations of the West German government. The long-range penetration procedure required the kinds of intellectual exercises that might be associated with three-dimensional chess, requiring strategies based on anticipations rather than on simple, current realities. In 1955, it was evident that the reemergence of Germany within the framework of NATO and the Western European Union was an unambiguous signal that World War II was over. It was also clear that the Western nations had, by this act, acknowledged that their collective security for the future was to be based on West Germany's participation.

Wolf's secondary, though no less important, target was the Federal

Republic's service (the BND), which was headed by General Reinhard Gehlen. In this case the SSD successfully optimized an "unplanned event" when a BND officer named Clemens offered to assist the SSD because of his lingering anger over the fact that his home city, Dresden, had been all but destroyed by a massive British-American bombing raid near the end of the war. Sensing the reliable motive of vengeance, the SSD moved quickly to the next question, "Are there any more at home like you?" Clemens then described his colleague, Heinz Felfe, another Dresdener harboring deep resentment toward the United States and Britain.

The SSD dutifully reported the event to the Soviets, who immediately seized control of the case. The East Germans assumed an operations support role to their Soviet controllers, who called all the plays. The East Germans and their Soviet masters directed Felfe's career carefully. They assisted him in breaking cases involving agents they considered expendable, and his career prospered. Thus, Felfe became one of the BND's most valuable senior agents.[12]

Finally, in 1961, the BND intercepted a KGB communication to Felfe that confirmed their now considerable conviction that the BND had been penetrated. Once arrested, Felfe confessed to having given the Soviets fifteen thousand frames of microfilmed BND documents and twenty reels of BND tape recordings. Most importantly, his actions had caused considerable loss of life among East Germans who had put themselves at great risk to assist the West in frustrating the Soviet espionage offensive in West Germany.

Felfe was sentenced to fourteen years in prison; Clemens, who cooperated, received a lesser sentence. When Gustav Heinemann, a socialist, became the minister of justice in the so-called grand coalition of 1966, he tried to have Felfe released "for humane reasons." Unsuccessful in this attempt, Heinemann finally did exchange Felfe for a mixed bag of prisoners held in East German jails. Clemens was by this time acutely aware of his destructive role and refused to be exchanged, preferring to remain in a West German prison rather than enjoy the "freedom" offered by the East.

In the 1950s, West Germany moved steadily in the direction of economic self-sufficiency and political stability, and it was clear that the country would become an important factor in the emerging East-West conflict. Wolf realized that the initial leadership was both elderly and transient and, in the longer-term, probably irrelevant to the future. The targets, then, lay in the younger politicians who would eventually hold power at the time West Germany became a more immediate threat.

The Adenauer regime was assessed in terms of the opportunities it might provide for penetrations of low-level people likely to achieve positions of greater importance in the future.

The Soviets agreed that once the aging, symbolic Chancellor Konrad Adenauer retired or died, his likely heir would become the leader of a powerful West Germany.

Of the many possibilities, the strongest candidate for succession was judged to be the mayor of Berlin, Willy Brandt. The SSD-KGB forecast did not differ in any significant degree from that of most of the Western political pundits. Casting about for the means of insinuating someone into Brandt's entourage, the Center came to Wolf's assistance.

Wolf's analysis of Brandt as a potential intelligence target revealed few vulnerabilities. As mayor of Berlin, Brandt was aware of the depredations among West Germans by the now hyperactive SSD. The competition among the various Allied intelligence services complicated the picture but may have provided the first opening for the East Germans to exploit. Brandt resented the sometimes patronizing attitudes of the Allied military government and the German High Commissioner's office.

In their analysis of Brandt as a target, the SSD, with the aid of the KGB, began at the beginning. Brandt seemed to be a "loner." He had few friends, as most had been killed by the Gestapo during the war.

The search did yield one name out of Brandt's past. It was that of Dr. Ernst Wilhelm Guillaume, who had at one time tended Brandt's wounds and sheltered him from capture. By 1954, Dr. Guillaume was a semi-invalid living in East Germany. Wolf's people sought him out and found that he, though infirm, remained a "good German," a staunch antifascist.

He lived with his daughter, Elsa, who cared for him and his son, Gunter. Elsa was resigned to life in the East, but young Gunter was deeply resentful of his lot. Elicitation by the recruiter established that Gunter despised the Allies and had a wholly tolerant view of the Soviet forces that had "liberated" and now occupied East Germany. Gunter was in his late teens when Hitler's dream ended in 1945. Like many young people of his generation, he regarded the Allied insistence on unconditional surrender as nothing more than a subterfuge for the planned destruction of the German people.

He was a dutiful son who contributed to the support of his ailing father and sister. Like many East Germans, he was forced into a life as a common laborer, one of those who daily crossed into West Berlin and worked under the direction of the Allied powers. To Gunter it was a degrading experience that only added to his resentment. This point in particular was carefully noted by the SSD recruiter and reported to the KGB.

The consensus in the SSD was that the young man could be recruited on two points: (1) his deep sense of obligation to his father and (2) his powerful antipathy toward the Allies. When the approach was made, Gunter was given assurances with respect to his father's continuing care and was offered a job in which he would be able to perform an important service for the East German government. His contempt for the Allies moved him readily to accept the SSD's assertions that the Soviet Union was now the dominant force in Western Europe and that it would be foolish for a promising young man to find himself on the losing side. The proposition was made as a skillful manipulation of the wants that had been identified in his earlier conversations with the SSD officer; a strong sense of familial duty, an intense, though peculiar, German nationalism, and a self-developed need for vengeance.

Gunter's commitment to the cause was easily won. His enthusiasm was carefully tempered by a tutorial in the essential skills. He was measured, tested, and continuously observed throughout the process. With thoughtful guidance provided by the SSD, he began to see the initially vague outline of the target. He was essentially an ideological recruit, and so it was imperative to reprogram his responses to political stimuli to ensure his own self-protection. He became a staunch anticommunist.

The first operational exercise Gunter ran under SSD direction was against his infirm father. He urged that Dr. Guillaume send a letter to his old friend and former patient, Willi Brandt, reminding Brandt of their last stressful meeting during the war, explaining his own state of declined health, and ending with a plea for Brandt to help his son. With Gunter's coaching, Dr. Guillaume pulled out all the stops. The old man explained that his son, a very able young man, was an indirect casualty of the war and desperately needed the chance to break out of the demeaning cycle of rubble-clearing.

Brandt was impressed with the letter and felt an obligation to Dr. Guillaume, for whom he had much respect. He thought of Gunter as the type of youngster who, in the normal course of events, would have gone on to a university education and a likely career in medicine had not Hitler led Germany to defeat.

From their first meeting in early 1955, Brandt was taken with Gunter. In a sense, Gunter might have been the son Brandt wanted but never had. Gunter became his "special assistant" during the period when Brandt was beginning to feel his way through the new German political jungle. Gunter found the fit of his job with Brandt to be perfect, and with extraordinary energy and skill he began the gradual process of making himself indispensable to his employer. Gunter was one of three special assistants but worked as if he were Brandt's sole support. "Energetic," "tireless," "available," and "prepared" were the words used to describe him. If Brandt arrived at his office at seven A.M., he would find that

Gunter had preceded him and was already dealing with the day's work in a quiet, efficient manner.

As Gunter's insinuation into Brandt's world continued, the SSD controller, now under Wolf's personal supervision, provided encouragement, reassurance, and praise. Gunter reported frequently and in interesting detail, but he was reminded, gently but often, that his primary objective was to become Brandt's most trusted confidant, dealing with the politically sensitive material that passed across his leader's desk. Gunter worked hard at his assigned task and came to be regarded by all as a diligent young man with a boundless capacity for details. He made a point of his devotion to duty by forgoing earned leave so that he could better tend Willy Brandt's interests.

By 1956, West Germany had become an integral element of the Atlantic Alliance, and Brandt had become a political power in his own right. Brandt's rise was a gratifying development for the SSD and the KGB elders at Karlshorst. From all appearances, they had put their money on the right horse, on the right track, at the right time.

It would be erroneous to dismiss Gunter as a "bad seed." He was simply the result of a painstaking recruitment based on a comprehensive assay of the forces that propelled him. The case is a tribute to clerical work, assiduous preparation, a clearly articulated objective, and constant psychological maintenance by a dedicated case officer.

Through the late fifties and early sixties, Willy Brandt was ascending rapidly through the ranks of West German politicians. His terms as mayor of Berlin had brought him into close contact with many Western leaders who found him politically adept, and he had great attraction for the new German electorate. Adenauer's immediate successor, Ludwig Erhard, was moving to strengthen his political base by focusing on the economy, but in 1966 his government collapsed because his Christian Democratic Party lost the support of the Free Democrats. A new government was formed in which the Christian Democrats coalesced with their parliamentary adversary, the Social Democratic Party (led by Willy Brandt), and became the "grand coalition" under Chancellor Kurt Georg Kiesinger.

The resultant political maneuvering was closely followed by the Center. Brandt, without his knowledge, even received some hidden assistance from the East that reinforced his success. With the departure of Kiesinger, Brandt rose to head a strong coalition government that embodied politically diverse views. In the perspective of the West, the Federal Republic under Willy Brandt was an acceptable expression of a novel form of democratic government.

From the Soviet point of view, each of Brandt's successes were Guillaume's successes. Gunter's access to increasingly sensitive information broadened with each elevation of his boss.

Brandt was an outspoken anticommunist and a loyal ally, and as the German economic "miracle" continued, he became even more important to the West. West Germany had joined NATO in 1955, and so Brandt's office dealt regularly with sensitive military information affecting all of the organization's members. As the Cold War continued, the Soviets were able to share in NATO's planning as an unseen, unrecognized, silent partner.

Guillaume had achieved continuing access to all West German data relating to West European defenses by rigorously discharging his role as Brandt's inexhaustible aide. Everything Brandt saw, Gunter saw first. The SSD at the direction of the KGB pressed Gunter *not* to take any initiative but to continue to absorb the daily traffic passively. In this way he was able to inform Wolf's people about summaries sent to Brandt that indicated, generally with great specificity, where additional information was to be found.

Such minutiae enabled the SSD to target particular NATO offices, using the growing group of suborned secretaries recruited by the SSD gigolos. As a West German counterintelligence officer who participated in the postmortem of the case remarked, Guillaume "functioned as a senior archivist and provided the SSD with maps showing precisely where the treasures were to be found."

The importance of the case lies in the fact that until 1974, when Guillaume's role was finally uncovered, he was able to provide the East with the information necessary to negate almost every substantive effort by the West. His worth to the Soviets was incalculable. As the twelfth man in every Western huddle for more than a decade, his cost to the Allies was also beyond reckoning.

The main lesson to be drawn from the Guillaume penetration is that it was developed as a systemic rather than a localized assault. The West German external intelligence service, *Bundesnachrichtendienst* (BND), had a strong interest in learning how Guillaume could have functioned with absolute impunity for so long a time. Their painstaking postmortem revealed that despite compartmentation, classification, and need-to-know strictures, Guillaume's main SSD function evolved into spotting the specific organizational sources of important data rather than attempting to acquire the data itself.

In doing this he used summaries of the Program of Cooperation (POC) transactions to provide exact targeting information to the SSD. The POC had been established in the late fifties as the vehicle by which highly classified military technology was provided to NATO members. The POC provided the basis for direct liaison among the NATO defense ministers and the various national military commands without the participation of the national foreign ministries.

The sweep and scope of the specifics of the POC transactions were routinely circulated to the chiefs of state, making it easy for Guillaume to get the information the SSD wanted. This targeting technique enabled the SSD to specify the documents to be stolen or copied by date, serial number, and title, thereby circumventing the dangers of indiscriminate collection by the suborned secretaries.

The overall effort was not an unalloyed success. The Soviets found themselves unable to exploit some of the technological intelligence collected by the SSD. For instance, at one point they acquired all the data relating to an inertial guidance system for an early prototype of a cruise missile. After study, the Soviets decided to construct a copy of the device. When tested, it not only failed to function as expected but killed and injured several engineers. Consistent with the KGB's adherence to the pirate's code, the accident was internally attributed to a foreign (in this case, U.S. or British) plot. Any suggestion that the work had been badly performed or that the engineers were incompetent or that the materials were defective might be misinterpreted as a "slander of socialism," and therefore the event had to be regarded as a diabolical provocation.

After a tip from an informant, Guillaume was arrested, tried, and convicted along with his wife. After several years in a West German prison, they were exchanged for a few West German citizens held in the East. He was awarded the Order of Lenin and, according to recent Soviet defectors, now lectures in the KGB's school complex.

Guillaume never looked back, and Willy Brandt, an honest politician, never fully comprehended the hurt inflicted by his personal Brutus.

The Guillaume case destroyed Brandt and caused great harm to NATO. The Felfe-Clemens case wounded the BND. All indications were that the bloc services deserved a place in the Soviet sun. The original proposal to entrust the satellites with KGB missions was now a matter of operational doctrine. In equivalent terms Guillaume, Felfe, and Clemens were second-generation penetrations on the Philby model,[13] each having been ideological recruits who rose within their national systems only to contribute to their destruction.

The Guillaume and Felfe cases reveal something about the Soviets' approach to sources and methods. Guillaume acted as a passive target spotter who was able to provide precise directions for use by the SSD's collection arm. His continuity in office and acute awareness of important issues greatly enhanced his general utility. Felfe's role was also vital to the KGB. As a counterintelligence officer, his reputation was, to a large degree, based on his successes. Although not recognized at the time, the Soviet and East German cases that he broke with such cunning and skill were mainly giveaways by the Soviets, calculated to build Felfe's importance and to ensure his promotions within the BND. By having a senior BND counterintelligence officer as a controlled Soviet agent, the KGB was able to shield its important operations and, simultaneously, occupy the Allies' full attentions with burned-out and bogus cases.

It was quite natural that General Gehlen, who headed the BND until 1968, diminished the importance of Felfe and suggested that the effect of Felfe's treason might have been overstated.[14] His comments served his own interests and they obscured the fact that a great number of Allied intelligence and counterintelligence officers had been identified to the Soviets and the SSD. This detailed knowledge enabled the organs not only to target those who were active but also, more importantly, to identify and continue the surveillance of intelligence contacts and sources and, in some instances, their replacements.

The Allies contributed to the problem illustrated by the Guillaume and Felfe cases by their often counterproductive competition in intelligence matters. Another factor that added to the Soviets' success was the fact of a divided Germany. The anomalous situation of an isolated Berlin, within which sectors and zones formed political frontiers, made Germany a counterintelligence nightmare. After the war, the area that became West Germany in 1949 was governed by British, French, and U.S. military governments and, later, by a high commissioner. The Federal Republic did not gain full independence until 1955. The political, social, and economic realities of an occupied, war-devastated, divided Germany were appalling. In general, the combat forces were quickly withdrawn and replaced by military government units. Most of the experienced, senior intelligence staffs were marked for early redeployment to the Far East, where both sides were preparing for the climactic final phase of the war—the assault on the Japanese home islands.

In the early stages, the line on the map that delineated the border between East and West Germany and marked the zones in Berlin did not stop the flow of refugees. It took the Red Army, with the help of its surrogate East German forces, several years to seal off the borders. Not until the Berlin Wall was erected in 1961 were the Eastern forces able to exert control. Even then, some East Germans were able to move to the West. Thus, in the mid-1980s East Germany's population stood at 17 million, about the same as it was in 1946. On the other hand, the population of West Germany has grown to close to 62 million—roughly a 40-percent increase over 1946. Berlin's population of a little over 3 million, East and West combined, has remained relatively stable.

All Germans were entitled to enter the Western zone and be received as citizens. Among the refugees were many coercive recruits (those with a mission who had families held hostage in the East), SSD-trained agents (who were charged with going through the process of applying for citizenship and, after a few months, returning to the East to report their experience and to surrender their recently acquired Western documents for later use by the SSD), and many others, including people like Guillaume, who lived in the East and worked in the West, with relatives and friends in both camps.

The Allies were unable to establish the bona fides of these hundreds of thousands of Germans who sought refuge. The dislocations, war damage, and incomplete, "removed," or destroyed records made West Germany and Berlin an exceedingly soft target for the introduction of thousands of agents.

The Soviets brought into play twenty-five years of experience, remarkable continuity, extensive files, and hundreds of trained and experienced multinational agents.

The Soviets also had clearly articulated objectives that were based on their official (i.e., Stalin's) view that the surrender of Germany marked the *beginning* of the great, and, perhaps, final war with the West. The main Allied efforts were spent in disarming troops, liberating POWs, denazifying Germans, bringing war criminals to trial, resettling refugees, and feeding, reconstructing, policing, and governing their respective sectors.

German troops in Soviet hands were marched off to camps where they remained for years after the war. The only "war criminals" in the Soviet zone were those Germans who were declared to be anti-Soviet and were summarily shot. Liberated Russian POWs, by having been captured, had already committed treason and were due no more than prompt execution. The displaced and homeless were transported to labor camps in the Soviet north. The meager food allocations to the remaining German people were rationed to ensure their submission and compliance. No reconstruction occurred in the Soviet zone, so that the Germans would live in the moonscape they had brought upon themselves by the war.

The East Germans performed a distinctive service for the West in 1953 by their unsuccessful attempt to revolt against Soviet rule. Though the uprising failed, it provided the trigger to the events that resulted in the arrest and execution of Beria.

In 1956, another attempted insurrection was also suppressed, but only after it had been artfully exploited by the organs. It was one more in a series of unplanned events that the Soviets were agile enough to convert to their own interest.

Unlike Germany, Hungary was undivided, as the Red Army had occupied most of the country by late 1944. The Soviet military occupation of Hungary and most other bloc states was imposed before the West fully realized what Stalin had done.

Faced with a fait accompli, there was little or no interest on the part of the West to react. In the rush to demobilize their forces, there seemed to be no conscious realization on the part of the West that the Soviets would take full title to the bloc countries overrun by Red Army troops. For that reason no one in the West was insisting on the need to "reliberate" Hungary.

The Soviet occupation was not without problems in Hungary. There was a latent opposition to communism stemming from a long history of a different kind of "socialist" advocacy. The principal issue, however, was the collapsed economy and Stalin's refusal to allow the Hungarians to apply for Marshall Plan aid from the United States.

Stalin remembered the politically destabilizing effects on Soviet society when Lenin acceded to Herbert Hoover's introduction of the American Relief Administration aid in the 1920s. Stalin was determined not to permit a U.S. role in Eastern Europe, even though his refusal imposed great hardships on the people. The Western powers, harboring the commendable illusion that well-fed people are happy and docile, overlooked the Soviet experience. The Bolsheviks had demonstrated in the USSR that starving people can be made even more docile. Happiness counts for nothing in the Soviet socialist scheme.

Stalin's decision in favor of Hungarian austerity produced no happy Hungarians, but the Red Army, the organs, and their Hungarian counterpart, the AVH, had no difficulty in maintaining internal security and public order. In Stalin's view that was all the situation required or demanded.

In 1953, the new Soviet-appointed Premier, Imre Nagy, presided over an uneasy Hungary. The populace was becoming increasingly restive, demanding a government policy that favored agriculture and consumer production. It was the classic socialist dilemma—the needs of the "state" versus the needs of the people. Nagy favored the policy advocated by the people, but the Kremlin did not. In one sense, Khrushchev and Malenkov, in the wake of Stalin's death, looked upon Hungary as the point in the bloc at which the Soviet regime might begin to unravel if the restraints on the people were lessened. There was also concern about the Hungarian Communist Party's insistence on an increased degree of autonomy in determining the methods of bolstering the national economy.

The new Soviet rulers, unsteady and fearful, opted for the more conservative decision—to tighten Soviet control over the Hungarian Communist Party and reinforce controls on the Hungarian people.

In executing this decision, a forty-year-old Chekist named Yuri Andropov was dispatched to Budapest in early 1954 as "counselor" at the Soviet embassy. His title suggested that he was a diplomat assigned by the Ministry of Foreign Affairs, although many were aware that he was a moderately important KGB officer. His function was to act as the "resident."

His assignment was routine and had no special portent except to identify him as a mid-level Chekist who had survived the post-Beria purges in the organs. His career up to that point was no more or less distinguished than others of his age, rank, and experience. His predecessor had blotted his copy book by allowing the Hungarian CP too long a leash and by not coming down hard on the first indications of popular dissent.

When Andropov reached Budapest, he found the situation to be far worse than he had been led to believe.[15] The domestic political situation was about as described, but the KGB station was in a shambles and had lost the prescribed steel grip on the AVH. In the course of the occupation, the KGB personnel had become slothful and self-indulgent. Budapest was filled with temptations that the Soviets found difficult to resist, and most of the station's personnel were summarily relieved and sent back to Moscow in disgrace.

It was clear that Andropov had, indeed, arrived in Budapest. Acting as a nerveless clinician, he excised the rot and removed the dead tissue from the station. His personnel purge produced a minor crisis when he dismissed a few officers who had thought they were inviolate on the strength of their previous loyalty to Stalin. The Center supported Andropov, and a replacement staff of tough new officers was assembled and sent into the breach. Andropov then moved quickly to snap the Hungarian Communist Party back on line and into absolute consonance with Moscow. The hierarchs of the Hungarian CP and the AVH might have imagined that they heard tumbrils rattling through the streets of Buda and Pest, as some prominent heads rolled and discipline was restored. The Center was pleased to congratulate Andropov four months later for his efficient "work."

Andropov assumed that Hungarian internal security was lax and could not be brought under proper control by resorting to Stalinist terror tactics. He saw the problem as requiring a more subtle approach and began a systematic penetration operation against actual and potential problem areas. The organized protestors represented an easy first step. This was followed by infiltration of the student political groups and labor elements. He understood that local Hungarian informants of the type used by the AVH could not succeed, and in their places he placed Soviet-trained agents under KGB control.

The tactics were conventional and involved penetration agents who could identify the protest leadership. The operation was unusual only because of the scale on which it was conducted. The Hungarian dissidents did not take even the most rudimentary steps to protect organizational security and did not understand the need for silence. They had no ideas about vetting new adherents and seemed to be willing to accept into the groups almost anyone who volunteered to participate in the "movement."

Andropov recommended to the Center that the time had come to teach Nagy a lesson in socialist humility. Nagy, though popular and possessing appropriate communist credentials, overestimated his importance to the new leaders in the Kremlin. When, on April 18, 1955, Andropov informed Nagy that he was to "step aside," the words came as a thunderbolt. Being without an alternative, Nagy complied, and Andropov's nominee, Erno Gero, took power as the Hungarian CP secretary, though without the title of premier.

Coincident with this event, Andropov was elevated and named as the Soviet ambassador to Hungary. He retained his post as resident but brought in Viktor Chebrikov to serve as his deputy and to run the station's day-to-day operations.[16]

Andropov was popular in Budapest's diplomatic circles. It was here that he gained his reputation as an urbane man of the world, in contradistinction to the humorless, run-of-the-mill Soviet apparatchiks in diplomatic suiting. Despite his duties, he became fluent in Hungarian, which not only broadened his popular base with the Hungarian CP, but also made it easier for him to discharge his more important tasks.

Gero continued to function as the Soviets' robot until mid-1956, when he fell into disfavor, and the Hungarian CP's rank and file called for his ouster and replacement by Nagy. The CP disliked his "collegial" approach to problem solving, and there was growing popular resentment over the party's policies.

KGB infiltrators confirmed the seriousness of the situation. In consequence, Andropov and the Kremlin agreed to reinstate Nagy in his former role as premier. This was to take effect on October 23, 1956. Gero was to remain as the party's general secretary, but with diminished powers. It was hoped that these changes would still popular discontent or, at least, buy time.

The plan didn't work. The demonstrations that had sputtered intermittently during the summer and early fall of 1956 erupted into open revolt by the second week in October. When the AVH opened fire on a demonstration, the shots signaled the beginning of the Hungarian "uprising." Whether the AVH opened fire on orders or in panic is not known. A darker view is that the Center's predilection for provocation was the basis for the action. The reasoning is that provocation is a little like cloud seeding—a way of bringing natural forces into resolution without getting your feet wet. In this version, Andropov judged mid-October as the most propitious time to eliminate the protest movement by the imposition of crushing new controls.

Gero, responding to the violence, called for assistance from the Soviet armed forces to crush the rioting. On October 18, when Nagy announced that the Soviet Union had agreed to withdraw its troops from Hungary, the insurrection appeared to be losing support. The Russian withdrawal began on October 19th, leaving the AVH to deal with a small mutinous residue. On October 23, the Nagy government announced that it was withdrawing from the Warsaw Pact and was appealing to the United Nations for help in regaining its national sovereignty. But neither the UN nor NATO took any action. Another Communist Party leader, Janos Kadar, quickly formed a rival government and called for Soviet military aid to end the revolt. The withdrawing Russian troops, augmented by heavy reinforcements, turned back and attacked Budapest on November 4. With a force estimated at near 250,000 men and 2,500 tanks, they quickly regained control of the city.

Andropov claimed that he had not been informed of the decision to attack; indeed, prior to its execution, he insisted to Nagy that such an attack would not occur. Then as now, Andropov's assurances were consistent with Lenin's argument that truth is a weapon to be used sparingly.

The popular movement was crushed with casualty estimates varying from 6,500 to 32,000 dead. Many who were later arrested were either executed or deported to the camps. Between 170,000 and 196,000 persons fled the country. The United States received 38,248 under a refugee emergency program, with other Western nations taking their share; 12,000 Hungarians were accepted by Great Britain.

Though there are conflicting analyses of Andropov's role in the Hungarian uprising,[17] the record is clear that it accelerated his ascent within the organs. A Western diplomat who served in Budapest in the 1950s said he thought that Andropov's eagerness to explore the true situation in Hungary was the key to his success in the months and years after the uprising. "When he came to Hungary, he was forty years old, a junior functionary, not even a member of the Central Committee," said the diplomat. "Then he became ambassador, which was in itself unusual, because few diplomats are ever promoted without changing posts. Then the country fell apart, which should have marked him for oblivion. Proconsuls who fail are usually deposed. However, Andropov kept on moving up. His big contribution—the thing that made his masters in Moscow respect him—must have been his tough accurate appraisals of the situation in Budapest. The key lesson of that episode is not the arrival of the Soviet tanks, which was obviously decided upon at a much higher level than the embassy, but what came after the tanks."[18]

What "came after the tanks" is an important factor to consider in understanding the KGB's effectiveness as well as Andropov's rise to head the organs. The subsequent events, though not the result of a formal plan, provided the KGB with an unprecedented opportunity to advance their "work."

The penetrations who had provided Andropov with the "tough accurate appraisals of the situation" in Budapest were now in unprecedented positions to carry on their work. Andropov's Hungarian agents had acquired the best cover the Center could have imagined, that of certified anticommunist "freedom fighters."

The violence of the Hungarian uprising was unanticipated by the Soviets, Western observers, and most of all by Hungarians. The AVH headquarters was attacked and burned, and many Hungarian state security officials were beaten to death or shot. Internal security communications were disrupted, leading hundreds of other AVH officers to conclude that they too were about to become victims of the searing vengeance of the people they had repressed and abused. Uniforms were discarded along with all identity documents, and, where possible, the frightened AVH survivors joined the thousands of Hungarians in flight to the Austrian border.

The Soviet-controlled penetrations who, in their own defense, had fought side by side with the insurrectionists also found themselves fleeing to the West when the Soviet military forces closed their grip on Budapest.

The tens of thousands of Hungarians in Austria were initially considered to be a homogeneous mob with a commonly shared seething antipathy to Soviet rule. International organizations such as the Red Cross, HIAS, and the UN, with substantial contributions from the West, provided essential food, shelter, and clothing in addition to assisting the refugees apply for visas to the Western countries that volunteered to accept them as immigrants.

The streams of escaped Hungarians that began to fan out into Western Europe and United States included defrocked AVH officers as well as Soviet penetration agents. With the reestablishment of Soviet control in Hungary, Andropov's preliminary assessment was that the uprising, however bloody, carried unintended collateral benefits for the organs. Never before had so many trained agents, with impenetrable cover, been distributed so widely in such a short time.

Since the days of Dzerzhinsky, the organs had been possessed of a special capacity for converting unexpected, fortuitous events into the obvious consequences of "prior planning." Andropov was able to report a triumph to the Center: Almost two hundred of his direct and indirect agents were en route to Canada, the United States, France, Italy, and Britain, all with the assistance of the Western governments and the international organizations.

The fact that the agents were out of contact and, in the case of many, wanted no further connection with the Soviets was of no consequence. Every one of them was vulnerable to being coerced back into Soviet service; the KGB would have no difficulty in recontacting them once they had settled into their new homes in the West. The prospects presented by this accidental victory produced a new regard for Andropov. It did much to enhance his personal status and prestige within the organs. In the curious world of Kremlin politics, meanwhile, Khrushchev had emerged as the leader. Both the army and the Central Committee reacted to the new opportunities with indifference, except to note that the tail of the organs seemed once again to be trying to wag the political dog. As cautious men, they were determined to restrain the organs and ensure that the KGB did not again become the dominant Soviet power. In the aftermath of Hungary, in December 1958, Khrushchev relieved Ivan Serov as KGB chairman and replaced him with Alexandr Shelepin.[19]

Despite continuing reservations about the role of the organs, the KGB continued to upgrade the quality of personnel and to introduce members of the "new breed." The most senior officers during this period had been very junior when Stalin purged the service in the thirties. Too junior to have been tried, shot, or sent to the forced labor camps, they had survived the hot war, been educated by the cold war, and were now more efficient, though much less ideological, than their predecessors.

Like well-rewarded bureaucrats everywhere, they were confronted with the pedestrian problem of ensuring that their growing children got a fair place in the sun. The route for these privileged ones was through the upper school system and university. Upward mobility for the sons and daughters of the apparatchiks was assured by the fact that few professors could summon the resolve to fail the son or daughter of a middling, let alone, senior KGB man.

Nepotism was unavoidable. Each year a somewhat larger crop of privileged graduates flooded the job market. The KGB has always had the advantage of the "pick of the litter," and since a growing number in each successive group were KGB-related, security and bona fides problems were minimal. Of the nonscientifically trained, the Foreign Ministry had second choice.

Life outside the Soviet Union brings many advantages, including access to Western consumer goods, which rank very high on the Soviet careerist's wish list. The accretion of foreign manufactured goods conveys the high probability that you, your father, brother, uncle, or son is a member of the organs.

By 1961, the organs had developed into a competent intelligence service. Shelepin's stewardship proved to be better than had been expected. Internal security was excellent, and the flow of quality intelligence through the Center to the party and the military was of sufficient quality for Khrushchev to conclude that the Soviet Union was well placed to make a dramatic move on the world stage.

The first small cloud in the Soviet sky appeared on January 20, 1961, when President John F. Kennedy gave his inaugural speech. The Center's psychological profiles of Kennedy and his likely appointees suggested that the relaxed and predictable days of the Eisenhower regime were at an end. The KGB's estimate was soon confirmed by additional evidence from the United States, Central America, and especially the new Cuban Intelligence service (DGI), which insisted that Kennedy would soon approve a plan for an invasion of Cuba.

Paradoxically, the more information about Cuba the Center passed on to Khrushchev, the less he believed. According to later defectors, Shelepin deferred to his political superiors on the relatively safe grounds that, although the intelligence indicated the plan was being advanced, it was not possible to draw firm and final conclusions about U.S. intentions.[20]

One Center asset with some American experience was a former S.I.S. officer, George Blake, who reportedly counseled that U.S. intentions should not be judged in terms of conventional Kremlin wisdom, because there had been a major change in American attitudes. Blake's interpretation was dismissed on the basis that he was judged to be hopelessly "out of touch."[21]

The Cuban invasion was indeed attempted, and one of the clear consequences of the event was that both Kennedy and Khrushchev felt betrayed by their respective intelligence services. Kennedy concluded that he had been seriously misled by Dulles.[22] Khrushchev was angered because Shelepin had failed to argue the KGB's case more forcefully.

Shelepin was disciplined as a result of Khrushchev's illogical reaction to unwanted intelligence. There was now nothing to be done except to continue to measure Kennedy's responses to the humiliation at the Bay of Pigs. A dependable interpretation was essential to construct an appropriate Soviet stance at the coming meeting between Kennedy and Khrushchev in Vienna. Some in the Central Committee argued that the meeting should be deferred, but the Soviet military leaders pressed Khrushchev to go ahead with the summit in order to reinforce the case with the new President that the USSR and its client states would not permit aggressive actions by the United States in Cuba or anywhere else in the world.

The meeting took place and resulted in some unanticipated consequences. The Soviet leaders concluded that Kennedy, still smarting from the Bay of Pigs, was now highly susceptible to intimidation. The Center was far from certain on this point; Shelepin gave voice to his reservations about probable American behavior. His view was derided and dismissed by the military. On the advice of "his" marshals, Khrushchev began the process that led to the shipment of Soviet nuclear delivery systems to Cuba.

Shelepin made one more attempt, arguing that it was dangerous and foolish to seek nuclear confrontation with the United States. But he was sacked by Khrushchev in November 1961 and replaced by Vladimir Yefimovich Semichastny. Then the situation turned out as Shelepin had forecast.

The events of the 1962 Cuban Missile Crisis are outside the scope of this account. The details have been exhaustively reported except for the comparative effects on the two national intelligence systems as well as the resultant changed relationship between Khrushchev and the Soviet military.

The organs were in a position to point to the correctness of their previous estimates, but the recently installed Semichastny curbed this inclination. The military sought scapegoats from its own ranks for the misadventure, thus surrendering some of its influence. Khrushchev came out of the confrontation with his reputation still relatively intact and boasting of the "special relationship" between himself and Kennedy.

Khrushchev's secret correspondence with Kennedy over the Cuban Missile Crisis reveals, among other things, that the two men had achieved a fragile *modus vivendi* that opened up new lines of communication between Moscow and Washington and lessened the threat of war by accident.[23]

In a sense, the confrontation worked to the advantage of both men. It enabled Khrushchev to pursue his economic policies somewhat at the expense of the Soviet military, whose influence was diminished by the Cuban crisis, and it gave Kennedy new support in the West.

In the Kremlin's scheme of things this didn't mean that the organs were committed to Khrushchev's public policy of "peaceful coexistence," particularly in the arena of foreign intelligence operations. Khrushchev had announced that the USSR would commit itself to the support of "wars of national liberation," and this public policy was to be put into effect by the organs. It was a new phase of war. It depended on clandestine means rather than conventional military forces. It also meant that the Soviet military adventurers were no longer tall in the policy saddle.

With a tug at its collective forelock, the Soviet military establishment accepted the assigned budget cuts and bided time. This role reversal was reported by Soviet defectors at the time, but the significance and accuracy of their information were disputed in Western intelligence circles, which were disposed to favor the probability of an ever-increasing Soviet "military threat."

The organs continued to report the U.S. position, although Khrushchev remained unconvinced that the American military "buildup" (presumed to have been a response to the Soviet "buildup") was a new threat or presaged any hostile action toward the USSR. Khrushchev had sensed a conservative strain in Kennedy's makeup and was prepared to act on that perception.

Although Khrushchev probably was correct in his assessment, conditions changed dramatically when Kennedy was assassinated on November 22, 1963. Khrushchev could no longer invoke his "special relationship," and Kennedy was no longer able to ameliorate or avoid new confrontation between the United States and the USSR. The public assumption of Soviet complicity in Kennedy's death continues, and the effects of the unexpected events contributed to Khrushchev's loss of power.

With the backing of the Soviet military, Leonid Brezhnev vowed not to be misled by American protestations of peaceful intent. The military collected part of the price for their support of Brezhnev in the ouster of Khrushchev through increases in the budget for the Soviet armed forces.

Restoration of the funds was not enough, however, since the technology essential to upgrade the military was lacking. Although the Soviet space program was in rough parity with the U.S. program it had provided little direct benefit to the Soviet military. Despite extensive KGB and GRU reporting on U.S. technological breakthroughs in the military field, little had been done to follow up and exploit the information by redirecting Soviet industry.

Although the KGB and GRU had their own scientific directorates, they were not able to organize and mount the kinds of expanded technical-intelligence collection missions that were needed. Much of the earlier work had involved the exploitation of material acquired by the Soviet "Purchasing Commission" during World War II. But the new technologies, especially those involving advanced electronics and underwater acoustics and guidance systems, required the attentions of more competent and better qualified scientists and technicians than were available to the services.

Early in Brezhnev's reign the specific deficiencies in the KGB and GRU programs were identified for correction. The results of this extensive audit formed the basis for the most recent changes in the organization and missions of the organs. First, the staffs of the KGB and GRU had to be augmented with personnel having the requisite scientific skills. Service in the organs was not an attractive prospect for those with marked ability in the scientific and technical fields, since such service invariably meant working under severe security controls with the concurrent loss of professional contacts among one's academic fellows. Outside the organs, the scientists enjoyed respected and secure positions in Soviet society, and most preferred the perquisites of their professions to the discipline and hazards of the intelligence trade.

Their objections could have been overcome if the scientists and technicians were needed only to serve as consultants to the KGB and GRU laboratories or as scientific "attachés" in foreign posts. However, the prospect of serving as "illegals" in clandestine foreign intelligence operations was frightening and unacceptable to many. The organs were empowered to compel the assignments, but they were acutely aware that such measures would not guarantee effective performance.

Further examination of the problem revealed that a major objection was the KGB/GRU practice of not permitting dependents to accompany agents assigned to foreign areas. The prohibition dated back to the beginning of Bolshevik history and was based on the conviction that it was essential to hold a clandestine agent's dependents hostage in the Soviet Union to assure his loyalty and to inhibit all thoughts of defection. In light of the organs' early experience with desertions, it was not a wholly unjustified approach.

By 1964 the need for technical intelligence was too acute not to consider the risk of altering the traditional policy. As a consequence, Brezhnev authorized dependents of clandestine agents to accompany their spouses. Later the same privilege was accorded to scientific officers, in an effort to induce their service in roles outside the USSR. Old Chekists expressed their reservations about the perils of the new regulations, but for the most part they tended to be the more senior officers who were without the most rudimentary comprehension of basic science.

The organs' increased emphasis on scientific and technical information required a shift in budgetary allocations. Defectors of the period estimate that as much as 50 percent of the new budget went to the technical-intelligence collection, with the remainder devoted to conventional espionage.

The first external sign of change was a marked increase in "scientific and cultural" exchanges, which were agreed to by President Johnson and Premier Brezhnev at their Glassboro, N.J., summit meeting in 1964. Shortly thereafter the United States was inundated with Soviet "scientists." It was evident to the FBI that these were scientific-intelligence collection agents in the diaphanous cover of forty-five-year-old "students." Because of their numbers, they presented a new challenge to the already thorny internal security problem in the United States.

Other Soviets were assigned to "commercial" activities and pursued their objectives by intense efforts to stimulate the promotion of "trade" in the fields of instrumentation, electronics, computers, sensors, communications switching, and other areas of military application.

The systematic theft of unpublished manuscripts and dissertations from university libraries throughout the United States can only be reckoned by the cost of the copying process. Several postdoctoral "students" focused on the central microfilm services, which regularly acquire theses from U.S. graduate institutions as an aid to research, and ordered microfilm copies by the hundreds. One "student" in particular spent over $14,000 in a three-month period, reproducing the scientific holdings of a major midwestern university at seven cents a page.

Unlike the spectacular potluck bonanza of the Purchasing Commission twenty years before, the scientific program was carefully planned and specifically targeted. The commercial network was concerned with the theft of industrial processes and instrumentation essential to exploit the scientific and technical intelligence concurrently acquired in other collection operations.

The foreign scientific collection program continued unabated and attacked all other advanced Western nations with considerable success. Despite the organs' exertions, however, Soviet industry proved incapable of achieving the expected advantage. Ineradicable *tufta* in the Soviet industrial establishment prevented change. To meet the problem, another reorganization took place within the KGB. But the bureaucratic momentum coupled with KGB oversight (provided by scientific and technical officers) still failed to improve the industrial system.

Nowhere was the problem more apparent than in the Soviet aviation ministry, where the leaders had enjoyed a relatively free hand for twenty years. Semichastny tried to achieve the Politburo's objectives with persuasion and the judicious invocation of Brezhnev's name and authority, but he was unable to cause the desired effect. Although Brezhnev had high personal regard for Semichastny, it became clear that his methods were unsuitable for the simple reason that he was not succeeding. Thus, in April 1967, Brezhnev replaced Semichastny with the Politburo's hatchetman Yuri V. Andropov. Though not a scientist or technician,[24] Andropov was first of all a Chekist. On the basis of his past performance he was the ideal choice to keep the organs on their appointed rounds while simultaneously force-feeding the bureaucrats of the military-industrial trusts with the KGB and GRU's technical intelligence. If anyone could modernize the Soviet Union's aviation ministry, it was thought to be Andropov. The Central Committee, including the Soviet military leadership, concurred in the need for draconian measures and agreed that Andropov was exactly the right man to devise, execute, and enforce the needed changes.

Brezhnev instructed Andropov to start at the top and eliminate the hierarchy, one by one, until he found the men and women who could convert the information acquired by the organs into practical application within the industry. It was not the first time that the KGB had played a key role in industry. In Beria's time there was no major manufacturing, construction, or extraction activity that wasn't under the control of the organs.

Thus ended an important era in the evolution of the organs. They had grown, expanded, and matured since the hectic days of Beria and were now poised, under the steady hand of Andropov, to enter an even more complex era than they had ever known in the past.

7 · The "Commercial" Stations

(1918–Present)

In some respects, the Bolsheviks had every reason to be confounded by
what they knew about the United States. President Wilson had advocated
a variety of benign measures including equal justice for friends and former enemies, thus putting himself at odds with his somewhat more vindictive British and French allies. He pressed for the establishment of
the League of Nations but was unable to persuade the Senate to ratify
the treaty. In the midst of his efforts to secure a just peace he authorized
the dispatch of American troops to Archangel and Vladivostok at the
instance of the British and French. The U.S. Vladivostok command, under General William S. Graves, a man of immense scrupulosity and even
greater naïveté, was charged with securing and safeguarding a portion of
the Trans-Siberian Railroad. Graves quite honestly believed that the Bolsheviks (with whom he had virtually no contact) were populists and deserving of his support. He was predisposed to dislike the anti-Bolshevik
forces of Admiral Kolchak as autocratic successors to the Czar. For this
reason he was at some pains to avoid involvement with the Kolchak government at Omsk. The State Department's man in Vladivostok, Consul
General Harris, the British General Sir Alfred Knox, and the Japanese
General Oi (with the largest force, numbering in excess of 72,000 Japanese troops) were all openly supporting Kolchak at the direction of their
respective governments.

In the west, the U.S. Archangel force (North Russian Expedition),
brigaded with the British, was engaged in combat with the Bolsheviks to
the extent that the Americans sustained significant casualties.[1]

How, then, could the United States advocate peace and simultaneously dispatch two military expeditions to "intervene"? How could
General Graves, in Siberia, refuse to comply with State Department pol-

icy and devote most of his time to warning Washington about the manip-
ulations of the British and the anti-Bolshevik actions of the allied
Japanese forces? How could the North Russian Expedition engage the
Soviets in warfare while Graves railed about the British, French, and
Japanese forces doing the same in the east? Like others before and since,
Lenin was having difficulty in divining the coherence and true nature of
U.S. foreign policy.

The later willingness of Washington to support the American Relief
Administration was another act that seemed to contradict assumed American attitudes. Many of Lenin's sources of information about the United
States were communists who had lived in small ethnic communities in
New York City, thus were able to give only the views of radical Russians,
Poles, Latvians, and Finns who, in the main, approved the removal and
execution of the Czar and welcomed the advent of what they took to be a
modern socialist state. These people resisted assimilation, continued to
speak their native languages, read foreign-language newspapers, and remained isolated from the older American communities. Many were East
European Jews,[2] socialists, anarchists, and political radicals who saw
their own plight in universal terms. Washington was just another oppressive and hostile government.

Even Lenin's American-born sources were not truly representative of
the United States. The John Reeds and Bill Haywoods came to Moscow
with their own peculiar politics and felt compelled to convey to Lenin
their convictions that the oppressed "working class" in the United States
was prepared to join the world revolution under the Bolshevik banner.
Distortions and exaggerations were the currencies they used to buy acceptance.

The anomalies of American history were not helpful to Lenin in his
effort to understand the United States, especially its relationship to Great
Britain. It was difficult to rationalize the connection between a former
colony and its original mother country, particularly when, after the
American Revolution, a second war was fought with Britain in 1812.

During the Crimean War the Russian government proposed a fictitious sale of Alaska to a U.S. company. The territory was vulnerable to
British attack, and it was hoped that such a sale would inflame the British
against the Americans. (The actual sale of Alaska to the U.S. government didn't occur until 1868, and because it was sold and not taken by
force of arms, the deal revealed nothing about U.S. expansionist aims.)

During the Civil War of the 1860s, the British clearly favored the
Confederate forces against the Union, yet Washington and London continued on good terms. It was evident to Lenin that U.S. behavior was
difficult to understand and impossible to predict.

The Spanish American War in 1898 was more comprehensible—the

United States defeated a weakened European power and took her colonies in the Philippines and Cuba. So now it was clear the United States was just another colonial power off to a slow start. This tentative assumption was turned on its head a few years later by U.S. behavior in China following the Boxer Rebellion. Of all of the intervening powers only the Americans refused to demand indemnities and territory from the prostrate Chinese. Instead, the monies that were due the United States were turned back to China to finance the educations of young Chinese. Such inconsistent behavior didn't lend itself to easy analysis.

The United States was a young and growing world power with a population nearly comparable to that of the USSR, and it could not be ignored in the context of the coming world revolution. Lenin had no reliable intelligence about American life and politics. The Bolsheviks' efforts to effect a relationship with the United States had failed because of their repudiation of the Russian foreign debt and a powerful disinclination on the part of the Congress and successive administrations to regard the Soviet government as much more than a bandit horde in temporary control of Russia.

When confronted with the same problems of distrust and suspicion in Europe, the Soviets found that by using "trade missions," "purchasing commissions," and small trading companies instead of insisting on diplomatic relations, it became possible to gain access to countries that saw advantages in trade but not in conceding Soviet respectability. The initial small numbers of Soviet "trade representatives" in Western Europe were able to generate important contacts in the fields of banking and manufacturing, since it was widely believed that the USSR, like China, would prove an insatiable market for European manufactured goods. Having trade representatives in the European capitals also provided a cover for a political reporting system that gradually assessed the host government's leadership personalities and the temperament of the masses and their state of readiness to join in the world revolution.

The use of commercial cover facilities for espionage purposes was pioneered by the GRU. At the same time, the Comintern labored to build myriad international organizations with the basic aims of promoting the national Communist parties, propagating the Soviet line, and developing political forces subservient to Moscow. The GRU's missions were directed toward military and industrial espionage.

The primary role of the Soviet commercial cover company was not only to establish a presence in those areas that were hostile toward the Soviet government, but also to penetrate the local community in a nonthreatening manner (by using other than Russian personnel) and to gain access to information not otherwise available to the government of the USSR. It was evident to the Soviets that "business" in the West was respectable, politically powerful, and usually could be depended upon to avert its gaze from unacceptable politics provided that the opportunities for profit were evident.

Then, as now, the business communities in Britain, Germany, France, and the United States exhibited a remarkable conviction that the USSR is a "market" to be exploited. Those with much to fear from the expansion of the Soviet state have tended to be the most vocal advocates of the illusion that, somehow, prosperity will flow from the Soviet "connection."

The Soviets needed intelligence about the U.S. government, the status of its armed forces, and its intentions with respect to the Bolshevik government. If there were indeed millions of workers in the United States looking to the Soviets to make a world revolution, they must be provided with guidance and leadership. If revolutionary ardor in the United States was to flourish, it must grow and prosper in the image of the Soviet party and would therefore need discipline and control.

In the 1920s prospect of the United States granting diplomatic recognition to the Soviet government was remote, but there was a possibility that "trade" could be used in the interim. If a commercial lodgment could be made in North America, Lenin could see three separable, though related, functions to be discharged: (1) The Comintern would be responsible for the development of a proper revolutionary climate through propaganda and organization; (2) the GRU's military intelligence mission would collect data regarding the U.S. armed forces, especially technical information that would accelerate Soviet industrial development for military purposes; and (3) the role of the GPU/OGPU would be its customary one of maintaining tight controls on counterintelligence, party loyalty, and Bolshevik discipline.

It was relatively simple to insinuate personnel into the United States by using false passports or stolen seamen's papers or simply by crossing the lightly patroled Canadian and Mexican borders. Once in the United States, by a variety of misrepresentations and through the cooperation of political sympathizers it was an easy matter to settle into virtual obscurity in any of the major cities. Foreign merchant vessels with Profintern crew members smuggled stowaways and accounted for the many bogus seamen who jumped ship in various U.S. ports.[3] With the missions and the personnel identified, all that was needed now was a commercial cover.

Soviet intelligence has had a long and profitable experience in the world of commerce. It started in Berlin in 1921, when the Fourth Department of the Red Army sent the brothers Aaron and Abraham Ehrenlieb to Berlin, with GRU money, to organize the Eastern Trading Company, or Wostwag (West-Osteuropaeische Warenaustausch Aktiengesellschaft) at #19, Schiffbauerdamm, Berlin NW 6. The Ehrenlieb brothers were Poles who had become Soviet citizens. Both were GRU staff officers.

Wostwag was supposed to handle the sale of Soviet products in Germany, but in 1921, not only were there few if any Soviet products to sell, there was very little money in Germany to be spent on imports of any kind. Yet, if you pretend that you are in business, it is necessary to look and act as if you know one end of a cash register from the other. To give the firm a few props and a small inventory, the Soviet trade mission in Berlin transferred its meager accounts to Wostwag.

By arrangement with Moscow the firm's income was to be used in the development of espionage nets. In 1925, the brothers were recalled to Moscow and replaced by another GRU officer named Uscher Zloczower. In 1926, Abraham Ehrenlieb was dispatched to the Far East, where he set up a new company at 49 Taku Road, Tientsin, called the Far Eastern Fur Trading Company.[4] His brother Aaron was sent to Urga, Mongolia, to open a branch of Wostwag. In 1935 Aaron was ordered to New York to open the American branch of Wostwag, but he was unable to secure a visa to enter the United States.

According to the rules, the GRU was to handle engineers, specialists, and others who had unique or technical information. Although the OGPU agreed to this division of labor, it seldom complied with the terms. The preemption of talent by the OGPU was a GRU grievance from 1923 onward.[5]

Staffing requirements for the "commercial" firms were met by searching through the numbers of Balts and Poles who had been in trouble in their own countries and had fled to the USSR. The Soviet trade delegations and purchasing commissions (operated and controlled by Torgpred) were under direction to "turn over" promising leads to the commercial companies. Prior to dispatch, the commercial agents were subjected to arduous training in covert methods. The training was intended to foster and reinforce, among other effects, the clandestine atmosphere that is so congenial to the Bolshevik temperament.

The first ray of hope on the U.S. commercial front was the arrival in Moscow of Armand Hammer, representing his father, Julius, who was temporarily in prison for performing an illegal abortion.[6] Hammer carried a letter of introduction from his father to Lenin, who quickly grasped the commercial and political implications of the Hammer family's initiative.[7] Julius Hammer had been a heavy contributor to the U.S. Socialist Labor Party, forerunner of the Communist Party (CPUSA). The fact that he was imprisoned in the United States certified his reliability, because it led Lenin to assume (erroneously) that his confinement attested to his revolutionary activity and made him appear a "barricades fighter" at a distance. To ensure that the Hammers profited from their initiative, Lenin endorsed Armand Hammer as a concessionaire and directed his staff to take all measures necessary to guarantee that he prospered. "Lenin approved the right of Hammer's employees to travel about Russia at will, granting them private railroad cars for that purpose. To combat the bureaucracy, Lenin told Hammer that he was forming a special 'Concessions Committee,' headed by Felix Dzerzhinsky, chief of the Soviet secret police so, if there were any problems, Dzerzhinsky would be the man to solve them. . . ."[8] With Lenin's approval and Dzerzhinsky (and the organs) at the ready to assist, it would have been difficult for Hammer to have failed.

The first major contract between the Hammers (on behalf of the Allied Drug and Chemical Company) and the Soviet government was signed by Maxim Litvinov and Petr Bogdanov,[9] who would later head the new commercial company in the United States.

On his return to New York, Hammer set up a Delaware corporation, Allied-American (Almerico), which by 1924 had gained the representation rights for thirty-seven major U.S. firms. As Almerico was preparing for aggressive action in the commercial area, the Labour government in Great Britain suddenly announced that diplomatic recognition had been accorded the Soviet government and that permission had also been granted for the establishment of a Soviet trading company in London.

The unexpected reversal by the British government was a spur to the U.S. advocates of recognition, who had failed in all previous attempts to persuade Washington to do the same. The most vocal and persistent advocate of diplomatic recognition, Ludwig C. K. Martens, had been deported earlier for his too enthusiastic efforts.[10]

The Soviet-American Chamber of Commerce was formed in the early 1920s to promote recognition, using the effective and now very familiar argument that trade with the pariah of nations would contribute to American prosperity. There was genuine concern among some U.S. bankers and businessmen that they would lose the Soviet "market" to the British.

The Soviets controlled a few small companies in New York, the most important of which were the Products Exchange Corporation (Prodexco) and Derutra. Both of these firms lobbied for recognition by sending their representatives to call on U.S. firms to explain the rewards of doing business with the Soviet government, pointing out that firms that were prepared to venture into agreements and to advance credits would be blessed with profitable returns as well as a high place in the esteem of the Soviet government. The third firm active in this effort was the Hammer family's Ural-American Refining and Trading Company (later incorporated into Almerico). At the time the Hammers were granted participation in this joint venture with the Soviet government, they were required to deposit $50,000 in gold in the new Soviet state bank as a "security deposit" and as palpable demonstration of their commitment to the future of Soviet-American trade.

Charles Recht, an American lawyer who had served as a legal adviser
to Ludwig Martens, now had the task of broadening the bases of Prodexco and Derutra so that the Soviet commercial presence in the United
States would be strengthened and extended. In collaboration with the
Hammers he merged Allied-American, Prodexco, and Derutra into a
new company, Amtorg, in May 1924.

For the first time the Soviets had a large and diverse "commercial"
presence in the United States. Amtorg was now able to operate as a fully
integrated Soviet foreign intelligence station with its own funding channels[11] and a relatively secure facility with good communications and
accommodations for hundreds of visiting "engineers," "inspectors," "ac-
countants," and "trade experts."

From its inception Amtorg conducted millions of dollars' worth of
legitimate business with U.S. companies. The corporation's reputation in
business and banking matters was routinely described by credit sources as
"satisfactory," though there were serious complaints about misrepresen-
tation and apparent business fraud in the early days.

As is the case in all Soviet organizations, a qualified individual acted
as the nominal head of the organization, brigaded by a resident representative of the organs who had the power to impose restrictions and redirect
or veto any activity initiated by the organization. The OGPU resident's
authority was exactly analogous to the OO representative's power in the
Red Army. Party members in Amtorg were required to meet regularly to
be reminded of their purpose and to be criticized and disciplined for any
infractions of the resident's code of approved behavior.

All business contacts, however casual, were reported to the resident,
who could, at his own election, demand an introduction to the American,
assign a specific intelligence mission to the Amtorg man, or require that
Amtorg initiate the further development of the American as a prospective recruit for the organs.

The GRU men assigned to Amtorg pursued conventional military intelligence missions, which were facilitated by the corporation's practice of
requiring plant inspections prior to making any contract with any U.S.
firm. Appointments for the inspectors were made by American employees of the corporation.

The Comintern representative saw to the liaison with the CPUSA.
Like the GRU man, the Comintern representative was subject to the
control of the OGPU resident. The Comintern man met with members of
the Control Commission of the CPUSA and gradually constructed the
funding mechanisms that would later channel money into Soviet propaganda vehicles (e.g., *The Daily Worker, The Forward, Daily Freiheit,
New Masses,* etc.), the financing of various organizations (e.g., Camp
Unity, Friends of the Soviet Union, League Against Fascism, etc.) and

several unions in which Communists had succeeded in gaining controlling positions.[12]

Three years after the founding of the Soviet trading corporation, there were still some American firms that would not do business with Amtorg. They saw it as a monopoly that did not allow for competition, and they didn't like the credit arrangements. Amtorg demanded credit terms that some U.S. companies found unacceptable because the financing of such contracts had unfavorable long-term consequences. With remarkable insight into the problem, Amtorg advanced a solution. Isaac J. Sherman, the corporation's treasurer and one of its founders, was directed to resign and form a new company, the Industrial Credit Corporation, to discount Amtorg acceptances and guarantee Amtorg notes. Sherman was thus able to convey the impression to prospective clients that he was independently taking all risks "to prevent Russian orders going to other countries." In a letter to prospective customers Sherman declared that he was investing $1 million of "his own money" in Industrial Credit and that he had another $3 million available should business develop. Sherman hoped to stay on good terms with Amtorg and stated that he would accomplish that end by maintaining active contact with Amtorg "through employees either related to his wife or others, actuated by self-interest."[13] The maneuver by Sherman was controlled, directed, and subsidized by Amtorg and was simply intended to provide access to that part of the U.S. business community that did not want to deal directly with Amtorg. It was a small but useful deception.

Arcos (All-Russian Cooperative Society), the new "trading company" in London, was described as having "foreign subsidiaries" in Germany (Wostwag) and in New York (Amtorg). With most of the world in an unstable economic state, the promise of large-volume Soviet trade was very attractive. To reassure Western businessmen, the Soviet companies were organized along conventional corporate lines, and officials referring to themselves as managing directors and vice presidents made their obeisance to the chairman of the board.

The fact, however, was that the trading companies were massive facilities designed to engage in industrial espionage. The Soviet government had not only repudiated all debt obligations to the Western countries, but had also induced the same countries to subsidize the wholesale removal of processes, machines, tools, and techniques that might aid in "the building of Socialism in one country."[14]

Within three years of its establishment in London, Arcos was raided by the police and its officers expelled from Britain, along with the Soviet embassy and all diplomatic personnel. The British government's findings, which detailed the hundreds of espionage, sabotage, and political actions directed from Arcos, were published and widely disseminated.[15] Several years later diplomatic relations were restored, and the Soviets were back in Britain largely on the basis of the resurgent myth that "Soviet trade" was essential to the British economy.

Arcos acquired a large building at 49 Mooregate and announced its purpose of establishing contact with prospective British producers who could assist in the construction of the new Soviet state. The Midland Bank held credits in excess of £50 million, and there was a general expectation that Soviet orders would begin to prime the pump of the ailing British economy and reduce the staggering unemployment figures. (The Midland Bank, in particular, has had a long involvement in trade with the USSR. In June 1983 its resident manager in Moscow was murdered in circumstances resembling the classical "artistic suicide" so long favored by the organs.[16])

The Arcos representatives began by systematically calling on manufacturing facilities to invite trade opportunities. The smaller firms and, for the most part, the least sophisticated in international trade were anxious to do business. The Arcos representatives examined the products offered by the British manufacturers and generally found them to be a little below the minimum standard set for Soviet purchases. In the course of discussions, the Arcos representatives alternately alluded to possible future orders amounting to hundreds of thousands of pounds and then returned to the inadequacies of the present product and its high price. The Arcos people gave assurances, however, that they would make an earnest effort to persuade Moscow that the product had utility. The British manufacturers were encouraged to believe that an arrangement might be made that would allow for the consignment of an order to the Soviet Union for demonstration and testing.

In time, Arcos uested that samples be sent to Moscow. The manufacturer, as a gesture of goodwill, was asked to include appropriate drawings and spare parts to ensure that a favorable demonstration of the product could take place. Once the goods were shipped, Arcos lost interest in the company. When no sale resulted, the manufacturer would attempt to recover the materials previously shipped. Of course, no record of such an order could be found in Arcos, and the trading firm simply suggested that the claim be taken up directly with Gostorg in Moscow.[17] It sometimes took as long as a year for the British manufacturer to realize that there had been no serious intention in the first instance to buy his products. The cost of shipping and the value of the finished goods and spare parts were irrecoverable losses. The Soviet embassy referred all complaints to Arcos, and Arcos, in turn, referred them to Moscow; Moscow didn't respond.

Like all confidence games, the "trade with the Soviet Union" gambit had a long and successful run in New York, London, and Berlin. The basic appeal was to the cupidity and greed of the intended victims, and the trade representatives were adept at leading the capitalist sheep to the shearing. Even the mighty industrial concerns of the West took turns submitting to the temptations of the great opportunities to contribute materials, machines, designs, and advanced technologies in expectation of trade that seldom materialized.

Quite aside from the success of Arcos in bilking English companies with promises of prosperity, a collateral effort was under way to investigate conditions in British industry, to effect contacts with disgruntled workers in the factories, and to locate Britons who were willing to engage in espionage on behalf of the Soviet Union.

Scotland Yard's Special Branch, working with M.I.5, maintained an effective watch on the peripatetic Soviets. Their secret allies in this effort were the officers of the Government Code and Cypher School, who patiently deciphered the wireless transmissions passing from Arcos and the Soviet embassy to Moscow.[18]

Among the Arcos messages in 1927 were several that related to specific acts of espionage about which M.I.5 had collateral information.[19] It was decided to maintain a conventional surveillance over an Arcos employee suspected of illegal contact with the cooperative Briton. Once it had been established that the material had been passed to the Arcos representative and that he had returned to 49 Mooregate, the Metropolitan police, led by Special Branch, would raid the premises, seize the stolen documents, and make arrests.

According to plan, the documents were observed to pass from the Briton to the Arcos man, who then set off under the watchful eyes of the hidden surveillants. The Soviet's deliberately serpentine trail eventually led back to 49 Mooregate. The Special Branch maintained a constant vigil until a force of seventy Metropolitan policemen, along with an assortment of M.I.5 and Special Branch officers, had converged on the entrance to the building. When the porter was shown a magistrate's warrant authorizing the search, he immediately slammed the door shut.

The police quickly broke the lock on the wooden outside door, but then found themselves in a vestibule, their further way obstructed by a great steel door. Repeated attempts to open it were unsuccessful. The door provided no purchase for levers and was impervious to their poundings. The police could hear shouting and running within the building, and it was clear that the warrant alone would not gain their entry. A few moments later they heard the sound of breaking glass and observed smoke coming from shattered windows on the upper floors. The fire brigade was summoned, and a team was sent off to get an acetylene torch to cut the bolts on the door.

After almost five hours of steady cutting, the bolts gave way, and the police entered the building along with the firemen. In virtually every room there was a smoldering fire, sometimes in the fireplace, more often in the middle of the floor. Arcos employees, all but overcome by smoke, were coughing and retching in the corridors. The temperature in the building was dangerously high. Some police and Special Branch officers went from room to room removing and extinguishing smoldering documents, while others collared Arcos workers and removed them from the building. Anton Miller, the chief cipher clerk of Arcos, and Robert Kopling (Kaulin), cipher clerk of the Soviet trade mission, were taken into custody. A search of Miller's person resulted in the British finding a comprehensive list of Soviet espionage and propaganda contacts located throughout the world who were subordinated to direction emanating from Arcos. The raid was dramatic and very successful even though the specific espionage document that was the target of the search was never recovered. The British hauled away several truckloads of compromising files, including the accounting for hundreds of thousands of pounds spent on espionage and subversion in England, the colonies, Canada, and the United States.[20] There could be no doubt that Arcos was the center for espionage in England, yet there were questions from the opposition in the House of Commons. At this point the Foreign Office was quite prepared to permit the Home Office to take full credit for the raid, and the Home Office was more than anxious to defer to the Foreign Office.

At last, Prime Minister Stanley Baldwin took up a question in Parliament and in his response committed what is generally regarded as the most egregious error in the history of communications intelligence. Baldwin asserted that the government had been reading the clear text of Soviet messages for years. He went on to compound his folly by reading a portion of a garbled text of a decripted Soviet message, thereby preserving in the Hansard, as a matter of public record, his blunder.[21] Of course, Soviet ciphers were immediately changed, worldwide. The British advantage had been lost by the Prime Minister himself.

In the aftermath of the Arcos raid, formal diplomatic relations between Great Britain and the Soviet Union were suspended. Ambassador Rakovsky (who was later succeeded by Ivan Maisky[22]) and his staff left England on June 3, 1927. Once the officials who represented Soviet authority had gone, most of the ordinary employees of the trade mission, Arcos, and the Soviet embassy—those who did not have diplomatic status—petitioned the British government for asylum. This group came to be known as the nonreturners (*nevozvrashchentsy*). Without exception, each took special pains to inform the British government of his or her direct knowledge of Soviet abuses of diplomatic status and, where known, the identities of the few Britons who had been in clandestine contact with Soviet intelligence.

With no base of operations in England, Soviet intelligence was compelled to work against the British from stations in continental Europe. Valerian Dovgalevsky, the new Soviet ambassador in Paris, was charged with the collateral duty of restoring the Soviet diplomatic presence in London. During the six months following the Arcos breach, Dovgalevsky made several visits to England in an effort to persuade the Foreign Office that the Arcos incident was the unfortunate result of provocateurs and "anti-Soviet elements" who had consciously plotted to make the Soviet government appear to be involved in "inadmissable" activities. For the moment, however, Dovgalevsky's entreaties were rejected by the British.

During this same period, the Soviet government's need for foreign exchange had grown desperate. Food production was just beginning to approach pre-World-War-I levels when Stalin ordered the export of grain and the forced collectivization of the lands. The combination of these two decisions inflicted such grave harm and terrible destruction that the effects are still felt, almost six decades later.

In solving the farm problem, Stalin identified the kulaks (peasant farmers who owned land and employed others) as the villains. The old established kulaks had sensed earlier that they would be driven off the land and had previously sold their holdings to others and moved to the cities: "as for their daughters, usually they tried to marry GPU men and become fine ladies . . ."[23] The imperceptive buyers of the larger farms, the "new" kulaks, were soon dispossessed and transported. Those who resisted were shot. Farms were looted and burned, and farmers were dispatched with such speed and violence that children and aged parents were abandoned to starve. Possessions of any sort were seen as badges of kulakism. Even looters of yesterday were shot as kulaks of the moment. It was a civil war, encouraged by the state, over goods and land, and in the end only the state won. The grain was sold in the foreign markets, the farms destroyed, the cattle slaughtered, and farmers killed or marched off to wilderness camps. The OGPU had won the day for Stalin's power as the Great Famine had won the millions of dead.

Without the ardent attentions of the OGPU Stalin's famine would have been a terrible scourge, but with OGPU's energetic assistance it was cataclysmic. The extent of the devastation of the country and its people is only now beginning to be understood. As the initial shock gradually diminished a few years later, it is estimated that there were at least 20 million fewer Russians to feed.[24] How was it possible to find people who would destroy their fellows with such enthusiasm? The oath of the Chekist required subordination of all to the will of the leader. The fact was that Stalin's irrational decision to sell grain and simultaneously destroy farmers had fewer troublesome consequences for the OGPU than would have any suggestion of compassion or disobedience. Just as the Red Army had learned at Tsaritsin that no enemy is as fearsome as the

Cheka, the Chekists already knew that fact from their own direct experience. Their allegiance was secured by the knowledge that Stalin always rewarded the OGPU and that as long as there was any grain left to seize, the Chekists would eat.

The Arcos raid and a raid on the Soviet Embassy in Peking convinced Stalin that the British were mobilizing anti-Soviet sentiment everywhere in the world. It would be typical of the British to use cat's-paws to do the bloody work, and the most likely sources of recruits were the pockets of monarchists in such cities as Warsaw, Sophia, Riga, Shanghai, Berlin, and Paris. It was time to strengthen the OGPU in Europe and Asia. The Foreign Ministry was instructed that some new diplomats with special responsibilities would be arriving soon at the more important embassies. The OGPU was going international.

The Arcos "nonreturners" pointed up the need to strengthen the controls on all Soviet citizens serving abroad, and Stalin, with his special ability to intimidate, told the chiefs of the organs that they would correct the problem or run the risk of becoming "one head shorter."

Yagoda's OGPU had the basic responsibility of vetting all personnel assigned to foreign posts. Exhaustive investigations were made to verify loyalty. In virtually all instances children and wives were held hostage in the USSR to guarantee the behavior of the husband. Unless the individual's rank was exalted and his politics pure, he would have no contact with the nationals in the country to which he was posted. Travelers were always accompanied by escorts who maintained constant watch against casual contacts on trains or ships. People assigned to sensitive positions in the embassy code rooms or registries were simply not allowed to leave the premises. But despite the elaborate precautions and iron discipline, the desertions had begun. Where the Romans might have inquired *Quis custodiet ipsos custodes?*, Stalin could have responded, "I do."

From the beginning, the OGPU was a vital part of every Soviet mission outside the USSR. The primary function of the Chekists was to ensure absolute compliance with party discipline among the diplomats and to detect incipient deserters before they had a chance to bolt. The mission was clear but difficult to discharge. In the last half of 1927, even OGPU officials were beginning to desert. Among the noteworthy defectors were Ibragimov,[25] the Soviet trade representative in Istanbul; Miasnikov, a senior member of the Armenian OGPU who slipped across the border into Persia; V. M. Bekenovsky, who escaped to Austria via Rumania; and Kozhevinkov, a lieutenant colonel in Soviet military intelligence (GRU). In China, following the Peking debacle, Saryan, an important Comintern agent, deserted, and in Stockholm Sobolev, naval attaché to the Soviet embassy, requested asylum from the Swedish government, explaining that he could not continue to serve under Stalin's brutal regime.

On the first day of 1928, Boris Bajanov crossed the Soviet border into Persia. By comparison, the other deserters were unimportant. Bajanov was Stalin's former personal secretary and thus had a unique view of Stalin's unlimited appetite for power. Bajanov was a skilled, intellectually disposed Central Committee bureaucrat. His daily contact with Stalin gave him a special appreciation of the incremental deceits that contributed to the general secretary's growing authority. Bajanov's flight personalized the problem for Stalin.

In the 1920s and up to the present day, when a Soviet official deserts a foreign post, the local ambassador's most fervent wish is that the official will be found dead within a few hours. If not dead, then let him at least be so injured or so ill that he dies within a few days, amid his grieving socialist comrades. To give substance to this hope, the indicated action is to scour the morgues and emergency rooms of the nearby hospitals. If no trace of the missing person is found, all available OGPU trustworthies are put on the street to visit every café, bar, and restaurant, hoping to find their quarry unconscious among the chair legs. Simultaneously, probes are made by Soviet-controlled police penetrations to determine if the official is being held. The next step is to assign search tasks to the locals who serve in the surveillance teams, the telephone operators, porters, maids, and others who make up the vast support apparatus of every Soviet mission.

The official line within the embassy after the official has been missing for twelve hours is that he has "met with foul play" or that he has been "unlawfully abducted by the police." All are exhorted to make a greater effort to locate the missing official. If, by reason of his rank, he has been accompanied by his wife and children, they are quickly sequestered within the embassy.

At the end of twenty-four hours an indignant note is handed to the local foreign ministry demanding the return of the missing official. The note alleges that the disappearance is the result of the host country's inability to restrain certain "anti-Soviet elements." A part of every note also makes clear the retributive steps that the USSR is considering. The notes are imperious, threatening, and rude. The Soviets have long recognized that legitimate diplomats are often flummoxed by raised voices and imperative demands. There will always be someone in the host government to concede that maybe the Soviet claim is at least partially justified. Another will point out that their own national embassy in Moscow will be beset with more restrictions and difficulties unless concessions are made to the Soviets.

If the host country has been approached by the official seeking asylum, internal problems arise. The moment the Soviet embassy knows that the official is enjoying the protection of the host government, the line abruptly changes. The official is transformed into a "moral degenerate," a "criminal personality," a "thief," an "embezzler," a "lunatic," or even someone who is wanted for complicity in the murders and molestations of children. The host country is transformed, as quickly, from a compassionate benefactor of a political refugee to a co-conspirator of a known felon and an active accomplice in his criminal acts. If there are weak hearts in the foreign ministry, they will pause and speculate on the possibility of truth in the Soviet's allegations.

In Moscow the organs simply turn up the heat. The local employees of the offending country's embassy are detained by the police. Attachés are manhandled and later given solemn "apologies." Embassy automobiles are damaged or impounded. Demonstrations are held in front of the embassy, and rocks are thrown through windows. A very utilitarian missile is the full bottle of purple ink that makes for semipermanent defacement of the building. Replacement glass is difficult to find in Moscow, but not as difficult as locating the glaziers to install it. The embassy cables its sorrows to the national capital, detailing the hostility of the Soviet government and the crowds that the organs have turned out.

If, in the interest of "fairness," the host country decides to allow Soviet representatives to meet with the official in an office of the ministry, what harm is there in that? The OGPU handles the arrangements. The official's wife, wherever located, writes a long, tear-stained letter as dictated by the OGPU. The most evocative family photographs are selected for inclusion with the note. The offending official's personnel file is examined for clues as to what might increase the leverage at the interview. The father dying of cancer in a remote village is propped up to express his personal grief at his son's irrational and villainous action. If the official's mother is still among the living, she will have a chance to go on record with an emotional appeal. Brothers and sisters who have not been in contact with one another for several years suddenly materialize with long lists of dreadful things that will happen to them and their families if the official refuses the forgiveness of the Soviet government.

The Soviet ambassador comes to the meeting bearing an unaccustomed burden of goodwill. His teeth, which have seldom seen the light of day, are in full view. His excessive affability is cloying. He is attended by his first secretary or counselor and two menacing Chekists, who stand at the ready like choke-chained Alsatians. As the official enters the room, the ambassador springs to his feet and gives his best impression of a warm and sincere welcome. He uses the form of address usually reserved for old close friends.

"*Dorogoymoy* [My dear], are you keeping well?" Despite the absence of a reply he says, "These are for you," and thrusts the letters into the official's hands.

The first secretary meanwhile engages the foreign ministry officials in a complicated discussion about the issues involving the deserter's status. The Soviet ambassador, rigid smile intact, then describes to the deserter, *sotto voce,* the wide variety of cruel punishments that await those who betray the socialist homeland. He goes on to enumerate the friends, relatives, and acquaintances who will suffer imprisonment and worse if the defector persists in his wrongheadedness. However, the ambassador is prepared to forgive this lapse that has endangered so many if only the official will return with him, immediately, to the Soviet embassy, where the matter can be sorted out and reported to Moscow.

If the deserter is resolved not to return to the socialist camp, the ambassador invokes the presence of the men from the organs and whispers sanctimonious apologies for his inability to restrain them. They will, he continues with mock remorse, hunt down and destroy those who have betrayed the trust of the Soviet people. There is no place to hide, they cannot be outrun, they invariably succeed in exacting "the most severe penalty" for treasonable acts. "Severe penalty" is a Soviet euphemism for death.

Once the confrontation is over, the Soviets do not accept defeat but set about to make their earlier threats credible. Each time the former official, perhaps with a new name and an altered appearance, moves to a new address, the Soviets are at pains to find him and signal that they are aware of his location and identity. This is intended as a psychological tickle, something to get the imagination racing.

On another level, using selected cutouts and what pass for double agents, the Soviets introduce a new thought—the deserter is really a senior Soviet intelligence official who, by feigning desertion, has penetrated the upper levels of the host government. As the U.S. military attaché in Riga put it: "There is a suspicion that this new custom of 'desertion' is simply a new method for getting OGPU agents into the confidence of the bourgeois circles."[26]

By the end of the twenties, with Stalin in complete control of the USSR, famine, mass murders, mass arrests, mass imprisonment, the gulag, population displacement, destruction of farms, crops, and animals, dekulakization, and collectivism were to be counted as his major accomplishments. Although no one disputed Stalin's authorship of the terrible successive blights visited on the Russian people, it must be admitted that it could not have been done without the organs, the "shield and sword" of the party.

In a very short period Stalin had demonstrated that his Peace was truly more destructive than any War, that Freedom in the Soviet Union was an abject form of Slavery, and that absolute mindless Ignorance of the past and present was an individual's only Strength against the commission of Crimes of Thought.

Before World War II, almost one quarter of the world was within the British Empire. The French, Dutch, and Belgian colonies were also extensive and populous. The Comintern had been designated to recruit among the East Indians, Malays, Burmans, and others, assuring these colonial peoples that a foremost objective of the USSR was to win their independence. (This thought was prevalent before the Soviet Union established its own colonies in East Germany, Hungary, Czechoslovakia, Bulgaria, Mongolia, Poland, Rumania, etc.) Access to these vast populations was possible only by the use of clandestine means. The USSR was still a diplomatic pariah in 1927 and had only limited entree into the Baltic states and parts of Western Europe.

The Soviet military intelligence (GRU) had, with considerable skill, already begun the construction of means to penetrate those areas to which Soviet access had been denied. Since it was generally accepted that the capitalist nations were salivating to get to the Soviet market, the trading companies set about to cultivate the dream. Once a trading company is established and foreign products are available for export, what could be more comprehensible than the building of a great Soviet maritime fleet to carry out the trade? The first Five-Year Plan for shipbuilding came and went without any ships having been built. To correct this problem, the Soviet government bought a number of near derelicts, some built before the turn of the century, and rechristened them, if the word can be used, with appropriate Revolutionary names. Now that the USSR had "shipping lines," it became necessary to establish offices in those ports at which the ships called. In a very short period the GRU had a presence in many of the great port cities of the world.

Among the USSR's "commercial" shipping companies were the Baltic Steamship Company, Union Steamship Company, Red Banner Fleet, White Sea Shipping Company, Baltic and Black Sea Steamship Company, Arcos Red Ensign Fleet, Nakhoda Steamship Company, Amur Steamship Company, and many others. There were almost as many steamship operating companies as there were Russian ships.

German communist strength was centered in the northern port cities of Bremen and Hamburg. Antwerp and Rotterdam were also considered to be controlled ports. The longshoremen's, dockworkers', and seamen's unions were under Soviet party control through the Profintern (the Red Trade Union International) rather than through the German or Dutch parties.[27] The Soviet ships, ostensibly operating as a transportation line, were able to distribute GRU and Comintern agents around the globe. Other vessels calling at the great northern European ports had Soviet maritime agents aboard, usually serving as couriers and sailing under foreign passports as regular crewmen. With these convenient transfer points and a virtually limitless supply of documents ranging from Nansen passports and Lascar sailing papers to passports from many different nations, Soviet agents could move about the world freely. In every foreign port of any consequence, money, documents, and assistance were available.

The Soviets' slow, rust-ridden merchant ships of the twenties and thirties are the direct lineal antecedents of the TU-134's of today's Aeroflot, which perform the same tasks at near-sonic speeds.

An agent boarding a Soviet vessel in Leningrad, Vladivostok, or Odessa carried a forged seaman's book identifying him as crew member. He then traveled to his destination port—Marseilles, New York, Shanghai, Vancouver, etc.—and went ashore, a seaman on leave. After making contact with the local GRU, the bogus seaman produced a second set of documents in a new identity that "verified" his citizenship in the nation to which he was assigned. If the local GRU had someone returning to the Soviet Union, the process was reversed. The seaman's book was reissued to the new traveler, along with instructions to board the vessel as a returning crew member. Most immigration services of the day were more concerned with numbers than identities. If twenty-four Soviet seamen went ashore, they were pleased to have at least that many rejoin the ship before she sailed.

Neither shippers nor passengers clamored for space on these ships. In the main, the Soviet lines were ignored by other lines as being noncompetitive. In 1927, 85 percent of the total Soviet merchant fleet consisted of ships under 3,500 gross tons, ideal for calling at out-of-the-way ports. The USSR was not a signatory nation to the shipping conventions, thus operated outside the international agreements. The Turks, in particular, reported numerous instances of Soviet ships in violations of the international rules of the sea that put other shipping at hazard in the Bosphorus. Soviet vessels avoided conventional sea lanes, violating territorial waters and restricted areas at will. The shipping lines were self-assuring, thus were under no obligation to disclose any information relative to their hulls, cargoes, or machinery for insurance purposes. In the twenties and thirties, even Lloyds' Register listed only those vessels that had been insured earlier by their prior owners.

The Soviets' obsessive secrecy and deception were necessary to shield the purposes of the merchant fleet, which were twofold: (1) foreign transportation for the Soviet intelligence and security services and the Comintern, and (2) justification for the establishment of commercial cover offices in foreign port cities.

When the OGPU was charged with "neutralizing" enemies of the state—those who had given offense to Stalin—the merchant ships that had transported GRU agents and Comintern acolytes out into the world could now be used to bring some of the misbehavers home.

Stalin was infuriated by the Soviet officials who defected from their foreign posts, particularly now that their numbers included members of Yagoda's OGPU. Thus, on November 21, 1929, Stalin issued a decree that was designed to stop the desertions. He ordered that those who did not respond within twenty-four hours to a summons from Moscow were to be "shot on recognition."[28]

The Soviet vice consul in London, within days of the restoration of diplomatic relations, issued ominous advice to the Soviet nationals serving in Britain:

> It is the right of the Consul of the Soviet Republic to order officials to proceed home when his government considers their presence here is no longer needed. . . .
>
> Those who refuse to comply with the Consul's orders, know perfectly well that, in accordance with the Decree of November 21, 1929, they will be subject to the severe penalty prescribed therein. . . . The penalties prescribed are well known, and those concerned well know the penalties involved by disobedience.[29]

The vice consul quite correctly assumed that the British government would learn of the Moscow threats and, out of a sense of delicacy, modified the text. The import of the word "severe" needed no clarification. When the Home Office received a copy of the full text, the Home Secretary issued a prompt rejoinder. He correctly pointed out that the Soviet Union's right to order home its officials rested wholly on the British Alien Law. The consul, according to the Home Secretary, could not carry out his order without the assistance of the British authorities. Further, the Home Secretary noted, "Every Russian employee of the Soviet in this country who may be 'ordered' home should know that the Consul's powers over him are not worth the paper they are written on . . ."[30]

With the delivery of the Home Office's crisp comment on forced repatriation, the British thought the matter of the nonreturners had been settled. Yagoda knew that Stalin was not impressed with what the British government had to say on this point. Stalin wanted the problem solved, and within weeks, clandestine action was under way. The immediate targets were those who had defected in years past.

To get the job done it was essential to arrange some form of transportation that would allow concealment, cover, and accommodations. Extrication of an individual by sea had been successfully employed in Germany on several occasions and, in at least one instance, at Hull, England, where an émigré was abducted in midday by a shipborne mobile group.[31]

This system of extracting apostates, nonreturners, and other deserters from foreign "protection" worked very effectively. The small Soviet tramps plying the lumber trade between Murmansk and the northern European ports called regularly at Hull. Abductions were carried out by the OGPU with transportation provided by the naval section of the GRU.[32] Collateral benefits of these operations included a reinforced realization on the part of the Russian expatriate communities throughout the world that the OGPU did, indeed, have long arms.

Included in the Soviet merchant fleet were more than thirty ships bought from the U.S. War Shipping Board in 1930 by Johann G. Ohsol of Amtorg.

At the time the ships were sold no one in the United States could have believed the uses to which they were to be put. Several were immediately pressed into service as prison ships, carrying hundreds of thousands of prisoners to the remote northern camps. Others were used by abduction teams in various parts of the world for the movement of contraband to Republican Spain, to ship stolen Spanish gold to the USSR, and for the transportation of OGPU, GRU, and Comintern agents to their foreign mission fields.

When the United States granted Lend-Lease to the Soviets during World War II, most of these vessels were returned to various U.S. ports for repair and, in some instances, complete rebuilding at considerable cost (as much as fifty times the original sales price). At the end of the war, the same ships were used by the Soviets for the new task of transporting German and Japanese prisoners of war to the northern forced labor camps. (See Appendix IV.)

Every ocean port of any consequence had a representative of the Profintern who could be called upon to respond to OGPU needs. In the early thirties, the docks, warehousing, and stevedoring in many European ports—including Marseilles, Amsterdam, Hamburg, Rotterdam, Toulon, Brest, and Le Havre—were under the absolute control of the Profintern, which was then headed by Solomon Lozovsky. Along with his American kinsman George Mink (an alias),[33] Lozovsky could ensure OGPU discipline in all maritime related matters. Each national Communist party had a section that was exclusively concerned with the infiltration of the maritime workers.

Soviet-controlled, nonofficial facilities began to multiply and divide. Intelligence collection was the responsibility of the naval section of the GRU. Propaganda, agitation, and organization were the charges of the Comintern. Internal discipline, counterintelligence, and operational control were missions of OGPU, which also held primacy in all matters.

In addition, a taste was developed for press-related activities when Tass reported the advantages of access that could be generated in the West by the use of press credentials. A logical next step was to dispatch additional "newsmen" from the major state-operated papers, and soon reporters from both *Pravda* and *Izvestia* began to appear in increasing numbers.

The disclosures stemming from the Arcos raid had repercussions in New York, where the Soviet "trading" firm Amtorg was beginning to come apart at the seams. A vice president, Boris Delgass, broke with the company and volunteered to testify before a Congressional committee. There were allegations of outrages, sinister behavior, and commercial fraud from the business community, and there was a growing public conviction that Amtorg was the locus of Soviet espionage in the United States.

Adverse press accounts abounded, like these in *The New York Times:* "G. Piatakoff (also known as J. Poliakoff [aka Polyakov, Poliakov], head of the Amtorg Moscow 'office') designated head of N.Y. office, denied visa in Berlin," "S. G. Bron, Chairman of Amtorg, denies Soviet arms purchase in U.S.," and other items that put the corporation in a questionable light. Amtorg responded to these reports with disdain and patiently pointed out that the company had ordered thousands of American-made tractors, railroad cars, and all kinds of machines, and the elemental fact was that the U.S. economy was a major beneficiary of Soviet trade.

In 1929, the company was accused of selling rare books in New York that had been confiscated from Russian Jews. In addition, AFL sources reported that Amtorg was dumping Soviet coal mined by slave workers. Petr A. Bogdanov, later "elected" chairman of the board, dismissed and denied all accusations.[34] It was only when Delgass quit Amtorg that the public was informed of the scope and size of the GRU/Cheka army occupying two sealed floors at 261 Fifth Avenue.

Confirmation of Delgass's charges came from an unexpected though highly qualified quarter when Mikhail Hendler, a former OGPU official, submitted a startling affidavit to a congressional committee chaired by Hamilton Fish. Dated November 29, 1930, the statement read:

> Early in 1922, I was sent to Greece to organize, by order of the GPU, a net of military and political espionage. On my way back to Russia, I stopped in Sophia, where, in the Hotel Bulgaria, I met some comrades from Moscow. Though they officially constituted the Soviet Red Cross Mission in Bulgaria, in fact, they were working under the orders of the military espionage division of the Red Army and the Foreign Division of the OGPU [c. August, 1923].
>
> The mission consisted of Koreehkov [Khoriakov], its chief representative, his two assistants, known under the names of comrades Boris and Chaikin and a number of official and undercover agents.
>
> Boris was in charge of operative work and military espionage (operative work means organization of terroristic acts, destruction of munition supplies, assassination of officials and so forth).

Chaikin was under the orders of the Foreign Division of the OGPU which consisted of political espionage and the fishing out and eliminating the officers of the Wrangel army.

During my sojourn in Bulgaria, Chaikin succeeded to induce General Pokrovsky and General Kutepov to come to the Serbia-Bulgarian frontier with the intention of killing them. He killed Pokrovsky. General Kutepov escaped through a window and fled to Serbia.

The episode was related to me by Chaikin and later, I verified it in the OGPU in Moscow.

While being an official member of the Soviet Red Cross, Chaikin, while bribing some Bulgarian police officers, obtained identification card and badge of Bulgarian secret police officer of high rank and was parading with it in Sophia.

During daily visits to the OGPU [c. October 1925], before leaving Moscow, I was requested by Trilisser to recommend to him an experienced and trustworthy man, to whom he could entrust the organization of undercover connections between Amtorg in New York and the Hamburg nuclei of the Berlin branch of the OGPU.

I presented to him a man who I knew under the name of Mikhail. This man received instructions and departed to New York which he entered illegally.

Before my last departure from Moscow in November 1926, I attended a secret meeting of the officials of the Foreign Department of the OGPU where it was decided to send to Amtorg, three employees—Chekists—who would fill, officially, posts in Amtorg but, who would actually work under orders of the OGPU, the military espionage department of the Red Army and the Comintern.

A secret connection between Mikhail and these men was arranged. Mikhail arrived, illegally, in New York in 1926, with the help of the Soviet embassy in Mexico, where a special organization for such purposes exists. He remained in New York when he was recalled to Moscow and left the United States.

When I came to Cuba, I visited the American embassy in Havana and informed them about the arrangement. Apparently the American embassy did not pay any attention to this.

I have been employed for several years as a responsible agent of the Military Espionage division and also the Foreign Division of the OGPU and therefore, I have a thorough knowledge of their organization, work and methods.

I can swear that nuclei of OGPU Military Espionage and Comintern exists, without exception, in *all* Soviet organizations abroad including all *embassies, commercial organizations and Red Cross Missions* [italics added].

The work of such nuclei is considered of primary importance and all other work is of secondary importance.
[signed] HENDLER

The director of U.S. naval intelligence passed a memorandum to the assistant chief of staff of the U.S. Army in which an ONI source reported: "At present, Amtorg are engaged in carrying out a survey of all companies on the [U.S.] Government's Procurement Planning and Industrial Mobilization Lists. Factory owners, in most cases, are glad to show the agents of Amtorg through their plants on the presumption that Amtorg is considering placing orders with them . . . [the source] infers this survey is being made for the purpose of being able to sabotage these factories in case of war or other emergency."

Amtorg was originally organized to provide a base in the United States in the absence of any official representation. Several of the earlier Soviet commercial firms, particularly the Product Exchange Corporation, which had been conveniently located in Ludwig Martens' office at 110 West 40th Street, were merged into the new company. The name Amtorg was an acronym of AMerican Trading ORGanization (AMerikanskaia TORGovaia) with "home offices" at #14 Kuznetsky Most, Moscow.

Earlier attempts to gain a commercial lodgment in the United States had been denied primarily because of two persistent problems: Soviet repudiation of Russian debts and the disruptive activities of the Comintern. A further problem devolved on the matter of payment should such trade be allowed. Both the United States and Great Britain had refused to accept Soviet gold because it consisted of recast czarist and other confiscated bullion against which the Allies had significant claims.

Amtorg was registered in New York State on the basis of an artfully inventive declaration of corporate purpose. The official fiction was that an American company called Amtorg had been successful in negotiating a contract with the people's commissar of foreign trade, Moisei Ilyitch Frumkin, which gave the chairman of the board of Amtorg, Isaya Yakovlevitch Hoorgin, exclusive license on all Soviet goods and materials exported to North and South America in addition to the exclusive rights to all goods imported to the USSR from North and South America.

For the purpose of avoiding any tax liability in the United States, a rubbery set of clauses was inserted into the contract with NKVT so that if Amtorg made a profit, it was remitted to Moscow as part of the license fee. If the company lost money, the people's commissariat would not only make up the deficit but would also contribute to the company's continuing sustenance. In addition, the NKVT determined the officers' salaries. Most comforting was the assurance that any disputes arising between NKVT and Amtorg would "be settled in the courts in Moscow."[35]

To sustain the illusion that the company had some vague American connection, it seemed useful to have at least one U.S. citizen in a management role. Thus, in 1924, a naturalized U.S. citizen named Johann G. Ohsol was appointed vice president. He had worked previously for the Products Export Corporation. Ohsol (sometimes referred to as Osolin), along with a Mr. Fox and a Mr. Sherman, held 15 percent of the company's outstanding stock. The remaining 85 percent was recorded as belonging to the State Import and Export Office, Gostorg, R.S.F.S.R.

Max Sachs, Amtorg accountant from 1924 to 1926, told a U.S. official in Riga that the Gostorgs were formed at the time of the New Economic Policy and were "given the status of a juridical person with the right to engage in foreign trade and to possess capital." At the time Sachs made his opaque disclosures, he was en route to Moscow to reorganize the accounting practices of Gostorg, R.S.F.S.R., the new owner of Amtorg. The Commissariat for Foreign and Domestic Trade (NKVT) receded into the background.[36]

Until the end of the 1920s, the U.S. government paid little heed to the activities of Amtorg. A few officials in the departments of State and Commerce were disposed to believe that there was mischief afoot, but they had difficulties in attracting the attention of their respective Secretaries. The problem of Amtorg was more real in New York, where the city police, on the basis of advice from Boris Delgass, raided J. B. Schafren's Manhattan drugstore in an attempt to capture "Mr. Filin" alias "Mr. Simeon," the OGPU resident in Manhattan. Filin/Simeon, a loyal Amtorg employee dating from 1926, could not be found. New York congressmen were becoming acutely aware of the sharp increase in Amtorg smoke, and Congressman Hamilton Fish called for hearings to search for the fire.

In Washington Secretary of State Henry Stimson was growing uneasy about the activities of the corporation and asked Andrew Mellon, Secretary of the Treasury, if Amtorg was known to his department. Yes, replied Secretary Mellon, but not much was known. Attached to his reply was a copy of a report from the supervising revenue agent of the Internal Revenue Bureau in New York that described the peculiar elastic nature of Amtorg, which seemed to allow it to metamorphose into a different form with each passing paragraph. The report ended with a cautionary note: ". . . evidence was not available to the examining officer as to the ownership of stock. All briefs and affidavits should be carefully checked as the officials of this corporation are extremely clever. . . . It is recommended that reports recently submitted [on the following companies] be handled by the same auditor, conferee and solicitor . . . :

Allied American Company[37]
AMTORG Trading Corporation

Products Exchange Corporation
DERUTRA
All-Russian Textile Syndicate
ARCOS Company . . ."

While the Internal Revenue Bureau, Congressman Fish, Secretary Mellon, and Secretary Stimson were each trying to read the Amtorg tea leaves, Johann G. Ohsol moved to his new office at 540 Fort Washington Avenue (though he continued to receive mail at the Amtorg office, Suite 1707, 165 Broadway, New York) and had some letterheads printed in his own name. He wrote to the U.S. Shipping Board, Merchant Fleet Corporation, Washington, D.C., and offered to buy thirty surplus steamships. In the opening sentence he declared his U.S. citizenship and went on to avoid any reference to his real employer. His offer included requests for a 2 percent discount for cash, permission to transfer the title of the vessels within six months, and the right to carry cargo from the United States on the delivery voyage.

Ohsol acquired his "Yankee know-how" by an unusual process. He was born in 1879, in Latvia to parents who were Imperial Russian subjects. As a young man he was politically active and was elected to the Second Duma in 1906 as a Social Democrat. Upon the dissolution of that body in 1907, he was arrested and indicted on charges of conspiracy. He managed to escape from his imprisonment and flee to the United States. He applied for naturalization and, later, took a doctorate in political science at Harvard. By 1919 he was a U.S. citizen and a minor employee of the Soviet government in New York City. Although on the payroll of the Products Exchange Corporation, his collateral duties consisted of working with several men who figured prominently in OGPU scams in the U.S.

By 1929 the U.S. Shipping Board had fifty-eight vessels of the same general type in lay-up and greeted Ohsol's offer with glad cries. On hearing of the proposed transaction, several American steamship companies complained in bitter terms about the sale of ships to the Soviets, only to be assured by the chairman of the Merchant Fleet Corporation that one of the ships ". . . is required for use as a canning ship with the others being used as feeder ships." In recommending approval of the sale, the president of the Merchant Fleet Corporation wrote: "As stated, Johann G. Ohsol is an American citizen, as is also the Amtorg Trading Corporation. . . . It is not considered therefore that an award such as is recommended would in any way conflict with the attitude of the State Department toward the Soviet government."

By March 1930 nineteen of the thirty ships awarded to Ohsol had been delivered. The outbound cargoes, Ohsol was happy to report, consisted of materials purchased by Amtorg for shipment to the Soviet Union. The certificates of ownership of the vessels issued by the Department of Commerce indicated that Ohsol executed the bills of sale "in favor of the Kamchatka Company, Ltd." Despite the fact that the terms of purchase of the vessels were guaranteed by Amtorg and the Russian Trade Limited Bank, the sales price of five Lake class ships was paid in cash.

On balance, the sale of the ships by Ohsol to Kamchatka to Amtorg appeared to please the interested parties. The U.S. Treasury took in a little over $2 million, the Shipping Board sold off thirty noncompetitive vessels, and the Russians got some cheap ships for their fleet. Ohsol, the ship-buying U.S. citizen, was free to resume his vice-presidential duties at Amtorg.

The sale also confirmed that the Five-Year Plan for shipbuilding was obviously in trouble or the Soviet government would not have spent hard currency to buy small, idle leftover vessels.

The end of the civil war and the defeat of the Soviet armies by Poland in 1920 found the Bolshevik government on the brink of total collapse. In February 1921 there was a bloody mutiny by the sailors at the Kronstadt naval fortress, suppressed by the Bolshevik leadership with more than necessary force. This was the first major instance of the new government being confronted by its own citizens demanding an end to the government's monopoly on grain. In the provinces peasants were resisting grain collections, and it was necessary to send Chekists and military forces to crush the outbreaks of antigovernment violence. The men who had previously advocated resistance, sabotage, and conflict found themselves the targets of revolution. It was necessary to act decisively to obviate the risk of being overcome by a truly popular rebellion. The compulsive breakers of all laws were suddenly cast into the role of repressive archconservatives who, with brutality exceeding anything known or experienced under the czars, arrested, imprisoned, and executed all who were thought to sympathize with the rebels.

From 1914 until the early 1920s there had been nearly continuous war. The people were exhausted, the land devastated. Then, finally, Lenin sensed that unless there was a retreat from Marxist experimentation, the Bolshevik coup would be lost.

The Soviet government cracked down on the internal dissenters with vengeance, and in the spring of 1921 the Bolsheviks gave the rest of the world to believe that by instituting the New Economic Policy (NEP), Karl Marx's panacea was under revision. The venerated writer Maxim Gorky was induced to appeal to the Western states for economic assistance, as was Patriarch Tikhon of the Russian Orthodox Church. The GPU was quick to realize that the strong international response to the plight of the starving Russians was an opportunity to be turned to their advantage. The compassionate and humanitarian instincts of the world were about to be converted into new Bolshevik weapons.

During World War I, the Russian Red Cross maintained offices in New York for the purposes of facilitating the relief of Russians who, because of the war, were starving and homeless. An additional service was to aid in reuniting thousands of families that had become separated during the Revolution, the Bolshevik coup, and the ensuing civil war. The contributions from the American Russian community in support of this merciful work were significant. In addition, the American Red Cross gave more than $3.5 million to the American Relief Administration and other large sums to the International Red Cross in Switzerland to be used in relieving the terrible suffering in Russia. After the 1918 coup, the Soviet government moved with some speed to capture this golden goose by repudiating the Russian Red Cross and declaring that the Soviet Russian Red Cross would now act as the exclusive agent for the management of relief funds.

Typically, the Soviet version of the Russian Red Cross had a central committee. The fiat establishing the Soviet organization was signed by "W. Ulianof (Lenin)" with Maxim Litvinov as a member of the central committee.[38] Included as the third organizational aim of the Soviet Russian Red Cross was a statement of ominous intent that dealt with: ". . . the measures to be taken relative to the liquidation of the institutions of the Red Cross into the regions into which the Society's activity formerly extended."

The second appendix to the Soviet "ordinance" began by asserting: "The Council of the Commissariates of the People has ordained: 1) The right to use the insignia of the Red Cross on a white background with the words 'Red Cross' or 'Geneva Cross' belongs exclusively: a) To the personnel and establishments of the Red Cross Society which is the only national society for relief of wounded or sick soldiers, duly recognized by the Soviet Federative Socialist Russian Government . . ." Just to tidy up the preemption, the paragraph outlined the sanctions: "Those who shall, either on land or on sea, make use of the Red Cross insignia or similar insignia without having been given authorization to do so, or who shall wrongfully use the words 'Red Cross,' shall be liable to a minimum punishment of imprisonment for three months, to be imposed by the courts of the People . . ."[39]

With the Soviet Red Cross established, Litvinov raced off to the International Red Cross in Switzerland to claim the U.S. millions. In addition, no time was lost in ordering the New York representative to start soliciting more money. The head of the Soviet Red Cross in the United

States was David Dubrowsky, a dentist, who announced that he was in full charge of Russian relief.[40] Dubrowsky's name first appeared in U.S. government files when he boasted to an assumed friend that he had successfully avoided conscription during the war by volunteering for the U.S. Army Dental Corps, adding that he knew the quota to be oversubscribed and ". . . there were 1,000 (dentists) ahead of me."

By sparing himself any exertions in the war, he was able to put his full energy into extracting relief funds from various organizations in the United States. For the sake of appearances Dubrowsky moved from the old familiar address of 110 West 40th Street to a new office at One Union Square. In the interest of promoting the Soviet cash flow, part of the office was devoted to selling "commodity drafts" in denominations of $5, $10, and $20. The drafts also carried 15 percent "service charges" of $.75, $1.50, and $3.00, respectively. It was explained to prospective buyers that one-third of the service charge went to expenses, two-thirds for "general relief in Russia by the Russian Red Cross." The drafts were said to be good for face value in commodities at any of the twenty-seven branches of the state universal stores (Torgsin) in the Soviet Union.

Dr. Dubrowsky assured clients that the five-dollar draft had a fixed valuation of ten gold rubles no matter what the rate of exchange. The Soviet Russian Red Cross noted in its solicitation letters, "The value of the American dollar will be computed in Russian rubles for this purpose at the mean average current rate of exchange for the three days prior to the presentation of this order."

The activities of the Russian Red Cross rang alarm bells among many genuine relief organizations, which then sought to check the bona fides of Dr. Dubrowsky with the American Red Cross and the American Relief Administration. There was no doubt that Dubrowsky was the duly appointed representative of the Soviet government. A familiar figure, in 1921 he was the official representative of the All-Russian Jewish Public Committee in America, which for a time occupied an office at 47 West 42nd Street, New York. This committee, among other things, offered to act as a transmitting agency for those who wished to send clothing and/or money to relatives and friends in the USSR. The Committee charged five dollars per package and had graduated fees for the transmission of money.

The legitimate Joint Distribution Committee of the American Fund for Jewish War Sufferers notified the American Red Cross:

> With Dr. Dubrowsky, we have found it impossible to establish any cooperative relations. His policies, in some important respects, have been such as were impossible for us to countenance. One branch of his activities has been the elicitation of funds for transmis-

sion to individuals in Russia. These funds he has endeavored to secure upon condition that they were to be exchanged into Russian funds at the rate of 250 rubles to the dollar; whereas it is well known that the prevalent rate of exchange is 5,000 rubles to the dollar; that is to say, twenty times the rate at which the funds listed by Dr. Dubrowsky are to be converted. The lack of substantiating information from the other side, the fact that the individual in receipt of supplies will receive a large amount of paper currency constantly depreciating in value and the fact that the one organized Jewish organization in this country does not cooperate with the Committee, may give one pause before using this Committee as a transmitting agent. . . . His [Dubrowsky's] methods were criticized a good deal and *he himself* tells us that a very small percentage of the remittances ever reach their proper destination [emphasis added].

The Soviet Russian Red Cross scam generated large sums of dollars that, for the most part, remained in Soviet-controlled bank accounts in New York City. Dubrowsky amassed an up-to-date, detailed exposition of the personal circumstances of thousands of Russian-Americans, from many of whom additional money could be extorted in the name of their Russian relatives. This also gave the Chekists the leverage to coerce people who sought only to relieve the distressed conditions of their families. The Soviet Russian Red Cross was far more effective in finding prospective victims than the Repatriation Unions in Europe, and best of all it turned a profit for the OGPU.

Johann Ohsol worked in close cooperation with Dubrowsky in the early days of the Russian Red Cross. The effusive Dubrowsky was given to heartrending descriptions of the plight of the starving and displaced Russians while his colleagues passed the hat. Posing as selfless humanitarians, they carefully noted the identities of the contributors for follow-up interviews. Moscow provided Dubrowsky with a secretary and chief assistant who were OGPU officers.

As the senior contact with the U.S. government, Ohsol was the man who explained that what the Soviets were doing was really aiding the U.S. economy. He tried to convey that those activities which might seem illegal, morally indefensible, and fundamentally criminal were simply instances in which the charges were based on false information, misunderstanding, and language difficulties.

When Whittaker Chambers decided to join the American Communist Party in New York in 1923, he looked for a guide into this exciting new world. By careful reasoning and with remarkable perspicacity, he concluded that the route led through the Soviet Russian Red Cross or Russian-American Relief. It was in the latter organization that he met Sender Garlin. Chambers's correct assumption was that since "Garlin had been associated with the Russian-American Relief, he would undoubtedly, know the location of the Communist Party in New York."[41] Russian-American Relief was on a dotted line with Dubrowsky's Russian Red Cross, having been set up to address the same appeals, but to a different segment of the American public.

A literate fellow like Chambers soon found himself writing for the *Daily Worker,* and within a span of only a few months he replaced Harry Freeman as editor. Freeman became the New York representative of the Soviet news agency, Tass. In an effort to preserve the familial atmosphere of the day, Freeman's apartment on Henry Street, Brooklyn, became a rendezvous for Tass employees, staffers from the *Daily Worker,* and of course the man from Amtorg, a Mr. Pavlov.

It was at one of the Henry Street tribal get-togethers that Chambers first meet Grace Lumpkin, a dedicated apparatchik who spent much of her time at the New York Public Library engaged in research in the fields of genealogy and infant mortality. Later he learned that Grace's dedication did not derive from any compassionate desire to lower the death rate; on the contrary, she might well have welcomed an upsurge in the numbers, since her only objective was to gather such data for the documentation of Soviet agents.

During her careful perusal of twenty-, thirty-, and forty-year-old death notices, Grace compiled lists of infant deaths and recorded all the particulars relating to family survivors, religious denomination, place of burial, and funeral home. Each survivor was then checked in the Greater New York telephone directories. If the funeral home was no longer in business, if the church or synagogue had moved, been demolished, or had a great fire—so much the better. The next step was to make a "premises observation," noting the character of the neighborhood and recording specific data relative to nearby grade and high schools, neighborhood shops, bus routes, subway stations, local streets, etc.

A collateral search was made using business directories and city directories, which were then commonplace references. The principal object was to find businesses that, like the babies, had died. Each expired company, loft, and shop was a prospective "former employer." With this accumulation of minutiae, it was not difficult to begin to construct a life history that would suit a newly arrived Soviet agent. By being born in a house (now demolished), in a neighborhood (now changed), to have attended a grade school (now consolidated), a high school (the student records of which had been destroyed in a 1919 fire), to have worked in a number of businesses (now defunct), combined to make a personal history that defied verification. By her faithful dedication to the task of inventing new lives for the old dead, Grace became one of the early "resurrectionists" for the Soviet service in New York.[42]

U.S. passports were blessed with many advantages. They could be used for easy travel to Great Britain and throughout Europe. You didn't have to speak much English to rightfully possess one, and, in the main, they were more honored and, at the time, less well known. The tens of thousands of immigrants who served in the U.S. forces during the First War were all entitled to apply for passports. The Soviets recognized the advantages and were quick to exploit the relative ease with which the passports could be obtained.

The OGPU, GRU, and Comintern appreciated the protection offered by a U.S. passport, and the document mills in Berlin and New York were pressed to the limits to turn them out in bulk. The travel documents collected from visitors to the USSR were not available in sufficient numbers to meet the demand.[43]

It was in this fevered atmosphere that two aspiring Soviet service recruits became world famous. The account of their unwanted prominence is best told by a direct witness in Moscow, Loy W. Henderson, who later became Under Secretary of State:

> We were conscious of the fact that the Soviet authorities were accustomed secretly to arrest, to interrogate, to try, to sentence, and to carry out the sentences on its own citizens and on citizens of other countries who happened to be in the Soviet Union. . . . The Division [East European Division, U.S. Department of State] therefore drafted a pledge for Litvinov to sign that would give U.S. citizens in the Soviet Union rights in the matter of legal protection that would be no less favorable than those that had been granted to German nationals. . . . We knew that the Soviet government was systematically failing to accord to German nationals the treatment promised in 1925 and that German nationals were disappearing mysteriously no less frequently than nationals of other countries. . . . On December 8, 1937, while I was in charge of the Embassy in the absence of Ambassador Davies, an American journalist stationed in Moscow told me that he had heard that an American citizen by the name of Robinson, who had been staying at the National Hotel, had been arrested and his wife was still at the hotel. I asked Angus Ward, who was in charge of the Consular Section, to go at once to the hotel, which was next door to the chancery, to ascertain whether or not a Mrs. Robinson was living there and, if she was, to call upon her and to make inquiries regarding her husband.

Upon his return from the hotel Ward told me that he had found that an American citizen by the name of Mrs. Donald Louis [Ruth Norma] Robinson was registered in the hotel and that he had had a talk with her in her room. In reply to his questions she had told him that her husband had become violently ill and had been removed to a hospital. She had been unable, however, to furnish the name of the hospital. When he had pressed her for details she had looked frightened and had become evasive. When he had asked to see her passport she had told him that she had turned it over to the hotel for registration with the Soviet authorities.

Disturbed by Ward's story, I went immediately with him to the hotel. When we asked to visit Mrs. Robinson, the assistant director of the hotel, who was believed by members of the Embassy to be a high official of the NKVD, objected. He tried to persuade us to postpone our visit. He said that she was in a nervous state and that it would be preferable for us to see her on the following morning. We insisted that we must see or talk to her at once. He accompanied us to her room and stayed with us so that he could overhear our conversation. During our talk with Mrs. Robinson, I tried to find out more about her—where she lived, who, if any, were her relatives in the United States. She answered my questions by saying that she was too tired and confused to talk with us about herself. She would feel more like talking in the morning.

While we were at the hotel, Ward and I requested the hotel personnel to let us see her passport or, at least, to give us the data relating to her that was in the passport. We were told that the passport was being registered with the authorities and was not, therefore, available, and that the hotel did not have any of the data contained in it in its possession.

When we called at the hotel to see Mrs. Robinson on the following morning we were informed that she had checked out without leaving a forwarding address. In view of the care in which all travel, particularly that of foreigners, in the Soviet Union was carefully controlled, we did not for a moment believe that she had been permitted to leave the hotel in order to go freely to some unknown destination. The attempts of the assistant director to prevent us from having a private talk with Mrs. Robinson and her apparent fright on the preceding evening caused us to believe that she was in serious trouble and that she might be under arrest. . . .

Ward was unable to obtain any information from NARKO-MINDEL [Soviet Ministry of Foreign Affairs]. . . . Vinogradov, the official in the third Western Division . . . told Ward that he had no knowledge whatsoever about any American nationals in the Soviet Union by the name of Robinson. . . .

I proposed therefore . . . that if no information regarding the Robinsons could be obtained by December 14, the Department authorize me to seek an interview with Litvinov. . . .

The Department in a telegram dated December 12, authorized me to make the call on Litvinov. It also informed me that the passports issued in the names of the Robinsons had been based on documents relating to dead persons and that, therefore, the documents had been fraudulently obtained. . . .

I made my call on Litvinov. . . . He was not at all pleased. He replied stiffly that he could not understand why the United States government should be interested in the case now that it seemed clear that the passports had been obtained fraudulently. . . . Furthermore, he stressed, it would appear that the couple had not requested our assistance and that Mrs. Robinson had left the hotel to avoid further contact with the Embassy. . . .

The Commissar said that he could not as yet definitely say that Mrs. Robinson had left the hotel voluntarily and that he could not as yet make any statement regarding the identity or whereabouts of the missing persons. . . .

On December 16, in response to a request of the Department, I telegraphed a description of Mrs. Robinson . . . that she seemed to us to be about twenty-eight years of age; that she had light brown hair and a round pleasant face with no distinguishing characteristics; that she was about five feet four inches in height; that she was plump without being stout and that her speech and gestures were typical of an American woman with at least a secondary education. . . .

Under date of January 3, 1938, the Department informed the Embassy that . . . it was forwarding the London Embassy copies of photographs that were attached to the applications of an Adolph Arnold Rubens and his wife, Ruth Marie Rubens. The telegram stated that the applications of Mr. Rubens and Mr. Robinson had appended to them fraudulent documents obtained from the County Clerk of New York County. . . . I telegraphed immediately that one of the photographs of the Rubenses was that of the woman to whom Ward and I had talked. . . .

On January 18 I gave Weinberg a letter requesting on behalf of the US government that a member of the Embassy be permitted to visit Mrs. Rubens at once. . . .

On January 21, Vinogradov told me by telephone that he had been instructed by Weinberg to advise me that it would be inconvenient for the personnel of the Embassy to visit Mrs. Rubens in prison until after the investigations of her case had been completed. . . .

When reminded of the terms of the Litvinov note agreeing to provide access to US nationals "without delay" and pointing out that Mrs. Robinson had been under investigation for five weeks, Vinogradov responded, in a few hours, with a new interpretation of the intent of the Litvinov promise.

I addressed on January 26, to Assistant Commissar Potemkin who, in the absence of Litvinov, was in charge of NARKO-MINDEL, the formal note which I had prepared in accordance with the Department's instruction. In reporting to the Department that I had done so, I stated that I had learned from members of other diplomatic missions in Moscow that "for some time at least, Soviet authorities have been refusing to permit representatives of foreign governments to visit their nationals in Soviet prisons until after investigations of such nationals had been completed. Although thousands of foreigners have been arrested during the last year, in apparently only a few instances have visits of diplomatic or consular officers been allowed." . . .

It was not until February 9 that I received a reply from Potemkin to my note of January 26. In his note, Potemkin stated that "as an exception, the competent authorities considered it possible for Ward and myself to have an interview with the woman in question on February 10 at 4 pm in the Butyrskaya Prison." The granting of the interview, he stressed, "cannot, of course, create a precedent." . . .

Ward and I entered the gates of the historic Butyrskaya Prison, punctually at 4 pm and were conducted to what appeared to be a room set aside for visitors. We found waiting for us the investigating magistrate, a Soviet official who acted as an interpreter and a representative of the Foreign Office. . . .[44]

The interview went very poorly. Mrs. Robinson seemed more concerned about giving answers that would please the investigator. She did admit that she had left New York City as Ruth Marie Rubens and traveled through Western Europe with her valid passport. When she entered the Soviet Union, however, she used the Robinson passport.[45]

When Ambassador Davies returned from his extended absence, he had a meeting with Litvinov, who told him that "complaints on the part of the Department represented a poor return for the exceptional manner in which the Soviet Union had gone out of its way to show the highest consideration for the United States."

Litvinov, not one to be embarrassed by a lie, made clear to Davies, in effect, that the Soviets were the victims of undue and unwarranted pressure from the embassy. Davies' comprehension of the issue was exceedingly limited, and he was disposed to believe the foreign minister. His brief from President Roosevelt was a simple sentence—"Get along with the Russians"—and he was prepared to swallow any improbability as long as it emanated from an elevated Soviet source.

Following the three visits to the embassy at Moscow in the summer of 1939, Mrs. Rubens/Robinson dropped from sight and broke off contact with her relatives in New York City.

The Rubenses did have a friend who remembered them. He recalled being introduced by J. Peters, a Soviet agent in New York, to a man using the work name "Richard." Peters explained that Richard was "engaged in a birth certificate and naturalization racket for the Soviets." As Peters pointed out, "it was a source of income." He met Richard again in the plaza of Rockefeller Center. Richard had a message from a mutual friend who had fled to Moscow,[46] under threat of arrest a few months before. Richard asked that arrangements be made with the fugitive's sister, who lived in an apartment on Riverside Drive in the Washington Heights area, to crate the friend's furniture and ship it to him, using Amtorg to handle the arrangements.

On another occasion, while having dinner with Peters at Zimmerman's Hungarian restaurant in lower Manhattan, he saw Richard at an adjacent table. Peters confided that Richard was disturbed about the purges then going on in the USSR, especially about the report that General Berzin (the GRU chief) had been shot. Later Peters remarked that Richard's spirits had improved and that he had just received an invitation to return to Russia for a celebration. According to Peters, the invitation was signed *Starik* ("Old Man"), the name by which Berzin was known to Richard.

Before Richard actually left New York for Moscow, he secured two additional American passports, one in the name of Rubens and the other in the name of Robinson. He got them both on the same day through the office of a New York City alderman without the necessity of going personally to the passport office. The friend recalled, "I later learned that there were two agents working in the alderman's office, and they arranged for the two passports to be issued on the same day."[47]

Rubens's "cover" for his last trip was as an official of the Gallian Press, a New York "publishing house devoted to assisting unpublished authors."

During the mid-twenties the Packard Motor Car Company began to build diesel aircraft engines having relatively favorable weight-to-horse-power ratios. The Liberty engine, which had been designed and built in record time by Packard during World War I, had established the company's reputation for engineering excellence. By the time the new diesels were under test, the depression struck, and prospective customers disappeared from the marketplace. The aircraft diesel, like everything else, was of interest to the Soviets, and Amtorg made a number of detailed inquiries regarding expected performance data, with the customary heavy implication that it was just about to place a large-scale order.

The head of the Packard diesel program made several trips to New York to promote and, if possible, accelerate the process. The Soviets didn't buy, but they became very friendly with the chief engineer. A few months later Packard was forced to cancel the diesel project, and the chief engineer found himself without a job.

In the belief that Amtorg might have need for his skills and experience, he wrote a letter to Markov, one of Bogdanov's vice presidents, declaring his availability and enclosing a résumé detailing his work experience and professional references. His letter went unacknowledged until four months later, when his home telephone rang. Without identifying himself, the caller said that he was a friend of Markov's and that he desired a meeting to discuss an important matter. The caller spoke with a heavy accent and insisted that they meet on a street corner in Detroit that evening. The engineer, who had been unemployed for many months, quickly agreed.

At the first meeting, the engineer was given a letter purportedly from Markov, assuring the engineer that he could speak with full confidence to the bearer, "Mr. Dmitrov." After the engineer read the letter, Dmitrov took it back and explained that it would be better if the engineer simply called him Bill, he in turn would call the engineer Jack. Bill then produced a list of questions to which Jack was to get answers. The questions concerned proprietary industrial processes and technical data relating to U.S. military hardware. Along with the questions Bill thoughtfully included $200 "for expenses and travel." As Jack collected the information, he was instructed to mail it to any one of six different addresses in New York City. Bill instructed him to vary the address with each letter, each address was serviced daily, so that all mail would get to Bill promptly. In transmitting the information, the engineer was instructed to use several specific coded phrases and to sign each transmittal with his new name, Jack.

One of Bill's most immediate questions was the exact nature of a new machine patented by the Budd Company for cold-rolling steel. Bill explained that the giant Soviet tractor manufacturers were extremely anxious to know this process so that disk wheels could be made without using the conventional heat process. In time, the engineer dutifully secured a cross-sectional drawing of the Budd machine and the associated engineering data essential to its construction and operation. The bulky letters went from Grosse Point, Michigan, to the New York addresses as instructed. From New York came packets of money, anywhere from $400 to $800—almost the price of a new Packard at this time—depending on the Soviets' estimate of the worth of the material.

Three months after the engineer undertook the first "order," he received a call from Bill insisting on another street-corner meeting that very evening. At this meeting, the engineer was introduced to a "Friend." Then Bill announced, "Jack, you have been given small stuff until now. We believe that you are trustworthy and are in a position to secure big stuff for us now," whereupon "Friend" began to recite his particular interests in detail:

"The U.S. Navy is making wide use of the Gidrophone [hydrophone], an acoustical apparatus for catching underwater sounds on ships and submarines. It is important that you obtain detailed plans and descriptions of this device. . . .

"When torpedoes are fired using compressed air, a large air bubble comes to the surface indicating the location of the submarine. We know the U.S. Navy is working on this problem. Learn what progress is being made. Also get complete information relative to air purifiers, water distillers and submarine diesel propulsion units. . . .

"We also know from your curriculum vitae that you are acquainted with the superintendent of the New London Boat and Engineering Corporation, which is building submarines for the U.S. Navy. Here is $140 in cash. You will proceed to New London, Connecticut, and contact the Superintendent at the submarine yard. Once you have had an initial talk with him, send a telegram to H. Mitchell, 219 Seventh Avenue, New York City. As soon as I receive your wire, I will join you in New London and make further plans . . ."[48]

The engineer's conscience finally made light contact with his intellect, and he was forced to conclude that he had been induced to join in a Soviet military intelligence operation and that no serious employment was in the offing. His initial rationalization of the Amtorg connection began to fade. He had taken the first money on the basis that the information was readily available to anyone with easy recourse to the technical and engineering publications that described new industrial techniques, patents, and processes. It was obvious to him from the outset that the Soviets' aims were to acquire new technology by theft rather than by license or purchase. Ordinarily, he would have refused to cooperate in such a venture, but his unexpected financial reverses, job loss, and the demands of the house at Grosse Point made industrial espionage appear as a better alternate than economic collapse.

Dmitrov and his "friend" had measured their man carefully and had exact knowledge of his precarious state. Their only businesslike exchanges were the scrupulously annotated receipts that he was required to sign after every cash payment. "Friend" seemed to have an amazing knowledge of the development work of the U.S. Navy, and the imperative tone of his instructions suggested that he now regarded the engineer as a *seksot*. Dmitrov's assurance that he believed the engineer to be "trustworthy" was simply a Soviet euphemism that literately meant: We think you are sufficiently compromised by the cash receipts and what you have already sent to us—concealing your identity, using a false name, and employing coded phrases—to guarantee your continued compliance with our demands.

The engineer agreed to meet with "Friend" in New London, but decided to tell U.S. authorities about this curious business of Amtorg vice presidents skulking on street corners in Detroit. His decision was reinforced by an unpleasant interview with the general counsel of the Budd Company, who put him on notice that Budd was aware of his theft of company data as well as of the fact that he had turned the information over to the Soviets. Within the week the engineer made an appointment with William Larsen, special agent in charge of the Detroit Office of the Federal Bureau of Investigation. They met in Larsen's office in the Lafayette Building, and the story was retold in full detail. Larsen prepared a lengthy report and forwarded it to Washington, where it was studied by the FBI and the criminal division of the Justice Department. At the time there was no federal statute dealing with such activity, and so the public record closed with a brief note from J. Edgar Hoover advising Assistant Attorney General Nugent Dodds that "The Bureau has taken no action with regard to the foregoing."

The engineer went to New London and later sent the telegram to "H. Mitchell." It seems reasonable that Bill, Jack, and "Friend" had no basis for believing that the U.S. authorities were interested in their "work." More important, it confirmed Bill's and "Friend's" contempt for the capitalist system, which did not have the will or the means to protect itself. Their evaluation of the bourgeois engineer was also unflattering—after all, they'd originally bought him for only $200.

The constant requirement for the cash needed to finance the expenses of Amtorg workers was a continuing source of vexation. Even ideologues had to pay full fare on the railroads. The Marxist-Leninists knew that the most satisfying sources of money were the intended victims; thus, the only remaining problem was to devise a means by which the U.S. industrial firms could be induced to contribute the money necessary to finance the theft of their own proprietary secrets. After careful consideration the answer became clear. Amtorg would go into the publishing business.

By the end of 1930, the publishing department had ten full-time workers and was experiencing great prosperity. Amtorg representatives called on hundreds of major U.S. manufacturers with the proposal that the firms buy advertising space in the Amtorg "business directory." The companies were informed that this was an unique opportunity to get their message to the appropriate people in the USSR, thus ensuring that their products would not be overlooked. To promote competitive buying the space salesmen made occasional "highly confidential" disclosures of how much space had been bought by rival businesses. The space rates were artificially high and had no relationship to circulation or readership data. The salesmen simply stressed the special character of the book and its obvious importance to any company trying to do business with the USSR. Many American businessmen, having been confounded previously by Soviet practices, were disposed to take the bait. Once a contract was signed, Amtorg wrote to the company and asked if it was the company's desire to have the ad appear, in the USSR, in English. If not, there was an additional charge for translation. Did the company wish to use photographs and drawings to illustrate the text? Again, the additional work required an increase in cost. Did the company wish to buy extra copies for its own distribution? Well, yes, they were available, though only in lots of twenty-four volumes. Further, the smiling salesmen reported, the Amtorg directory was certain to be a raging success, and in recognition of that fact the board of directors already saw the need to make it an annual publication. Of course, no one from Amtorg told the advertisers that there would be no distribution in the USSR. In the land of central planning there is no need for multiple copies.

With the lofty title *Catalogue of American Industry and Trade,* the bulky print rolled off a nonunion press in New York City. The fourth edition contained 734 pages, almost 600 of which were display ads by large American manufacturing firms. The space rates were in excess of $600 per page, with additional translation and graphics fees bringing the average page cost to $750. For those who couldn't or wouldn't buy display ads there were various gradations of listings under a variety of headings that could be bought for less.

In the first pages of the catalog tribute was paid to "V. F. Prosin, the initiator and organizer of the work done by the Publications Division of Amtorg."[49] Mr. I. V. Boyeff, chairman of the board of Amtorg, wrote the introduction, which is easily seen as a cryptic message to his state security superiors in Moscow. His introduction ended with the wry comment: "I wish to express the hope that the benefits derived by the Soviet readers of this catalog will more than counter-balance any shortcomings it may have."[50] Boyeff had a taste for irony, but it wasn't only the inside joke and the net of a quarter of a million tax-free dollars that pleased him. The real satisfaction came from knowing that American businessmen had shown their willingness to subsidize industrial espionage against their own interests.

After the war, Prosin's creation exceeded all expectations. When the 1946 version of the catalog appeared, it consisted of 5,000 pages in three volumes.

It can only be hoped that "Friend's" trip to New London was not paid for out of the advertising budget of the New London Boat and Engineering Company.

In 1930, Union Tours of 261 Fifth Avenue appeared to be a conventional New York travel bureau where one could book a week in the Catskills or a trip to Albany on the Hudson River Day Line. Once inside the door, however, it became clear that Union was something special. It was one of the very few agencies in New York that could make arrangements for a visit to the USSR. Union agents knew all about Intourist, hotels, visas, and routes, and they were able to give prospective travelers detailed instructions on how to get to—and, once there, how get into— the USSR.

Since there was no Soviet embassy in Washington and no consulate in New York, the U.S. government took the position that the Soviet Union was diplomatic *terra incognita* and tried to caution those who were determined to go that there was no official U.S. representation in Moscow or anywhere else in the Soviet Union. Thus, the Department of State was unable to provide the advice and protection normally available to U.S. citizens abroad.

Union travelers came from a variety of sources and fell into several distinct classes. There were those who went on "business"—delegates to the unending series of conferences and conventions sponsored directly or indirectly by the Comintern. The Profintern concentrated on the selection of U.S. labor representatives of acceptable political views who were thought to have the organizational and leadership talents necessary to eventually gain control of the American unions. The labor elements of most immediate concern to the Profintern were the longshoremen, warehousemen, and all seagoing maritime workers, with particular emphasis on ship's radio operators.

Another group consisted of representatives of various national groups who had been led to believe that they and their followers would be welcomed in the USSR as immigrant workers in the struggle for justice and freedom. (Several thousand Finnish-Americans, with all their machinery, tools, possessions, and savings, paid their own passage on the strength of a never-to-be fulfilled promise that, on arrival, they would be given land and encouragement in the building of a new, socialist Karelia.)

Young people were induced to believe that going to the USSR was roughly analogous to joining a Crusade. Despite the hardships to be endured, the joys and rewards of participation were certain to be boundless. Furthermore, unlike the Crusades, the International Movement consisted wholly of those who were bold, egalitarian, democratic, liberated, socially advanced, and intellectually strong. It was heady medicine laced with evocative appeals to the emotions. The USSR was the only place on the globe that celebrated the common man, a place where each human was met with equal dignity and respect and where purity of purpose was a given. Not to have traveled to the USSR was a little like being consigned to Limbo, never to know the absolute bliss of an ascension to Bolshevik Heaven.

Despite the utter cynicism of these deliberate misrepresentations, Union arranged passage to the promised land for hundreds of young people. Part of the process required the provision of much personal and family data. It was explained to the traveler that such information was necessary for the issuance of a Soviet visa. The applications were very detailed, and since the visas could only be granted in the USSR, several months were required for the processing and movement of the applications by sea mail. A copy was retained in the U.S., and the OGPU in New York screened the applicants by arranging their inclusion in study groups concerned with Russian language, Russian culture, and Karl Marx. Each study group was controlled and monitored by an OGPU agent, who assessed the motivations of the participants. Those who failed to give a convincing demonstration of their witlessness were not issued visas. Those who showed appropriate revolutionary zeal and who were not obvious degenerates or lunatics found themselves en route within a few months.

During the hiatus in British-Soviet diplomatic relations following the police raid on Arcos, the first port of call was Helsinki or a north German or French port, from which overland transportation was available. Although the practice varied from place to place, Soviet visas were generally issued as separate documents, and no note or entry was made in the traveler's passport. The OGPU arranged for the collection of foreign passports at the Soviet border and issued substitute identity documents in their stead. The process allowed OGPU technicians to replicate signatures, cachets, and endorsements for future use in the authentication of altered passports issued by the organs. It was usual to remove a page or more from the genuine documents and to substitute counterfeit pages. In this way OGPU accumulated stores of paper produced by the U.S. Bureau of Printing and Engraving for later use in the fabrication of spurious passports.

In a number of instances the traveler leaving the USSR was simply told that his or her passport had been lost or inadvertently destroyed. The Soviets would lament the failure of their new bureaucracy and suggest that the traveler could be put across the border into Latvia or Lithuania, there to approach a U.S. consular office and apply for a replacement. The proposal was made unofficially and with a hint of naughtiness. Travelers who agreed to this collusion with agents of the state security were then cautioned about the need to conceal their visit to the USSR. OGPU assisted them in the development of a minor "legend," which included a detailed account of the circumstances under which the passport was lost. Once in Riga or Vilnius, a traveler would give the false statement, under oath or affirmation, and would be issued a new document. The OGPU now had evidence of the commission of federal crimes—passport violation and giving false and misleading statements to a consular officer under oath.

Amtorg was being pressed by the Fish Committee to explain why, on July, 15, 1930, it was necessary for Amtorg to have 578 Soviet nationals taking inspection tours of U.S. industrial firms. The Amtorg census did not include several hundred U.S. citizens working for the firm in facilitating the plant visits of the itinerant "inspectors." Johann Ohsol and Peter Bogdanov responded by lecturing the committee on the economic benefits that were bound to accrue to the United States as a consequence of the *next* Five-Year Plan. The witness Bogdanov did not reply to the questions and deferred, in every instance, to his "American" vice president. The committee was incredulous and growing impatient with Ohsol's flummery. In an effort to get back to the point of the hearings, Committee Counsel Nelson turned to Bogdanov and asked:

"Mr. Bogdanov, I understand that the Soviet government is opposed to the capitalistic system. Is that correct?"
(Bogdanov interpreted by Ohsol) No.
(N) It is not?
(B/O) No, I wish to explain what I mean.
(N) I wish you would, for there is a general misconception in this country that it is.
(B/O) The Soviet government considers possible the collaboration with capitalistic governments, as has been declared at the Geneva International Economic Conference.
(N) That is fine. Now I ask the witness if the Soviet government does not stand for the principle of abolition of the capitalistic system, and he can answer that yes or no and we will keep on going.
(B/O) It does not stand for abolition.
(N) Does not stand for the abolition of the capitalistic system?
(B/O) No, sir, it does not.

(N) You stated yesterday that it did.

(B/O) I stated yesterday that the Communist Party stands for it.

(N) But the Soviet government is in accord with the Communist Party on that point, is it not?

(B/O) The Soviet government has nothing in common with the Communist Party.[51]

In the end the committee was frustrated, bored, confused, and fatigued by the insistent techniques of "Never admit, seldom deny, and always distinguish." Amtorg, which proved to have greater stamina than the committee, went on and on, and the New York hearings ground to a close.

The number of Amtorg-associated travelers reached two thousand per year by the late thirties, and Union Tours prospered. The U.S. Post Office also contributed to the financial well-being of Union Tours by distributing a letter from the acting second assistant postmaster general, J. W. Cole, which instructed postmasters to recommend that "persons seeking to send merchandise to relatives in the USSR avail themselves of the authority given to the Amtorg Trading Corporation of 261 Fifth Avenue, by the Soviet government to issue licenses prepaying import duties on merchandise being sent to the Union of Soviet Socialist Republics. . . . For the convenience of senders in this country, the duty prepaid licenses may be obtained through the following named firms and banks, who will attend to the matter of collecting the fee for the license . . . as well as a fee for their own services."[52] The second name on the list was Union Tours, conveniently co-located with Amtorg at 261 Fifth Avenue.

In the late 1920s, the Soviet leaders came up with another scheme, which was aimed at bringing large amounts of hard currency into the Kremlin's coffers while at the same time exerting a destabilizing effect on the U.S. dollar. The plan first came to light in Vienna, Austria, when the police were summoned to the Central Bank to interview a teller who had accepted some counterfeit U.S. currency.

The teller thought the man was "dark, medium height," and in sum not very memorable. He had presented some French francs, three British pounds, and a $100 U.S. Federal Reserve note for conversion into schillings. In the course of the transaction, he remarked on the weather and told the teller that he hoped 1930 would be a better year than '29. When he was given the schillings, he wished the teller a Happy Christmas.

The $100 note was counterfeit.

Within a month several of the large casinos in Havana accepted $100 Federal Reserve notes that, when deposited in Havana banks, were declared counterfeit. Again, the recollections of the cashiers failed to provide an adequate description of those who passed the notes. After all, the $100 bill was a fairly common item in the casinos, even in a world depression.

In April 1930 the Bulgarian Central Bank received a wire from its New York correspondent bank that four of the $100 notes it had submitted for exchange were bogus and had been surrendered, under law, to the U.S. Treasury.

In the office of the newly installed president of the old Berlin banking house of Sass & Martini, Mr. Dorn and Mr. Zimmons were discussing the future.[53] It was late December 1929. The old bank had been dormant for many years, but it had just been bought by a syndicate that planned to revitalize it to promote interest in securities the group owned. German law of the day required a direct bank association for any brokerage firm offering stocks to the public. Dorn was an experienced dealer in all sorts of stocks and bonds and was at this very moment sojourning in Germany while certain of his earlier investment promotions in the United States were in the process of "cooling."

It was three days before the official opening of the bank under its new management. Another bank officer, Mr. Eckert, came in through the gilded doors of #23 Taubenstrasse with the bank's first prospective customer on his arm. Eckert went directly into Zimmons's office, leaving the client in the anteroom.

"He wants to cash some American dollars, and if we can accommodate him, he's in a position to give the bank a lot of business."

Dorn stepped out of the private office and looked at the man. He recognized him as the fellow he'd seen dining with Eckert in a restaurant the night before.

Returning to Zimmons's office, the three men discussed the transaction and decided to accommodate the new client. Eckert left the room and returned a moment later with a packet consisting of fifty $100 notes. They decided to dispatch the chief cashier to the Deutschebank with the bills. The cashier was instructed to warn the Deutschebank to examine the notes carefully to ensure that they were genuine. A half hour later the cashier returned to Taubenstrasse and reported that the notes had been examined and accepted by the Deutschebank as a routine exchange transaction.[54]

The press of other business took Dorn to Paris in the early weeks of 1930. The day following his return to Berlin, Sass & Martini was raided by the Berlin police. Earlier on that same day the Deutschebank had received an urgent cable from the Federal Reserve Bank in New York stating that most of the $100 notes forwarded by the Deutschebank and now arriving in the United States were counterfeit.

Dorn, having no appetite for association with the Berlin police, kept a respectable distance from Sass & Martini and stayed away from 23 Taubenstrasse. It was only later that he established that the first bills had been genuine and that the subsequent and much larger transactions, made in his absence, had consisted entirely of the counterfeit notes. Dorn immediately recognized the technique as the traditional practice of confidence men everywhere always to salt the game with a little substance.

Many years later, after completing his sentence as a convicted swindler at the federal prison in Lewisburg,[55] Dorn told the U.S. authorities that after the Sass & Martini raid, he had seen the same "client" on several occasions at the Circle Hausemann in Paris in March 1930. According to Dorn, the man was gambling with large-denomination chips. Ten years later, Dorn saw a photograph of the man in *The New York Times* book review section, with a caption identifying him as Walter G. Krivitsky.[56]

Stalin's concept of the world banking system had led him to assume that counterfeiting might be an effective way of achieving several of his most immediate goals. The Soviets were desperately short of foreign exchange. By exchanging counterfeit U.S. currency, he thought, the Soviets would benefit directly from the francs, guilders, pounds, and marks that would result from the trade. The second advantage lay in the appealing idea that the success of the plan would reduce confidence in the U.S. dollar, and best of all, the U.S. dollar, the building block of the bastion of capitalism, would become a secret subsidy to the Soviet government.

Counterfeiting is not an easy business because all currencies are proofed against unlawful replication. The technical problems of imitating inks, watermarks, and paper are in themselves exceedingly complex. The extraordinary draftsmanship of the engravers and the precision of the machines essential to the process are additional factors.

Assuming success in this technical phase, intelligence regarding series numbers, coded serial numbers, scaled exemplars of the various signators and the dates of their service, and many other factors reduce the possibilities of a successful large-scale counterfeit issue to zero. When these obstacles were presented to Stalin, he took them as evidence of lack of imagination and small-mindedness on the part of his lieutenants. The technical problems would be overcome, he insisted; these objections were no more than incidental details about which he wanted to hear no more.

The selection of the denomination to be copied also required careful consideration. If the amount was too high, the note would automatically come under close scrutiny. If the denomination of the bills was too low, it might be possible to insinuate them into an economy with relative ease, but with the obvious need to pass more notes and thus increase the risk of discovery. In addition, small-denomination bills, in the necessary volume, would be more difficult to secrete, store, and transport. Even if it were possible to solve all the technical problems, there was still another, almost insurmountable problem: How could a large volume of currency be introduced into exchange channels?

The OGPU chiefs were unable to dissuade Stalin from this deranged notion, and so they found themselves working under great pressure to implement it. The paper experts and highly skilled engravers associated with the passport mill in Berlin were given the imperative to commence an immediate study of U.S. currency. Paper stock, always a counterfeiter's nemesis, promised to be the most critical item.

Fine traces of colored silk were introduced into the U.S. paper stock before it was pressed, marked, and sized for printing. Duplication of the process was technically impossible. An alternative would be to locate the source of the paper and obtain the necessary stocks by theft. The countervailing argument was that if Soviet agents were successful in stealing the paper, U.S. authorities would be alerted to the fact that some enterprising counterfeiters were about to introduce a new line of bogus bills. Besides, no one knew where the U.S. paper was made and stored.[57]

The German laboratory began to experiment with the possibility that small-denomination genuine bills could be washed and bleached and then used as the stock for counterfeit higher-denomination bills. To accelerate the process, it was thought that low-denomination bills could be reduced, cooked, and bleached in one continuous process, with the resulting pulp being relaid, marked, sized, ready for the printing phase. But this work was demanding, and the results were unsatisfactory.

At the time, Nicholas Dozenberg was working around New York City as a GRU support agent.[58] He'd been recruited, in 1926, to do odd jobs at $35 per week for Alfred Tilton, then the GRU chief in New York.[59] By 1928, Dozenberg was a valuable factotum and courier, Tilton's link with the burgeoning Soviet military intelligence nets in the area. Dozenberg arranged for the GRU to lease, for nocturnal use, part of the premises of a photographer named Joseph Tourin. Once the deal was made, Dozenberg bought a large photostat machine and set it up in Tourin's shop at 67 West 119th Street. Initially, Tourin had been in financial difficulties, which was the main reason for Dozenberg's approach. Now, with the photostat machine in place, Tourin began to raise the price of his services. Tilton, annoyed with Tourin's lack of ideological fervor, gave Dozenberg the money to buy Tourin out.

Dozenberg minded the store while Lydia Stahl operated the machine and performed a variety of other photographic and other tasks for Amtorg.[60] Among her collateral duties was the purchase of scientific and technical publications for shipment to Moscow. By day Lydia accumulated the items on the Soviet shopping list; by night Dozenberg crated the instruments, machines, books, and documents for export. To ease the problem of the chronic short supply of money, the Comintern sent twelve crates of books to Dozenberg for sale in the United States. The books were mostly turgid theoretical tracts from Moscow and Berlin, and Dozenberg was unable to sell them at retail. He finally sold the lot for pulp to a paper concern in New Jersey.

Dozenberg's first clear view of Tilton's military-intelligence collection effort occurred when Tilton's newly arrived associate, Boris Davyatkin, acquired engineering drawings of the British battleship HMS *Royal Oak,* which were being taken by courier from Ottawa to Washington. Tilton told Dozenberg that they had gained access to the documents through a cooperative and venal American officer. The group worked throughout the night reproducing the blueprints, and in the early morning the drawings were returned to the courier without incident.

Both Dozenberg and Tilton used the offices of a dentist, Dr. Philip Rosenbliett,[61] for operational contacts and meetings with the seaman couriers from the North German Lloyd Lines, who maintained still another link with Moscow.

A former member of the Communist Party Control Commission[62] in New York City later testified that, in the late thirties, Dozenberg approached him and asked "to learn the secret process of the serialization of numbers on American money."[63] The request was quite beyond the everyday incidental knowledge of the Control Commission, and Dozenberg was directed to look elsewhere.

Both Dozenberg and Burtan had made extensive efforts to cultivate several employees of the U.S. Bureau of Printing and Engraving. The employees were entertained, given gifts, and invited to bring their special skills to the USSR, where they would be treated with the respect their work deserved and rewarded handsomely simply for taking charge of the modern Soviet facility being built in Moscow to handle specie printing and engraving for the Soviet government. Then the problem was turned over to an enterprising executive in New York named Polyakov. (As J. Poliakoff he had been denied a U.S. visa in Berlin on an earlier application. With a slightly altered version of his *nom d'espion* he was later successful in taking up an assignment to Amtorg in New York.)

Polyakov aggressively followed up the leads and met with considerable success. Several employees were induced to provide technical intelligence, and one in particular actually assisted the Soviets in acquiring a large stock of U.S. banknote paper. Two other Printing and Engraving employees quit their jobs in Washington and presented themselves for transportation to the USSR at Polyakov's office in New York. He was easy to locate. They simply went to Amtorg and asked for "Engineer Polyakov."

When W. H. Moran, chief of the Secret Service Division of the Treasury Department, saw the first Soviet counterfeit, he knew it was not the product of a schoolyard gang. The laboratory confirmed his first impression that it was printed from intaglio plates on bleached genuine paper.

Quite apart from the minor errors and faulty bits of engraving, obvious only to a trained examiner, the Soviets were off to a good start. Their craftsmanship had won the attention of Secret Service, and a circular letter issued from Washington conceded: "This is an extremely dangerous counterfeit . . . unusually deceptive, and great care should be exercised in handling notes of this variety and denomination. . . ."

The first note had been detected in March 1929, and by the following June the new, improved Soviet edition was the subject of another Secret Service warning circular. It was basically the same note except that "this production, exceptionally dangerous, is printed from finely etched photomechanical plates on bleached genuine paper and is the handiwork of the counterfeiters responsible for the $100 Federal Reserve Note described in Circular Letter #602. . . ." Still another new note, this one purporting to be on the Federal Reserve Bank of Philadelphia, prompted an even stronger cautionary injunction from Moran: "These counterfeits will deceive even the wary handlers of currency and great care should be exercised in examining notes of this denomination. . . ." By February 1930 three additional types of Franklin counterfeits, all "originating" with the same source, were added to the growing Soviet product line. All of the notes produced by the Soviets were Federal Reserve notes of the old, large size, bearing Franklin's portrait.[64]

In retrospect the big bill was an odd choice because every bank in the world was anticipating a change in the appearance of U.S. currency. Unfounded rumors persisted during this period that the large old bills would have to be presented for exchange within ninety days of the appearance of the small replacement bills and that after the exchange period lapsed, the old notes would not be honored. The Department of State had a sufficient number of inquiries from foreign holders of the old currency to warrant a request to the Treasury Department for a statement relative to the proposed redemption rules governing the old currency.[65]

If the Soviets had devoted the same skill, money, and effort to the manufacture of the new small note, they might have benefited from the mass exchange that later occurred, with the added advantage that the foreign banking community was unfamiliar with the new, small notes, the first of which appeared on July 10, 1929.

Dr. Valentine Gregory Burtan was one of the very few Soviet intelligence agents who shared Stalin's admiration for the counterfeiting project. Burtan saw it as a chance to show Stalin that at least one of his men in New York was imaginative, ambitious, and capable. It occurred to Burtan that the ideal solution for disposing of large amounts of the coun-

terfeit money was to locate a corruptible finance minister in Central or
South America who would agree to substitute the Soviet product for genuine currency stored in vaults in the central bank. In this way Burtan
hoped to avoid the tedious business of hundreds of small transactions in
favor of one big one.

To aid him in this adventure, he had among his marginal contacts an
experienced German con man who spoke Spanish and Portuguese. According to the German's own assertions, he was widely connected with
men of influence in the upper reaches of various Latin American countries. Burtan was attracted by the prospect of using the German to negotiate the switch and found that the German's name of the moment, Count
Enrique von Bulow (or "von Buelow"), was just the right touch to lend
the project a little panache.[66]

Burtan's entrepreneurial instincts and his need for recognition were
very strong. Before the counterfeiting scam came along, he had made
several unsuccessful attempts to persuade Amtorg that he was just the
man to conduct the Soviet purchasing program in the United States. During this period, the pressures on the various Soviet agents in the United
States were considerable, with the result that many organizational discipline and security practices were seriously neglected. Burtan worked for
the GRU and at the same time maintained contacts with three Control
Commission members, Gitlow, Lovestone, and Dirba. He was also in
direct contact with Amtorg and maintained connections with other GRU
and OGPU agents in Manhattan.

With the redoubtable von Bulow, Burtan traveled south to Mexico
and Central America. Burtan sat in various hotel lobbies while the count
tried to find a finance minister who was prepared to make a currency
switch. According to von Bulow, the problem was not discovering avarice
and venality among the finance ministers, it was finding one whose price
was affordable. Burtan was angered by the fact that the few who were
agreeable to the plan wanted most of the proceeds for themselves. With
the inverted morality of a practiced Soviet agent he pronounced them all
thieves and returned to New York.

Burtan had a little less than $125,000 in counterfeit bills, and from
that he was supposed to raise at least $60,000 in genuine currency to
finance Dozenberg's newest commercial cover company, the Romanian-
American Film Company. Burtan was beginning to find the counterfeit
currency a burden, but it was not his style to go from bank to bank at the
retail level of crime. He continued his search for a suitable wholesale
connection to take the bogus notes off his hands.

Within a month von Bulow suggested that Burtan accompany him to
Chicago to meet a friend who might have some thoughts on how the
money could be exchanged. The friend was a private detective named

Smiley who maintained wide associations among the lower levels of Chicago crookdom and knew a few who were available to take a chance at a "big score." Burtan and von Bulow put up at the Drake Hotel. Later in the day, the count made his presentation to Smiley, who was rapt when the count finished his preamble and stupefied when he saw the goods.

Smiley wanted a few samples to "test," and the count gave him several notes and a warning to keep the matter "confidential." Having broad experience with marginal operators, Smiley immediately betrayed his trust and met with his lawyer, whose tiny clientele consisted entirely of unsuccessful minor criminals. As Smiley had estimated the price of von Bulow's desperation, his lawyer was furiously calculating the cost to Smiley of his opinion. By late afternoon, the count was interviewing a knot of petty gamblers, touts, and minor hoodlums in the lounge of the Croydon Hotel. The conspiracy had expanded 800 percent since the count's earlier meeting with Smiley.

The aggregate technical competence of the Chicago conspirators (or, as they might have been known, the original Smiley's people) was roughly equivalent to that of a doorknob. None had sufficient confidence in himself (and certainly not in his colleagues) to present the first note without reassurance that it was reasonably safe to do so. One in the group was inspired—he knew an unemployed former bank teller who could give an expert opinion. It was agreed that they would make the contact and collectively secure his evaluation. Now that the ranks of the conspiracy were swelling, the lawyers discreetly removed themselves to a respectable distance, reserving their participating shares should the project succeed. Throughout the day von Bulow had been awarding 7 percent shares in the undertaking to each of his new associates, and it was time to close the syndicate before his own participation evaporated completely.

The new partners agreed that the bank teller would be entitled to a fee but not a percentage of the net, even though he was going to be a prime mover in passing the bogus bills. In the time-honored tradition, the man with the skills who assumed the burden of risk was to be the least rewarded. The meeting with the out-of-work teller took place in the white-tiled and brightly illuminated nearby Thompson's restaurant. Four hangers-on from the Croydon lounge, the count, and the teller arranged themselves (in overcoats and wide-brimmed fedoras) around the composition-covered table in a nervous scuffling of bent cane chairs. Cold coffee stood in the quarter-pound utility mugs while they watched the former teller eat his first full meal in days.

When he had finished, the count pushed a piece of the goods across the table as the others hunched up expectantly. The teller hadn't seen a note of this denomination for some time but, recalling his past training, began to look for the conventional telltales of the counterfeit. Finding none, he pronounced the bill genuine.

When the count judged that the plan was proceeding, he arranged for Burtan to meet with his local distributors in the mezzanine of the La Salle Hotel in the Loop. Burtan, as "Mr. Smith," had previously hit on the idea that he would promote the notion that the currency was a part of the Arnold Rothstein hoard and in that way convey the impression that it was genuine, though "hot." He expected that American mobsters would immediately nod with understanding and not put too fine a point on the origins of the money. Suggesting that he, himself, had been entrusted to unload the bundle conferred a certain status on Burtan in the eyes of Smiley's friends. Rothstein was a major New York gangster then under heavy federal and local police scrutiny for his involvement in a number of major rackets, wholesale bootlegging, and most recently the armed robbery of a U.S. Treasury truck. The Chicagoans displayed appropriate reverence for Rothstein's reputation, and the glow of admiration for Rothstein enveloped Burtan. Rothstein had a cash problem, according to Burtan, and needed the assistance of understanding friends elsewhere to aid in its solution. The specifics were simply that he wished to get rid of some money acquired in New York because the police had most of the serial numbers. Using the money in New York might make new problems for Rothstein, so he decided to sell it at substantial discount to a few deserving out-of-state beneficiaries.

The balance of the meeting concerned the price and Burtan discreetly failed to mention that the notes were counterfeit. The Croydon gang didn't doubt Burtan's genuineness because they knew that if someone tried to sting the mob, there would be no place to hide. No one who wasn't a confirmed psychopath with a rampant death wish would even consider it. The part about Rothstein's trouble was true, and it was likely that Arnold did have a supply of money that was no good in New York. The recurrent problems of "hot" money were familiar, but the idea of "queer" money hadn't occurred to anyone.

In Burtan's view there was no ideological objection to a temporary alignment with some picturesque native-born criminals, and by the end of the first meeting, he had set in motion the "deal" that launched him on his ten-year tour of the federal penitentiary at Lewisburg, Pennsylvania, and a small but secure place in the annals of Chicago crime.

Burtan returned to New York, and the count rounded out his distribution gang. By mid-December 1932, Johnson, the out-of-work teller, was energetically pushing the "goods" at the Harris Trust & Savings Bank, the First National Bank, the West Side Trust & Savings Bank, and the Northern Trust Company. On a repeat visit to the First National he attempted to convert one hundred Soviet-made Ben Franklins for $10,000 in genuine bills. The cashier balked and said that the notes would have to be examined. Johnson, believing the notes to be genuine, went off in search of one of the Croydon Hotel gang, who was waiting in the streets outside the bank. His aim was to explain that there was a delay in the transaction, but his chum had vanished.

A call from the bank to the Chicago office of the Secret Service produced an immediate response, and a few minutes later Johnson was arrested while searching the bank lobby for the man who had given him the money to exchange. News of Johnson's arrest spread quickly, and within a few hours a stream of volunteer witnesses began to flow into the office of Thomas J. Callaghan, the Secret Service chief in Chicago. The volunteers simply wanted to assist the government in getting to the bottom of the counterfeit ring. Within forty-eight hours of Johnson's arrest two lawyers, one contractor, Johnson, four boulevardiers from the Croydon, and Frank Smiley, the private detective, offered themselves up as government witnesses.

The count was taken into custody on his arrival in New York. He immediately informed the Secret Service that he had been duped into the affair by the mysterious Dr. Burtan, who was the sole source of the "goods." Burtan, who was never very good at remembering his own aliases, had used one when he met the amateur distributors in Chicago, and, of course, he realized that at least five of them could recognize him on sight no matter what name he had used. He must also have had reservations about the count's dedication to the cause now that he was in U.S. custody on a major federal felony charge. So Burtan struck his tent and headed for Montreal, but after a few nervous days he returned to New York, where he was arrested and charged.

Nicholas Dozenberg, whose new movie company, Romanian-American Films, had been due to get $60,000 of needed financing from Burtan, bought his steamship ticket and prepared for a hasty departure. Dozenberg's wholly innocent wife read about Burtan's arrest and wanted to call Mrs. Burtan to express her sympathy, but she was enjoined from doing so by Dozenberg. He thought it best not to recollect the Burtans if asked.

A few days later Dozenberg sailed from U.S. jurisdiction and returned to Moscow "for consultation." Burtan refused to make any admissions and, like Robert Osman, a U.S. Army corporal who was court-martialed for espionage that same year, insisted that he was being prosecuted only because he was a Jew. His attitude in the face of the evidence moved the jury to an easy decision. Burtan was sentenced to fifteen years in the federal penitentiary.

Each successive time that Burtan was eligible for parole the director of the Federal Bureau of Prisons solicited responses from the various agencies concerned. The unanimous opinion was that parole not be granted because of his recalcitrant behavior. During World War II Burtan "offered to serve *his* country" as a physician. It was a relatively safe political bet because the United States was allied with the USSR, but his offer was declined.

Burtan is another of the hundreds of tragic figures who devoted their whole lives to an illusion. The proponents of the counterfeiting scheme had, by this time, all been executed by Stalin. The secret Burtan guarded with his silence was revealed and confirmed by many others. The Soviets would never want him back because he had been in the custody of the U.S. authorities and, by Stalin's lights, had been "turned."

Although not recognized at the time, there was a collateral benefit to the Soviet services in allowing some of the more senior Amtorg employees to be accompanied by their wives and families. The children of these people grew up in the Bronx or Brooklyn and attended the New York public schools as Americans. They were thus ideal future illegals. The point was made conclusively when the Royal Canadian Mounted Police came into contact with an illegal who had entered Canada using the alias David Soboloff, who had been raised in the Bronx as the son of an Amtorg employee.[67]

Returned Amtorg employees and dependents also contributed to the tutorials given to Soviet illegals bound for the United States. Among them was Fainna Solasko, the daughter of a Russian woman who for years "served in the United States as a courtesan to KGB officers and visiting Soviet officials. Fainna had grown up in New York, where her mother was assigned to Amtorg. After studying at Columbia and New York universities, she entered into an unhappy marriage with an American employee of Tass. In 1955, she slipped away to Moscow, ideally suited by background, intellect and disposition to teach spies about the United States. . . ."[68]

As of 1985, there are a number of Amtorg children still residing in the United States. Several have married, become derivative U.S. citizens, and achieved some prominence. One or two have become influential journalists, and it is very difficult for their American colleagues to accept the possibility that they are still connected to the organs. Insistence on the proposal that the sins of the parent should not be visited on the child might well be amended to exclude, in most instances, the children of Amtorg.

In the course of promoting the international trade myth, the USSR has permitted the social philosophers in the West to conclude that commercial relationships are the most effective means of taming Soviet aggressive attitudes. If there were only more consumer goods available in the USSR, perhaps the contentment that comes with owning a toaster would begin to subdue the urge to destroy Afghanistan. Such assumptions, based on mirror-imaging, fail to note that the Soviet hierarchs already have access to all the Western goods that interest them. The wants and needs of the "people" are irrelevant to any question of government policy, and the Soviet public has been out of the participating political loop for close to seven decades.

Since the end of World War II the USSR has succeeded in building powerful economic dependencies and constituencies in other countries. The prosperity of the U.S. wheat farmer has become, increasingly, a function of decisions made in Moscow rather than in Washington. Their case is simply put: If we don't sell them the wheat, the Canadians, Argentinians, or someone else will! Today all economic sanctions available to the U.S. government must be measured against their effect on many large American banks, which have, in quest of high returns, overextended themselves in granting credits to the USSR and her impoverished satellites.

The great Soviet pipeline captured an enormous European constituency and provided tens of thousands of jobs in West Germany and elsewhere. The undertaking has put billions of dollars of capital goods in Soviet hands, secured only by the promise of eventual payback in natural gas. Politicians have always been able to see the merit in strange alliances as ways of easing unemployment and improving economies. The great metalworking industries in West Germany supported the pipeline plan in return for Soviet agreement to allow the West Germans to manufacture the necessary large-diameter pipe in Germany, provided the cost was to be financed by the Germans.

Businessmen, sometimes considered the intellectual superiors of politicians and frequently characterized as shrewd and hardheaded, have somehow always led the list of easy gulls. Success in U.S. corporate life doesn't mean that one will succeed in negotiations with the Soviets. If anything, the high-velocity American businesspeople are made more vulnerable by their reputation for "getting things done." When they go to a country where nothing "gets done" until every conceivable political implication has been weighed on the scales of Marx (as amended) and examined under the intense, searching lamp of the organs, it is no longer business. Associated with the hyper-attitudes are the numerous little disabling conceits having to do with image, prestige, imagined power, and "success."

The Soviets understand that Americans are rewarded for "getting results," and since the outcome of negotiations depends on the Moscow political bureaucracy, the Soviets control the results. The experience of Donald Kendall, chairman of Pepsico, illustrates the point. While allied with Richard Nixon, Kendall rode the crest of a small, highly carbonated wave of political euphoria and planted the corporate flag in the USSR. Kendall demonstrated to his competitors and others that a successful business deal with the Soviets was just a matter of knowing how. Of course, Kendall's deal was dependent on his reciprocal acceptance of a line of premium Soviet vodka for sale in the United States—dollar for dollar and ruble for ruble. The reaction to the Red Air Force shooting down of a South Korean civil airliner in 1983 had the additional unintended effect of simultaneously shooting down the sales of Stolichnaya vodka. In fifteen states laws were passed to forbid such sales.

The delusion of "trade with the USSR" persists, and U.S. businessmen are still anxious to stand in line in expectation that, once at bat, they will somehow reverse the course of history and win the day for the old firm. As a service to commercial aspirants attending any of the business schools in the United States, the curriculum might be revised to include a course on Soviet-American business successes. It would be exceedingly short and undemanding but well worth knowing, especially if the students learned nothing more than the useful fact that the inventors of the non-person and the non-book also hold the basic patent on the non-deal.

Robert Lee Johnson (left): convicted for espionage on behalf of the USSR. (Washington Star *photo*)

Army Lieutenant Colonel William Henry Whalen (below), highest ranking U.S. military officer convicted of espionage on behalf of the USSR. *(Department of Defense file photo)*

Joseph G. Helmich, Jr. (left): convicted for espionage on behalf of the USSR. *(AP)*

Boris N. Ponomarev, former member of the Executive Committee of the Comintern (1936–1943), head of Sovinformburo (1948–1949), and chief of the international section of the Central Committee Secretariat, CPSU. Here he is seen auditing a conference in a U.S. Senate office building in 1978. *(Washington Post staff photo)*

Marc Zborowski: implicated in the Trotsky assassination; indicted for perjury in the United States.

Stanislav A. Androsov, reported KGB resident, Washington, D.C., 1983–1985.

Valentin M. Ivanov: first secretary of the Soviet embassy in Washington, D.C., and KGB chief. *(UPI)*

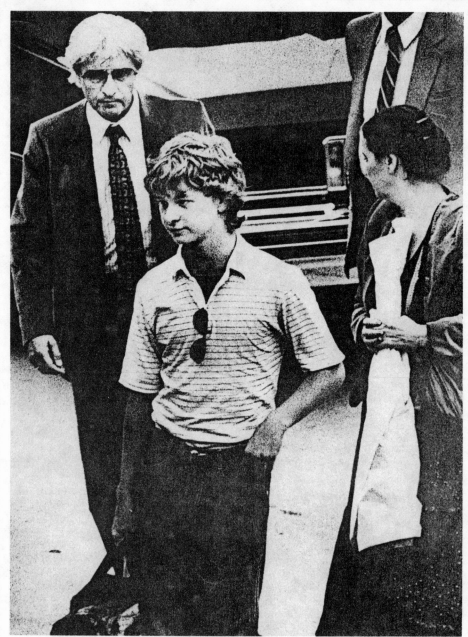

Veteran KGB officer Valentin Berezhkov, known as "the man with the Long Tail." Berezhkov served the NKVD in Berlin as a *Tass*man in 1940. He reappeared in Washington more than forty years later as the scholar in residence at the Soviet embassy, where he represented Goergi Arbatov's Institute for the Study of the U.S.A. and Canada. In August 1983, his son, Andrei, wrote President Reagan a letter asking for asylum in the United States. Quickly taken in hand by his father, Andrei denied his request for asylum and was returned to the USSR. *(*Washington Post*)*

Petr Bogdanov, who served as head of Amtorg in New York from 1930 until 1935, returned to the USSR, where he was arrested, "investigated," and shot for harboring "Trotskyite sympathies." As far as is known, Bogdanov was the first chief executive officer of a "U.S." firm to be executed for the commission of an alleged political crime. *(Official Soviet photo)*

Juliet Stuart Glaser Poyntz (aka Points) dropped out of the overt CPUSA to "work" in New York for the GRU. Later, she came under NKVD control and specialized in exploiting intellectual circles at Columbia University and verifying Stalinist loyalties among recruited faculty members. Poyntz was thought to have been abducted from her New York apartment on June 3, 1937 and taken aboard a Soviet ship in the East River for the voyage to Leningrad. No public notice of the event appeared until December 18, 1937. *(FBI photo)*

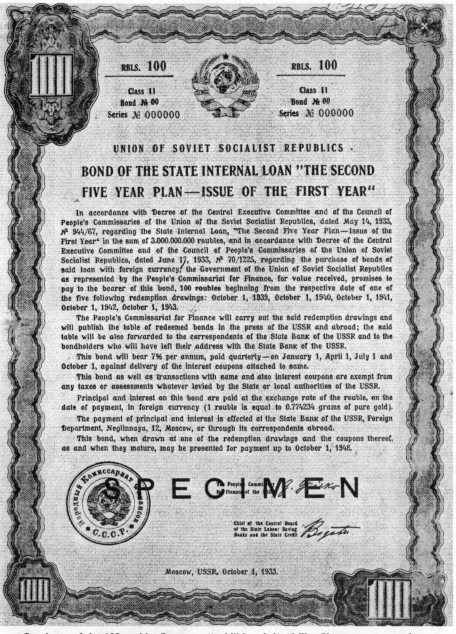

RBLS. **100**

Class II
Bond № 00
Series № 000000

RBLS. **100**

Class II
Bond № 00
Series № 000000

UNION OF SOVIET SOCIALIST REPUBLICS ·

BOND OF THE STATE INTERNAL LOAN "THE SECOND
FIVE YEAR PLAN—ISSUE OF THE FIRST YEAR"

In accordance with Decree of the Central Executive Committee and of the Council of People's Commissaries of the Union of the Soviet Socialist Republics, dated May 14, 1933, № 944/67, regarding the State Internal Loan, "The Second Five Year Plan—Issue of the First Year" in the sum of 3.000.000.000 roubles, and in accordance with Decree of the Central Executive Committee and of the Council of People's Commissaries of the Union of Soviet Socialist Republics, dated June 17, 1933, № 70/1225, regarding the purchase of bonds of said loan with foreign currency, the Government of the Union of Soviet Socialist Republics as represented by the People's Commissariat for Finance, for value received, promises to pay to the bearer of this bond, 100 roubles beginning from the respective date of one of the five following redemption drawings: October 1, 1939, October 1, 1940, October 1, 1941, October 1, 1942, October 1, 1943.

The People's Commissariat for Finance will carry out the said redemption drawings and will publish the table of redeemed bonds in the press of the USSR and abroad; the said table will be also forwarded to the correspondents of the State Bank of the USSR and to the bondholders who will have left their address with the State Bank of the USSR.

This bond will bear 7% per annum, paid quarterly—on January 1, April 1, July 1 and October 1, against delivery of the interest coupons attached to same.

This bond as well as transactions with same and also interest coupons are exempt from any taxes or assessments whatever levied by the State or local authorities of the USSR.

Principal and interest on this bond are paid at the exchange rate of the rouble, on the date of payment, in foreign currency (1 rouble is equal to 0.774234 grams of pure gold).

The payment of principal and interest is effected at the State Bank of the USSR, Foreign Department, Neglinnaya, 12, Moscow, or through its correspondents abroad.

This bond, when drawn at one of the redemption drawings and the coupons thereof, as and when they mature, may be presented for payment up to October 1, 1948.

SPECIMEN

People's Commissar for Finance of the USSR

Chief of the Central Board of the State Labour Saving Banks and the State Credit

Moscow, USSR, October 1, 1933.

Specimen of the 100 rouble, 7 percent "gold" bond that Miles Sherover promoted as "President of Soviet-American Securities Corporation, 20 Broad Street, New York." The sales were halted by the U.S. government. The Chase Bank, which had been the original New York paying agent, continued to redeem the bonds until 1948. After his brief career on Wall Street, Sherover dropped out of sight, only to reappear in 1936 as "President of the Hanover Corporation," a Soviet-run commercial "cover" company that acted as the purchasing agent of war materials and machinery for the Loyalist forces in Spain. (*Courtesy of Chase Bank*)

Nikolay Ogorodnikov (above): under indictment for Soviet espionage, 1984. *(Illustration by Dave Rose, AP)*

Svetlana Ogorodnikova (above): under indictment for Soviet espionage, 1984. *(Illustration by Dave Rose, AP)*

FBI agent Richard W. Miller (below): under indictment for Soviet espionage, 1984. *(Yearbook photo)*

Karl F. Koecher (below): under indictment for Soviet espionage, 1984. *(David Brookstaver, AP)*

8 · From Andropov (1967) On: The New KGB

When Yuri Andropov became chairman of the KGB in April 1967, he was seen by many in Western intelligence circles as a lackluster party hack rather than a professional intelligence officer. They did not know or, perhaps, had forgotten about his performance in Hungary from 1953 to 1957 and his labors on behalf of the organs in the Central Committee between 1957 and 1967. During that decade, though nominally in charge of the Socialist Countries Department, his actual role was that of coordinating the organs and providing supervision and direction of the bloc states' intelligence services.

During this early period, Brezhnev saw Andropov as an essential ally in his plan to force Khrushchev from power. Brezhnev had already won the support of the military leaders by his promise to restore the military budget. The generals felt that they had been slighted by Khrushchev's grandiose economic development plans and were quick to throw their influence to Brezhnev in exchange for his commitment to meet their demands for an increased budget.

In 1964, neither the organs nor the party could exert full authority without the endorsement of the military. Brezhnev came to power on the basis of his acceptance of the Soviet military's make-or-break terms. He had no quarrel with the military and agreed with their contention that the USSR must rearm, at least to the point of military parity with the United States.

Vladimir Semichastny, who was still head of the KGB, willingly accepted the concessions to the military. He continued to act as though the organs should stay out of the line of political fire and get on with their assigned tasks. His experience should have told him that, in Soviet politics, neutrality is considered to be a form of hostility by all contending sides. Thus, in 1967, he was dismissed, a victim of the military's charge that the organs had not met their demands for advanced technological information and equipment. A collateral charge was his failure to prevent the defection of Stalin's daughter, Svetlana Alliluyeva, to the West.

Andropov was not the unanimous choice of the Politburo and Semichastny's deputy, Alexandr Ivanovich Perepelitsyn, had expectations of his own. Brezhnev's sponsorship and strong personal endorsement won the day, and Andropov was appointed KGB chairman. Perepelitsyn was personally affronted, because he had served as Semichastny's deputy for eight years and had "earned" the right to the chairmanship. He took his plaint about the decision to Brezhnev, and in the curious world of Kremlin politics, he was dismissed and allowed to drift into obscure retirement. To replace Perepelitsyn, Brezhnev selected his brother-in-law, General Semen Tsvigun, whose appointment served two obvious purposes. First, it maintained "peace" in Brezhnev's extended family. More importantly, it gave Brezhnev another pair of high-level eyes on Andropov to see that he continued to be an apolitical Chekist.

Once in office, Andropov was expected to fill the Soviet military's technical and scientific needs. He was also told to keep the KGB out of party and Politburo politics. Accepting these terms, he produced a plan that was so far-reaching that it sent tremors throughout the civil ministries of the Soviet Union. It was a technical-intelligence collection program, precisely targeted and divided into sections of direct concern to the military.

The program addressed specific areas in which the civil ministries had failed. One was the growing need for high-grade avionics, the electronic packages that enable aircraft to fly and fight at speeds of Mach 2. A second area of inadequacy was in the development of helicopters, which had, to a degree, taken over the role of conventional air support of ground troops. It was a clear indictment of the ravages of *tufta*. It specifically pointed up the disabilities and extravagances of the ministries that had not achieved their objectives.

Andropov avoided taking sides in the internecine battles within the Red Army, Air Force, and Navy. Instead, he directed the KGB to redouble all efforts to acquire the devices, instruments, and information that the Soviet Aviation Ministry had not been able to produce. In so doing, he made important friends among the senior officers, especially those who held operational commands. Andropov knew that he was winning a constituency in the Soviet armed forces. They had been so sorely tried by the party hacks during the Khrushchev period that they were willing to embrace him as an influential friend who understood that their needs could not be met simply by spending more rubles.

Soviet spending, for international prestige purposes, had been directed to the highly visible space program, which produced only marginal military benefits. This deflection of manpower and money aided in creating a strategic deception as to the state of Soviet science. But it also had the effect of putting the Soviet armed forces in a remote second place in their quest for modernization. It was in this context that the organs, under Andropov, became the Soviet military's natural ally. Although Andropov was obliged to answer to many masters in the Politburo, he did it with facility, and since many members were Brezhnev cronies more concerned with their individual "franchises" than with the tedious issues arising out of the East-West conflict, Andropov was able to press ahead with more important work.

It is useful to recall that, despite what has been said in the volumes of biographic minutiae published on Andropov, his succession as head of state in 1982 was an inevitability firmly rooted in Soviet political realities.[1] Although he was the first head of the organs to make it to the top of the Kremlin, he was not the first to try. Andropov was not a man from the shadows but a fundamental Chekist who could claim direct lineal ties back to Felix Dzerzhinsky. He had known no life other than the organs. To have achieved the chairmanship of the KGB was in itself a measure of his comprehension of the functions of repression. Starting with his early days under Stalin, he exhibited the chill, dispassionate mind that was, for forty-five years, fully engaged in the techniques of the accretion of power. To dismiss him as a "spymaster" or "secret policeman" is as misleading as it is to represent him as a Kremlin "dove" or "closet liberal." To understand the man and his long-term effect on the future, it is essential to examine his accomplishments during the fifteen years he headed the organs. Only in this way is it possible to begin to see Andropov as the most highly distilled product of the Soviet power elite.

The first years of Andropov's stewardship over the KGB were exceedingly active. Instead of going through the usual ritualistic reorganization, he pursued a program that made mission assignments more precise and lines of authority more evident. By delegating authority and auditing the results he was able to measure the competence of the personnel and accurately judge true intelligence capabilities. His own survival was based on his ability to increase the efficiency of the organs and to avoid political involvement. Andropov's dedication to his duties in no way diminished his interest in the mechanics of Kremlin politics and his growing awareness of the vulnerabilities of his political superiors.

In 1967, when the KGB was presented with the task of providing the Red armed forces with much of the technical and operational intelligence they required, the United States was heavily involved in the war in Vietnam. Thus, it was natural that the introduction and field testing of new

U.S. equipment would form the basis for a major Soviet intelligence effort. The Soviets' problem was complicated by the need to depend on the North Vietnamese (and their agents in South Vietnam), who, though willing, were not experienced or well suited to carrying out technical-intelligence collection operations. Despite these admitted deficiencies the KGB was able to acquire not only matériel, equipment, and new weapons but also detailed reports on the new tactics dictated by their use. War matériel and equipment were removed from Vietnam to the USSR in large volume, so that the prototypes could be studied, tested, and replicated by Soviet scientists and engineers.

Department T, the second largest element in the KGB's First Chief Directorate (scientific and technical intelligence collection),[2] and the GRU were directed to mount a three-pronged operation in Vietnam. One phase was limited to the theft of high-tech military equipment deployed by the United States throughout Southeast Asia. The work was carried out by North Vietnamese agents and with the aid of communist agents in the government and the army of South Vietnam. Captured and stolen material made its way to Department T's research institute, located near the Belyourski Railroad Station in Moscow, by a variety of routes and means. Some went overland from South Vietnam via the Ho Chi Minh Trail to Hanoi and thence to Moscow by air or by sea to Vladivostok. These "exports" were dispatched under many guises, ranging from military equipment concealed as "construction machinery in need of repair" to "household goods."

The second phase was a bit more sophisticated. It involved the exploitation of intelligence information that the KGB had acquired several years earlier from an American traitor, Joseph George Helmich, an Army cryptographer. While serving in Paris in 1963, Helmich had sold the Soviets confidential maintenance and operations instructions, top-secret "key lists," and highly classified technical details of the rotors of the KL7 cryptographic system.[3] At that time the information was a valuable acquisition for the Eighth Chief Directorate, which was responsible for cipher and cryptographic systems for the KGB and the Ministry of Foreign Affairs. The information became priceless a few years later when U.S. combat forces became heavily committed in Vietnam. The data from Helmich were then used by the Soviets to intercept U.S. military communications, including situation, order-of-battle, and after-action summaries.

The Eighth Chief Directorate was thus in a position to make a major contribution to Andropov's calls for scientific and technical information. In addition, the cryptographic material provided by Helmich enabled the Soviets to know, with some accuracy, just how the war was going. It was most likely that Helmich's contribution was never fully shared by the

Soviets with their North Vietnamese surrogates. It was essential for the protection of the system that the North Vietnamese take their full share of surprises and casualties to cloak the Soviet success. With this low-cost facility ($131,000 was paid to Helmich) in place, the Soviets were able to make detailed measurements of the U.S. forces' combat effectiveness. This information, especially as it affected the evaluation of new military technology and equipment, was crucial to the Kremlin's military modernization decisions.

The third phase of the collection plan was more indirect in its contribution to the collection mission. It involved the application of a block of additional data sold to the KGB in 1964 by another American traitor, Robert Lee Johnson, an alcoholic career soldier with severe marital problems. Johnson made his first indirect approach to the Soviets in Berlin on Christmas Day, 1952. He was eventually recruited and trained; later, while stationed outside Paris, he passed "more than ninety large envelopes filled with documents and cipher systems" to the KGB.[4] More documents were passed to KGB agents in Paris, where Johnson later worked at a courier center for the U.S. Army in Europe. Sergeant Johnson was arrested on the basis of information provided by a Soviet defector in 1965 and sentenced to twenty-five years' imprisonment. (In 1972 Johnson's son, a Vietnam veteran, visited his father at the federal prison at Lewisburg, Pennsylvania, and, during the meeting, produced a knife that he used to stab his father to death.)

One set of documents was extremely important to the Soviets. They purported to show how the United States would go to war under a variety of situations and scenarios. As such, they represented U.S. doctrinal thinking and plans. Their worth to Andropov's technical intelligence mission was as a base line from which it was possible to measure the effectiveness of the doctrine and to deduce what changes the Vietnam combat results would suggest.

Although generals have been accused of fighting the next war in terms of the last, microchip technology has had a "deprogramming" effect on strategy. Based on the information provided to the KGB by both Helmich and Johnson, it was possible for the Soviets to examine the U.S. experience in Vietnam in such a way as to avoid the trial-and-error costs that attend the development, production, and utilization of new weapons systems.

The process was analogous to the old Soviet Purchasing Commission's success in the acquisition of atomic weapons technology. With the data gathered in the exploitation of two low-ranking members of the U.S. Army, Andropov presented the Soviet armed forces with a guide to the upgrading of conventional forces without the considerable attendant research and development costs. The success of the KGB's espionage strengthened Andropov's credibility with the Soviet military leaders.

There was easy acceptance of the intelligence on technical items, but there was a strong institutional resistance to change in most tactical matters. It wasn't until the invasion of Afghanistan and a string of bloody failures that the Soviets came to modify their tactics to conform more with the doctrinal line set forth in the documents provided by Sergeant Johnson.

Andropov's understanding and advocacy of the role of scientific and technical information was carefully tempered by his realization that he could not mount a direct assault on the patrons of the Soviet military-industrial complex without goring a great herd of political oxen. Instead, he tutored Brezhnev on the need to bring the aging marshals of the Soviet armed forces to the discomfiting discipline of cost-effective management.

Despite the workmanlike performance of the KGB in directing the intelligence programs in Vietnam, the military was still reluctant to act on much of the data. The usual response to the KGB's broad-scale entry into the GRU's domain was expressed in the conservative tones of the marshals: The KGB has told us much, if true, but there is much we haven't been told which lessens the value of the early information. It was a way of conveying the common belief that, in military matters, Andropov was a talented amateur.

Andropov took no umbrage at the slight, and the KGB persisted in mining the rich Vietnam vein. Only a year later, in February 1968, there was an opportunity, and his effective exploitation of events enabled Andropov to gain new respect among the military leaders and to simultaneously muzzle his former critics.

It involved the North Koreans' seizure of the USS *Pueblo*. For several months before the action occurred, the chief of the Eighth Directorate reported that the Helmich data had taken them as far as could be reasonably expected. Quite obviously, American communications intelligence had not been idle since the Helmich caper in 1963, and there was a new and growing need to ascertain the present state of the art in the U.S. military. Although Helmich's information had been useful, as it pertained to the procedures, equipment, and techniques (many of which were still in use), there was a need to know about improved versions that had come into limited use. For this reason the *Pueblo* became a high-priority target.

Andropov and his deputy Viktor Chebrikov became convinced that the *Pueblo* could be induced to respond to certain stimuli and gently drawn into a trap. In anticipation of such an event personnel from the Eighth Chief Directorate were dispatched to the Far East to be on hand when and if the trap snapped shut. Within the KGB the decision was not widely supported. Other members of the organs looked upon the members of the Eighth Chief Directorate as prima donnas who pretended a kind of superiority. This attitude abraded the other, more pedestrian Chekists.

What the Soviets knew about the *Pueblo* and how they knew it remains classified and is outside the scope of this account. The fact remains that a KGB detachment was on the ground and in a state of readiness, prepared to supervise the taking of the ship and the removal and salvage of the electronic equipment. When the *Pueblo* was towed into North Korea, all documents, instruments, antennas, and electronic processing machinery were removed and shipped to Moscow. The loss of the equipment was a damaging blow to the United States. Of greater importance was that Andropov increased his credibility among the Soviet military hierarchs by adding much new and important data relative to U.S. capabilities in the field of electronic intelligence.

Commander Lloyd Bucher, captain of the *Pueblo*,[5] and the Board of Inquiry that recommended his court-martial, conceded that there was little the North Korean captors and Soviet interrogators did not know about the *Pueblo*'s mission. The obvious breach of operational security could not be attributable to anything Commander Bucher did or failed to do. It was more of a tribute to the tailors and the bar girls in Yokosuka, the Japanese port from which the *Pueblo* sailed, who knew as much about U.S. fleet movements as those in the naval command staff who plotted them on acetate overlays.

The Soviet interrogators who dealt with the *Pueblo*'s crew demonstrated a high level of technical competence in carrying out the initial field interrogation. While the shock of capture was still high, the Soviets pressed for answers to those questions that would aid the Eighth Chief Directorate's detailed assay of the equipment, documents, and data seized from the ship. The exploitation of the *Pueblo*, in terms of intelligence yield, was a stunning vindication of Andropov's decision to place a specialist team in North Korea in anticipation of the event.

With the adroit analysis of the product of the *Pueblo* case, the Soviets were able, once again, to reduce the U.S. advantage. Quite apart from the technical booty, the *Pueblo* had significant value as a propaganda tool. Department A of the First Chief Directorate, which specializes in disinformation, arranged for the North Korean clients to claim full credit for repelling the "attack" on Korean sovereignty by the *Pueblo*. The hulk of the ship, the manacled crew members, and the victorious North Koreans were filmed at length, and the Soviets provided voice-over narration in at least twenty different languages. The films were distributed worldwide.

The films and commentaries were of a quality quite beyond the capacity of the North Korean government to produce. Yet, nowhere was there the slightest indication of Soviet involvement. It was simply another documented instance of U.S. aggression against a "small, peace-loving nation." Since the Soviets were signators to the Geneva Conventions and the North Koreans were not, it was important to avoid any reference to the USSR's participation. Nonsignator surrogates like North Korea and North Vietnam have been important adjuncts to Department A's program of propaganda. The nonsignators can abuse and exploit prisoners of war with impunity. In the case of the *Pueblo* crew, the coercion was brutal and blatant, yet it failed to ignite any sense of outrage in the U.S. and West European press.

The Soviet press, pretending objectivity, was forced to conclude that Bucher and his crew were the aggressors and that what happened to them at the hands of the North Koreans was "justified" in light of their "crime." The Soviet stories were played and replayed in the West, with much of the free-world press playing an undiscerning role. It was as much an indictment of Western gullibility as it was a measure of the effectiveness of the KGB's disinformation skills.

Andropov basked in the warm glow of the approbation of the Soviet leadership. The principals in the Eighth Directorate were awarded appropriate promotions, medals, and commendations. Brezhnev was pleased to have his original selection of Andropov vindicated.

It is difficult to overstate the importance of the capture of the *Pueblo,* which came at a time of great turbulence in American politics. It was a signal event of greater import to the United States than Lyndon Johnson's abrupt decision not to run for reelection. Information taken from the *Pueblo* enabled the Soviets to gain more than five years in the continuing race with the United States for supremacy in the field of communications intelligence. Much of that gain, like that associated with the Soviets' atomic espionage effort, was attributable to their finding out for sure what procedures and equipment modifications actually worked, thereby curtailing the heavy R&D costs associated with communications intelligence. The Soviets were also advantaged by the aftermath of the event, in which the U.S. Far Eastern command structure was seen to have outdated operating procedures and somewhat garbled missions. Bucher left the Navy, and there was sufficient doubt raised as to further reduce public confidence in the U.S. armed forces. In every respect Andropov had a right to Brezhnev's praise.

Brezhnev, perhaps, like Lenin before him, thought he had found the model Chekist. Andropov reinforced Brezhnev's appreciation by not forcing himself or his opinions into the policy-decision loop. His apparent apolitical stance and spartan conduct attracted the interest of Mikhail Suslov, the party's ideologue, who gradually concluded that Andropov, like himself, was a Marxist ascetic, a man to be admired. Suslov was the arbiter, in terms of Marxist-Leninist orthodoxy, of all that was proposed. He thus looked upon the nepotic Brezhnev's *banda* as corrupt and saw Andropov as a convicted believer in the grand tradition of Dzerzhinsky. Though there are no indications of Andropov's initiative in the relationship with Suslov, it is clear that he welcomed the embrace of the party's doctrinal guru.

In late spring 1968, Brezhnev had a serious problem: the natives in Czechoslovakia were becoming increasingly restless. None of his close political associates was of any use in handling this problem, mostly because of their preoccupation with the accretions of personal wealth. (Under Brezhnev, the corrosive acid of grand-scale *tufta* had been permitted to leach into the Central Committee.) By traditional calculus the Czechs were subverting socialism and must be crushed before others in the bloc began to rattle their chains. In Bolshevik terms, the Czechs were "threatening the security of the USSR."

Brezhnev traveled to Prague to meet with the Czech leaders. Instead of being accompanied by the Central Committee members having nominal responsibility for national parties, Brezhnev took as his principal aide Yuri Andropov. His selection can be rationalized by the fact that in his previous position Andropov had extensive dealings with foreign Communist parties.

From another point of view, it marked Andropov's first game as a major player in the Soviet Union's policy determination. Out of the several meetings there emerged what has come to be called the Brezhnev Doctrine (i.e., that the Soviets reserve the right to intervene in any state that decides to reject the Soviet way). But the Czechs misread Brezhnev's statements, thinking, like others before them, that they could travel another route. Andropov watched, listened, and said little. His silence might have added to the Czechs' belief that they could pursue a "middle way" and still stay aligned with the USSR.

Brezhnev and Andropov returned to Moscow leaving the impression among the Czech communists that the problem had been solved and that their proposed changes were satisfactory to the Kremlin. But the Czechs had made a fundamental error. They thought that they were part of a "fraternal body" and that they were thus enabled to argue, on behalf of their members, as equals among equals. It was then, as now, a foolish delusion. The Czechs, like the native Russians, were expected to do as they were told by the Bolsheviks. The Czechs did not realize that the visit by Brezhnev and Andropov was simply to take a final measure of the potential for disorder and that the conciliatory "negotiations" were only a cover for the Soviets' true purpose.

In August 1968, troops from Russia, Bulgaria, East Germany, Hungary, and Poland invaded Czechosolovakia. It was the Soviets' hypocritical version of the "United Nations forces," but it was effective nonetheless. Andropov understood the Czechs and was willing to bet his future on the probability that they would rather demonstrate than make war and that a Soviet show of force would be sufficient to intimidate the renegades. A few Molotov cocktails were thrown, and there was sporadic small-arms fire. However, as organized resistance is defined, the Czech opponents were never a serious challenge to the Soviet military.

In calling the turn on the Czechs, Andropov was on sure ground. He knew that the Czech resistors had no stomach for armed confrontation. Thus, the Soviet "invasion" was structured in symbolic terms, with Soviet armor in the van. The sight of such force prompted discussions within NATO regarding improvement of the Western defenses. On closer examination it became evident that the tanks had run out of fuel in the streets of Prague and that the much vaunted Soviet armor was caught in a gridlock rivaling anything seen in Manhattan. The military fumble was not news to Andropov, because he had direct knowledge that the Soviet ground forces of 1968 were hollow, far from combat-ready, and a military threat in name only.

The Czech invasion provided him with another opportunity to duplicate his earlier success in Hungary. In his previous role as the enforcer of compliance within the bloc, he had promoted the "salting" of dissident factions with *seksots,* who might find themselves caught up in an uprising followed by a mass escape. Since they were thoroughly compromised by the Soviets prior to insertion into the groups, they could be reactivated readily at a later date in their new foreign environs. It was a low-cost maneuver, easily accomplished.

Skilled and educated Czech communists who broke ranks and became certified anticommunists could be converted to valuable KGB assets once they arrived in their Western safe havens. The number of Czechs who fled as "anticommunist freedom fighters" was much lower than the total number of Hungarians who left their country in 1956. The educational level and technical experience of those who were sent to the United States and Britain was considerably higher, however. The U.S. ambassador to Czechoslovakia at the time, Shirley Temple Black, was outraged by the Soviet invasion and put her own personal imprimatur on the heroism of the anticommunist Czechs. Her reports coupled with the general Western repugnance toward the Soviet actions were sufficient to give some "anticommunist" Czechs visas they might not have deserved.

There were of course many Czechs who genuinely opposed the Soviets. However, the question in the West was and is how to distinguish legitimate expressions of hope and belief in freedom from the legends constructed for KGB-run penetration agents.

The success of the Hungarian and Czech "freedom fighters" (and successive waves of Cuban refugees) in making penetrations has provided the KGB with an embarrassment of riches. Though no intelligence service ever believes that it has too many agents, such prosperity exacts a price. Having more assets than can be effectively controlled is far worse than having too few. A lean organization is more likely to exercise greater care in ordering its priorities and generally avoids confusing "nice to know" with "need to know."

Considerable care was taken in expanding the number of case officers to run the Hungarian and Czech penetrations. It was far better to let the agents remain inactive than to bring them on line under less than satisfactory control conditions. The problem was to find the right kinds of personnel, to improve agent communication techniques, and to determine the effective limit on the number of people who could be controlled by a single case officer. The predictors of success in this task, unlike those developed over the years by Dzerzhinsky and Beria, were much less reliable.

The difficulties in this kind of personnel selection are revealed in two failed KGB cases. Each collapsed for different reasons, and both illustrate parts of the selection problem. The first case is that of Yuri Loginov, a KGB illegal, and the second concerns a KGB official who served in the London embassy, Oleg Lyalin.

No final conclusion can be drawn from the Loginov and Lyalin cases. On one level, it appears that the organs erred in their selection of both men, who were found wanting when it came to an issue of critical importance. On another level, the Loginov case, in particular, suggests a second order of subtlety wherein his capture by the South African security forces might appear as a planned deflection of attention from a major (still unrecognized) Soviet security failure elsewhere or a high-risk ploy to insinuate disinformation into Western counterintelligence channels. Based on the paucity of declassified evidence in the Loginov case, there has been some speculation on the improbable prospect that he is still alive, well, and "working" again under a new identity somewhere in the United States or Canada. Too much time and effort were expended in preparing Loginov to reject his further use. So goes the story. Such suggestions by the press are helpful in adorning the illusion that KGB operations do not fail unless the failure itself is deliberately arranged to further another objective.

As we have said earlier, but wish to emphasize again, when Andropov assumed the chairmanship of the KGB, he came to the job with a carefully thought-out long-range plan and a determination to professionalize the organs. He was acutely aware that Brezhnev's regime was weak, corrupt, and, almost imperceptibly, losing control. The *banda* of Brezhnev cronies was pillaging the USSR as no other administration had, and the level of abuse had risen to the point of becoming a matter of widespread public knowledge.[6]

Andropov made no effort to confront the issue in the Central Committee but, instead, used his energies to make the organs a better-coordinated and more effective institution that could meet the growing internal and external security challenges to the Soviet state. He was, as M.I.5's one-time director-general, Sir Percy Sillitoe, was once characterized, seen as an "honest cop."

Many in the organs shared Andropov's sense of purpose. They had fought in the Cold War and retained a strong dedication to their principles. They are not to be underestimated or dismissed on the grounds that they have been stifled by the dogmas of Marxism-Leninism. Instead of Marx, who lost his relevance years ago, the men of the organs today are protecting "a way of life" in which their association with the KGB brings the tangible rewards of good housing, plentiful food, consumer goods, educational opportunities for their young, social privilege, and, sometimes, foreign travel. In this very concrete context, a KGBnik's way of life is well worth the day-to-day dedication to repression in the name of the party.

Yuri Nickolaevich Loginov was arrested by the South African Bureau of State Security (BOSS) in 1967. It seemed odd, at the time, that a KGB illegal who had been trained for eight years could have been so easily found by the relatively inexperienced South Africans. The exact time of his arrest is not publicly known. Nor is it certain how long he was held before Barbara Carr, a journalist with no special credentials, was invited to write a book based on material provided by BOSS. Her book did little to account for either the South African role in the affair or the purpose of Loginov's mission.[7] But it did much to raise new questions.

After two years Loginov was exchanged for eleven West German "agents" held in the East. The chief of BOSS, General Henrik van den Berg, was quoted as saying that Loginov, while in the control of BOSS, disclosed information on spy networks in twenty-three countries. In another public statement he beclouded the matter by saying that in his own view, Loginov had "not told all there is to know."[8]

The case became highly politicized in South Africa. Critics of the government were outraged that Ms. Carr had been given special access and that no official report was made to the public. The handling of the Loginov case points up the problem of small inexperienced services, with limited capacities and resources, to deal with Soviet cases. It also suggests the small service's vulnerability to deception and confusion.

Loginov had entered South Africa using a Canadian passport in the

name of Edmund Trinka. He was arrested while photographing a building that had formerly been occupied by the South African police. As the
Soviets would say, his behavior was "provocative." Once in custody, he
quickly told his captors, among other things, that he had been tutored as
an illegal by "Colonel Abel," that his wife Niri was also a KGB agent
who had failed in her assignment in Havana and had been withdrawn to
be disciplined, and that South Africa was simply a way station on his
circuitous route to the United States.

Soon after Loginov's arrest, press officers in the Soviet embassies
around the world moved quickly to confide in their media contacts that
the Loginov story "sounded fishy" and "should be treated with reserve."
The opposition press in South Africa joined the chorus in an effort to
force disclosures from BOSS. Reporters pursued leads in Australia, Canada, Britain, and the United States. They tended to confirm what was
already known or suspected about Soviets serving in embassies, trade
missions and commercial-cover companies in those countries.

Meanwhile, in the United States, the issue of the bona fides of Yuri
Nosenko, another KGB defector (1964), were still in dispute. In August
1978, Edward Jay Epstein wrote that Loginov's information additionally
supported and confirmed Nosenko's story and that once the information
had been passed to the United States, "Loginov redefected."[9] The implications of Epstein's thesis suggested that Loginov's central purpose was
to buttress the reputations of Soviet agents who were still providing
"intelligence" to the United States. The issues now involved the bona
fides of several "sources" and had the effect of reversing the polarity once
again on the Soviet spy circuits, with yesterday's good guys becoming
today's bad guys.

In the end, it can be safely asserted that the distrust, suspicion, and
loss of confidence arising out of these uncertainties were the result of a
clear KGB purpose that aimed at politicizing the issues, inflicting damage, and weakening both the internal and external intelligence services of
the United States. Loginov's mite contributed to the problem rather than
the solution. In the view of some experts his "failed" mission was in fact a
dramatic success. To keep the equation in balance, it was pointed out in
countervailing terms that Loginov had provided useful and accurate data
that was damaging to the USSR.

In the other case, Oleg Adolfovich Lyalin seemed to be prospering as
a member of the Soviet trade delegation in London when he suddenly
defected in 1971. His action heartened Her Majesty's Government to
take the first significant steps to counter Soviet espionage and subversion
in Britain since the Arcos raid, forty-four years earlier. This time, ninety
Soviets were expelled and fifteen more were barred from reentering the
UK. It was not a case of "rounding up the usual suspects." The operation

was specifically directed at the Soviet espionage professionals, whose ranks had grown from 138 in 1950 to 550 at the time of Lyalin's disclosures.

Employees of the trade delegation (which had been granted diplomatic status under a trade treaty of 1934), Aeroflot, the Moscow Narodny Bank, the Soviet Wood Agency, and the Soviet Travel Agency were among the ranks of the expellees, along with a troop from the Soviet embassy. Tass (which lost a "reporter") solemnly noted that the British action was a "relapse into the Cold War." When British Foreign Secretary Sir Alec Douglas-Home warned the Soviet Foreign Minister, the durable Andrei Gromyko, that British patience with Soviet espionage was wearing thin, Gromyko dismissively replied, "Write me a letter."

The Soviets had been greatly emboldened by the damage already inflicted on the British security and intelligence services by Philby, Maclean, Burgess, and the loss of public confidence that followed. The Soviets were no longer skulking around London with secretaries and clerks; they were devoting their energies to "developing" politicians, bankers, and industrialists in the course of lavish entertainments.

High-level recruitments all eventually depend on support mechanisms to protect security and communications. The London resident, consistent with the usual pattern of Soviet support operations, had a penetration in the Greater London Council's vehicle licensing department who was on Lyalin's direct payroll. The man was able to assist in verifying ownership of cars so that surveillance vehicles could be identified to the KGB. The fact that a license number appeared on the "special list" was sufficient for the Soviets to conclude that the car was used by Scotland Yard's Special Branch or the security services.

Another near-victim was a young Asian woman who worked for the Royal Navy. Three years before, she had taken a cruise aboard a Soviet "love boat" to Leningrad. The assistant purser made such persistent attempts to cultivate her that she later reported the matter to the Royal Navy security officials. Since the frontal approach had failed, the license clerk in London was given the young woman's address and instructions to attempt to develop her "as a source." For his exertions the clerk was rewarded with small amounts of money, a wristwatch, a toilet set, and a portable radio. In all, it was small beer exchanged for the three-year prison term he later served.

Lyalin's defection did not result from his careful analysis of lofty ideological conundrums but because he had become involved with his secretary, Irina, who joined him in asylum. Without delay, the Soviet Foreign Ministry bombarded Irina with emotional letters from her mother, relatives, and friends urging her to return home at once. In addition to attempting to induce her redefection, the appeals were useful elsewhere in support of the suggestion that Irina was being held against her will by the British.

It is unfortunate that partisan politics often plays an interfering role not only in international relations but also in matters of security and intelligence. The British Labour Party leader at this time, Harold Wilson, denounced the Conservative government for its decision to expel the ninety Soviets. Wilson characterized the action as "a Tory political plot" and went on to put his own imprimatur on unfettered espionage, saying, "Of course we know that spying goes on. It goes on between consenting adults so far as advanced nations are concerned."

Dennis Healey, another Labour Party leader, not to be surpassed in fecklessness, opined that the action had been based on the Tories' assumption that it would "secure a narrow scrape victory in a by-election." Both Wilson and Healey were subsequently quoted, in many languages, by Radio Moscow.

The dilapidated Soviet cruise ship *Baltika* moved into the Tilbury docks in London to board the departing spies. The loudspeaker blared "If I Were a Rich Man" as the impenitent Soviets boarded and their claque of well-wishers saw them off to Leningrad. Meanwhile, a few hundred miles to the east, the Belgian authorities found an automobile abandoned by Anatoli Chebotarev, who had the previous day deserted his position in the Soviet trade mission in Brussels.

In Moscow, a decision was made to announce the identities of seven British diplomats who were identified by Philby as "intelligence agents" in the Middle East. By this time Philby's veracity had slipped off the scale of finite measurement; the "revelations" produced widespread ennui.

Reino Hayhayen, "Colonel Hermann," Lyalin, and a hundred others had already made the case for the difficulties of personnel selection by the organs. With the Soviet internal security problem growing more acute and complex, there were more pressures and greater opportunities to break ranks. It has often been remarked that Stalin's greatest mistake was to permit his troops to see Europe. Although once said in jest, there is growing evidence that the subsequent walls, mined borders, and relentless application of fear have failed to keep out the general realization that the Russian people are captives of the Bolshevik dynasty and not just fraternal fellows in the socialist camp.

Andropov's comprehension of this dread shared by all imperial rulers made him redirect his attentions to the reimposition of the absolutism of Stalin. Andropov understood that the Soviet system is not capable, by itself, of generating the scientific and technological base to compete successfully with the West over the long term. The Soviet space program was a tremendous effort and a visible success, but it was done at terrible cost to the already inadequate industrial and scientific base. And by completely controlling the release of information concerning the programs, the Soviets managed to hide the tragedies, failures, and collateral costs from public view.

Andropov was never confused or deluded by the display. Nor were the Soviet generals. An industry that could not produce a reliable automobile battery for the Chaika limousine was not quite ready to take on the world. The significance of the fact that Brezhnev's Central Committee observed the tapes of later rocket launches on Sony VCRs and listened to the in-flight chatter on their Seimens radios was not lost on Andropov.

In the sixties, U.S. business was beginning to enjoy the advantages of a new commercial development that promised to revolutionize the rapid reproduction of all forms of paper carrying text, drawings, and photographs. By using charged selenium plates, it was possible to make inexpensive copies of almost anything. The process was called xerography, and it changed the way we lived.

Within a few years the machines appeared in libraries, archives, universities, and research facilities all over the United States. The concept of such a device is antithetical to the basic tenets of Bolshevism. Where the United States was exploring new techniques to propagate information, the USSR focused on new ways to choke it off.

The information "explosion" occasioned by the new copy devices made the arduous task of retyping (as in Whittaker Chambers's "pumpkin papers"[10]) and photocopying (as in the Cicero case[11]) obsolete. Now, anyone with the instincts of a Stakhanovite and a few minutes access to classified documents can make thousands of dry, clear copies according to their own political compulsions (as in the "Pentagon Papers"). The obvious security implications were as threatening to the West as they were joyously received in the East.

A year's production by a surreptitious agent with a minicamera couldn't begin to approach the monthly output levels of Sergeants Johnson, Mintkinbaugh, or Dunlap after xerographic machines came into common use around 1960. If there was no available machine, there was always a copy center nearby. The devices made no distinction as to class and were used by secretaries as well as bosses. The machines were also as illiterate as they were classless. Not being able to comprehend the print they were copying, they regarded "Top Secret" and copyright warnings as simply more words to be reproduced. Xerography also offered the advantage of reducing the stresses associated with espionage by making the process so widespread and commonplace that a practiced spy doing a large volume of "work" could permit another person to use the machine for a few urgent copies while he stood by collating the material in hand.

In the period before xerography, copies reflected distribution, and symbols clearly indicated the identities of the "info" addressees. With only one original and a few carbon copies, the task of recovering a version for copy was both difficult and extremely dangerous. With xerography, any version could be instantly reproduced without any visible indication that yet another copy had been made.

The first element of the Soviet bureaucracy to have a xerographic machine was, of course, the KGB. The device was technically wondrous but, by Soviet standards, as threatening as a bomb. It was inconceivable that any Western office dealing in defense secrets would allow such a frightening hazard in the premises. Used carbon paper had been a significant danger, but this device was a source of unmitigated terror.

The case of Geoffrey Arthur Prime, which is discussed more fully later on, illustrates in stark terms a new meaning of the words "sources and methods" and suggests a further evolution in Soviet methodology. The secretaries and the sergeants had worked with great effect as sources of documents. Most were ill equipped to comment on, amplify, or interpret the substance of what they stole. They had as their principal attraction for the Soviets access to classified data and the means of copying documents. All lived in environments over which they had little control. The secretaries were shifted without warning, and the sergeants, reassigned at the end of their duty tours, might find themselves transferred from the heart of the command center to a remote motor pool.

For KGB officials, a possible solution to this problem might be found in examining the feasibility of training and equipping an agent who, if successful, could not only gain important access but also have the background to do something about improving it. It's a very old idea, probably predating John Thurloe's first use of the term "mole" in the mid-17th century.

It had been tried in New York in the thirties when a "disassociated" CP member took the New York City examination for selection as a police officer. The Soviets had a City Hall contact who was able to ensure that the candidate did well in the competitive examination by providing him with the correct answers beforehand.

Once through training, the new officer took the sergeant's exam as soon as he was eligible to do so. Again the answer man was able to facilitate the process, and the policeman found himself high on the list of new sergeants. He was a diligent, hard-working officer and, again, once qualified in terms of service, took the examination for police lieutenant.

He not only made the list but placed in the top group. Here was a man on the way up. Each promotion meant a transfer, and soon it was rumored that he would easily make captain and, in time, probably become chief inspector if not commissioner. It will be remembered that Governor Franklin Roosevelt had gone from the state house in Albany to the White House in Washington, and the popular wisdom of the day held that the route to national power led through the State of New York. It was hoped that with his excellent record and continued meteoric rise, he might become a prospective replacement for J. Edgar Hoover as director of the FBI.

In 1940, the City Hall contact was caught (an unplanned event), and the young lieutenant was brought before a police board and dismissed. Because there was no violation of federal law, the case was handled as a misdemeanor at an administrative level, and the Soviets' nominee for the directorship of the FBI was out of the running. The ex-lieutenant subsided back into one of the boroughs of New York, where he still lives, forty-five years later, as an abandoned, failed case.

In the late seventies, David Barnett, a CIA officer serving in the Far East, resigned from the service to go into business. After a period of time, he met with economic setbacks. In the belief that he could raise needed cash, he approached the local Soviet embassy and proposed a bilateral agreement in which he would provide his recollections of the agency and its operations in exchange for cash. The scenario bore a strong resemblance to the British Foreign Office clerk's adventure with Voynovich in Paris.

Self-selected, motivated by money, confident that as an individual he could deal with an organization, and deluding himself into believing that he could impose limits on his cooperation, Barnett had already lost the game when he made his first contact. As in other cases, he started with a historical reprise and went on from there. Once the local Soviets were persuaded that Barnett was prepared to cooperate, he was sent to Vienna to meet higher-level Soviet officials, then returned to Indonesia.

The plans relating to clandestine communications were worked out, and Barnett soon returned to the United States to look for a job. His assigned case officer was the ubiquitous "Igor," who was, in fact, Vladimir V. Popov, third secretary in the Soviet embassy, Washington. Barnett was offered a contract position with the CIA and was surprised when Popov failed to share his enthusiasm. Popov proposed and encouraged him to seek a job on Capitol Hill, preferably with either the House or the Senate Intelligence committee.[12]

The stresses accumulated, and the Popov-Barnett connection became known to the FBI. In April 1980, agents arrested Barnett, whose wife had no knowledge of his Soviet involvement. She suffered a stroke following the disclosure, and Barnett was indicted, pleaded guilty to accepting $92,600 from the KGB, and was sent to a federal prison. Pópov had an easy exit. He was, after all, a "diplomat" and was able to make his way safely back to Moscow, where he could prepare for his next assignment. In the KGB being declared *persona non grata* and expelled from the "enemy camp" is a small badge of honor.

A KGB officer preparing for a next assignment is a bit like a child getting ready for Halloween or an actor casting himself in a part. Depending on the "work," he might have to pick up a new false name and a suitable passport. Instead of an altered document, his will be furnished by the Ministry of Foreign Affairs of the USSR. He might be dispatched as a "trade representative," an Amtorg "inspector," a stringer for Tass or *Pravda*. Perhaps he will man the ticket counter of the Aeroflot office in Paris, be a freight agent for Morflot in Antwerp, join the United Nations staff in New York, Geneva, or elsewhere. If "all the world's a stage," the KGB might be seen as central casting.

The Barnett case is noteworthy only in its ordinariness. Traces of all other Soviet cases are found therein. It does have one innovative thread, and that is Popov's taking a controlled ex-CIA officer and attempting to use him against the more tempting congressional target. It may be assumed that, if hired, Barnett would have been seen as more of an "expert" on the hill (hence more consultations and access) than he would have been at the CIA.*

Following World War II, intelligence became a growth industry in which hundreds of thousands of individuals now routinely prepare, handle, transport, file, classify, manage, access, evaluate, and occasionally read the nation's "secrets."[13] The sheer volume tends to explain how files are "lost," "misplaced," and certified as "destroyed." With xerography, a clerk can always assume that "there's another copy around here somewhere." The prosperity of the firms that sell paper, machines, file cabinets, and safes is invariably shared by the Soviet organs, which have also benefited from the "information explosion."

The disclosures relative to the Prime case in the United Kingdom repeat some of the lessons already learned. They point up how a series of routine decisions, ordinary events, and intermittent inattention led to a tiny chink in the British defenses through which an important penetration was made. The Prime case has been dealt with in only a minor way, if at all, by other sources. Yet, the case is of great significance, not only because of the damage Prime did to British national security, but also because it is such a good example of a successful and fruitful KGB operation. The Soviets had the proper personnel on hand to deal expeditiously with the opportunities offered by Prime.

The report of the Security Commission details the dismal process in

---

*Editor's note: In truth, the CIA is a low-priority target of the KGB. The CIA holds few secrets in its own right that are of interest to the KGB. On the other hand, the committees of Congress in connection with their closed-door sessions and briefings by defense, scientific, and economic officials are a prime KGB target. The importance, for example, of the details of a new inertial guidance system for missiles is infinitely greater than the CIA's plans for covert actions or the operations of its Counterintelligence/Security Division. Hence, Capitol Hill is the prime location for the KGB either to get leads to real secrets or to acquire them by one means or another from Congressional sources.

stark terms, which are all the more striking by their clarity and force.[14] In 1956, Prime began to meet the National Service requirement by his entry into the Royal Air Force. He had hoped to be selected for training as a crewman, but he was rejected for color-blindness. He then applied for a course in the Russian language, as he believed that he had linguistic ability and motivating interest. After committing himself to a nine-year enlistment, Prime was posted to Crail, Scotland, in 1956 to begin his studies. He failed the first course at Crail but passed the second, and in April 1957, he was promoted to Aircraftsman I. The following month he was given acting sergeant rank and sent to London University for advanced language training. However, due to substandard academic performance, he returned to the RAF after only three months.

He automatically lost his rank of acting sergeant and became a storeman—or supply clerk—in which capacity he served from 1957 until 1963. In 1958, he was promoted successively to leading aircraftsman, senior aircraftsman, and corporal. He served at RAF St. Eval, Cornwall; Aden; 16 Maintenance Unit, Stafford; and, between September 1959 and April 1962, at RAF Eastleigh, in Kenya.

In April 1962, Prime returned to England and was assigned to the Air Ministry Unit (Group Headquarters) at Kenley, Surrey. He subsequently decided to reapply for a Russian language course. Between May 1963 and May 1964, he attended the Joint Language School at RAF Tangmere, Surrey, where he qualified in Russian.

In May 1964, Prime was posted to RAF Gatow, in Berlin, where he was engaged until July 1968 in intelligence duties as a voice radio operator. In May 1968, he was promoted to sergeant and, at the beginning of July, was returned to England to spend the last part of his service at RAF Innsworth. On separation, he applied for employment in the Government Communications Headquarters (GCHQ) at Cheltenham. Following interviews and a test of his linguistic skills, he was offered a post as a linguistic specialist (grade IV), which he accepted.

When he took up employment with GCHQ on September 30, 1968, he was assigned to the London Processing Group in St. Dunstan's Hill. The LPG was a specialist transcription organization, and for most of his first year, Prime was engaged in transcription training.

On June 30, 1969, having passed the Linguist Special Open Competition, Prime was given established civil service status. Soon afterward, he completed his training and began work as a transcriber. During his period at LPG, he also spent several months in "Control," the area where transcripts were finally checked before being passed to headquarters at Cheltenham.

The LPG was formed in 1958 from part of a transcriber force formerly employed but no longer needed by another intelligence agency. Almost all of the transcribers were Baltic State émigrés with homes and families in London. It was decided to keep the unit in London, partly because such a large influx of foreigners to Cheltenham would have attracted attention, and partly because many of the staff would have been unwilling to move their homes and it would have been difficult to find recruits to replace them. For reasons of security LPG continued to be run as an independent and completely isolated cell. Supervision and liaison with Cheltenham were in the hands of a very small group of British civil servants who, mostly, had been transferred to London from Cheltenham.

From 1973 to 1977, the work of LPG was progressively transferred to Cheltenham. Prime was moved on March 22, 1976, but no change in his type of work was involved. GCHQ at Cheltenham employed a staff of thousands with a wide range of technical and linguistic skills. The work included two major functions: (1) signals intelligence and (2) communications security. Prime was engaged in the former work throughout his time at Cheltenham and thus had access to material of the highest sensitivity.

On June 30, 1976, he was promoted to higher linguistic specialist and became the leader of a small team of transcribers. He was responsible for allocating work, exercising quality control of transcripts, and redoing tapes of particular difficulty. This work continued until November 1, 1976, when he was transferred to another branch with responsibility for analysis, as opposed to transcription, of signals intelligence material. In this section, he was in charge of seven linguists.

In September 1977, Prime suddenly resigned from GCHQ. Part of his duties at the time involved giving lectures, a task that made him extremely nervous. On September 22, he was required to give a lecture, but he failed to report for duty and shortly afterward tendered his resignation. Following his resignation from GCHQ, he obtained employment as a taxi driver and as a wine salesman.

Such are the bare bones of Prime's career with the RAF and GCHQ. There are no indications in his record that he was on a fast track to the top of either organization. Perhaps the only factor that would commend him to anyone's attention was his access to sensitive sources and his awareness of special methods.

From the Soviet viewpoint he was a political "progressive" who advocated change in the vague hope that he would somehow benefit. Additionally, he had limited social abilities and was sometimes disposed to molest female children. It was a certainty that this morose, lonely, and friendless individual would come up on the KGB's screen by any number of routes.

His posting to RAF, Gatow, was proximate to Berlin. In the period of his tenure there (May 1964 through August 1968), there was ample time and much opportunity for the Soviets to pick up the spoor. Like many young servicemen assigned to communications intelligence in overseas posts, Prime was isolated from the usual camaraderie found in military line organizations, a condition that increased his vulnerability. The inhibitors and stresses that affect the lives of enlisted operators in military intelligence organizations are so well known to the Soviets that they do not permit their own personnel to have *any* contact outside their structured and disciplined units.[15] The harsh and unyielding restrictions applied to Soviet personnel allow for no exposure to outside temptations and, hence, a greatly reduced danger to the unit.

The common thread in most of these cases is the matter of vulnerability. In some instances, it derives from financial problems; in others, it involves psychological or emotional weaknesses frequently associated with narcotics and alcohol. In this context, the KGB seeks victims who can be bought or coerced into directed espionage, and the organs have been adept at both recognizing and exploiting indications of weakness wherever found.

Prime exhibited most of the disabilities on the KGB check list and more than qualified as a target for recruitment. A loner, a young man with sexual problems, and someone who, by his own admission, believed that the downtrodden of the world would fare better under communism. Such symptoms and attitudes assured that, at an appropriate moment, he would fall into the Soviet bag. The case is not a tribute to the Soviets' prescience but another instance of their readiness for an event such as Prime's self-selection, their single-minded patience, clerical effort, and corps of competent case officers who were trained and fully aware of what their jobs entailed.

In Berlin the Soviet support nets are massive. In addition to surveillants, drivers, couriers, police, and postal employees, they include "swallows" who specialize in foreigners who enjoy mild or other forms of perversion. In fact, every Western military base from the Azores to Zanzibar has its own street of Butterfly Bars outside the gates. Depending on the sensitivity of the base, the KGB's "girls" (most of whom are unaware of the identity of their true employer) provide the organs with volumes of information about their clients.

They are also encouraged to steal ID cards, passes, military orders, and family documents (letters, driver's licenses, photographs of wives and children, etc.) while the client sleeps. The process has been under way for a thousand years, but the KGB is the first customer to offer to pay for paper debris that has no intrinsic value and can't be sold elsewhere.

This river of authentic pocket and wallet litter is dredged for its operational intelligence content, such as identity of unit, family data, home address, and, in the case of orders, military occupational specialties, rank, and assignment. The girls are also alerted to spot the six "d's"—

discontent, disaffection, depression, drunkenness, desperation, and sexual dysfunction—any one of which might provide a future lever.

It is usual for members of the same military unit to develop a sense of belonging by using a particular club or by frequenting the same bar. Over a period of time a covey of attentive bargirls can construct an order-of-battle outline that might be more current and complete than the one in the chief of staff's safe. The girls' knowledge of the RAF personnel at Gatow was available to the KGB for a price, as is comparable data at Yokosuka, Manila, Bangkok, Alexandria, and all around the free world. The girls for the most part are apolitical and see themselves as entrepreneurs or, more simply, as vendors.

The report of the British Security Commission does not deal with the precise factors that motivated Prime to offer his services to the Soviets, except to confirm that he was another self-selected individual who presented the Soviets an unplanned target of opportunity. Prime claimed that it all began in January 1968. While returning from Christmas leave, he passed through a checkpoint prior to entering West Berlin and, in the process, handed a note to the Soviet officer who was inspecting documents. In the message he stated that he wished the Russian intelligence services to contact him and designated a rendezvous at a restaurant on the Liebnitzstrasse. Although no one met him, he later discovered a magnetic cylinder on his car door handle instructing him to travel to the Friedrichstrasse S-Bahn station in East Berlin.

At the first meeting, he was briefly asked his particulars, occupation, and what he wanted to do. At following meetings, he was requested to explain his function at Gatow in detail. He stated that he was sympathetic to communism. The Soviets emphasized the need to establish that he was not a double agent, which he accepted. Though Prime considered himself ideologically motivated, he also accepted (under protest, he insisted) £30 or £40 at each of the East Berlin meetings. This mandatory payment or gift was wholly consistent with approved Soviet methodology. The cash serves as the "small hook" to be set at the earliest possible moment.

Prime's tour with the RAF was due to end in August 1968. He discussed his future employment with the Soviets and mentioned the prospect of applying to GCHQ, an idea that he was encouraged to pursue. At his last meeting, a senior officer thanked him for his help and asked him to return to Berlin during his terminal leave.

In August, after leaving the RAF, Prime returned to Berlin, changing planes, as instructed, at Amsterdam. He spent a week in a flat near Karlshorst—Soviet headquarters in East Germany—while being trained in the receipt of radio transmissions, secret writing, encryption, use of ciphers and microdots, operation of a miniature camera, and the use of dead drops. Training was carried out by two Soviets through an interpreter.

Prime was an apt pupil, and when the KGB learned that he had been accepted for employment by the GCHQ, his training was accelerated and intensified. It was essential that the neophyte agent have the tools of the trade well in hand before he left Karlshorst.

Prime was not allowed to leave the Berlin flat alone, and after each day's instruction he was locked in for the night. He was given a recognition phrase for exchange with his contacts and told that no meetings would be held in the United Kingdom, but only in neutral countries. He was told to choose between Finland and Austria, and he opted for the latter. At the end of his training, he was supplied with a set of one-time pads—a letter-sized tablet containing secret writing carbons—and £400, all concealed in the secret compartment of a briefcase.

He flew back to London, changing planes at Hamburg. On arrival at Heathrow he posted a card as a signal to indicate that he had encountered no problems. As the Security Commission report notes, Prime's training in spycraft by the KGB took place at precisely the same time that GCHQ was clearing him for access to sensitive intelligence information. The concurrence of these events in no way reflected failure by the British security authorities, as their investigation was limited to examining his past life rather than his current activities.

The development of the case suggests that the KGB made haste slowly. His case officers were like watchful cooks. Prime was already in the stew. They were willing to wait for the broth to boil. The KGB understood that while on transcription training Prime would have little opportunity for espionage. During his apprenticeship, he reported to the Soviets by secret writing that he had begun training. He also provided the names and his personal estimate of his colleagues. In reply, he received his first broadcast message instructing him to continue to report.

At first glance, his early reports might appear benign, but they were not. His identification and assessment of his co-workers was potentially as damaging as his own treason. The key to acquiring additional assets has always been in the hands of those on the inside. On the basis of frequent contact and shared experience, they are able to assess the vulnerabilities and attitudes of their associates.

A strong parallel can be drawn to the earlier case of "Hans," the Soviet agent who successfully learned from the Foreign Office clerk, Scott, that he indeed had a colleague who shared his desperate financial circumstances. It was at that point that the clerk nominated and later, introduced John Herbert King, who was eventually recruited by the Soviets. Prime was an agent in his own right, but by virtue of his training and posting, he was also an important talent spotter.

After beginning operational work in 1969, Prime sent several letters in secret writing to the Center. He listened for broadcasts every other weekend, and in the autumn of 1969 he was instructed to clear a dead drop in the Esher area. When he did so, he found a message of congratulations and £400. Prime was now functioning effectively, and the organs were quick to provide him with a generous reward.

For the next eight years, his service followed a familiar pattern. As his access to more sensitive intelligence increased, so did the KGB's interest. His communications with his controllers became more frequent. Following his resignation from GCHQ, Prime gave up listening to the shortwave broadcasts that were used to give him additional orders and information. Twice in the summer of 1977 he made plans to defect to Russia, but each time he changed his mind.

His behavior in this regard warrants comment, because it reflects directly on a method by which the KGB attempts to maintain control over sources. Just as there is a "psychology of defection"—a set of principles that tend to explain the action of someone who elects to defect—there is a psychology associated with those who, for whatever reason, betray their own countries. It is a major part of the case controller's responsibility to anticipate and assuage the betrayer's anxieties and fears, and to recognize the periods of depression that invariably occur. These symptoms become evident in every case, and if ignored or not recognized, they will almost certainly result in disaster. To avoid or mitigate the problem, the KGB generally provides the betrayers with a promise of an escape to the socialist sanctuary in the USSR should the going get too tough or if the agent is about to be exposed. It is a standard offer that, curiously, is seldom accepted. Relatively few foreign agents have exercised the option, preferring prison at home to "freedom" in the USSR.

The KGB made no effort, in 1977, to persuade Prime not to resign from GCHQ. In fact, he had no contact with the KGB until April 1980, when a foreign-accented male telephoned his sister to obtain his current number and then called him, asking him to come to Vienna. He readily agreed, making the excuse to his wife that he had to pick up a repaired car in Vienna for a friend.

At the meeting, according to Prime, the Soviets did not censure him for quitting the GCHQ but encouraged him to rejoin. Though Prime was unwilling, the Soviets paid him £600 in appreciation of his having come to Vienna to provide them with what material he had retained since leaving GCHQ.

His next and final contact with the KGB was in November 1981, when he was called by telephone to a meeting in East Berlin. Though he had no more information to give the Soviets, he again readily agreed to the meeting. After arriving in East Berlin, he was driven to Potsdam, where he met his controller, who had flown in from Moscow. He was questioned in detail about the material he had provided during previous year, but he was unable to answer many of the controller's questions. It was suggested that he might find work at the Royal Army Education Corps, Beaconsfield, as a teacher of Russian, presumably to act again as a "talent spotter." At the end of the meeting, he was paid £4000.

Prime's reason(s) for rejecting this final suggestion by the KGB are, in spite of extensive psychiatric examinations conducted by the British government, still unclear. From November 1981 to November 1982 Prime continued to work as a taxi driver and wine salesman. The "case" came to a close on November 10, 1982, when he pleaded guilty at the Central Criminal Court to seven counts of an indictment charging offenses under Section 1 of the Official Secrets Act 1911 and to three counts of a separate indictment charging indecent assaults on young girls aged eleven, thirteen, and fourteen. He was sentenced to a total of thirty-five years imprisonment for the Official Secrets Act offenses and to three years (to be consecutively served) for the sexual offenses.*

The British government made no effort to represent Prime as a low-level employee; instead, the Security Commission concluded that the damage inflicted by him on the British and U.S. intelligence organizations (GCHQ and the National Security Agency) was of a "very high order." As in previous instances, the commission found that security provisions were not all that the authorities thought them to be. Better methods of screening as well as follow-up investigations were recommended. The predictable (though tardy) response of the security bureaucracy was essentially reactive and devolved more on new procedures to avert future Primes than it did on the Soviet methodologies that produce agent recruitments.

The passivity of Western security systems is predicated on respect for human rights. There is great reluctance to take action against security and intelligence personnel who, at some point, evince behaviorial defects. Because the economic implications for wayward individuals are grave, solutions are sometimes found in transfers to less sensitive duties—there is no other *fair and just* provision for dealing with such cases. The inhibitions

---

*Editor's note: Though Prime's guilty plea eliminated the necessity for a trial, in camera or in public, this action did not resolve all the problems associated with Prime's perfidy. The report of the Security Commission mentioned herein did not, for example, delineate Prime's role as a taxi driver. Here, still working in behalf of the KGB, Prime used his taxi driver cover to function as a courier who picked up secret documents, had them photocopied, and returned the originals by way of a "witting" fare. In many respects, it is difficult to assess whether Prime did more damage to U.K. and U.S. intelligence interests when he was "inside" rather than when he was outside driving a taxicab on the streets of London. Although Prime was a loner, he also was a KGB talent spotter, and all of those he spotted have not been discovered to date.

of the managers are based on social and moral considerations that, in the aggregate, operate against the interests of security.[16]

The kinds of indicative behavior that illustrate high vulnerability to recruitment are rarely sufficient grounds on which to recommend separation. Intelligence and security officers have the same decay rate as other humans, and incipient problems frequently do not become apparent for many years. Acceptance of this regrettable fact makes constant review of all personnel a security imperative. If there are wounded in the herd, the Soviet predators will find them. The damage they do is so appalling and affects so many lives that the indulgence of such waywards becomes a serious crime in itself.

Prime's *modus operandi* is illustrative of earlier remarks about photography and xerography. According to the Security Commission, Prime admitted to retaining and taking home to photograph documents that, both in London and at Cheltenham, should have been returned at the end of each day to a secure vault. At Cheltenham Prime worked in an office in a compartmented spur in B Block with controlled access. At both establishments all entrances were manned by a security officer at all times. But searches, regular or random, were not made of GCHQ personnel, their bags, briefcases, or automobiles.

The vault was located in the same spur. It was locked at 4:30 P.M. daily. The combination to the vault was known only to three officers, of whom Prime was one from November 1976 until his resignation. The vault could not be opened after 5:00 P.M. without setting off an alarm, but between 4:30 and 5:00 it was theoretically possible to reopen it without detection. It is unlikely that Prime attempted to do so. He had free access to the material throughout the working day and could easily hold back documents without being observed or suspected. To reopen the vault between 4:30 and 5:00 would have been a peculiar action likely to attract attention, which he was always anxious to avoid.

There was some material that Prime was not able to remove from the office with ease because it was in circulation and had to be passed on quickly. He reproduced material of this kind, using a copier situated in the small administration office across the corridor from his own office. He did this about fifteen to twenty times during the lunch break, when the administration office was unoccupied. The copier had a lockable immobilization switch, but during the lunch hour it was not immobilized, nor was the administration office locked.

It was the practice then for personnel to do their own copying, entering the details in the copy register. Alternatively, the copying was done on request by a clerical assistant who worked in the administration office. Prime did not make any entry in the register for the material he reproduced. The copying machine had a counter that measured how much paper was used. If this had been checked regularly, it would have shown the discrepancy between the entries in the register and the amount of paper used.

The foregoing is cited simply to suggest the extent of absolute dependence by the public on the patriotism and high motivation of security and intelligence personnel and their obligation to protect the public's national trust. Although xerography has been a valuable enabling agent to the Soviets, it is still necessary for them to find the person with access who will succumb to recruitment. The best defense against a case such as Prime's is a common responsibility that is shared by every citizen, because its failure affects their lives.

One of the most depressing aspects of the Prime case was the distorted and unwarranted sense of this obligation on the part of many who observed or knew of Prime's peculiarities, yet failed to come forward. It was a reprise of the cases involving Burgess, Maclean, Philby, and others when *many* friends and associates came forward in the aftermath and claimed to have had information that might have prevented or at least reduced the stunning, successive blows to British and U.S. national security.

During Andropov's fifteen-year tenure as KGB chairman, he was careful to maintain balance among the various elements of the organs. The virtue of his method was the avoidance of the kind of internecine bureaucratic warfare that in the past had dominated the resource allocations to intelligence and internal security elements.

By the mid-seventies, his crash program to acquire the technical intelligence needed to modernize the Soviet armed forces was stabilized. The collection program had been greatly extended by the spread of all kinds of Soviet trade delegations, missions, and representatives. The Nixon-Brezhnev meeting in 1972 provided for the massive propagation of Soviet trade representatives within the United States. On the Soviet side, a U.S. trade office, staffed by one officer from the Department of Commerce, was established in Moscow, and the public was assured that multiple benefits would flow from the reciprocal arrangements.

With White House endorsement, large delegations of American businessmen flocked to Moscow to stake their claims to the promised prosperity. In the United States, meanwhile, the new Soviet "traders" broadened and intensified their purchases of desperately needed American technology. (See Appendix IV for data relating to the number and location of Soviet trade representatives.)

The Soviet industrial espionage and illegal-procurement systems gradually fell into three distinct but related categories. The first level of high-technology espionage is quite obvious and requires only occasional resort to clandestine method. It consists of the collection of all scientific and technical material published in the United States (including doctoral and postdoctoral work at universities and publications of research and development facilities and corporations engaged in any defense-related work).

For targeting purposes it was and is essential for the Soviets to relate the names of the principal workers to their specializations. The move five years later of key people to the Livermore Laboratory or to White Sands would suggest a change of emphasis or convey early warning of a shift in U.S. defense priorities. This indexing of names and correlation with specialties is another labor-intensive clerical chore. The collection phase has been carried out by persons who, if their relationship to the Soviet Union was known, would have been denied the information.

In the collection of scientific and technical data, as distinguished from the acquisition of machines, equipment, and materials, the approach is all-inclusive. The Center's dicta is simple: "Get everything." In this context, "everything" includes: open publications, dissertations, papers delivered at technical and professional association meetings, patents and patent applications, trade journals, textbooks, software, etc.

The information is initially screened and processed in New York and Washington. Amtorg and the Soviet trade delegations provide offices to KGB officers from Directorate T, who identify promising leads relating to new products, processes, and manufacturing firms. With the aid of telephone books, trade association registers, access to credit bureaus, banks, law firms, and other common sources of commercial data, the KGB has been able to intensify its focus. If indicated, a further reconnaissance can be made, and the mammoth clerical matching process is begun to determine if there are assets available who can be used in the next phase.

Substantive material collected in this effort that does not have direct or immediate intelligence application is sent to Moscow for distribution to the appropriate scientific and technical institutions. In one sense the documents are essentially library acquisitions. Though Soviets assigned to diplomatic missions and consular offices are generally denied ordinary access to some published materials such as certain patents and a few highly specialized association journals, the problem is readily overcome by having a Soviet "international civil servant" assigned to the UN join the associations and collect the data.

Such individuals, because of their status, are not precluded from such actions. Similarly, they are also allowed to travel freely in the United States, thus enabling them to attend conferences and join associations. In addition to Russians, this extensive group includes all of the Soviet-bloc nationals who hold international civil service status at the pleasure of the Soviets. Because there are no restraints on these people, they constitute an almost unmanageable counterintelligence problem for the United States. At present there are no effective means of preventing these officers and co-optees of the organs from talent spotting and assessing personnel in the U.S. scientific and technical community.

A National Academy of Sciences report contends that the free flow of ideas does not threaten our national security.[17] Though this assertion is true in the context of the report—we would lose as a nation by attempting to precensor scientific dialogue and discourse falling outside legitimate security classifications—the report does not address the hazards of the KGB's free operational access to American scientists.

In the last twenty years, many American scientists have developed legitimate and important relationships with U.S. industry. These connections allow them to pursue their own research and concurrently to work on classified defense projects. Like all useful citizens, they value intellectual freedom and the right to form and express their political views. They customarily attend international meetings and conferences at which the KGB is also present. Under the auspices of prestigious sponsors, the attendees are met, assessed, and gently elicited on their areas of study. The KGB's assets at these meetings are co-optees and coerced agents of high technical competence who are drawn from many nations. Keeping a wary eye on the Soviets usually misses the point, because such operations might be conducted by a West European or even an American colleague. To suggest that the record reflects a degree of past political naïveté among some prominent U.S. scientists in no way denigrates these men and women of exceptional gifts. It is simply a fact that a few have been compromised, and many have been exploited.

Individuals who have spent most of their adult lives plumbing the depths of such fields as plasma physics, astrophysics, and magnetohydrodynamics are sometimes less than aware of the nuances and realities of the Soviet version of continuing war and are fundamentally disposed to reject the notion as unreasonable. Personal convictions of the highest moral tone are not always an adequate asepsis against exploitation by false-flag methods. Prominent U.S. scientists who have been openly anti-Soviet and who have advocated strong measures to restrict the organs' corruption of international scientific exchange have been subjected to attacks by the KGB that have been piously replayed in the national media. The most obvious example is the now popular characterization of Dr. Edward Teller. There can be no doubt about his critical contribution to U.S. security; however, thirty years later he is represented in the press as the basely motivated nemesis who destroyed the reputation of Robert Oppenheimer and as a demented devotee of thermonuclear war.

The second track of KGB espionage in science and technology is more narrowly focused. It proceeds in large measure from the information acquired from the first track, which identifies areas of research, manufacture, and expected utilization. These data, enhanced with information from more sensitive, clandestine operations and evaluations made by Department T, result in the formulation of an ultratech shopping list. These distilled requirements, in turn, serve as the basis for formulating operational approaches to both the physical and personnel targets.

Court documents filed by the FBI in connection with an espionage case in the 1970s include a master list of wanted Western technology as compiled in Moscow by Soviet engineers and scientists.[18] In some cases such needs can be met by legal means. For example, the Kama Truck Plant was built over a period of seven years with imports of more than $1.5 billion worth of U.S. and West European automotive production equipment and technology.[19] Large numbers of military trucks produced there are in current use by Soviet forces in Afghanistan and by Soviet military units in Eastern Europe opposite the NATO forces. Similarly, large Soviet purchases of printed circuit board technology and numerically controlled machine tools from the West already have benefited the Soviet military manufacturing sectors.

When Soviet technological needs cannot be met by legal means, there is no hesitation on the part of the KGB to resort to illegal means. The great bulk of this effort is carried out through illegal trade channels. The processes by which this is done, though known and understood by the U.S. government, are difficult to detect and monitor. For example, the diversion of controlled technology from legitimate trade channels to proscribed destinations is accomplished in four general ways: through U.S. and foreign firms willing to engage in profitable impropriety; through agents in place in U.S. firms or their foreign subsidiaries; through Soviet and East European firms locally chartered in the West; and through foreign purchasing agents (including arms dealers).

The basic *modus operandi* of the KGB's use of illegal means to evade U.S. and other Western export controls is a variation on the Amtorg scams described in Chapter 7.[20] The most successful current stratagem involves the establishment of dummy corporations in the United States or Western Europe that purchase or place orders for sophisticated microelectronic manufacturing equipment.[21] The extremely competitive nature of this industry is sufficient to dull the security concerns of many American firms. This makes it easy for the Soviet selling companies to make a "buy." Once in hand, the equipment is shipped or reshipped, sometimes with the knowledge of individuals in the selling companies, to conceal eventual destinations in the Soviet Union or Eastern Europe. Both the KGB and the Warsaw Pact intelligence services are the sole proprietors of these firms specializing in the flow of illegal technological trade.

The dimensions of this traffic can be measured only indirectly. Public

attention has been drawn to instances in which the illegal acquisition of
U.S. technology has been successfully thwarted.[22] These isolated instances obscure the fact that the illegal trade continues largely unabated
and is part of a coherent process. The Soviet intelligence effort against
Western defense contractors poses a serious problem in itself. With more
than 11,000 such corporations in the United States and hundreds of subsidiaries abroad, U.S. counterintelligence assets are inadequate to the
task. Meanwhile, the protection of U.S. firms abroad from hostile intelligence threats is the responsibility of host governments, but they, too,
are feeling the burden of artfully orchestrated Soviet-bloc attentions.
(These problems are particularly acute in Japan.) It is evident that Western industrial security, both defense and commercial, will be even more
severely attacked by the Soviet intelligence services and their surrogates
during the late 1980s.[23]

The problem is essentially political. It is compounded by the pressures
of honest, highly motivated Americans whose personal experiences have
led them to an unalterable view that the excesses of the Soviet are overstated and that it is inconceivable for any nation to pursue such aggressive
and destructive policies. The "Russian people" are frequently invoked as
a likely restraint against Soviet adventurism. The fact that the Russian
people and their thoughts are irrelevant to the operations of the Soviet
government is looked upon as incredible by those who promote the mirror-imaging illusion that people are people everywhere. We are encouraged to accept the flummeries of those who insist that it is only the
bellicosity of the U.S. government that produces tensions in the world
and that the Soviet policy is simply reactive to our chronic, wrongheaded
belligerence.

The joyous heralding of détente served Soviet interests by assuaging
the critics and their followers while the Soviets pursued a high-velocity
catchup program of technical theft. The "trade" treaties, instead of producing better opportunities for peace, have simply accelerated the Soviets' ability to improve their military capacities. The SALT Agreements,
which the Soviets have violated consistently, continue to be regarded by
many as having some relationship to disarmament and peace. The key to
success in this process has been the Soviets' ability to manipulate public
opinion and, systematically, to disinform. When the national media are
induced to play a Soviet theme, the later realization of that fact presents
the patriarchs of the Fourth Estate with the unpleasant digital options of
declaring themselves either fools or knaves.

The nonprofit nature of Soviet trade should be evident to the business
community by this time, but it is not. The real point, which is seldom
made, is that the combined effect of the legal and illegal acquisition of
U.S. technology by the KGB is devastating to the national security inter-

ests of the United States. Our inability or unwillingness to stop the hemorrhaging of vital information to the Soviets is a threat to every individual American. Business, in this sense, should not be conducted as usual.

The combined effect of legal and illegal acquisition of U.S. technology, especially through the trade scams, is deadly. Since the successful interdiction of this system is wholly within the capacity of the business community and cooperating banks, this raises the question of the credibility of those who profess that they would not do anything to damage the interests of the United States by aiding Soviet military modernization. Despite these sincere protestations of patriotic intent, the KGB's looting of U.S. technological treasure would not be possible without the cooperation of willing Americans. Specific targets that have been subjected to intense KGB/GRU collection efforts have been identified by the CIA to the Congress, to wit:

SELECTED SOVIET AND EAST EUROPEAN LEGAL

AND ILLEGAL ACQUISITIONS FROM THE WEST AFFECTING KEY AREAS

OF SOVIET MILITARY TECHNOLOGY

Key Technology Area, Notable Successes

Computers: Purchases and acquisitions of complete systems designs, concepts, hardware, and software, including a wide variety of Western general-purpose computers and minicomputers for military applications.

Microelectronics: Complete industrial processes and semiconductor manufacturing equipment capable of meeting all Soviet military requirements, if acquisitions were combined.

Signal processing: Acquisitions of processing equipment and know-how.

Manufacturing: Acquisitions of automated and precision manufacturing equipment for electronics and optical and laser weapons technology; acquisitions of information on manufacturing technology related to weapons, ammunition, and aircraft parts, including turbine blades, computers, and electronic components; acquisitions of machine tools for cutting large gears for ship propulsion systems.

Communications: Acquisitions of low-power, low-noise, high-sensitivity receivers.

Lasers: Acquisitions of optical pulsed power sources and other laser-related components, including special optical mirrors and mirror technology suitable for future laser weapons.

Guidance and navigation: Acquisitions of marine and other navigation

receivers, advanced inertial-guidance components, including miniature and laser gyros; acquisitions of missile guidance subsystems; acquisitions of precision machinery to make ball bearings for missiles
and other applications; acquisitions of missile test-range instrumentation systems and documentation and precision cinetheodolites for
collecting data critical to postflight ballistic missile analysis.

Structural materials: Purchases and acquisitions of Western titanium alloys, welding equipment, and furnaces for producing titanium plate
of large size applicable to submarine construction.

Propulsion: Missile technology; some ground propulsion technology (diesels, turbines, and rotaries); purchases and acquisitions of advanced
jet engine fabrication technology and jet engine design information.

Acoustical sensors: Acquisitions of underwater navigation direction-find-
ing equipment.

Electro-optical sensors: Acquisitions of information on satellite technology, laser range finders, and underwater low-light-level television
cameras and systems for remote operation.

Radars: Acquisitions and exploitations of air-defense radars and antenna
designs for missile systems.

Behind each of these "notable successes" is an explanation based on
the hoary "too little and too late" syndrome. Unfortunately, the KGB
"acquisitions" we know about came to official attention after the fact of
their appearance in the Soviet military. For every Soviet illegal trade
scam detected there are probably fifteen or twenty that go unnoticed.
These estimates do not reflect on the U.S. internal-security and enforcement elements so much as they demonstrate the scale and intensity of the
Soviet effort and the indifference of the U.S. citizenry.

These are serious matters. It is specious to berate the FBI, customs
officials, and local law-enforcement agencies for the failure to staunch the
outflow of U.S. technology. The men and women who enforce U.S. laws
in this vital area are caught between a burgeoning unregulated Soviet
presence in the United States and a somnolent public. As Soviet and
satellite numbers of agents have grown, the FBI's internal-security force
has become less experienced and less numerous than in past years. This
force suffered significant damage from the indictment of senior Bureau
officials who had worked in the field for many years. In fact, internal
security is no longer looked upon as a desirable assignment for FBI
agents interested in career advancement. The action today seems to be in
organized crime control. Correction of the problem seems to be repeatedly deferred in the fragile hope that the Soviet leadership will undergo a
change in attitude, despite the overwhelming evidence that it has been an
immutable marvel of consistency for almost seventy years.

The attitude toward "illegal" technology transfer to the Soviet Union bears some resemblance to the dismissive popular response to the rise of smuggling in the Prohibition period, when public indifference allowed organized crime to develop and grow into an almost ineradicable blight. The current lack of public support in choking off the flow of technology has encouraged the KGB. In addition, Andropov's understanding of the diffuse nature of American technological development enabled the Soviets to gain much of what they needed from the small innovative firms and energetic entrepreneurs rather than from the more obvious major firms.

Of course, the large companies, like large bureaucracies, tend to be impersonal and anonymous. Loyalty to the profit center in which an individual currently passes the workday is apt not to flourish. Occasionally, an individual breaks trust for a variety of highly subjective reasons. Security classification and control procedures are commonly seen as limiting personal freedom. Others who are at ideological odds with the hand that feeds them disregard security as a form of political statement.

Consistent with a forty-five-year-old trend, the U.S. government no longer manufactures ships, aircraft, or armaments. Virtually all defense equipment and supplies are manufactured by the private sector. In exchange for this shift to nongovernment production of defense goods, contractors have pledged compliance with security regulations governing the part of their activity that consists of classified work.

The KGB has taken special notice of what they describe as "workplace discontent." On closer examination such attitudes do not necessarily translate into a willingness to aid the Soviets; rather, they relate to strong sentiment in favor of staggered work hours, day-care centers, job reclassification, and, of course, more pay. There have been several documented instances of Soviet approaches, based on such erroneous assumptions, that have resulted in the discontented worker reporting the recruitment overture to the FBI. There have been other instances in which the organs have succeeded.

The treason of Christopher John Boyce and Andrew Daulton Lee reveals a worst-case instance of the discontented in the workplace. The process has been carefully described by Robert Lindsey in *The Falcon and the Snowman*. Of recurring interest are the principles of the unplanned event and the Soviets' ability to exploit opportunity. It also points up another truth: Potential KGB assets come in all shapes and sizes.[24]

Boyce and Lee were privileged residents of Palos Verdes in Southern California. They served together as altar boys and shared a passion for falconry. Both were "affected deeply by an unpopular war, the rise of the flower children, LSD and a festering disenchantment with old standards and Watergate."

Though bright (an IQ of 142), intense, idealistic, and religious, Boyce drifted aimlessly from one college to the next, brooding about the state of the nation and flying his falcons. Lee was a small, incredibly ambitious, highly successful drug dealer. They lived "in a social millieu where ambition was a religion and money was the ultimate laurel of success." On the surface, "they had everything—including boredom."

In July 1974, Boyce's father, a former FBI agent, helped his son get a job at the Redondo Beach branch of TRW, an aerospace company. Within five months Boyce learned that "TRW was developing and manufacturing satellites used by the CIA to collect secret intelligence information from space." Initially hired as a clerk, Boyce was soon assigned to work in the communications room, sometimes referred to as the Black Vault. He was twenty-one years old, earned $140 a week, and had a top secret clearance.

This situation highlights the fact that in many cases it is no longer possible to limit access to highly sensitive information to one or two thoroughly vetted people. Often, secrets are entrusted to low-level, poorly paid employees who are not closely supervised. These workers are perhaps the most vulnerable of corporate targets. Their low status, relative seclusion from the mainstream, and physical separation from others—and often periods of inactivity—all contribute to the problem. As in any job, drugs are a continuing menace. Boyce represented only one of many potential national security disasters in the making.

One night early in April 1975, following an extended session with cocaine, Boyce suddenly confided to Lee that he had access to certain material that could be worth a lot of money to a foreign country. Lee was interested, and they made a plan. A week later, Lee flew to Mexico City, went directly to the Soviet embassy, and announced that he had information of interest to the Soviets. Within minutes, Lee and Boyce were on their way to becoming two more self-selected Soviet sources.[25]

After Lee's second visit to the Soviet embassy, he was "handed off" to a new control, a man identified only as Grishin, a work name that has been used by the Soviets much like a rented tuxedo. Although Robert Lindsey identifies the Boyce-Lee handler as "Boris Alexei Grishin," this is inconclusive in establishing the KGB man's true identity. According to confidential sources, Grishin was actually Boris Skaggs, a graduate of Moscow's Polytechnic Institute with a specialty in electronics. No matter what his true name was, it is accurate to note that Grishin did in fact possess a high level of technical expertise, so that he was able to exploit the Boyce-Lee connection promptly and thoroughly. Grishin's purpose was to assess Lee, to make a competent field evaluation of the material gathered, and to redirect his sources in their collection efforts. The importance of the technique of using technically qualified case officers to direct ultratech espionage cannot be overstated.

It was obvious from the onset that the Soviets knew that they were dealing with young amateurs who would have a predictably short run before detection. It was therefore imperative that the technical officer attempt to optimize the access they represented. Grishin was able to reduce the communications turnaround time from Mexico City to the Center in Moscow to a bare minimum.

Eventually, they were arrested, indicted, and convicted on charges of espionage. For most Americans the Boyce-Lee case has remained an anomaly; in actuality it was not unique. The case is noteworthy principally because it reveals the intensity of the KGB's response to technical intelligence opportunities. As stated earlier, the decision to recruit and dispatch technically competent individuals to serve in the foreign KGB residencies had already been made in Moscow, and the Boyce-Lee case served to confirm the remarkable utility of that decision.

Boyce-Lee and the later case of William Holden Bell's recruitment[26] by the Soviets' Polish proxies resulted in the loss of classified reports relating to:

The F-15 look-down-shoot-down radar system; the quiet radar system for the B-1 and Stealth bombers; an all-weather radar system for tanks; an experimental radar system for the navy; the Phoenix air-to-air missile; shipborne surveillance radar; the Patriot surface-to-air missile; a towed-array submarine sonar system; a new air-to-air missile; the improved HAWK surface-to-air missile; and a NATO air-defense system.

The information in these documents put in jeopardy existing weapons and future advanced-weapons systems of the United States and its allies. The acquisition of this information saved the Soviet government hundreds of millions of rubles in research and development by permitting the immediate utilization of proven designs developed by the United States and by fielding operational counterpart systems in a much shorter time period. Other data relating to specifications on current and future U.S. weapons systems have also facilitated the rapid development of defensive countermeasure systems.

The Boyce-Lee and Bell cases are noteworthy not only in terms of damage to the United States but also for what they reveal about Soviet methods. Regrettably, the clock cannot be rolled back. The only salvage available from the two cases consists of a few familiar lessons. Vulnerabilities of the individuals were exploited with unerring accuracy, vital material was lost, and more victims were strewn about the terrain. The sources were self-selected and motivated by money, though in the case of Boyce there were also vague, undeveloped social and political factors. The Soviets' response to the unplanned events was quick, certain, and highly professional. Perhaps the most noteworthy point was that the

KGB's technical competence was prepositioned in the large Soviet embassy in Mexico City and prepared to act.*

It is difficult not to attribute much of this success to Andropov personally. The organizational planning, the recruitment of technical officers, and the recognition of both the needs of the Soviets and the opportunities in the West, occurred during his chairmanship of the KGB. It is also clear that Andropov acted on the reports, analyses, and recommendations of KGB personnel whom he respected.

Because of the gradual realization of the scope of the ultratech theft problem, it has been useful for the Soviets to pour oil on the troubled waters. There is probably no better qualified pourer of oil than Georgi Arbatov, head of the Institute for the Study of the USA and Canada. The institute purports to be the West's "window into the Kremlin." Arbatov effectively promotes the fiction that his group consists entirely of scholars who are desperately trying to ameliorate the differences between East and West. He spends most of his time talking with influential Americans and U.S.-Soviet scholars who believe that they, too, share his concerns.

Arbatov is the perennial Russian uncle trying to induce a "feast of reason and a flow of soul." He is lavish with his invitations to various American scholars to visit the institute in Moscow. He has developed a broad U.S. constituency that believes him to be "a guy we can talk with." Arbatov is consciously so unlike the standard Soviet in his seemingly pliant, moderate, scholarly, and objective attitudes that he serves as a living example of the popular American thesis that, in the process of learning about the United States, most Soviet citizens would, quite naturally, aspire to U.S. citizenship.

One of his specialties is the "unguarded moment," in which he confides to his foreign visitors that his is a difficult, uphill struggle, but that he is beginning to make some progress in making reasonable men out of the gargoyles on the Central Committee.[27] The whispered insight is followed by the injunction that much patience and understanding will be

---

*Editor's Note: In this regard, KGB, GRU, and satellite intelligence personnel with scientific and technical expertise, as a consequence of Andropov's order, have been routinely assigned to the network of Soviet trading organizations and consular offices and as exchange students at U.S. universities. Their cover varies from trader to bureaucrat to student. They are generally found in close proximity to defense plants associated with the so-called military-industrial complex, in areas where there is a great deal of ultratech research such as California's Silicon Valley, and near sensitive installations such as the National Security Agency's headquarters at Fort Meade, outside Washington, D.C. Although the Soviets in this group carry out scientific/technical espionage operations in their own right, they also can be called upon to serve as controllers of Americans who have been developed by other agents of the KGB. This element of the KGB/GRU apparat in the United States numbers between four and eight thousand, according to U.S. intelligence sources. As such, it constitutes a scientific/technical "fifth column" unprecedented in scope in the history of Soviet espionage operations.

necessary in getting the Kremlin and the White House to make sense, and that it is "our" duty to defuse explosive issues and cool the fevered brows of the benighted nonintellectuals. Several visitors have described the somewhat furtive exchanges with Arbatov outside the Institute's offices and conference rooms. In all cases he has given the impression that the information discussed is strictly off the record, a personal confidence to be respected.

Even sensible scholars, blessed with such a confidence, feel a fierce determination to protect Arbatov's image. They insist that he is the one Soviet deserving of trust. Professing expertise on Soviet matters requires that serious academics make periodic visits to the font, adding a further inducement to believe Arbatov, since he can exert controls on visits and introductions. The institute is one of the few Moscow organizations with subscriptions to Western magazines. Yet in the so-called open library of the institute, *Time* and *Newsweek* are treated as classified documents available only to appropriately cleared members of Arbatov's staff.

Arbatov came close to becoming a media personality in the United States, when one of the major TV networks planned to put him on the air nightly to comment on the 1980 election campaign process. Fortunately, this particular hare was caught and caged before Arbatov saw the red lights of the cameras.

Though a sycophant of Brezhnev's, Arbatov had the agility to make the transition to Andropov without missing a beat in resuming his Comrade Congeniality role with the new tenant. He is a sympathetic listener and a superb judge of fools. When required, he can drop his scholarly mien and procure compliant companions for visiting U.S. officials after a long day of reconstructing the world at the conference table.

His utility is evident because of his wide American acquaintanceship and his remarkable degree of familiarity with the U.S. decision-making process. He is one of the best sources—if not the only source, in the Soviet scheme of things—able to provide the Kremlin leadership with personalized, accurate, and timely measures of the attitudes of the U.S. leadership. There are very few among the American political elite, in or out of office, who don't know Arbatov (each on a *highly personal and privileged basis*). Georgi Arbatov is considered by many leaders of American public opinion to be an honest broker trying to build bridges between the United States and the Soviet Union. To suggest that Arbatov is an agent whose purpose is to probe for weaknesses and areas of indecision and irresolution is, at best, a serious social gaffe if not an obvious fascist calumny.

Ordinarily, Arbatov might be thought wrongly accused, except that his institute's Washington representatives have impugned his objectivity by their repeated exposure as KGBniks. Despite the KGB's careful vetting of nominees for posts in the United States, two of Arbatov's best "scholars" recently fell out of their diplomatic tree.

Georgi Mamedov, a golden son of the Bolshevik elite, impressed some in Washington as a tireless advocate of disarmament and détente. He argued the case with considerable skill, not as a Soviet diplomat but as a dedicated scholar representing the Institute for the Study of the USA and Canada. He had one unfortunate habit. When he became bored, tired, or drunk, he took vengeance on his young wife and beat her to restore his flagging spirits.

In April 1982, a badly bruised Madame Mamedova escaped from the Soviet compound and spent the weekend with the FBI. Apparently, she had no intention to defect, just an urge to give Georgi something to think about. Returning to the compound early in the next week, she was immediately found to be "overwrought" and was bustled aboard Aeroflot for the long ride to the psychiatric ward of the Serbsky. Georgi returned to Moscow, where it is generally accepted that he was diagnosed by the KGB as requiring discipline, a new wife, and a much shorter leash.

More recently, Arbatov's scholar in residence at the Soviet embassy in Washington, Valentin Mikhailovich Berezhkov, an old-line Chekist, was described by Peter Deriabin, a former KGB colleague, as a man who "wears a long tail." His forty-five-year career in Soviet espionage began under Stalin and continued under Andropov. In the period of the Nazi-Soviet nonaggression pact, he was attached to the Soviet trade mission in Berlin, not as a scholar but as an engineer. He dropped engineering and took up "interpreting," so that he was on hand for the Teheran Conference and the early organization of the United Nations. Finding little stimulation in interpreting, Berezhkov switched to journalism and became a "special correspondent" for the KGB-run *Novoye Vremya (New Times)*. Another former KGB officer, Stanislav A. Levchenko, has pointed out that *New Times* reserves twelve of its fourteen foreign bureaus for the exclusive use of the organs. Berezhkov's former boss and role model, Vladimir Dekanozov, was executed along with Beria. By the 1960s, Berezhkov felt the tug of academe and moved to Arbatov's institute.

He was assigned to the Soviet embassy in Washington and was avidly pursuing his studies when, in the late summer of 1983, he was subjected to unwanted exposure in the matter of a letter to *The New York Times* from his sixteen-year-old son, who expressed a desire to defect. His exalted rank notwithstanding, Valentin was removed along with his errant son to Moscow to explain why an "Honored Chekist" with "a long tail" can't control an enterprising teenager. As W. S. Gilbert noted years ago, "A policeman's lot is not a happy one."

Arbatov's "confidential exchanges" usually induce the beneficiary to reciprocate with one of his own, making Georgi one of the best informed

Soviet experts on the U.S. political system and its players. When President Reagan was deciding whether or not to withdraw the sanctions applied to European firms that exported U.S. equipment to the USSR for use in building the Soviet gas pipeline, Arbatov was dispatched to Washington to lobby in favor of the "rational" decision. The President changed his mind, withdrew the sanctions, and the Soviets got what they needed. A few days later, Arbatov returned to Moscow having earned another "well done, good and faithful servant" award from the Kremlin.

Arbatov is an effective vaudevillist and produces remarkable shows for visiting U.S. academics, politicians, and businessmen. Through his magic of melding rhetoric and reality, reasonably intelligent visitors have returned after a seance at the institute to voice Arbatov's tendentious justifications for the Soviet invasion of Afghanistan. Machiavelli's Prince could envy his charlatan's arts in deception and manipulation.

Others have written much about KGB disinformation and its effectiveness.[28] Although disinformation has been used extensively in support of Soviet objectives, it is frequently trivialized as a threat and accorded little importance by Western observers. A clear distinction must be made between Soviet disinformation and Soviet propaganda. The latter might be described as directly attributable to the Soviets, the satellites, the client states, or the obviously predisposed. Disinformation is seldom attributable to these sources and depends on its false attribution to an ally, to "discovered" classified documents that purport to reveal plans to attack the USSR, and to other rumors, forgeries, and orchestrated deceptions with enough verifiable content to raise serious doubt among allies. For example, the conflicting accounts of new "evidence" in the papal assassination plot succeeded for a time in diffusing public attention and deflecting focus from the USSR.

Another among the valued means of war available to the Soviets is terrorism. No nation in the world can claim parity with the USSR in this bloody arena. The Soviet leaders, having practiced and refined the art in their war against the Russian people, know more about this vicious and dangerous tool than anyone else on the globe.

Outside the USSR, terrorism is at best a tactic of limited applicability. It is only a potentially contributory means to accomplish political and military ends. Quite often, it can prove to be counterproductive, because it tends to provoke increased security measures in the target country, and it intimidates those the Soviets want to win over to their side. Yet, trained terrorists under effective discipline can function in support of Soviet policy, especially when they are used selectively to eliminate those who constitute a genuine threat to long-term Soviet objectives.

Political assassination, as the Soviet and other experience indicates, is an unpredictable weapon. Its use frequently creates martyrs and gives the political opposition renewed momentum at a time when its power would otherwise diminish. Also, political assassination must depend on flawless execution at the propitious moment. It cannot be undertaken too early, nor can it be delayed, because of the ever-present threat of detection, retaliation, and other unintended consequences.

Andropov has always been aware of the subtleties and nuances of terrorism. Such was his experience and his proven attitudes that the circumstantial case alleging his direct knowledge of the attempt on the life of Pope John Paul II is highly credible. The decision, obviously, was not Andropov's alone to make. It required approval by Brezhnev and the benediction of Suslov, the party's ideologist, who justified the act as he had the invasion of Afghanistan. With the consent of the leadership the planning, direction, and timing was assigned to the KGB. The act itself was relatively straightforward, so that the burden of the planning concerned itself with the contingencies that might arise from failure. Such a plan usually provides for the extrication or murder of the assassin. In this instance the trial of attribution was so indistinct that initial assertions that Agca was a "right-wing fanatic" or a "Muslim fundamentalist" deflected the world press and served the Soviet interest. The assassin's control was exerted by the KGB through successive echelons of Bulgarians, right-wing Turks, and religious fundamentalists, ensuring that no Soviet telltales would emerge and that any reaction or reprisal would be confused.

The rationale of the attack was based on the Soviets' conviction that the Pope's support of Lech Walesa and the unprecedented Solidarity movement threatened the Soviets' continued control of the Polish state. The Pope's open letter declaring his determination to go to Poland, if necessary, to resist Soviet armed intervention raised the stakes. A Soviet decision to act would produce unpredictable consequences, and risk is not a component of Soviet decision making. It was conceivable that sending Soviet armed forces into Poland to "pacify" the Poles might provoke widespread resistance by the people and by a disaffected Polish army, thus opening the way to other counteractions that could lead to a war. Brezhnev and Andropov had reason to fear this scenario. The Soviet leadership, unlike some Western leaders, knew the true state of readiness of the Soviet armed forces.

Here again an unplanned event came to the aid of Andropov and the organs. This time it was the failed assassination attempt on President Reagan. Following Hinckley's shooting of the President, Secretary of State Alexander Haig made an overly anxious, nonreassuring statement that he was in control of the government. Haig's ill-considered assumptions confirmed to Andropov that no one was really in charge, that no one was able to take or order decisive action against the Soviet Union. The situation was not materially different during the President's convalescence.

The hiatus provided the "window of opportunity" needed to launch the Bulgarian proxies and others in an attempt to kill Pope John Paul. It is probable that if the President had been fit and in command, the Soviets would not have run the risk of the attack, despite their carefully planned program of denial. With Reagan *hors de combat,* the risk entailed in an attempt on the Pope was considerably reduced while retaining its potentially high payoff. Even with the failure of the assassination, Andropov's advocacy has been vindicated. Soviet tanks did not have to roll into Warsaw, and Solidarity has gone off the boil to a less threatening simmer.

Andropov demonstrated that he was a man of many talents and not another gray, faceless drudge from the depths of the organs. He more closely resembled Dzerzhinsky than any of his predecessors, as evidenced by his redefining of the USSR in ways that the West has been slow to recognize. A source who knew Andropov both socially and professionally (circa 1969), described the way in which he began to make himself and his ideas known to the young KGB novitiates as they took up their places in the organs. Like Dzerzhinsky before him, Andropov knew the kinds of men and women he was looking for, and he showed unexpected personal concern with the selection of young officers. Today these men and women are the majors, lieutenant colonels, and colonels of a thoroughly reinvigorated service. Discipline and loyalty are the prevailing virtues, originally defined by Dzerzhinsky and reaffirmed by Andropov. In the main, these officers are skilled, motivated, and professional. *Tufta,* the endemic curse of the Bolsheviks, has been offset somewhat by perks, benefits, and status. By no measure can the organs be certified as "clean" in anything other than a Soviet context. The distribution of the Andropov recruits throughout the organs ensured a kind of compliance that no leader has had since Stalin.

Unlike Stalin, who promoted toadies and hacks, Andropov concentrated on promoting "up" rather than the customary inclination of leaders to promote "down." This procedure entails the leader's effort to identify people who are more intelligent and better qualified than he. Frequently, when such ability is found in a bureaucracy, the talent is punished rather than rewarded. The less well equipped tend to rise because they, like the leaders, seek homogeneity, ease of administration, and the other reassuring traits that guarantee a puddinglike consistency of median efficiency.

Within the most politically oriented society in the world, Andropov was able to put his men and women into positions of great and growing power. The group cannot be seen as resembling political hacks or "ticket punchers" of the sort seen in the past. Rather, they are the "best and the toughest" the Soviet system has been able to produce in nearly seven decades. The aim was reinforced dedication to achieving primacy in the world for the USSR—the goal envisioned by Dzerzhinsky.

Andropov did not stand in isolation. His rise required the efforts of loyalists who willingly served his interests. Their names are not familiar to the general public, but they have captured the attention of some Kremlinologists.

First among Andropov's "eagles" was Viktor M. Chebrikov. His official biography runs to twelve lines in the official Soviet yearbook, revealing only that he trained as a metallurgical engineer, served in the army in World War II, and rose to prominence in Dnepropetrovsk, the Ukrainian city where Brezhnev was once party chief. Chebrikov was a young lieutenant under Brezhenv and, as such, became acutely aware of the corruption of the boss and his cronies (most of whom later went on to important positions during the Brezhnev era). Chebrikov was a dutiful officer but was at some pains to avoid being drawn into the morass of political *tufta*. His aberrant behavior was attributed to juvenile idealism and not considered a fatal flaw. Brezhnev liked Chebrikov and enjoyed the young man, who professed all the ideals Brezhnev had outgrown. In the immediate postwar period the Ukrainian people were severely punished for their ambivalent loyalty during the war, and the area was awash in punitive pillaging led by the party's man, Brezhnev.

Caught up in the milieu of Brezhnev's intrigues, Chebrikov was in a curious position. He knew the methods of personal enrichment that were used, but his youth and subordinate position made it difficult for him to exploit the knowledge. In consequence, his willingness to "go along to get along" while remaining silent commended him to Brezhnev in a way that was more important than any demonstration of soldierly virtue or heroism.

Brezhnev seemed to be in Stalin's favor; Chebrikov shared in the glow. Early in the fifties, by random occurrence, he served on a junior-to mid-level promotion panel. Quite by chance, Andropov was detailed to the same assignment. The work was dreary, demanding, and boring to the degree that all of the panel members were anxious to be elsewhere. In the course of the assignment the two men found that they shared many interests and strong ideological cants that were surprisingly congruent. Out of the chance meeting and the curious personal chemistry Andropov and Chebrikov became friends. Though ten years older, Andropov felt a kinship with Chebrikov that he had not found among his peers.

The duty lasted for only two weeks, at which time both men returned to their regular duties in the compartmentalized warrens of the organs. Years later, when Andropov was designated resident in Hungary and soon became ambassador, he requested that Chebrikov be sent to Budapest as his deputy.

With Brezhnev's confidence and Andropov's sponsorship, Chebrikov was a relatively young man on an exceedingly fast track. By 1971, he was named a delegate to the 24th Party Congress, a position that had been routinely denied other members of the organs. Like Andropov, he seemed to have broken tradition when, in 1973, at the age of forty-seven, he was "elected" a candidate member of the Central Committee of the 25th Party Congress. Two years later, at the 26th Party Congress, Chebrikov was elevated to full membership in the Central Committee. In 1983, he was promoted to the rank of full general and chairman of the KGB. His rapid promotions were without precedent, suggesting that Andropov had already decided who would control the organs in the future. Chebrikov's only major political statement does little more than echo a strong party line, more consistent with the aims of Dzerzhinsky than of Brezhnev.[29]

Second among Andropov's "eagles" was Vitali V. Fedorchuk. In May 1982, when Andropov moved from the KGB to take up the post of Communist Party General Secretary in anticipation of his takeover in the wake of Brezhnev's death, he selected Fedorchuk as his replacement. Fedorchuk was also from the Ukraine, where he had headed the KGB since 1970. Andropov's decision was based on the need to give Fedorchuk some Moscow experience before his next assignment, Minister of Internal Affairs (MVD). This appointment was made on December 17, 1982, one month after Brezhnev's death and Andropov's elevation to General Secretary. At the same time Chebrikov succeeded Fedorchuk as chairman of the KGB.

The significance of these bureaucratic moves can be seen in the fact that it took Stalin almost seven years to bring the organs and the MVD under full and effective control, whereas Andropov accomplished the same feat in seven months. Fedorchuk's mission was simply stated: To crack down on corruption and fraud in the Soviet Union. Within weeks bureaucratic heads began rolling quietly in the corridors of the great Soviet bureaucracy, and the *tufta* men were in full flight. Andropov's dedication to this problem was genuine for the elemental reason that the Soviet Union was (and is still) more severely threatened by internal corruption than by any external menace. Fedorchuk is described as a humorless, unrelenting purger with an unforgiving nature. Just the right man to fight corruption.

Two others qualified as "eaglets" in Andropov's aviary. One is Gaidar Aliyev, another KGB officer who was appointed as first deputy prime minister in November 1982. The second, Dmitri I. Yakushkin, was brought back from the United States in late 1981 to oversee a major restructuring of the KGB's foreign operations. Yakushkin carried out the role previously played by Andropov in managing the KGB's multinational assets. Because of his extensive service in the United States—from

1963 to 1969, in the Soviet UN delegation as head of KGB operations, and from 1975 to 1981 as the "legal" (diplomatic) resident in the Soviet embassy in Washington—he is extraordinarily qualified to do the job.

In Yakushkin, the Kremlin leaders have what has been sorely lacking in the Center for more than a decade—someone with sufficient hands-on experience and rank to deal with matters affecting the USSR in its relationship to the United States.

These, then, are some of the key persons selected by Andropov to control the USSR and to operate the organs. They will exert real power in the years ahead, and each of them shares Andropov's legacy of a new sense of purpose and discipline. Whether the eaglets will be corrupted eventually by their new power cannot be known. In the meantime we can be certain that the organs have been fully restored as the sword and shield of the party, and that the party is under KGB control.

The death of Andropov in early February 1984, and the emergence of Konstantin Ustinovich Chernenko as his successor, gave rise to speculation in the West about the expected future behavior of the USSR. It was confidently stated by some that Andropov's "confrontational policies" had failed, so that the world could now expect a return to a pro-détente policy of accommodation. Others insisted that, since the USSR must have Western credits to meet imperative domestic economic needs, the prospects of new, rational trade relationships were bound to follow.

These cheery and not unfamiliar promises for the future were predicated on the fundamental assumption that the powerful conservatism of the Soviet leadership has succeeded in maintaining its primacy, and that Chernenko emerged as a bona fide Soviet leader. A familiar old party fixture, Chernenko is best remembered for his long and faithful service to Brezhnev as drinking companion, factotum, and valet. He can be considered by most measurements as perhaps the most inexperienced man in the Kremlin. He is without background in industry, the military, science, art, agriculture, party organization, or, for that matter, as a competent Marxist-Leninist ideologue.

His limited involvement in government included a period when, under Brezhnev's patronage, he was a ranking party official in Moldavia. Before Andropov's death, *Pravda* directed the world's attention to the astonishing levels of corruption recently discovered by the vigilant KGB in the Moldavian SSR. The *Pravda* story was interpreted by knowing Soviets as a signal that Chernenko was likely to become a compromised casualty of the anticorruption campaign then under way.

The fact that Chernenko exhibited no known skills or high-level experience, that he owed his all to Brezhnev, and that he had a reputation in his own right as a participant in wide-scale Moldavian corruption, made his later selection as General Secretary of the Soviet Communist Party an improbable event. Additionally, he was chronically ill with circulatory and lung ailments of a near critical nature. Yet, this least able, most compromised man was named to act as the operative head of the Soviet government.

News of Chernenko's appointment was interpreted by Russian black marketeers (as it was by Western diplomats) as a clear sign of a veering away from Andropov's steely version of neo-Stalinism. His ascension also gave the general appearance that the collegial will of the party still prevailed and that the spirit of Brezhnev lived. The promotion and propagation of such impressions among foreign and domestic observers was tactically important to the Soviet leadership. It bought time so that when significant changes do occur in the future, they will appear as part of the familiar evolutionary process rather than a sharp decision for change.

The coalition of military and KGB representatives previously elevated to the Central Committee and Politburo by Andropov now control the essential levers of Soviet power. Men in their late seventies, such as Premier Nikolai Tikhonov, the late Defense Minister Marshal Dmitri Ustinov, and Andrei Gromyko, the durable Foreign Minister, were, apart from their own limited and personal constituencies, powerless to muster any effective opposition, even if so disposed, to the ambitions of the younger men in their midst.

In a historical context Tikhonov gave the regime the same sense of continuity that Stalin promoted in his use of Voroshilov. It has always been important to have someone handy who can attest to the days on the barricades and the revolutionary struggle under Lenin even if as a teenager.

Ustinov, until his death, offered important strengths to the regime, since he represented a rare combination of talents. Though trained as an engineer, he carried a marshal's baton and, despite the fact that he was not a professional soldier, enjoyed wide acceptance among the ranking military leaders. His instincts were highly developed, and his comprehension of internal Soviet political realities made him a valuable and effective adjunct to the regime.

Gromyko, a technician with unparalleled experience in foreign affairs, has played an essential role as foreign minister and *consigliere* to the Politburo on matters relating to the outside world. From his uninterrupted, forty-five-year-long perch near the top, Gromyko, like Ustinov, is nothing if not a practical man.

Gromyko's detailed comprehension of U.S. men and mores, when coupled with the special insights of the KGB's Dmitri Yakushkin and Georgi Arbatov of the Institute for the Study of the USA and Canada, has provided extraordinary depth, strength, clarity, and realism to any new policy formations by the Politburo on matters affecting the United States.

Yakushkin, on assuming his new duties, followed in Andropov's trail and began to tighten the control, coordination, and discipline among the satellite intelligence services, especially in connection with their respective roles in the scientific and technical collection missions targeted against the United States. As deputy chairman of the KGB, with broad personal experience in conducting operations in the United States, Yakushkin is the KGB's resident expert on the subject of the United States (or, as the KGB prefers, the "main adversary").

The elder statesmen, along with Chernenko, were absolutely essential to support the illusions of gradualism, collegiality, and continuity, while the younger Andropov eaglets—Chebrikov, Aliyev, Vorotnikov, Gorbachev, and Romanov—decide on the future.

The outward calm and consistency of the change of power have reinforced the biases of those (black marketeers and foreign diplomats) who wanted to believe that Chernenko signaled a return to the calm of the Brezhnev era. Nowhere was this absurdity more evident than in the minds of the apparatchiks in the higher reaches of the Soviet international bureaucracies. The senior ambassadors, delegation heads, and the beneficiaries of Brezhnev who were serving in foreign diplomatic posts, the UN, or elsewhere now know that the old standards of competence and loyalty by which Soviet success is gauged are under revision. The shift of power had changed the system that was built and nurtured on the security of symmetry. The introduction of new and unknown factors regarding alignments, repudiated policies, personal associations, sponsors and the unending accountability for all previous words and actions was a paralytic agent familiar to all senior Soviet officials. All of these men had direct knowledge of the swing of the KGB's sword, and all know that they are vulnerable to attack.

Several Western pundits urged an immediate summit meeting with Chernenko, demonstrating U.S. goodwill and an earnest desire to facilitate constructive new understandings. During the process of realignment within the Politburo, however, such a meeting would have the same substantive content as a half-hour conference with Peter Rabbit or the Tin Woodman.

The 1953 execution of Beria and the separation of the MVD from the minister of state security's portfolio were actions taken by frightened men following the death of Stalin. At the time it was intended that no other man gain the oppressive powers of Beria.

When Chebrikov succeeded Fedorchuk as KGB chairman and was elected as an alternate member of the Politburo, two other KGB men, Gaidar Aliyev and Vitali Vorotnikov, were also made members of the

Politburo by Andropov. The two key jobs in the Central Committee, personnel chief and secretary, were also filled by KGB apparatchiks. Like Stalin, Andropov, Fedorchuk, Chebrikov understood the power of clerical work.

With the pragmatic old men, the recently elected military members, the new KGB members, a KGB secretariat, and the guiding hand of Viktor Chebrikov, the USSR no longer resembles any previously known form. The party, supported by the KGB and the armed forces, no longer retains its comforting *primus inter partes* symmetry. The KGB now operates the USSR, and Chebrikov heads the KGB. The lessons of Marshal Beria's fatal attempt at power have been fully absorbed by the eaglets who now control the engine of Soviet power.

EPILOGUE

January 11, 1984. The Supreme Soviet Presidium approved a decree that strengthened and broadened the provisions of the old laws dealing with treason, sabotage, anti-Soviet agitation and propaganda, the transmittal of "work-related secrets" and economic data to foreigners, and discipline in corrective labor camps. The decree was signed by Andropov and entered into force on February 1, 1984.

The new definition of treason allows virtually any political offender to be charged with treason, given the all-encompassing meaning of "state security" in Soviet usage. The specified punishments (fifteen years' imprisonment plus five years of internal exile and confiscation of personal property, or death) remain unchanged.

The charge of sabotage (rarely invoked since Stalin's death) now includes aircraft hijacking, political terrorism, or responsibility for disasters *including major environment pollution,* and the penalty remains the same as for treason.

Under the new formulation, the author or owner of any written material, reproduction, object, or art form deemed to be "anti-Soviet" can be prosecuted even if it was not shown or given to another person.

The maximum penalty has been increased from seven to ten years' imprisonment. Those at risk include independent writers who receive payments from foreign publishers; recipients and distributors of aid from the Russian Social Fund to Aid Political Prisoners and Their Families (also known as the Solzhenitsyn Fund), and so-called refuseniks who receive parcels or other aid from Western Jewish organizations or private individuals, including foreign citizens who provide such aid while visiting the USSR. Such foreigners need not even be members of foreign organizations—it is enough if they are found to be "acting in the interest" of foreign organizations.

The new article (13.1) has expanded the definition of "state secret" to include the concept of "work-related secrets" (*sluzhebnaya tayna*) and has criminalized contacts between activists and foreigners. Depending on the political realities of the moment, enforcement can be expanded to include almost anyone. The purpose is to disrupt all contacts between foreigners and activists. All information about the Soviet Union is a state secret unless it has been approved for official release. The language of the article is designed to serve as the basis for prosecuting anyone for divulging any kind of information acquired in any way whatever; it makes any Soviet citizen having contact with a foreigner (including diplomats, journalists, academics, and businessmen) vulnerable to criminal charges.

Article 14.1 is designed to protect prison-camp informers (i.e., those who have "entered on the path of reform") from reprisals by inmates, including political prisoners. It can also be used to punish inmates for any show of solidarity or organized opposition to the camp administration, whether by joint protest, hunger strike, or the preparation of signed declarations.

April 19, 1984. Konstantin Chernenko bestowed the rank of marshal and the Order of Lenin on KGB Chairman Viktor Chebrikov. On the same occasion, Minister of Defense Ustinov and Politburo member Mikhail Solomentsev (a Brezhnev antagonist and supporter of Andropov's) were also honored.

May 24, 1984. C. William Verity, Jr., cochairman of the U.S.-USSR Trade and Economic Council, a private organization of 220 American companies and 125 Soviet foreign trade enterprises, said "trade is trade" and should be separated from political issues.

The two-day council meeting in New York was attended by a Soviet trade and economic mission led by Vladimir N. Shushkov (also cochairman of the council) and the Soviet ambassador to the United States, Anatoli Dobrynin. Donald M. Kendall, chairman of Pepsico, was on the dais.

Verity claimed that American companies are losing $10 billion a year in sales because of U.S. government restrictions. Shushkov said trade between the United States and the USSR *could* be in the $22–$25 billion range (emphasis added).—*The New York Times,* May 25, 1984.

May, 1984. KGB Chairman Viktor Chebrikov visited East Berlin and Prague to discuss "questions of mutual cooperation among friendly security corps."

May, 1984. Vitali Levin, known in the West as Victor Louis, first announced that the USSR would boycott the 1984 Olympic Games. Levin is remembered as the journalist who "leaked" the first account of Premier Khrushchev's ouster. Andrea Lee, author of *Russian Journal,* writes that in 1978 she was warned, prior to a visit to Levin's stately home outside Moscow, that "Viktor Louis is KGB, how else could a Soviet journalist write for Western papers?"—*Washington Times,* September 18, 1984.

May 25, 1984. A new decree, effective July 1, 1984, specified fines for Soviet citizens who provide foreigners with "housing or means of transportation or . . . other services in violation of the established [undefined] regulations." The decree is intended to discourage Soviet citizens from inviting foreigners to stay overnight in their homes without the required preliminary registration with authorities or providing foreigners with other services, such as the use of a car or assistance in purchasing train or airline tickets.

The decree can be used against "stateless persons" (Soviet Jews who have renounced Soviet citizenship as a condition of immigration and who have not yet departed the USSR). Such persons, having lost their internal passport, employment, personal possessions, former apartments, and even their right to remain in the locality of their former residence, are particularly at risk under the new decree, as are any friends or relatives who extend help to "stateless persons."

During Stalin's time, labor camp commanders had the authority to resentence and extend the confinement of political prisoners to prevent their release. New Article 188.3 of the Russian Republic (RSFSR) criminal code has been added to restore such authority to the administrators of the corrective labor camps and other penal institutions. Under the provisions of 188.3, camp and prison commanders can charge inmates with "malicious disobedience to its lawful demands" and administratively extend the prisoner's period of confinement. Conviction under the new decree carries a punishment of an additional three to five years—Based on July 1984 *Foreign Affairs Note,* prepared by the Department of State.

May 27, 1984. The Amtorg Trading Company in New York celebrated sixty years of continuous operations as the oldest commercial cover station outside the USSR.

May 1984. The KGB, in an effort to improve its image, has offered prizes for the best books, motion pictures, and television programs that deal with its activities in internal security and foreign intelligence. The competition was announced in connection with plans for its seventieth anniversary in late 1987.—*The New York Times,* May, 30, 1984.

September 11, 1984. Stalin's daughter, Svetlana Alliluyeva, was put into contact with the Soviet embassy in London to "request" permission to return to the USSR.

September 18, 1984. Fifteen states refused to traffic in the sale of Soviet-made Stolichnaya vodka after the shooting down of Korean airliner 007 on September 1, 1983, but eight have resumed sales. A spokesman for the distributor explained that sales are "back to where we were before the Korean incident and we're growing very well." (The firm expects 1984 imports to reach 1,605,000 gallons, with an estimated contribution to the Soviet government of $64 million.)

September 24, 1984. The wife of the first secretary of the Soviet embassy at Oslo, Norway, was detained by the Norwegian police after she had attempted to exchange a U.S. $500 bill of a series that went out of circulation in 1937. The woman was released on the grounds of diplomatic immunity.

September 24, 1984. Secretary General Chernenko was awarded the Order of Lenin for service to the CPUSSR on his seventy-third birthday.

September 1984. West German authorities arrested and charged with commiting espionage Manfred Rotsch, a sixty-year-old aircraft designer and planning manager for Messerschmidt-Belkow-Blohm (MBB), West Germany's premier aerospace company. It is reported that Rotsch's espionage has jeopardized the effectiveness of the Tornado fighter aircraft being built in West Germany, Italy, and Britain. Rotsch was caught in the act of retrieving secret MBB documents from a dead drop in a forest. Also believed compromised are the Transall military transport aircraft, the Roland, the Milan, and the Hot missiles made by MBB.—*Washington Post,* October 24, 1984.

September 1984. Marshal Nikolai Ogarkov, First Deputy Defense Minister and Chief of the Soviet General Staff, was abruptly removed from his post and reassigned. Ogarkov is the official who explained, on worldwide television, why Soviet defense considerations required the shooting down of the Korean Air Lines flight 007.

October 2, 1984. FBI agent Richard W. Miller was arrested in Los Angeles along with Svetlana Ogorodnikova and her husband Nikolai Ogorodnikov. All were charged with violations of the Espionage Act. Also involved in the case were "diplomatic" officers Alexsander Chikvaidze and vice-consul Viktor Zonev, both of whom are assigned to the Soviet consulate in San Francisco. (It is invariable that KGB espionage cases are supervised and operated only by KGB officers.)

October 2, 1984. Alice Michelson was arrested and charged with espionage by the FBI prior to her departure from Kennedy International airport for Europe. Michelson was carrying information and materials received from a U.S. Army sergeant. KGB officers "Misha," "Dima," and "Konstantinov" of the Soviet embassy in Mexico City were involved in inducing the sergeant to sell defense data. The sergeant had reported the approaches made to him in Germany in 1981, and was instructed to maintain contact with the KGB officers. The Army worked with the FBI in operating the case during the three-year period.

November 2, 1984. Zdzislaw M. Rurarz, former Polish ambassador to Japan who defected to the West after General Jaruzelski declared martial law in December 1981, stated that "as a former member of the Polish communist party, with over thirty-six years as a government and party official, twenty-five of which were in association with military intelligence, I can say with certainty that the SB (Polish intelligence) is penetrated and guided by the KGB. The SB is strictly forbidden to wage operations without KGB approval, whereas the KGB has a free hand to do what ever it deems necessary to maintain order in Poland."—*Wall Street Journal,* November 2, 1984.

November 3, 1984. No date has been set for the trial of Richard Craig Smith, a former U.S. Army counterintelligence officer accused of providing the identities of six American double agents to a Soviet intelligence officer for $11,000.

The spirit and, certainly, the remains of Joseph Stalin have been on the move since his death in 1953. The body, first entombed with Lenin's in the great Mausoleum in Red Square, was removed in 1961 and later interred near the Kremlin wall. The move followed a two-day denouncement of Stalin and his crimes by Khrushchev in a marathon speech before the Twentieth Party Congress. The concrete slab on Stalin's new resting place bears only his name, date of birth, and date of death.

In 1970, a bust of Stalin was added in a first, tentative effort to rehabilitate the reputation of the bloodiest of tyrants. Contemporary Soviet history had been heavily edited after his death, and references to his long (1927–1953) rule were expunged or minimized to the extent that very few Russians under the age of forty know who he was and what he did. Older citizens who survived his depredations look back with a strange nostalgia to the period, when the revolution was vibrantly alive along with their hopes for the future. The kindness of time has diffused and diminished recollections of the terror, the trials, the war, and the terrible torments of their lives. Instead, they contrast the corrupt, inefficient Soviet government of today with an imperfectly recalled sense of the excitement and political dynamics of Stalin's time.

It is precisely the effect of this bleak comparison that energized Andropov and his KGB successors to attempt to reverse the internal decay that is destroying the USSR. The KGB's co-opting of the MVD, the recently promulgated laws (harsher than any known since Stalin), the internal war against *tufta* in industry, agriculture, and the bloated bureaucracy, are clear imperatives for survival of the present Soviet power elite.

In anticipation of the fortieth anniversary of the end of the war with Germany, Stalin's ghost is emerging from the crypt. This time Stalin is seen as the commander-in-chief of the Red armies that destroyed Hitler and as the diplomatist whose wise counsel guided the USSR to its present role as a great power.

It is apparent that his resurrection is judged essential to the current regime because it provides a paradigm of strong, purposeful leadership at a time when it is desperately needed. The induced return of his daughter* was important to the process, to ensure that his carefully crafted new image would not be subjected to more of her acidic revelations. The regime's return to "Stalinism" (once a perjorative term) is necessary to permit the imposition of even more stringent controls in the USSR. The apathetic Soviet citizens have long been willing to exchange their commitment to world revolution and the march to socialism for any small improvement in their lives or food ration. A move toward Stalinism bodes ill for all, but the incumbent leaders have exhausted their options; they must devise means to recapture the 270 million Russian people or sit in witness of the certain, though gradual, disintegration of the Soviet Empire.

Thirty years ago, in the brief period of relaxation after Stalin's death, Yevgenni Yevtushenko, a celebrated Russian poet wrote a prophetic warning for the world:

Mute was the marble. Mutely glimmered the glass.
Mute stood the sentries, bronzed by the breeze.
Thin wisps of smoke curled over the coffin. And breath seeped through the chinks
As they bore him out the mausoleum doors.
Slowly the coffin floated, grazing the fixed bayonets.
He was also mute—he also—mute and dead.
Grimly clenching his embalmed fists,
Just pretending to be dead, he watched from inside . . .
He was scheming. Had merely dozed off.
And I, appealing to our government, petitioned them
to double, and treble, the sentries guarding this slab,
and stop Stalin from ever rising again and, with Stalin, the past . . .

From *The Poetry of Yevgenni Yevtushenko,* trans. George Reavey (New York: October House Inc., 1965, 1969), p. 161.

*The KGB's role in inducing her decision to return to the USSR could only have gladdened the hearts of those who remember that, at the time of her defection in 1967, the KGB was blamed for failing to stop her and the then chairman, Vladimir Semichastny, was dismissed from his post.

November 7, 1984. Marshal Dmitri F. Ustinov, USSR Minister of Defense, failed to appear at the Red Square celebration marking the sixty-seventh anniversary of the Bolshevik seizure of power. He was last seen in public on September 27.

November 12, 1984. Five Romanian "diplomats" were expelled from West Germany in connection with a plan to bomb the headquarters of Radio Free Europe in Munich. The diplomats were all identified by the German police as Romanian secret police officials.

November 26, 1984. Karl F. Koecher was arrested by the FBI enroute to board a flight from Kennedy International Airport to Europe. Koecher was charged with espionage. It was alleged that he had been trained by the Czech intelligence service as an "illegal" assigned to operate in the United States. For a brief period Koecher was a CIA contract employee.

December 3, 1984. Konstantin Chernenko, who did not serve in the Soviet armed forces during the Great Patriotic War, was celebrated in a new film, *Outpost of Youth. Pravda* reports that the film evokes "with emotion, those unforgettable years (1930–1933)" when Chernenko was a private in the Kazakhstan OGPU Border Guards—*Washington Post,* December 3, 1984.

December 7, 1984. Dr. Armand Hammer pronounced Konstantin Chernenko "very much the boss" when he met him in Moscow on December 4, 1984. Hammer said Soviet officials had told him "the human rights situation in their country would change if relations with the superpowers improved." Hammer again urged President Reagan to consider signing a treaty with the Soviet Union in which both countries agreed not to use force—Reuters, December 7, 1984.

December 16, 1984. Mikhail Sergeevich Gorbachev met with British Prime Minister Thatcher for five hours of discussion of East-West issues. Gorbachev's selection to lead the eighteen-member Soviet delegation to the InterParliamentary Union meeting in London provided an informal means to confirm his nominal new roles as both the heir-apparent to Chernenko as well as the youngest and brightest member of the Politburo. His long and intimate association with a succession of major failures in Soviet agricultural programs does not seem to impair his new image.

Gorbachev is reputed to be a pragmatic, technically competent leader who carries only a light ideological burden and is an ideal counterweight to the granitelike implacability of Gromyko. While in England, he displayed great skill in repeatedly stressing the point that resolve on the part of the United States to pursue the research and development of the Strategic Defense Initiative was an intolerable menace not only to the USSR but to all of Western Europe as well. In a large measure, the U.S. media can claim credit for the now almost universal use of the nondescriptive, misleading, and frightening term "Star Wars," which the Soviets have been quick to incorporate into their standard lexicon. "Star Wars" has come to be thought of by hundreds of millions of people as a system that is offensive in nature and wholly unpredictable in its consequences. It now implies a future of high-tech terror with an irresponsible American finger on the trigger.

During the visit, Gorbachev made a point of stressing the benefits of expanded trade with the USSR, a gambit which has lost none of its appeal over the years. The visit to the United Kingdom is best seen as an "Off-Broadway" opening. The English-language press faithfully quoted the Prime Minister's gracious remarks about him and Gorbachev's public persona succeeded in softening some public perceptions of the character and intentions of the new Soviet leadership.

Throughout Soviet history, deception has always been the state's most formidable weapon. It has been used to gain allies, to discourage enemies, and to control internal affairs. In the past, every member of the Soviet leadership who has been accused of advocating liberalization and "reform" within the Bolshevik ranks has been found later to have only played a role in the attainment of some other fundamental Soviet objectives. Litvinov, Mikoyan, and even Khrushchev have had major speaking parts in the Soviet international theater, yet none of their advocated reforms was put into effect.

Manifestations of Soviet goodwill and a disposition to negotiate are perhaps the most accurate indications of the scope of the genuine internal problems of insufficient food, pressing nationality issues, and an inefficient and failing economy which cannot be concealed, particularly from the 270 million apathetic Soviet citizens who live within the system.

With the gradual but certain consolidation of the KGB's dominance of the Politburo, the Central Committee, and the military, there is no rational argument on which to base expectations of any concessions or reforms in the future. Disruption of cohesion among the Western allies, the deferral or cancellation of the United States' Strategic Defense Initiative, and sufficient respite in which to institute new internal controls are the preoccupations of the ruling elite.

NOTES

CHAPTER 1

1. *Izvestia,* December 10, 1917, quoted in G. A. Belov et al., eds., *Iz istoril Vserossiikoi Chrezychainoi Komissii* (1917–1921 gg.) (Moscow: Sbornik dokumetov, 1958), p. 84. The dates are somewhat confusing here because the Soviets modernized the Russian calendar on January 31, 1918, which they declared to be February 14, 1918. This latter is the new-style date. Thus, the event that occurred on December 7, 1917, and was reported on December 10, 1917, actually took place on December 20, according to the new calendar.

2. "Dzons Rids, Luiza Braijanta un parejei Oktobra draugi" ("John Reed, Louise Bryant and Other Friends of the October Revolution") (Riga), *Karogs,* No. 10, October 1967, pp. 186–87. See also Barbara Gelb, *So Short a Time* (New York: Berkley Publishing Corp., 1973), which further delineates Bryant's relationship with Reed. The film *Reds* ends with Reed's death from typhus in 1920. Bryant then became active in the U.S. Communist Party, which Reed had helped found. She later married William C. Bullitt, who served as the first U.S. ambassador to the Soviet Union in 1934. Bryant's marriage foundered because of her then chronic alcoholism. For her effect on Bullitt's attitudes toward the Bolshevik state, see F. Fomin, "Pervyy Chekist" ("The First Chekist") (Riga), *Sovetskaya Latviya,* October 1, 1966, pp. 232–35; on p. 4 there is a description of those present at the celebration of the VChK's founding.

3. *Bolshaia Lubianka 2,* Peters, 1927, *Zashchita Revoliutsii,* p. 169.

4. John Reed, *Ten Days That Shook the World* (New York: Random House, 1960), p. 67.

5. Curzio Malaparte, *Coup D'état* (London: The Macmillan Co., 1936), esp. chaps. I, II, and IV, which advance the theory that the essence of the coup d'état was the seizure of the main utilities. If the hydroelectric plants, railway stations, airports, and post offices fell into the hands of the rebels, he argued, the coup was bound to succeed. Trotsky seized these objectives and pointed out that Malaparte had mistaken the relatively unimportant side effects of the coup for the coup itself. In essence, Trotsky looked upon the coup d'état as a social dynamic or fait accompli that those who were dialecticians rather than fighters were incapable of opposing. Trotsky was particularly scornful of many Bolsheviks on the grounds that they seemed to prefer to talk their opponents to death rather than to dispose of them by military action. See esp. L. D. Trotsky, *Our Revolution* (New York:

Henry Holt, 1918); *Between Red and White* (London: Communist Party of Great Britain, 1922); and *History of the Russian Revolution,* 3 vols. (London: Gollanez, 1932–33); see also Nikolai Lenin, *Towards the Seizure of Power* (London: International Publishers, 1933).

6. See esp. Granville Hicks, *John Reed: The Making of a Revolutionary* (New York: Blom & Ayer, 1936), which describes some of the doubts entertained by Reed concerning the course of the revolution in Russia. Hicks, an acknowledged Communist who later came to understand the nature of the Bolshevik system, argues that Reed, at the time of his death, was preparing to disavow Lenin and his revolution.

7. Throughout his career Nikolai V. Krylenko exhibited a less than balanced mind. His severity, prejudices, and ideological excesses made him an unlikely source of justice. Like so many of his colleagues, he was eventually arrested and executed by Stalin. Roy A. Medvedev quotes M. V. Ostrogorskii: "The former Commissar of Justice, N. V. Krylenko, gave in only after cruel tortures. He asked for some paper in his cell, and there, in the presence of his comrades in misfortune, he began to create his counterrevolutionary organization. He would mumble: 'Ivanov? No, he's a good official and a man. I won't put him down. But, Petrov, he's a louse; let's sign him up.' . . ." *Let History Judge* (New York: Alfred A. Knopf, 1972), p. 268.

8. The rapid and absolute collapse of the Romanoff regime has been extensively studied. See esp. George Vernadsky, *A History of Russia* (New Haven, Conn.: Yale University Press, 1929), pp. 232–33, for an exposition of the view that the collapse was caused by bureaucratic rather than systemic failure of the czarist government. Regardless of one's point of view, the fact remains that the government lacked the capacity to manage and organize the Russian economy as well as direct its participation in the 20th century's first modern war.

9. "Its punitive rights were strictly limited; initially, the Cheka did not even have powers of arrest, though these were quickly enough conferred upon it (along with other investigation commissions), by decree of the Commissariat of Justice on December 29, 1917, and the sphere of its responsibilities rapidly expanded to meet the mounting challenge of counter-revolution." George Leggett, *The Cheka: Lenin's Political Police* (Oxford University Press, 1981), p. 18.

10. See V. I. Alidin et al., eds., *Chk: iz ostproo Moskovskoi Chrezychainoi komissii* (1918–1922 gg.) (Moscow: Sbornik dokumetov, 1978), p. 4, and P.G. Sofimov, *Ocehrki istoril vserissusior Chrezvyhassinoit komissii* (1917–1922 gg.) (Moscow: 1950), p. 39, which put the Cheka's move at March 10; however, Belov, op. cit., p. 478 and *Ezhenedelnik,* No. 6, October 27, 1918, give the date as March 12, 1918. For a particularly entertaining account of the move from Petrograd to Moscow, see E. Hanbergs, "4001. iebrauca vakara . . ." ("The 4001 Arrived in the Evening . . .") (Riga), *Cina,* December 24, 1966, p. 2. The article quotes Eduards Smilgas, an old Chekist, who was only twenty years old on March 10, 1918, when he and other Latvian Red riflemen were ordered to guard train 4001, which brought Lenin and the Soviet government from Petrograd to Moscow. Smilgas, in the twilight of his life, reminisced with some humor about the fears and trepidations of the "great" Lenin and the "heroes" who made up his entourage. Smilgas is typical of the irreverent private soldier who observes his

frightened general in a less than commanding posture. The account is an antidote for those who have romanticized the early days of the revolution. Smilgas's recollections underscore the basic insecurity of Lenin and the other Bolshevik leaders. The image of a cowering Lenin is obviously not a part of the Bolshevik legend; nonetheless, Smilgas was there.

11. V. M. Chernov, Che-ka: *Materialy po deiateinosti Chrezvychainois Komissii Izdanie tsentratnogo biuro partii sotsialistov-revoliutsionerov* (Berlin: 1922), pp. 152–53.

12. *Khoziastvennyi Otdel Vserossiliski Chrezvychainois komissil po borbe s kontr-revolutsiei I spekuliatsiei. Vedenie khoziaistva v Chrezvychainkhy Komissilakh* in *Organizastia ChK, 1918,* p. 38. The expansion of the Cheka organization was wholly consistent with the additional counterrevolutionary mission given Dzerzhinsky by Lenin.

13. *Dekrety Sovetskoi Vlasti,* Vol. III, pp. 450–51; *Izvestia,* October 26, 1918. Also *Kontrolno-revizionnai komissiia,* the formation of which was announced on September 29, 1918. These bureaucratic concessions to public opinion were meaningless. By late 1918, Dzerzhinsky's Cheka had Lenin's unswerving support as well as a dynamic of its own, which none of Lenin's enemies fully comprehended.

14. Kaplan's unsuccessful attempt to assassinate Lenin prompted a massive propaganda effort to represent the attack as the work of an international conspiracy designed to bring down the fledgling Bolshevik state, rather than the individual action of a fellow "socialist" who decided that Lenin had "betrayed" the revolution. Lenin's avowed ideological enemies could not be used to whip up the population and justify the mass terror that was directed against those who had tacitly accepted the Bolshevik regime.—Leggett, op. cit., p. 117. See esp. *Pravda,* January 3, 1918 (text in Belov, op. cit., p. 87), *Pokushenie na V. I. Lenina 1 ianvaria, 1918,* pp. 257–73. This particular attempt on Lenin's life was investigated by Red Army commander Kliment Voroshilov. The alleged assassin, Lt. Shtyrev, was a czarist and the kind of man whose enmity could be expected. Kaplan, on the other hand, was one of those who had made the revolution succeed and only later realized it as a brutal sham and betrayal.

15. *Izvestia,* September 4, 1918. See also, *Ezhenedelnik,* VChK, No. 6, October 27, 1918, p. 27. Kaplan was included as number thirty-three on a list of ninety persons executed by the Cheka for "crimes against the state." Some of those on the list were executed for criticizing the failure of the Bolsheviks to distribute grain in accordance with "Socialist principles." Those who believed in the revolution, supported it, and later came to resent the creation of Lenin's "new class" of privileged party members were considered among the most dangerous of the so-called counterrevolutionaries.

16. See Adam B Ulam, *The Bolsheviks* (New York: Viking Press, 1965), p. 422.

17. *Severnaia kommuna,* No. 109, September 19, 1918, p. 2. Also, Latsis in *Krasyni Terror,* No. 1, Kazan, November 1, 1918, quoted in Bertram Wolfe, *The Bridge and the Abyss* (New York: Greenwood Press, 1967), p. 82.

18. Lenin (5), Vol. XXXVII, p. 410, first published in *Pravda,* November 6, 1926. Lenin's acceptance and adoption of the tactic of mass terror to facilitate the

revolution continues to disturb Soviet scholars. Soviet apologists insist that the text is frequently misread. Whatever the interpretation, Lenin exhibits a pragmatic disregard for the residual humanistic goals of the revolution. Once presented with the opportunity to control a police state, he abandoned all pretense of idealism.

19. *Newsweek,* January 1, 1968. Interview with H.A.R. (Kim) Philby in Moscow:

"Question: 'I have a straightforward question Comrade Kim: Are you happy?'

"Philby: 'Looking back over the years I don't think I've lived them in vain. Yes, I am happy. I would like to repeat the words of Felix Dzerzhinsky, the Knight of the Revolution, that great humanist, 'If I had to begin my life again I would begin it just as I did.'"

Dzerzhinsky was indeed known as Felix of the Golden Heart. His "humanism" had its limits, however; reportedly, he wept as he signed death warrants during 1917–1926, when he headed the Soviet organs.

20. See esp. "There Are No Written Laws of Civil War," *Izvestia,* August 23, 1918. The writer was Martyn Ianovich Latsis (alias of Ian Fridrikhovich Sudrabs), who was Dzerzhinsky's trusted deputy and alter ego in the Cheka:

"In almost all epochs, among almost all peoples, established customs assumed the form of written laws. Capitalist war has its written laws, formulated in various concepts. . . . But, in civil war . . . you will look ludicrous if you apply or demand the observance of such customs and laws. . . . This is the law of civil war—slaughter all those wounded fighting against you. And so it is. That is the practice. It is essential not merely to destroy the active forces of the enemy, but also to demonstrate that anyone raising the sword against the existing order will perish by the sword. That is the meaning of civil war which is well observed by the bourgeoisie. . . . We have not learned these rules. Our people are shot in hundreds and thousands, we execute singly and after long deliberations in commissions and tribunals. In civil war there are no courts of law for the enemy. It is a life-and-death struggle. If you do not kill, you will be killed. Therefore kill, that you may not be killed."

21. John Erickson, *The Soviet High Command* (London: Archon Books, 1962), pp. 45, 58. The "military specialists," who were recruited by Trotsky from the Imperial Army's professional ranks, were clearly the enabling factor that allowed the Reds to prevail over the Whites in the Civil War. They were, by any standard of definition, patriots and professional soldiers who later found themselves prosecuted as "counterrevolutionaries." Trotsky himself did not protect or intercede on their behalf once the war had been won. See esp. Trotsky, 1969, Vol. II, pp. 111–12, for his latter-day recognition of the role of these military men and his failure to stand up to Lenin in their defense.

22. George A. Vernadsky, *A History of Russia* (New Haven, Conn.: Yale University Press, 1929), pp. 280–83.

23. S.U.R. 1919, No. 6:58, *Izvestia,* February 21, 1919, text in Belov, op. cit., pp. 259–61. The significance of this bureaucratic maneuver was scarcely appreciated at the time. It was, nonetheless, the most important of the powers given to the Cheka because it provided the mechanism to ensure the obedience and loyalty

of the armed forces to the Bolshevik government. In evaluating the OOs' performance in the post-civil-war period, Leggett (op. cit., p. 96) noted:

"In building a conscript army on a basis of discipline and professionialism, Trotsky had chosen to rely on a central core of ex-Czarist officers who were prepared to accept the Bolshevik regime; in the Red Army they were closely supervised by political commissars, i.e., the OOs. During 1918, the Bolsheviks succeeded in attracting over 22,000 of these so-called 'military specialists' to serve in the Red Army; in 1919, they constituted four-fifths of Red Army Commanders and they continued to outnumber commanders of proletarian origin throughout the Civil War."

24. The OOs have never been without their detractors, yet their mission, as conceived by Dzerzhinsky, neutralized the political potential of the Red armed forces. The OO responsibility remains an integral part of the KGB's system of "internal security."

In this regard, the appointment in 1982 of V. Fedorchuk to replace Yuri Andropov as head of the KGB illustrated the continuing Bolshevik concern about the loyalty of the military.

Contrary to many Western analyses, Fedorchuk is a hard-line Bolshevik whose specialty had been ensuring the political reliability and obedience of the Red armed forces. Chebrikov is another old Chekist who can be depended upon to enforce compliance

25. See esp. Louis B. Ely, *The Red Army Today* (Harrisburg, Pa.: Military Service Publishing Co., 1949). Though long out of print, Col. Ely's work remains among the more important published works on the Soviet Army. Ely provides an objective analysis of the influences and effects of the OOs on the Soviet armed forces.

26. Interview with "Colonel BSK," who was imprisoned during the early Stalin era and later served as an army field commander in World War II. After the war he was an officer in military intelligence, or GRU *(Glavnoye Razvedovatelnoye Upravlenie.)* Many of the Soviets' major intelligence coups can be attributed to the GRU and its military personnel rather than to the more powerful and favored KGB. The significance of this variation in operational effectiveness is sometimes not evident to Western observers, who have been inclined to accept Soviet security and intelligence services as indistinguishable components of an operational monolith. The GRU continues to be an effective element of the Soviet intelligence system, though it does not have the political power of the KGB. Even in decisions that involve the Soviet armed forces, such as the invasion of Afghanistan, political considerations overcame the GRU's recommendations (in Afghanistan, against the military action).

27. "The Soviet Army: Assets and Failings of the Ground Forces," *The Times* (London), October 6, 1950, p. 7. See also Maj. Gen. Richard Hilton, "The Soviet Armed Forces," *Royal United Service Institute Journal,* Vol. 94, No. 576, November 1949, pp. 552–56.

28. Leggett, op. cit., p. 114, quotes Latsis, chairman of the Eastern Front VChK, writing in the Cheka periodical, *Krasnyni Terror (Red Terror),* November 1918:

"We are not waging war against individual persons. We are exterminating the bourgeoisie as a class. During the investigation, do not look for evidence that the accused acted in deed or word against Soviet power. The first questions you ought to put are: To what class does he belong? What is his origin? What is his education or profession? And it is these questions that ought to determine the fate of the accused. In this lies the significance and essence of the Red Terror." (Quoted in Wolfe, op. cit., p. 82.)

29. A. Myagkov, *Rossiiski Demokrat* (Paris), September 1947.

30. "Interim Report of the Committee to Collect Information on Russia," 1920, p. 11.

31. J. D. Atkinson, *The Edge of War* (Chicago: Henry Regnery, 1960), p. 223.

32. Isaac Don Levine, *Stalin's Great Secret* (New York: Coward, McCann, 1956), and Alexander Orlov, "The Sensational Secret Behind the Damnation of Stalin," *Life,* April 23, 1956.

33. Anton Ovseyenko, *The Time of Stalin* (New York: Harper & Row, 1981).

34. Maj. Gen. V. O. Firstenko, *Polveka boyevoy vakhty* ("Half a Century on Guard") (Kiev), *Rabochaya Gazeta,* May 28, 1968, p. 1.

35. *Dekrety Sovetskoy vlasti, 1 aprelya–31 iyulya 1919, g. Tom V (Decrees of the Soviet Government,* April 1–July 31, 1919, Vol. V) (Moscow: Politizdat, 1971).

36. Sergei Melgounov, *The Red Terror in Russia* (London: J. M. Dent, 1925), p. 253. See also Vasili Ivanovich Ardamatsky, *Vozmesdiye* (Retribution) (Moscow: Molodaya Gavardiya, 1968). This is the first comprehensive account published in the Soviet Union concerning the GPU provocation operation that induced Boris Viktorovich Savinkov to reenter the USSR in 1924. He was led to believe that there was, within the USSR, a powerful anti-Soviet organization in need of an experienced leader. This pseudo-organization was operated and staffed by the GPU. After Savinkov crossed the border into the USSR from Finland, he was arrested and tried. A number of his associates, some unwittingly and others under GPU coercion, collaborated with the Soviet service in the deception.

37. John Barron, *KGB: The Secret Work of Soviet Secret Agents* (New York: Reader's Digest, Press, 1973), p. 78.

38. Soviet Intelligence and Security Services, 94th Congress, 1st Session, Committee on the Judiciary, U.S. Senate.

39. A. Myagkov, *Rossiiskii Demokrat* (Paris), September 1947, pp. 44–45.

40. An aide to Congressman John Conyers, Neil Kotler, reported the appearance at his hotel room in Moscow of a Soviet citizen who spoke "excellent English" and purported to be a long-lost relative of his father, who had emigrated from the Soviet Union in 1910. Kotler was sensitive to the Soviet's "soft" sell, "designed to determine my sympathies towards the Soviet Union and to play on the familial connection to the 'Motherland'." Further, because of Kotler's position in the Congress, the Soviet "friend of the family" was able to cut the bureaucratic red tape and enable Kotler to see "the real Russia" and its "real citizens."

41. E. Van Der Rhoer, *The Shadow Network* (New York: Charles Scribner's, 1983), pp. 63–64.

42. W. H. Chamberlin, *The Russian Revolution, 1917–1921* (London: Ayer & Co., 1935), Vol. II, pp. 68–69. Professor Chamberlin's analysis of the Lockhart affair puts it into perspective and illustrates the comic-opera approach of the Allies to the deadly game of trying to topple a revolutionary government without intelligence, plan, or trained personnel.

43. *Izvestia,* September 5, 1918. The terse announcement makes it appear that Captain Cromie was murdered more in sorrow than in anger, as if he were an innocent bystander who happened to be at the scene of a violent crime and became an unintended, accidental casualty.

44. Mikhail Maklyarsky, "Zagovor poslov" ("Conspiracy of the Ambassadors") (Moscow), *Ogonek,* No. 51, December 1967, pp. 6–7.

45. R. B. Lockhart, *The Diaries of Sir Robert Bruce Lockhart,* Vol. I, 1915–1938, Kenneth Young, ed. (New York: St. Martin's Press, 1973), p. 257.

46. *Izvestia,* December 17, 1918.

47. Documentation on this point is controversial and obscure. The Soviet Union has given Lenin credit for sparing the life of Kalamatiano. See esp. I. Cirulis, "Lenina gvarde uz ekrana" ("Lenin's Guards on the Screen") (Riga), *Cina,* February 26, 1966, p. 4. The reviewer states that this movie is based only on facts. Every step in the production was decided upon only after careful study designed to re-create the events as close to reality as possible. In this case, Lenin is granted the "wisdom" to realize the potential worth of Kalamatiano in future dealings with the U.S. government, hence the decision to spare Kalamatiano's life.

48. Department of State cables: from Quarton in Viborg to SecState, November 12, 1920: from SecState to American Legation, Christiania, November 20, 1920, for Dr. Nansen. Fridtjof Nansen was a Norwegian statesman and humanitarian who negotiated the repatriation of 500,000 war prisoners. The League of Nations was not recognized by the Soviet government, but Nansen was regarded as an acceptable envoy. He acted as high commissioner for International Red Cross famine relief missions in the USSR and was awarded the Nobel Peace Prize in 1922.

49. Golinkov, 1971, pp. 274–79, and Kuskova, *Volia Rossii,* 1928, No. 3, pp. 58–69.

50. Unshlikht, p. 99; Belov, op. cit., pp. 443–44, quotes Dzerzhinsky's letter to the Cheka of July 12, 1921; Lenin (5), Vol. LIV, p. 810; Fisher, pp. 117–19.

51. *New York Times,* August 11, 1921.

52. Ibid.

53. Office of the Commissioner of the United States, Riga, Cable #1165, August 23, 1921, to the Secretary of State, Washington.

54. Interviews with Culver Military Academy authorities, memorial tribute to Kalamatiano in Culver yearbook, and miscellaneous personnel documents in Culver's files.

55. The former GRU officer BSK (1938), and state security officers EPS (194?), GHO (195?), GMI (196?), and IPO (197?), each have confirmed the difficulty of the Kalamatiano case in terms of integrating their own understanding of the case with the party line of the moment. Initials used for identification only. Sources are necessarily anonymous.

56. Despite the difficulties cited in note 55, these same ex-officers maintain that this has in no way altered the basic counterespionage doctrine established by Dzerzhinsky. In fact, they contend that the doctrine has been reinforced by the emphasis placed on the Kalamatiano case.

57. Lenin (5), Vol. XLII, p. 62. Lenin's speech on December 6, 1920.

58. Simon Wolin and Robert Slusser, *The Soviet Secret Police* (New York: Frederick A. Praeger, 1957), p. 376.

59. Alexandr Fedorovich Khatskevich, *Soldat velikikh boyev (Soldier of Great Battles)* (Minsk: Nauka i Tekhnika, 1965), pp. 237–45; S. Krlov, "Rytsar revolyutsii" ("Knight of the Revolution") (Moscow), *Voyenno Istoricheskiy Zhurnal,* No. 9, September, 1962, pp. 67–73.

60. Georges S. Agabekov, *OGPU: The Russian Soviet Terror* (New York: Brentano's, 1931), pp. 15–16. See also Agabekov's *GPU: Zapiski chekista* (Berlin: 1930) and *Cheka za rabotsi* (Berlin: 1931), for further descriptions of early INO methods and overseas operations.

61. Georgi Frolov, "Znizn, otdannaya revolutsyii" ("A Life Devoted to the Revolution") (Riga), *Sovetskaya Latviya,* November 21, 1971, p. 2, tells the latter-day story of one of Dzerzhinsky's most able "singleton" agents, Yan Mikhailovich Bikson, who "came in out of the cold" in the late 1920s and was chief of the state security's operative section from 1932 until 1934. See also Gordon Arnold Lonsdale, *Spy: Twenty Years in Soviet Secret Service* (New York: Hawthorn Books, 1965), pp. 123–42; Vladimir M. and Evdokia Petrov, *Empire of Fear* (New York: Frederick A. Praeger, 1956), pp. 63–68. See also R. Abel, N. Agayants, G. Axelrod, et al., *Chekisty Sbornik (Chekists, Collected Stories)* (Moscow: Molodaya, 1970), and *Dipkuryery. Ocherki o perkvykh Sovetskikh diplomatucheskikh kuryerakh (Diplomatic Couriers. Narratives About the First Soviet Diplomatic Couriers)* (Izdatelstvo Politcheskoy Literatury, 1970). Reference in these narratives clearly establishes the meaning of Dzerzhinsky's concept of the "need to know."

62. *Sovetskoye gosudarstvo i pravo v period stroitelstva sotsializma (The Soviet State and the Law During the Building of Socialism)* (Moscow; Nauka, 1968).

63. Corson, *The Armies of Ignorance* (New York: Dial Press, 1977), pp. ix–xvi.

64. Leggett, op. cit., p. 44. The event is further described by Chamberlin, op. cit., Vol. I, pp. 368–69.

65. Maxim Gorky, *Untimely Thoughts* (London: Paul Erickson, 1970), pp. 124–25.

66. Leggett, op. cit., chap. IV, "The Left Socialist Revolutionary Uprising." Leggett points out that the LSRs, led by Maria Spiridonova (1886–1918), were the only effective political opposition to the Bolsheviks' attempt to "steal the revolution." At Lenin's order, the Cheka arrested and executed most of the LSR leadership.

67. Most notable among these are: Alexandr Fedorovich Khatskevich, *Soldat velikikh boyev (Soldier of Great Battles)* (Minsk: Nauka i Teknika, 1965); S. Krylov, "Rystar revoliutsii" ("Knight of the Revolution") (Moscow) *Voyenno Istoricheskiy Zhurnal,* No. 9, September 1962; M. F. Rozvadovskaya and V. M. Slutskaya, *Rystar revoliutsii. Vospominaniya sovremennikov of Felikse Edmun-*

doviche Dzerzhinskom (Knight of Revolution. Reminiscences About Felix Edmuṅ-dovich Dzerzhinsky by Contemporaries) (Moscow: Gosudarstvennoye Izdateltsvo Politicheskoy Literatury, 1967), and Nikolay Ivanovich Zubov, *F. E. Dzerzhinsky* (Moscow: Izdatelstvo Politicheskoy Literatury, 1965).

68. Khatskevich, op. cit., pp. 5, 9, 17. Also, Ulam, *The Bolsheviks* (New York: Viking, 1965), p. 4.

69. Feliks Dzerzinskis, "Vestules masai no cietumien un trimdas" ("Letters to Sister from Prisons and Forced Exile") (Riga), *Padomju Jaunatne,* September 10, 1972. See esp. pp. 3–4, which reflect Dzerzhinsky's agonies over the personal conflict between his Catholicism and his belief in socialism.

70. Khatskevich, op. cit., p. 17, makes the point, as does Tomash, p. 91; however, neither author specifies the nature of Dzerzhinsky's troubles with the school authorities.

71. G. Buravkin, "Tak srazhalis Dzerzhinskye" ("How the Dzerzhinskyites Fought"), *Pravda,* June 13, 1968, p. 6.

72. *Vospominaniia o Dzerzinskom,* pp. 41–43.

73. Zubov (1965), p. 194; Voroshilov, p. 85.

74. Dzerzinskaia, 1965, pp. 267–71.

75. Alfred Senn, *Diplomacy and Revolution* (South Bend, Ind.: Univ. of Notre Dame Press, 1974), p. 171.

76. Marguerite Harrison, *Chicago Tribune,* August 1, 1926. Ms. Harrison, imprisoned as an "enemy of the Soviet State," was greatly impressed by Dzerzhinsky. As a trained journalist, she attempted to convey her observations of Dzerzhinsky and his influence and power to her employer. Her efforts were un-availing, and her direct observations were largely dismissed as less than objective.

77. S.U.R. 1922, No. 16:160, February 6, 1922; *Izvestia,* February 8, 1922 (text in Belov, op. cit., pp. 471–74).

CHAPTER 2

1. "Manifesto of the Communist International to the Proletariat of the Entire World," March 1919. Written by Leon Trotsky; English translation in Jane De-gras, ed., *The Communist International, 1919–1943, Documents* (London: Oxford University Press, 1956), Vol. I, pp. 38, 41–45, 47.

The International Workingmen's Association, or First International, was formed in St. Martin's Hall, London, on September 28, 1864, by representatives of the British trades unions, French labor organizations, Italian Mazzinists, and individual Poles and Germans.

Karl Marx became a member of its first general council and drafted the first public address. The International was supported by Marx and Engels despite its heterogeneous composition. Because of their perseverance and intellectual supe-riority, they soon became its leaders and spokesmen.

The defeat of the Paris Commune in 1871 presaged the collapse of the First International. Its decline had already been hastened by the increasingly violent conflicts between the followers of Marx and the supporters of the Russian anar-chist Mikhail Bakunin. The Hague Conference of the International in 1872 was marked by the victory of the Marxists over the Bakuninists and the decision to transfer the seat of the International to the United States. The last conference was held in Philadelphia on July 15, 1876. The Bakuninists continued to consider themselves the International, held several ineffectual congresses, and then also disbanded.

In contrast to the revolutionary trend of the First International and its centralized character, the Second International was a loose association of national socialist parties of all varieties. Its date of formation is generally accepted as 1889, when the French and German Marxist groups, together with several others, gathered at Paris.

The International Socialist Bureau, the only central organ of the Second International, was established in 1900 with headquarters in Brussels. The revolutionary high-water mark of the Second International was the Amsterdam Conference of 1904, at which the revisionism of Bernstein and the ministerialism of Milleran-Jaures were both condemned. Despite the formal condemnations, the practice and theory of reformism was gradually gaining the upper hand in the Second International.

The start of World War I marked the apex of the International's influence; thereafter, it fragmented into its national constituent parts. After the war, and following the formation of the Third International, efforts were made to revive the Second. This was finally accomplished at Hamburg in 1923, when the International of the extreme reformist parties fused with the "Vienna International." The latter was led by the Austrian social democrats, who had remained outside and to the left of the principal socialist parties.

The Hamburg fusion was effected entirely on the basis of the classic reformist positions. This obscure bit of organizational history has been useful to the Soviets for what it implies—legitimate parental antecedents that led to the distillate called Bolshevism. For a time, invoking the word "International" was extensive because it conveyed another impression—utterly false—of universality. The practice has gone out of vogue as it is no longer useful.

2. Conditions of Admission to the Communist International, Approved by the Second Comintern Congress, August 1920. *The Communist International Documents,* Vol. I, pp. 168–72.

3. Gregori Zinoviev, *Problems of the German Revolution,* 1923; excerpts translated in *Xenia.* J. Eudin and Harold H. Fisher, *Soviet Russia and the West* (Palo Alto, Calif.: Stanford University Press, 1957), pp. 214–15.

4. Narkomindel is the acronym for *Narodyni Komissariat Inostrannykh Del,* the Peoples' Commissariat for Foreign Affairs.

5. Aino Kuusinen, *The Rings of Destiny* (New York: William Morrow, 1975).

6. *The Historical Journal* (Cambridge University Press), Vol. 20, September 3, 1977. *The British Secret Service and Anglo-Soviet Relations in the 1920s.* Part I: From the Trade Negotiations to the Zinoviev Letter, p. 678. Christopher Andrew cites Peters to MacDonald, No. 1027, November 4, 1924, FO 373/10479.

7. Kuusinen, op. cit., pp. 47–52.

8. Oleg Penkovsky, *The Penkovsky Papers* (Garden City, N.Y.: Doubleday & Co., 1965).

9. The Kuomintang was admitted to the Comintern as a "sympathizing party"

early in 1926. When the vote approving the admission was taken by the Soviet Central Committee, the sole dissenter was Trotsky. Hu Han-min, right-wing Kuomintang leader, was a "fraternal delegate" to the Sixth Plenum of the ECCI in February 1926. At the same meeting, Chiang Kai-shek was made an "honorary" member of the Comintern—a pragmatic measure of the Bolsheviks' standard of ideological purity.

10. The Declaration of the Eighty-four (May 1927); see "Trotskyists of the Comintern," Trotsky Archives, New York Public Library. Also reprinted in *Fourth International* (New York: The New International, July 1934).

11. Gunther Nollau, *International Communism and World Revolution* (New York: Frederick A. Praeger, 1961), p. 162, and Julius Braunthal, *The History of the International* (New York: Frederick A. Praeger, 1967), pp. 147–68.

12. "To the wild and vague discussions of the USA Committee, I listened with indifference. They had absolutely no political significance and made the impression of boxing matches with the monopoly of party leadership as a prize. . . . In the beginning, I was inclined to regard the rudeness of the American communists as an expression of their unbridled political temperaments. Once it looked as if one of them, purple in the face, would smother his adversary who had just called him an inspeakable name. I jumped up to prevent a fist fight. My friend Lapinsky, a gentle Polish economist who had some understanding of America and Americans, motioned me back to my seat. . . . 'They are only trying to impress us in order to get one more vote for themselves—they'll do anything for that.'

"In the end, the naive over-shrewdness of the leading American communists led to their own downfall. They fell for all the traps set for them by Stalin's court intriguers and, at the same time, lost Stalin's favor and their influence in the party. . . ." Ypsilon, *Pattern for World Revolution* (Chicago: Ziff-Davis, 1947), pp. 119–20.

13. *The Washington Post* of April 23, 1939, pointed out that ". . . the *Daily Worker* was the only publication in the United States not to print Monday night a single line about the fact that Hitler and Stalin had announced plans for a nonaggression treaty. For years the newspaper has been calling Hitler and the Nazis names as vile as can appear in print.

"The *Daily Worker* explained that it had cabled Moscow for confirmation and that nothing would be published until word was received from Moscow. . . ."

14. Consolidated Statement of Whittaker Chambers, FBI Item 3220.

15. The Soviets persisted in the fiction that the Comintern had no connection whatsoever with the Soviet government and that the USSR simply provided a meeting hall for these like-minded fellows in Moscow out of fraternal sentiment.

At the time of the Comintern meeting in August 1935, the U.S. Department of State lodged a formal protest with Moscow in which it was pointed out that Soviet sponsorship of the Comintern was in violation of the U.S.-USSR (Litvinov-Roosevelt) agreement of the year before. Litvinov blandly responded that "The Soviet government cannot take upon itself and has not taken on itself obligations of any kind with regard to the Communist International."—Basil Rauch, *Roosevelt: Munich to Pearl Harbor* (New York: Creative Age Press, 1950), p. 65.

On May 15, 1943, the Soviet government dissolved the Third International (Comintern); the demise was officially announced on May 22, 1943. The text of the Soviet government's bulletin "declares the autonomy of Communist parties outside the USSR." Some auditors had the impression that Litvinov had said that eight years before.

16. The "Chinese" Nguen Ai Quac later became better known as Ho Chi Minh. His contribution of one of the two clues that led to Noulens's arrest and the eventual smashing of a major Comintern net in China is not a part of his official biography.

17. NA, RG 263, Shanghai Municipal Police file D 2527/41.

18. The Far Eastern Branch of the Comintern and the Pan-Pacific Trade Union Secretariat were co-located in Noulens's accountings, a serious break in the rules governing compartmentation and security. The incident illustrates the problem of handling large sums of money in clandestine circuits. Had Noulens failed to keep detailed records, he would have been thought an embezzler. By his scrupulosity, he managed to make the undeniable connection between these two branches of the Soviet apparatus, the Comintern's FEB and the PPTUS.

19. The names Beuret and Ruegg were supposed to have been those of Swiss nationals. As a matter of fact, they were found to belong to actual persons who were living in Europe at the time the Noulenses were arrested. The Swiss nationality had been selected because the Swiss passport officer in Basel, who had access to the records and could adjust them, was employed by the Soviets.

As far back as the early thirties and well into the war, the Soviet intelligence services had an inside agent in the passport office in Basel. He worked through a female cutout and, for his services, was paid 150 francs a month as a retainer, with an additional 100 francs for each passport he provided.

The procedure for obtaining a Swiss passport was simple. Moscow supplied the passport officer with the physical details of the person for whom the passport was required. The passport officer then consulted the files of various Basel citizens and chose a suitable identity for the new passport holder. The details included date and place of birth, parentage, profession, and so forth—all the details normally required for a passport in any country. Moscow forged the necessary certificates so that a passport application form could be completed in the name of the agent. The passport officer, in a routine way, passed the form in with a batch of other forms for signature to the chief of police (who is responsible for issuing Swiss passports).

The false passports could be prolonged at any Swiss consulate abroad. If the consular authorities were suspicious and queried Basel, then the particulars, tallying in every detail, were in the passport records there.

Richard Sorge, a Soviet agent arrested by the Japanese late in 1941, testified at his trial in Tokyo that Noulens was in charge of the organizational apparatus in Shanghai in the early thirties. Hede Massing, a former Soviet agent and one-time wife of Gerhart Eisler, also knew Noulens through Eisler, who was then in Shanghai as Noulens's "political adviser" in the Comintern net in China.

20. Hearings, Permanent Select Committee on Intelligence, U.S. House of Representatives, July 13–14, 1982. These transcripts include testimony from CIA and FBI experts on the subject, showing that the Nuclear Freeze movement is a follow-on to the campaign against the "neutron bomb" of the late 1970s.

21. Hitler purged the ranks of his own adherents within a year of taking

power. Among those arrested and shot were Ernst Rohm, leader of the SA; Gregor Strasser, formerly Hitler's chief aide in the Nazi Party; Gen. Kurt von Schleicher, and Gustav von Kahr, who had earlier quashed the beer-hall putsch. The Fuehrer had a long memory and a deadly compulsion to avenge himself on his enemies.

Hitler's "night of the long knives" must have been an inspiration to Stalin. Within six months, the Russian dictator arranged for the "assassination" of Sergei M. Kirov, whom he regarded as an incipient political rival with strong party support. Later, just as Hitler confronted his army leaders and drove Gen. Kurt von Schleicher to his death and Gen. Hans von Seekt to a battlefield suicide, Stalin arrested Marshal M. N. Tukhachevsky and seven generals and saw them through a speedy public trial and execution as members of an imagined conspiracy.

22. Isaac Don Levine, *Letters from Russian Prisons.*

23. Isaac Don Levine, *Eyewitness to History* (New York: Hawthorn Books, 1973), p. 170. Kindness of Ruth Levine (Mrs. I. D.). Published collections of Einstein's correspondence generally do not include his exchanges with Levine.

24. Peter Deriabin and Frank Gibney, *The Secret World* (New York: Doubleday, 1959), p. 100: ". . . the Soviet regime is pledged to a particularly vicious form of anti-Semitism." p. 219: ". . . the Great Russian racial consciousness is unfriendly to Jews, Georgians and Poles." p. 126: ". . . several of the doctors involved [in the "Doctor's Plot"] were Jewish, a fact which gave the regime an excuse for showing off its always latent anti-Semitism." And ". . . until 1949 there were almost 150 Jews in the [Kremlin] Guard. Almost overnight they were released from their jobs."

"B.D.," *The Russian Jew Yesterday and Today;* quoted by Roy A. Medvedev in *On Stalin and Stalinism* (New York: Oxford University Press, 1979), p. 114: "Although Jews were in no sense intended as a special target, they suffered greater injury in the rebound of the purges than any other national group." p. 146: "After the 'Leningrad affair' . . . thousands of 'cosmopolitans' were arrested, or, in plain language, Jews, members of Jewish cultural organizations which had suddenly been condemned and dissolved." p. 147: "And when the mass arrest of prominent Jewish cultural figures was carried out in 1949–50, it was largely done in secret and nothing appeared in the press, official Soviet agencies abroad receiving instructions to rebut the 'rumors' of the arrest of Jewish writers and performers." p. 153: "The 'Doctors' Plot, the arrest of Minister of State Security Abakumov, the arrest of the chief of the MGB in Georgia—these events and others like them were intended to prepare the ground not only for the deportation of the Jews but for a new wave of terror . . . his [Stalin's] sudden death intervened." p. 159: "According to Ehrenburg, the plan to deport the Jews began to take on reality at the end of 1952 and the beginning of 1953. They had already completed the construction of temporary barracks somewhere in the East. Before the deportation was inaugurated, it was intended to publish 'An Appeal to the Jewish People' signed by the most famous members of the intelligentsia of Jewish origin, calling on all Soviet Jews to submit to the decision. Ehrenburg refused to sign [the document] which already bore the signatures of the editor of *Pravda,* the Minister of State Control, the members of the Central Committee, Lev Mekhlis and the prominent historian, Isaak Mints. Mekhlis sent for Ehrenburg and spent

many hours trying to induce him to sign, but when persuasions and threats were of no avail, he went to the safe and took out the draft text of the 'Appeal' with handwritten notes by Stalin and asked 'Do you know whose handwriting this is?'"
p. 189: "Nor is there any need to mention Stalin's revival of Great Russian chauvinism, his deportation of many peoples of the USSR from their native lands, or his anti-Semitic policies which led to the physical destruction of the most brilliant representatives of Jewish culture and his plans for the deportation of all Jews to remote regions of the USSR."

Stephen Graham, *Stalin* (New York: Kennikat Press, 1970), p. 81. "[In 1927] Stalin intended to play one Jew off against another in the Politburo and he succeeded."

Daniel M. Jacobs, *Borodin, Stalin's Man in China* (Cambridge, Mass.: Harvard University Press, 1981), p. 324: ". . . in 1949 when Golda Meir, the first ambassador to the USSR from the State of Israel, appeared in Moscow and was greeted by 50,000 of her co-religionists, Stalin's anti-Semitism had long been apparent. Now this outpouring of emotion by a large section of Moscow Jewry proved to Stalin that Jews were disloyal to the Soviet Union. Nationalism was an enemy; Jews were nationalists; hence Jews were enemies."

Louis Fischer, an admiring biographer of Stalin's, gave the essence of the Soviet legend on anti-Semitism in his *Men and Politics* (New York: Duell, Sloun and Pearce, 1941), pp. 247–49: "I told them that the Russian Jews were equal. A rabbi was persecuted in the same manner as a minister, priest or mullah. Any Jew could join the proletariat and thereby become equal . . . others persist in long ingrained habits and I told friends in Jerusalem of the case I knew of a Jew in Kursk who collects old tin cans and stamps crosses out of them and sells them, secretly, to peasants or, wholesale, to priests for anywhere from 5 to 50 Rubles. He markets about 2,000 crosses a month and has been in business for about a year. Sometimes he visits Moscow looking for tin cans. When he is caught, as he inevitably will be, he will be punished not as a Jew but as an illicit businessman."
p. 248: "Anti-Semitism in Soviet Russia, I told them, was counter-revolutionary. Anti-Semitism is a hardy plant and Czarism had fed it well. But the Bolsheviks cut it down and tore out its roots one by one. . . . Bolshevism is essentially a doctrine of internationalism. Nationalism and nationalistic hates are foreign to its conception . . . the Soviet policies of no Russian nationalism, no discrimination between nationalities, no foreign conquests and no anti-Semitism are all tied together, all part of the same cloth. This was the lesson I preached in Jerusalem in 1934."

Petr G. Grigorenko, *Grigorenko Memoirs* (New York: W. W. Norton, 1982), makes frequent reference to arrests and beatings of Jews.

See also Roy Medvedev, *Let History Judge* (New York: Alfred A. Knopf, 1972), pp. 493–97; John Barron, *KGB* (New York: Reader's Digest Press, 1973), pp. 4–5, 16, 75, 84–85, 97, 92n, 99n; Tolstoy, *Stalin's Secret War*, pp. 24, 27, 32, 44, 247, 373, 444; H. M. Hyde, *Stalin* (New York: Popular Library, 1971), pp. 65, 84, 352, 577, 588–90; Isaac Deutscher, *Stalin* (New York: Oxford University Press, 1950), pp. 91, 604–609, 618–22, 627.

25. T. Weingartner, *Stalin und der Aufstieg Hitlers*, 1970, p. 115.

26. Walter Krivitsky, *I Was Stalin's Agent* (London: Hamish Hamilton, 1939), pp. 21–22.

27. *Ryndschau,* No. 39, July 5, 1934, pp. 1541–43.

28. E. H. Carr, *Twilight of the Comintern* (New York: Pantheon Books, 1983), pp. 123–24.

29. Vyacheslar Molotov, "The Meaning of the Soviet-German Non-Aggression Pact." Speech to the Supreme Soviet, August 31, 1939; English translation in *Strategy and Tactics of World Communism,* Supplement I, "One Hundred Years of Communism," U.S. House of Representatives, Doc. #619, 80th Congress, 2nd Session, (Washington: U.S. Government Printing Office, 1948), pp. 158, 160–63.

30. Heinz Guderian, personal interview, 1956.

31. E. H. Carr, op. cit., pp. 151–52.

32. Anthony Cave-Brown, and Charles B. MacDonald, *On a Field of Red: The Communist International and the Coming of World War II* (New York: G. P. Putnam's Sons, 1981), pp. 615–16.

33. Leon Lazarevich Felbin, or Orlov, as OGPU chief in Spain, applied himself to the execution of Stalin's orders. By the summer of 1938 it was evident that Soviet intervention in Spain had failed and that the Republican government was doomed. Additionally, Stalin had been purging the OGPU, and Felbin knew that he would not survive a return to Moscow. He made his way to Paris and, with the aid of French contacts, was able eventually to enter the United States along with his wife and young daughter. Felbin had used various work names, including Alexandr Nikolsky, Schwed, Lyova, Leon Nikolaev, Stein, and General Alexandr Orlov.

The family lived in seclusion in Cleveland, Ohio, for fifteen years until Stalin's death in 1953, at which time he prepared a series of articles for *Life* magazine.

Felbin was extraordinarily informed on matters concerning the operations of the GPU, OGPU, and NKVD throughout the world.

34. Stalin insisted that his fraternal gesture in support of the Spanish Republican government be paid for with Spanish treasure. Each cathedral, church, monastery, rectory, great home, or castle that fell into Loyalist hands was to be stripped of valuable paintings and other items that could be readily sold, with the proceeds going to the Soviets. (During this period, one wartime British M.I. officer functioned as a prospering art dealer, specializing in Spanish treasure, and another, in London, occasionally acted in a consultative capacity to verify and ascribe value to the stolen property. Both were later revealed to have been Soviet agents.)

Felbin's tally of Spanish gold was "168 lorry loads, comprising 7,900 crates of gold." The bullion was loaded on four Soviet vessels and shipped to Odessa. The Spanish government is still trying to recover the stolen hoard.—Gordon Brook-Sheperd, *The Storm Petrels* (London: Collins, 1977), p. 200.

35. Molotov, op. cit., pp. 12–13.

36. Resolution of the Presidium of the Executive Committee of the Communist International, May 22, 1943, proposing the dissolution of the International (English translation in *Strategy and Tactics of World Communism,* op. cit.)

37. OSS Weekly Survey, March 10–17, 1943.

38. Memo, Communist Party in the United States, Brig. Gen. Clayton Bissell, G-2, to Lt. Gen. T. T. Handy, OPD, Russia, 1944, NA RG 165.

39. Thaddeus Wittlin, *Commissar: The Life and Death of Lavrenty Pavlovitch Beria* (New York: Frederick A. Praeger, 1973), p. 247.

CHAPTER 3

1. "Organs" is the generic term used by Russian writers to refer to the collective Soviet state security and intelligence services. That is, the KGB, GRU, militia, and law-enforcement elements of the Ministry of Interior. See esp. Anton Antonovich Ovseyenko, *The Time of Stalin: Portrait of a Tyranny* (New York: Harper & Row, 1981), pp. 111–12, 121–24, 126.

2. Ibid., pp. 21–24. Ovseyenko makes clear that Lenin's final testament included a warning and admonition to his colleagues to bar Stalin's access to power.

3. Col. Ivan Okhridsky, Committee for State Security at the Ministry of International Affairs, Moscow. Broadcast from Sofia Domestic Service, in Bulgarian, 1830 GMT, December 29, 1963.

4. Felix Dzerzhinsky's demise at 8:40 P.M. on July 20, 1926, is one more in a long list of inadequately explained deaths of Soviet hierarchs; most of the clues point in the direction of Stalin. According to Ovseyenko, op. cit., pp. 44–45, Dzerzhinsky declared "I will not permit a coup!" at the Joint Plenum of the Central Committee and Central Control Commission on July 20, 1926, in reference to feuding within the party. Within a few hours of his speech Dzerzhinsky was dead. Ovseyenko asks, "Was it just a heart attack? No one had time to tell him, 'Alas Comrade Felix, the coup has already taken place.' " Another version alleges that after completing his speech he said he felt faint and the "doctors" in attendance injected a stimulant. According to this account, Dzerzhinsky unwillingly returned to his Kremlin apartment but refused to go to bed. He then turned suddenly to his wife and said, "I think after all I will lie down," staggered toward a couch, and fell across it dead. See Walter Duranty's article in *The New York Times*, August 2, 1926. No matter the truth of "Who Killed Dzerzhinsky?" the fact of his death removed a major obstacle in Stalin's ascent to total power in the Soviet state.

5. S. Vladimir Krulich, *Los Angeles Times*, March 6, 1977.

6. For instance, a Soviet rug was presented, at the direction of Boris Bykov, to Nathan Silvermaster. Swiss Brig. Gen. Jean Louis Jeanmarie, who worked for the Soviets for more than twelve years, had elegant gold cuff links to mark the KGB's appreciation. Dr. Alan Nunn May, Canadian physicist convicted of complicity in Soviet espionage in Canada, refused money but accepted "$200 stuffed into a whisky bottle."—Alan Moorhead, *The Traitors* (London: Hamish Hamilton, 1952), p. 28.

7. Milovan Djilas, *Conversations with Stalin* (New York: Frederick A. Praeger, 1957), p. 148.

8. Ibid., p. 171.

9. Vladimir Voynovich, who operated under many aliases, enjoyed a broad reputation in the Cheka for bold, unconventional operations. His aplomb in dealing with "Scott" might be attributed to his coup in stealing the Italian ciphers. Voynovich's wife was also an experienced Chekist.

During his assignment in Paris, he was one of those who supervised the abduction of General Kutepov, which occurred on the streets of Paris in broad daylight.

This kidnapping was never officially resolved by the police, and the prime suspects were allowed sufficient time to leave France before being sought. One Soviet woman employed by the trade mission was detained in connection with her husband's probable complicity. Released on a bond posted by the Soviet embassy, she immediately fled to the USSR.

Voynovich was recalled to Moscow in connection with the "Scott" case, and there his sponsor, a Hungarian Communist named Karl Pauker, was able to intervene on his behalf and block his arrest. In the mid-thirties, Voynovich served as Stalin's chauffeur and as one of his personal bodyguards. In late 1936, Stalin decided that both Voynovich and Pauker were too well informed about his affairs and set the stage for their arrests, which occurred in early 1937. They were held prisoner, exhaustively interrogated for a year, and then executed. See Peter Deriabin, *Watchdogs of Terror* (New Rochelle, N.Y., Arlington House, 1972), pp. 203, 298.

Voynovich was rewarded for his work with the Italian, his success with Kutepov, and initially his swindle of "Scott." His failure to identify "Scott" for recontact was later regarded as "reckless" and hurtful. For a time, Stalin seemed to enjoy Voynovich's bloody-minded taste for action. Voynovich also used the names Yanovich, Janovich, and Volovich.

During this period, Walter Krivitsky was in Holland working to intercept German military communications. The fact that Gustave Bertrand, the French cryptographic expert, noted that "nothing much came of it" suggests the possibility that the Soviets had more to lose than to gain in any collaboration with the French on German military cipher systems. Although he admitted using many aliases, there is no record of his declared use of the name "Scott" in connection with French intelligence contacts. Krivitsky's true name was Samuel Ginsberg/ Ghinsberg, and his aliases included Eduard Miller, Dr. Martin Lessner, Walter Poref, and Walter Thomas. In a warning letter to the wife of his close friend Ingnace Reiss, after her husband was assassinated by the NKVD, Krivitsky used the name "Krusia," an esoteric reference to a mutual childhood friend, to convey his identity and bona fides.

Voynovich's assistants in Paris were Ivans (an alias), who posed as an inspector at the Soviet trade mission in the Rue de la Ville-l'Eveque; Ellert (an alias), who was documented as an official of the Naphtha Syndicate in the Rue Louis le Grand; and Leon Helfand (alias Lev B. Gelfand, alias Schober, alias Hoffmann). Helfand served in Germany as early as 1921, where he used the names Hoffmann and Schober. He was sent to Paris to replace Kopp (alias Victor Prassolov), who was reported to have lost 10 million francs of OGPU money at the gaming tables in Deauville and had been returned to the USSR for "investigation."

Helfand played a key role in the Kutepov abduction and was later posted to the Soviet embassy at Rome. In the summer of 1940 he was ordered to Moscow. Fearing arrest and possible execution, he deserted his post and, with the aid of Italian Foreign Minister, Count Galeazzo Ciano, fled to the United States. There is no available record of his later contact by American authorities.

Kopp served in China in 1926 and 1927, then entered France illegally. He set up an OGPU commercial cover firm at 4 Rue Mondetour with Soviet subsidies. Called "Société Française de Commerce Exterieur," the firm was very profitable, and Kopp became less attentive to his primary OGPU duties. He entertained and gambled and otherwise offended his spartan masters. Moscow, fearing that he might desert his post and seek the protection of the French police, decided to abduct him. While at a casino in Deauville, he was approached by one of his assistants, who informed him that his only son was dangerously ill. Without reflection, Kopp entered an automobile and was at once overpowered by OGPU agents, who arranged for his delivery to a Soviet vessel waiting in the harbor at Hamburg. He was tried at Leningrad. Because of his sister's marriage to an important Soviet official, received an unexpectedly gentle sentence of ten years at Solovetsky Island, which he did not survive.

Voynovich/Volovich/Janovich/Yanovich is sometimes referred to under the additional alias Vladimir Borisovich Ianovich. In an earlier post in Turkey he used the name Viliansky.

Bessedovsky depreciated Voynovich by writing "In the old days, his services would have been employed in the local police courts of a provincial town." Later, Bessedovsky conceded that "He was well acquainted with the technicalities of his profession and organized his section well in the Embassy."—Encl. #3, Department of State dispatch #578, from Paris, May 20, 1930.

Mme. Voynovich, young and attractive, was a trained photographer who also kept the confidential books of the Paris KGB residency. She was an experienced clandestine operator and had previously filled various cover assignments, posing as a Hungarian countess, the wife of a Persian diplomat in Austria, and the widow of a rich diamond merchant in Czechoslovakia.

Surreptitious photography was in its infancy in 1930. Hand-held cameras, slow shutter speeds, and even slower film speeds made for poor results in the presence of any motion, however slow. Films of higher speeds and reduced graininess were not available in Europe until late 1931. Miniature cameras with relatively fast lenses first became widely available in the United States during the early thirties. It was Mme. Voynovich who took the picture of "Scott" approaching the embassy.

10. The Grand Hotel d'Estrees was constructed in 1713 by Robert de Cotte for the Duchesse d'Estrees, who lived there until her death in 1737. Later it was the home of Charlotte-Aglae d'Orleans, daughter of the Regent and wife of the Prince d'Est. It was acquired by the Imperial Russian government and, for a brief period, was the Paris residence of Czar Nicholas II (1886). After the Russian Revolution, the structure was claimed by the Bolshevik government as the intended Soviet embassy in Paris. In 1930, the offices of the Cheka were at 79 rue de Grenelle, overlooking the embassy garden and house. Known as "Petit hotel d'Estrees," number 79 was originally occupied by the Duchesse d'Estrees while number 81 was being built. The Cheka also occupied several offices in the embassy. Four rooms at number 79 were used for document photography, another for the fabrication and forging of documents; there was also a small secret writing laboratory and a room for the monitoring of embassy phones. A disused pantry in the main building was used as a primitive photographic darkroom.

Malcolm Muggeridge records impressions of the building as seen in 1944:

"Quite suddenly Kim [Philby] said: 'Let's go to the Rue de Grenelle.' I didn't know then (though I should have) that this was where the Soviet Embassy was situated, and supposed he might have in mind some favorite cafe or night spot. Anyway, I was in a good mood to go anywhere, so we set off. Kim now began at last to talk about his new responsibilities, and I realized, at the time without any particular amazement, that we were making for the Soviet Embassy. How are we going to get in there? Kim kept saying, and went on to expiate upon the special difficulties of penetrating a Soviet Embassy as compared with others . . . no chance of planting a servant when all the staff, down to the lowest kitchen maids and porters and chauffeurs, are imported from the USSR, and sometimes, in reality, hold quite senior positions in the Intelligence apparat. Tremendous obstacles, too, in the way of bugging the place; they never let foreign electricians or builders, or anyone like that, into the Embassy. Listening devices, observation posts, inside agents, all ruled out; the staff themselves, high and low, rigidly controlled, only certain picked members allowed to circulate freely, and even they are often kept under surveillance. Look at it!—by this time we were in the Rue de Grenelle—every blind drawn, every door locked, every window with its iron grating, the very fire escape contained in steel netting; even so, behind the doors and windows, round-the-clock guards, burglar alarms, every imaginable and unimaginable security precaution. . . .

"He carried on like this in an almost demented way; not exactly shaking his fists, but gesticulating and shouting at the hermetically sealed Embassy, standing so insulated and isolated in a Paris street, as though it had been just dropped there out of the sky, to be removed, intact, when its purpose had been served." Malcolm Muggeridge, *The Infernal Grove, Chronicles of Wasted Time* (New York: William Morrow, 1974), Vol. II, pp. 250–251.

11. When the first Soviet ambassador was installed, the entablatured pediment was concealed by a canvas screen bearing a bright painting of the national emblem of the USSR. The painting and hand-lettered signs applied to the exterior walls gave the Soviet embassy an audacious and temporary character. NA Paris *Times* Collection, photo #9317.

12. Valerian Dovgalevsky's career was blighted by the effects of OGPU/GRU activities and by the indiscipline of subordinates who worked under him in the three embassies at which he served as ambassador. He was first sent to Sweden in 1926. The next year, in December the GRU naval attaché, an Estonian named Pavl Yurevich Oras, was expelled from the country for espionage involving a reserve lieutenant in the Swedish Army. Dovgalevsky was left to tidy up relations with the forgiving Swedes. He was then sent to Japan, where he found the Japanese less cordial and where his reputation for brooking if not directing espionage had preceded him. When Rakovsky was abruptly recalled from France in 1927, Dovgalevsky replaced him and was given the task of negotiating the restoration of Anglo-Soviet relations, which had terminated with the Arcos raid. He nominated Bessedovsky to act in his stead while he attempted to assuage the British across the Channel.

13. We are indebted to Gordon Brook-Sheperd for providing the details of Dovgalevsky's meeting with Arthur Henderson, the British foreign secretary Henderson ". . . was at Brighton that week, attending the annual conference of the Socialist party. Dovgalevsky also repaired to Brighton 'for his health.' But, for extra secrecy, the two men had met at the White Hart Hotel in Lewes, where

the final agreement was hammered out."—*The Storm Petrels* (London: Collins, 1977), p. 99.

It was during this visit that Dovgalevsky learned that Bessedovsky had bolted; thus, his success in England was overtaken by the debacle in Paris. When he returned to France, public outrage was at such a pitch that he feared the Soviet embassy would be overrun and sacked. According to Alexander Graf (alias Alexander G. Barmine) of the Soviet trade mission, the ambassador armed the embassy staff in anticipation of the attack, which did not occur.

Dovgalevsky returned to the USSR and dropped from sight. The official *Annuaire Diplomatique du Commissariat du Peuple pour les Affaires Etrangeres* for the years 1933–36 does not reflect another posting for Dovgalevsky. It is possible that the cumulative effect of his problems in Sweden, Japan, and, in particular, the Bessedovsky affair in France led to his becoming an early non-person.

14. The Foreign Office list to which the permanent under secretary referred cited among the Scotts the redoubtable Ambassador Sir Oswald Scott, a distinguished diplomatist.

Fifty-one years later, on the November 29, 1981, Sir Oswald's son, Edward Jervoise Scott, publicly admitted that while in the British Foreign Service *he* had worked for the Czech intelligence service, which, since its postwar inception, has been the KGB's most profitable subsidiary.

From the end of the war until 1969, the Czechs were considered the most adept of the East Europeans in the espionage game. However, the loss of many defectors to the West in '69 put the Czech service into chaos. Internal investigations, transfers, and other changes made at the direction of the KGB further reduced its utility.

At about the same time that the Czechs lost the confidence of the Soviets, the East Germans were beginning to score significant victories against NATO and the Federal Republic.

E. J. Scott was a product of Eton and Cambridge, and it would be difficult to make the case that he was an oppressed member of the toiling masses. Involvement with a Czech female agent, Irena Pecova, put him in a vulnerable position for coercive recruitment. With astonishing panache, he explained to the British press that he had colluded with the Czechs in order to get an exit visa for Peckova. "If you like, the payment for her visa was my letting the Czechs believe that in the long run they might have caught a useful fish." —*Daily Telegraph,* November 30, 1981.

Scott must be accorded a unique place in history for his extraordinary capacity to trivialize the implications of his service to the KGB. Like so many others before, the theme of double deception is present. His bland assertion about "letting the Czechs believe" suggests that his confidence in his own manipulative skills remained intact.

15. Stalin's preoccupying fear of the British was evident in many of his decisions. He assumed that the British were responsible for his failures in China. They were certainly behind the Peking raid, and the colonial police in Malaya, Burma, and India were extremely effective against Soviet efforts to propagate revolution.

There seems to be general agreement that attempts to warn Stalin of the likelihood of a German attack were seriously discounted by Stalin, since he invariably sensed deception and degraded the sources as "British plants."

Hitler confided to Stalin that it was possible that some of his own senior military officers might attempt an armed provocation against the USSR. He assured the Generalissimo that if such an incident occurred, he would take prompt disciplinary action. Stalin had just finished his purge of the Red Army and was disposed to believe Hitler's calculated suggestion that the senior officers of the German Army were likely to be "politically unreliable." Perhaps his lingering confidence in his fellow tyrant was at the root of his near-catatonic state on June 22, 1941, when the Nazis invaded.

Initially, Stalin was more fearful of the millions in the concentration camps, whom he regarded as a more immediate threat than the Germans. Before he focused on the invasion, he gave the orders to the NKVD camp commandants to begin mass executions of the prisoners.

16. Beginning in 1926 the Chekists were given the added mission of executing deserters and others who had earned the enmity of Stalin. For the most part, "wet" operations were the exclusive domain of the state security service.

Among the more widely known KGB "hits" are the murders of Rudolf Klement in Paris and, of course, Leon Trotsky in Mexico.

The Comintern executed a number of disaffected associates in the Far East and especially in Spain during the civil war (1936–37).

A GRU officer, Valentin Markin, alias "Oscar," was murdered in New York City, not because he had been unfaithful to Stalin but for other reasons according to Walter Krivitsky. Krivitsky stated that the New York records reflected the fact that Markin's death resulted from "a brawl in a speakeasy."—FBI file 100–11146, Sec. 2.

A popular theory on the reason for Markin's death holds that he had written a letter criticizing GRU operations in New York directly to Molotov, thereby embarrassing his superior, Gen. Berzin, who was then GRU chief. Markin was later killed by his GRU colleagues in an event that involved the use of a New York city taxicab. The Markin killing was represented as an act of retribution for his disloyalty to the GRU rather than for his betrayal of Stalin.

Krivitsky states that Markin had recently been moved from the GRU to the OGPU.

Hede Massing, who worked for Markin, described him as "a youngish man, with high cheekbones, bad teeth, and a brush-like mop of brown hair. His complexion was gray, his eyes cold. He struck one from the very beginning as a man who, with great energy, withheld his real self from observation. He was the personification of the Russian careerist. . . . It was a fascinating character combination, one of extreme sentimentality when drunk and relaxed, and extreme cruelty when sober and on the job. His moral and ethical standards were typical of the young Soviet man; it is not the human being that counts, but the idea!"—Hede Massing, *This Deception* (New York: Duell, Sloan & Pearce, 1951), pp 154–55.

17. Studnikov and Pauker served in the foreign division under Trilisser with responsibilities for the successful conduct of "special operations" such as the abduction of Gen. Kutepov. Studnikov not only survived the purges, the execution of his boss (Trilisser), World War II, and the death of Stalin, but he retired as

chief of the old Spetsburo, or the Thirteenth Department of the KGB, as it became known in 1954.

Little is known about Pauker except that he was arrested in December 1932, while attempting to cross Holland posing as a chauffeur. His "passenger" was a woman whose documents were found to be false, and the Dutch border police took the two into custody. A subsequent investigation by the Dutch traced the false passports to a Soviet-run passport factory in Berlin.

Pauker's taste in passports was no better than his selection of a wife. Ana Pauker, by reason of her boundless capacity for intrigue, deception, and brutality, rose to head the Romanian Communist Party. While Ana was ascending in the party, she demonstrated her absolute fidelity to Stalin by denouncing her husband as a Trotskyite.

After World War II, in the aftermath of Tito's break with the Soviets, the East European satellite parties conducted extensive purges. Ana Pauker was shot to death.

In the early thirties, E. Y. Pauker worked for Amtorg in New York City, where he was known as "Marcel" to Mrs. Whittaker Chambers, who had taken a job with the corporation as a receptionist. She remembered him as "white-haired, slight build and dark complected." FBI file 74–1333–3220.

Pauker was executed in Moscow in 1937.—David J. Dallin, *Soviet Espionage* (New Haven: Yale University Press, 1955), p. 100.

18. The "officials," who had diplomatic passports, regarded the "illegals" with fear and loathing. The fact that there were representatives of state security, the GRU, and the Comintern, operating in parallel and not always known to the resident in the embassy, made the officials very nervous. In many respects, the multiple systems were insurance against excessive corruption, fabrication of reporting sources, indiscipline, and party disloyalty. In the Soviet system, it is not always possible to distinguish an umpire from a ballplayer without a program. This institutionalized uncertainty has the effect of keeping the officials alert, active, and focused on their assigned targets.

The illegals lived in constant fear because their status denied them the comfort of fraternal contact with like-minded souls. For the most part, they operated in hostile environments with no protection except their wits. The possibility of betrayal, compromise, or accidental arrest was and is a constant, palpable threat.

Their lives were completely structured, with direction coming from a single source of authority. The operational objectives of many of their activities were never fully disclosed to them, making their concept of the "unknown" infinite in its bounds. An illegal's role is demanding, dangerous, and sometimes lethal.

19. Hans Galleni was an early member of the illegal Swiss Communist Party. In 1921 he "dropped out" to join the GRU. After a few years in France and Belgium, he moved to The Hague, where he worked against German targets.

Galleni spoke French, Italian, German, Dutch, and English. He had the manners and speech of a sophisticated European businessman. His many years of service in The Hague gave him a solid cover and a rational contact with another GRU agent who "worked" as a bona fide artist in Holland.

Galleni dropped from sight in 1936, and there was no subsequent trace of him in Western Europe. It is very likely that he was caught up in the purge of the Soviet services and executed.

In 1940 Krivitsky informed the British of J. H. King, and King, after his arrest, identified "Scott." An effort was then made to identify "Scott's recruiter. Although "Scott" had been dead for seven years, his wife Lucy was still living in London at Newton Mansions, Queen's Club Gardens, Kensington. Because she knew Galleni as a result of seeing him on several occasions in 1931 and 1932, arrangements were made to seek her cooperation in providing confirmation of Hans's identity from photographs and drawings. Regrettably, she died in London a few days before the meeting with the authorities could take place.

Galleni, whatever his fate, can claim credit for the first significant penetration of the British Foreign Office. His courage and discipline as a solitary illegal in undertaking an exceedingly dangerous mission to London is noteworthy. At the time of his first visit, in fact, Britain was, from the Soviet viewpoint, a "denied area."

In the spate of official Soviet writings issued on the fiftieth anniversary of the founding of the Cheka, Galleni is not mentioned, nor is there any evidence that he has been "rehabilitated." A number of his GRU colleagues deserted in 1937 and 1938 and were accused of having been in the pay of the British or Germans— which would have been sufficient basis for his execution.

20. The organs' resident in London at that time (c. 1930) was Theodore Maly, who returned a few years later as Paul Hardt, Stevens, and Peters to play a stellar role in the Woolwich Arsenal case.

Maly was a chaplain in the Hungarian army during World War I and was taken prisoner by the Russians. He became a strident Bolshevik in his POW camp, renounced the cloth, and took up espionage as his new vocation. He worked with some effect against the British but very nearly became the victim of an M.I.5 counter-espionage operation. With feline agility he avoided arrest, escaped Britain, and disappeared into France.

The prosecution of the Woolwich Arsenal case revealed that the British, too, had very effectively penetrated several Soviet organizations and facilities. Thus, like so many other Soviet security and intelligence officers working in foreign areas, Maly came under Soviet suspicion on several counts: (1) he wasn't a Russian; (2) his net had been penetrated; and (3) the British had scored a significant public coup. It is assumed that he was arrested and executed along with hundreds of other GRU and NKVD officers in 1937–38, though this has not been confirmed by other sources.

21. Until January 1, 1960, Article 58 referred to the provision, under Soviet law, for charges against those engaged in sedition, counterrevolutionary activity, slander and libel of Soviet leaders, espionage, antisocial behavior, etc. The provisions of Article 58 were broad, and the interpretations allowed to the state security were virtually infinite.

The new penal code promulgated in January 1960 was not a revision of the fourteen paragraphs of Article 58 but was made up of several new, individual articles and definitions. The term "counterrevolutionary" was replaced by "anti-Soviet," for instance. All of the original articles were slightly revised and assigned new numbers.

The changes in no way diminished the law's breadth and punitive power. As before, every individual in the USSR was and is in violation of one or more of the interpretations of the revised Article 58, so it is solely a question of how the authorities opt to apply and enforce the laws.

22. "'Nonsense,' said the indignant camp official to a prisoner serving a twenty-five-year sentence. The prisoner had insisted that he had done 'nothing' to deserve such a term.

"'For "nothing" you only get ten years.'"—Alexandr I. Solzhenitsyn, *The Gulag Archipelago 1918–1956* (New York: Harper & Row, 1956).

23. Literally, *Abwehr* means "defense, warding off, guarding against." The Abwehr in its original form constituted the secret intelligence service of the German High Command. From 1925 on, the Abwehr operated within and against the Netherlands from a base in Cologne. The OGPU and GRU succeeded in penetrating the Abwehr, and many of its agents, particularly those involved in maritime intelligence collection, were well known to the Soviet services. See Jan Valtin (pseudonym of Richard Julius Herman Krebs, alias E. Holmberg), *Out of the Night,* which describes the conflicts between the Germans and the Soviets over control of the merchant seamen and dockworkers in Amsterdam and Rotterdam in the 1920s and '30s.

24. "Cobblers" or "shoemakers" were euphemistic references to those who manufactured or altered documents. The Comintern term for passport was *sapog* (boot). Soviet services have a truly gigantic need for examples of cachets, rubber stamps, seals, and original signatures taken from valid documents. Initially, the primary facility for document preparation was in Berlin. Aside from the highly skilled engravers and printers, artists, and photographers there, an even larger group was devoted to the collection and current posting of intelligence regarding the documents themselves. For instance: What is the name of the Uruguayan consul who served in Lyon in 1924? Is his signature on file? When did the Belgian government increase visa fees? Do British Commonwealth passport serials indicate coded information relating to the bearer? What is the precise nature of the application questionnaire necessary to file for a Nansen passport? How do the Italians affix photographs to documents? What solvents can be used to remove them without disturbing the inks?

Another element was concerned with the theft of documents. The Soviets made a market with thieves and pickpockets, offering to buy documents and identity papers, which otherwise had little value.

The Berlin shop was a fully integrated factory capable of making paper and inks and of engraving, printing, and binding passports of eight to ten different countries on demand.

All passengers arriving in the USSR by train surrendered their passports to the border guards, to be returned on arrival at the passenger's destination. On board Soviet passenger or tourist ships the foreign passports are routinely photographed for the cobblers' files.

Foreigners sympathetic to the USSR have been asked to offer their passports and be quiet about it. In these cases, the photograph of the donor was removed and that of the new bearer affixed. Next, the new bearer learned the curriculum vitae of the donor and any peculiarities that would aid the impersonation. The details of the donor were meticulously noted and filed with the altered passport for reference. The donor system was widely used in the Comintern.

25. Since July 17, 1861, the U.S. government has issued paper currency. During President Taft's term in office (1909–1913), Secretary of the Treasury Franklin MacVeagh proposed that a committee be established to study the economies that would result from the issuance of smaller-sized notes. The study concluded that more than $500,000 in savings would accrue each year if the bills were reduced in size. The Bureau of Printing and Engraving was given the order to issue the new bills just at the time of a change in administrations. William McAdoo succeeded MacVeagh and, though not opposed to the order, deferred its execution.

In 1925, Secretary of the Treasury Andrew Mellon restudied the question, and in May 1927, he ordered the production of the new bills. The smaller-sized U.S. currency was not in general circulation until after July 10, 1929.

The $100 Federal Reserve note bearing the likeness of Benjamin Franklin (pre-WWI series) was to figure prominently in another Soviet operation that was wholly devoted to the counterfeiting of U.S. currency.

26. Techniques of agent communication in Europe during the 1930s were by personal contact and the disciplined use of the postal systems. The telegraph and telephone systems were only lightly used because they were government operated and under official surveillance. A part of the agent-communications support structure required the generation of a large number of cooperative addressees who would agree to accept mail. Most, if not all, of the innocent addressees were told only that the mail dealt with correspondence of a romantic nature that, if sent direct, would complicate domestic life. The letters were usually put into a second preaddressed, prepaid envelope for remailing. Sometimes a single letter passed through several remailings before being seen by the intended reader.

The letters themselves carried enciphered sections so that, even if read, nothing compromising was disclosed. Secret inks were also used, but these were more difficult to prepare and sometimes required chemical processing to make them visible. All letters passing through these circuits contained hidden systems that would reveal if the seal had been disturbed or the contents removed for inspection. Although the techniques were rudimentary, they were generally effective.

The terms "mail accommodation," "accommodation address," and "letter drop" are used interchangeably.

27. In late 1943, Klaus Fuchs was sent to the United States from the University of Birmingham as a member of the Joint American-British-Canadian team working on the development of barrier technology essential in the gaseous diffusion-separation method of concentrating U-235. Prior to his departure from Great Britain Fuchs took the initiative and made contact with Jurgen Kuczynski (see below), who passed the word to his Soviet contact, Simon Davidovich Kremer, an assistant to the military attaché in the Soviet embassy. Kremer, an experienced GRU officer, arranged for a less visible contact, Sonia Kuczynski, to pick up the case. She instructed Fuchs, on arrival in the United States, to go to a specified intersection on the Lower East Side of New York City on successive Saturdays carrying a tennis ball in his right hand. His Soviet contact, Henryk Golodnotzky (alias Harry Gold or Raymond), would carry a green-bound book, wear gloves, and carry a second pair of gloves in the same hand as the book.

Both men were subsequently arrested in 1950. Gold was convicted in the United States and was sentenced to thirty years. He died in prison. Fuchs was arrested in Britain, tried, convicted, and sentenced to fourteen years' imprisonment. On his release in 1959, Fuchs returned to East Germany, where he was appointed deputy director of the Central Institute for Nuclear Physics at Dresden.

Kremer's counterpart in the United States used the alias or "work" name of Anatoli A. Yakolev (his true name was Yatskov). He was attached to the Soviet consulate in New York City from 1941 to 1946. One of the people he tried to recruit was Thomas L. Black, an American party member who worked for Amtorg. Black declined but suggested Gold. The interview took place in Yakolev's second office, located within the Amtorg complex.

When Yakolev was indicted by a federal grand jury, he hastily departed the United States for France, where he took up a position in the Soviet embassy in Paris as "a scientific and technical officer." Like many of his diligent predecessors, Yakolev found himself in trouble on his return to Moscow in 1948 "because of relatives."—*New York Times,* December 5, 1975.

The man who put Klaus Fuchs in contact with the GRU in London, Juergen Kuczynski, was the son of a professor at the London School of Economics. Juergen's sister Ursula, with her husband of convenience, Leon Buerton, had recently arrived in England from Switzerland. Ursula used the names Buerton and Hamburger but is best known in the trade as Sonia.

She was a GRU officer in China from 1930 to 1935. She worked for the KPD in Germany until 1938, at which time she and her then husband, Rudolph Hamburger, were sent to Switzerland. In early 1940, she divorced Hamburger and married a British radio operator named Leon Buerton, so that she could acquire British citizenship for use in her next assignment, Romania. But the assignment was canceled, and she moved to England in February 1941. She is currently living in East Germany, where she has published a book purporting to tell of her adventures on behalf of "the peace-loving people of the world."

CHAPTER 4

1. Constitutional Acts 1922–1936; Collection of Laws 1934–1941; *Bolshaya Sovietskaya Ensiklopedia;* Soviet press reports.

2. To qualify for the distinction of being named an Honored Chekist required ten years of service in the organs. The entire first group to be nominated consisted of veterans of the civil war.

3. Thaddeus Wittlin, *Commissar: The Life and Death of Lavrenty Pavlovich Beria* (New York: The Macmillan Co., 1972), p. 74.

CHAPTER 5

1. Thaddeus Wittlin, *Commissar: The Life and Death of Lavrenty Pavlovich Beria* (New York: The Macmillan Co., 1972), p. 217.

2. Ibid., pp. 261–62.

3. See esp. Lavrenti P. Beria, *Stalin's Early Writings and Activities: On the*

History of the Bolshevik Organization in Transcaucasia (Moscow: Foreign Language Publishing House, 1939). The first edition of Beria's work was published in Russian in 1935; the final, ninth edition was published in 1952. Careful reading of these successive paeans to the "Great Stalin's role in the revolution" strongly suggests the basis of Orwell's parody on Big Brother's appetite for historical revisionism. Concurrent with Beria's rewrite, competing versions of the events were eradicated, as were many of those with firsthand knowledge and, in some cases, the actual performers of the heroic deeds attributed to Stalin by Beria.

It should be noted that after Beria's execution, one of the first acts of his successor, Sergey N. Kruglov, was to order the elimination of all copies of Beria's fictional history. The collection, as Orwell might have put it, became non-books.

4. See esp. "Thirty-fourth Anniversary of the Great October Socialist Revolution," address of L. P. Beria at the Solemn Session of the Moscow Soviet on November 6, 1951 (FBIS Report #242, USSR, November 13, 1951). Beria's speech literally turns economics upside down. The exaggerated claims of increased production, expanded capital investment, and improvements in individual welfare are well beyond the credulity of all but the most slavish ideologue.

It is unfortunate that Soviet "political statistics" still form the basis for some comparative economic studies by U.S. academics who seek to derive an understanding of the performance of the Soviet economy.

5. J. Bernard Hutton, *School for Spies* (New York: Coward-McCann, 1962), pp. 55–62.

6. Wittlin, op. cit., p. 298.

7. Aleksei Myagkov, *Inside the KGB* (New York: Arlington House, 1976) pp. 61–75.

8. Once he became General Secretary of the CPSU, Stalin became the sole judge of what Soviet communism was. A few years before, Jan Sten, prominent Marxist philosopher, had been called to direct Stalin's study of dialectics. Sten later told E. P. Frolov about his student's inability to master Marx's *Capital* and Hegel's *Phenomenology of Mind:*

> His [Stalin's] inclination towards administrative fiat, towards coercion instead of convincing, his oversimplified and mechanistic approach to complex political problems, his crude pragmatism and inability to foresee the consequences of alternative actions, his vicious nature and unparalleled ambition—all these qualities of Stalin seriously complicated the solutions of problems that were overwhelming to begin with.

Lenin's wife, N. K. Krupskaya, charged Stalin with "insincerity" in a 1930 speech in which she said, "Collectivization, as carried out by Stalin, has nothing in common with Lenin's plan for developing cooperatives."

With few exceptions, the old Bolsheviks were destroyed in their attempts to defend the ideals of Marxism-Leninism from Stalin's ideological corruption. Walter Krivitsky cited Stalin's contempt for the Comintern (a Lenin-Trotsky creation) in the dictator's reference to the International as *Lavoehka,* a "gyp joint." From

1927 on, Marxism-Leninism became a weapon of repression instead of a philosophical base for the body politic. There are hundreds of other sources who decried Stalin's perversions of the ideals of Marxism-Leninism, his disregard of the goal of "world revolution," and his betrayal of the Russian revolution.

9. We use a theoretical example here because U.S. government agencies have so far refused to acknowledge the existence of these cases.

10. John Barron, *KGB Today: The Hidden Hand* (New York: Reader's Digest Press, 1983), p. 390; see also pp. 230–55 for an account of "Colonel" Hermann's experience at Bykova and the proposed Soviet plan to recruit his son.

11. Staff interviews with Nikolai Khokhlov (1954) and Yevgeny V. Runge (February 1970). Subcommittee to Investigate the Administration of the Internal Security Act and Other Internal Security Laws, Committee of the Judiciary, U.S. Senate.

12. Staff interviews, op. cit. with Ladislaw Bittman (1971).

13. Peter Deriabin, *Watchdogs of Terror* (New Rochelle, N.Y.: Arlington House, 1972), pp. 219–20. "Among those executed were Marshal Tukhachevsky and his comrades in arms, Marshals Kork, Uborevich, Yakir, Feldman, Primakov, Eideman, and Putna, who were accused of being fascists.

"A short time later, Chief of the Red Air Forces, Alsknis, and the Commander in Chief of the Red Navy, Admiral Orolov were condemned to death as were Marshals Yegorov, Rokossovsky and Army Commander Belov and General Gorbatov, along with many other leading officers were deported to Siberia. The insane purges in the Red Army reduced the Soviet military forces by at least 30 percent. For the men who were familiar with the situation it was no secret that 60 to 70 percent of the officers were arrested; 11 Adjutant Commissars of War and 71 out of 80 members of the High Council disappeared, being deported to hard labor camps in Siberia. They were aware also that 90 percent of the generals and 80 percent of the colonels were eliminated. All told, between 30,000 and 35,000 men, including the Specialist Officer Corps, were exterminated." In terms of the United States, this act of madness would have been equivalent to the elimination of 80 percent of the armed forces' officer corps above the rank of major, just prior to the attack on Pearl Harbor.

14. Richard Sorge, a doctor of political science and a GRU agent, arranged to be accredited as the Far East correspondent of the *Frankfurter Zeitung*. As a Soviet agent, Sorge avoided all association with the KPD (German Communist Party) and was able to insinuate himself into the German National Socialist fringe.

He became a member of the Nazi Party and a personal friend of Joseph Goebbels, the propaganda minister, who introduced him to the Fuehrer. General Ott, the German military attaché and, later, ambassador of Japan, nominated Sorge as press attaché of the Tokyo embassy. The Soviets could not have had a more competent or better-placed clandestine operator than Sorge in the center of the official German community in Japan immediately prior to World War II.

15. W. R. Corson, *The Armies of Ignorance,* (New York: Dial Press, 1977), pp. 84–87.

16. Wittlin, op. cit., pp. 295–96.

17. Although the term Smersh was not in use after 1946, the organizational

tasks are still provided for within the present KGB. For information about such activities during the years 1950–1970, see Vincent and Nan Buranelli, *Spy-Counterspy* (New York: McGraw-Hill, 1982), p. 294, "The function for which SMERSH is most notorious in the West is the killing, kidnapping, blackmailing, or otherwise disposing of selected opponents of the regime who live abroad. To facilitate murder when the murderer must quickly escape, SMERSH invented an array of lethal gadgets and concoctions, from electric guns to poisons both highly potent and difficult to detect. Its murder laboratory is one of the world's most effective research facilities.

"Detailed information about SMERSH and its methods reached Western intelligence mainly through KGB agents who defected, especially through Nicolai Khokhlov and Bogdan Stashinsky. Both testified to the organization's skill in scientific murder. Khokhlov, for instance, was armed with a miniature electric gun firing cyanide pellets, while Stashinsky had a small tube that sprayed prussic acid. Both men claimed to have been horrified by their assignments and deserted rather than obey their superiors."

18. Raymond N. Dawson, *The Decision to Aid the USSR* (Chapel Hill: University of North Carolina Press, 1959), pp. xi–xii.

19. See esp. Roberta Wohlstetter, *Pearl Harbor, Warning and Decision* (Palo Alto, Calif.: Stanford University Press, 1962). Mrs. Wohlstetter makes the point that, as devastating as the Japanese attack itself was, once it occurred, the U.S. political and military commanders were stunned, temporarily, into inactivity, which prevented or delayed prompt reactive measures.

20. David Kahn, *Hitler's Spies: German Military Intelligence in WWII* (New York: Macmillan, 1978), esp. chap. 5, "The Military Attaché."

21. Sir Edward L. Spears, *Assignment to Catastrophe.* Vol. 2: *The Fall of France June 1940* (New York: A. A. Wyn, 1955). Maj. Gen. Spears makes clear that the German victory against the French and British forces was more a "live firing exercise" than a real contest for terrain, position, and physical defeat of the enemy forces. Spears' detailed account discusses the "fifth column" myth, which was used to explain and, in some ways, justify the failure of French arms. There was no fifth column. The French Army, having been conditioned to expect defeat, was emotionally prepared to surrender after a few insignificant engagements.

22. FBI file 65–6515.

23. William H. Standley, *Admiral Ambassador to Russia* (Chicago: Henry Regnery, 1955), pp. 35, 39–40; Capt. William D. Puleston to CO, USS *Saratoga,* June 21, 1934, Box D25, Day File.

24. Peer DeSilva, *Sub Rosa: The CIA and the Uses of Intelligence* (New York: Times Books, 1978), pp. 72–74.

25. Some headlines from Walter Duranty's *New York Times* stories are indicative: "Soviets Growing Spirit of Compromise," March 27, 1927, II, 1:2; "Dawning of Friendlier Days," March 27, 1927, II, 1:2; "Romance Returns to Moscow Markets," March 30, 1927, 8:1; "Russia's Hate for Britain, Actuated by Fear of British Plot to Destroy Soviet State," June 28, 1927, 5:2; "Marxist Dogma of Economic Basis of All Wars Spurs Belief in World's Jealousy of Russia," July 4, 1927, 6:1; and, in particular, "2% Grain Surplus for State Grain Collection Program. Winter Wheat is 4½% Larger Than Last Year," December 22, 1929, III, 8:1.

See Marco Carynnyk, "The Famine the *Times* Couldn't Find," *Commentary*, November 1983, p. 32. Carynnyk quotes the announcement of Duranty's Pulitzer Prize: "[His dispatches] were 'marked by scholarship, profundity, impartiality, sound judgment and exceptional clarity.' Malcolm Muggeridge regarded Duranty as 'the greatest liar of any journalist that I have met in fifty years of journalism.' Joseph Alsop echoed Muggeridge by observing that Duranty 'lied like a trooper.' Stalin is quoted as telling Duranty 'You have done a good job in your reporting of the USSR, although you are not a Marxist, because you tried to tell the truth about our country and explain it to your readers." At the time, Stalin was referring to the 1933 opposition to recognition of the USSR. Among the points raised by the oppositionists was Stalin's manufactured famine, which Carynnyk describes as one of the greatest crimes of the 20th century.

Neither the *Times* nor the Pulitzer Prize committee have acknowledged their respective, though unwitting, roles in propagating Soviet disinformation and simultaneously rewarding the vehicle of the deception.

26. Standley, op. cit., p. 41.

27. Anthony Cave Brown and Charles B. MacDonald, *On a Field of Red* (New York: G. P. Putnam's Sons, 1981), pp. 9–10.

28. *Nash,* the Russian word for "our." Used esoterically in the organs to convey that an individual is "trustworthy and disciplined."

29. Reino Andrey Hayhanen, alias Eugene Maki, "worked" (though not very effectively) under William Fisher, alias "Col. Abel," the doyen of Soviet illegals in the United States. The money was to go to Helen Sobell, whose husband Morton was also under prosecution by federal authorities. (Sobell was sentenced to thirty years imprisonment on March 29, 1951.) The hapless Hayhanen was eventually recalled to Moscow. En route he stopped off at the U.S. embassy in Paris and requested asylum. One of the "gifts" he brought to U.S. intelligence was the identification of Abel, who had been in the United States as an illegal since 1948. Abel was arrested in New York City in June 1958. After a trial in which the defense called no witnesses but relied on questioning the legality of searches and seizures of Abel's property, the Soviet agent was sentenced to thirty years in federal prison. In February 1962 he was exchanged for captured U-2 pilot Francis Gary Powers.

30. Ronald Radosh and Joyce Milton, *The Rosenberg File* (New York: Holt, Rinehart and Winston, 1983).

31. Wittlin, op. cit., pp. 328–29.

32. Staff interviews, Subcommittee to Investigate the Administration of the Internal Security Act, 1972.

33. Corson, op. cit., pp. 279–84.

34. Wittlin, op. cit., p. 326.

35. Hearings before the Select Committee of the U.S. House of Representatives, 82nd Congress, Part 7, Exhibit 24 (Washington, D.C.: U.S. Government Printing Office, 1952).

36. Hearings before the Select Committee to Conduct an Investigation of the Facts, Evidence and Circumstances of the Katyn Forest Massacre, 82nd Congress, 2nd Session, Part 7, June 3, 4, November 11, 12, 13, 14 (Washington D.C.: U.S. Government Printing Office, 1952).

37. Ibid.

38. Telephone interview, October 1983, kindness of T. Wittlin.

39. Corson, op. cit., pp. 291–329.

40. Thomas F. Troy, *Donovan and the CIA* (Washington, D.C.: The Central Intelligence Agency, 1981).

41. Corson, op. cit., pp. 333–34.

42. William Manchester, *American Caesar* (Boston: Little, Brown, 1978), pp. 596–97.

43. Ibid.

44. Wittlin, op. cit., pp. 375–76. According to this source, on the night of March 1, 1953, Stalin was alone with Beria at his country home, Blizhny at Kuntsevo, ". . . standing with his back to his subordinate, the Dictator displayed his short neck and above it the weak spot just under the right ear and the bone behind. One swift, precise stroke with the blackjack Beria always carried in his pocket could cause the effect he had achieved so many times when practicing on victims in the cellars of the Lubyanka prison. The right and perhaps the only moment came. Did Beria seize the chance? Nobody can tell for certain." Wittlin supports his scenario by citing his conviction that Beria had sufficient motive to kill Stalin. Beria's subsequent actions indicated that he had already, consciously, prepared a plan to seize power.

45. On December 24, 1953, *Pravda* announced the formal indictment and the sentence as well as the execution of Beria and his codefendants as follows:

"IN THE SUPREME COURT OF THE USSR

"From the 18th to the 23rd of December 1953, the Special Judicial Session of the Supreme Court of the USSR consisting of:

"I. S. Konev, Marshal of the Soviet Union, Presiding Justice of the Special Judicial Session of the Supreme Court and members of the Special Session: N. M. Shvernik, Chairman of the All-Union Central Council of Trade Unions; E. L. Zeydin, First Deputy Chairman of the Supreme Court of the USSR; K. S. Moskalenko, General of the Army; N. A. Mikhaylov, Secretary of the Moscow Region of the Communist Party of the Soviet Union; M. I. Kuchava, Chairman of the Council of Trade Unions in Georgia; L. A. Gromov, Chairman of the Moscow Municipal Court; K. F. Lunev, First Deputy Minister of Internal Affairs of the USSR sitting in a Secret Session, *in camera,* duly constituted according to procedure established by law of 1 December 1934, examined the criminal case of L. P. Beria and others.

"In accordance with the indictment, L. P. Beria was brought to trial under charges specified by Articles 58–1B, 58–8, 58–13, 58–11 of the Criminal Code of the Russian Soviet Federated Socialist Republic; V. N. Merkulov, V. G. Dekanozov, B. Z. Kobulov, S. A. Goglidze, P. Y. Meshik, L. E. Vlodzimirsky, under the indictment for crimes specified by articles 58–1B, 58–8, 58–11 of the Criminal Code of the Russian Soviet Federated Socialist Republic.

"The judicial investigation fully confirmed the finding of the preliminary investigation, presented to all defendants in the indictment.

"The Court has determined that having betrayed the Country and acting in the interest of foreign capital, Beria organized a treacherous group of conspirators, hostile to the Soviet State, consisting of defendants, V. N. Merkulov, V. G. Dekanozov, B. Z. Kobulov, S. A. Goglidze, P. Y. Meshik and L. E. Vlodzimirsky, tied with Beria in joint criminal activities in the course of several years. The criminal intent of the conspirators was to use the organs of the Ministry of Internal Affairs against the Communist Party and the Government of the USSR; to elevate the Ministry of Internal Affairs above the Party and the Government in order to seize power; to destroy the Soviet Workers' and Peasants' System; to revive capitalism and to restore the rule of the bourgeoisie.

"The Court has found that the beginning of the criminal, treacherous acts of L. P. Beria and the establishment of secret communication with foreign services dates dates back to 1919, the time of Civil War, when L. P. Beria, residing in Baku, committed treason by working as a secret agent for the Intelligence of the counter-revolutionary Mussavat government in Azerbaijan, operating under the British intelligence network.

"In 1920, L. P. Beria was living in Georgia, where again he committed treason by establishing a clandestine communication with the Secret Political Police of the Georgia Menshevik Government, the latter being also a cell of British Intelligence.

"In the following years, L. P. Beria continued and widened his secret connections with the foreign Intelligence until the moment of his arrest.

"In the course of several years, L. P. Beria and his accomplices carefully concealed and camouflaged their hostile activities.

"Following the death of J. V. Stalin, counting on the intensification of efforts against the Soviet Government by the reactionary imperialist forces, L. P. Beria increased his efforts in order to accomplish his anti-Soviet treacherous designs, which facilitated in a short time the unmasking of Beria as well as of his accomplices, thus putting an end to their criminal activities.

"When he became the Minister of Internal Affairs of the USSR in March 1953, the defendant L. P. Beria, preparing for a seizure of power, began to promote intensely the members of his conspiratorial group to positions of leadership in the Central as well as in the local organs of the Ministry of Internal Affairs. L. P. Beria and his accomplices persecuted the honest employees of the Ministry of Internal Affairs who refused to carry out criminal orders of the conspirators.

"To achieve their anti-Soviet treacherous goals. L. P. Beria and his accomplices undertook a number of criminal measures in order to revive the remnants of the bourgeois and nationalist elements in the Soviet Republics, to spread hostility and mistrust among the nations of the USSR, the first before all to undermine the friendship of the nations of the USSR with the great Russian Nation.

"Acting as foul enemy of the Soviet Nation, and intending to create problems in the Country's food supply system, the defendant L. P. Beria sabotaged and hampered the implementation of important measures undertaken by the Party with the view of improving the economy of collective and State farms and constantly raising the prosperity of the Soviet people.

"It has been established that by concealing and camouflaging their criminal activities, defendants L. P. Beria and his accomplices perpetrated acts of terror upon persons by whom they feared to be exposed. Slander, intrigues, and various forms of provocation were among the basic methods used by the conspirators against honest Party and Soviet Government workers who stood in the way of the hostile designs against the Soviet State of L. P. Beria and his accomplices, and who were hindering their thrust for power.

"The Court has determined that defendants L. P. Beria; V. N. Merkulov; V. G. Dekanozov; B. Z. Kobulov; S. A. Goglidze; P. Y. Meshik and L. E. Vlodzimirsky, using their official positions in the organs of the People's Commissariat of Internal Affairs, NKVD; the Ministry of State Security, MGB; and the Ministry of Internal Affairs, MVD; perpretrated a number of grave crimes with the intention of destroying honest cadres who were dedicated to the Communist Party and the Soviet Government.

"The Court has also established that L. P. Beria committed crimes which testify to his moral degeneration; and that he committed acts of criminal greediness, self-aggrandizement and an abuse of power.

"Guilt of all defendants was proven in Court on the basis of genuine documents, material evidence, records in their own handwriting, and testimony of many witnesses.

"Being exposed by the evidence in Court, defendants L. P. Beria, V. N. Merkulov, V. G. Dekanozov, B. Z. Kobulov, S. A. Goglidze, P. Y. Meshik and L. E. Vlodzimirsky, corroborated the evidence with which they were confronted during the preliminary hearing and confessed being guilty of perpetrating a number of acts of high treason.

"A Special Judicial Session of the Supreme Court of the USSR has found L. P. Beria guilty of treason against the country for organizing the anti-Soviet group of conspirators aiming to seize the power and to restore the rule of bourgeoisie; for committing acts of terror against political leaders devoted to the Communist Party and to the Nations of the Soviet Union; for actively opposing the revolutionary workers' movement in Baku in 1919, when Beria was a secret agent working for the Intelligence of the counter-revolutionary Mussavat government in Azerbaijan, where he made connections with the foreign Intelligence Service, and subsequently for maintaining and expanding his contacts with the foreign Intelligence until the time of his exposure and arrest, that is for the offenses specified by Articles 58–1B, 58–8, 58–13, 58–11 of the Criminal Code of the Russian Soviet Federated Socialist Republic.

"The Court established the guilt of the defendants . . .

"The Special Judicial Session of the Supreme Court of the USSR decided to sentence L. P. Beria, V. N. Merkulov, V. G. Dekanozov, B. Z. Kobulov, S. A. Goglidze, P. Y. Meshik, L. E. Vlodzimirsky to the highest degree of penalty— execution by firing squad, confiscations of their personal property, forfeiture of military titles and decorations.

"The Sentence is final, without right of appeal.

"EXECUTION OF THE SENTENCE

"Yesterday, on 23 of December, the Sentence passed by the Special Session of the Supreme Court of the USSR, condemning L. P. Beria, V. N. Merkulov, V. G. Dekanozov, B. Z. Kobulov, S. A. Goglidze, P. Y. Meshik and L. E. Vlodzimirsky to the highest degree of punishment—execution by a firing squad was carried out."

(Note: Although the bogus indictment, trial, and sentence came as no surprise to the defendants, it did surprise the British to have the Soviets pay such high tribute to M.I.6. By official Soviet reckoning, Beria was the *third* head of the organs to serve as a secret British agent. The U.S. press interpreted the remarkable statement in *Pravda* by tersely observing, "Soviet Spymaster Is Dropped.")

46. On or about December, 27, 1953, Boris Nikolaevski further identified the executed:

Sergei Goglidze, colonel general, old Caucasian Chekist, close friend of Beria's and about same age. Since 1939–40, head of Far East intelligence (China, Japan, and Korea). A Georgian who handled particularly "complex" matters for Beria.

Vsevolod Merkulov, army general. Served with Beria in the Caucasian Cheka. Head of main the administration of state security of the People's Commissariat of Internal Affairs (GUGB NKVD), which was changed from "people's commissariat" to "ministry" in March 1946. Since 1938–39, People's Commissar of State Security (since 1946, Minister), when state security became an independent People's Commissariat in 1941. Was later replaced by V. Abakumov. Last post was that of minister for state inspection.

Bogdan Kobulov, colonel general, long-standing deputy to Merkulov in various posts.

Lev Vlodzimirski, lieutenant general, head of one of the main administrations of state security.

Vladimir Dekanozov, former chief of the Foreign Department, Internal Affairs, People's Commissariat, Republic of Georgia. Since 1939, in the People's Commissariat for Foreign Affairs of the USSR. Ambassador to Nazi Germany. Last post was minister of internal affairs, Soviet Republic of Georgia.

Pavel Menshik. First public mention was in May or June 1953; ex-minister of internal affairs, Soviet Republic of the Ukraine.

The names Goglidze, Merkulov, Kobulov, and Dekanozov suggest Caucasian (not Georgian) origins. The typical Russian first names suggest a willing attempt at Russification.

CHAPTER 6

1. The death sentences of Merkulov, Dekanozov, Kobulov, Goglidze, Meshik, and Vlodzimirsky in connection with Beria's attempted coup were unprecedented in the history of the organs. These men were, respectively, the unchallenged heads of the organs. They actually controlled the Soviet Union's internal security and worldwide espionage apparatus. Their abrupt executions and the arrests and removal of their principal deputies by Kruglov resembled Stalin's earlier purge of the Red Army's principal commanders. The action, though justified in terms of the necessity to reestablish the party's control, effectively decapitated the organs.

2. While Beria was using the NKVD to operate technical surveillance against the telephones of the senior party officials in his one-man effort to seize control, Kruglov, using trusted MVD men, wired Beria's office and phones on orders from

Stalin.—Peter Deriabin and Frank Gibney, *The Secret World* (New York: Doubleday, 1959), p. 170.

Beria's main charge against Kruglov was that Kruglov was "disloyal" (to Beria) at a time when Beria was being disloyal (to the party). See John Barron, *KGB: The Secret Work of Soviet Agents* (New York: Reader's Digest Press, 1973), p. 341.

3. Brian Freemantle, *KGB: Inside the World's Largest Intelligence Network* (New York: Holt, Rinehart and Winston, 1982), pp. 38–59.

4. The fact that Marshal Konev presided over the trial of Beria and the others had significance beyond the charade of the trial itself. His role unambiguously conveyed the message that the Soviet military had weighed in behind Malenkov and Khrushchev and was supporting the party in its action to purge itself. Having Marshal Konev in the judge's chair gave the purging of Beria a kind of legitimacy that could never have been achieved in an ordinary civil court or party tribunal.

5. Brian Freemantle, op cit.

6. House Committee on Un-American Activities, Staff interview with Captain Nikolai Fedorovich Artamanov (1960).

7. Brian Freemantle, op. cit., p. 70.

8. R. Dan Richardson, *The Comintern Army* (Lexington: The University Press of Kentucky, 1982), p. 70.

9. Dallin, David J., *Soviet Espionage* (New Haven, Conn.: Yale University Press, 1955), p. 127.

10. Wollweber's sabotage group was dependent on penetrations of the maritime unions for access to the ships. The twenty-man team that operated under his direction consisted of old KPD bombers who were well known and much sought after by the Gestapo. See Heintz Hohne, *Canaris* (New York: Doubleday & Co., 1976), p. 241.

11. See David J. Dallin, op. cit., pp. 126–29. Dallin quotes a memo from Heydrich to Himmler stating that sixteen German, three Italian, and two Japanese ships were attacked by the Wollweber organization.

12. In 1944, Philby was appointed to organize an element within S.I.S. that would focus on the Soviets. Like Felfe, he systematically deceived his superiors by suppressing information damaging to Moscow. Felfe went beyond this by inserting disinformation into the Allied intelligence channels. Philby occasionally went into the field on secret missions. On one of these occasions, he traveled to Turkey to receive a Soviet intelligence officer who had informed the British of his intention to defect. Prior to his departure from London, Philby notified his Soviet controller, who warned Moscow. When Philby arrived in Turkey, the incipient defector, Konstantin Volkov, had already been returned to the USSR under duress.

Three years later, Philby was assigned to the British embassy in Washington, where he was able to function as a high level penetration agent at the very heart of Anglo-American intelligence. Felfe was able to make his highly significant contribution to the Soviets without leaving his base in West Germany.

13. Philby, a Soviet-controlled penetration of British intelligence, inflicted severe damage on the Western services from 1939 through the mid-1950s. Just as he aided the Soviets by his subtle frustration of British actions, they contributed to

building his reputation by giving him several "successes." Fifteen years later, Felfe rose rapidly in the BND by his adroit use of information provided by his Soviet case officer.

14. The career of Reinhard Gehlen bears directly on any objective assessment of the organs' sources, methods, and effectiveness. Gehlen was prototypical of those who came early to the anticommunist cause, had a change of mind, and as the political climate changed, once again embraced anticommunism as it returned to vogue under Hitler. Gehlen was an "Army brat," born in 1902. His father, like many who served the Kaiser in peace and then in war, was returned to civilian life after Germany's defeat in 1918. He became a job printer and managed to earn a modest income. Young Reinhard, influenced by the "stab-in-the-back theory," decided upon a military career instead of following his father into printing. He joined the 100,000-man *Truppenamt* (provided for by the Versailles Treaty), in 1920. Gehlen attended officer candidates school and was commissioned as a lieutenant of artillery. This was a curious appointment, since under the provisions of Versailles, the Germans were not allowed to have "offensive" weapons such as artillery. In 1933, Gehlen entered the new War Academy, which had been opened to provide staff officers to a Wehrmacht that lacked international legitimacy. While Gehlen was at the academy, Hitler came to power, repudiated the Versailles Treaty, and directed the rearmament of Germany. By 1939, Gehlen was a commander of troops in one of the divisions that led the way in the German's invasion of Poland. Destined for more important posts, it was not long before he was reassigned to the German High Command, which was planning the campaigns against France and the Soviet Union.

Had Gehlen remained a troop commander, he likely would not have been an important figure in the war. However, at the urging of Marshal Von Paulus, he accepted an assignment in 1942 as the head of military intelligence with Foreign Armies East, the German forces in the USSR. Even then, intelligence was considered an undesirable posting for a professional officer who aspired to a field marshal's baton. In the course of the next two years, he developed an excellent espionage organization, assembled massive documentation on the Soviets, and produced remarkable intelligence reporting regarding their operations. These accomplishments, however, counted for very little in the final outcome on the Eastern front. Gehlen displayed an uncommon grasp of intelligence, which might have made some difference had Hitler been disposed to believe his staff warnings.

When Hitler's impending defeat became evident to Gehlen, he began to see to his own safety by preparing to make himself, his trusted personnel, and his files available to the Western Allies. Accordingly the records were hidden in the Bavarian mountains, safely out of the way of the Russian advance. At the time of his surrender to the U.S. forces, he notified his captors of what he had done.

In fairness to Gehlen, he had several noteworthy successes against the USSR. As was learned later, the principal weaknesses of his organization were inadequately vetted personnel and other security-related problems.

Gehlen weathered the storm of Felfe's exposure and remained as chief of the BND until he retired in 1968. He wrote a self-serving account of his three careers—as a Nazi, as an Allied and West German officer, and as an intelligence chief. For conflicting treatment of the Gehlen phenomenon, see Heinz Hohne and Hermann Zolling, *The General Was a Spy: The Truth About General Gehlen and His Spy Ring* (New York: Coward, McCann, 1972); Edward Spiro, *Gehlen, Spy of the Century* (New York: Random House, 1972); and Gehlen's own book, *The Service: Memoirs of General Reinhard Gehlen* (New York: World, 1972). See esp. Louis Hagen, *The Secret War for Europe: A Dossier of Espionage* (1968), and Bernard Hutton, *How Russian Spies and Other Iron Curtain Spies Operate* (1969). Both these volumes make it clear that Felfe's contributions to the organs were substantial, thorough, and devastating in their effects on Western intelligence. Gehlen, op. cit., pp. 165–74.

15. Interview with "Frank O'Brien" (pseudonym), a Hungarian "freedom fighter" who was recruited under Andropov to infiltrate the Hungarian protest movement. "O'Brien" lives in the eastern United States and is currently employed by the federal government in a nonsensitive position.

16. O'Brien, op. cit., "Chebrikov was a true SOB. In Church terms he was Andropov's Torquemada. From those who were taken we learned that Chebrikov was without compassion or remorse and barely shrugged when one of the fighters died at the hands of the Russian interrogators. . . . They [Andropov and Chebrikov] used to look at each other as if they had some special kind of secret. Like jackals who enjoyed killing penned sheep."

17. See esp. David Irving, *Uprising* (1982), for an analysis of what Andropov knew and when he knew it. The decision to eliminate the Hungarian dissidents/protesters/rebels revealed much about officially sanctioned murders by the Soviets. It is another signal that was lost in the noise of détente.

18. Quoted in the *New York Times,* December 28, 1982.

19. Ivan Serov was the last of the notorious Soviet espionage chiefs. He was dismissed while faithfully carrying out his role as the head of the organs. Born at Sokal in Western Russia in 1905, Serov came from a peasant family, joined the Red Army, and in World War II was put in charge of deporting hundreds of thousands of people from Eastern Europe. He is also reported by Polish survivors as the executor, under Beria's orders, of the Katyn Forest massacre. Serov was named by Malenkov to head the KGB in 1954. His fall from grace probably occurred in 1956, when he went to England to prepare the way for a visit by Khrushchev and Bulganin. While there, the British press attacked him with unaccustomed fury, referring to him as "Ivan the Terrible" and forcing his recall. The event came at a time when Khrushchev was trying to portray the image of the "reasonable Russian." As a consequence, Serov was removed from the KGB on the specious grounds of failing to detect a move by Khrushchev's political enemies against him. Serov slipped down the Soviet ladder of power and in 1963 dropped off Western intelligence screens. There are no indications to support the view that he was "eliminated."

See also Gerald Kurland, *Nikita Sergeivich Khrushchev: Modern Dictator of the USSR* (Charlottesville, N.Y.: Sam Har Press, 1972), p. 74, which describes how Khrushchev disposed of Serov.

20. See esp. Peter Wyden, *Bay of Pigs: The Untold Story* (New York: Simon & Schuster, 1979), for an accurate perception of the invasion as it appeared from the Soviet and Cuban points of view.

21. According to Vincent and Nan Branellie in *Spy-Counterspy: An Encyclo-*

pedia of Espionage (New York: McGraw-Hill, 1982), pp. 35–36, Blake was a Dutch national of Jewish origins, born in Rotterdam as George Behar. He was interned by the Germans in 1940, escaped, and served in the Dutch Resistance for three years (1940–1943). When the German counterintelligence was about to arrest him, he was exfiltrated by an established escape and evasion net, eventually crossing the Pyrenees into neutral Spain. There he volunteered his assistance to the British and was permitted to enter England to enlist.

After training, he was commissioned in the Royal Navy Reserve and assigned to the Dutch branch of the Special Operations Executive (SOE). After D day, he served at Allied headquarters on the Continent and, later, with British naval intelligence in Hamburg.

By now a naturalized British citizen, Blake was recruited by S.I.S. and, in 1947, assigned to the British embassy at Seoul, Korea.

Captured by North Korean troops in June 1950, he spent the next three years in various prison camps. While a prisoner, he was contacted by the Soviets, who were aware of his former familial and operational contacts with the Soviet-operated nets in the Netherlands and France.

It is entirely possible that his uncle, Henri Curiel, alerted the Soviets to his internment by the North Koreans. Blake presented a very attractive possibility to the organs. His release, along with other diplomatic and civilian prisoners (both British and U.S.), was arranged. On his return to London, he was credited with a number of decent and patriotic acts by his fellow prisoners and taken back into the SIS fold. (Stalin's dictum of never trusting anyone who had suffered even one hour in the confinement of the enemy was not a part of the British operating system of the day.)

Blake was assigned to West Berlin in 1955 and there engaged in highly sensitive double-agent operations. His betrayal was particularly damaging because, as a British official, he had liaison contacts with the Gehlen organization and was able to inform the Soviets of the identities of West German agents, tactics, and current cases. In this respect, Blake reinforced and confirmed Felfe's information, and the disclosures resulted in serious casualties to the West.

Blake is also credited with informing the Soviets about the Berlin Tunnel, which the U.S. and British used to tap Soviet communications lines leading to Moscow from Karlshorst. By 1956, the Soviets decided to end their telephone deception and arranged for the "discovery" of the tunnel by the East Germans.

In 1959, Blake was identified by a Gehlen agent named Horst Eitner, who also had been doubled by the Soviets. Two years later, another defector confirmed the charge, and Blake was brought back from Beirut, where he was attending the British Mid-East School, and arrested.

Blake's treason concerned matters so closely connected with British national security that most of his trial was held in camera. He was convicted and sentenced to forty-two years but served only six before he escaped. He reached sanctuary in Moscow, where his services were rewarded with a job in the KGB, conducting seminars on the penetration of Allied intelligence organizations.

See also Norman Lucas, *The Great Spy Ring* (London: Barker, 1966), and E. H. Cookridge (pseud. Edward Spiro), *The Many Sides of George Blake Esq.: The Complete Dossier* (Princeton, N.J.: Vertex Books, 1970).

22. Corson, op. cit., pp. 381–86.

23. In addition to the hot line between the White House and the Kremlin, which was installed following the Cuban Missile Crisis, a more relevant comment was that of Khrushchev in *Khrushchev Remembers* (Boston: Little, Brown, 1970), p. 289: "When I raise a question with Eisenhower he puts it on a piece of paper and hands it to Dulles [John Foster] before he answers, if he answers at all. In the case of Kennedy when I ask him a question I get an answer without equivocation and delay."

24. Andropov was not completely lacking in technical skills. Besides being a skilled c-w radio operator (one who could send and receive high-speed Morse code transmissions), he also knew a great deal about the technical aspects of communications intelligence, including communications security, cryptography techniques, and related technology. In essence, his own familiarity with all aspects of communications intelligence protected him from being overwhelmed by experts in the field, who occasionally lay claim to a higher order of knowledge or expertise than those who labor at conventional intelligence duties.

CHAPTER 7

1. Adjutant General's List of Officers and Enlisted Men Reported Killed and Missing in Action in the North Russia Expedition, Archangel. NA RG 165 10110–2623/4.

2. The cultural and social factors that produced the early prominence of East European Jews in the extreme radical Left movements is convincingly explained and documented in S. Rothman and S. R. Lichter, *Roots of Radicalism: Jews, Christians and the New Left* (New York: Oxford University Press, 1982).

3. One of these was Fritz Karklin, an OGPU man who assisted Ohsol as an interpreter at the time of the indirect sale of U.S. vessels by the U.S. Shipping Board to the Soviet government. In entering the United States, Karklin jumped ship in Baltimore, where he later served as the OGPU man. His chief was Grigori P. Grafpen, vice president and general manager of Amtorg. NA RG 165 10110–2623.

4. As late as 1940, Uscher Zloczower, posing as an Austrian, had a "business" address in care of the Pacific Merchandise Company, 132 West 34th Street, New York City. His long-time GRU associate, Rubin Glucksmann (true name: Rubin Gidoni, also posing as an Austrian), was arrested by the British while acting as the London manager of the Far East Fur Trading Company. Glucksmann's books included a letter signed Frank Kleges, an identity previously bought from a New Jersey undertaker for $40. Kleges firm, Société Anonme Française pour l'Importation de Legumes Secs, was located in Paris and provided the GRU with cover in France. A third associate, Adam Purpiss, a friend of Glucksmann and Kleges, was also in New York as the head of the Oriental Trading and Engineering Corporation. Purpiss had come to New York after serving as the manager of Wostwag in Shanghai.

Keeping one's cover straight wasn't always easy. Glucksmann told the British that a man named Ernst Czucka (whose name was found in his files) was a former friend who worked in Wostwag in Berlin and, later, worked with Glucksmann and Zloczower in Paris. Unknown to Glucksmann, the British had already arrested Czucka for taking photographs in an area prohibited to aliens. At the time of his arrest, Czucka claimed to be a Dutchman representing another cover firm, the ADA Press Service or Anglo-French-American Press Agency of Amsterdam.

While detailing his contacts to the British, Glucksmann also identified Philip Rosenbliett, a New York dentist who, by then, had already been recalled to Moscow and executed.

5. In a statement to the Sovnarkom on December 9, 1923, Dzerzhinsky stressed the great service the GPU had rendered the Red Army. On the other hand, the General Staff resented the encroachment of the GPU into matters of military concern. Two high-level defectors, Grigori Agabekov, in 1930, and Walter Krivitsky, in 1940, both made a point mentioning this "chronic feud" between the two services.

At various times, the GPU urged the Central Committee to abolish the GRU and turn all intelligence collection over to the GPU's foreign department (INO). The issue was resolved by a typical conservative decision born out of insecurity—keep both active and let them compete. The INO, as a collateral duty, "watched" the GRU. There was general agreement among former officers of the organs who deserted the services at various times that the quality of GRU reporting was consistently superior to that produced by the INO.

6. Joseph Finder, "Dr. Armand Hammer's Medicine Show," *Harper's,* July 1983, p. 30. Armand Hammer, octogenarian chairman of Occidental Petroleum Corporation, has been a consistently ardent advocate of trade with the USSR. He has personally known every Soviet leader since Lenin.

7. Trotsky did not share Lenin's regard for the leaders of American socialism, among whom Julius Hammer was an important figure. Trotsky wrote, after his visit to New York in 1917: "To this day I smile as I recall the leaders of American Socialism . . . successful and semi-successful doctors, lawyers, dentists, engineers, and the like who divide their precious hours of rest between concerts by European celebrities and the American Socialist Party. Since they all have automobiles, they are invariably elected to the important committees, commissions, and delegations of the Party. . . . And, properly speaking, they are simply variants of "Babbitt" [in Sinclair Lewis's novel], who supplements his commercial activities with dull Sunday meditations on the future of humanity. These people live in small national clans, in which the solidarity of ideas usually serves as a screen for business connections. Each clan has its own leader, usually the most prosperous of the Babbits. They tolerate all ideas, provided they do not undermine their traditional authority, and do not threaten—God forbid!—their personal comfort." Joseph Finder, *Red Carpet* (New York: Holt, Rinehart and Winston, 1983), pp 14–15.

8. Ibid., p. 35.

9. Ibid., p. 34. Bogdanov was a former president of the Soviet Supreme Economic Council and, in 1930, a principal though reluctant and uncooperative witness before the Fish Committee. Following his return to the USSR, Bogdanov was arrested, "investigated," and executed in the 1937–1938 purges. Insofar as is

known, Bogdanov has the distinction of being the first board chairman of a U.S. corporation to be executed by a foreign government.

10. Ludwig Christian Alexander Karlovich Martens (aka Maertens) was born at Bachmut, Yekaterinoslav, Russia, in 1875. His father and mother were born in Germany, and they were at some pains to register his birth with the German consul to ensure his German citizenship. He finished the gymnasium at Kursk and received an engineering degree from the Technological Institute at Petrograd in 1896.

In the same year, he was arrested for revolutionary activities and sentenced to three years in prison, following which he was deported to Berlin. He served in the German Army in 1899. In 1901, he met both Lenin and Trotsky in Berlin. After receiving an advanced engineering degree from the Polytechnical Institute at Charlottenbourg in 1905, he returned to Russia. However, when Lenin was arrested, Martens fled to England, where he set up a machine shop in High Street, Hoxton, London. His associates were Yacov Peters, Fritz Swartz, and an Italian anarchist named Enrico Malatesta. In 1915, he left England for the United States via the SS *St Louis* on Christmas Eve (NA RG 165, 10110–1194).

In the United States, Martens organized the "Russian Mission," and on March 20, 1919, he made a public announcement that he was the absolute, sole representative of the Russian Soviet Government in the United States. His office was on the third floor of the World Tower Building at 110 West 40th Street in New York City. His legal counsel at the time was Charles Recht, who also maintained his office in the Russian Soviet Bureau.—*The New York Call*, March 21, 1919.

One of the itinerant Soviet agents who gave Martens an assist at this time was Mikhail Borodin, who at the time was using the aliases Michael Berg and Adolf Berg. Martens declared himself the Soviet ambassador, and another associate, Santeri Nuorteva, was named consul general in New York. Dr. David H. Dubrowsky was appointed secretary. The first order of business was to eliminate the competitors for leadership of the U.S. Communist Party, which each of them had joined using an alias. An earnest attempt to compromise and denounce Louis Fraina, the general secretary of the fledgling party, was attempted without success. In 1921, the U.S. Immigration Service issued deportation warrants against Martens and Nuorteva, and they were expelled. Dubrowsky, who had joined the party as David Ivanov, was a naturalized citizen and not easily deportable. As the sole remaining representative of the unofficial Soviet embassy, he was acutely underemployed until, while on a visit to Moscow, he was named as the head of the Soviet Russian Red Cross in the United States—Jacob Spolansky, *The Communist Trail in America* (New York: The Macmillan Co., 1951), p. 171.

Dubrowsky raced back to New York and quickly organized the Soviet Russian Red Cross, which proved to be of inestimable value to the Cheka, particularly in the financing of espionage and in the identification of Russians in the United States who could be coerced into the service of the Cheka.

11. In the mode of W. C. Fields, Amtorg opened many different bank accounts in several New York and neighboring locales. In 1930, the corporation used Equitable Trust Company (two accounts), Chase National Bank (two accounts), Bank of the United States (two accounts), Irving Bank, and Columbia Trust, State Bank of New York, Amalgamated Bank of New York (two ac-

counts), Chatham & Phoenix National Bank (two accounts plus a payroll account), and the Bank for Russian Trade (London).

The process required that "Amtorg draw on the Arcos Company (London) for amounts necessary to cover specific shipments. Amtorg also draws drafts on Gostorg through the Bank of Russian Trade (London). These amounts are then placed to the credit of Amtorg in bank A and the checks in payment of purchases by Amtorg are drawn on banks B, C and D, etc. Amtorg has various accounts through which they pay for their purchases and they have other accounts in which they deposit drafts drawn on Gostorg through the Bank for Russian Trade (London) . . ." NA RG 165 2655–H–260/19. By maintaining many and varied accounts in the United States, Canada, Germany, and England, Amtorg was able to move the large sums of money required to finance espionage and subversion in the United States.

12. By the mid-thirties, Amtorg alone was giving in excess of $5 million per year to Soviet-controlled organizations in the United States. A detailed listing of individuals, publications, organizations, and amounts (based on Amtorg files) was provided to the War Department by an Amtorg employee. NA RG 165 2515–D–135/21.

13. The unwary U.S. businessman now found himself in contact with *two* Soviet-controlled companies rather than with Amtorg alone. NA RG 165 2347–D–66/2.

14. "Socialism in one country" was a departure from the previous objective of "world revolution." The debacles in Germany and China suggested to the pragmatic Stalin that the world wasn't quite ready for a workers' revolution, nor was the Comintern. The new, modified goal also conveyed to the attentive the fact that Trotsky had been repudiated and that the Comintern had been subdued.

15. *Documents Illustrating the Hostile Activities of the Soviet Government and the Third International Against Great Britain, Presented to Parliament by Command of His Majesty* (London: His Majesty's Stationery Office, 1927), PRO, CMD 2874.

16. The Midland Bank representative in Moscow, Dennis Skinner, was found dead after a fall from his eleventh-floor apartment on Leninsky Prospekt in Moscow on the morning of June 17, 1983. The event occurred a few days before Skinner was to leave after fifteen years as Midland's man in Moscow. A British embassy physician who viewed the body at a Soviet morgue concluded that the injuries were consistent with those that are associated with what he termed a "judicial hanging." Skinner was concerned for his life. Thirty hours before his death, he had written a note to the British authorities stating that he had information concerning a "Soviet spy within the British embassy."

The last line of Skinner's note read: "For God's sake, do this or I'm dead." A coroner's jury in London concluded that Skinner had been "unlawfully killed," and Coroner Mary McHugh noted: "It's a strange coincidence that death should have called on him so shortly after writing this note." Information from the *Wall Street Journal*, May 17, 1984.

17. Article 1 of the charter of Gostorg states: "For the purpose of organizing all import and export operations of the People's Commissariat of Foreign Trade there shall be established the *Gostorg* which shall act under the general direction

and under the control of the People's Commissariat of Foreign Trade and its local organs." —*Collection of Decrees and Resolutions Concerning Foreign Trade up to June 1, 1922* (Moscow: Narkomvneshtorg, 1922), Vol. 1, p. 39.

18. By 1920, Feterljain was chief of the Russian section of the GC&CS. According to Lord Hankey: ". . . the Russians [émigrés] were the first to introduce us to this system of decoding, and I believe one of our most skillful experts was and is of Russian origin. . . ." (Letter to Lloyd George, September 8, 1920, Davidson manuscript.) Also see "The Christopher M. Andrew, British Secret Service and Anglo-Soviet Relations in the 1920's," Part I. *The Historical Journal,* Cambridge University Press, Vol. XX, September 3, 1977.

Feterljain's former principal assistant, Vladimir Krivosh, remained in Moscow and became chief of the cryptographic division of the Cheka. Vladimir Mikhailovich Petrov, *Empire of Fear* (New York: Frederich A. Praeger, 1956), p. 157.

19. The Arcos raid was prompted by the initiative of a Briton named George Monkland, who was employed as an underwriter at Lloyds. Monkland was approached by Wilfred McCartney and asked to provide information on arms shipments to Lithuania and Poland. Monkland gave some data to McCartney, and McCartney insisted that Monkland accept twenty-five pounds for his efforts. Monkland immediately contacted Sir Reginald Hall, the former director of naval intelligence, who alerted Guy Liddell of Scotland Yard's Special Branch and Sir Vernon Kell, director general of M.I.5. McCartney then asked Monkland to collect data concerning a secret RAF manual that included aircraft performance reports. McCartney advised Monkland that, if he succeeded, he was to take the material to the Soviet embassy, ask for one of the attachés, and introduce himself by saying, "I am one of the firm."

The raid was carried out under the direction of Major General Sir Wyndham Childs, assistant commissioner of the metropolitan police. The warrant was issued by a London magistrate on the strength of information presented to him by Home Secretary Sir William Joynson Hicks, who had conferred with the Foreign Secretary and the Prime Minister. Rosengoltz, the Soviet chargé d'affaires at the time, later served as Soviet commissar of foreign trade. (During the period March 2–13, 1938, Bukharin, Rosengoltz, Rykov, OGPU chief Yagoda, and Ambassadors Rakovsky and Krestinsky along with many others were "tried" in the great Moscow show trials and executed.)

On the day of the Arcos raid, McCartney phoned Monkland and instructed him to "get rid of the documents." He also said to Monkland that he had been successful in warning Arcos of the impending raid.

The passport office in London had previously issued a passport to McCartney, but a search of the official files after the raid revealed that McCartney's letters of application and photographs had disappeared from the office files. US MA London Rept No. 20664, December 5, 1927. NA RG 165 10058–M–34. (The forewarning of Arcos and the withdrawal of McCartney's passport file fueled speculation that the Soviets had achieved effective penetration of the Metropolitan police, the Special Branch, and possibly M.I.5.)

McCartney was unable to get out in time, however. He was tried and convicted under the Official Secrets Act: On his release from prison, he went to

Spain and took command of the British battalion of the XV Brigade, which, according to a subsequent commander of the battalion, consisted of "a mixed mob—ex-servicemen, hunger marchers, political enthusiasts and honest toughs and queer 'uns." (Thomas Wintringham, *English Captain*, p. 91, cited in R. Dan Richardson's excellent *Comintern Army: The International Brigades and the Spanish Civil War* (Lexington: University Press of Kentucky, 1982).

Before going into combat, McCartney was shot in the leg by Peter Kerrigan, the British political commissar. Comintern policy did not allow nonparty members to lead battalions of the International Brigades.

After World War II, McCartney was again convicted, the Official Secrets Act, this time for his collaboration with Eddie Chapman in the publication of a book entitled *Zigzag*. Convicted on the same charge was Sir Compton Mackenzie, World War I M.I.6 officer and author of the intelligence classic *Water on the Brain*. It was the second conviction for both Mackenzie and McCartney.

Arcos, like Amtorg in the United States and Wostwag in Berlin, conducted conventional trade involving millions of dollars. The legitimate trade provided cover accommodation for hundreds of Soviet state security and GRU officers. Host governments were inclined to be cautious about taking direct action even in instances where palpable evidence of Soviet espionage activity was discovered, because it was believed by some that the loss of the Soviet state as a customer might prove more serious than a little misguided spying. In fact, at the time of the Arcos raid, the trade balance strongly favored the Soviets. Irrefutable evidence in the form of documents, communications intercepts, counterespionage penetrations, and the abundant testimonies of former employees failed to cause the British, German, and American public to focus on the organic ties between the Soviet trading companies and the GRU and Cheka.

20. On May 24, 1927, Prime Minister Stanley Baldwin said: "The evidence now in the hands of the authorities proves that both military espionage and subversive activities throughout the British Empire and North and South America was directed and carried out from Soviet houses . . ." London *Times,* May 25, 1927. The term "Soviet houses" refers to the buildings in which the Soviet trade delegation and Arcos were located.

See *Documents Illustrating the Hostile Activities . . .* op. cit.

In Riga, Latvia, a Soviet agent called Lange was secretary to the Soviet military attaché, V. T. Sukhorukov. Lange was arrested by the Latvians while actually engaged in extorting classified information from a lieutenant in the Latvian Army. (Sukhorukov, through a police penetration, learned that Lange's arrest was imminent and fled across the border into the USSR.) After Lange had been held in jail for two days, the Soviet minister, Lorenz, threatened economic reprisals and the arrest of Latvians in the USSR unless Lange was released into his custody. The Latvian government acceded to Lorenz's demands, and Lange was released on condition that he not leave the country. On the day of his release, Lange was immediately flown to the USSR in an aircraft sent to Riga for that purpose.

In his dealings with the Latvian foreign office, Lorenz used the Arcos case as a precedent, pointing out that ". . . even the English had not dared to arrest Soviet citizens . . . under similar circumstances." NA RG 165, MA Rept from Riga, July 13, 1928, 9944–D–37.

Ten Latvian frontier guards were found guilty of espionage for the Soviets under the direction of Sukhorukov/Lange, and four were executed. Sukhorukov eventually returned to Riga to take up his attaché duties. Dr. Bilmanis, the Latvian minister in Moscow, stated that Sukhorukov was a close friend of Voroshilov's and enjoyed the general's patronage.

Despite his elevated sponsorship, in the late thirties Sukhorukov fell victim to a Bulgarian counterintelligence operation that eventually cost him his life. The Bulgarians were able to plant documents within the OGPU that incriminated the Soviet military attaché, his staff, and most of the Soviet embassy in Sophia. They were arrested by the OGPU and subjected to harsh treatment. Sukhorukov did not survive. —Roy A. Medvedev, *Let History Judge* (New York: Alfred Knopf, 1972).

21. Professor R. V. Jones notes: "Part of the evidence on which the raid had been based had come from the GC&CS success in breaking the Russian diplomatic code. Stung by the Socialist attack, Baldwin gave the Parliament a full statement of the evidence on which the raid had been based, including reading out verbatim the text of the decoded messages. The story as I heard it from the cryptographers was that he even read out at one point "group mutilated" the standard cryptographic indication of an error in receiving the message). But, *Hansard* (Vol. 206, Column 1848) records him as saying at the relevant point ". . . There is one word missing . . . The result, of course, was gratis information to the Russians that we were reading their diplomatic codes, which were changed a fortnight later and were not since readable, at least up to the time that I left MI6 in 1946. And this from a Prime Minister who had achieved a reputation for discretion with the phrase 'my lips are sealed'. . . ." R. V. Jones, *Intelligence in a Democracy*. Paper presented to the Department of State, Washington, D.C., December 4, 1975.

22. Ivan Maisky succeeded Rakovsky as the Soviet ambassador to Great Britain, a post he held until 1942. Maisky started his political career as a Menshevik. When Lenin prevailed, he became an enthusiastic Bolshevik. His first official position in the Soviet government was as a press officer in the Ministry of Foreign Affairs in 1921. Maisky's long survival within the Soviet system attests to his remarkable ability to adapt to shifting currents. When his benefactor Stalin died in 1953, Maisky promptly wrote several long attacks on Stalin's "cult of the personality," a wholly acceptable theme to the new Moscow leadership.

Harold Nicholson called on Maisky at the end of March 1941: "He sat there in his ugly Victorian study like a little gnome in an armchair, twiddling his thumbs, twinkling his eyes and giving the impression his feet do not touch the floor." *The War Years, 1939–1945* (New York: Atheneum, 1967), p. 155.

23. Anton Antonovich-Ovseyenko, *The Time of Stalin* (New York: Harper & Row, 1981), p. 66.

24. "Executed or died in prison during the postrevolutionary
period (1919-1923). 500,000
Executed during the Stalin Terror. 2,000,000
Died in camps during the pre-Yezhov period of Stalin's rule
(1930-1936) 3,500,000

Died in forced labor camps during the Stalin-Yezhov terror 12,000,000
Died in the politically organized famine during forced collectivization 3,500,000
            Total: 21,500,000

Source: *U.S. Senate, Commission on the Judiciary Report,* 91st Congress, Second Session, pp. 1-2.

The estimates are attributed to Soviet expert and author Robert Conquest and do not include:

Lost in the civil war because of military actions, mass executions, preventable diseases (e.g., typhus, due in large part
  to political famine)....................................... 9,000,000
Additional casualties as a result of the 1921-1923
  famine... 5,000,000
Noncombat losses in the Finnish war............................ 400,000
Noncombat losses in World War II (including camp executions, camp deaths, population displacement, suppression
  operations against Poles, Ukrainians, Balts, etc.).......... 5,000,000
Japanese and German POW deaths............................... 500,000
            Grand total: 41,400,000
(Does not include the estimated 3,000,000 unborn due to famine 1921-1923
  or the "missing" millions in the most conservative demographic extrapolations over the decades of Soviet rule.)

25. On August 4, 1928, *Borba za Rossiyu* (Paris) reported that Ibragimov, the Soviet trade delegate in Istanbul, took money and documents with him at the time of his departure in late 1927. He offered to return the documents in ex-change for a "safe-conduct" guarantee.

The same edition also reported the "escape" of A. Saryan, chairman of the executive committee of the Comintern from Samarkand to Sinkiang in northwest China.

Miasnikov's desertion was the basis for Agebekov's first direct meeting with Beria.

In September 1927, *Algemeine Zeitung,* an Austrian newspaper, reported the arrest in Vienna of a "Soviet agent, Bekenovsky," who confessed to having been a member of a Soviet spy agency. The account was republished in *Borba za Rossiyu* (No. 47, October 1927). Bekenovsky declared that "he decided to leave this organization several years before, but other members threatened to kill him." He claimed to have escaped from the USSR through Odessa to Bucharest and then to Vienna.

GRU Lt. Col. Yevgenni Kozhevinko deserted on May 18, 1927, in China. Better known as Eugene Pick, Kozhevinko was in China as an attaché to Mikhail Borodin, who was the principal Soviet adviser to the Chinese Nationalist govern-ment in Canton. In February 1927 a Chinese Communist leader, Koo Chen-Chang, defected to the Nationalists and reported while serving as chief of ". . . Borodin's bodyguard and secret service in Hankow and Wuhang, I dis-covered that Eugene Pick, who was serving under Borodin as adjutant, had stolen from his master a diary and a report regarding the foreign warships at Hankow and sold them to the French Consul and that Pick was acting as a spy for the Foreign Consulates generally. Pick was arrested and placed under detention in a Foreign house from which he escaped by jumping over four verandahs. As he ran away, shots were fired at him and he was wounded. . . ."—Shanghai Municipal Police Special Branch file 2911/8, 1931.

Pick then joined the Nationalist Chinese foreign office as a recruiter of Russian instructors for the Chinese Army and dabbled in document forgery and various confidence tricks on the side.

Not being encumbered by ideological convictions, he found it comfortable to take up new duties as a counterintelligence agent for the Japanese in 1937. On February 5, 1938, two defective Japanese-made hand grenades were thrown into his room at 317 Rue Bourgeat in the old French Concession in Shanghai. With his felinelike supply of lives, Pick survived.

On September 14, 1941, Pick was charged with arranging the assassination of Sergei Ivanovich Mamontoff in Shanghai. It was demonstrated in court that he had employed a Chinese assassin to dispatch Mamontoff, alias Riabchenko, himself a member of the anti-Soviet fascist organization in China. Pick was sentenced to fifteen years' imprisonment. There is no indication in the files that Pick went to prison.

By 1944, the Shanghai police had a report that "secret Germans" intended to murder Pick. It was also reported to the police that even though his desertion in a hail of bullets gave him a certain credibility, he had, in fact, later come back under the influence and control of the Soviets. Still later, in 1945, there were reports that he had been abducted or murdered in Macao.

In 1946, he turned up in Japan and wrote several long letters to General MacArthur, suggesting that he could be of great assistance in defeating Soviet influence in Japan and asking that he be authorized to organize intelligence nets to seek out the Japanese Communist Party agents the military government had just released from prison. His offer was declined.

Among some of the names used by this enterprising Soviet agent/defector/provacteur, as reflected in the extensive files of the Shanghai police, are Eugene Pick, E. M. Hovens, Carl von Klige, Capt. E. Pick, Hovansky, Kojevnikoff, and Mr. Dick. Among the governments he purported to serve were the Soviet, British, German, U.S., Chinese, Japanese, and French.

26. NA RG 165, US MA Riga (Major George E. Arneman), Rept #7485, April 17, 1930.

27. The Red Trade Union International (Profintern) was organized in Moscow in 1921 with Solomon Abramovich Dridzo, alias S. Lozovsky or Arnold Lozovosky, as head. Its objective was to break the left-wing labor unions away from the Social Democratic Federation of Trade Unions. The organization endured until 1937, when a change in Soviet policy—the shift to a "united front" against fascism—required its dissolution.

The Soviet government, being always on the lookout for good men, converted the venerable apparatchik Dridzo to His Excellency, S. A. Lozovsky, assistant peoples commissar for foreign affairs, on July 14, 1941.

Both the Cheka and the GRU had need of maritime support organizations throughout the world. The seamen's clubs in every port city were highly organized and brought into a coherent body in 1930 with the establishment of the International of Seamen and Harbor Workers (ISH). The ISH provided men to proselytize among the crews of merchant ships, to sabotage vessels and cargos, to act as couriers and propagandists, and, most important, to operate the transport system that allowed the Cheka, GRU, and Comintern to move their operatives to any point on the globe.

Particular emphasis was placed on organizing the Pacific Ocean area under the Pan-Pacific Trade Union Secretariat (PPTUS).

The wife of a former luminary in the Profintern and the PPTUS observed: "In a sprawling, colonnaded white building on the banks of the Moscow river, the Profintern was to its affiliated, independent Left federations in 61 countries very much what the Comintern was to the Communist parties abroad, with perhaps less disciplined, organizational clout than the Comintern. Its territorial Sections, like those of the Comintern, were staffed by representatives sent from the movements of each country." Peggy Dennis, *American Communist* (Westport, Conn.: Lawrence Hill & Co., Berkeley, Calif.: Creative Arts Book Co., 1977).

The Royal Navy was a continuing target of the Soviets. In September 1931 British sailors from the Atlantic Fleet whose ships were anchored at Invergordon, Scotland, mutinied in protest of a 10 percent pay cut. The cut was part of a national austerity program announced by Ramsay MacDonald's newly formed coalition government. Two of the leaders of the mutiny were Wilfred McCartney, who was soon to be involved in the Arcos scandal described earlier in this chapter, and Len Wincott, who later openly joined the British Communist Party in 1934. He was invited to the USSR and honored as a "Symbol of the British Working Classes." Soon thereafter, Wincott was declared "A Hero of the Soviet Union" For his work as a Profintern employee operating seamen's clubs in Leningrad with the object of suborning British merchant seamen. But then, in 1936, Wincott was arrested by the Soviets as a British spy and sentenced to ten years in a labor camp. When he was released twenty years later, he offered to return to Great Britain to assist Harry Pollitt in running the party there. His offer was declined. Wincott then went to work with Donald Maclean, and in 1974, he made a three-week visit to the UK. On being interviewed by the press in London, Wincott insisted that he had not renounced his British citizenship but had lost it during the war because of "a provision in the Soviet law." Wincott died in Moscow in January 1983.

28. Stalin's demand for absolute compliance in responding to a summons from Moscow came to be referred to as the "Bessedovsky decree." John C. Wiley, the U.S. chargé ad interim at Warsaw, described one case: "Michel Naumov, an important member of the Soviet Trade Delegation in Paris, was suddenly recalled to Moscow at the end of May 1930. He had been an active Communist Party member since 1918. His wife, also employed at the Trade Delegation, was ordered to remain in Paris.

While en route, Naumov suddenly realized that he was under surveillance by the OGPU and jumped from the train in the vicinity of Biala Podlaska. After barely escaping a train coming from the opposite direction, he proceeded on foot to the railroad station. He was taken to a police station where he declared his intention to remain in Poland or return to France. While awaiting a decision by the Polish authorities, he slashed himself with a pocket knife and was transported to a local hospital. . . ."—Dispatch to the Department of State from the U.S. embassy, Warsaw, June 14, 1930.

29. The full text of the Soviet instruction is given in the *Saturday Review* (London), September 11, 1936.

30. Ibid.

31. Shipborne abduction teams were very active in the Thames, at Hull, Shanghai, New York, and elsewhere. In some instances, the misbehavers were taken by force, though it was always "more satisfying" to the teams to take them by deception. The usual process involved a reception, celebration, or dinner aboard a Soviet vessel. The food and/or drink were enhanced with an emetic, and the victim became too ill to realize what was occurring and too weak to protest. After a few days at sea, the victim was put on a regimen to ensure his readiness for the investigation that would begin on his arrival in Moscow.

If the intended victim could not be found, a mother, wife, or child was taken in expectation that the wanted victim would voluntarily follow at a later date.

32. The maritime-intelligence collection activity was the domain of the GRU (naval section) representative on board. The merchant crew men, for the most part, were under the Profintern; as usual the OGPU/NKVD/KGB maintained political discipline.

Although Smersh was officially disbanded at the end of World War II, the naval Smersh continued to operate in the Baltic and Sea of Japan, using fishing trawlers to carry out abduction and assassination missions.

The search for seamen couriers was continuous, and when prospects were initially identified through Profintern agents aboard the ships, they were interviewed under some pretext. If they demonstrated a convincing ideological bent, they were brought to the attention of the prospective clandestine employers, who later, if appropriate, approached them for recruitment.

Aboard ship, the couriers scrupulously avoided all association with crew members who openly advocated any political position. Their duties were to convey instructions and funds to the representatives of the organs in the foreign port cities at which their ship regularly called. The North German Lloyd Line was a preferred company simply because of the strength of the Profintern in Hamburg and the speed and regular schedules of the ships. In addition to acting as couriers, many sailors had additional reporting responsibilities, such as surveillance of designated passengers and the provision of annotated passenger manifests to clandestine contacts on arrival in port.

33. As early as 1930, the U.S. branch of the ISH was headed by a relative of Lozovsky's, who used the names George Mink, George Hirsh, or Alfred (Boris) Hertz.

"Mink was dispatched to Copenhagen [in 1934]. In 1935, he was arrested at his hotel there for attempted rape of a chambermaid. Codes, addresses and false passports were found in his possession. . . . Mink served a term of 18 months and on his release went to Moscow.

"In Moscow he had to explain the adventure which had proved so detrimental to the Soviet secret service abroad. Again, he managed to inspire confidence. . . . Mink took the blame and was pardoned.

"In 1937 he was sent to Spain to keep watch on the Lincoln Brigade. . . . William McCuiston, a close friend of Mink's until 1936, testified later that he had been present when two GB men, George Mink and Tony Del Maio, killed two members of the Brigade."—David J. Dallin, *Soviet Espionage* (New Haven, Conn.: Yale University Press, 1955), p. 410.

While in Spain, Mink handled other, documented Cheka executions in the International Brigades. "There were two International Brigades in Spain, the military unit of that name and a horde of Comintern gangsters and gunmen—the Cheka . . ."—R. Dan Richardson, *The Comintern Army in Spain* (Lexington: The University Press of Kentucky, 1982), p. 163. As the prospects of a Soviet proxy victory in Spain began to fade in late 1937, there were increased desertions in the brigades of the French, British, and American volunteers. One group of Americans witnessed "the arrest of some twenty-five Americans who had left the front and reported to headquarters for discharges because their contracts had expired. After a fake court-martial the twenty-five had been taken back to the front under guard and executed. . . . The Brigade press also began to attack the problem of desertion . . . [with] an article entitled 'The Battalion Gets Cleaned up of Cowards'" (p 166).

34. Peter Bogdanov, or Petr Alexeevich Bogdanov, was "born 20 May 1882 in Moscow. Arrested in February 1902 and imprisoned at Wyschnevoltzk. Active in the subversive underground organization of the [Imperial] army. Member of the Executive Committee of the Moscow Bolshevik Party . . ."—N. Bukharin, ed., *Great Soviet Encyclopedia,* Vol. VI, pp. 585–86. Bogdanov was chairman of the board of Amtorg during the period that the Bessedovsky accusations of OGPU activity in the United States were published in Europe. Amtorg documents, made public by the former Amtorg executive Delgass, were presented to a congressional committee chaired by Hamilton Fish. Bessedovsky asserted that the GRU resident in New York from 1926 to 1930 was Semion Filin, alias Semen Firin.— G. Z. Bessedovsky, *Na Putyakh K Termidoru.* Published in English as *On the way to the Thermidor* (Paris: 1930).

The New York police under Commissioner Grover Whalen attempted to arrest Filin, but he had already left the United States via Canada using yet another alias—M. Gordon, "manager of the Amtorg art department." That department handled, for resale in the United States, gemstones, rare books, and works of art confiscated by the OGPU in the Soviet Union.

Filin was transferred from the GRU to the OGPU in 1934 and become deputy in charge of the hundreds of thousands of forced-labor prisoners who built the Moscow-Volga Canal. He was reported to have been arrested and executed on the eve of the opening of the canal.—David J. Dallin and Boris I. Nicolaevsky, *Forced Labor in Soviet Russia* (New Haven, Conn.: Yale University Press, 1947), pp. 208, 316.

During the Fish hearings, John G. Ohsol was introduced to the committee as Bogdanov's interpreter, without reference to the fact that Ohsol was also an Amtorg employee and Bogdanov's subordinate. It seemed that Bogdanov, who had been traveling throughout the United States making trade promotional speeches in English, had suddenly lost his tongue. Ohsol stated to the committee that Bogdanov "was a businessman and not an expert on politics . . ."

Other topics touched upon by the committee related to Amtorg's connection to Arcos in London. After much dithering and faulty translations of opaque responses, Bogdanov conceded that there had been such a relationship. On the matter of the Soviet Russian Red Cross and its U.S. head, Dr. David Dubrowsky, Ohsol and Bogdanov admitted knowing of the doctor and his good works but denied that he had any direct connection to Amtorg. Ohsol gave a concise description of Dubrowsky's purpose that might have been the specific mission directive issued by Yagoda: "The Russian Red Cross is looking for Soviet citizens, relatives, for those who are in distress, for those who desire any relief in connection with having served in the [U.S.] army during the World War, and establishing their connections with their native country . . ."

Although Bogdanov "affirmed," Ohsol testified under oath. The hearings from which material has been quoted were held in New York on July 22, 1930.—Special Committee to Investigate Communist Propaganda in the United States, Hamilton Fish, Chairman. Part 3, Vol. 3, LC HX 653, .A5 1930.

The fact that Bogdanov and Ohsol were not charged with contempt and/or perjury was seen as a measure of U.S. tolerence of the deliberate deceptive policies of the Soviet Union.—*New York Times,* July 20, 1930, pp. 1–2.

35. Letter from Moisei Ilyitch Frumkin, acting peoples' commissar for foreign trade, to the chairman of the board of the Amtorg Trading Corporation, Isaya Yakolevitch Hoorgin, November 28, 1924. Presented to the Office of the General Counsel of the Bureau of Internal Revenue.

36. Memorandum to the Department of State, "Notes on Conversation with Mr. Max Sachs," accountant for the Amtorg Trading Corporation, from F. W. B. Coleman, Riga, Latvia, April 16, 1928. NA RG State decimal file 661.1115.

37. Allied American Corporation (Alamerico), originally the Ural-American Refining and Trading Company, was formed in 1921 by Armand Hammer on his return from Soviet Russia, with offices at 165 Broadway, New York City. Charles Recht, who represented numerous "beneficiaries" in the Veterans Bureau scam (see note 40), was a New York lawyer who had assisted Ludwig Martens and Julius Hammer's earlier efforts in the formative U.S. Communist Party. "By the middle of 1924, all American business was transferred from Allied-American to the new, wholly Soviet-owned enterprise called Amtorg."—Joseph Finder, *Red Carpet* (New York: Holt, Rinehart and Winston, 1983), pp. 30, 47.

38. Meer Genokh Moiseevitch Wallach, using the alias Maxim Litvinov, served Stalin as foreign minister and, later, as ambassador to the United States. As early as 1919, he was appointed to the central committee of the (Soviet) Russian Red Cross, though his primary duties were in the international field. The apex of his career was his successful meetings with President Roosevelt in 1933, which formed the basis for U.S. recognition of the Soviet Union.

Stalin replaced Litvinov, a Jew, with his home-grown aryan, Vyacheslav Molotov, as a concession to Hitler at the time of the German-Soviet nonaggression pact in 1939.

In his youth, Litvinov played an important role in prerevolutionary history following the "expropriation raids" (a Bolshevik euphemism for armed robberies in which millions of rubles were taken) in Tiflis on June 23, 1907. It fell to his lot to try to exchange the stolen banknotes, some of which were of very large denomination, in Western Europe. Litvinov, along with several others, was arrested.—Isaac Deutscher, *Stalin* (New York: Oxford University Press, 1967), p. 87.

Bessedovsky claimed that shortly before Stalin named him foreign minister, Litvinov was in Prague using a forged passport in the name of Mikhail Maximoff. An incredulous State Department asked the American minister in Prague to comment on the allegation. The minister, after consultation with the chief of police at Prague, reported that Litvinov and his wife stayed at Marienbad during July 1927 and that he had a diplomatic passport in the name of Maximoff.

When Litvinov returned to the United States in 1941 as the Soviet ambassador, he made clear to Harry Hopkins and Eleanor Roosevelt that with Loy W. Henderson advising on Soviet policy matters in the Department of State, "no satisfactory progress could be made in US-Soviet relations." Henderson, who had been on the staff of the U.S. embassy in Moscow when it was opened in 1934, knew Litvinov well and had seen him repeatedly engage in a variety of deceptions as Soviet foreign minister. Henderson's well-founded reservations regarding the integrity of the oleaginous Litvinov made him one of the few senior U.S. officials to comprehend Soviet realities of the day. His experience in Soviet affairs had been the basic reason for his selection by Secretary Hull to act as the East European Division's link with the Soviet embassy, Washington.

At Litivinov's instigation, both Mrs. Roosevelt and Hopkins attempted to pressure Hull to reassign Henderson. Hull refused to accede, but then the President himself directed that Henderson be removed to a position in which the Soviets would not object.—Interview with Loy W. Henderson, September 14, 1982.

Having manipulated the departure of Henderson, Litvinov informed Secretary of the Treasury Henry Morgenthau in January 1942 that the Japanese would attack the USSR within two months and for that reason the United States ought to "slow down" the $500 million loan to the Chinese Nationalist government. Such a slowdown would help the Chinese Communists, who would be able to turn their full attention to fighting the Japanese.

Chen Li-fu, minister of organization in the Nationalist government, stated that the USSR's modest military aid to China abruptly ceased the moment Japan attacked the United States. Dr. Chen was in Moscow in the first week of December 1941, attempting to persuade the Soviet government to provide additional aid to the Nationalist government so that China could try to go on the offensive against the Japanese. The Nationalists had been receiving Soviet military assistance since 1937, but the attack on Pearl Harbor made this "no longer necessary" from the Soviets' point of view. With the United States at war with Japan, Soviet policy shifted to starvation of the Nationalists and support for the then Moscow-controlled Eighth Route Army under Mao Tse-tung.—Interview with Chen Li-fu, March 14, 1951.

The Litvinov line at the Treasury Department was actively advanced by Morgenthau's principal aides, Harry Dexter White and Frank Coe, who encouraged the secretary, in a memorandum, "to wriggle out" of the China commitment. Their efforts were not successful.

White, identified under oath as a Soviet agent, died in 1948. Coe was an assistant to White, as was Nathan Gregory Silvermaster, also identified under oath as a Soviet agent. Litvinov's imagined Japanese attack on the USSR never occurred. The USSR entered the war with Japan two weeks before it ended.—U.S. Senate Internal Security Subcommittee release of portions of Secretary Morgenthau's diary, May 21, 1956. Also *New York Herald Tribune,* May 22, 1956.

After World War II, in separate interviews with Cyrus Sulzberger, Richard C. Hottelet, and Alexander Werth, Litvinov gave voice to startlingly heretical views, particularly when he said to Hottelet: "If the West acceded to the current Soviet demands it would be faced, after a more or less short time, with the next series of demands . . ."

Twenty-five years later, ". . .Khrushchev, by then himself out of grace and confiding his own unconventional views to a tape recorder for posterity's sake . . . reported that when secret files had been examined and police officers questioned after Stalin's death [it was] revealed that "Beria's men" [NKVD] had devised a plan to dispose of Litivinov in a particularly dastardly way: like his fellow Jew, actor Solomon M. Mikhoels, he was to be thrown in front of a truck and run over."—Vojtech Mastny, "The Cassandra in the Foreign Commissariat. Maxim Litvinov and the Cold War, Foreign Affairs, January 1976, p. 366.

Several years after Litvinov's death, his British-born wife, Ivy, returned to England, where she died. In 1974, his grandson Pavel Litvinov was told by the KGB to "go West or go East"—meaning Siberia. He opted for the West in the hope that he could continue efforts to assist friends remaining in the USSR.— *Times* (London), March 21, 1974, p. 5.

39. *International Red Cross Circular # 206,* Geneva, October 15, 1921, to which is appended *Ordinance of the Soviet Council of the Peoples Commissars,* dated August 7, 1918, and signed "Ulianof (Lenin)." NA RG 200, American Red Cross, 900.02, Russia/31.

40. David H. Dubrowsky, according to a classmate from the same small town in Russia, joined the Bolshevik Party in 1905. He later studied in the United States, took a degree in dentistry, and became a citizen. Dubrowsky came to the attention of U.S. authorities during World War I, when he became an active Soviet agent. He made several concerted efforts to be appointed to one of the five major U.S. commissions sent to Russia after the war. Unable to arrange for his inclusion in any of these commissions, Dubrowsky proceeded to Moscow on other resources. It was during this first visit that he was instructed to put his energies into the establishment of the Russian Red Cross in the United States.

On his return to New York, the British reported "that a certain Dr. Doubrovski [sic], member of the Communist Party, has been sent to the United States to watch over the development of the work of Bolshevik agents. . . . Doubrovski is leaving as representative of the Committee for the Relief of the Starving with the mission of organizing branches of the Committee at New York, Philadelphia, Boston, etc, In reality, he will represent the Executive Committee of the Third International and will take charge of the distribution of secret funds and instructions from Moscow."—NA RG 165 245–52, November 5, 1921.

By the end of December 1921, Dubrowsky agents were traveling throughout the United States in a highly organized collection program on behalf of the "Red Cross." When this fact became known to the American Red Cross, H. J. Hughes, assistant to the chairman of the ARC, wrote a strong letter of objection to Dubrowsky. The familiar interlocutor, Johann G. Ohsol of Amtorg, responded that he "took the matter up at once with Dr. D. H. Dubrowsky and . . . pointed out the impropriety and inadvisability of carrying on any relief work under the Red Cross emblem in this country." On the same day, Dubrowsky wrote to Hughes explaining that incident had been another innocent misunderstanding and that he had taken "steps everywhere in accordance with the desires of the American Red Cross." The fact that Dubrowsky's pledge not to use the Red Cross emblem was written on letterhead imprinted with a large Red Cross emblem could not have given Hughes much confidence.

Dubrowsky's collaboration with Charles Recht is noted elsewhere in this chapter. In 1928, Dubrowsky began to feel the pressures of the OGPU to the extent that he was being pushed out of his New York office by new arrivals from Moscow, who soon made the Russian Red Cross in the United States an important outstation for the OGPU. Either genuine misgivings or the need for vengeance moved him to detail these activities to the American Red Cross and the U.S. Congress. Like others, Dubrowsky testified at length before various congressional committees as the victim of Soviet deceit. In view of the fact that he had served the Bolshevik cause in a number of ways continuously since 1905, even the most forgiving would have to concede that Dubrowsky's motivation in apostasy might have been somewhat self-serving.

The Moscow Municipal Credit Association (referred to as the Credit Bureau in the United States) was a cover office of the Trust, a major Soviet provocation operation designed to neutralize foreign-subsidized efforts directed against the USSR. At one time Trust agents succeeded in gaining the support of ten governments, including Great Britain, France, Poland, and Bulgaria, who were interested in purchasing intelligence about the USSR and in destablizing the Soviet government. Among other duties, the bureau fabricated false insurance claims for presentation to the U.S. Veterans Bureau. Dubrowsky testified before the congressional committee examining this additional manifestation of official Soviet government's criminal fraud, stating that ". . . there were 56,000 Russian families of veterans, Russian nationals, in the American Expeditionary Forces . . . [and] the lump sum due each and every beneficiary . . . was substantial. . . . It usually amounted to $57.50 per month for a duration of 20 years. . . . We had thousands of claims. In addition to the insurance benefits, there were benefits paid to dependent parents, to dependent widows, to dependent minors—bonuses; all the benefits which the American native veteran was legally entitled. . . . The OGPU confiscated the funds [because] the moment they [the true claimants] received it, they were transferred from real, honest-to-goodness proletarians into kulaks. . . . The desire for the dollar was stronger than the principles involved and so they have overlooked the fact that we were creating a middle class. . . . The Credit Bureau is to notify the police department, which is quite centralized and quite efficient, almost as efficient as the Gestapo, and they begin to go to the region where the man has supposedly migrated from and sooner or later, they will discover some relatives, you may rest assured. . . . Documents are prepared; the heirs are in a great many cases quite illiterate, and they will make and execute a power of attorney to Mr. Charles Recht, so he has an absolute monopoly of all estates in the United States and Canada, so far as the Russians are concerned. . . . The documents he receives and he collects the funds and sends them, if you please, to that central organization in Moscow, irrespective of the fact whether the individual lives in Moscow or 5,000 miles away in Vladivostok, or anywhere else. . . . No individual in Russia can afford the luxury to state to any official body in Russia that 'I do not feel like signing the document' without being suspected of being a spy. . . . The income from the estates which I handled amounted to more than a million dollars a year."—House Committee on Un-American Propaganda Activities, 1939, Vol. 8, pp. 5162–67 and 5241–43.

Dubrowsky died in New York in 1950, as noted in a *New York Times* obituary on June 24, 1950 (13:4). Years later, his widow applied to the American Red Cross for whatever "pension" Dubrowsky's survivors were entitled to. Mrs. Dubrowsky was of the opinion that her husband had devoted his life to the Red Cross; like so many others, she failed to realize the distinctions between the American Red Cross and the Cheka-run Russian Red Cross. NA RG 200, 900.02.

41. Consolidated Report of Whittaker Chambers, FBI document 74-133-3220.

42. For a number of years, Jacob Raisen, using the alias of Jacob Golos (work name "Timmy"), maintained a stable of resurrectionists at the New York Public Library. During his reign as head of the U.S. documentation mill, he also ran Globe Travel (a follow-on version of Union Tours).

Golos was a later member of the U.S. Control Commission (see note 62, this chapter). In the passport business, he displayed rather advanced marketing techniques by providing genuine U.S. passports on short notice to the GRU and Comintern at considerably more than the manufacturer's cost.

The North American record for resurrectionists was set by a hapless, friendless Canadian named George Victor Spencer. Employed five days a week by the Canadian Post Office, Spencer passed the balance of his time over a period of many years traveling around remote settlements and logging camps recording premature deaths. He photographed hundreds of tombstones and laboriously copied death registers, then forwarded the results of his researches to his NKVD/KGB case officer.

When Spencer was retired against his will in 1964, by the Post Office, he wrote a pathetic letter of appeal to the Prime Minister, asking that consideration be given to his long and faithful work in the service of the Soviet Union, Canada's wartime ally, which continued to call on him for assistance. The letter was referred to the RCMP, and two incredulous officers had several long sessions with the dying Spencer. He detailed his resurrectionist work for the Soviets, day by day, over a period of about fifteen years. In the aggregate, it has been estimated that Spencer produced documentation for as many as *several thousand* Canadian "ghosts" for use by the KGB elsewhere in the world.

43. Walter Krivitsky estimated that the documentation of a single OGPU officer involved in a major European case might require as many as nine or ten different passports. (Testimony before the Dies Committee, 1939.) In the Noulens case in Shanghai, it was established that Noulens/Ruegg had nine active indentities, all documented, and as many as eight more that were never fully confirmed. (Shanghai Municipal Police File # D-2510/7.)

44. The quoted parts of the Rubens/Robinson case have been taken from the exhaustively documented, unpublished memoirs of Loy W. Henderson. Ambassador Henderson served in Moscow under Ambassadors Bullitt and Davies and was a direct participant in the examination of the Rubens/Robinson case.

45. In July 1938, Mrs. Rubens was still undergoing "investigation." On April 15, 1939, the State Department asked that she be released or brought to trial. On June 7, Stuart Grummon, chargé d'affaires in the Moscow embassy, was informed that a judgment would be made soon in the Rubens case. At midnight on July 8, he was advised that the trial would take place the following day at the Moscow Municipal Court. Mrs. Rubens pleaded guilty to entering the Soviet Union illegally and was sentenced to eighteen months, the term to start on the day of her arrest. She was released on the day following the trial. Ten days later, she called at the embassy and executed an affidavit relating to her passport. She said that she had decided to remain in the Soviet Union in order to be able to visit her husband, who was reportedly serving a sentence in a labor camp. On October 10, 1939, she renounced her U.S. citizenship and became a Soviet citizen in her maiden name of Boerger.

The investigation in the United States confirmed that the Rubens-Robinson couple were Soviet agents. There is no doubt that Mrs. Rubens was fully informed and active on her own behalf. Rubens is reported to have delivered approximately 150 passports to the Soviet security service on his last visit.

The case developed at the time that all foreign agents of the NKVD, GRU, or Comintern who happened to be in Moscow were subject to investigation, arrest, prison, or execution. Very few (e.g., Hede Massing, Nicholas Dozenberg) were able to escape the bloody, rampaging terror that swept through the Soviet security and intelligence services of the day.

46. The fugitive friend was one of three Tamer brothers who were in the "work" in New York. One had been an apprentice in the house that printed the *Daily Worker,* another worked in a New Jersey water works, and the third was employed at the Crucible Steel Company, also in New Jersey. The Tamers' uncle, Sam Shoyet, was the assistant foreman at Crucible and an experienced Soviet agent who had served in Tokyo and Paris in the twenties. Shoyet's daughter Azia was a bacteriologist studying at Hunter College. In the early thirties, both father and daughter moved to the Far East, where Sam Shoyet took over as the GRU resident in Mukden.

Mrs. Samuel Shoyet, with an expired U.S. passport, posed as a missionary who traveled between Dairen and Liaoyang. Her function at the time was to provide liaison and courier service to Soviet-controlled Chinese nets operating against the Japanese in Manchukuo.

Harry Tamer, the brother who worked for Crucible Steel, was discovered to have removed technical documents from the company as well as personal identity papers from the personnel file. To avoid arrest, he fled via Canada to Europe and then went on to Moscow. When his wife, Rose, attempted to renew her U.S. passport, she was questioned about her husband's role in an earlier passport fraud. She denied all knowledge and with her young daughter, Arva, arrived (via the *Queen Mary*) at Southampton on August 16, 1937. She informed the British that she was a tourist en route to the USSR.

Rose Tamer said that she could not explain her husband's abrupt departure from the United States in March 1935, insisting that she knew nothing about his "business affairs." She volunteered the fact that her husband had taken Soviet citizenship "at the behest of the Russian authorities."—NA Department of State Decimal 800.B/Tamer.

47. FBI file #74–133–3220 Whittaker Chambers. Chambers added: "I might observe that this procedure is somewhat contrary to underground methods and I believe that Rubens probably did this so as to be sure he left a trail when he went to Russia."

Hede Massing had left no clear trail when she left New York for Moscow, but when the R/R case broke, she wished she had. Massing was also a guest at the Metropole Hotel and had good reason to believe that she might suffer the same fate as Mrs. Rubens. To protect herself, she took advantage of the presence in Moscow of Mr. and Mrs. Corliss Lamont, whom she had met at *New Masses* fund-raising parties in New York. Massing recounts:

"As much as I hated to disturb Corliss' equilibrium, I saw a chance to send a message through him to our friend, Roger Baldwin, at that time director of the [American] Civil Liberties Union and an outstanding liberal. I began giving him the names of literally dozens of prominent German Communists who had fled from the vengeance of Hitler and were imprisoned or shot by the Soviets. He was startled, looked at me guardedly from the corner of his eyes. When I kept on in the same vein, he moved a little away from me, as if to get a better look at 'that insane woman.' He is a well-bred and polite man, and I would guess, hesitant to contradict people. He had not previously heard any of the facts that I told him this evening and he was completely unprepared to be told them by someone he knew to be a 'party functionary.' When I tried to make him understand our personal predicament, he looked aghast, as though I had really lost my mind.

"In spite of his obvious disbelief in what I had told him, I asked him to notify Roger Baldwin when he got back home so that Roger could notify the State Department if we were to disappear. All that he delivered of my message, I learned later, was to say, 'You know, Roger, I had dinner with Hede. My! She has gone sour. . . .'" Hede Massing, *This Deception* (New York: Duell, Sloan and Pearce, 1951), pp. 382–83.

On June 28, 1939, Walter Krivitsky told a representative of the Department of State:

"Rubens was sent to the United States to get genuine American passports which could be used with no alteration, preferably, or with merely a change of photographs. Until the change in U.S. passports, it had been possible to manufacture, in Moscow, the needed passports by taking apart the passport without leaving noticeable marks. Rubens was in the country more than a year actively endeavoring to get birth certificates, naturalization certificates and taking steps which would put him in a position of getting a supply of passports. He was in charge of the job himself and had possibly 20 persons under his direction. . . ."

Krivitsky claimed to have seen Rubens's Soviet personnel file and recalled seeing the names Rutowski and Rudewicz in the file. Krivitsky knew him as Ewert.

"Mrs. Rubens was an established and trusted member of the Communist Party before Rubens met her. She was 'assigned' to Rubens by the Party authorities and their living together and their marriage were agreeable to the Party officials."

Krivitsky estimated the strength of the Soviet security and intelligence services in New York alone (that is, exclusive of those in diplomatic guise) to be fifteen key officers with an additional 250–300 "workers" on the periphery. FBI file 100–11146–82.

48. Letter to Headquarters, Federal Bureau of Investigation, from William Larson, special agent in charge, Detroit field office, July 14, 1932. NA Department of Justice file 207600–280.

49. *Catalog of American Industry and Trade,* published by Amtorg, c. 1931. RG 242 1542 RS 3685.

50. *Catalog of American Industry and Trade,* published by Amtorg, 1937, 735 pp., 4th edition. NA RG 242 1542 RS 3685.

51. Report to the House of Representatives by the Special Committee to Investigate Communist Propaganda in the United States, July 22, 1930. Library of Congress HX 653.AS 1930a, Part 3, Vol. 3.

52. Notice to Postmasters I P B-G, 170/5, Division of National Postal Service, Washington, D.C., undated. Signed: J. W. Cole, Acting Second Assistant Postmaster General.

53. Sass & Martini was founded in 1852 as a small banking partnership in Berlin. The founders had passed from the scene long before World War I, and the bank had become dormant. However, the charter had been maintained over the years.

In discussing the true ownership of the bank around 1930, Walter Krivitsky named Franz Fisher as one of the key officers at the time of the currency switch. But Joseph Dorn insisted that he was directly involved in the reorganization of the bank at that time and had never heard of a Franz Fisher. Dorn was not *nash,* however, and therefore was not likely to know the identities of the true owners. Several photographs of Franz Fisher are included in the U.S. Secret Service files relating to the Sass & Martini affair. National Records Center, Suitland, Maryland.

Joseph Edward Dorn, released on probation from the federal penitentiary at Lewisburg, Pennsylvania, was staying at the Barbizon Plaza Hotel in New York City when he first read the Krivitsky articles in the *Saturday Evening Post.* He felt compelled to correct certain impressions given by Krivitsky relative to his role in the Sass & Martini affair. A condition of his cooperation with the FBI was the assurance that his parole, which was to expire in August 1941, not be prejudiced.—FBI file #100–11146, Sec. 2, February 12, 1941, interview with Joseph Dorn.

54. Many years later in 1941, Joseph Dorn insisted that the first packet of fifty hundred-dollar notes exchanged at Sass & Martini contained the new small notes. He was confident of the accuracy of his statement and said that he remembered them "vividly" because they were the first such notes he had seen, although he had been aware of the impending change in U.S. currency.—Ibid., Sec. 6.

55. Dorn, Dozenberg, and Burtan were simultaneously at the federal penitentiary at Lewisburg. The first two cooperated with the authorities, while Burtan did not. Dozenberg and Dorn claimed that Burtan tried to elicit information from them while in prison, but both men insisted that they made special efforts to avoid contact with him.

56. Krivitsky insisted that Dorn was in error and that Dorn had mistakenly identified Krivitsky as another Soviet some three inches taller.

57. The technique of currency-stock theft had been raised to its highest level by an English counterfeiter, James Burnet, who managed to steal genuine Bank of England paper from the mills at Laverstock in the late 1850s. Burnet's feat put

him in possession of stock that had not been sized, however; thus, despite the excellence of his plates, the paper did not accept the inks, and Burnet was caught. S. Cole, *Counterfeit* (New York, Abelard-Schuman, 1955), p. 198.

58. In the fall of 1929, Dozenberg was recalled to Moscow, where he was met by his old boss, Alfred Tilton, and taken to the GRU headquarters for a meeting with General Berzin, then director of Soviet military intelligence. As was customary, Dozenberg traveled with two passports, one in the name of Nicholas Dozenberg to be used in travel to the Soviet frontier, another in the name of Nicholas Dallant for use within the USSR.

Berzin outlined the task that Dozenberg was to undertake on his return to the United States: assisting a senior GRU officer called John Kirchenstein to document himself with a genuine U.S. pasport and other papers.

Back in New York, Dozenberg found that Tilton had already ordered Herbert Newmark to take the first step in the transformation of Kirchenstein. Newmark had contacted an undertaker in New Jersey from whom he bought the citizenship papers of a deceased American soldier, Frank E. Kleges, for forty dollars. Using the dead man's papers, Kirchenstein applied for and received a genuine U.S. passport.

Dozenberg was again recalled to Moscow in 1931, and this time Berzin ordered him to Romania to survey new commercial cover opportunities for the GRU. On leaving Moscow, he made his way to Bucharest via Berlin and Vienna, where he conferred with the local GRU staffs relative to their cover needs.

In Romania, he represented himself as an American movie mogul and was able to persuade the government to grant him a concession to produce and exhibit Romanian-American films. After several months of photographing everything in Romania he thought to be of interest to the Soviet military intelligence (including films of Magda Lepescu frolicking in the nude), he returned to Berlin. There he received an order to sail for New York, where he was to contact Aleksandr Burkan and get the $60,000 necessary to fund his film projects. On Dozenberg's arrival in New York, Burkan informed him that there would be a delay in getting the funds as "they were temporarily tied up in a deal with a German individual that had certain South American ramifications."—Unpublished mss. by a close contact of Dozenberg's, in author's possession.

Dozenberg's later admissions to the U.S. authorities were designed to put himself in a very distant place each time the subject of counterfeiting came up. He knew that Burtan had been sentenced to fifteen years in connection with counterfeiting, and Dozenberg showed a natural preference for the year-and-one-day sentence he had been given for passport fraud. He was at some pains to avoid any admissions of complicity in the more serious crime.—FBI file 61–6670–65.

59. Alfred Tilton (aka Tiltin), alias Joseph Paquette, was the GRU chief in New York City; his major intelligence targets at the time were military. Tilton's ranking associate in New York was Maj. Gen. Sergei Gusev—alias Drobkin and Green; according to Michael Straight, "Mr. Green" was the alias used by his Soviet contact in Washington in the thirties—who specialized in political intelligence.

Tilton was a Latvian who came to the United States in early 1928 and then, after a few months, returned to Europe. Five weeks later, he was back in New York with a new assistant, Lydia, the Baroness Stahl.

Tilton's wife, Maria, was on assignment for the GRU in Finland, where she was eventually discovered, arrested, and sentenced to ten years for espionage under the name Mary Louise Martin.

Tilton was arrested and shot in Moscow in May 1937.—FBI file 100–11146, Sec. 2.

60. Lydia Chkalov, much better known as Lydia, the Baroness Stahl, "was born in Kozlov in 1885, married a landed baron in the Crimea, divorced him in Constantinople, took her degree of master of arts at Columbia and her doctor of law at the Sorbonne, was a polyglot who spoke English, French, German, some Russian and Ukrainian and had prepared a thesis on Confucian culture from original sources.

"At the moment when they arrested her [in Paris], she was studiously occupied with a Chinese translation—of Japanese war plans. . . ."—A contemporary, romantic account by Janet Flanner (Genet), *Paris Was Yesterday* (New York: Viking Press, 1933), p. 121.

Stahl's counterpart in Amtorg was the mysterious Comrade Lisa in whom the Fish Committee had a deep interest. Years later, it was determined that Comrade Lisa was Elizaveta Zubilin. While in New York, she had meetings with Hede Massing to assess her reliability. Massing recalled her most distinctive features as "large feet, ugly hands, poor posture, and excellent English." "Lisa" also operated the photostat machine in Amtorg and by night assisted Baroness Stahl in copy work in the rear of Tourin's Photo Company at 67 West 119th Street, New York City.

Stahl was a highly intelligent woman and an extremely competent Soviet agent. Despite the collapse of her Paris operation, there are no indications that she provided French counterintelligence with any useful data. Had she cooperated, under French law her sentence could have been reduced or even suspended. Instead, Stahl went to prison and began her four-year sentence for espionage in silence.

61. According to the record, Philip A. Rosenbliet, D.D.S., with offices at 1440 Broadway, New York City, was only slightly better at conspiracy than he was at dentistry. Among the more important Soviet agents, he was the most garrulous. As for dentistry, Whittaker Chambers sat in his dental chair intermittently for seven years and then, at the time of the Hiss trial, was subjected to the embarrassment of having Alger Hiss peer into his mouth in an effort to remember "George Crosley" by his remarkably bad teeth.

In the early thirties, Rosenbliett was Chambers's case officer and mentor. For reasons of his own, he broke all the rules of conspiracy and detailed information relative to identities and activities. These accounts took up permanent lodgment in Chambers's memory. Rosenbliett's behavior is unaccountable since it is axiomatic in the Soviet service that there is no such thing as trust.

Hede Massing put it simply: ". . . the Soviet mind; a mind that assumes that everybody a priori is a spy and not to be trusted unless he can prove otherwise. Mistrust is the most essential feature in the Soviet character make-up. For one who shows trust—the Soviet feels only contempt."—Hede Massing, op. cit., p. 116.

Whittaker Chambers described Rosenbliett's waiting room as being somewhat unusual:

"I have often sat in the doctor's office with a half dozen other patients while he tended an earlier arrival inside. The doctor's patients were a miscelleanous lot, though all of them seemed to be Europeans. I noticed that most of them shared one peculiar habit. Most patients enter a waiting room, look a little dismayed at those ahead of them, pick up a magazine, sit down, riffle through it, put it down and take up another. The doctor's patients almost always entered the waiting room without glancing at anybody. They went directly to the magazine pile, picked up a magazine and buried themselves so deeply in it that it was sometimes almost impossible to see their faces."—Whittaker Chambers, *Witness* (South Bend, Ind.: Regnery/Gateway, 1979), p. 307.

Rosenbliett's problems took a turn when his brother-in-law, Joe Cannon, threw in with the Trotskyites. On one occasion, a seaman courier, just arrived in New York, was held up in the streets en route to the doctor's office; the $9,000 that he carried was taken from him. The Control Commission suspected that this was the work of agents under the direction of Cannon. Rosenbliett was under a strict injunction from that point onward to have absolutely no contact with the Cannon family.

He left New York for Moscow in late 1936 and returned a year later, this time as a purchasing agent for the Soviet-backed Loyalist government in Spain. His mission was to locate and purchase automatic munitions loading equipment. While in the United States, he made what he thought was a secret visit to the Cannon home. He failed to accept the near certainty that the Cannons were still under surveillance by order of the Control Commission, and he was observed going into the house. Within a few days, he received a cable instructing him to return to Moscow at once. Failing to realize that his visit to the Cannons was already known to Moscow, he sailed from New York on the first available ship. On arrival in Moscow, Rosenbliett was arrested and shot.

62. Each national Communist party had a control commission (sometimes consisting of only one member) that was charged with ensuring compliance with the Moscow line. In New York, the commission supervised the collection of dues, publication of the *Daily Worker,* and coordination and funding of various support organizations (fronts), along with maintaining clandestine contact with Amtorg. The commission was the final arbiter of disputes and spoke with infallibility in matters of doctrine and party discipline. More than once, the CC was late in receiving notice that Moscow had precipitately reversed itself on a critical issue. On these occasions, such as in the case of the Soviet-German nonaggression pact, the *Daily Worker* distinguished itself by a series of journalistic grotesqueries. Hitler had come in for the most bitterly vituperative attacks from the left, but when he became Stalin's ally, the Communists' tune changed overnight, with the *Worker* coming in only on the last chorus.

As indicated elsewhere, the foreign division of the OGPU had responsibility for counterintelligence in the Comintern. As a consequence, the CC had well-organized control lines from Moscow. The CC was also involved with recruitment of OGPU and GRU agents within the U.S. party. The decision to tap an overt party member for "disassociation" in preparation for clandestine work was made and approved by the Control Commission.

63. Dozenberg, consistent with his determination to avoid any possible charge of complicity in the counterfeiting operation, denied Gitlow's assertions.

64. The first description of the counterfeit Soviet $100 Federal Reserve note was issued by Secret Service in Circular Letter #602, May 8, 1928, which described only one of the notes. A second circular letter (#626), June 8, 1929, described the others. A detailed description of the flaws in each of the notes appeared in a supplement to CL #626 and was issued February 20, 1930, to aid in identification of the counterfeits.

65. The Department of State propagated a Treasury Department Circular (#415, June 10, 1929, signed by A. W. Mellon), which advised that new $1, $2, $5, $10, and $20 bills were being introduced as of June 10, 1929, and that bills of larger denomination would be introduced at a later, though unspecified date. NA RG 59, 851.5.

66. Count Enrique von Bulow, or von Buelow, was one of the more elegant aliases used by a petty criminal named Hans Dechow. As the Count, he claimed, among other things, to have served as a senior officer in the Kaiser's Uhlans and to be the former owner of vast Baltic estates. Burtan had a notion that the count was just the man to aid in the counterfeit swindle. The count saw Burtan as his lead into the upper reaches of crime. Together, they comprised a not very formidable team.

The count cooperated fully with the U.S. authorities and aided in the prosecution of Burtan. As late as 1941, the count was reported as still an active (though minor) stock promoter in Latin America.

67. The RCMP referred to the individual as "Gideon" and attempted to run him against the Soviets. "Gideon had learned English as a boy while his father was stationed in New York with the Russian Trading Company Amtorg." John Sawatsky, *For Services Rendered* (Toronto: Doubleday Canada, Ltd., 1982), p. 34.

68. John Barron, *KGB: The Secret Work of Soviet Secret Agents* (New York: Reader's Digest Press, 1974), p. 269.

CHAPTER 8

1. Among these are: Arnold Beichman and Mikhail S. Bernstam, *Andropov: New Challenge to the West. A Political Biography* (New York: Stein & Day, 1983); Zhores Medvedev, *Andropov* (New York: W. W. Norton, 1983); Martin Ebon, *The Andropov File. The Life and Ideas of Yuri V. Andropov, General Secretary of the Communist Party of the Soviet Union* (New York: Macmillan, 1983); Vladimir Solovyov and Elena Klepikova, *Yuri Andropov: A Secret Passage into the Kremlin* (New York: Macmillan, 1983).

2. John Barron, *KGB: The Secret Work of Soviet Secret Agents* (New York: Reader's Digest Press, 1974), p. 223, and *KGB Today: The Hidden Hand* (New York: Reader's Digest Press, 1983), p. 445. See also Brian Freemantle, *KGB: Inside the World's Largest Intelligence Network* (New York: Holt, Rinehart and Winston, 1982), pp. 40–41.

3. Joseph George Helmich, who was indicted on espionage charges by a federal grand jury on July 15, 1981, is a typical case of KGB targeting methods. In the first instance, Helmich was a self-selected agent of a type the organs have shown considerable flair in developing and exploiting. In Helmich's case, the

workman was worthy of his hire. According to the charges, Helmich received $131,000 from the KGB for information regarding the KL7 cryptographic system and was awarded the title of "colonel" in the Soviet Army. He further agreed to provide the Soviets with information about future "anticipated hostilities."

It is not possible here to assess the full extent of the damage done to U.S. interests by Helmich's act. It is, however, feasible to place his case in the KGB's overall perspective. It was evident in the course of the trial that Helmich did not fully realize the significance of the data he sold the KGB.

The enormity of the act derives from the earlier defections, in August 1960, of William H. Martin and Bernon F. Mitchell. Both were employees of the National Security Agency. (See William Corson, *Armies of Ignorance* [New York: Dial Press, 1977], pp. 402–4.) Martin and Mitchell did not go to the Soviet Union emptyhanded. Along with their considerable technical skills they took as much documentation as they could carry.

As the subsequent congressional investigation revealed, there were gaps in what they had managed to convey. See U.S. House of Representatives, Un-American Activities Committee, "Security Practices in the National Security Agency (defection of Bernon F. Mitchell and William H. Martin)" (Washington: U.S. Government Printing Office, August 13, 1962). To a large measure, the gaps in the Soviets' knowledge were closed by Helmich's contributions. With the complementary data from Helmich and the technical aid of Martin and Mitchell, the KGB was able to compromise the KL7 crypto system. Though Martin and Mitchell had considerable experience with the KL7 system, they could not have replicated it from memory. With Helmich's information in hand, the problem yielded. The case illustrates both the patience of the KGB as well as the organs' willingness and ability to exploit unplanned events.

4. The Johnson case pointed up another aspect of the KGB's devotion to the principle of "rendering" all parts of each opportunity. In addition to vital data, Johnson included copies and examplars of official U.S. correspondence. The legitimate letterheads and appropriate signatures were then used to produce forged intelligence documents that revealed discord among the Western allies. It is relatively simple to find press outlets for disinformation when it is based on authenticated forgeries.

As in similar espionage cases, the full extent of Johnson's treachery was not disclosed. The United States does not conduct internal-security trials in camera, so it is usual for the prosecution to disclose only information necessary to secure a conviction. A standard part of these proceedings is the denigration of the traitor's access or status. This is thought to be reassuring to the public. In many respects, however, the policy of minimizing disclosure serves only to spare embarrassment to the particular bureaucracy that had jurisdiction over the defendant's security and access.

The policy also contributes to the KGB's well-being by conveying the popular impression that an insignificant, low-level employee was caught in some kind of misbehavior and severely punished. The public and the Congress are induced to accept the fact that the damage has been repaired and that suitable steps have been taken to prevent its recurrence.

The Martin-Mitchell investigation was a notable exception to this practice, but only because Speaker of the House John McCormack, who had a clearer, broader comprehension of internal-security matters than almost all his colleagues combined, was not taken in by the suggestion that the defectors were low-level employees of the NSA with no significant access or knowledge.

After the KGB knew that Johnson had been caught by the FBI, it decided to get a little more advantage out of the stolen documents. The then head of the KGB's Department A of the First Chief Directorate (disinformation), Ivan Ivanovich Agayants, alias Ivan Avalov, arranged to leak some of the documents to selected publications in Italy and West Germany in early 1968. The planted stories resulted in a disappointing reaction because of their turgid military jargon, which made them virtually unintelligible to the general reader. Undismayed, Agayants tried again. According to Phillip Knightley and Antony Terry writing the *Sunday Times* of London on June 22, 1980, Agayants consulted Heinz Felfe, the KGB's expert on West Germany. Felfe suggested concentrating on a single document that purported to be the plan for a guerrilla operations in which U.S. Green Berets were to be dropped behind Soviet lines equipped with tactical nuclear weapons and the equipment for biological and chemical warfare. The document, with its top-secret designation, appeared in the September 1970 issue of the German newsmagazine *Der Spiegel,* with a letter from an anonymous contributor writing from Rome.

The letter said the documents had been supplied by the deputy chief of the West German counterintelligence service, Horst Wendland, who had committed suicide on October 8, 1968. The Pentagon immediately explained the plans were out of date and had been changed. This account was made believable only by revealing the true source of the documents and their chronology. Under pressure from the angry Germans, the United States was forced to admit the whole sorry story of Johnson and his treachery.

It was one for the KGB and zero for the United States. The story of the documents passed by Sergeant Johnson did not end there. It appeared once again when some documents were sent to members of Britain's Parliament and the British press on the day after the Secretary of State for Defense, Sir Francis Pym, announced the sites in Britain that would accommodate 160 U.S.-produced cruise missiles (June 18, 1980). The Americans and the Soviets both knew that Johnson's documents were still alive and altered even though Johnson himself had been stabbed to death by his son eight years before.

There was no serious attempt to conceal the identity of the source of the documents. The KGB's doctrine in these matters calls for the exploitation of sources, and protection is only provided to those who have continued utility. Johnson probably would have been accepted in the Soviet Union if he had elected to take the "defection" option. But failure to seek shelter in the USSR canceled the KGB's obligations, and he became expendable.

5. See esp. Trevor Armbrister, *A Matter of Accountability: The True Story of the Pueblo Affair* (New York: Coward, McCann, 1970). As Armbrister notes (p. 11): "Communications Technician First Class Francis J. Ginther wondered, that despite all the secrecy—these bar girls all seemed to know what *Pueblo*'s mission was, when and where she was sailing and the date she was due back in port. Even among the crew, only the CT's and the men on the navigation detail were sup-

posed to know that. Ginther suddenly had a 'weird feeling' about his forthcoming voyage. 'Something,' he sensed, 'was going to go wrong.'"

6. Brezhnev's *banda* consisted of seven top security officials in the KGB and the MVD who had been intimates and protégés of Brezhnev when he was party boss in the city of Dnepropetrovsk.

The *banda* included Semen Kuzmich Tsvigun, who was named first deputy chairman of the KGB in 1967 (at which time Andropov was named chairman) and given the Army rank of full general in December 1978; Georgi Karpovich Tsinev and Viktor Mikhailovich Chebrikov, two of the five other deputy chairmen of the KGB; General Vadim Matrosov, chief of the KGB border guards; General Nikolay A. Shchlokov, minister of internal affairs (MVD) and another of Brezhnev's old cronies from his time on the Dnieper River; Lieutenant General V. S. Paputin, first deputy minister of the MVD; and Lieutenant General Yuri M. Churbanov the next man in the MVD's chain of command.

These men were the principal members of the family that Brezhnev designated for promotion and full participation in the rape of the Russian people. To Andropov, the corruption of the *banda* was an appealing vulnerability. With Chebrikov as Brezhnev's Brutus, the other six members were either killed or "retired." Perhaps, at some interminable party congress in the future, the extent of the corruption of Brezhnev and the *banda* will be revealed.

7. Barbara Carr, *Spy in the Sun* (Capetown; Timmins, 1969).

8. South Africa Cape *Times,* September 13, 1967.

9. Edward Jay Epstein, *The New York Times Magazine,* September 28, 1980.

10. Chambers hid photo negatives of retyped State Department documents in a hollowed-out pumpkin on his Maryland farm. He had acquired these documents in the months before he left the Soviet service, believing that they would be important proofs not only of his relationship with the Soviets but also of his connection with Alger Hiss, from whom he claimed to have received the documents.

11. "Cicero" was the code name for an Albanian named Elyesa Bazna, who served as valet to Sir Hughe Knatchbull-Hugresen, British ambassador to Turkey in 1943 and 1944. Bazna photographed hundreds of secret papers he took from the ambassador's safe and sold the film to the Nazis.

12. Barnett was aided in his search for employment in the Congress by several members who provided letters of recommendation.

13. The Reagan administration, in connection with its proposed prepublication review requirement (with a lifetime obligation) for those who have or had access to "compartmented intelligence information"—i.e., intelligence with various gradations of sensitivity as well as conventional security classifications—has indicated that the number of individuals with current access to these types of information is approximately 120,000! An incredible number, indicating a three-to-four-thousand-percent increase in the last thirty-five years.

14. *Report of the Security Commission May 1983.* Presented to Parliament by the Prime Minister by Command of Her Majesty, May 1983 (London: Her Majesty's Stationery office, CMnd 8876).

15. Two U.S. cases that correspond to the screening problem in the Prime case are those of Sergeant Jack Dunlap, who earned a modest fortune in the early 1960s by reproducing thousands of secret U.S. documents for the Soviets, and

Lieutenant Colonel William H. Whalen. Dunlap was recruited by the GRU while on duty with the U.S. Embassy in Moscow, where the organs noted his proclivities for "wild women and strong drink." His alcoholism made him such an easy recruit that the sexual entrapment was almost unnecessary.

On his return to the United States, Dunlap was assigned to the National Security Agency, from whence he passed documents, to the Soviets in exchange for $60,000. Included in his transmittals were top-secret CIA estimates of Soviet military, naval, and nuclear capabilities. Dunlap committed suicide when U.S. counterintelligence initiated an investigation of his activities.

William H. Whalen had a long career in intelligence before being exposed as a Soviet agent. He came under FBI surveillance in 1959, when he was routinely observed meeting with two Soviet embassy officials, First Secretary Mikhail M. Shumaev and Colonel Sergei A. Edenski. Whalen is believed to have become acquainted with one of the Soviet military attachés in 1955 and the other in 1959. One of them was promoted by the GRU to two-star general rank for his handling of this case. Whalen was arrested by FBI agents in July 1966.—See FBI Report, William Henry Whalen: Espionage, Washington, D.C., August 30, 1968, p. 21.

At the time of his arrest, Whalen had the distinction of being the only U.S. commissioned officer ever charged with espionage on behalf of the Soviets. He was recruited "in place" while serving with the Joint Chiefs of Staff in the Pentagon. Whalen was charged with passing to the Soviets "information pertaining to atomic weaponry, missiles, military plans for the Defense of Europe, information concerning the retaliation plans of the U.S. Strategic Air Command, and information pertaining to troop movements, documents and writings relating to the National Defense of the United States." (See Joseph Newman, ed., *Famous Soviet Spies* (Washington, D.C.: U.S. News & World Report, 1973), pp. 20, 174.

The Dunlap and Whalen cases received relatively little attention in the U.S. intelligence community. Both were dismissed on the "occasional rotten apple" theory rather than their illumination of systemic weakness. The KGB's attention to the observation of specific target's vulnerabilities, identifiable in the course of "innocent" social exchanges, and the noting of behaviorial excesses in certain U.S. officials, paid off handsomely.

16. The vetting, or close evaluation, of intelligence personnel is one of the most difficult issues faced by security officers in the West. In the KGB and the Soviet-bloc services, of course, there is no real problem. No one is above and beyond suspicion or immune to dismissal, no matter how high the position or how many years of faithful services have been rendered. This is not the case in the United States and Great Britain. In addition, Western reliance on polygraph tests does not take full account of the fact that the "black box" can be confounded by someone with adequate training and experience.

17. *Scientific Communication and National Security,* Vols. I-II, National Academy of Sciences, National Academy of Engineering, Institute of Medicine. (Washington, D.C.: National Academy Press, 1982).

18. On October 23, 1974, Werner Jurgen Bruchausen, a thirty-four-year-old West German residing in Los Angeles, incorporated four companies for the purpose of buying and selling sophisticated electronic equipment. The firms all used

the address of 4676 Admiralty Way in Marina Del Rey. Subsequently, Bruchausen incorporated eight other entities in Southern California.

Of the four companies organized in 1974, the principal enterprise was California Technology Corporation (CTC). From its inception through 1980, CTC used eighteen other trade names, twelve of which were incorporated in California. From 1977 to 1980, CTC and its variants, under the direction of Anatoli Maluta and Sabrina Dorn Tittel, purchased high-technology electronic equipment, peripherals, and components valued in excess of $10.5 million. Most of the items they purchased were classified as strategic commodities, controlled for national security purposes and requiring U.S. export licenses from the State and Commerce departments.

In the same four-year period, CTC exported to the Soviet Union, East Germany, and other satellites more than three hundred shipments of strategic commodities. None had proper export licenses. The shipments were documented with fraudulent U.S. shipper's export declarations. Most of the exports were sent to West Germany, consigned to companies controlled by, or associated with, Bruchausen. From West Germany most were transshipped to Switzerland or Austria or other intermediate countries, then reshipped to the USSR or another Warsaw Pact nation.

19. Central Intelligence Agency report, "Soviet Acquisition of Western Technology" (U), prepared for the House Committee on Science and Technology: Subcommittee on Investigations and Oversight (Washington, D.C.: April 1982).

20. The Coordinating Committee (COCOM) was established in 1949 to develop a system of strategic export controls. It is composed of the United States, the United Kingdom, Turkey, Protugal, Norway, the Netherlands, Luxembourg, Japan, Italy, Greece, France, the Federal Republic of Germany, Denmark, Canada, and Belgium.

21. *Christian Science Monitor,* January 4, 1983, p. 30.

22. In the late 1970s, a former East European intelligence officer revealed organizational and targeting details related to direct Soviet acquisition of Western technology through the East European intelligence services. Of particular priority were military-industrial manufacturing technologies. Many technologies were acquired through dummy firms established in Western Europe. These firms succeeded in acquiring some of the most advanced technologies in the West, including computer, microelectronic, nuclear, and chemical technologies. See esp. staff statement of Fred Asselin, investigator, Permanent Subcommittee on Investigations, U.S. Senate, May 4, 1982.

23. Central Intelligence Agency report, op. cit., p. 12.

24. Robert Lindsey, *The Falcon and the Snowman* (New York: Simon & Schuster, 1979).

25. A KGB variation in exploitation might be termed the "indulgence of Walter Mitty ploy." For example, the case of a former low-level CIA employee, William Kampiles, who sold the KGB a manual for the KH-11 satellite. Kampiles' defense at his trial involved his stated conviction that he was only trying to gain access to the Soviets so that he could work as a U.S. penetration of the KGB. This case is not unique. In fact, the KGB welcomes such feckless amateur endeavors with open arms.

26. William Holden Bell, a radar project engineer at the Hughes Aircraft Company, was recruited by Marian Zacharski, an officer of the Polish intelligence organization *Sluzba Bezpieczenstwa* —(SB). Zacharski operated under cover as a vice president of Polamco, which was incorporated in Illinois and Delaware as a subsidiary of the Polish Government corporation. Polamco began as an importer/exporter of machinery, parts, and tools and as a consultant to firms exporting these products to Polland. The recruitment began as a simple friendship between neighbors with mutual sporting interests and grew quickly to include their families, then to proving Bell's credentials by showing a classified document to Zacharski, and finally to passing microfilm copies of classified reports at meeting places in the United States, Switzerland, and Austria. Bell was in financial straits and was easily influenced by the cash proferred—a total of $110,000 over the three-year period 1978–1981. In all, over twenty highly classified reports on advanced future U.S. weapons systems and components were passed by Bell to the SB and thence on to the KGB for additional exploitation.

27. The "unguarded moment" ploy is by far one of the most effective tactics in the KGB's bag of disinformation tricks. Through its millions of informers and surveillance teams, the KGB maintains close control over the few thousands of Soviet citizens who are in any regular official or semiofficial contact with foreigners, especially U.S. citizens who have any claim to influence. As Khrushchev himself put it, in repudiating the idea that he had spoken out of turn to the late Senator Hubert Humphrey in 1958 on the subject of Chinese communes: "The mere suggestion that I might have confidential contact with a man who boasts of having spent twenty years fighting communism can only give rise to laughter. Anyone who understands anything at all about politics, to say nothing of Marxism-Leninism, will realise that a confidential talk with Mr. Humphrey about the policies of communist parties and relations with our best friends, the leaders of the Communist Party of China, is inconceivable."—Documentary record of the Extraordinary Twenty-first CPSU Congress, in Leo Gruliow, ed., *Current Soviet Policies,* Vol. 3, January 1959 (New York: Frederick A. Praeger), p. 206.

The ex-KGB officer Anatoliy Golitsyn writes, "Yet many Western observers and scholars claim to have benefitted from such disclosures. In the preface to his book *The Soviet Bloc: Unity and Conflict,* Zbigniew Brezinski wrote: 'I am also grateful to several officials of various communist states, for their willingness to discuss matters they should not have discussed with me.' No explanation is offered in the book of the reasons why communist officials should have been willing to speak frankly to a prominent anticommunist scholar and citizen of the leading 'imperialist' power, nor is any reference made in the book to the possibilities of disinformation. *But if the existence of a disinformation program is taken into account, together with the control over the communist officials in contact with foreigners, the explanation for these indiscretions is obvious* [italics added].—*New Lies for Old* (New York: Dodd, Mead, 1984), p. 100.

The "closet liberal" description of Yuri Andropov has interesting antecedents:

"The fact that a propaganda campaign to popularize Andropov in the West was being conducted on the Soviet side was acknowledged by my old friend G. A. Arbatov, a member of the Central Committee, during a conversation with the American journalist Joseph Kraft. Arbatov did explain, however, that the opera-

tion was the 'work of volunteers.' Arbatov himself belonged to their number, and
the co-workers from his institute—but not only them! Among Soviet intellectuals
there were of course volunteers who considered the pragmatic Andropov the best
of possible candidates for Secretary General. . . . In the Kraft interview, Arbatov
said that he [Andropov] made the KGB different from what it had been. Under
him its reputation improved. It no longer fitted the stereotype of an organ of
terror. Still, it is not a welfare organization. . . ."—Michael Voslensky,
Nomenklatura: Anatomy of the Soviet Ruling Class (London: The Bodley Head,
1984), pp. 378–379.

Arbatov's confidence was duly reported by Kraft. Confirmation of Andropov's
attributes was not long in coming. Dusko Doder, the *Washington Post*'s man in
Moscow, reported that he had learned from highly placed Soviet sources (volunteers?) of Andropov's benign temperament and developed tastes in rock music,
Scotch whisky, and tailored suits.

28. The works of John Barron, Claire Sterling, and Brian Freemantle, previously cited, provide an overview of KGB tactics and techniques of disinformation.

29. V. N. Chebrikov (deputy chairman of the KGB), "Vigilance—A Well
Tried Weapon," *Molodoy Kommunist*, No. 4, April 1981. This article, based on a
speech, was a clear indication of the "high moral ground" that Chebrikov and
Andropov were staking out in anticipation of their control of the Soviet power
center.

APPENDIX I

OPERATIONS OF THE AMTORG CORPORATION

With a Partial List of Individuals Associated with It

Including Some Who Were Active Operatives of the Soviet Espionage and Security Services in the United States

"From 1927 on, the USSR refused to release patents. One of Amtorg's functions, in the name of 'war-time cooperation' with the U.S., was to send teams of technical experts to the U.S. Patent Office who were provided with any and all patents requested. After the war, the Four Continent Book Company took over the mass reproduction of free U.S. patents on behalf of the Soviet government. The practice was finally terminated on December 13th, 1949."—George R. Jordan, *Major Jordan's Diaries* (New York; Harcourt Brace, 1952), p. 136.

The largest request for U.S. patents came from the "innocuous-sounding firm called the 'Four Continent Book Corporation' described as 'importers of new, old and rare books from the Soviet Union.' On January 2, 1945, this communist-created puppet placed its order with the U.S. Government Patent Office for 60,000 patents, enclosing its check for $6,000. That order was signed by Cyril Lambkin."—Jacob Spolansky, *The Communist Trail in America* (New York: Macmillan, 1951), p. 147.

In the mid-thirties, "Many puzzled American firms, unaware of the Soviets' game, were mystified when contracts containing a unique provision began to pour in for American goods. No orders would be accepted, the contract said, unless a Russian representative had the right to inspect the plant at which the goods were made. Thus, a stream of thousands of 'inspections' was set in motion. Sitting back as commander of this army was Cyril Lambkin, an official of the Amtorg Trading Corporation."—Spolansky, p. 146.

In 1930, the Amtorg staff numbered 489, 105 of whom were Soviet citizens; in addition, 61 were Soviet citizens who had applied for U.S. naturalization, 305 were U.S. citizens, and 18 others were of uncertain status. "Inspectors" from the USSR came in ever-increasing numbers: 66 arrived in 1926; 171 arrived in 1927; 220 arrived in 1928; 552 arrived in 1929; 575 arrived in 1930. The total for the year 1930 was 1,064 people in the United States who were either employed or sponsored by Amtorg.

Lambkin and Leon Josephson, legal adviser to the International Labor Defense, are credited with developing the "inspection" system in the United States.

Andrei Shevchenko, a graduate of the Aviation Institute of Moscow, arrived in the United States in June 1942 to take up his duties with the Soviet Purchasing Commission. Shevchenko was assigned as the Soviet liaison officer to the Bell Aircraft Corporation, Buffalo, New York, for a period of three years. He made a concentrated effort to develop a close relationship with a couple named Franey. She was employed by Bell as a librarian, and he worked for the Hooker Chemical Corporation. Shevchenko attempted to persuade Mr. and Mrs. Franey that by providing him with classified data (principally reports from the National Advisory Committee for Aeronautics), they could make considerable money. The Franeys, in cooperation with the FBI, provided Shevchenko with misleading reports. In July 1945, the Franeys met with Shevchenko in his office at the Amtorg Trading Corporation.

"The Amtorg Trading Corporation, which set up offices in New York in 1924, controlled the first real Soviet espionage effort against the United States. Communications with the Soviet Union were, naturally, carried on in code, and whatever system was used, it effectively protected the secrets of their American spies. Representative Hamilton Fish Jr. of New York subpoenaed 3,000 coded Amtorg telegrams in 1930. The cryptanalysts of the Navy's Code and Signal Section, to which he submitted the cryptograms, reported that 'The cipher used by the Amtorg is the most complicated and possesses the greatest secrecy within their [the Navy cryptanalysts] knowledge.'"—David Kahn, *The Codebreakers* (New York: Macmillan, 1967), p. 635. The security of the Soviet cipher system owed much to British Prime Minister Stanley Baldwin's public disclosures following the Arcos raid.

Although total figures on the number of Soviets and non-Soviets assigned and/or employed by Amtorg are not publicly available, it has been estimated by U.S. intelligence authorities that the mix between Soviets and others remains in the 40 to 60 percent range. The non-Soviets generally carry out the legitimate administrative tasks associated with the nonespionage activities of Amtorg. As such, these persons help to maintain the fiction that Amtorg is simply another trading organization.

As FBI Director William Webster has noted there are approximately 1,000 Soviet staff intelligence officers currently operating in the US. The number of Soviets, Poles, Czechs, Bulgarians, East Germans, Cubans, Romanians, Libyans, and Syrians, when added to the unnumbered illegals of varying nationalities now operating in the United States, gives a total professional strength well in excess of 3,000. In the last thirty years, they have turned up in every large city and small town, and the chances are excellent that tens of thousands of citizens have been in "unwitting" contact with these representatives of the organs.

The precise number of current Amtorg employees is not publicly available. As in the past, the staff is comprised of both U.S. and Soviet citizens, with the former mainly concerned with the legitimate purposes of the organization and the latter with the supervision of the more important Soviet espionage operations in the United States.

The FBI has estimated that a minimum of 40 percent of *all* personnel assigned or attached to Soviet establishments outside the USSR are trained intelligence officers. Included in the estimate are all embassies, consulates, missions, UN organizations, trade representations and delegations, *Tass,* Novosti, *Pravda,* Aeroflot, Intourist, and all "commercial firms" such as Amtorg.

This massive espionage effort draws heavily on the satellite services and, of course, the additional thousands of Soviet and satellite dependents in New York, Washington, and the West Coast who are also in the United States and available to perform operational support roles, such as surveillance and investigations of U.S. citizens, the identification and servicing of impersonal communication systems (i.e., "dead drops"), and the research essential to the selection of those industrial, scientific, and technical targets of highest interest to Moscow.

Among the individuals and their associated organizations that contributed to the establishment of Soviet commercial operations in the U.S.:
Martens, Ludwig C. K.   1919-. Deported from the United States in 1921, having failed in his efforts to gain recognition for the Soviet government.

Recht, Charles   1919-. Adviser to Prodexco. In 1924 he assisted in the formation of the Amtorg Corporation. Later, represented Soviet citizens with claims against the U.S. Veterans Bureau (now Veterans Administration). (Congressional testimony of Dr. David Dubrowsky, 1939; also Spolansky and [1])*

Sherman, Isaac   1919-mid-1930s. First employed by Prodexco and later as a director and stockholder of Amtorg. (Department of State decimal files, subject: Amtorg; also [7])

---

*In parentheses following most of the annotations are the sources for the information cited. For easy reference many of the basic sources are referred to by a bracketed number, as follows:

[1] David J. Dallin, *Soviet Espionage* (New Haven: Yale University Press, 1953).
[2] Georges Agabekov, *OGPU: The Russian Secret Terror* (New York: Brentano's, 1931).
[3] Whittaker Chambers, *Witness* (New York: Random House, 1952).
[4] Louis Budenz, testimony.
[5] Department of State, decimal files.
[6] John Barron, *KGB: The Secret Work of Soviet Secret Agents* (New York: Reader's Digest Press, 1973).
[7] Joseph Finder, *Red Carpet* (New York: Holt, Rinehart and Winston, 1983).
[8] Elizabeth Bentley, congressional testimony.
[9] John Sawatsky, *For Services Rendered* (Toronto: Doubleday, 1982).
[10] George R. Jordan, *Major Jordan's Diaries* (New York: Harcourt Brace, 1982).
[11] Thaddeus Wittlin, *Commissar: The Life and Death of Lavrenty Pavlovitch Beria* (New York: Macmillan, 1973).
[12] Roy A. Medvedev, *Let History Judge: The Origins and Consequences of Stalinism* (New York: Alfred A. Knopf, 1971).
[13] Peggy Dennis, *American Communist* (Westport, Conn.: Lawrence Hill; Berkeley, Cal.: Creative Arts, 1977).
[14] Isaac Don Levine, *Stalin's Greatest Secret* (New York: Coward, McCann, 1956).
[15] John Barron, *KGB Today: The Hidden Hand* (New York: Reader's Digest Press, 1983).
[16] Dan N. Jacobs, *Borodin: Stalin's Man in China* (Cambridge: Harvard University Press, 1981).
[17] Jacob Spolansky, *The Communist Trail in America* (New York: Macmillan, 1951).
[18] N. M. Borodin, *One Man in His Time* (London: Constable & Co., 1955).

Adams, Arthur A.   1927-. Came to the United States as a representative of the Soviet Automobile Trust. Returned in 1932 as an agent of the Soviet Aviation Trust under Amtorg sponsorship. In 1938 Adams established a "technical laboratory" in New York City, and in 1942 he became a buyer of chemicals. ([1]; Department of State decimal files, subject Adams; various congressional citations)

Hammer, Dr. Julius   1921-. Active in the American Labor Party, forerunner of the CPUSA. Aided in the establishment of Amtorg. (Congressional citations and [7])

Hammer, Dr. Armand   1921-. Assisted in the establishment of Amtorg in 1924. Concessionaire in the USSR until the early thirties. Prominent U.S. businessman. ([7] and Department of State decimal files, subject: Amtorg)

Chatski (Tschatsky)   1925-1928. Reportedly the first GPU/OGPU resident in Amtorg. (Hendler, [1] and [2])

Wolf, ("Felix")   1924-1929. Wolf was the first GRU resident in New York City and operated under Amtorg-related commercial cover. ([8])

Rosenbliett, Dr. Philip   1926-1937. GRU officer in New York City and operational contact of Whittaker Chambers. Acted as purchasing agent (within an Amtorg subsidiary) for the Loyalist forces during the Spanish civil war. Recalled to the USSR in 1937 and executed for alleged Trotskyite sympathies. (FBI Consolidated Report of Whittaker Chambers and [1])

Fox, I.   1924-1927. Officer in Prodexco at the time of the formation of Amtorg. Served as one of three Amtorg directors and stockholders. (Department of State decimal files, subject: Amtorg; Treasury Department, Internal Revenue Reports; various U.S. Army, G-2 reports, NA RG 165)

Tilton, Alfred ("Paquett")   1928-1930. Senior GRU officer in New York City. Recruiter of Dozenberg. Husband of "Mary Louise Martin," who was arrested along with Arvid Jacobson and convicted of espionage in Finland in 1933. Maintained an Amtorg-related commercial cover office in New York. Reportedly executed in the USSR in 1937. ([1] and U.S. Army, G-2 reports, NA RG 165)

Tourin, Joseph   1928-1931. Recruited by Nicholas Dozenberg to provide a "commercial" cover for a GRU photostat facility in New York. (FBI)

"Charlie," alias of Leon Minster   1928-. GRU officer in New York. ([1] and [8])

Davyatkin ("Murzin"-"Dick")   1928-1931. GRU officer in New York in contact with Elizabeth Bentley and Jacob Golos; known to Whittaker Chambers. ([1], [8], and FBI)

Stahl, Lydia (nee Chkalov)   1926-. GRU officer associated with Tourin and Dozenberg; maintained intermittent contact with Amtorg-based resident. Reassigned to Paris in 1931. Arrested along with Robert Switz and his wife. Stahl was convicted of espionage against France in 1933 and imprisoned. While in New York she specialized in managing GRU nets within Columbia University. (FBI, and [1])

Martin, M. L. (Mrs. Tilton)   1929-1933. GRU officer in New York. Wife of resident. Reassigned. Arrested, convicted, and imprisoned in 1933 for espionage against Finland. (NA RG 165, U.S. Army, G-2 files, [1])

Jacobson, Arvid V. 1932-1933. Reportedly recruited by Whittaker Chambers for the GRU. Arrested, convicted, and imprisoned for espionage against Finland in 1933. (NA RG 165, U.S. Army, G-2 files, [1])

Tretiakoff, N. 1929-1930. Cipher clerk assigned to Amtorg. Attempted defection in New York. (HR Committee Hearings, NYC, June 1930, chaired by Hon. Hamilton Fish)

Sedov, F. 1928-1930. Cipher clerk assigned to Amtorg. Attempted defection in New York. (Ibid.)

Shulga, A. 1929-1930. Cipher clerk assigned to Amtorg. Attempted defection in New York. (Ibid.)

Rykoff, A. 1930-. Cipher clerk assigned to Amtorg. Attempted defection in New York. (Ibid.)

Levin, O. A. 1929-1930. Cipher clerk assigned to Amtorg. Attempted defection in New York. (Ibid.)

"Michael" 1935-1937. NKVD officer assigned to Amtorg. ([1])

Budenz, Louis 1930-1945. Worked under Dr. G. Rabinovitz of the Russian Red Cross. Broke with the Soviets in 1945. ([8], [13], [14], and thirty-four congressional citations)

Gitlow, B. 1920-. Member of the Control Commission of the CPUSA. Broke with the party. ([1] and eighteen congressional citations including references to Amtorg)

Dirba, Charles 1920-. Member of the Control Commission of the CPUSA. (Ibid.)

Massing, Hede 1923-1945. GRU officer in New York. Worked for Jacob Golos. Operated commercial shipping and freight forwarding cover company related to Amtorg. Also took over most of the GRU net operating in the U.S. government previously handled by Whittaker Chambers. Broke with the GRU in 1945 and cooperated with the FBI. ([1], [8], and eight congressional citations including extensive testimony)

Josephson, Leon Legal adviser to the International Labor Defense and to Amtorg. ([1] and nineteen congressional citations including testimony in 1952)

Asaturov, Vladimir 1929-1930. OGPU resident in New York City and Amtorg official. ([1] and Fish Committee files including Amtorg personnel list)

Filin, Semion 1928-1930. OGPU officer in New York and employee of Amtorg. Fled the United States in 1930 and was reported to have been executed in 1934. (NYT, [1] and [17])

Pogany, Joseph (alias John Pepper) 1923-. OGPU officer in New York with extensive contacts with the Control Commission and Amtorg. Reported to have been executed in the mid-thirties. (Congressional citations and FBI)

Hoorgin, I. Served as chairman of the board of Amtorg from 1924 to 1925, when his body was found in Lake George. The circumstances surrounding his death were never established to the satisfaction of the New York police. Two of his former associates gave sworn statements that Hoorgin's death was a political murder.

Ziavkin, Feodor   1929-1931. A senior OGPU officer who posed in New York as an Amtorg official. ([1] and congressional citations)

"Comrade Liza" (Elizaveta Zubilin)   An experienced OGPU/NKVD officer and wife of Vasili Zubilin. Liza worked in Amtorg in 1929 and 1930. Left the United States and returned in 1934, remaining until 1944. Known to Elizabeth Bentley. (FBI, Fish Committee hearings 1930, [1], [8], and numerous congressional citations)

Pavlov, Alexander   1928-1930. GRU officer serving as an Amtorg employee who maintained contact with Whittaker Chambers. (FBI, Consolidated Report, Whittaker Chambers)

Hendler, Mikhail   1922-1925. Defected GPU officer who provided the Fish Committee with detailed information regarding the Soviets' use of trade missions, the Red Cross, and the commercial companies, such as Amtorg, as covert espionage facilities. (Congressional hearings, 1930)

Delgass, Boris   1927-1930. Resigned as a vice president of Amtorg in July 1930. Testified before the Fish Committee: "I have seen information regarding the army and naval defenses of the United States that has been gathered by Amtorg's agents and transmitted to Russia." (Congressional citations and [1])

Markin, Valentin   1933-1934. Originally a GRU officer in New York City with Amtorg connections. In an out-of-channel message, Markin complained to Moscow that the GRU in the United States was badly managed. He was reassigned to the OGPU/NKVD resident in New York and found murdered a few months later. (FBI, Department of State decimal file, subject: Krivitsky; [1] and [8])

Shpak, Boris   1936-1937. Senior NKVD officer operating illegal nets out of Amtorg-related commercial firms. (Congressional citations)

Raina, Ivan A.   1940-1944. Senior NKVD officer assigned to Amtorg at the time the Soviet Purchasing Commission was set up in Washington. The early staff of the commission consisted of Amtorg employees. After the end of the war, Raina was identified as the senior Soviet intelligence adviser to Mao Tse-tung. (Congressional citations)

Ovakimian, Gaik   1932-1941. OGPU/NKVD resident in New York. When arrested by the FBI in 1941, Ovakimian claimed diplomatic immunity as an Amtorg employee. At the time, the Soviet government detained six American citizens who were traveling in the USSR. Ovakimian was exchanged for the Americans. Among his subordinates in the New York net were Julius Rosenberg and Harry Gold. (FBI, [5], [8], [14], Department of Justice case files, and numerous congressional citations)

Pitcoff, Robert   Amtorg employee who was subjected to intense recruitment pressures by the NKVD. He resigned from Amtorg, quit the CPUSA in 1934, and later (1939) testified before the HUAC. (Congressional citations and [1])

Lambkin, Cyril 1933-1945. Amtorg employee credited with devising the "inspection" system used to such great effect in Amtorg's industrial espionage work. ([1], [17], [4], and congressional citations)

Frankfurter, Gerda GRU officer in New York, 1934-1936. Contact of Bentley's. ([8])

Gorskaia, Lydia OGPU officer assigned to Amtorg, 1929-1930. She served in England in the late thirties and was later (1944) posted to the Soviet consulate in New York. ([1] and congressional citations)

Gorsky, Anatoli (alias Professor Nikitin, alias Anatoli Gromov) Husband of Lydia Gorskaia and case officer for Philby, Burgess, and Maclean. Followed Maclean to Washington in 1944. ([8], [15], and numerous congressional citations)

Grinke, Walter (alias Bill) GRU officer assigned to Amtorg in 1934. Contact of Bentley's.

Bron, Saul G. 1925-1927. Chairman of the board of Amtorg during his assignment to New York.

Bazarov, Boris (known to Bentley as "Fred") In New York from 1935 to 1937. Previously served as a GRU officer in Berlin (1927) and in various Balkan posts in 1929 and 1930. Recalled from the U.S. and executed in 1937. ([1] and [8])

Dozenberg, Nicholas ("Arthur") An active GRU officer from 1927 until 1939, at which time he was arrested, tried, and convicted of passport fraud and sentenced to one year in a federal prison. In 1927, Dozenberg operated on directions from Amtorg. Later, he was warned repeatedly by his GRU superiors to avoid all direct contact with Amtorg in the future. ([1], FBI, congressional citations, Secret Service files, Bureau of Prisons files, and Department of Justice records)

Burtan, Dr. Valentine From 1927 until his arrest in 1933, Burtan maintained close contacts with the GRU officers in Amtorg. In 1934, he was sentenced to fifteen years' imprisonment following his conviction for counterfeiting. (FBI, Secret Service, Bureau of Prisons files and records)

Kirchenstein, John GRU illegal who came to New York in 1929 and remained until 1931, when he was reassigned to Paris. Dozenberg and others assisted in providing him with a new identity and with a commercial cover for his European activities. (FBI, Department of State decimal files, and [1])

Stern, Moishe (known as "General Kleber" in Spain and Zilbert in New York) From 1927 until his sudden departure in 1931, Stern operated out of Amtorg and directed military espionage by attempting the recruitment of an employee of the Arma Corporation then engaged in classified work for the U.S. Navy. The Arma employee assisted the Office of Naval Intelligence and the FBI in defeating this particular GRU effort. Stern fled the United States via Canada, then reappeared a few years later in Spain where he commanded one of the International Brigades. In 1937, he was recalled to the USSR and executed. (FBI, NA RG 165, G-2 reports and ONI files)

Ulanovsky, Alexander (known as "Walter" and "Ulrich")   GRU officer in New York, 1932-1933. Served as Whittaker Chambers's case officer. Reportedly arrested and sent into a forced labor camp from which he was released in 1956.

Ulanovskaya, Nadya (known to Chambers as "Elaine")   Served with her husband in New York, 1932-1933. During the war, she was assigned as an interpreter to various Western journalists then in Moscow. One in particular was Godfrey Blunden, an Australian who was later to write a novel based on information provided to him by Nadya. Despite his efforts to conceal his source, Nadya was arrested, convicted of treason, and sent off to a coercive labor camp. Her husband, Alexander, protested her arrest in a letter to Stalin and was, in turn, arrested and sentenced to ten years in the camps. Their teenage daughter, Maya, was later arrested and sentenced to twenty-five years. The family was released following the Twentieth Party Congress, and to a degree the Ulanovskys were "rehabilitated." Alexander died, and Maya along with her younger brother Alexander emigrated to Israel in 1973. Nadya joined her children there in 1975.

Switz, Robert Gordon   Recruited to the GRU in New York. Trained as a photographer and replacement for Lydia Stahl. Sent to the Canal Zone to recruit and handle a young Army corporal named Osmon who was assigned as a clerk. Osmon had been identified to Switz as a former Young Communist League activist in New York. A misdirected communication from Osmon to a mail cut-out in New York led to the corporal's arrest and court-martial. Switz was reassigned to Paris with his wife Marjory, where he again worked at Stahl's direction. Stahl and the Switzes were arrested by the French (owing to a trade-craft error by Switz) and brought to trial. The Switzes volunteered to assist in the prosecution of Stahl and were later released by the French. (U.S. military attaché, Paris, NA RG 165, [1], FBI files)

Switz, Marjory (Tilly)   wife of Robert G. Switz.

Osmon, Corporal Robert   Charged, in 1933, with violating the U.S. Army regulation on espionage. Osmon was tried, convicted and sentenced to two years, a dishonorable discharge, forfeiture of all pay and allowances due, and a $10,000 fine, the maximum penalty. (At the time, a $10,000 fine was the equivalent of eighteen years of imprisonment; each day in a military prison counted as $1.50.) The case was reviewed at the national level on three separate occasions, and each time, the verdict of the original court was upheld. In 1934, President Roosevelt was informed that Osmon had been victimized by the Army because he was Jewish. Roosevelt ordered a new trial. This time Osmon was represented by the distinguished labor lawyer, Louis Waldman. Three members of the newly convened court voted "guilty," and two members voted "not guilty." Osmon was acquitted because the court-martial rules required a two-thirds majority for a conviction. Osmon was given an honorable discharge, back pay, $1,000, and transportation back to New York. (U.S. Army court-martial transcript, in possession)

Sterngluss, Dr. Jacob Arrived in New York in 1933 to take up his duties with the Russian Red Cross. Sterngluss was a senior OGPU/NKVD officer and worked with Dr. David Dubrowsky until 1935, when the latter quit the RRC. Sterngluss remained until 1937, when he was recalled to the USSR. Dubrowsky testified before a congressional committee in 1939 and described Sterngluss's role in the RRC as that of a secret police officer and intelligence operative. ([1], Department of State decimal file: Sterngluss; congressional citations)

Rabinovich, Dr. Grigori Assigned to the Russian Red Cross in New York in 1934. Rabinovich's wife was employed by Amtorg and was known as Miss Schwartz. (Rabinovich numbered among his many aliases the name Dr. Robert Schwartz.) FBI files state that Elizabeth Bentley, Thomas L. Black, and Louis Budenz all identified Rabinovich in connection with Amtorg. It was his custom in 1937 and 1938 to spend an hour or two at the RRC office each day and the balance of his time at his office in Amtorg. Rabinovich's principal mission was to organize and direct the several major separate NKVD operations aimed at the assassination of Trotsky. The team that finally succeeded in murdering Trotsky in 1940 was able to penetrate the Trotsky stronghold in Mexico by the extensive use of American personnel recruited in New York. Rabinovich's secondary mission was to work for the "disintegration" of the Socialist Workers Party through the extensive use of penetration agents. ([1], FBI files, [14])

Dubrowsky, Dr. David Original head of the Russian Red Cross in the U.S. Served in that capacity from 1921 until 1935, when he broke with the Soviets. (In 1934, the RRC had been taken over by professional NKVD officers.) He waited five more years before notifying U.S. authorities of his convictions that the RRC had been converted to a NKVD outpost in New York. Through his early involvement in parcel forwarding and "commodity drafts," two services offered by the RRC, Dubrowsky was reliant on Amtorg for technical support. ([1], G-2, NA RG 165, [17], congressional testimony)

Mink, George An ex-Philadelphia cab driver related to Solomon Dridzo (alias Lozovsky), who headed the Profintern. In 1928, Mink worked as an organizer and disciplinarian in the Soviet-controlled maritime unions. He was in Spain during the civil war and is reliably credited with the execution of several Americans who had lost their revolutionary fervor while serving in the International Brigades. He was arrested for attempted rape of a chambermaid in a Danish hotel and imprisoned. Following his release, he returned to the USSR and dropped from sight. In the view of some of his contemporaries in the service, he was executed or died in the purges. ([1] FBI files)

Raisen, Jacob (alias Golos) Member of the Control Commission in New York City and operator of the travel company known as World Tourists. As a senior intelligence officer, Golos served in New York from 1925 until his death in 1943. He maintained liaison with Amtorg and directed the activities of Elizabeth Bentley. A second commercial endeavor operated by Golos and Bentley was the freight forwarding company, U.S. Service and Shipping Co. ([1], FBI files)

Rosenberg, Julius and Ethel Related to Amtorg by the fact that their principal source of direction originated with Gaik Ovakimian, who maintained an office within the firm and was described as an Amtorg employee by the Soviet embassy in Washington. The Rosenbergs were executed following their conviction under the Espionage Act.

Brothman, Abraham   Convicted of espionage at the time of the Rosenberg trial and sentenced to seven years' imprisonment. Brothman was identified by the Director of the FBI as a Soviet agent maintaining close links and frequent contact with officials of Amtorg. (FBI files)

Bentley, Elizabeth   Confessed Soviet agent who managed some of the penetration agents in the U.S. government who had been formerly operated by Whittaker Chambers. Bentley broke with the Soviets and cooperated extensively with the FBI. ([8] and FBI files)

Zborowski, Mark   Confidant of Leon Sedov (Trotsky's son) in Paris at the time of Sedov's mysterious death. Zborowski was also circumstantially involved in the theft of the Trotsky archives in Paris. Later, in Mexico, he became a trusted member of the Trotsky household on the basis of having been Leon Sedov's close friend. In a letter to Trotsky, General Orlov (Felbin) described Zborowski as a Soviet penetration agent. The warning was ignored. Eighteen years later, Zborowski was arrested in New York, tried, and convicted of perjury and given the maximum five-year sentence in December 1958. He was linked to the OGPU/NKVD/KGB from 1927 to 1958, and was specifically identified by his boss, Jack Soble (who was arrested on January 25, 1957). Soble and his wife Myra were convicted of espionage and sentenced to only seven and one-half years in prison because of their "valuable assistance" to the government. (FBI files and press)

Poyntz, Juliet   An early enthusiast who was recruited into the GRU in the twenties. In the mid-thirties, Poyntz was co-opted by the NKVD and assigned to operate as a talent scout and recruiter at Columbia University and Hunter College in New York. In 1935, Poyntz directed a Polish-born woman who was a coercive NKVD recruit. The woman's mission in the U.S. failed, and she attempted suicide. Poyntz arranged for her extrication from the United States and her return to Europe, where the wounded woman was taken in hand by the NKVD. Poyntz, reportedly, became disenchanted with her NKVD role and was rumored to be writing an exposé of the Soviets. In the summer of 1936, she disappeared from her apartment and her body was never found. When her death was finally reported in December 1936, her non-Soviet associates concluded that she had been abducted and removed from the United States. A friend of Poyntz, Carlo Tresca, testified before a congressional committee that Poyntz had been abducted and taken aboard a Soviet vessel. Within a few months following his appearance before the committee, Tresca himself became the object of one more unsolved political murder. (FBI files, congressional testimony, and public record)

Pauker, D. ("Marcel")   Assigned as a GRU officer and Amtorg employee during 1936 and 1937. ([3])

Markov, Nancy   Identified in State Department documents as an OGPU officer assigned to Amtorg in 1930. (NA RG 165 and Department of State decimal files)

Grafpen, Gregori   Senior employee of Amtorg, 1928-1931, identified in G-2 files as the OGPU officer controlling an agent named Fritz Karklin, who had entered the U.S. by jumping ship in the port of Baltimore. (G-2 files, NA RG 165)

Stashevich   GRU officer, chief of the Fur Section of Torgpred, 1925-1934. Assigned to Amtorg, 1935-1936. (G-2 files, NA RG 165)

Bogdanov, Peter A.   Chairman of the board of Amtorg, 1928-1930. Testified before the Fish Committee in 1930. Returned to the USSR and was executed. ([12], Fish committee hearings, public record)

Bykov, Boris   GRU officer in contact with Whittaker Chambers from 1936 to 1938. Maintained Amtorg contacts. Returned to the USSR and was reportedly executed. (FBI files and [3])

Gromov, Anatoli   Soviet resident and senior NKVD officer in the United States in 1943. In contact with Bentley and Golos. (FBI files, congressional testimony, and [8])

Gorin, Mikhail   West coast representative of Intourist/Amtorg in 1939. Arrested by the FBI along with Hafis Salich and charged with espionage. Gorin was permitted to leave the country, and Salich was tried, convicted, and imprisoned. (Departments of Justice and State files, FBI files)

Salich, Hafis   Civilian employee of the Office of Naval Intelligence who was recruited by Gorin to provide ONI files from the 13th Naval District. (Ibid.)

"Gideon"   Soviet illegal and "son of Amtorg," who defected to the Royal Canadian Mounted Police. Gideon learned to speak English by attending grade school in New York (1936-1940) where his father was employed by Amtorg. The RCMP "turned" Gideon, then lost him through the betrayal of an RCMP officer. ([9])

Adamov, Joe   One of *Radio Moscow*'s premier English-speaking reporters and a "son of Amtorg" who attended grade school in New York.

Posner, Victor   Soviet reporter and television commentator with extensive contacts in the American media. Learned to speak English while in New York, where his father was employed in the film industry. *(Parade* magazine, October 1984)

Cohen, Morris (also known as Peter John Kroger, known in Spain as Israel Altman)   He and his wife Lorna (nee Petka), also known as Mary Jane Smith, were Amtorg employees in the 1930s. Morris Cohen was then assigned to Spain in 1936-1937, and after World War II, the couple served in New Zealand (1950) before their assignment to Britain, where they acted as the communications link for Konon Trifonovich Molody (aliases: Alec Johnson, Gordon Lonsdale, and Georgi Lonov). The Cohens, Lonsdale, Harry Houghton, and Ethel Gee were arrested by the British and imprisoned. Before expiration of their sentences, the Cohens and Lonsdale were exchanged, while the two British subjects, Houghton and Gee, served out their terms. Lonsdale died, and the Cohens are reportedly living in Prague. (British press, FBI files, and many congressional citations)

Solasko, Faina   NKVD officer assigned to Amtorg, 1940-1946. Her daughter was educated in the United States and has since returned to the USSR, where she is reportedly engaged as a tutor for Soviet illegals being trained for U.S. assignments. ([6] and [15])

Peters, J.   OGPU/NKVD officer and member of the Control Commission who maintained contact with Amtorg through his brother, who was an employee of the trading firm, 1933-1941. (Congressional citations and hearings before the Immigration subcommittee)

Chambers, Mrs. Whittaker   Employee of Amtorg for a brief period in the thirties. (FBI consolidated report)

Gusev, Sergei (aka Drobkin)   NKVD officer assigned to Amtorg, 1941-1945. (FBI files and congressional citations)

Semenov, S. A. "George"   NKVD officer assigned to Amtorg, 1938-1944. (FBI files and [8])

Golodnotzky, Henryk, also known as Harry Gold and "Raymond"   Identified by Klaus Fuchs as his U.S. case officer. When arrested, Gold named Greenglass (brother of Ethel Rosenberg) as a Soviet agent, leading to an investigation and the arrest and ultimate execution of the Rosenbergs. Golodnotzky was originally recruited in 1933 by Semon M. Semonov of Amtorg. Golodnotzky was released from prison in 1966 and died on August 28, 1972. (FBI files and Department of Justice files)

Gubichev, Valentin   Arrested in New York in the company of Judith Coplon, Department of Justice employee. Both were brought to trial, but the case was dismissed owing to a government error. Gubichev was allowed to leave the country. At the time of his arrest, he was in active contact with Amtorg. (Department of Justice files, and FBI files)

Zubilin, Elizaveta   See "Comrade Liza."

Shevchenko, V.   GRU officer and Amtorg employee (1942), later assigned (1943-1945) to Bell Aircraft Corporation as the Soviet Purchasing Commission representative. Attempted the recruitment of an American couple, who made contact with the FBI. (FBI and Departments of Justice and State files)

Borodin, Lt. Col. Nikolai M.   Amtorg employee in New York, 1946-1948. Reassigned to London, where he defected from the Soviet service. ([18])

Klimov   Identified by N. M. Borodin as a NKVD officer assigned to Amtorg, 1945-1946. Klimov was responsible for the security of the "Soviet colony" in Amtorg. ([18])

Akimov, Anatoli I.   Amtorg employee and GRU officer in New York, 1962-1966. Expelled from the United States for his involvement in espionage.

Ivanov, I. A.   Amtorg employee from 1963 until his arrest in 1974. Tried and convicted in the Butenko case and ordered deported from the United States. (State Department records)

Maximov, V.   KGB officer assigned as an Amtorg employee from 1972 until

1975, at which time he was expelled from the United States for his involvement in espionage. (Department of State record)

A number of "sons and daughters" of Amtorg are currently in the United States as naturalized U.S. citizens working in areas of some influence, particularly in the field of journalism.

"Amtorg is not only a trading organization but also a spying organization. Amtorg depends for its source of information upon sympathizers or members of the local party. . . . Amtorg depends upon the acquisition of information from such of its employees as chauffeurs . . ."—Kirill Mikhailovich Alexeev, ex-commercial air attaché, Soviet embassy, Mexico, May 12, 1949. Part 1, House Subcommittee on Immigration and Naturalization.

"Miss Bentley: Mr. Golos was in constant contact with several people in the Soviet Purchasing Commission who were engaged in that work (espionage), also in the Amtorg Corporation. One of my contacts, who was my Soviet superior, was the wife of the man who was then head of the Tass agency. . . . She herself had a position in Amtorg. . . . My main contact after Mr. Golos' death was the first secretary of the Russian embassy, who was the head of the Russian secret police in this country. The man's name is Anatoli Gromov. . . . He told me that it was the policy that the First Secretary of the Russian embassy was the NKVD man. That is, the Russian secret police."—Testimony before Senate Subcommittee on Immigration and Naturalization, May 13, 1949, p. 110.

"Miss Bentley: . . . the only espionage they trust to Americans is the sort of thing where they cannot use anyone but Americans, in other words, government employment, for example. But the links beyond that and your higher ups are all Russian-trained people. They may be from satellite countries, because the Russians do not trust Americans. That has been told me over and over again. Back in 1945, I was told that there would eventually be a war between this country and Russia, and I was told by the First Secretary of the Russian embassy again and again that what worried them most was the fact that they didn't know that they could count on an American communist, no matter how corrupted or no matter how 'steeled,' as they called it, in the event of war between the United States and Russia. . . . Every member of the Russian embassy and consulates is working in espionage of various sorts, whether it is commercial or military or Russian secret police. The same is true of the Russian nationals in Amtorg and Tass.

"Chairman: What was the source of your information? You say 'I was told.'

"Bentley: I was told this by Mr. Golos and I was told this by Mr. Anatoli Gromov, the First Secretary of the Russian embassy . . ." p. 113

Medical doctors and dentists have always played significant roles in Soviet espionage. They can take their cover with them wherever they are assigned; their "patients" have easy access to their offices; they can lease property and operate clinics for use as safehouses; and they can provide medical and dental services (cosmetic surgery, etc.). In addition, they have high status in the community, good credit, and social respectability.

Physicians and dentists associated with various Soviet activities in the United States:

Dr. Robert Soblen   Indicted for espionage. Unsuccessful suicide attempt (using table knife) while in custody of U.S. marshals aboard a commercial aircraft. Later succeeded in securing lethal drugs while in close custody in Great Britain.

Dr. Julius Hammer   Chairman of the board of Allied American Corporation, which was absorbed into Amtorg in 1924.

Dr. David H. Dubrowsky   Broke with Soviets, testified before congressional committee in 1939.

Dr. Valentine G. Burtan   Served sentence in U.S. federal penitentiaries. Denied parole on the basis of his refusal to cooperate with prison authorities.

Dr. Phillip Rosenbliett   Recalled to the USSR in 1937. Thought by his superiors to be in contact with his brother-in-law, the U.S. Trotskyite Joseph Cannon. Was tricked into believing that his U.S. mission had been canceled and that he was urgently needed in Moscow. He returned immediately and was arrested and executed.

Dr. Joseph Benjamin Stenbuck   Acted as New York addressee in the Osmon-Switz case.

Dr. Gregor Rabinowitz   Took over the direction of the Russian Red Cross from Dubrowsky. Later recalled to Moscow and executed.

Dr. Julius Littinsky   In complicity with Juliet Poyntz, assisted in the coercive removal of a spoiled Soviet agent from the United States. (FBI file 100-206683-45)

"Dr." Jacob Sterngluss   OGPU/NKVD officer assigned to the New York office of the Russian Red Cross.

APPENDIX II

PARTIAL LIST OF CASES INVOLVING AMTORG AND OTHER SOVIET QUASI-OFFICIAL ORGANIZATIONS

Of course, all Soviet organizations are official in the sense that no activity can occur in the USSR without the direct sponsorship of the government. There is no legal "private sector," there are no entrepreneurs, no commercial agents, no "independent" business owners. Only clandestine deals can be contemplated without the Soviet government's participation at every step. When it is in the interest of the Soviet government, major transactions occur. As is the case with China, it is possible to do business *with* the USSR but never *in* the USSR. Legal foreign exchange is controlled by the government banks, as are all export/import approvals.

Soviet press representatives serving outside the USSR are Soviet government employees, with a high percentage being either officers of the organs or individuals who have been co-opted by the organs to perform assigned tasks. This statement applies to representatives of Tass, Novosti, *Pravda,* and *Izvestia* in addition to Soviet radio, films, television, etc.

A great many of the correspondents assigned to Novosti *(Agentsvo Pechati Novosti),* or Press News Agency (PNA), are given additional status as minor diplomats attached to the Soviet embassies in the countries in which they serve. This practice allows the Novosti representative to have all of the benefits and privileges of a legitimate member of the press and, if he is found to be engaged in espionage, diplomatic immunity. Novosti provides informational items about the USSR, including articles, films, photos, tapes, and other propaganda materials intended for "progressive students of the USSR."

Soviet-flag carriers providing international transportation by sea and air are operated, without exception, by crews whose functions are, in a dominant way, governed by the organs. The merchant fleet of Morflot as well as the planes of the air carrier Aeroflot are adjuncts of the Soviet Navy and Air Force and continue to provide transportation of goods and personnel in support of, and at the direction of, the organs.

All trade delegations, missions, and other representatives specialize in scientific, technical, and industrial espionage as well as commercial and banking intelligence. These elements were originally organized under the umbrella administration of Torgpred, which draws its authority from the Ministry of Foreign Trade. The extent to which all the trade missions, representatives, and delegations have been directly involved in espionage is a measure of the organs' employment of commercial cover for noncommercial uses.

SOVIET "COMMERCIAL" BRIEFS

In May 1977, two foreigners coming out of a noodle house in a seedy section of Tokyo were stopped by the Japanese police and asked for identification. One produced his, which identified him as a U.S. Navy petty officer assigned to the aircraft carrier *Midway*. The other man bolted. The Japanese soon overtook him and subdued him (the Soviets claimed that he was "brutally beaten"). The prisoner was identified as Aleksandr Matchekhin, correspondent of the Novosti Press Agency. Three days later, the Japanese called a press conference and declared that Matchekhin was not a newspaperman but a middle-ranking GRU officer. He had previously served in Bangkok, where he was well known to the Thai counterintelligence forces. On the evening of his arrest, he had spent $1,500 entertaining the U.S. sailor and had offered an additional $1,000 for classified information. Matchekhin had arrived in Tokyo in October 1974 and had never been known to file a news story. A few days later, the Japanese released Matchekhin "out of diplomatic considerations," and he was put aboard an Aeroflot flight for Moscow.—Murray Sayle, *New Statesman,* June 11, 1976; John Saar, *Washington Post,* May 15, 1976.

In late September 1974, Boris Moiseyev, a Tass correspondent, disappeared from Dar es Salaam, Tanzania. The Tanzanian police posted his picture in hotels and public places under the word WANTED! His espionage business had been going badly and was now complicated by an automobile accident in which Moiseyev was not even involved. He was a KGB officer, and so it was easy for him to depart with little or no notice. Aeroflot customarily kept a turboprop aircraft waiting for such quick travel on the tarmac at the Dar es Salaam airport.—*Los Angeles Times,* October 6, 1974.

In December 1975, Vladimir Kozlov took up his duties as the Tass man in Dublin. His reputation preceded him, since he was a very well-known officer of the Fifth Chief Directorate of the KGB. The Irish were stunned by the effrontery of the Soviets in sending Kozlov to Dublin so soon after the reestablishment of diplomatic relations. When the KGB agent Lyalin defected in London in 1971, he had described Kozlov as a principal officer in the KGB element that specializes in terror and assassination. (The Soviets had provided arms to the IRA terrorists through Czechoslovakia.) Kozlov's predecessor, Yuriy Ustimenko, another Tass correspondent, maintained regular contacts with Michael O'Riordan, general secretary of the Irish Communist Party.

When the Soviets returned to Dublin in 1974, they built a masonry wall around their compound that was two feet higher than allowed by law. Irish protesters have blown holes in the wall and have deposited barbed-wire wreaths at the Soviet embassy entrance.—Christopher Dobson, *The London Sunday Telegram,* December 7, 1975.

Viktor Anizimov, a Tass representative, "took over handling and training" a forty-two-year-old Swedish naval petty officer, Andersson, in 1947. Andersson was arrested in 1952 and sentenced to life imprisonment. At the time of his arrest, he was working at the direction of the Soviet military attaché, Orlov, who had diplomatic immunity. Anizimov had returned to the USSR just before the arrest of Andersson.—Austin Goodrich, *The New Leader,* May 1952.

From September 1964 to June 1965, Boris P. Netrebsky attended Harvard University as an important part of his training as a young officer in the organs. He was then assigned to the Soviet Ministry of Foreign Affairs and took on the cover of a Soviet diplomat. Netrebsky was assigned to The Hague, where he had the collateral function of representing Novosti. On February 17, 1970, Netrebsky and a fellow diplomat, V. S. Sherevatov, skidded off the road into a canal in the town of Hoofddorp. Both were able to extricate themselves from the car, but when the police later recovered the vehicle from the canal bottom, they found maps detailing the Dutch military's provisions for the storage of weapons, new construction at the Fokker aircraft plant, and cryptic notes relating to strategic communications centers in the Netherlands. Soviet Ambassador Lavrov quickly lodged the standard denials and filed a protest with the Dutch government describing the discovery at Hoofddorp as "a serious provocation, which is not conducive to the development of friendly relations between the Netherlands and the Soviet Union." Netrebsky was put aboard a train for the Soviet Union, and thirty enthusiastic members of the Soviet embassy staff, as well as the ambassador and his wife, bearing a gigantic bunch of tulips, saw him off at the Hook of Holland Railway Station.—M. W. van Eijk, *Algemeen Dagblad,* The Hague, May 8, 1970.

On November 23, 1963, a Novosti correspondent, B. Keknazar-Jouzbachev, and two other Soviets were expelled from the People's Republic of the Congo for espionage. The incident led to the breaking of diplomatic relations.—M. W. van Eijk, *Algemeen Dagblad,* The Hague, May 9, 1970.

In April 1966, Yuriy Kouritsine, the Novosti representative, and three other Soviets were expelled from Kenya for espionage. Kouritsine was specifically charged with funding leftist student clubs, collecting intelligence information, and engaging in antigovernment actions.—Ibid.

On June 6, 1967, A. Kanzansev, the Novosti correspondent in Ghana, was expelled for espionage and the promotion of clandestine political actions to bring about the return of the Soviet client, and former head of state, Kwame Nkrumah.—Ibid.

In 1964, G. N. Soekachev, a Novosti correspondent in Cairo, was expelled as a Soviet espionage agent. He had previously served in The Hague in 1958, from whence he, the Soviet naval attaché, Capt. K. S. Zenin, and Col. L. J. Chernov were expelled as GRU officers.—Ibid.

The Dutch expelled the Tass correspondent Pissarev on December 23, 1952. The Soviet press attaché, Vasiliy Drankov, was arrested and expelled on January 18, 1957. A year later, on January 30, 1958, Zenin (the naval attaché), Chernov (the air attaché), and Soekachev, an "interpreter," were also expelled. On July 6, 1960, Peter W. Smirnov, a Soviet student at the Institute for Social Studies in The Hague, using the alias Serge Petrov, together with a fully recruited German associate, Karl Heinz Richter, tried to penetrate the Dutch security service (BVD). Smirnov was arrested in the Netherlands on a charge of espionage and expelled. Richter was later arrested in Germany.—Ibid.

In February 1970, Italy ordered the expulsion of Vladimir Aleksandrov, secretary to the Soviet military attaché, and Lolli Zamoisky, a correspondent for *Izvestia*. The two Soviets had received secret information from an Italian noncommissioned officer, who was arrested.

Concurrently, Switzerland expelled Nikolai Savine and Alexander Sterlikov for their role in one of the most serious espionage cases in recent years. (Alexander Gratchev, also involved, had departed a few months before.) Also arrested was a Swiss official, Marcel Buttex, who was in charge of immigration and residence permits in Lausanne. Buttex provided the Soviets with documents and Swiss passports that would allow Soviet agents to travel throughout the world as Swiss citizens.—*Washington Post,* February 13, 1970.

The September 17, 1951, issue of *Time* raised the question "Newsmen or Spies?" and went on to detail the facts: "The representatives of Russia's Tass news agency make a great show of acting like reporters . . . (e.g., Washington Tasser Euphemia Virden, daughter of a Cleveland capitalist, married the *Daily Worker* correspondent, Bob Hall). But publicly, Tassmen take care to avoid contact with U.S. communists or with Manhattan's *Daily Worker*. If they write for it they use assumed names.

"A typical Tassman on the U.S. scene is 32-year-old Mikhail Federov, aeronautical engineer by education, by calling, chief of Tass's Washington bureau. Washington newsmen quickly awoke to the fact that puppy-friendly Federov, obviously no trained reporter, had a strange way of covering stories. During the Gubichev-Coplon spy trial, he spent most of his time working cross-word puzzles and taking no notes. But when the testimony got round to the slips by which the spies betrayed themselves, Federov scribbled busily. . . . Federov, like all Tassmen, can count on traditional U.S. freedoms to give him press privileges. . . . And he can always depend on sincere Americans to defend his right to these privileges. . . . In last week's furore, the good grey New York *Times* warned against any retaliation against Tass because of Russia's restrictions on Western newsmen. . . . Neither the [New York] *Times* nor the [Washington] *Star* seemed to get the point. . . . If Tassmen are Russian intelligence agents and not bona fide correspondents, then they are not entitled to the privileges of the working press.

"In the U.S., where Tass admits to spending $25,000 per month [1951] on its coverage, the main headquarters is in Manhattan's A.P. Building in Rockefeller Center. It is bossed by a poker-faced Russian, Ivan Beglov, 47, who came here a year ago, describes himself as a 'historical science specialist.' Second in command is affable, Brooklyn-born Harry Freeman, for twenty years a Tass news-desk man and its No. 1 American staffer. Of Tass's 22 U.S. editorial staffers, eight are Russians, one a Briton, and one a Canadian. The other 12 are U.S. citizens who have all been vouched for as 'reliable' by the National Cadre and Review Commission of the U.S. Communist Party.

"Under the cover name of 'Martin,' Tass 'correspondent' Nicolai Zheivinov was a member of Canada's atomic spy ring uncovered in 1945. He skipped home to Russia to avoid arrest.

"In Tokyo, Tassman Evgeny Egorov* has never been known to turn in a story for clearance by UN censors; he is presumed to send all of his material either by diplomatic pouch or by radio code from the Russian embassy.

"In Teheran, Tass's representative has never been seen to visit Radio Pahlevi from which all other correspondents transmit their copy. He too, is getting his reports out by diplomatic pouch.

"In many countries, the Russians no longer make any pretense at maintaining Tass as a newsgathering agency. In Montevideo, for example, the Tassman does not even have a phone, gets messages only through the Soviet embassy."—*Time,* September 17, 1951.

"[As of 1971], The last Soviet official to have been expelled from Thailand was Viktor V. Mizin who was declared persona non grata in 1971 for having stolen documents concerning U.S. air bases in Thailand and for having tried to recruit American personnel. Others expelled before him included Tass correspondents Yuriy Fedorovich Trushkin and Khairulla Mukhanovich Shalkharov (1958); assistant press attaché K. Sahagorov and Tass correspondent I. Garuchin (1960); the manager of the Singapore-based Silver Star Motion Picture Company, T. P. Bulgakhov (1962); attaché (and GRU officer) Alexei Obukhov and Trade Representative Leonid Aleksandrovich Mamurin (1966); and Vasiliy Ilich Khopyanov (1971)."—*Far Eastern Economic Review,* September 26, 1975, p. 23.

The prestigious London-based Institute for the Study of Conflict, in a work entitled "The Peace Strategy of the Soviet Union," estimated (in 1973) that 72 percent of the 2,146 Soviet diplomats posted to NATO capitals have been trained in espionage techniques, as have 45 percent of the staffs of Soviet trade missions, Intourist, Aeroflot, and the press agencies Novosti, Tass, *Pravda,* and *Izvestia.*

In August 1965, Ingeborg Lygren, a fifty-two-year-old secretary in the Norwegian Defense Department, applied for a second assignment to Moscow. She

---

*Egorov was able to give Moscow advanced and detailed reporting on the exact scope and timing of the U.S. invasion at Inchon. He gathered the information simply by talking in the Tokyo Press Club to U.S. newsmen who were preparing to leave Tokyo aboard U.S. Navy vessels participating in the landings.

had served there from 1956 to 1959 as secretary to the Norwegian ambassador. Ingaborg Lygren was a Soviet agent then being operated by Alexsandr Bardin, the Novosti representative in Oslo. Bardin fled to the Soviet Union a few days before Lygren's arrest.—Lasse Bangtsson, *Expressen,* Stockholm, September 29, 1965, p. 13.

On January 9, 1972, Kurashvile Merab, a thirty-six-year-old Soviet exchange student, was forcibly transported to the USSR by Soviet authorities in New York City. While he was being taken to Kennedy Airport, Merab jumped from the car and cut his throat and wrists with a razor blade. The local police took him to a hospital in Jamaica, New York, but Dr. Unid, a Soviet physician to the Soviet community in New York, insisted on Merab's immediate release, even before his wounds could be treated.—*Washington Post,* January 10, 1972, p. A-3.

In November 1971, Anatole Chebotarev of the Soviet trade mission in Brussels was reported missing. His disappearance was linked to the defection, in Britain, of Oleg Lyalin, the principal KGB officer in the Soviet trade mission in London. Lyalin's disclosures led to the expulsion of 105 Soviets and their families from Great Britain. In fact, Chebotarev had defected to the Belgians, who expelled thirty-seven Soviets, including Konstantin I. Leontev, commercial director of a Soviet trade company called Belso, and two employees of Aeroflot, Oleg Gluchenko and Yuri Parefenov. Leontev was identified as a GRU colonel. Chebotarev was identified as a Soviet intelligence officer who later returned to the USSR.—Manchester *Guardian,* November 5, 1971; London *Times,* October 19, 1971.

In 1967, when NATO moved its headquarters from Paris to Brussels, the Soviets built the Skaldia-Volga automobile assembly plant, which they hailed as an important commercial venture. The most important feature of the plant was the huge aerial installed on the roof, in a location thought ideal for the interception of NATO shortwave radio traffic. The Belgians countered by jamming the transmissions. Skaldia-Volga keeps a few automobile parts around as props and hopes for the day that its antennas will produce information worth the capital investment in the sham auto plant.

Following the Lyalin/Chebotarev actions, in 1971, Benjamin Welles conducted a survey of *New York Times* correspondents and reported that the total number of Soviet diplomats legally in the United States was 1,380, with half the men employed as agents of the GRU or KGB. In these instances, the Soviet wives are also trained to provide "operational support" to their husbands. Illegal Soviet agents in the United States outnumber the diplomats: 800-900 are in the New York area alone, including 120-150 in the Soviet mission to the UN, 150-160 international civil servants in the UN, 10-20 at Amtorg, 10-20 working for Aeroflot and Intourist, and 10-20 working for Tass, *Izvestia, Pravda,* and Novosti.

"The KGB, an arm of the Soviet Communist Party's Central Committee, headed by Yuri Andropov, a close ally of that party leader, Leonid Brezhnev, dominates Soviet foreign operations, security men say. 'There's no question about Andropov asking Gromyko for a number of cover-slots in some embassy or Intourist office,' one said. 'The Central Committee tells Andropov it wants expanded coverage of the U.S., Britain or some other area—and Andropov tells Gromyko how many slots he'll need.'

"Among those ordered to leave Britain was Anatoly I. Akimov, a GRU agent in the Amtorg office in New York from 1962-66. (Eight others expelled by the British had served previously in the U.S.)

"At the height of the Lyalin affair, the Soviets nominated B. G. Glushchenko to the post of First Secretary of the Soviet embassy in London. The British Foreign office replied: 'This man was in Britain from 1964-1968. At that time he was described as the representative of Aviaexport at the Soviet trade delegation. Mr. Glushchenko's activities, however, had little to do with the sale of aircraft. He came to our notice on various occasions; for example, he offered a large sum of money to a British businessman if he would obtain details of certain British military equipment. This is the man whom some Soviet organization has nominated to serve as First Secretary at your embassy in London. You will hardly be surprised to learn that I am not prepared to permit such a person to return to this country.

"'And I am told that a visa application had recently been submitted for A. P. Safronov whom we know to have engaged in inadmissible activities when he worked at the Soviet trade delegation between 1962 and 1966. They have included the running of agents, instruction in the use of clandestine techniques, the offer and payment of considerable sums of money to persons resident in this country either to suborn them or secure their help in obtaining classified information (both official and commercial) or commodities subject to embargo or other restrictions.'" (British Foreign Secretary Alec Douglas-Home to Soviet Foreign Minister Andrei A. Gromyko, September 25, 1971.)—Benjamin Welles, *New York Times*, October 3, 1971.

Igor Nikolayevich Bryantsev, GRU agent and member of the Soviet trade mission in Cologne, who was taken into investigative custody in November, was exchanged for Kurt Bade, a fitter from Cottbus who had been sentenced to life imprisonment in East Germany. (April 3, 1977, Hamburg DPA, broadcast in German, 1941 GMT.) Bryantsev and a man disguised as a sailor, who was arrested in Bremen last December as an officer of the GRU, are no longer inmates of prisons in the Federal Republic.—*Frankfurter Rundschau*, February 16, 1977.

In October 1972, Longinas Morkunas, a fifty-five-year-old electrical engineer from Vilnius, defected from the Soviet trade delegation in Genoa, Italy, and asked the Italian government for asylum.—*Laiks*, New York, October 21, 1972.

Nikolai Mikhailovich Borodin, while working for Amtorg in New York, found his two assistants quarreling. One kept telling Borodin that the other was anti-Soviet and probably an enemy spy. Borodin did not report this even though Soviet rules of procedure made it imperative for him to do so. Later, he was called into the office of Klimov, an Amtorg expert who was actually a representative of the Central Committee of the Soviet Communist Party. Although his lame excuse apparently was accepted, Borodin knew he would be called to strict account when he returned to Moscow.

By the time Borodin went to England to negotiate with British firms, he was becoming disaffected with the Soviet system because any criticism of the regime was tantamount to high treason. In August 1948, he was recalled to Moscow, and at that time, he defected.—N. M. Borodin, *One Man in His Time,* London: Constable & Co., 1955.

On January 26, 1966, Cecil W. V. Mulvena, a dual citizen living in Britain, was sentenced to four years in prison for aiding Soviet espionage. The man had been cultivated by a Soviet from the trade mission, Pevchenko, and another from Morflot, "Sergei." Hoping to expand his own shipping business, Mulvena was led to believe Sergei's tale about a nephew "who needed documents in order to get out of the Soviet Union." Mulvena obtained a British passport in the name of John Henry de Lancey Foreman, an English engineer who was fatally ill at the time. By the time Mulvena was arrested, both Sergei and Pevchenko had departed the UK.—*Washington Post,* November 3, 1966.

Igor A. Ivanov, chauffeur for Amtorg, and two Soviet diplomats, Gleb A. Pavlov and Yuri A. Romashin, from the Soviet UN mission, met with John Butenko, an American employed by ITT, in the parking lot of a train station in Englewood, New Jersey. They were apprehended, along with a third Soviet, Vladimir I. Olenev. The two diplomats were released, but Ivanov and Butenko were held for trial. In December 1964, Ivanov was convicted and sentenced to twenty years in prison (he could have been executed for the crime of receiving secret information concerning communications and counterstrike operations of the Strategic Air Command). The Soviet government posted a $100,000 bond, and Ivanov was released pending appeal. In 1971, still out on appeal and living at the Soviet compound at Glen Cove, New York, Ivanov was allowed to board an Aeroflot flight and return to Moscow. Soviet Ambassador Dobrynin promised that if Ivanov lost his appeal, he would be returned to the United States to serve his term in prison. Ivanov lost the appeal and has not returned. Soviet officials insisted that no "deal" had been made and instead warned that they could not guarantee the safety of Americans in the USSR because of "recent harassment of Soviet citizens and attacks on the Soviet missions in the United States as part of the agitation over treatment of Soviet Jews." A U.S. spokesman remarked that Ivanov was allowed to leave the country "in the interest of détente." Butenko was convicted of espionage and sentenced to thirty years in prison; Olenev was expelled.—Alfred Robbins, *New York Journal American,* October 31, 1963; *New York Times,* November 16, 1963.

In 1961, in France, the Soviets set up an engineering company under a naturalized Frenchman named Serge Fabiew. The company did military work for the French government for fourteen years before it was discovered that the company's more important business was providing the Soviets with information on NATO's early-warning system, the French military and commercial aircraft industry, a variety of military projects, and the defense systems of French airports. In 1965, the manager of Aeroflot in Paris, Sergei Pavlov, was expelled for stealing Concorde secrets. In this case, however, the guiding hand was a Soviet assigned to UNESCO in Paris. The French were reluctant to name the Soviet because Brezhnev was expected to visit Paris in June to talk about the Helsinki Agreement. Pavlov was sentenced, in absentia, to a twenty-year prison term for espionage.—James F. Clarity, *New York Times,* March 23, 1977.

At the end of April 1969, the Austrian government arrested Aloise Kahr, a cipher clerk in the Foreign Ministry. The investigation disclosed that Kahr had worked for the preceding ten years for the Soviet government as an agent. In the course of his career, Kahr served a tour of duty in Moscow. The Austrians concluded that Kahr had been coercively recruited while in the USSR and, at the time of his arrest, was working for money. Kahr's Soviet case officer at the time of his arrest was Gennadiy Fedorenko of the Soviet trade mission. The Austrians demanded Fedorenko's immediate recall after Kahr's arrest.—*Los Angeles Times,* April 29, 1969.

In early July 1971, a Russian interpreter accompanying a team of visiting Soviet military officers attempted to seek asylum in Stockholm. He was attacked by three men in the street while he was en route to the Stockholm police headquarters to ask for asylum. The three assailants knocked him to the ground, kicked him, and tried to drag him to a waiting car. Passersby and Swedish policemen came to his assistance, and the three men fled on foot. The driver of the waiting car, asked to identify himself, showed a Soviet diplomatic passport. Another car in which the attackers were later seen cruising in the area was traced to the Soviet trade mission.—*Algemeen Dagblad,* May 9, 1970.

"Soviet operations in Thailand have not always gone smoothly. In May 1971, A. V. Krestianinikov, an engineering specialist with the Min Sen Company, died in mysterious circumstances. The Soviet authorities claimed that he committed suicide by hanging himself in his apartment in the Soviet trade mission, and quickly sent the body back to Moscow. But, before it was removed, a Thai doctor was able to examine it and he found that, apart from a concentration of blood in the brain, there were no other indications that the man had died by hanging. It was generally believed that Krestianinikov was discovered while trying to defect."—*Far Eastern Economic Review,* September 26, 1965.

In September 1939, M.I.5 surveillance of A. A. Doschenko of the Soviet trade delegation in London led to a small market town, Leighton Buzzard. Doschenko was observed making contact with another man, who was later found to be employed at the British communications center at Bletchley Park. The investigation resulted in several arrests and prosecutions. At the time that Doschenko made the contact, the Soviets maintained an intelligence exchange with their most recent allies, the Nazi German government.—Anthony Cave Brown, *Bodyguard of Lies,* pp. 66-67.

In December 1967, Viktor Kozolapov and Aleksandr Selikh were two seemingly honest citizens living in Belgium with their wives and children. A few days later, they vanished without a trace. They were, until their departure, representatives of the Soviet trade mission in Brussels and Morflot, the Soviet shipping line. They had diplomatic status a little beneath that of consular diplomats.—*'t Pallieterke,* Flemish weekly, December 7, 1967.

When the Soviet agent Yuriy Nikolayevich Loginov confessed to the South Africans, his cover story led back to Belgium. Loginov stated that he had come into Antwerp on a Soviet vessel and that Kozolapov and Selikh, the men from Morflot, smuggled him into Belgium and supplied him with a Canadian passport in the name of Trenka.

All of this happened behind the modest facades of Brussels apartment houses and in the cabins of certain Soviet vessels in Antwerp. The Soviets have a preference for Antwerp because it is regarded as having the poorest port security in Western Europe.—London *Times,* September 11, 1967.

Loginov named Anatoliy Kosalapov, director of the Baltic Steamship Line in the Netherlands, as a KGB officer. Baltic is one of scores of steamship lines operated by Morflot, the marine equivalent of the Soviet state airline, Aeroflot.

Loginov also confirmed what has been a customary practice in the assignment of KGB officers to Soviet embassies abroad—the use of official aliases. For example, a senior KGB officer, Vitaliy Pavlov, was posted to a new assignment in which the Soviet Foreign Ministry informed the host country that his name was Nikolai Kedrov, and Boris Ansimovich Skoridov was scheduled to be sent to London as Boris Zhiltov. This practice is intended to allow the Soviets to use KGB officers who have been expelled from one country in a different country. By simply using a new identity, the host country might not recognize the visa application as relating to an individual who would be automatically barred from taking up a diplomatic post. It is also a measure of the degree of control the KGB has with regard to assignments by the Soviet Foreign Ministry.

There is nothing quite so decadent as taking a cruise on a luxurious oceangoing vessel. Some exceptions, of course, were the early Soviet Stakhanovites, who were nominated by their unions for overfulfilling production norms. Still later, Komsomol and union members who were paid up in terms of exemplary work habits and flawless political outlook became eligible for trips aboard the few Soviet liners. It was customary to provide superior accommodations for the Soviet power elite in the way of better quarters, separate dining rooms, and easy access to the sea breezes. (The seagoing Soviets are hardly classless.) It was on such a voyage that the Soviet cruise ship *Litva,* operated by Morflot, called at Beirut harbor on October 16, 1966. Olga Farmakovskya debarked and made her way directly to the U.S. embassy, where she asked for protection. The embassy was somewhat skeptical because Olga was the wife of Vadim Vadimovich Farmakovsky, earlier identified by Oleg Penkovsky as a highly placed official in the GRU. She claimed to be disillusioned with the Soviet system and personally unhappy with her marriage. Both the Lebanese and American officials resisted the Soviets' efforts to take her back into their custody. Mrs. Farmakovsky, with a suitable new name, now resides in North America.—John K. Cooley, "Soviet Espionage," *Christian Science Monitor,* April 9, April 18, 1968.

After years of practicing on Soviet passengers, the ex-Morflot-, now Sovinflot-, operated line's *Mikhail Lermontov* * is currently offering to haul non-Soviet

---

*Mikhail Yurevich Lermontov (1814-1841), a Russian poet and novelist, sometimes referred to as the "Russian Byron." (It is of passing interest that some of Lermontov's poetry has not been published in the USSR since 1918 because of its antiauthoritarian flavor.)

passengers on round-the-world cruises. It is no longer necessary to be approved by your union or endorsed by your local Komsomol to reserve a cabin on the *Lermontov,* and as a concession to the capitalists, tipping is permitted.

In April 1967, Vladimir Alexandr Glukhov, head of the Aeroflot office in Amsterdam, was arrested by Dutch security officers while carrying special materials and equipment for use in espionage. The Dutch arresting officer described Glukhov as "a well-trained spy and a danger to the national security of the state." Despite the fact that Glukhov did not have diplomatic immunity, he was released by the Dutch and expelled from the Netherlands five days later. In Moscow, following word of the Glukhov arrest, KGB officers had seized the Royal Dutch Airline (KLM) manager in a busy Moscow street. The Dutchman was held without charge, for his arrest was simply in retribution for the Aeroflot arrest in Amsterdam. Glukhov was the third Aeroflot employee to have been involved in the plot.

"The arrests brought to 35 the number of persons known to have been picked up in Italy, Greece, Cyprus, the Netherlands, and Norway. Soviet diplomats have either been expelled from—or have hastily left—Italy, Cyprus, Switzerland, Morocco, and Japan."—*A.N.P.* news bulletin, The Hague, May 9, 1970.

In April 1967, Belgian counterintelligence announced that Anatoliy Trifonovich Ogorodnikov, a Tass journalist, was taken into custody and escorted to a Moscow-bound Aeroflot plane. Ogorodnikov's job was to "run" a Belgian woman who had been recruited by the Soviets in Africa in 1962. The woman had been instructed to seek employment at the U.S. embassy in Brussels or, failing that, NATO. Also implicated in the unsuccessful operation was Vitaliy Dmitrievich Balachov, a third secretary in the Soviet embassy at Brussels. Ogorodnikov's arrest and expulsion followed by one week the arrest and expulsion of the Aeroflot manager in Brussels, Vladimir A. Glukhov, and his deputy, Vladimir Cheretun (aka Sheretun). In retaliation, the Belgian Airline representative in Moscow, Lucien Thoye, was arrested and expelled for "inadmissable activities."—New York *Daily News,* April 20, 1967; *Washington Star,* April 19, 1967.

On January 23, 1970, for the first time in modern British history, a member of the House of Commons was arrested on a charge of betraying secret information potentially useful to an enemy. The accused was William James Owen, a Labour Party backbencher who was induced to promote friendship with East Germany and to accept directorship of a tourist agency called Berolina Travel in 1964. During his long service in Parliament, Owen had access to much highly classified information relating to Britain's defense establishment. Owen was developed by a Czech commercial attaché named Robert Husak. During the period, Owen visited East Germany three times and the USSR on one occasion. He was paid 2,300 pounds by the Czechs, entertained, and given presents. The Czechs were particularly interested in Owen's parliamentary colleagues, and he was pressed for information "on sex, money difficulties, abnormalities and perversions of sex." Owen was maneuvered by the Czechs into believing that they would inform the British security service if he refused to cooperate. Owen was quoted as saying, "They squeezed and squeezed until I finally defected." After a thirteen-day trial, the seventy-year-old Owen was directed to pay 2,000 pounds toward the legal costs and acquitted.

By 1969, Britain was awash in Czech intelligence officers who had joined the defectors after the Soviet armed intervention in Czechoslovakia in the "Prague Spring." Among these was one who claimed that he had targeted a British MP and was told by his superior that the MP was "a horse from another stable," a euphemistic warning that the target had been recruited by the Soviet service. The Czech made clear the fact that the Czech service invariably deferred to the primacy of the Soviets in the coordination of all operations involving the satellite intelligence services.—Malcolm Dean, *The Guardian,* June 16, 1970.

In 1953, Otto Verber and his brother-in-law, Kurt Ponger, were sentenced to prison on their conviction as Soviet agents. Both had served in the U.S. Army during World War II. Following their release from service, the two set up the Central European Press and Literary Agency with a leased telephone answering service and office address at 100 West 42nd Street in New York City. The men were arrested in Vienna, returned to the United States, and charged with fourteen counts of espionage. Also arrested was Walter Lauber, another "employee" of CEPIA, who was held as a material witness. All three men were attending school in Austria under the GI Bill. Their Soviet contact in the United States, Yuriy V. Novikov, second secretary at the Soviet embassy in Washington, was expelled.—Fred Blumenthal and J. Anderson, *Parade,* January 6, 1954.

Novikov became the third Soviet to be declared *persona non grata* since the end of the war in 1945. Jacob Lomakin, Soviet consul general in New York, was ordered to leave after a Russian teacher, Oksana Kasenkina, leaped from the second-floor window of the consulate in Manhattan to frustrate efforts to forcibly return her to the USSR, and Valentine A. Gubichev was arrested in New York with Judith Coplon, an employee of the Justice Department.

In 1945, the Australian government was concerned that the postwar emigration might be penetrated by Soviet agents. Security officials prevailed upon a Polish doctor, Michael Bialoguski, who had served honorably in the Australian army, to maintain contacts in the Australian Society for Friendship with the Soviet Union and the Russian Social Club. Both organizations had a Soviet-controlled core of subversive members. It was at the Russian Social Club that Bialoguski met Ivan Mikhailovich Pakhomov, the Tass representative in Australia, and then Pakhomov's successor, Viktor Nikolayevich Antonov. In 1951, the Tass representatives frequented the clubs looking for prospective recruits among the Australians. It is certain that the Soviets regarded Bialoguski as a potentially useful Soviet agent. Antonov introduced Bialoguski to Vladimir Mikhailovich Petrov, third secretary of the Soviet embassy in Canberra, the capital, and head of the MVD in Australia. Over a period of two years, the doctor and the MVD chief became friends. In 1953, Petrov's fortunes took a turn with the death of Stalin and the execution of Petrov's personal patron, Beria. Bialoguski gradually induced Petrov to confront the fact that there had been a dramatic change in the Moscow climate and that Petrov, should he return, might not survive. Petrov eventually defected to the Australians in 1954, but his wife, Yevdokia Alekseyevna (Dusya), a captain in the MVD and cipher clerk, was immediately seized and held in the Soviet embassy to prevent her joining her husband. A group of MVD heavyweights was sent to Australia to bring Mrs. Petrov back to the Soviet Union. On leaving Canberra, it was necessary to take an Australian domestic airline to the coast in order to make international connections. Mrs. Petrov was closely guarded in flight, but a resourceful Australian stewardess succeeded in separating her from her keepers and explained to her that she had the right to remain in Australia if she chose to do so. Mrs. Petrov elected to stay, and when the plane landed, the Australian police forcibly restrained the Soviet strongarm guards, and Mrs. Petrov was given asylum along with her husband.—Report of the Royal Commission on Espionage, Commonwealth of Australia, Sydney, 1955.

On March 15, 1967, an Italian skydiver, thirty-nine-year-old Giorgio Rinaldi, was arrested as a GRU agent operating against NATO. The Italian counterintelligence made a connection between clandestine radio communications directed to Italy from a station outside Moscow and the travels of Rinaldi's chauffeur, Armando Girard. After Girard was arrested, he confessed and implicated Rinaldi, who was then arrested. Rinaldi told the Italian authorities that he had deposited materials intended for his Soviet controller in a dead drop. On the following day, Yuri Kuzmich Pavlenko, unaware of Rinaldi's cooperation with the Italian authorities, attempted to empty the cache, was photographed and arrested. Rinaldi told the Italian authorities that more than ten years before, heavily in debt, he had approached Alexei Solovov in the Soviet embassy, Rome, and that he had agreed to take up espionage for pay. (Alexei Solovov had been expelled by the Italian government in 1958.) Two months before Rinaldi's arrest, the Belgians had arrested and expelled Vladimir Cheretun (Sheretun), the Aeroflot representative. A few weeks later, Ivan Yakolovich Petrov, chief Soviet delegate to the International Telecommunications Union in Geneva, was ordered out of Switzerland for attempting to recruit a senior Swiss official. On March 24th, on Cyprus, the Soviet cultural attaché, Boris Petrin, and the Aeroflot manager, Nicolai Ranov, were arrested and expelled. Arrested along with Ranov and Petrin, was Vikentios Boutros, a telecommunications worker who was able to provide the Soviets with copies of cable and telephone messages exchanged between foreign missions in Cyprus and their home governments. Three days later, the Greeks expelled two Soviet diplomats, Igor Ochurkov and Albert Zacharova. On the following day, the Austrians made several arrests in Vienna, and the senior GRU officer, Col. Mikhail Ilich Badin, departed without notifying the Austrian government. In the second week in April, Norway arrested three men on charges of Soviet espionage.—*U.S. News & World Report,* April 24, 1967.

In 1936, before the nonaggression pact with the USSR, the German anti-Nazi group led by Harro Schulze-Boysen reported German plans for military operations against Republican Spain. Schulze-Boysen's only intermediate contact with the Soviets in Berlin was a KPD veteran, Gisela von Poellnitz. In an attempt to conceal her link to the group, von Poellnitz pushed the Shulze-Boysen reports "through the letter box of the Soviet trade delegation at 11, Lietzenburgen Strasse, Berlin."—*The Rote Kawpelle: The CIA's History of Soviet Intelligence and Espionage Networks in Western Europe, 1936-1945* (Frederick, Md.: University Publications of America, 1979), p. 142.

In August 1956, Peter Mironinikov of the Soviet trade delegation in Stockholm was expelled from Sweden for espionage. The charge was based on the arrest of a Swedish instrument maker, Anatole Ericcson, who pleaded guilty to supplying the Soviets, through Mironinikov, with information on Swedish air defense radar equipment. Ericcson was sentenced to twelve years' penal servitude, and Mironinikov departed Stockholm on the next scheduled Aeroflot flight.—*The Times* (London), October 7, 1957.

In 1962, a young industrial scientist in West Germany was told that he could buy the freedom of his wife (then held in East Germany) if he would agree to provide certain materials on electronic research and nuclear energy. He was given a special camera and trained in its use. His original agreement with the East German intelligence was for one year of cooperation. Four years later, he found that he was really working for the Soviets (his wife finally had been permitted to join him in 1964). Following his arrest, it was disclosed that he had provided sixteen scientific reports prepared by the West German, British, and U.S. governments to the Soviets and had been paid $1,500. The Soviets who controlled the agent were Michael S. Spagin, Boris Saryschev, and Albert Kuzemenzov, all three employed in the Soviet trade mission in Cologne. Also among his Soviet controllers were Igor Jakowiew of Tass and Igor Modnov of the Soviet Radio and TV Service in Bonn. The German government called only for the expulsion of Spagin. Public disclosure of the case in Germany was opposed by members of the Bonn government because "the expulsion of three trade mission officials, two Soviet embassy attaches, one Tass man and the sole representative of the Soviet Radio and TV Service could cause the Soviets to retaliate against the West German embassy in Moscow."—*Washington Post*, January 22, 1966.

In 1964, the Ottawa correspondent for *Izvestia*, Vasiliy Tarasov, was expelled by the Canadian government after he was caught trying to buy classified industrial secrets from a government employee. (The secrets involved U.S. defense contracts with Canadian firms.) With Tarasov's departure, the Canadian press corps was informed that Tarasov's "beat will be covered by the Tass representative, Aleksandr Zhigulev, and Leon Bagramov, who represents Selskaja-Zhizn," a Soviet agricultural paper. When Vladimir Petrov defected from the Soviet embassy in Canberra in 1954, he testified that "every correspondent of the Soviet news agency Tass is an officer in the Soviet secret police." In 1953, the Canadians admitted Tass correspondent Ivan Tsvetskov to the Parliamentary press gallery in Ottawa despite the fact that he was attached to the Soviet embassy and had diplomatic immunity. Having been granted gallery credentials, Tsvetskov went immediately to Canadair for a tour of the plant. He was an aeronautical engineer and had no press experience. Tsvetskov's immediate predecessor in Ottawa was N. Zhevelnov, who hastily left Canada a few days before he was named in the Canadian spy trials that followed the defection of Igor Gouzenko. Tarasov had previously served as the *Izvestia* representative in Australia, New Zealand, and Pakistan.—*Chicago Tribune,* July 12, 1964, February 18, 1968; *Montreal Star,* April 30, 1964.

In October 1971, the Swedish security police finally determined that the Soviet automobile sales company Matreco A. B. was really a Soviet espionage cover company. Matreco was set up in Sweden in 1957 to sell Moskvich, Yalta, and Volga cars. From 1965 to 1969, annual sales averaged about 200 vehicles, but the company staff increased from 56 to more than 200. Profits were nonexistent. Swedish authorities estimated that the firm had lost 680,000 pounds over a period of several years. Despite sagging sales, new branches were set up in Luleaa, Gaevle, Malmo, and Gothenburg. The Luleaa office had a large radio installation and was in contact with Soviet ships operating off the Swedish coast. The head office of the company in Bromma, a Stockholm suburb, sported an aerial that was amplified with a concealed loop to facilitate radio transmissions over great distances.—Elga Elraser, *Daily Telegraph,* October 22, 1971.

Following the Lyalin defection in Britain and the expulsion of 105 Soviets, Viktor Ivanov, head of the Soviet trade delegation in London, told the Russo-British Chamber of Commerce that "unfortunate and unjust allegations" had been made against his group. "History has shown a lot of attempts to raise artificial obstacles to trade between our countries."—*Daily Telegraph,* October 22, 1971.

On June 16, 1975, a Romanian intelligence agent, Virgil Tipanudt, third secretary in the Romanian embassy in Copenhagen, defected to the Danes and identified forty other industrial spies in Soviet and bloc embassies in Oslo, Copenhagen, Bonn, London, and Stockholm. As a KGB surrogate, the Romanian service was charged with collecting scientific data in four main fields:
1. The most recent developments in nuclear technology.
2. All aspects of computer technology as well as the acquisition of CMOS designs and manufacturing processes.
3. The heavy chemical industry.
4. The pharmaceutical industry.
COCOM, the Paris-based committee that determines what will be allowed for shipment to the USSR and bloc countries, prohibited the export of IBM 370s. It is known, however, that at least one of these computers was flown to the USSR from Schipol Airport in Amsterdam via Aeroflot. An IBM 370 was later shipped to the Soviet Union via Sweden, where it was reloaded onto an Aeroflot flight for Moscow. A Soviet firm called Elorg, with offices in Belgium, Luxembourg, the Netherlands, Finland, and Monaco, made plans to expand into France and Italy. Elorg's "business" consists of underbidding all competitors in the computer servicing field. A company agreeing to buy Elorg services is, in effect, contributing the identities of its employees, the names of its clients, and, in the course of normal business, making many unintended disclosures of proprietary information directly to the Soviet government.—*Washington Post,* August 30, 1975.

A German employee of the large IBM factory in Stuttgart was found dead in the streets one evening. The man had apparently been struck by a car. Subsequent investigation established that he had been lured from a restaurant by a phone call and murdered. That same night, another man entered the IBM facility, using the dead employee's key and identity card. Soviet industrial espionage is no less brutal or deadly than is military espionage.—John M. Goshko, *Washington Post,* January 16, 1975; *New York Times,* January 16, 1975; Reuters, January 16, 1975; *Daily Telegraph,* January 15, 1975.

By 1975, the Soviets had a team of fifteen officers working on Capitol Hill, of which Yuriy Barsakov and Stanislov Kondrahov of *Izvestia* were two of the most experienced operatives. Senator Frank Church of Idaho, a presidential hopeful, saw a floodlit hearing room, national television exposure, and a chance to intrude into every home in the land with his wrathfully pious inquiry into the failings of the CIA and FBI. The Soviets could scarcely believe that an investigation of the U.S. internal security and intelligence agencies would compete with *As the World Turns* on daytime TV. A good part of Church's indignation and outrage might have been directed, more accurately, to the Congress itself for having failed, assiduously, to discharge its oversight responsibilities but the coming national elections made any effort to depoliticize the hearings unacceptable. What was wanted was high drama in which Senator Church would be seen leading the forces of good against the dark and malevolent armies of intelligence and security. Vice President Nelson Rockefeller expressed his personal concern that the Congress had been penetrated by Soviet agents. Senator Barry Goldwater, in a subsequent talk with newsmen, stated flatly that the offices of seven senators had been infiltrated. As a result of the Goldwater statement, fifty-two members of Congress signed a letter asking Church to look into the matter. Church passed the matter to the FBI, which reported that there was no evidence that the Soviets had *succeeded* in penetrating congressional staffs; however, in a second, highly sensitive report, the FBI informed Church of the many unsuccessful Soviet attempts at recruitment in the staffs, which the Bureau had successfully "doubled." Church ignored the sensitive report and announced that "the allegations about Soviet spying have been put to rest." The Church Committee did not investigate the matter of the Soviet "electronic bug" that fell out of a chair in the House Foreign Affairs Committee room. The chair would not have been a suitable witness to harangue and intimidate. After all the drama and excitement of the hearings, Senator Church was rejected by his party as a credible nominee. The Church Committee hearings boomeranged to the degree that he, himself, was defeated in his home state in the race for what had been his secure senatorial seat. In addition to the men from *Izvestia,* others on the roster of the Soviet intelligence team "working" the Hill during the period were:

Igor Bubnov, Soviet embassy counselor
Anatoliy Davidov (aka Davydov), second secretary
Viktor F. Iaskov, minister-counselor
Vadim Kuznetsov, counselor
Vladimir V. Vikoulov, attaché

Anatoliy Kotov, attaché
Ikav Zavrazhnov, secretary
Alexandr Kokorev, secretary
Alexandr Freskovsky, official
Aledsadr Romanov, employee
Valeriy Ivanov, first secretary
Victor Trifonov, counselor
Andrei Kokoshin, librarian

As of late 1984, Viktor Iaskov, Vadim Kuznetsov, Aledsadr Romanov, Valeriy Ivanov, and Victor Trifonov were still operating out of the Soviet embassy in Washington.

In 1978, an officer in the Royal Canadian Mounted Police was offered "unlimited funds" by a Soviet official in exchange for information on Canadian intelligence personnel and methods. The RCMP officer accepted $30,500 from the Soviet and provided him with spurious material. After a year of manipulating the Russians, Canadian Secretary of State for Foreign Affairs Donald C. Jamieson called Soviet Ambassador Aleksandr N. Yakolev to his office, where an aide to Jamieson informed him that eleven Soviet officials were to leave Canada within forty-eight hours. Heading the list was Igor P. Vartarian, first secretary of the embassy, who made the initial offer to the RCMP officer. The operation ran for about a year and involved the wives of several of the Soviet officials. Two of the Soviets named were out of Canada, and the expulsion order simply indicated that they would be barred from returning. The second man on the list was Anatoliy A. Mikhalin of the Soviet trade office in Canada.—*Time* and *Newsweek,* February 20, 1978.

On February 25, 1969, Igor Petrovich Sobolev, a senior KGB man who was deputy chief of the Soviet trade mission in Cologne, gave his KGB boss and colleague, Yuriy Nikanorovich Verontsov, a festive lunch. Verontsov had a bad heart, diabetes, and circulatory disorders, none of which tempered his ingestion of too much food and much too much alcohol. After lunch, Verontsov drove his black Mercedes into an oncoming car and died a few moments later. The Soviet embassy physician, Tatiana Serbina, confirmed that the KGB chief for West Germany was a drunk-driving casualty. Sobolev was called to the embassy by Alexandr P. Bondarenko and severely rebuked. Next, Sobolev was subjected to three days of intense interrogation by his KGB seniors, who concluded that he had:

(1) encouraged Vorontsov to drink during their meeting in Cologne and had thereby endangered the Moscow espionage networks in West Germany;

(2) violated all rules of conspiracy at the scene of the accident by ostentatiously securing Vorontsov's radio receiver, safe keys, briefcase, and umbrella;

(3) broken the cover of several agent meeting places, by his negligence and lack of circumspection, so that the West German authorities were able to identify safe houses and meeting places in Cologne that, previously, had been thought secure.

By his actions, Sobolev had clearly (once again) made the connection between the KGB and the Soviet trade mission on Aachener Street in Cologne. Also publicized after the death of Vorontsov was the Black Sea and Baltic Sea Transportation Insurance Co. (Sovag), with offices at 37, Schwanenwick in Hamburg. A former director of Black Sea, Dmitriy Ivanovich Kirpichev, had been arrested by the West Germans for espionage in 1961. The Soviet trade mission had also lost Valentine Aleksandrovich Pripolstev (1962), Mikhail Shpagin (1966), Boris Leoniovich Zarychev (1966), and Albert Mikhailovich Kusnetsov (1966) to espionage arrests. In 1966, Tass had lost Igor Yakolev and Igor Semenovich Modnov. In Berlin, Serge Wjakin, the Intourist representative, was arrested and expelled in 1976.—Peter Schmitt, *Daily Telegraph,* March 18, 1969.

In early 1925, the first resident director of the organs in the United States was Mikhail Chatsky (aka Tchatsky, Tschazky), probably the enterprising GPU man identified to Trilisser by Hendler. His cover, like that of so many OGPU men who were to follow, was as a senior member of the Amtorg staff.

Before Chatsky's arrival, Arthur Alexandrivich Adams had done the original scouting for the organs in 1921. He returned later in the 1920s, and in the '30s and '40s, to manage several major nets in the United States. Adams entered the country on a fraudulent Canadian birth certificate that had been provided him by M. S. Milestone of Toronto. (Milestone was later identified in the Canadian spy trials of 1946.) On each of his tours in the United States, Adams relied on Amtorg for communications, funding, and cover.

One of the senior "outside" men for the organs was J. Peters (alias Goldberger, alias Isidor Boorstein), who entered the United States on February 10, 1924, and took up station in New York City. Peters is generally credited with the operation of the Harold Ware group, which had remarkable success in penetrating the upper reaches of the U.S. government during the thirties and especially during World War II. Several members of the Ware group, which included Alger Hiss and E. C. Carter of the State Department, maintained clandestine contact with the Washington Tass representative (and senior NKVD man), Vladimir Rogoff, facilitating his access to other State Department personnel.—*Washington Post,* October 29, 1953.

In the spring of 1941, before the German attack on the USSR, a decision was made in the NKVD to transfer, wherever possible, all Soviet espionage operations from the military attachés and other officers assigned to Western European Soviet embassies to the Soviet trade missions, particularly in Belgium and France. This decision was based on the assumption that if the military attachés or the embassy officers were found to be actively engaged in espionage, their credibility would be affected adversely. At the same time, it was believed that espionage by the trade missions probably could be suppressed without the need for Soviet diplomatic intervention.

Leopold Trepper (true name: Leo Domb), "the grand chief" of the wartime Soviet nets in Western Europe, made a personal inspection of the breakthrough of the Maginot Line at Sedan as well as the battlefield at Abbeville and the beaches of Dunkirk. He then prepared a typewritten report of sixty pages, which was forwarded to Moscow via the Soviet trade mission in Belgium.—Leopold

Trepper, *The Great Game: Memoirs of the Spy Hitler Couldn't Silence* (New York: McGraw-Hill Book Co., 1977).

On July 4, 1923, the Turkish police arrested Vasiliy Novikov and M. Azlkind of the Soviet trade office in Constantinople. A few weeks earlier, thirty-five Soviet agents were arrested in Ankara for espionage and attempting the overthrow of the Turkish government. The Turkish authorities linked the thirty-five who were being brought to trial with the two Bolsheviks in the trade office.—*New York Times,* July 5, 1923.

In January 1939, Natasha Gorin, wife of Mikhail Gorin of the Intourist office in Los Angeles, was arrested and charged with active complicity in her husband's espionage attempt against the U.S. naval intelligence office in Los Angeles. (The Gorins were later said to be under Amtorg supervision and, from the Soviet viewpoint, deserving of diplomatic immunity.) A naturalized American, Hafis Salich, was arrested with the Gorins and went to prison, but the Gorins were permitted to leave the country.—Dept. of Justice file 95-400-3.

In 1939, Inrekiama, the advertising subsidiary of Amtorg, reportedly took $3 million per year away from U.S. firms wanting to do business with the USSR. Inrekiama charged three to five percent of the dollar amount of all business done through Amtorg for the cost of "advertising" the American products in the USSR. There was no advertising, of course, and the Inrekiama billing to the U.S. companies was simply a kickback racket. Bookniga, another firm operating under Amtorg, made between $1 and $2 million per year selling propaganda materials and books to the U.S. Communist Party, thereby allowing the affluent comrades to pay their own way. Amkino, another Amtorg creature, imported Soviet films and netted $4-$5 million annually in sales and rentals.—Dept. of Justice file on prosecution under the Foreign Agents Registration Act.

The Soviet-American Securities Corporation was set up by Amtorg after the U.S. bank moratorium in the early 1930s. Soviet-American Securities sold several millions of dollars in Soviet "gold" bonds on the assurance "that a sovereign state [the USSR] cannot fail like an American bank." The corporation was promptly put out of business by the U.S. Department of Justice, although the Chase Bank in New York continued to act as paying agent for the bonds until October 1, 1948.—Dept. of State decimal file EE 861.51; ltr. to author from The Chase Manhattan Bank, N.A., May 13, 1983.

In early 1940, the U.S. government began to crack down on the growing espionage that was under way throughout the country. The Soviets and Germans were still allied, and the federal efforts tended to put more emphasis on closing out the Nazis, who were generally easier to deal with. They were less well trained, maintained poor security, and in many ways were obvious in their espionage attempts. The Germans had nothing to compare with the long-standing Soviet nets. The few non-German Nazi ideologues were useless in any kind of clandestine context. Based on the distribution of the U.S. investigative effort during the period of the nonaggression pact, it appears that the Soviets "shopped" a number of German cases to the United States through their various respectable American citizen contacts. Of special value were the residual antifascist organiza-- tions (many with covert Soviet funding), which collected and maintained files on suspect Germans.

One of the few actions directed at the Soviets during the period was in a charge filed by Attorney General Frank Murphy in Federal District Court in Washington on January 3, 1940, in which he named three "commercial companies" and eight individuals. The individuals were charged with espionage on behalf of the USSR, and the companies were identified as being wholly subsidized and controlled by the Soviet government as espionage covers. The individuals were Alexander Trachtenberg, Abraham A. Heller, Joseph R. Brodsky, J. N. Golos, Robert Minor, Wallace E. Douglas, Rebecca Grecht, and Israel Amster. The companies were World Tourist, International Publishers, and Workers Library Publishing. Golos (true name: Jacob Raisen) was the common-law husband of Elizabeth Bentley and a member of the Control Commission of the CPUSA. He was also the sole stockholder in World Tourists. Golos pleaded guilty to failing to register as an agent of the Soviet government. Amtorg immediately disassociated itself from Golos, and the parent company of World Tourists was confessed to be the USSR Travel Company of Moscow, which, of course, was conveniently outside the jurisdiction of the court. Golos was fined $500, as was the USSR Travel Company of Moscow. The fine was waived in the case of the Soviet parent company, and the hastily organized USSR Travel Company of Moscow disappeared without a trace. No record of that company appears anywhere except in the record of the Golos violation of the Foreign Agents Registration Act case of March 1940.—Department of Justice files on prosecutions under the Foreign Agents Registration Act.

The Swiss government, having established the identities of the NKVD assassins of Ignace Reiss, a senior NKVD official in Western Europe who defected from his service in 1937, asked that they be extradited from France. Three were identified as being in the Soviet trade mission in Paris, and two were working in the same city for the Union for the Repatriation of Russians. By the time the French responded, all had fled France, save the wife of one. The woman, Lydia Groskovska, who had played an active role in planning the assassination, denied all knowledge of the event and claimed never to have heard of Reiss. She feigned illness and was put in the charge of the Soviet embassy after easily posting a 50,000-franc bond. When called to appear for a second hearing, the Soviet embassy explained that she had suddenly left for Moscow and could not be contacted.—David J. Dallin, *Soviet Espionage* (New Haven, Conn.: Yale University Press, 1955), p. 69.

In 1959, the Argentine government arrested and later expelled for espionage Vasiliy Grigorevich Ivashov of the Soviet Commercial Mission in Buenos Aires.— Roster of sixty-two Soviet officials publicly declared *persona non grata,* dated September 1, 1961, in possession of author.

On August 23, 1961, the West German government arrested and expelled (on a charge of espionage) the *Izvestia* correspondent Oleg Yakolevich Yenakiev.—Ibid.

In February 1953, Lev Konstantinovich Pissarev, the Tass correspondent in The Hague, was expelled on a charge of espionage.—Ibid.; also *New York Times,* December 25, 1953.

In August 1956, Petr Sergeyevich Miroshnikov was expelled from Sweden. Miroshnikov was a senior official of the Soviet trade delegation in Stockholm.—Ibid.; also *The Times* (London), October 7, 1957.

On October 10, 1960, Vladimir Kurkurin, the manager of a Soviet export company, was expelled from Bern, Switzerland, for espionage.—Ibid.

Yuriy Fedorovich Trushin, a Tass correspondent in Bangkok, was expelled for espionage and subversion in October 1958.—Ibid.; also *New York Times,* October 2, 1975.

In May 1941, former chief of the Fourth Section of the GRU, came to Germany under the alias of Georgi Petrovich Nikolayev and using the utilitarian cover of Tass. After the German invasion a few weeks later, he was ordered to Ankara to resume espionage operations against the Germans. In the following year, when he was recalled to Moscow, he promptly deserted the Soviet service. His true name was Ismail Gusseynovich Akhmedov, which he changed to I. G. Ege. During the war, he made several attempts to contact U.S. officials without success. In 1948, he finally effected a contact with both the British and the Americans. In the normal course of establishing his bona fides, Akhmedov was debriefed in exhaustive detail by H. A. R. Philby, a consequential NKVD officer moonlighting as the M.I.6 station chief. Akhmedov somehow survived Philby's ministrations * and later came to the United States, where he provided important, detailed information regarding the operations of the Soviets and, in particular, his past, direct supervisory role over two GRU officers then in New York under Amtorg cover.—Russell Porter, *New York Times,* October 29, 1953.

---

* An earlier Soviet service defector in Turkey, Konstantin Volkov, was abducted and murdered by the Soviets with Philby's aid.

APPENDIX III

PARTIAL LIST OF SOVIET PRISON SHIPS REHABILITATED BY THE UNITED STATES UNDER LEND-LEASE

The *Nevastroi* was built at Tacoma, Washington, in 1918 as the *Bellingham*. She was 379 feet in length and was listed at 4,837 gross tons. After being sold to Johann Ohsol, acting as agent for Amtorg, she was renamed the *Navastroi*, and Odessa became her home port. Following her role in the Kutepov abduction, she was put into service as a prison ship. Robert Conquest in his book *Kolyma* has noted that in the year 1938 alone, the *Nevastroi* transported between three and four thousand prisoners per voyage to the Kolyma camps.

During World War II, she made four voyages to the United States, one to New York (1941), one to San Francisco (1942), and two to Seattle (1943-1944). While in the United States, the *Navastroi* was repaired and refitted at a cost of $84,203.99 under the terms of Lend-Lease. In 1945, she returned to the USSR and was put in service transporting Japanese military prisoners to the northern camps.

The *Indigirka* was only 2,336 gross tons and, by 1932, was already in service as a prison ship, with Vladivostok as her home port. She was wrecked and foundered in the Pacific Far East in December 1939. A second vessel, *Indigirka II* (formerly the *Commercial Quaker,* built in 1920 in Manitowoc, Wisconsin, at 2,960 gross tons), also operated as a prison ship, with Nagayevno as her home port.

Among the prison vessels identified by Conquest are several of the ships sold to Johann G. Ohsol by the U.S. War Shipping Board in 1929-1930. The World War II voyages to the United States have been added to the list:

Dalstroi: Prison ship, 6,948 gross tons, ex-*Yagoda*, ex-U.S. *Arnelo*, built at Flushing, New York, in 1918. Transported six to nine thousand prisoners per voyage in 1937 and seven thousand average in 1939. In 1942-1943, she made at least four visits to the United States, during one of which she was repaired and refitted at a cost of $1,376,189.15. In all, the *Dalstroi* made eight voyages in 1944-1945 with additional repair costs of $13,240. The *Dalstroi* was blown up in 1946. At the time, she was loading ammonal (ammonium nitrate, TNT, and powdered aluminum) at Vanino, when Latvian prisoners succeeded in detonating the cargo, which was intended for the mines.

Dneprostroi: Prison ship, 4,756 gross tons. Built at Tacoma, Washington, in 1918. Home port at Vladivostok. Transported three to four thousand prisoners per voyage in 1939. During the war, she made six voyages to New York, New Orleans, San Francisco, and Seattle; repairs and refitting cost, $243,737.89.

Dzhurma (Djurma): Prison ship, 6,908 gross tons. Built at Schiedam in 1921. Home port at Nagayevo. Transported three to four thousand prisoners per voyage in 1938, six to nine thousand prisoners per voyage in 1939-1940. In service as a prison ship since 1932. The *Dzhurma* made several refit and repair voyages to the United States during World War II. Lend-Lease rehabilitation costs to the United States were $305,255.97. After the war, she was returned to prisoner transportation. Robert Conquest* describes an earlier voyage: ". . . first reported in these waters in 1933 when she sailed, ladened with an above-capacity load of prisoners said to have numbered as many as 12,000, from Vladivostok through the Bering Straits to Ambarchik at the mouth of the Kolyma. Reaching the Arctic ocean too late in the season, she was caught in the pack ice near Wrangel Island for the whole winter, arriving the following spring with no survivors among the prisoners." In 1939, according to three witnesses, ". . . a fire broke out. The male criminals seized the opportunity to try to break out and were battened down into a corner of the hold. When they went on rioting, the crew hosed them down to keep them quiet. Then they forgot about them. As the fire was still burning, the water boiled and the wretched men died in it. For a long time afterwards the *Dzhurma* stank intolerably."†

Felix Dzerzhinsky: Prison ship, built at Newcastle as the 9,180-gross-ton cable ship *Dominia* in 1926. Originally based at Vladivostok, later at Nagayevo. After the Soviets acquired the *Dominia,* she was renamed the *Nikolai Yezov,* in honor of the chief of the OGPU. When Yezov fell afoul of Stalin in 1934 and was executed, the *Nikolai Yezov* became the *Felix Dzerzhinsky,* a tribute to the conveniently dead founder of the Cheka. From 1937 to 1940, she carried six to nine thousand prisoners per voyage. She was replaced by a newer vessel, the *Felix Dzerzhinsky II,* of only 3,767 gross tons, built as a cargo carrier in 1929. This vessel made six repair and refit voyages to the United States during 1942 and 1943. The materials and labor costs to the United States were $206,035.04. By 1945, she had made fourteen round-trips to the United States and had run up an additional $37,040.00 in repair bills. At the end of the war, she returned to the transportation of Japanese and German prisoners to the Arctic camps.

Igarka: Prison ship, 2,900 gross tons, 321 feet in overall length. Built at Teeside, England, in 1936 as a cargo vessel. Home port at Vladivostok. Prisoner transportation in 1940-1941, carrying an average of seven thousand prisoners per voyage. During World War II, she visited San Francisco and Seattle for repair work. Being a relatively new ship, the work was not major, and the costs borne by the United States amounted to $24,110.00.

Kiev: Prison ship, of 3,283 gross tons. Built as the *Ramschied* at Flensburg in 1917 as a cargo vessel. In service as a prison ship in 1940, carrying an average of seven thousand prisoners per voyage. Home port at Odessa. She made one visit to Boston in November 1941; repairs cost the United States $71,635.00. The *Kiev*

---

*Robert Conquest, *Kolyma* (New York: Oxford University Press, 1979), p. 25.
†Ibid., p. 34.

was subsequently lost at sea and replaced by the *Kiev II,* the U.S.-built *Coast Miller,* which, in three repair visits to San Francisco, Portland, and Seattle, required equipment and repairs amounting to $107,816.21. On her eighth U.S. voyage in 1945, she underwent additional repairs at a cost of $65,283.04.

Kim: Prison ship, 5,114 gross tons. One of the very few Soviet-built vessels. Built at Leningrad in 1933. She operated in the Pacific Far East with Vladivostok as her home port. In 1942-1943, she made six repair voyages to Portland, Seattle, and New York at a cost of $231,777.20. On one of her return voyages (June 28, 1943), she carried a complete Douglas oil refining plant valued at $1 million from Los Angeles to Vladivostok via the Kurile and Tatary straits. By 1947, she was back on the prison run, carrying an average of three thousand prisoners per voyage. The *Kim* had a long successful run out of the port of New York, carrying several thousand Americans on Communist International Youth tours. The *Kim* was the first Soviet-flag vessel to visit New York in twenty-four years, and on her arrival, Amtorg arranged for a reception on board with Ambassador Umansky and the elder Troyanovsky (father of the Soviet UN delegate) as the guests of honor.

Komsomolsk: Prison ship, 2,900 gross tons. Built at Teeside, England, as a cargo ship in 1936. Home port at Vladivostok. In 1940-1941, the average number of prisoners transported per voyage was seven thousand. During the war, she made four voyages to Seattle and Portland for cargo and repairs. The refit/repair costs in 1942-1943 on this vessel were $288,471.42.

Kulu: Prison ship, 6,492 gross tons. Built in Holland as the cargo ship *Bitoe* in 1917. In 1938, she carried an average of three to four thousand prisoners per voyage. Home port at Nagayevo. In 1942-1943, the *Kulu* made five voyages to Portland and San Francisco, where she was repaired/refitted at a cost of $222,381.96.

Minsk: Prison ship, 5,949 gross tons. Built as the cargo vessel *Murla* at Flensburg in 1918. Home port at Nakhoda. Average number of prisoners transported per voyage in 1940-1941 was seven thousand. Five voyages to the United States (Seattle, San Francisco) in 1942-1943 for repair/refit at a cost of $91,987.09.

Rabochy: Prison ship, 2,513 gross tons. Built at Leningrad in 1923 as a cargo vessel. Although Leningrad was her registered home port, she carried prisoners on the Archangel-Ambarchik route in 1933.

Shaturstroi: Prison ship, 4,905 gross tons. U.S.-built as the cargo ship *Aledo* at Shooters Island in 1918. Home port at Vladivostok. In prisoner transportation as early as 1932. During 1941-1942, she made five repair/refit voyages to Seattle and Portland, costing the United States $185,711.25; at the time of her eleventh voyage, additional work amounting to $24,795.00 was completed at Portland.

Sovietskaya Gavan: Prison ship, lost and later replaced by the new, American-built EC-2 *Samuel A. Worcester.* Soviet-demanded alterations and additions cost $40,000 in addition to the cost of the vessel.

Sovietskaya Latvia (also listed as *Sovlatvia*): Prison ship, 4,117 gross tons. Built as the *Hercogz Jacob,* a cargo vessel, at Malmo, Sweden, in 1926, for the Latvian government. The ship was confiscated by the Soviets at the time the USSR occupied Latvia. Immediately put into service transporting prisoners. Home port at Nagayevo. Transported an average of six to nine thousand prisoners per voyage in 1940. Conquest refers to the *Dzhurma, Dalstroi,* and *Sovlatvia* as "the core of the slave fleet."* In 1942-1943, the *Sovlatvia* was repaired and refitted at a cost to the United States of $460,032.08. By 1949, she was back on the prison run, averaging five thousand prisoners per voyage.

Svirstroi: Prison ship, 4,768 gross tons. U.S.-built as the *Puget Sound* at Tacoma, Washington in 1918. Home port at Odessa. In service as a prison ship in 1932. Bought for Amtorg by Ohsol.

Uritsky: Prison ship, 2,336 gross tons. Built at Leningrad in 1929. Home port at Vladivostok. Transported an average of seven thousand prisoners per voyage in 1940-1941. During 1942-1943, she made four voyages to the United States (San Francisco, Baltimore, Portland, and Seattle) and was refitted and repaired at a cost of $299,253.71. By 1946, she had returned to the transportation of prisoners to the Arctic camps.

Volkhovstroi: Prison ship, 4,943 gross tons. Built at Shooters Island as the *Galesburg* in 1918. Went into service transporting prisoners in 1932. During 1942-1943, she made five repair/refit voyages to Seattle and Portland at a cost to the United States of $312,888.21. The *Galesburg* was another Ohsol purchase on behalf of Amtorg.

Information elicited from Soviet shipmasters on the U.S. West Coast confirmed that there was evidence of regular sailings between the USSR and Japan during the war.

An Amtorg official, inspecting a West Coast cargo depot, was asked directly if he believed that the Japanese were receiving any Lend-Lease material. He replied, "Of course, how else do you think it would be possible for us to carry goods into Vladivostok unmolested?"

On April 10, 1943, Harry Lundberg, secretary of the Sailor's Union of the Pacific, put the case with his customary vehemence: "While talking about the Russian ships, I think they are doublecrossing us, as they are probably discharging about 75 percent of their Lend-Lease cargos in Japan."†

Consistent with the Soviet policy of keeping everything close to the vest, the *Sergei Kirov,* in 1942, refused to respond to a signal request for identification (IFF—Identification, friend or foe?) and was, consequently, bombed by U.S. aircraft.

Another Soviet vessel, the *Erivan,* made several trips to New York in the thirties and was widely heralded as the "Russian Red Cross ship." The *Erivan* was also used in an abduction in Shanghai in the twenties and, with the *Kim,* reportedly was involved in the abduction of Juliet Poyntz from New York.

*Ibid., p. 25.
†ONI Summary for 1943, Soviet Merchant Shipping. RG 165, NA, Old Navy Branch.

APPENDIX IV

SOVIET "TRADE" REPRESENTATIVES WORLDWIDE

Afghanistan	4	Germany, West	6	New Zealand	1
Algeria	3	Ghana	2	Nigeria	2
Angola	2	Greece	3	Norway	3
Argentina	2	Guinea	4	Pakistan	7
Australia	3	Guyana	3	Peru	4
Austria	5	Hungary	5	Philippines	2
Bangladesh	5	Iceland	3	Poland	4
Belgium	3	India	16	Portugal	2
Benin	1	Indonesia	4	Romania	5
Bolivia	1	Iran	3	Rwanda	1
Bourkina Fasso	1	Iraq	3	Senegal	2
Brazil	4	Ireland	1	Sierra Leone	1
Bulgaria	5	Italy	7	Singapore	2
Burma	3	Jamaica	2	Somalia	2
Burundi	1	Japan	3	Spain	4
Cameroon	2	Jordan	2	Sri Lanka	2
Canada	3	Kampuchea	1	Sudan	3
Cape Verde	3	Kenya	1	Sweden	4
Central African Republic	2	Korea, North	4	Switzerland	3
Chad	2	Kuwait	3	Syria	4
China	5	Laos	3	Tanzania	2
Colombia	2	Lebanon	3	Thailand	2
Congo	1	Liberia	1	Togo	1
Costa Rica	2	Libya	2	Tunisia	2
Cuba	10	Luxembourg	1	Turkey	6
Cyprus	1	Malaysia	4	Uganda	4
Czechoslovakia	8	Mali	2	United Kingdom	2
Denmark	3	Malta	2	United States	129
Ecuador	3	Mauritania	1	Uruguay	1
Egypt	4	Mauritius	1	Venezuela	4
Equatorial Guinea	1	Mexico	2	Vietnam	2
Ethiopia	2	Mongolia	4	Yemen	2
Fiji	2	Morocco	4	Yemen, Southern	4
Finland	5	Mozambique	5	Yugoslavia	4
France	5	Nepal	2	Zaire	1
Germany, East	7	Netherlands	3	Zambia	2
				TOTAL:	458

Source: CIA publication, *Directory of USSR Foreign Trade Organizations and Officials,* March 1980.

Out of the total number of identifiable Soviet trade representatives, only 376 are in nonbloc, nonclient states. The list shows 129 trade representatives in the United States, but another 19 Soviets, who represent special interests (such as the Kama River Purchasing Commission or the Belarus Machinery Co.), should be included. This means that the number of "trade" or "commercial" representatives located in the United States total 148, or approximately 40 percent of the entire number operating outside the USSR, its satellites, and its client states.

Once again, Amtorg, at 750 Third Avenue, New York City, leads the list with eighty-seven Soviets on its roster. The current office, a marked improvement from the previous several floors at 355 Lexington Avenue, also had a satellite at the World Trade Center called the Amtorg information center. As is customary, most of the Amtorg employees "belong" to some other Soviet activity; Amtorg simply provides office space, administrative support, etc. This artifice becomes important should an Amtorg man be caught flagrante delicto. The corporation does what it has always done, and that is to disavow knowledge of the miscreant's wayward conduct and to explain that Amtorg accepted him sight unseen on the recommendation of Moscow. Whatever he is accused of doing has no bearing on Amtorg, which in all circumstances resolutely maintains its ignorant innocence.

In plush offices at 805 Third Avenue sits the US-USSR Trade and Economic Council, where there are seven additional Soviet "commercial" representatives who engage in stimulating the profit motives of local bankers and financiers with embellishments of the hoary old trade myth.

In California, the Soviet traders are represented through the Soviet consulate general, and three hyperactive men from the commercial consul's office at 2790 Green Street, San Francisco, buy expensive meals for locals who want to learn more about the advantages of "building trade bridges" with the USSR.

In Seattle, the Soviets can be found at the US-USSR Marine Resources Company, 4215 21st Avenue West. It is worth noting that the Soviets now incorporate "U.S." or "United States" in their corporate titles. Presumably, it is a minor deception intended to suggest that what they are doing has official U.S. government support.) The Seattle corporation is run by a vice president assisted by a "third director" and a "representative to the U.S." No one seems to be able or willing to disclose where the home office is located or to identify the chairman or president or, perhaps most intriguing of all, whatever became of the "first and second directors."

Milwaukee, Wisconsin, the home of some famous American beers, is less well known as the operating locus of Belarus Machinery of the USA, Inc. Belarus is less fortunate than US-USSR Marine Resources Company, for it does not have any corporate officers on the premises nor a nearby home office—there are just four Soviet "engineers" who operate out of 7075 West Parkland Court, Milwaukee. If you ask where the chairman of Belarus is located, you will be told to contact him at 450 Park Avenue, New York City, where he sits with the deputy chairman and, of course, another "engineer." (Belarus stands for Byelorussia Machinery Company, USA.)

Washington, D.C., which is famous for its lack of industry, boasts the largest concentration of Soviet "traders" outside of Moscow. Where Washington has more than thirty Soviets operating out of the magnificent former Lothrop mansion at 2001 Connecticut Avenue, N.W., London has only two Soviet commercial representatives in the whole of Great Britain.

At 767 Fifth Avenue, New York City, you'll find the Kama River Purchasing Commission, with eleven Soviet "engineers" at the ready.

From the viewpoint of the Soviet services, these commercial covers provide access to parts of the United States that are denied to Soviet officials. It is also possible for the commercials to travel with fewer restraints than are placed on the "officials" and diplomats. By keeping their heads down, they are able to get on with the "work." In most respects, the commercials are in a better position to service illegal agents and to perform handling tasks that are potentially too compromising for the officials. It is also expected that, should the United States react against the USSR and order Soviet representation out of the country, the commercials might be overlooked, as has happened before in other countries.

The Soviets have directed some of the satellite services to pursue "commercial" cover. Among these, the Czechs were the most adept at first. However, at the time of the armed Soviet intervention in Czechoslovakia in 1968, there were a great many desertions by senior officers of the Czechoslovak intelligence service (STB). As a consequence, by 1969 the STB had lost its position of trust with the KGB and is very much less evident today. The Polish intelligence service (SB) has been successfully used with great effect in the United States in recent years, with various agents operating under the cover of representatives of the Polish Ministry of Machine Industry, the Polish-American Machinery Company, and other Polish firms doing business in the United States.

It has been with the instrumentality of the Polish intelligence that the Soviets have made spectacular inroads into Silicon Valley. The process has been greatly aided by the recurrent boom-and-bust cycle that has afflicted the personal fortunes of many of the people and firms involved in high-tech research, development, and manufacturing.

The principal cause of individual and corporate financial failure has always been undercapitalization. Sometimes, just meeting one more payroll or holding creditors in check for a few more days is thought to be the difference between millions in profits and bankruptcy. The prospect of an interim loan, an unexpected chance to profit from a drug deal, a large, unanticipated foreign order, the unauthorized sale of proprietary data, the theft and sale of classified government documents, acting as the procurement agent in an illegal transaction involving embargoed computer hardware or software—all these and more become serious options for a desperate individual to consider.

The Soviet and satellite recruiters have been taught to look for the symptoms with the dedication of the Mayo Clinic. Too much alcohol and too-evident angst are two of the most reliable indicators of readiness for an approach. The first fact, essential to the process, is confirmation of access to the knowledge or equipment that is wanted. Once that connection has been verified, the individual undergoes a change from just another loser to target of the week.

The recruiter then casually introduces the addictive ingredient of hope with the certain knowledge that it will be leaped upon like a fumbled punt. The target's discernment and judgment, if ever present, depart, and a dependency on the recruiter for the production of the financial deus ex machina grows insistently.

The process isn't limited by geography to poorly lit California saloons; it has also played well at board rooms in Ohio and exclusive clubs in New York. The recruiter's affability is calculated to disarm the target and, in most instances, to promote the notion that the target, in addition to being more clever, maintains freedom of action and can delimit the terms should they become too demanding. The propositions of financial aid come in packages clearly marked "one-time-only," and with that bogus proviso, the target takes the hook along with the worm.

Once the target has violated the law or proprietary confidence or accepted money in the form of consulting fees, retainers, or whatever euphemism is used, he is on his way to full recruitment. Self-extrication seldom occurs because the mind that consented in the first instance can't contemplate the contempt with which, he imagines, his admissions will be received. In the end, he continues to respond to indirect Soviet direction while he plays the role of Mr. Micawber, vaguely hoping that "something will turn up."

Something always does turn up. The senior Soviet or satellite intelligence officer who deserts his service always brings gifts of information to his accommodating hosts. The best presents are those that deal with current espionage, and, in time, the feckless recruit and his satellite case officers become just two more inmates in a federal penitentiary.

The recent adventure of the president of the Polish-American Machinery Corporation (Polamco), home office in Elk Grove, Illinois, is just another tedious reprise of the same set of facts with only minor changes in the locations, victims, and targets involved. Marian W. Zacharski represented the Polish subsidiary of the KGB, the SB. The victim was William Holden Bell, a radar specialist employed at Hughes Aircraft Corporation. The instruments were money, booze, and a fast life. The locations were Vienna, Warsaw, and Los Angeles.

Taking a note from Amtorg, Polamco is really "controlled" by Metalexport, which is owned by the Polish government and inconveniently located in Warsaw. Since the operation was couched in commercial fiction, Zacharski paid Bell "commissions" in a businesslike manner. Bell's testimony was important to Zacharski's conviction, and Bell himself, in his sixties, is currently serving an eight-year sentence.

Responsibility for the internal security of the United States is a primary function of the Federal Bureau of Investigation. The competence and sophistication of the FBI in these matters is truly astonishing; however, the bureau's ability to defeat Soviet espionage in the United States is directly related to the support it receives from citizens.

Until the Congress or the several states take serious steps to exclude the commercial cover companies and limit the bloated official Soviet and satellite "diplomatic missions," there is nothing between the American citizen and the Soviet services except the FBI.

The effectiveness of any intelligence or internal-security organization is directly related to its reputation. When there is public confidence, the organizations tend to attract first-rate applicants and are seen as worthy, necessary, and important parts of the popular government. The depredations of the Church and Pike congressional committees of the seventies debased, ridiculed, and partially destroyed the intelligence and security services of the United States *without* conceding that both organizations are creatures of the Congress, agents of the Executive, and servants of the public.

The FBI is charged with the enforcement of a great many federal statutes, and the CIA's functions are detailed in the National Security Act of 1947, as amended, with directives formulated in the National Security Council. Neither organization deserved Senator Church's characterization of "rogue elephant," yet large segments of the public, aided by the media, formed strong, adverse attitudes that, though intended to enhance Church's presidential candidacy, served only to aid the interests of the Soviet service.

In the course of the hearings, the term "department of dirty tricks" was repeatedly used in reference to the Operations Directorate of the CIA. The press, long aware of the reference, persisted in using it in the belief that it revealed some close familiarity with the work of the directorate. The term was manufactured by the KGB's disinformation section and was first used, in English, in an East German publication in 1960. When the unawareness of the chairman of a Senate committee and the lack of discernment by the national press allows the insinuation of a Soviet term deliberately calculated to damage U.S. interests, it is a victory of considerable moment for the KGB.

In an effort to convey the impression that Soviet foreign trade is diverse and dynamic, the foreign trade organizations of the USSR are listed, each with a distinctive logo, in an Amtorg publication released on May 27, 1974. Nineteen of the "major" trade organizations are on the same Moscow telephone number, and six, including VAO Intourist, do not even list a phone number.

Name	Telephone	Name	Telephone
V/O AVIAEXPORT	121200	V/O PROMMASHIMPORT	121200
V/O ELECTRONORGTECHNIKA	121200	V/O RAZNOIMPORT	122200
V/O EXPORTLES	121200	V/O SOJUZGASEXPORT	122200
V/O EXPORTKHLEB	121200	V/O SOJUZNEFTEEXPORT	122200
V/O PRODINTORG	121200	V/O STANKOIMPORT	122200
V/O METALLURGIMPORT	121200	V/O SOVFRACHT	122200
V/O MACHPRIBORINTORG	121200	V/O SOJUZPROMEXPORT	122200
V/O MACHINOIMPORT	121200	V/O SOJUZPLODOIMPORT	122200
V/O TECHNOPROMIMPORT	121200	V/O TECHMASHIMPORT	122200
V/O TECHSNABEXPORT	121200		

In some respects, it really doesn't matter: In Moscow, any number dialed by a foreign businessman will get the prompt attention of the organs.

PARTIAL LIST OF SOVIET AGENTS IN INTERNATIONAL ORGANIZATIONS INCLUDING THE UNITED NATIONS HEADQUARTERS IN NEW YORK

The formation of the UN in San Francisco and the later establishment of its headquarters in New York City opened up new opportunities for the organs. The Soviets were well aware of the joys of international organizations from their brief (from September 1937 until their expulsion on December 14, 1939, following the Soviet attack on Finland) membership in the League of Nations in Switzerland. Despite the fact that the USSR concurrently owned and operated its own International, the prospect of a protected base in Western Europe was too appealing to forgo.

The Swiss, ever cheerful hosts, were disposed to regard expectorating on the sidewalk as a more serious crime than espionage, which ranked with, but after, a driver's failure to signal a turn. By attracting various international organizations, the Swiss embarked on a policy of serving the high-minded world institutions by seeing that they were well housed and well fed. Swiss neutrality in all things, a scenic and congenial locale, and good transportation and communications made international peace a new and profitable Swiss industry.

The Soviets found that, in addition to the national delegations in the League of Nations, there were many subsidiary organizations and a growing class of international civil servants (ICSs). Participating members had the right to nominate expert personnel to these positions on the basis of their contribution to the League's support. The ICSs were accorded tax-free status and, since the beginnings, international documentation that effectively cloaked their true nationality and purported to make these selfless servants of peace into neutral supernationals whose loyalties were exclusively devoted to the governing covenants of the League.

Articles 23 and 24 of the Covenant of the League of Nations provided for the inclusion of the Universal Postal Union, establishment of the International Labor Organization, and support of the International Red Cross. Later, the Permanent Court of International Justice, the International Intellectual Co-Operation Organization, the International Financial Organization, and the International Organization for Communications and Transit were added. Each had its own staff of ICSs.

A penetration of the International Red Cross could (and did) easily use the organization's facilities to locate former prisoners of war, reconcile families, and find missing persons for subsequent, unattributed action by the organs.

Experts from member countries, distinguished authorities, and men and women of extraordinary competence contributed their services without cost, and the League began to perform useful work of ever increasing importance.

The first significant event involving aggression by one member nation against another was the armed attack by Japan against China in December 1931. By the time the League organized a commission to examine the issues, the Japanese had already formed the new state of Manchukuo. The League's later report condemned the Japanese aggression, but Japan rejected the findings and simply withdrew from the League.

The worldwide economic depression had the effect of destroying the purpose of the League's financial organization and pointed up widespread dissent among the member nations.

Throughout the thirties and during World War II, the International Labor Organization served as a secure base for various Soviet operations run in Western Europe.

Initially, the USSR viewed the League and its purposes as vain, ridiculous, and mainly exploitative measures by the failing Western governments, which were in the final stages of their "historically imperative" decay. With the ascendancy of Hitler, however, Stalin reversed the line, and the USSR petitioned for membership.

When Italy attacked and later annexed Ethiopia, the League's economic sanctions proved inadequate to stop or even delay the action. In 1933, Germany withdrew from membership in the League; the Nazis went on to rearm and to annex Czechoslovakia and Austria. The Spanish Civil War was also beyond the League's ability to influence. In 1939, with the German attack on Poland and the Soviet attack on Finland, the debilitated League no longer was able to play any role in international affairs.

The League secretariat continued to operate, in Switzerland, though on a reduced scale. Finally, in 1946, the chattels, the Palaise des Nations, and the residual ICSs were transferred to the supervision of the United Nations.

By now, the Soviets had a certain grasp on the operating principles of maneuver within international organizations, and they moved quickly to stake out the UN Secretariat. There, on the high ground, the KGB and GRU representatives took the standard oath of loyalty to the United Nations and swore not to accept direction from *any* member government. In exchange for their commitment to the UN, they were declared immune to legal process by any member nation and immune from being taxed by any member nation, along with other grants of privilege. In addition to providing the land (donated by the Rockefeller family) and the building, the United States was permitted to make an initial contribution of 49 percent of the UN budget.

The Secretariat's personnel, communications, finance, and general administration have had the unrelenting attention of the three hundred Soviet ICSs. Although Britain and the United States are entitled to a proportionate share of staff positions, the tax exemption and the "prestige" associated with such employment has not been an inducement to qualified Americans. As members, the Czechs, Poles, Bulgarians, and other Soviet proxies have quotas of their own in the Secretariat, thus giving the controlled and disciplined Soviet espionage the multiplication effect mentioned elsewhere.

The counterintelligence implications of the penetrations of the Secretariat by the Soviet and bloc ICS agents have been publicly demonstrated, yet the UN sanctions have proved meaningless. To this core element of employees must be added the wives and dependents, many of whom are trained agents and all of whom can be called upon as support agents. The Soviet mission to the UN, with its large staff, supports the Soviet delegation to the UN, adding hundreds more to the KGB army, making it an almost impenetrable phalanx.

The Soviet and bloc personnel who are employed as international civil servants have two additional advantages. First, since they are technically supernationals, they are not subjected to the same travel restraints as they would be as Soviet, Czech, or other bloc citizens and are therefore free to travel anywhere in the United States, at any time. Soviet and bloc diplomatic officials are enjoined from restricted areas and are bound to—though frequently they do not comply with—a system of formal notification to the Department of State, but those with ICS status are in no way limited.

The second advantage is that, because of their special status, the ICSs are free to join professional associations, to subscribe to technical journals, and to enjoy other forms of access to information that specifically exclude Soviet citizens.

The following list consists *only* of the few Soviet citizens assigned to international organizations who have been identified, most recently by the Department of State, the FBI, and the Department of Justice, as being active KGB and GRU officers; it does not include satellite service members, wives, or dependents:

Alexandrov, Andrei M.	New York 1957
Alipov, Ivan V.	New York 1955
Amosov, Igor A.	Washington 1954*
Ananyev, Georgi	New York 1967
Andreyev, Igor L.	New York 1969*
Anissenko, Mikhail	Paris 1972
Antipov, Mikhail M.	New York 1972
Barmyantsev, Yevgenni	New York 1983*
Baulin, Vladimir I.	New York 1973
Belorussets, Roman S.	Paris 1971
Bogachev, Alexandr M.	Paris 1968
Borisov, Ivan D.	New York 1973
Bragin, Lev A.	New York 1968
Bubchikov, Ivan A.	Washington 1956
Burdyukov, Lev	New York 1957
Burov, Nikolai I.	New York 1961
Bykov, Yuri V.	New York 1967
Charchyan, Eduard B.	New York 1975
Chernyayev, Rudolf P.	New York 1978†
Chernyshev, Viktor A.	Washington 1973*

Chitov, Vasili	Washington 1982*
Chuchkin, Vladimir A.	New York 1961
Davidov, Alexandr	Paris 1967
Demin, Konstantin A.	New York 1965
Doronkin, Kiril S.	New York 1959*
Dovolev, Leonid A.	New York 1959*
Dyachenko, Oleg	Paris 1966
Dzhirkvelov, Ilya G. defected from World Health Orgn Geneva 1967	
Ekimov, Konstantin P.	New York 1956*
Enger, Valdik A.	New York 1978†
Fateyev, Albert G.	Vienna 1967
Filatov, Vladimir G.	New York 1966
Filipov, Yuri V.	New York 1970*
Fochine, Nikolai	New York 1977
Fomenko, Viktor and Galina	Paris 1970
Fomin, Andrei A.	New York 1959
Gadzhiyev, Abdulkhalik H.	New York 1975
Galkin, Alexei I.	New York 1963‡
Gapon, Vsevolod I.	New York 1958
Gladkov, Boris F.	New York 1956*
Golubov, Sergei M.	New York 1961*
Grusha, Vladimir A. (1st Secretary, UN)	New York 1957*
Gladkov, Boris F.	New York 1956*
Golubov, Sergei M.	New York 1961
Grechanin, Vladimir P.	Washington 1964*
Grusha, Vladimir A.	New York 1957*
Gubichev, Valentin A.	New York 1949*
Guryanov, Alexandr K.	New York 1956*
Ikonnikov, Alexei	Paris 1971
Isakov, Vadim A.	New York 1966*
Ivanov, Felix	Paris 1965
Ivanov, Valentin M.	Washington 1960*
Kalinkin, Georgi	New York 1967*
Kaptsov, Nikolai	New York 1959
Karpov, Yevgenni P.	New York 1977*
Karpovich, Boris V.	New York 1965*
Kashlev, Yuri B.	Vienna 1960*
Kharlamov, Mikhail A.	New York 1978
Kharkovets, Georgi I.	Bern 1962
Khrenov, Vladimir M.	New York 1971
Kireyev, Anatoli T.	New York 1967
Kirilyuk, Vadim A.	New York 1959*
Kirsanov, Stefan M.	Washington 1965*
Kleymonov, Mikhail F.	Geneva 1967
Klimov, Anatoli	Vienna 1973
Klokov, Vladimir V.	New York 1962*
Kochegarov, Yevgenni M.	Geneva 1969*

Kochubey, Yuri N.	New York 1968
Konstantinov, Oleg	New York 1983*
Kostikov, Lev	Paris 1967
Kotchoubei, Yuri	New York 1962
Kotschegarov, Yevgenni	Geneva 1969
Kovalev, Alexandr P.	New York 1954*
Kovalev, Leonid A.	New York 1960
Krassilov, Alexandr F.	Paris 1962
Krestnikov, Nikolai T.	New York 1957
Krivtsov, Yuri I.	Paris 1969
Kroupnov, Viktor	New York 1978
Krylov, Yuri P.	Washington 1957*
Kudashkin, Fedor D.	New York 1963‡
Kudryavtsev, Sergei M.	Paris 1972
Kukhar, Alexandr A.	Washington 1979*
Kulikov, Ivan A.	Paris 1957*
Kurochkin, Nikolai I.	Washington 1958*
Kuzin, Vladimir	New York 1963
Kuzmin, Vlacheslav	New York 1978
Kvashnin, Yuri D.	New York 1959
Leonov, Yuri P.	Washington 1983*
Lessiovsky, Viktor (aide to General Secy)	New York 1959-1978
Lisenko, Igor A.	New York 1971
Lishinsky, Imants	New York 1978
Lomakin, Yakov I.	New York 1948*
Lukyanov, Pavl P.	New York 1961
Lukyantsev, Yevgenni F.	New York 1978
Makarov, Vasili G.	New York 1971
Malik, Yakov A.	New York 1971
Malinin, Alexei R.	Washington 1966*
Manuilski, Dmitri	New York 1972
Marakhovsky, Yuri	Washington 1981*
Markelov, Valeri I.	New York 1972*
Martinov, Maxim G.	New York 1955*
Mashkantsev, Gennadi F.	Washington 1957*
Maslennikov, Petr E. (1st Secretary, UN)	New York 1963‡
Mayorov, Ivan S.	Geneva 1962
Melekh, Igor Y.	New York 1961*
Miakushko, Vasili	Paris 1960*
Mikheyev, Alexandr	New York 1983*
Mishukov, Yuri A.	New York 1962*
Mitropolsky, Yuri A.	Geneva 1971
Molchanov, Alexandr A.	Geneva 1973
Molev, Vasili M.	Washington 1957*
Morozov, Ivan Y.	Geneva 1972
Nikulin, Leonid N.	New York 1966
Novikov, Nikolai S.	New York 1962

Novikov, Yuri V.	Washington 1953*
Okulov, Vasili N.	Geneva 1972
Olenev, Vladimir I.	New York 1963*
Orlov, Vladimir N.	New York 1967
Parail, Vladimir A.	Paris 1972
Pavlichenko, Vladimir P.	New York 1968
Pavlov, Yevgenni V.	New York 1962*
Pavlov, Gleb	New York 1963*
Petrosyan, Petros (UN delegate)	New York 1975*‡
Petrov, Ivan Y.	Geneva 1967*
Petrov, Viktor I.	New York 1956*
Petrov, Yuri	New York 1972
Petukhov, Alexei D.	New York 1957
Pivnev, Leonid I.	Washington 1954*
Ponomarev, Vasili	Paris 1964
Popov, Nikolai F.	Washington 1969‡
Popov, Vladimir V.	Washington 1980‡
Prikhodko, Ivan Y.	New York 1955
Prokhorov, Yevgenni M.	New York 1962*
Rabinovich, G.	Geneva 1927-1940
Radchenko, Vsevolod	Geneva 1972
Ratnikov, Valentin M.	New York 1964
Redin, Nikolai G.	New York 1946*
Revin, Valentin A.	Washington 1966
Rezun, Vladimir	Geneva 1978
Romanov, Leonid	New York 1978
Romashin, Yuri A.	New York 1963*
Rybatchenko, Vladimir	Paris 1977*
Ryabkov, Yuri M.	New York 1973
Ryzhkov, Konstantin P.	Washington 1946*
Sanko, Vasili F.	New York 1967
Savelev, Mikhail S.	New York 1962‡
Serebryanikov, Fedor D.	New York 1973
Sevastyanov, Gennadi G.	Washington 1963*
Shapovalov, Rotislav Y.	New York 1956*
Shatrov, Vadim A.	New York 1960*
Shepenin, Mikhail S.	Geneva 1972
Sheskin, Vladimir F.	Geneva 1969
Silkin, Galena T.	New York 1960
Skripko, Anatoli Y.	Washington 1983*
Skvortsov, Nikolai S.	New York 1952*
Smirnov, Viktor P.	Geneva 1969
Sobolev, Arkadi A.	New York 1953
Sorokin, Alexandr	New York 1963
Sorokin, Stanislav I.	Paris 1971
Sorokin, Vadim V.	New York 1962‡
Stepanov, Svyatoslav A.	New York 1976‡

Stura, Melor	New York 1982
Sumskoy, Mikhail	New York 1956
Suslev, Vladimir	New York 1958
Svirin, Mikhail N.	New York 1957
Tiblayshin, Alexei	Paris 1971
Tikhomirov, Alexandr V.	New York 1970‡
Tulayev, Vladimir	Vienna 1965
Tumantsev, Yevgenni	New York 1968
Turkin, Nikolai F.	New York 1956*
Udalov, Alexandr V.	Washington 1964*
Vakhrushev, Vasili	New York 1974
Vakula, Vladimir	New York 1965*
Vaygauskas, Richardas K.	New York 1962*
Vetrov, Yuri P.	New York 1968
Vinogradov, Sergei A.	New York 1965
Volkov. Nikolai F.	New York 1961
Vyrodov, Ivan Y.	New York 1962*
Yakolev, Alexandr A.	New York 1975‡
Yatsyna, Vladimir	New York 1961
Yegorov, Ivan D.	New York 1963*
Yekimov, Konstantin P.	New York 1956*
Yemelyanov, Vladimir V.	Geneva 1969
Yazhov, Petr Y.	Washington 1960
Zabivkin, Leonid V.	New York 1965
Zadvinsky, Vasili V.	Washington 1964*
Zakharov, Albert P.	Paris 1968
Zaostrovtsev, Yevgenni A.	New York 1959*
Zaytsev, Valentin A.	New York 1953
Zaytsev, Yuri V.	New York 1962*
Zhimzhin, Vladimir	New York 1984§
Zinyakin, Vladimir P.	New York 1978*

All of the individuals listed served in international organizations, including UN headquarters in New York, the International Labor Organization (ILO) in Geneva, the International Atomic Energy Agency in Vienna, the World Health Organization, UNESCO in Paris, etc. Many of those listed also served tours in foreign areas as diplomats attached to Soviet embassies, consulates, missions, etc. The list omits the names of satellite intelligence officers, agent recruits from among nonbloc nationals, and the many hundreds of Soviet and satellite diplomats expelled from the United States and other Western countries.

*Individuals who were expelled from the host country on charges of espionage.
†Chernayev, the UN personnel officer, and Enger, assistant to the UN secretary-general, were both convicted of espionage in 1978.
‡Indicates "voluntary" departure instead of expulsion.
§The most recent publicized case of Soviet espionage at the UN involved Vladimir Zhimzhim and a Norwegian, Arne Treholt, serving in his government's delegation. The investigation, which lasted five years, required extensive effort in Oslo, New York, and Vienna.

APPENDIX VI

ORGANIZATION OF STATE SECURITY (INCLUDES CHEKA, GPU, OGPU, NKVD, NKGB, MVD, MGB, AND KGB)*

CHAIRMEN

Cheka-VCheka	Dzerzhinsky, Felix Edmundovich	12/20/1917
GPU-OGPU	Dzerzhinsky, Felix Edmundovich	7/19/1926
VCheka	Peters, Yakov Khristoforovich	7/1917–8/1917
OGPU	Menzhinsky, Vyacheslav R.	7/1926–5/1934
NKVD	Yagoda, Genrikh Grigorevich	7/1934–6/1936
NKVD	Yezhov, Nikolai Ivanovich	9/1936–8/1938
NKVD	Beria, Lavrenti Pavlovich	8/1938–1/1941
NKGB	Merkulov, Vsevolod Nikolaevich	2/1941–7/1941
NKVD	Beria, Lavrenti Pavlovich	7/1941–7/1945
NKVD	Kruglov, Sergei Nikforovich	7/1945–3/1946
NKGB	Merkulov, Vsevolod, Nikolaevich	4/1943–3/1946
MVD	Kruglov, Sergei Nikforovich	3/1946–3/1953
MGB	Merkulov, Vsevolod Nikolaevich	3/1946–1950
MGB	Abakumov, Viktor Semenovich	1950–1951
MVD	Beria, Lavrenti Pavlovich	3/1953–6/1953
MVD	Kruglov, Sergei Nikforovich	6/1953–3/1954
KGB	Serov, Ivan Alexandrovich	3/1954–12/1958
KGB	Shelepin, Alexandr Nikolaevich	12/1958–11/1961
KGB	Semichastny, Vladimir Yefimovich	11/1961–4/1967
KGB	Andropov, Yuri Vladimirovich	4/1967–6/1982
KGB	Fedorchuk, Vitali	5/1982–12/1982
KGB	Chebrikov, Viktor Mikhailovich	12/1982–

*These names and dates are taken from available open literature. Additional information may be found in other public sources. Without access to Soviet records, however, the information cannot be fully qualified and confirmed.

DEPUTIES

Vcheka	Alexandrovich, Vyacheslav	12/1917–7/1918
	Peters, Yakov Khristoforovich	1917–1919
	Latsis, Martyn Yanovich	1918–
	Panyuskin, Vasili Lukich	1918–
	Zaks, Grigori	1918–
	Yevseyev, D. G.	1918–
	Ksenofontov, Ivan Ksenofontovich	1919–1920
	Brenner, M. V.	1920–
	Peterson, Karl Andreevich	1920–
GPU	Unshlikht, Iosif Stanislavovich	1921–1923
GPU	Menzhinsky, Vyacheslav Rudolfovich	1923–1926
OGPU	Trilisser, Mikhail Abramovich	1926–1930
OGPU	Yagoda, Genrikh Grigorevich	1926–1934
OGPU	Messing, Stanislav, Adamovich	–1931
OGPU	Akulov, Ivan Alessevich	1931–1932
OGPU	Balitsky, Valerian Apollonovich	1931–
OGPU-NKVD	Agranov, Yakov Saulovich	1933–1936
NKVD	Prokofyev, Georgi Yevgennevich	–1936
NKVD	Belski, Lev Nikolaevich	1934–1937
NKVD	Ryzhov, Mikhail Ivanovich	1934–1937
NKVD	Mironov, Lev G.	1936–
NKVD	Frinovsky, Mikhail Petrovich	1936–1937
NKVD	Berman, Mtvey Davydovich	1936–1937
NKVD	Bulanov, Pavl Petrovich	1936–1938
NKVD	Zakovsky, Leonid Mikhailovich	1938–
NKVD	Zhukovsky, Semen Borisovich	1938–1939
NKVD	Filaretov, G.	1939–
NKVD	Maslennikov, Ivan Ivanovich	1939–
NKVD	Merkulov, Vsevolod Nikolaevich	1939–1941
NKVD	Abakumov, Viktor Semenovich	1941–
NKVD	Chernyshov, Vasili Vasilevich	1941–1952
NKGB	Gribov, Mikhail Vasilevich	1941–
NKGB	Kobulov, Bogdan Zakharovich	1941–
NKVD	Kruglov, Sergei Nikiforovich	1941–1945
NKVD	Obruchnikov, Boris Pavlovich	1941–
NKVD	Safrazyan, Leon Bogdanovich	1941–
NKVD	Sokolov, Grigori Grigorevich	1941–
NKGB	Serov, Ivan Alexandrovich	1941–1954
NKVD	Svinelupov, Mikhail Georgievich	1941–
NKVD	Nedosekin	–1942
NKVD	Apollonov, Arakdi Nikolaevich	1942–1944
NKVD	Zavenyagin, Avraami Pavlovich	1944–1946
MVD	Bogdanov, Nikolai Kuzmich	1945–
MGB	Ogoltsov, Sergei Ivanovich	1951–
MGB	Yepishev, Alexey Alesxeevich	1951–1953

MGB	Ryumin, Mikhail D.	1952–1953
MVD	Lunev, Konstantin Fedorovich	1953–1959
KGB	Tikunov, Vadim Stepanovich	1958–1961
KGB	Belchenko, Sergei Savich	1958–1965
KGB	Ivashutin, Petr Ivanovich	1962–1963
KGB	Zakharov, Nikolai Stepanovich	1962–
KGB	Rogov, Mikhail Stepanovich	1966–
KGB	Pankratov, Lev Ivanovich	1967–
KGB	Perepelitsyn, Alexandr Ivanovich	1959–1967
KGB	Tsvigun, Semen Kuzmich (1st)	1967–1982
KGB	Malygin, Ardalion Nikolaevich	1968–
KGB	Chebrikov, Viktor Mikhailovich (Special Assistant to Chairman KGB)	1969–1981
KGB	Pirozhkov, Vladimir Petrovich	1971–
KGB	Tsinev, Georgi Karpovich	1971–1982
KGB	Yemokhonov, N. P. (1st)	1974–
KGB	Antonov, Sergei Nikolaevich	1974–
KGB	Kryuchkov, Vladimir Alexandrovich	1978–
KGB	Grigorenko, Grigori Filippovich	1978–
KGB	Chebrikov, Viktor Mikhailovich	1981–1982
KGB	Ageev, Genii Evgenevich	1983–
KGB	Bobkov, Filipp Denisovich	1983–

HEADQUARTERS ELEMENTS

First Chief Directorate
(Formerly Foreign Department)

CHIEFS

Davtyan, Yakov Khristoforovich	1918–1919
Mogilevsky, Solomon Grigorevich	1919–1920
Lifshits, Yakov	1920–
Trilisser, Mikhail Abramovich	1920–1930
Messing, Stanislav Adamovich	1930–
Artuzov, Artur Khristianovich	–1935
Slutsky, Abram Aronovich	1935–1938
Shpigelglass, Alexandr	1938–1939
Dekanozov, Vladimir Grigorevich	1939–
Fitin, Pavl Mikhailovich	1943–1944
Pitovranov, Yevgenni Petrovich	1944–
Savchenko, Sergei Romanovich	1952–
Kobulov, Bogdan Zakharovich	–1953
Ryasnov, Vasili Stepanovich	1953–
Panyushkin, Alexandr Semenovich	1953–
Sakharovsky, Alexandr Mikhailovich	1965–

DEPUTIES

Loginov	1930–
Berman, Boris Davydovich	–1937
Shpigelglas, Alexandr	1937–1938
Zubilin, Vasili Mikhailovich	1947–1948
Fedotov, Petr Vasilevich	1948–
Korotkov, Alexandr Mikhailovich	–1954

SECRETARY

Lebedinsky	1930–

TREASURER

Klyucharev, Ivan	1921–

Executive Action Department
(Also known as Operations Department)

CHIEFS

Artuzov, Artur Khristianovich	1919–
Plyat	–1923
Ksenofontov, Ivan Ksenofontovich	1923–
Kaul, Alexandr Iosifovich	1929–
Pauker, Karl Viktorovich	1935–1937
Volovich, Z. I.	1937–
Raykhman, Leonid Fedorovich	1941–

DEPUTIES

Volovich, Z. I.	–1937
Novikov	1944–

Executive Action Section*

CHIEFS

Sudoplatov, Pavl Anatolevich	1942–1953
Studnikov, L. I.	1953–1954
Rodin, Nikolai Borisovich	1962–

---

*Wet Operations—directed assassinations, abductions, and special executions—remain within the purview of the First Chief Directorate's Executive Action Section.

Passport Section

CHIEF

Myuller, Georg   1936–

Press Section

CHIEFS

Klyavin, Yan Yurevich   1918–1922
Kravchenko, Vladimir Fedorovich   1970–

Second Chief Directorate
(Internal Security)

CHIEFS

Fedotov, Petr Vasilevich   1953–
Gribanov, Oleg Mikhailovich   1965–

Counterintelligence Department
(KRO)

CHIEFS

Latsis, Martyn Yanovich   1918–
Artuzov, Artur Khristianovich   1922–
Olsky, Yakov   1928–
Volynsky, S. G.   1934–

DEPUTIES

Styrne, Vladimir Andreevich   1920–1937
Puzitsky, Sergei Vasilevich   1922–
Pilyar, Roman Alexandrovich   1922–1924

Department D
(Disinformation)

CHIEF

Agayants, Ivan Ivanovich   –1967

DEPUTIES

Sitnikov, Vasili Romanovich   1965–

Kondrashev, Sergei Alexandrovich 1965–

Secret Political Department (SPO)

CHIEFS

Peters, Yakov Khristoforovich	1917–1918
Kedrov, Mikhail Sergeevich	1918–
Skrypnik, Nikola Alexeevich	1918–
Yakovela, Varvara Nikolaevna	1918–1919
Agarbekov, Georgi Alexandrovich	1919–1920
Mukomol, Yakov V.	1920–
Latsis, Martyn Yanovich	1920–
Menzhinsky, Vyacheslav Rudolfovich	1920–
Samsonov, Timofey Petrovich	1921–1924
Meshcheryakov, N.	1924–
Deribas, Terenti Dmitrievich	1924–1934
Molchanov, Georgi Alexandrovich	1935–1937
Fedotov, Petr Vailevich	1942–

DEPUTIES

Tuchkov, A.N.	1918–
Romanovsky	1920–
Andreyeva	1922–
Syunnerberg, S. K.	1923–
Lyushkov, Genrikh Samoylovich	1934–1936

SECRETARY

Gerson, V. L.

Section for Extraordinary Matters

CHIEF

Shapiro, Isaak Ilich 1937–

Records Section

CHIEF

Fomin, Vasili Vasilevich 1923–

Third Chief Directorate
(Military Counterintelligence)*

CHIEFS

Kedrov, Mikhail Sergeevich	1919–
Pavlunoovsky, Ivan Petrovich	1919–
Dzerzhinsky, Felix Edmundovich	1919–1920
Menzhinsky, Vyacheslav Rudolfovich	1920–
Popov	1920–
Boky, Gleb Ivanovich	1921–1923
Yagoda, Genrikh Grigorevich	1923–1930
Firin, Semen Grigorevich	1930–
Gay, Mark I.	1935–1937
Mochanov, Georgi Alexandrovich	1937–1939
Shevelev, Ivan Grigorevich	–1941
Gladkov, Petr Andreevich (Smersh Navy)†	1943–1946
Chernyshov, Vasili Vasilevich (Smersh Army)†	1942–1943
Abakumov, Viktor Semenovich (Smersh Army)†	1943–1946
Chernyshov, Vasili Vasilevich	1946–
Fadeykin, Ivan Anisimovich	1967–

DEPUTIES

Pavlunovsky, Ivan Petrovich	1919–1920
Budnikov, Vladimir	1921–
Lyubimov	1936–
Shevelev, Ivan Grigorevich	1941–
Chernyshov, Vasili Vadilevich	1943–1946
Belkin	1946–
Fadeykin, Ivan Anisimovich	–1967

VCheka Joint Commission

CHIEF

Stuchka, Petr Ivanovich

DEPUTY

Ikhnovsky

---

*Formerly Extraordinary or Special Department—Osobye Otdel (OO).
†Smersh (*Smert Shpionam,* "Death to Spies") operated from April 1942 until March 1946. Smersh was established as an extraordinary or special department directly subordinate to the Soviet Supreme Commander in Chief, J. V. Stalin.

BOARD MEMBERS

Svidersky, Alexey Ivanovich
Avanesov, Varlaam Alexandrovich

Agent Section

CHIEF

Kats	1923–

Eastern Department

CHIEFS

Peters, Yakov Khristoforovich	1922–1928
Triandofilov, V.	1928–
Dyakov	1928

Chief Directorate of Border Guards (GUPVO; including Internal Troops (GUPVVO) 1947–1953)

CHIEFS

Mokasey-Shibinsky, G.	1918–
Shamshev, S. G.	1918–
Frolov, Vladimir D.	1918–
Fedotov, Petr Frolovich	1918–
Mukomol, Yakov V.	1922–
Olskiy, Yakov	1923–1925
Katsnelson, Zinovi Borisovich	1925–
Velezhev	1929–
Vorontsov	1930–1932
Bystrykh, N. M.	1932–
Frinovsky, Mikhail Petrovich	1936–1937
Maslennikov, Ivan Ivanovich	1938–1942
Stakanov, Nikolai Pavlovich	1942–
Zyryanov, Pavl Ivanovich	1954–
Matrosov, Vadim Alexandrovich	1974–

DEPUTIES

Kogan	1926–
Bobryshev	1931–
Yatsenko, Nikolai Ivanovich	1941–1945
Petrov, Gavriil Alexandrovich	–1961
Bannykh, Stepan Anisimovich	1961–1963

Reznichenko, Yakov Terentevich	–1969
Ionov, Petr Ivanovich	1969–
Vlasenko, Grigori Ivanovich	1974–
Dalmatov, N.	1974–

FIELD COMMANDERS

Kruchinkin, N. K.	1937–1938
Kovalev, Alexandr Antonovich	1938–1939
Sokolov, Grigori Grigorevich	1939–

DEPUTY FIELD COMMANDERS

Kruchinkin, N. K.	1932–1937
Sokolov, Grigori Grigorevich	1938–1939
Voytenkov	1938–
Apollonov, Arkadi Nikolaevich	1939–

CHIEFS OF STAFF

Yatsenko, Nikolai Ivanovich	1939–
Sekretarev, Konstantin Fedorovich	1963–
Matrosov, Vadim Alexandrovich	1967–1974

Internal Troop Department
(GUVVO; a separate chief directorate under MVD since 1966)

COMMANDING OFFICERS

Popov, D.	1918–
Valobuyev, Konstantin Maximovich	1919–
Kornev, Vasili Stepanovich	1920–1921
Studinkin, P. K.	1921–
Kadomtsev, Ezram Samuilovich	1922–
Aplok	1923–
Golubev, Alexandr Nikolaevich	–1934
Prokofyev, Georgi Yevgennevich	1936–
Apollonov, Arkadi Nikolaevich	1941–
Gerbatyuk	1944–

DEPUTIES

Spilnchenko	1921–
Mogilsky, Boris Yefimovich	1936–
Yatsenko, Nikolai Ivanovich	1943–
Kiryushin, Ivan Nikiforovich	–1944
Grebennik, Kuzma Yevdokimovich	1956–

Bunkov, Stepan Mikhailovich   −1970
Yakolev, I. K.   1971−

Administrative Department

CHIEFS

Chayvanov, Vladimir Nikolaevich   1922−
Morozov   1923−

Eighth Chief Directorate*

CHIEFS

Rostovtsev, F. V.   1918−
Fomin, Vasili Vasilevich   1919−
Zhukov, Nikolai Alexandrovich   1920−
Karyakin   1923−
Blagonravov, Georgi Ivanovich   1923−1927
Shanin, Alexandr   1935−
Fedorov, Vsevolod Tikhonovich   1941−
Lyalin, Serafim Nikolaevich   1967−

DEPUTIES

Slyusarenko   1920−
Nikolsky, Lev   1936−

Investigation Division

CHIEFS

Kingisepp, Viktor Eduardovich   1918−
Lukashin, Sergei Lukyanovich   1918−
Galbanis, Robert   1918−
Moroz, Grigori Semenovich   1920−
Gorb, Mikhail   −1937
Leonov, A. G.   1946−1951
Ryumin, Mikhail D.   1951−1953
Vlodzimirsky, Lev Yemelyanovich   −1953
Paramonov   1953−
Volkov, Alexandr Fedorovich   1970−

*Formerly Road and Transportation Department, also Railways and Sea Transportation Department.

DEPUTIES

Valeskalin, Peteris	1920–
Komarov, V. I.	–1953
Likhacev, M. T.	

Prison Department (GULAG)

CHIEFS

Kedrov, Mikhail Sergeevich	1920–
Katsnelson, Zinovi Borisovich	1922–
Dukis, K. Yakov	1929–
Yagoda, Genrikh Grigorevich	1930–
Popov	1933–
Berman, Matvey Davydovich	–1937
Ryzhov, Mikhail Ivanovich	1937–
Nedosekin	1942–
Maltsev, Mikhail Mitrofanovich	1944–
Bogdanov, Nikolai Kuzmich	1945–

DEPUTIES

Firin, Semen Grigorevich	1934–1937
Pliner, I. I.	–1937
Rapoport, Yakov Davydovich	–1937
Yermakov, A. P.	1937–
Kravchenko, Valentin Alexandrovich	1941–

Economic Department (EKO)

CHIEFS

Krylenko, Nikolai Vasilevich	1921–
Katsnelson, Zinovi Borisovich	1922–
Prokofyev, Georgi Yevgennevich	1929–1934
Mironov, Lev G.	1934–1936
Ostrovskiy, I. M.	1936–

DEPUTIES

Nikolsky, Lev	1924–1925
Mironov, Lev G.	1925–

Ninth Chief Directorate

CHIEFS

Avanesov, Varlaam A.	1917–
Bykov, Fedor A.	1917–
Berzin, Eduard P.	1917–1918
Nikitin, I. I.	1918–1921
Borisov, Ilya I.	1918–
Belensky, Abram Yakov*	1918–1926
Pauker, Karl Viktorovich	1926–1935
Pavlov	1935–1938
Gulst, Venyamin N.	1941–
Vlasik, Nikolai Sidorovich	1941–
Kapandze, Andrei P.	1946–
Kuznetsov, Alexandr K.	1946–1947
Rakov, Alexandr M.	1947–
Shadrin, Dmitri Nikolaevich	1947–
Vlasik, Nikolai Sidorovich	1947–1952
Ignatyev, Semen Denisovich	1952–
Martynov	1953–
Novik, Nikolai P.	1953–
Kuzmichev, Sergei F.	1953–
Lenev, Alexandr M.	1953–1954
Ustinov, Vladimir Ivanovich	1954–1957
Zakharov, Nikolai Stepanovich	1957–1967
Tsvigun, Semen Kuzmich	1967–1982

DEPUTIES

Chertok	1936–
Valovich, Vladimir V.	1936–
Vlasik, Nikolai Sidorovich	–1947
Lynko, Vladimir Semenovich	1947–1952
Goryshev, Serafim Vasilevich	1947–1952
Grishkov	1947–1950

KREMLIN COMMANDANTS

Malkov, Pavl Dmitrevich	1917–1920
Peterson, Rudolf Avgustovich	1920–1935
Tkalun	1935–1937
Rogov	1938–1939
Spiridonov, Nikolai K.	1939–1953
Vedenin, Andrei Yakov	1953–1967
Shornikov, Sergei S.	1967–

*Also special assistant to the chairman of the OGPU.

ASSISTANT COMMANDANTS

Martinov, Mikhail I.	1918–1920
Kosynkin, Petr Yevgenni	1941–

Provincial Department

CHIEF

Fomin, Vasili Vasilevich	1918–

Registration Department

CHIEF

Rotsen	1920–

Training Department

CHIEF

Savinov, V. I.	1919–

Technical Department

CHIEF

Goryanov	1931–

Chief Directorate for Railway Construction Camps*

CHIEF

Safrazyan, Leon Bogdanovich	1941–

DEPUTIES

Buyanov, Leonid Sergeevich	1941–
Khudyakov, Pavl Vasilevich	1941–

Chief Directorate for Mines and Steel Works*

CHIEF

Zakharov, Petr Andreevich	1943–

*During World War II only.

Chief Directorate for Airfield Construction *

CHIEF

Safrazyan, Leon Bogdanovich	1941–

DEPUTIES

Pachkin, Vasili Alexeevich	1941–
Pavlov, Nikolai Ivanovich	1941–
Vasilyev, Nikolai Pavlovich	1941–

Antispeculation Department

CHIEF

Fomin, Vasili Vasilevich	1918–

Organizational Department

CHIEF

Vanyukov, Alexandr Alexeevich	1921–
Vorontsov, I.	1922–1928

Managerial and Supply Department

CHIEFS

Pogrebinsky, Matvey S.	–1922
Ambayn, Z. I.	1922–
Sidorov	1925–

Information Department

CHIEFS

Peters, Yakov Khristoforovich	1918–
Antipov-Levyy	1923–
Alexeyev	1928–

DEPUTY

Zaporozhets, Ivan V.	1928–

* During World War II only.

Finance Department

CHIEFS

Berzin, R.	1920–
Ulrikh, Vasili Danilovich	1920–
Diets	1923–
Lurye, A. Yakov	–1938

Special Section

CHIEFS

Ter-Gabriyelyan, Saak Mirzoyevich	1919–
Bokiy, Gleb Ivanovich	1923–1937
Meshik, Pavel Yakovlevich	1953–

The dates given correlate with the violent changes that occurred in the Soviet government under Stalin. The rewards and punishments of the system are evident in the dates of appointments and of dismissals and arrests. In some cases, the beginning date marks the time that an individual was appointed to a specific position. The absence of a second date indicates only that the date of dismissal, death, retirement, or arrest is not given and must be adduced. Similarly, the date marking the end of an individual's tenure in a given post is cited in the absence of the date on which he was first appointed. Some individuals display considerable bureaucratic longevity by their ability to jump from one directorate to another.

Also, some departments and sections established early in the regime no longer exist in their original form or title; for example, "Antispeculation" is now a generalized function carried out by the Third Chief Directorate in its efforts to stamp out "waste, abuse, fraud and corruption" in the Soviet government.

APPENDIX VII

PARTIAL LIST OF INTELLIGENCE AND SECURITY SERVICE ABBREVIATIONS

AVB   *Allami Vedelmi Batosag;* Hungarian; ex-AVH.

BCRA   *Bureau Central de Renseignements et d'Accion;* London-based Free French in World War II.

BfV   *Bundesamt fur Verfassungsschutz;* West German Federal Internal Security Office.

BND   *Bundesnachrichtendienst;* West German Federal Intelligence Service.

BOSS   Bureau of State Security; South African.

DGI   *Dirección General de Inteligencia;* Cuban.

DS   *Drzaven Sigurnost;* Bulgarian Department of Security.

DSE   Cuban Department of State Security.

DST   *Direction de la Surveillance du Territoire;* French internal service.

FEB   Far Eastern Bureau of the Comintern; Soviet.

GPU   *Glavnoye Gosudarstvenno Politcheskoye Upravleni;* Soviet.

GRU   *Glavnoye Razvedyvatelnoye Upravleniye;* Soviet military intelligence.

HVA   *Hauptverwaltung fur Aufklarung;* East German external service.

INO   *Inostranny Otdel;* Soviet Foreign Department (from 1922, including GPU, OGPU, and NKVD).

INU   *Inostrannoye Upravleniye;* Soviet Foreign Administration (from 1941, including NKGB-MGB).

KGB   *Komitet Gosudarstvennoy Bezopasnosti;* Soviet Committee for State Security.

KI   *Komitet Informatsii;* Soviet Committee for Information.

MAD   *Militarischer Abschirmdienst;* West German Military Security Service.

MfS   *Ministerium fur Staatssicherheit;* East German Ministry for State Security.

MVD   *Ministerstvo Vnutrennikh Del;* Soviet Ministry of Internal Affairs.

NKGB   *Narodnyi Kommissariat Gosudarstvennoi Bezopasnosti;* Soviet People's Commissariat for State Security.

NKVD   *Narodnyi Kommissariat Vnutrennikh Del;* Soviet People's Commissariat for Internal Affairs.

OGPU   *Obiedinennoye Gosudarstvennoye Politicheskoye Upravlenie;* State Political Administration; Soviet.

OMS   *Otdel Mezhdunarodnoi Sviazi;* Soviet Comintern liaison office.

OO   *Osobye Otdele;* Special sections, Soviet military counterintelligence units; with wartime augmentation and extended powers, 1943-1946, came to be referred to as Smersh.

OSZ   *Otdel Spetsialnikh Zadanii;* Special Tasks Branch of Soviet GRU.

ROVS   *Russikiy Obshcho Voyenskiy Soyuz;* Russian Armed Services Union; early anti-Soviet émigré organization.

RSHA   *Reichssicherheitzhauptamt;* Reich Central Security Office, Nazi Germany.

SB   *Sluzba Bezpieczenstwa;* Polish intelligence service.

SDECE   *Service de Documentation Exterieure et de Contre-Espionage;* French, after World War II.

SMERSH   *Smert'shipionam;* "Death to Spies"; Soviet military counterintelligence units.

SSD   *Staatssicherheitsdienst;* East German intelligence service.

STB   *Statni Tajna Bezpecnost;* Czech intelligence service.

VChK   *Vserosiiskaya Chrezvychainaya Kommissiya;* VChK or Cheka; Soviet.

WEB   West European Bureau of the Comintern; Soviet.

Ze-2   Polish military intelligence.

AMTORG: ANNOTATED BIBLIOGRAPHY

American Banker's Association, Commission on Commerce and Marine *Industry, Government, Finance and Foreign Trade in Soviet Russia.* N.Y. (1926), pp. 22-24.

In its discussion of Amtorg, this pamphlet provides a version of the firm's history and trading operations. Amtorg is described as the purchasing and sales agent, publisher, advertiser, tourist agency, and general promoter of relations between the United States and the USSR.

American Mercury. "Utopia on Fifth Avenue (January 1940), pp. 75-82.

Amtorg Trading Corporation. *American Engineering,* Vol. 1 (New York), November 1924.

A Russian-language magazine, published in the United States, devoted to science, engineering, and manufacturing developments in the United States. Intended to acquaint Soviet officials with American technical developments.

———. *Economic Review of the Soviet Union* (New York), 1927, 1933, 1934, and 1935.

Semimonthly magazine featuring economic developments in the USSR. Contains articles that reflect the Soviet government's view of industry, agriculture, labor, and the efficacy of cooperatives.

———. *Economic Statistics of the Soviet Union* (New York), 1st ed., March 1928; 2nd ed., June 1928.

Pamphlet consisting of compiled statistics on the USSR economy; based on data provided by the Soviet government.

———. *Russian Gold* (New York), May 1928.

Pamphlet consisting of articles, newspaper editorials, and statistical data on the Soviet gold reserves and gold shipments; based on information provided by the Soviet government.

———. *Soviet Oil Industry* (New York), February 6, 1927.

Pamphlet including statements of Sir Henry Deterding of the Royal Dutch Shell Group, Chairman Saul G. Bron of Amtorg, and representatives of the Standard Oil Company on the signing of contracts to buy Soviet oil. Appendix with statistics on Soviet oil production.

Bron, Saul G. "Address Delivered at the Luncheon Meeting of the Export Manager's Club of New York," November 27, 1928.

Discusses growth of Soviet industry in the USSR and affirms stability of the Soviet government and its ability to meet payments.

Business Week. "Buying for Moscow" (July 13, 1935), pp. 30-32.

Describes procedure by which Amtorg handles Soviet commercial transactions. Describes Soviet trade as a government monopoly. Each industry must apply to the Commissariat for Foreign Trade for a license to make a purchase of sale abroad. If licensed, the request is forwarded to the appropriate foreign trading agent (Amtorg in the United States), which receives a fixed commission on each transaction.

Farago, Ladislas. "Amtorg: Its Business Is Business with Russia." *United Nations World* (July 1947), pp. 29-31.

This overview of Amtorg's history and operations cites various accusations made against the firm. The U.S. Congress has charged it with operating a vast industrial espionage network. Under the Republican administrations of the 1920s, Amtorg suffered numerous political attacks. In 1930, Amtorg in the person of its newly appointed chairman, Petr Bogdanov, was investigated by a Congressional Committee.

Feinstein, J. M. Tatcher. *Fifty Years of US-Soviet Trade*. New York: Symposium Press, 1974.

Feinstein, who was employed by Amtorg for forty-five years, claims to have produced the book on his own initiative and without Soviet sponsorship. The text suggests otherwise. Of particular interest are the photographs of Petr A. Bogdanov and various early Amtorg board members who were subsequently executed by Stalin. There is also a photograph of a reception aboard the "Soviet flagship *Kim*" in New York harbor in 1934, which features the first Soviet ambassador to the United States, Konstantin Umanskiy. The same photographs, with altered captions, appear in the official publication issued by Amtorg in celebration of its fiftieth anniversary. There is no suggestion that the *Kim,* having been rebuilt during World War II with Lend-Lease funds, returned to service as a prison ship on the Kolyma run.

Flagler, J. M. "Visit to Amtorg." *The New York Times Magazine* VI (May 9, 1954), pp. 42-43.

This guided tour of Amtorg cites the fact that the FBI considers that not all Amtorg employees are involved in commerce and refers to the Harry Gold espionage case, in which Amtorg served as a source of intelligence direction.

Fortune. Note (May 1930).

Three-paragraph account of Amtorg's attempt to secure petroleum cracking plant from the McKee Corporation.

Literary Digest. "Agent Amtorg: Soviet Reduces Purchases Through Famed Business Firm" (April 10, 1937), p. 43.

Newsweek. "Amtorg: Soviet Union Spent $25,000,000 in US This Year" (August 17, 1935), pp. 33-34.

Historical overview of Amtorg. Names Isaiah Hoorgin as first chairman, succeeded by Paul Ziev, Saul Bron, Petr Bogdanov, and, in 1934, Ivan Boyeff. Soviet purchases reached a high of over $110 million in 1930, only to suffer a 90 percent decrease in 1934 because of restrictions on Soviet imports and charges of dumping.

————. "What Makes Nicolai Run?" (February 9, 1959), pp. 68 et seq.

Amtorg is the USSR's sole commercial agent in the United States. Although it claims to have no ties with the Soviet government, it has been involved in espionage (the Harry Gold case) and has been repeatedly charged as the "clearing house for Soviet espionage."

Scholastic. "Soviet Agency Indicted" (November 2, 1949), p. 14.

U.S. Congress. House Report 1229, January 8, 1952 (originally released December 29, 1951).

"With the founding of Amtorg, the Soviet Union had for the first time a legitimate cover for its espionage activities in the United States." (p. 6.)

Wood, Junius B. "How Russia Trades With Us." *Nation's Business* (March 1945), pp. 42 et seq.

In this contemporaneous historical overview, Amtorg's political activity is discussed. The company has been accused of being a propaganda center, though the Justice and Commerce departments have opted not to take action. According to the Treasury Department, Amtorg is under sole control of the Soviet government, which owns most of its shares. Amtorg receives 2½ percent commission on every transaction but must remit 50-60 percent of its net receipts to the USSR. There are a few other, more specialized firms in New York that have the same form as Amtorg, including Sovfoto and Artkino.

Zelchenko, H. L. "Stealing America's Know-How." *American Mercury* (February 1952), pp. 75-84.

New York Times News Items

March 4, 1930, 16:3. M. Woll charges that Amtorg is channel for Communist propaganda in the United States and predicts congressional inquiry.

March 7, 1930, 6:1. On Russian engineers in the United States.

May 7, 1930, 5:4. Twenty Russians arrive in New York to study engineering.

July 18, 1930, 1:6. M. Woll says safety of United States is jeopardized by maintenance of trade relations with Amtorg.

July 25, 1930, 4:3. Amtorg representative held in Mexico City on suspicion of communist propaganda activity.

July 29, 1930, 12:5. Attorney General Tuttle denies any official statement linking Amtorg to smuggling operations.

July 30, 1930, 2:3; July 31, 1930, 1:3. New York City Police raid drugstore in search of man named Filin, alias Simeon, said to head two Soviet espionage organizations claimed to be operating under cover of Amtorg.

August 3, 1930, 2:2. P. A. Bogdanov, president of Amtorg, speaks on its activities.

April 4, 1931, 2:5. G. R. Bernardsky, anticommunist, asks for investigation of Amtorg on the grounds that A. I. Pogojeff might have been slain by Soviet agents.

January 18, 1932, 18:1. Amtorg denounced by Representative Eslick.

December 4, 1935, 11:1. Montevideo branch of Amtorg accused of aiding revolt in Brazil.

December 31, 1936, 1:1. Amtorg's connection with Cuse airplane shipment to Spain denied by the Soviet embassy in Washington.

September 8, 1939, 1:2. At Dies Committee hearing, Benjamin Gitlow charges that the U.S. Communist Party got kickbacks from New York Amtorg employees.

October 15, 1939, 28:1. Robert C. Pitcoff links Amtorg to OGPU at Dies Committee hearing.

March 22, 1940, 6:2. U.S. National Munitions Control Board reports blocking Amtorg plane shipments intended for Loyalist Spain in 1939.

March 5, 1947, 5:1. Representative J. Parnell Thomas reports that Amtorg buys U.S. patents for USSR. Corporate attorney denies charge.

July 29, 1948, 29:3. Amtorg staff cuts noted. Aide reveals that reported mysterious shipping crates are for employees returning to the USSR.

April 29, 1949, 11:3. Regarding Coplon spy trial, false atom bomb data connected with Amtorg was planted as trap for Coplon, the prosecution reveals.

April 30, 1949, 6:7. Defense tries to prove that Coplon urged prosecution of Amtorg for nonregistration as a foreign agent.

June 14, 1949, 12:3. At Coplon spy trial, FBI agent testifies that Amtorg employees function as espionage agents; Amtorg issues denial.

June 16, 1950, 1:7. In Harry Gold spy trial, two unnamed persons indicted with Gold are believed to be A. A. Yakovlev, formerly of the USSR consulate in New York City, and S. M. Semenov of Amtorg.

July 30, 1950, 1:1. New York federal grand jury indicts A. Brothman and M. Moscowitz; Brothman is linked to Gold and Amtorg official Semenov; J. Edgar Hoover calls Semenov head of a Soviet spy ring.

November 16, 1950, 1:7; November 17, 1950, 16:3. Gold testifies in the Brothman-Moscowitz trial about Semenov and Amtorg's role.

June 3, 1950, 1:4. Senator Joseph McCarthy says that Amtorg fur sales provide the Soviet Union with income for espionage purposes.

October 30, 1953, 8:4, 7. A. Svenchansky testifies before Senate Subcommittee on Internal Security; he refuses to say whether he introduced A. Brothman to an Amtorg aide for espionage purposes.

October 31, 1953, 6:7. Gold states that Brothman told him Svenchansky worked for Amtorg.

December 27, 1953, 16:2. Before the Senate Permanent Investigations Subcommittee, Ege testifies that Soviet spy rings include twenty "legal" organizations such as Tass and Amtorg.

June 22, 1961, 11:1. In Robert A. Soblen spy trial, his brother, Jack Soble, tells of reporting to Amtorg.

October 31, 1963, through December 24, 1964. Numerous articles on the spy trial of John W. Butenko and I. A. Ivanov. The latter was an Amtorg aide.

APPENDIX IX

PARTIAL LIST OF THE "REVOLUTIONARY" OR "PARTY" NAMES OF PROMINENT SOVIET LEADERS

True name	*Party name*
Djugashvili, Joseph Vissarionovich	Stalin, J. V.
Rosenfeld, Lev Borisovich	Kamenev, L.
Ulyanov, Vladimir Ilyich	Lenin, V. I.
Wallach, Maxim Maximovich	Litvinov, M.
Skryabin, Vyacheslav Mikhailovich	Molotov, V.
Sobelsohn, K.	Radek, K.
Brilliant, Gregory	Sokolnikov, G.
Bronstein, Lev	Trotsky, L.
Radomylsky, Gregory Yevseyevich	Zinoviev, G.
Gruzenberg, Mikhail Markovich	Borodin, M.
Kogan, Lazar	Kaganovich, L.
Bogdanov, Alexandr	Malinovsky, R.

BIBLIOGRAPHY

Accoce, Pierre, and Pierre Quet. *A Man Called Lucy,* trans. A. M. Sheridan Smith. New York: Coward, McCann, 1967.

Agabekov, Georges. *OGPU: The Russian Secret Terror.* New York: Brentano's, 1931.

Akhmedov, Ismail. *In and Out of Stalin's GRU.* Frederick, Md.: University Publications of America, 1984.

Alexandrov, Victor. *The Tukhachevsky Affair.* Englewood Cliffs, N. J.: Prentice Hall, 1964.

Amalrik, Andrei. *Will the Soviet Union Survive Until 1984?* New York: Harper & Row, 1970.

Anders, Wladislav. *An Army in Exile.* London: Macmillan & Co., 1949.

Bailey, Geoffrey. *The Conspirators.* New York: Harper & Row, 1960.

Bargghoorn, Frederick C. *The Security Police. Interest Groups in Soviet Politics.* Princeton, N.J.: Princeton University Press, 1971.

Barron, John. *KGB: The Secret Work of Soviet Secret Agents.* New York: Reader's Digest Press, 1973.

―――. *KGB TODAY: The Hidden Hand.* New York: Reader's Digest Press, 1983.

Baschanov (Bajanov), Boris. *Ich war Stalins Sekretar (I Was Stalin's Secretary).* Frankfurt/Main: Ullstein, 1977.

Beck, F., and W. Godin. *The Russian Purge and the Extraction of Confession.* New York: Viking Press, 1951.

Beria, Lavrenti P. *On the History of the Bolshevik Organizations in Transcaucasia.* Moscow: Foreign Languages Publishing House, 1939.

Bernikow, Louise. *Abel.* New York: Trident Press, 1970.

Bialoguski, Michael. *The Case of Colonel Petrov.* New York: McGraw-Hill Book Co., 1955.

Bittman, Ladislav. *Deception Game: Czechoslovak Intelligence in Soviet Political Warfare.* Syracuse, N.Y.: Syracuse University Research Corporation, 1972.

Boyle, Andrew. *The Climate of Treason.* London: Hutchinson, 1979; as *The Fourth Man.* New York: Dial Press, 1980.

Brown, Anthony Cave, and Charles B. MacDonald. *On a Field of Red.* New York: G.P. Putnam's Sons, 1981.

_____. *Bodyguard of Lies.* New York: Harper & Row, 1975.

Burnham, James. *The Web of Subversion.* New York: John Day, 1954.

Byrnes, Robert F. "American Scholars in Russia Soon Learn About the KGB." *New York Times Magazine,* Nov. 16, 1969.

Bullock, John, and Henry Miller. *Spy Ring.* London: Secker & Warburg, 1961.

Carpozi, George, Jr. *Red Spies in Washington.* New York: Pocket Books, 1969.

Carr, Edward H. *The Bolshevik Revolution, 1917–1923.* Baltimore: Penguin Books, 1950.

_____. *Twilight of the Comintern.* New York: Pantheon Books, 1983.

_____. "The Origin and Status of the Cheka." *Soviet Studies* (London), Vol. X, No. 1 (July 1958).

Chamberlin, W. H. *The Russian Revolution, 1917–1921.* London and New York: Ayer & Co., 1935.

Chambers, Whittaker. *Witness.* New York: Random House, 1952.

Chester, Lewis, Stephen Fay, and Hugo Young. *The Zinoviev Letter.* Philadelphia: J.B. Lippincott Co., 1968.

Chiang Kai-shek. *Soviet Russia in China.* New York: Farrar, Straus and Cudahy, 1957.

Colton, Timothy J. *Commissars, Commanders and Civilian Authority. The Structure of Soviet Military Politics.* Cambridge, Mass.: Harvard University Press, 1949.

Conquest, Robert. *The Great Terror: Stalin's Purges of the Thirties.* New York: The Macmillan Co., 1968.

_____. Robert, ed. *Justice and the Legal System in the USSR.* London: The Bodley Head, 1968.

_____. *The Soviet Police System.* New York: Frederick A. Praeger, 1968.

_____. *The Soviet Deportation of Nationalities.* New York: St. Martin's Press, 1960.

Constantinides, George C. *Intelligence and Espionage: An Analytical Bibliography.* Boulder, Co.: Westview Press, 1983.

Cookridge, E. H. (pseudonym for Edward Spiro). *The Third Man.* New York: G.P. Putnam's Sons, 1968.

Corson, William R. *The Armies of Ignorance: The Rise of the American Intelligence Empire.* New York: Dial Press, 1977.

Crankshaw, Edward. *Russia Without Stalin.* New York: Viking Press, 1956.

Dallin, David J. *Soviet Espionage.* New Haven, Conn.: Yale University Press, 1953.

_____. *The Changing World of Soviet Russia.* New Haven, Conn.: Yale University Press, 1956.

_____. *From Purge to Coexistence.* Chicago, Ill.: Henry S. Regnery Co., 1964.

_____, and Boris I. Nicolaevsky. *Forced Labor in Soviet Russia.* New Haven, Conn.: Yale University Press, 1968.

Deakin, F. W., and G. R. Storry. *The Case of Richard Sorge.* New York: Harper & Row, 1966.

_____. *The Brutal Friendship*. New York: Harper & Row, 1962.

Delmer, Sefton. *The Counterfeit Spy*. New York: Harper & Row, 1971.

Deriabin, Peter. *Watchdogs of Terror*. New Rochelle, N.Y.: Arlington House, 1972.

_____, and Frank Gibney. *The Secret World*. New York: Doubleday & Co., 1959.

Deutscher, Isaac. *Stalin*. New York: Oxford University Press, 1950.

_____. *The Unfinished Revolution*. New York: Oxford University Press, 1969.

Djilas, Milovan. *The New Class*. New York: Frederick A. Praeger, 1957.

_____. *Conversations with Stalin*. New York: Harcourt, Brace, 1962.

Dulles, Allen. *The Craft of Intelligence*. New York: Harper & Row, 1963.

Duranty, Walter. *Stalin and Co*. New York: William Sloane Associates, 1949.

Ebon, Martin. *Svetlana*. New York: New American Library, 1967.

_____. *The Andropov File*. New York: McGraw-Hill Book Co., 1983.

Ely, Louis B. *The Red Army Today*. Harrisburg, Pa.: Military Press, 1949.

Erickson, John. *The Soviet High Command: A Military Political History, 1918–1941*. London: Archon Books, 1962.

Foote, Alexander. *Handbook for Spies*. Garden City, N.Y.: Doubleday & Co., 1969.

Freemantle, Brian. *KGB*. New York: Holt, Rinehart and Winston, 1982.

Gehlen, Reinhard. *The Service*, trans. David Irving. New York: Popular Library, 1972.

Gelb, Barbara. *So Short a Time*. New York: Berkley Books, 1973.

Ginzburg, Evgenia Semyonovna. *Into the Whirlwind*. New York: Harcourt, Brace, 1967.

Gorbatov, A. V. *Years off My Life,* trans. Gordon Clough and Anthony Cash. London: Constable & Co., 1964.

Gorkin, Julian. *L'Assassinat de Trotsky*. Paris: Juilliard, 1970.

Gorky, Maxim. *Untimely Thoughts: Essays on Revolution, Culture and the Bolsheviks, 1917–1918,* ed. and trans. Herman Ermolaev. London: Paul Eriksson, 1970.

Gouzenko, Igor. *The Iron Curtain*. New York: E.P. Dutton, 1948.

Graham, Stephen. *Stalin*. New York & London: Kennikat Press, 1931 (reissued, 1970).

Granovsky, Anatoli. *I Was a Soviet Spy*. New York: Paperback Library, 1963.

Graves, William S. *America's Siberian Adventure*. New York: Jonathan Cape and Harrison Smith, 1931.

Guillermaz, Jacques. *A History of the Chinese Communist Party, 1921–1949*. New York: Random House, 1972.

Heilbrunn, Otto. *The Soviet Secret Services*. London: George Allen & Unwin, 1956.

Hicks, Granville. *John Reed: The Making of a Revolutionary*. New York: Blom & Ayer, 1936.

Hingley, Ronald. *The Russian Secret Police: Muscovite, Imperial Russian and Soviet Political Security Operations, 1556–1970*. New York: Simon and Schuster, 1970.

Hirsch, Richard. *The Soviet Spies*. London: Nicholas Kaye, 1947.

Historia Hors Serie, Histoire de L'Espionage 1945–1971. Paris: Librarie Tallan-
    dier, 1971.

Hutton, J. Bernard. *School for Spies.* New York: Coward-McCann, 1962.

———. *Stalin: The Miraculous Georgian.* London: Neville Spearman, 1961.

Hyde, H. Montgomery. *Stalin: The History of a Dictator.* New York: Popular
    Library, 1971.

John, Otto. *Twice Through the Lines.* New York: Harper & Row, 1972.

Karski, Jan. *Story of a Secret State.* Boston: Houghton Mifflin Co., 1944.

Kaznacheev, Alexandr. *Inside a Soviet Embassy.* Philadelphia: J. B. Lippincott
    Co., 1962.

Khokhlov, Nikolai. *In the Name of Conscience,* translated from the Russian
    Pravo na Sovest. Frankfurt: Possev Verlag, 1957; New York: David
    McKay, 1959.

Khrushchev, Nikita. *Khrushchev Remembers,* ed. and trans. Strobe Talbott.
    Boston: Little, Brown & Co., 1970.

Koestler, Arthur. *Darkness at Noon.* London: Jonathan Cape, 1951.

Kravchenko, Victor. *I Chose Freedom.* New York: Charles Scribner's Sons, 1946.

Krivitsky, Walter G. *I Was Stalin's Agent.* London, Hamish Hamilton, 1940.

———. *In Stalin's Secret Service.* New York: Harper & Row, 1941.

Laqueur, Walter Z. *The Fate of the Revolution.* New York: The Macmillan Co.,
    1967.

Lazitch, Branko, and Milorad M. Drachkovitch. *Biographical Dictionary of the
    Comintern.* Palo Alto, Calif.: Hoover Institution Press, 1973.

Leggett, George. *The Cheka: Lenin's Political Police.* Oxford: Oxford University
    Press, 1981.

Levine, Isaac Don. *The Mind of an Assassin.* New York: Farrar, Straus &
    Cudahy, 1959.

———. *Stalin's Great Secret.* New York: Coward-McCann, 1956.

Lewis, Flora. *Red Pawn.* New York: Doubleday & Co., 1967.

———. "Who Killed Krivitsky?" *Washington Post,* February 13, 1966.

Lindsey, Robert. *The Falcon and the Snowman.* New York: Simon & Schuster,
    1979.

Lockhart, Robin Bruce. *Ace of Spies.* New York: Stein and Day, 1967.

———. *Memoirs of a British Agent.* London: G. P. Putnam and Sons, 1932.

Lonsdale, Gordon. *Spy: Twenty Years in the Soviet Secret Service,* London: Ne-
    ville Spearman, 1965.

Malaparte, Curzio. *Kaputt.* New York: E. P. Dutton, 1946.

———. *Coup d'etat.* London: Macmillan & Co., 1936.

Masterman, J. C. *The Double Cross System in the War of 1939–1945.* New
    Haven, Conn.: Yale University Press, 1972.

Medvedev, Roy. *Let History Judge: The Origins and Consequences of Stalinism.*
    New York: Alfred A. Knopf, 1972.

———, and Zhores Medvedev. *A Question of Madness.* New York: Alfred A.
    Knopf, 1971.

Moorehead, Alan. *The Traitors.* New York: Harper & Row, 1952.

Morros, Boris. *My Ten Years as a Counterspy.* New York: Viking Press, 1959.

Orlov, Alexander. *Handbook of Intelligence and Guerrilla Warfare.* Ann Arbor: University of Michigan Press, 1965.

————. *The Secret History of Stalin's Crimes.* New York: Random House, 1953.

Ovseyenko, Anton Antonov. *The Time of Stalin.* New York: Harper & Row, 1981.

Page, Bruce, David Leitch, and Phillip Knightley. *The Philby Conspiracy.* New York: Doubleday & Co., 1968.

Pares, Bernard. *A History of Russia.* New York: Alfred A. Knopf, 1951.

Penkovsky, Oleg. *The Penkovsky Papers,* trans. Peter Deriabin. Garden City, N.Y.: Doubleday & Co., 1965.

Perrault, Gilles. *The Red Orchestra.* New York: Simon & Schuster, 1969.

Petrov, Vladimir and Evdokia. *Empire of Fear.* New York: Frederick A. Praeger, 1956.

Philby, Eleanor. *The Spy I Married.* New York: Ballantine Books, 1968.

Philby, Harold Adrian Russell. *My Silent War.* New York: Grove Press, 1968.

Pincher, Chapman. *Their Trade Is Treachery.* London: Sidgwick & Jackson, 1981.

————. Too Secret Too Long. New York: St. Martin's Press, 1984.

Pipes, Richard. *The Formation of the Soviet Union.* Cambridge, Mass.: Harvard University Press, 1964.

Reed, John. *Ten Days That Shook the World.* New York: Random House, 1960.

Report of the Royal Commission on Espionage, Commonwealth of Australia. Sydney: Government Printer for New South Wales, 1955.

Rositzke, Harry. *The KGB: The Eyes of Russia.* New York: Doubleday & Co., 1981.

Sawatsky, John. *For Services Rendered.* Toronto: Doubleday Canada, Ltd., 1982.

Scott, E. J. *Soviet Affairs, "The Cheka."* St. Antony's Papers No. 1. London: Chatto & Windus, 1956.

Senn, Alfred Erich. *Diplomacy and Revolution: The Soviet Mission to Switzerland, 1918.* South Bend, Ind.: University of Notre Dame Press, 1974.

Seth, Ronald. *Unmasked: The Story of Soviet Espionage.* New York: Hawthorn Books, 1965.

————. *Spies at Work.* New York: Philosophical Library, 1954.

Smith, Walter Bedell. *My Three Years in Moscow.* Philadelphia: J. B. Lippincott, Co., 1950.

Soviet Spies in the Scientific and Technical Fields. Wavre, Belgium: Ligue de la Liberté, 1968.

Soviet Spies in the Shadow of the UN. Wavre, Belgium: Ligue de la Liberté, 1968.

Sterling, Claire. *Masaryk Case.* New York: Harper & Row, 1969.

————. *The Terror Network.* New York: Holt, Rinehart and Winston, 1981.

Tietjen, Arthur. *Soviet Spy Ring.* New York: Coward-McCann, 1961.

Trotsky, Leon. *The First Five Years of the Communist International,* Vol. 1. New York: Pioneer Books, 1945.

————. *Stalin.* New York: Stein and Day, 1967.

Tucker, Robert C., and Stephen F. Cohen, eds. *The Great Purge Trial. Verbatim Report of the 1938 Moscow Trial.* New York: Grosset & Dunlap, 1965.

Ulam, Adam B. *Stalin: The Man and His Era.* New York: Viking Press, 1973.

_____. *The Bolsheviks: The Intellectual and Political History of the Triumph of Communism in Russia*. New York: Viking Press, 1965.

Van Der Rhoer, Edward. *The Shadow Network*. New York: Charles Scribner's Sons, 1983.

_____. *Master Spy*. New York: Charles Scribner's Sons, 1981.

Vernadsky, George A. *A History of Russia*. New Haven, Conn.: Yale University Press, 1929.

Weinstein, Allen. *Perjury: The Hiss Chambers Case*. New York: Alfred A. Knopf, 1978.

West, Rebecca. *A Train of Powder*. New York: Viking Press, 1955.

_____. *The New Meaning of Treason*. New York: Viking Press, 1964.

White, John Baker. *The Soviet Spy System*. London: Falcon Press, 1948.

Whiteside, Thomas. *An Agent in Place*. New York: Viking Press, 1966.

Wittlin, Thaddeus. *Commissar: The Life and Death of Lavrenty Pavlovitch Beria*. New York: The Macmillan Co., 1973.

Wolfe, Bertram D. *Khrushchev and Stalin's Ghost*. New York: Frederick A. Praeger, 1967.

_____. *Three Who Made a Revolution*. New York: Dial Press, 1948.

_____. *The Bridge and the Abyss: The Troubling Friendship of Maxim Gorky and V. I. Lenin*. New York: Greenwood Press, 1967.

Wolin, Simon, and Robert M. Slusser. *The Soviet Secret Police*. New York: Frederick A. Praeger, 1957.

Young, Kenneth, ed. *The Diaries of Sir Robert Bruce Lockhart, 1915–1938*. London: Macmillan & Co., 1973.

Ypsilon (pseudonym of Karl Volk and J. Humbert Droz). *Pattern for World Revolution*. Chicago: Ziff-Davis, 1947.

SELECTED WORKS IN RUSSIAN

Alidin, V. I., et al., eds., *MChK: Iz istorii Moskovskoi chrezvychainoi komissii (1918–1921 gg.)*. Sbornik dokumentov, Moscow, 1978.

Belov, G. A., et al. eds. *Iz istoril Vserossiiskoi Chrezychainoi komissii (1917–21 gg.)*. Moscow: *Sbornik dokumentov*, 1958.

Bol'shaya Sovetskya Entsiklopediya (Great Soviet Encyclopedia), 2nd ed. Moscow: 1957.

Chernov, V. M., ed. *Che-Ka: Materialy po deiatelnosti chrezvychainoi komissii* (Izdanie tsentralnogo biuro partii sotisialistov-revoliutsionerov), Berlin, 1922.

Golinkov, D. L. *Krakh vraazheskogo podpolia: is istoril borbys kontrrevoliutsieei v Sovetskov Rossii v 1917–24 gg*. Moscow: 1971.

Krylenko, N. V. *Sudoustroistov RSFRE: Lekstii po terroistorii sudousttoistva*. Moscow: 1924.

Kuskova, E. Mesiats. "Soglashateslstva" in *Volia Rossii*. Moscow: 1928.

Lenin, V. I. *Collected Works*.

References to the "complete works of V. I. Lenin" must be viewed with reservation. His name is customarily involved with, and his imprimatur given to, the solutions of problems not even envisioned during his lifetime. Sixty years after his death, the regime continues to remark on his prescience to an absurd degree. The bulk of the writings that generally can be attributed to Lenin include:

Sobranie sochinenirr, 20 vols., Moscow, 1920–1926.
Sochineniia, 30 vols., Moscow, 1925–1932.
Sochineniia, 30 vols., Moscow, 1935–1937.
Sochineniia, 35 vols., Moscow, 1941, 1946–1950.
Polnoe sobraanie sochinenii, 58 vols., Moscow, 1958–1966.

These intermittent, sequential editions of Lenin's "complete works" pose some problems for Soviet and Western scholars in that editorial license has been used to make his wisdom conform to the political realities of the moment. Though the sweep and general tenor of Lenin's thought remains in the most recent, expanded series of his works, the Soviet attempt to make Lenin omniscient and correct in every specific, forever more, requires careful reference to the date on which the original work was published, announced, or otherwise became part of the Bolsheviks' official library.

Peters, Y. K. "Vospominaniia o rabote v VChK v pervyi god revoliutsii" in *Proletarskaia revoliutsiia,* 1924, No. 10 (33), pp. 5–32.

———. "1905 god v Libave i ee okrestnostiakh" in *Proletarskaia revoliutsiia,* 1925, No. 11 (46), pp. 194–203.

———. Ia., "Zashchita revoliutsii" in *Desiat let sovetskogo stroitelstva,* L. Riabinin, ed., Leningrad, pp. 167–90 (Peters, 1927, "Zashchita revoliutsii").

———. Ia., "Bolshaia Lubianka, 2" in *Dni,* No. 1275, December 22, 1927, reprinted from *Komsomolskaia Pravda,* December 16, 1927 (Peters, 1927, "Bolshaia Lubianka, 2").

———. Ia., "Neistovyi Feliks" in *Feliks Dzerzhinskii. 1926–1931,* q.v., pp. 144–59.

Sofinov, P. G. *Ocehrki istoril vserissusior chrezvyhassinoit komissii 1917–22 gg.* Moscow: 1950.

Unshlikht, I. S. "Vospominanuuai o Vladimire Iliche." *Voprsoy istorrii KPSS,* No. 4. Moscow: 1965.

INDEX